POLITICS
IN POST-WAR
FRANCE

POLITICS IN POST-WAR FRANCE

*Parties and the Constitution
in the Fourth Republic*

by

PHILIP WILLIAMS

LONGMANS, GREEN AND CO
LONDON · NEW YORK · TORONTO

LONGMANS, GREEN AND CO LTD
6 & 7 CLIFFORD STREET, LONDON W 1
ALSO AT MELBOURNE AND CAPE TOWN

LONGMANS, GREEN AND CO INC
55 FIFTH AVENUE, NEW YORK 3

LONGMANS, GREEN AND CO
215 VICTORIA STREET, TORONTO 1

ORIENT LONGMANS LTD
BOMBAY CALCUTTA MADRAS

First Published 1954

342.44
W 674 p

Nov. 17, 1954
J. Gov.

PRINTED IN GREAT BRITAIN BY THE WHITEFRIARS PRESS LTD
LONDON AND TONBRIDGE

PREFACE

This book has a large but limited theme: the parliamentary machinery of the Fourth Republic and the combinations of men who operate or obstruct it. It describes each of the principal parties and political institutions of the country, and analyses the working of the parliamentary system as a whole. Many important and interesting subjects have had to be omitted. Administration, justice, and 'France overseas' fall outside its scope. Institutions not mentioned in the constitution are not discussed; those which are mentioned, but which do not impinge on domestic politics, receive only the briefest notice. The social and philosophical background is not treated; significant and revealing episodes like the worker-priest movement, or the protest against the Rosenberg executions, find no place. The influence of press and army, universities and trade unions, is touched on only incidentally. Problems of policy are mentioned only when necessary to explain their impact on institutions or parties.

The period covered is approximately the term of office of the first President of the Fourth Republic, from the beginning of 1947 to the end of 1953; but it cannot be made intelligible without much discussion of the preceding years. The period has been regarded as a whole; for example more space has been devoted to the R.P.F. than to its rivals, in spite of its present decline. A volcano remains interesting when the eruption is over.

The sources most likely to be available in Britain have been quoted wherever possible.

In one important respect the French practice has been followed. In writing about politics, the British academic tradition is one of complete detachment: the French (despite state control of the universities) are less concerned to avoid the appearance of taking sides. There is much to be said for both approaches: there is nothing to be said for professing one and practising the other. Bias is dangerous only when it is concealed—or unconscious. In studying French affairs I have tried to appreciate all points of view; but I have neither found it possible, nor felt it desirable to avoid acquiring preferences and prejudices. The reader is, therefore, entitled to know my political standpoint, which is that of a supporter of the moderate wing of the Labour party.

My principal debt of gratitude is to the Warden and Fellows of Nuffield College, Oxford, both for making it possible for this book to be written and for much encouragement and stimulus in the writing of it. Mr. David Butler and Mr. Asa Briggs read the manuscript and gave much helpful advice and criticism in the formative stages, as did M. Jean Blondel and Mr. J. W. Saxe later; and I am also most grateful to Mr. Butler for advice about the diagrams, and to the draughtsman for his work on them. I am very particularly indebted to M. Léo Hamon, Senator for the Seine, for sparing time to read a large part of the text and for making most thorough and valuable comments on it.

I wish also to thank most warmly a large number of politicians and party or state officials who were very generous with their time: M. Hibon of the *Maison française* at Oxford, M. Meynaud of the *Fondation nationale des sciences politiques* at Paris, and their staffs, for their unfailing helpfulness: M. André Imbert of the National Assembly staff, for supplying a great deal of information on the parliamentary side: Miss Macdonald of the French Embassy, and M. Collin of the *Institut français d'opinion publique*, for providing other information at very short notice: Mrs. Yates for typing: Mr. Robert Shackleton for reading the proofs: and Mr. R. R. Farquharson and Mr. A. C. Whitby for invaluable help with the index. My debt to M. Jacques Fauvet, M. François Goguel, and other French writers on the subject, will be plain to anyone who consults the footnotes; to both of them, and to M. Hamon, I am very grateful for their help and encouragement.

I am, of course, solely responsible both for the views expressed, and for the lurking errors which, no doubt, it will be the duty and pleasure of reviewers to correct.

PHILIP WILLIAMS

OXFORD,
March 1954

CONTENTS

	PAGE
PREFACE	v
LIST OF WORKS CITED	ix
ABBREVIATIONS	xiii

PART I. THE BACKGROUND
1. The Basis of French Politics. 1
2. The War and its Aftermath, 1940–1947. 11
3. The Search for a Majority, 1947–1953. 27

PART II. THE PARTIES
4. The Communist Party. 44
5. The Socialist Party. 60
6. The *Mouvement Républicain Populaire*. 77
7. The Radical Party. 90
8. The Conservative Groups. 107
9. The *Rassemblement du Peuple Français*. 118
10. The Minor Parties. 140

PART III. THE CONSTITUTION
11. The Constitutional Problem. 154
12. The Presidency and the Premiership. 169
13. The National Assembly. 191
14. The Assembly and the Government. 211
15. The Committee System. 234
16. The Budget. 252
17. The Council of the Republic. 267
18. The other Constitutional Organs. 287

PART IV. THE POLITICAL SYSTEM
19. The Electoral Laws. 309
20. The Pressure Groups. 327
21. The Parties and Elections. 342
22. The Parties and Parliament. 359
23. The Parties and the Government. 374
24. Conclusion. 396

EPILOGUE 408

Appendices

		PAGE
I.	THE CONSTITUTION	423

(Text of the Constitution of the Fourth Republic, authorized English translation.)

II.	THE PREMIERS	436

(List of Governments, 1944–53.)

III.	THE MINISTERS	*facing* 436

(Composition of Governments, 1944–53.)

IV.	THE OPPOSITION	438

(Principal votes in the Assembly, 1945–53 : Parties opposing the Government.)

V.	THE VERDICT OF THE ELECTORATE	440

(Referendums and General Elections, 1945–51; Strength of Parties in the Four Assemblies.)

VI.	THE DETAILED WORKING OF THE ELECTORAL LAWS	442
VII.	THE COMPOSITION AND OUTLOOK OF THE PARTIES	446

Index

449

Diagrams

Figure 1.	Party alignments, 1945–6.	15
,, 2.	Governments, 1945–53: the instability of ministries.	28
,, 3.	,, ,, the stability of ministers.	30–31
,, 4.	Party alignments, 1951–3.	43

Maps

1. Distribution of Industry, 1946.	417
2. The Left, 1932 Election.	418
3. R.P.F. strength, 1951 Election.	419
4. Communist strength, 1951 Election.	420
5. Electoral Coalitions, 1951.	421

LIST OF WORKS CITED

No attempt has been made to compile a complete bibliography for the Third Republic; but one or two works on the subsequent period have been included, although not cited in the text. These books are starred.

In the case of particularly useful or significant works, the author's name appears in large capitals.

I. Works in English dealing mainly with the Third Republic and the war years.

BODLEY, J. E. C. France. Macmillan, 1898, 2 vols.
BROGAN, D. W. Development of modern France. Hamilton, 1940.
EHRMANN, H. W. French Labour from Popular Front to Liberation. O.U.P., New York, 1940.
ENSOR, R. C. K. Courts and Judges in England, France, and Germany. O.U.P., 1933.
GOOCH, R. K. French Parliamentary Committee System. Appleton-Century, 1935.
JACKSON, J. H. Clemenceau and the Third Republic. Hodder & Stoughton, 1946.
MAILLAUD, P. France. O.U.P., 1945.
MIDDLETON, W. L. French Political System. Benn, 1932.
*PICKLES, D. M. France between the Republics. Contact Books, 1946.
SAIT, E. M. Government and politics of France. World Book Co., 1920.
SHARP, W. R. Government of the French Republic. Van Nostrand, 1938.
SIEGHART, M. Government by decree. Stevens, 1950.
THOMSON, D. Democratic Ideal in France and England. C.U.P., 1940.
THOMSON, D. Democracy in France. O.U.P., 1946.
*TISSIER, P. Government of Vichy. Harrap, 1942.
WERTH, A. Destiny of France. Hamilton, 1937.
WERTH, A. Twilight of France. Hamilton, 1942.

II. Works in English dealing mainly with the Fourth Republic.

ANON. A Constitution for the Fourth Republic. Foundation for Foreign Affairs, Washington, D.C., 1947.
CHAPMAN, B. Introduction to French Local Government. Allen & Unwin, 1953.
EARLE, E. M., ed. Modern France. Princeton U.P., 1951.
EINAUDI, M. AND GOGUEL, F. Christian Democracy in Italy and France. Cornell U. P., 1952.
GOGUEL, F. France under the Fourth Republic. Cornell U.P., 1952.
LIDDERDALE, D. W. S. The Parliament of France. Hansard Society, 1951.
PICKLES, D. French Politics. Royal Institute of International Affairs, 1953.
*TAYLOR, O. R. The Fourth Republic of France. Royal Institute of International Affairs, 1951.
WRIGHT, G. Reshaping of French Democracy. Methuen, 1950.

III. Works in French dealing mainly with the Third Republic and the war years.

ALAIN (EMILE CHARTIER). Éléments d'une doctrine radicale. Gallimard, 1933 ed.
Augé-Laribé, M. La Politique agricole de la France. Presses Universitaires, 1950.
Auriol, V. Hier . . . demain. Charlot, 1945, 2 vols.
Barthélemy, J. Essai sur le travail parlementaire et le système des commissions. Delagrave, 1934.
Barthélemy, J. Le Gouvernement de la France. Payot, 1939.
Blum, L. La Réforme gouvernementale. Grasset, 1936 (first published anonymously in 1919).
Frédérix, P. État des forces en France. Gallimard, 1935.
Galtier-Boissiére, J. Mon journal sous l'occupation. Gallimard, 1945.
Giraud, Gen. H. Un seul but, la Victoire. Julliard, 1949.
Goguel, F. La Politique des partis sous la Troisième République. Éd. du Seuil, 1946.
Halévy, D. La République des comités. Grasset, 1934.
Jouvenel, R. de. La République des camarades. Grasset, 1914 ed.
Rossi, A. Physiologie du parti communiste français. Éd. Self, 1948.
Siegfried, A. Tableau des partis en France. Grasset, 1930.
Soulier, A. L'Instabilité ministérielle sous la Troisième République. Sirey, 1939.
Tardieu, A. Le Souverain captif. Flammarion, 1936.
Tardieu, A. La Profession parlementaire. Flammarion, 1937.
Thibaudet, A. Les Idées politiques de la France. Lib. Stock, 1932.
Thorez, M. Fils du peuple. Éd. Sociales, 1949.
Walter, G. Histoire du parti communiste français. Somogy, 1948.

IV. Works in French dealing with the Fourth Republic.

Aron, R. Le Grand Schisme. Gallimard, 1948.
Arrighi, P. Le Statut des partis politiques. Pichon & Durand-Auzias, 1947.
Brayance, A. Anatomie du parti communiste français. Denoël, 1952.
Debré, M. La Mort de l'état républicain. Gallimard, 1947.
Debû-Bridel, J. Les Partis contre Charles de Gaulle. Somogy, 1948.
Duverger, M., ed. L'Influence des systèmes électoraux sur la vie politique. Colin, 1950.
Duverger, M. Manuel de droit constitutionnel et de science politique. Presses Universitaires, 1948.
Duverger, M. Les Partis politiques. Colin, 1951.
Fauvet, J. Les Forces politiques en France. Le Monde, 1951.
*Fauvet, J. Les Partis politiques dans la France actuelle. Le Monde, 1947.
Gaulle, Gen. C. de La France sera la France. R.P.F., 1951.
George, P., etc. Études sur la banlieue de Paris. Colin, 1950.
Goguel, F. Géographie des élections françaises. Colin, 1951.
Goguel, F. Encyclopédie politique de la France et du monde, vol. 1. (Section on French parties.) Éds. de l'Encyclopédie coloniale et maritime, 1950–51, 4 vols.
Husson, R. Élections et referendums des 21 octobre 1945, 5 mai 1946, et 2 juin 1946. Le Monde, 1946.
Husson, R. Élections et referendums des 13 octobre, 10 novembre, 24 novembre et 8 décembre, 1946. Le Monde, 1947.
Lachapelle, G. Les Régimes électoraux. Colin, 1934.

LAFERRIÈRE, J. Manuel de droit constitutionnel. Donat-Montchrestien, 1947.
MARABUTO, P. Partis politiques et mouvements sociaux. Sirey, 1948.
MEYER, J. La Question de confiance. Albin Michel, 1948.
MORAZÉ, C., ED. Études de sociologie électorale. Colin, 1951.
MOTTIN, J. Histoire politique de la presse. Bilans hebdomadaires, 1949.
PRÉLOT, M. Précis de droit constitutionnel. Dalloz, 1949.
PRIOURET, R. A. La République des partis. Éd. l'Élan, 1948.
ROUGIER, L. La France à la recherche d'une constitution. Sirey, 1952.
THERY, J. Le Gouvernement de la Quatrième Republique. Pichon & Durand-Auzias, 1949.
VEDEL, G. Manuel élémentaire de droit constitutionnel. Sirey, 1949.
WALINE, M. Les Partis contre la République. Rousseau, 1948.

ABBREVIATIONS

I. *Political parties*

(Those starred have, or have had since the war, a separate group in the National Assembly. Most are discussed in Chapter 10.)

A.D.	Alliance démocratique.
*A.R.S.	Action républicaine et sociale.
*M.R.P.	Mouvement républicain populaire.
P.C.I.	Parti communiste internationaliste.
P.D.P.	Parti démocrate populaire. (Third Republic.)
*P.R.L.	Parti républicain de la liberté. (Defunct.)
P.S.D.	Parti socialiste démocratique.
R.F.	Réconciliation française.
R.G.R.	Rassemblement des gauches républicaines.
R.G.R.I.F.	Rassemblement des groupes républicaines et indépendants français. (Temporary combination for 1951 election.)
*R.P.F.	Rassemblement du peuple français.
*S.F.I.O.	Section française de l'internationale ouvrière. (Official title of the Socialist party.)
*U.D.I.	Union démocratique des indépendants. (Defunct.)
*U.D.S.R.	Union démocratique et socialiste de la résistance.
U.N.I.R.	Union nationale et des indépendants républicains. (1951 election.)
*U.R.A.S.	Union des républicains et d'action sociale. (Temporary name adopted by R.P.F. group in May 1953; not used in text.)
*U.R.P.	Union des républicains progressistes.
*I.O.M.	Indépendants d'outre-mer.
*M.T.L.D.	Mouvement du triomphe des libertés démocratiques.
*R.D.A.	Rassemblement démocratique africain.
*U.D.M.A.	Union démocratique du manifeste algérien.

II. *Other organizations*

A.C.J.F.	Association catholique de la jeunesse française.
A.P.L.E.	Association parlementaire pour la liberté de l'enseignement.
C.F.T.C.	Confédération française des travailleurs chrétiens.
C.G.A.	Confédération générale de l'agriculture.
C.G.C.	Confédération générale des cadres.
C.G.S.I.	Confédération générale des syndicats indépendants.
C.G.T.	Confédération générale du travail.
C.G.T.-F.O. / F-O.	Confédération générale du travail (Force ouvrière).
C.N.P.F.	Confédération nationale du patronat français.
F.N.S.E.A.	Fédération nationale des syndicats d'exploitants agricoles.
I.G.A.M.E.	Inspecteurs-généraux de l'administration en mission extraordinaire. ('Super-prefects'.)
J.A.C.	Jeunesse agricole chrétienne.
J.O.C.	Jeunesse ouvrière chrétienne.
M.L.N.	Mouvement de libération nationale. (Resistance movement.)
O.C.M.	Organisation civile et militaire. (Resistance movement.)
P.M.E.	Petites et moyennes entreprises.

III. Publications

A.N.., Doc. no. . . .	Documents published by the National Assembly.
A.P.	*L'Année politique*, published annually since 1944–45 by Éditions du grand siècle.
B.C.	*Bulletin des commissions* (published by the National Assembly).
J.O.	*Journal officiel de la République française.* Unless otherwise stated the series referred to is that of *Débats parlementaires* either of the Constituent or of the National Assembly according to the date. The date shown is that of the debate, not that of publication.
J.O. (*C.R.*).	*Journal officiel . . . Débats parlementaires, Conseil de la République.*
J.O. (*A.U.F.*).	*Journal officiel . . . Débats de l'Assemblée de l'Union française.*
J.O. (*A.C.E.*).	*Journal officiel . . . Avis et rapports du Conseil économique.*
B.C.E.	*Bulletin du Conseil économique.*
R.D.P.	*Revue du droit public et de la science politique.*
S.C.C., I.	*Séances de la commission de la constitution, Comptes rendus analytiques.* (First Constituent Assembly.)
S.C.C., II.	*Séances . . .*, etc. (Second Constituent Assembly.)

Part I. THE BACKGROUND

Chapter 1

THE BASIS OF FRENCH POLITICS

1. FRANCE AND BRITAIN: THE BACKGROUND

THE British have never had much respect for the political capacity of their nearest neighbour. Official and ministerial circles too often share the view of the man in the street, that the French are congenitally incapable of governing themselves properly, or even that the descendants of the men of 1789 are unable to manage a democratic system at all, and had better revert to autocracy. There is little understanding of the deep differences between the British and the French outlook on politics, or of the fundamental reasons for these differences. The faults in the political structure of France are the result of her historical and geographical background. No country can rid itself of its past.

In the first place, the Reformation failed on the other side of the Channel. The Catholic Church remains active and powerful, and retains the allegiance of a substantial proportion of the population. The position of the Church is consequently, as in all Catholic countries, still a political issue of the first importance. Education is as explosive a political issue as it was in Britain in the last century. But the conflict is even more bitter because the issues are more clear cut—as Bodley put it, the group structure of French politics is found in Britain in the religious sphere, while the clear and straightforward British party system is paralleled in France by the struggle between clericals and anti-clericals.[1]

In the second place, the form of the state is still open to question. Frenchmen are used to expecting not merely changes of government, but changes of the whole political regime. The British practice of revolutionizing the reality, while retaining the name and the façade, is reversed in France: there the fundamentals of life continue with comparatively little change over large regions of the country, while the political surface is immensely volatile. The stability and resilience of French life below that surface are unfortunately less striking than the apparent chaos at the top. The well-known story of the Paris bookseller regretting that he could not supply a copy of the constitution ' because we do not deal in periodical literature ' is, after all, over a hundred years old: its modern counterpart could be seen in the huge posters in the Metro in the summer of 1948—' The Republics pass: X's paint remains.'

Thirdly, though the political form of the state may be open to

---

[1] J. E. C. Bodley, *France*, i, p. 138 ; ii, p. 457.

question and change, its administrative structure has stood without fundamental alteration since the reforms of Napoleon. It is a tightly centralized system, based on a uniform pattern and closely controlled from Paris. The police, in particular, are under the direct authority of the ministry of the Interior. The degree of central control involved is far greater than in Britain, where similar complaints are heard. Moreover, the powers of the French police are much greater than those of the British. The centralized administrative and police system is reinforced by a centralized judicial organization under the ministry of Justice, and protected by an army much stronger than the British, for France has three land frontiers. The Vichy leaders found the seizure of power a relatively simple matter, for in the words of Deschanel 'We have the Republic on top and the Empire underneath.'

The Frenchman's approach to the problem of political authority is consequently shaped by three crucial factors: a political struggle which has always been waged with sectarian bitterness and thoroughness, sparing no sector of the country's organized life: an experience of governments abusing their authority to maintain their position: and an immensely powerful administrative machine, which provides a standing temptation to such abuse. There is a latent totalitarianism in the French attitude to politics, which makes French democrats fear the power of government, and regard it as a source of potential dangers rather than of potential benefits.

The historical factors are reinforced by geographic and demographic ones. The stationary population and the experience of an invasion in every generation have both engendered an uncertainty about the future which provides fertile soil for defeatism and disillusionment. British observers who see in this state of mind further confirmation of their country's moral superiority might reflect that our own illusions, wishful thinking and ill-timed fits of conscience were largely responsible for failing to avoid two wars in which, on both occasions, the French paid a far heavier price in lives lost, in resources destroyed, and in domestic unity compromised.

Most of all, France is still, politically speaking, a country of small enterprise. The importance of agriculture is very much greater than in Britain: France has only one industrial worker for every agricultural worker, while Britain has nine. Moreover, small towns and small industry still predominate. There are sixty-one towns with a population of 100,000 in Britain, only twenty-two in France. Twenty years ago, 60 per cent. of French industrial workers were still employed by firms having less than twenty workers. In 1946, almost half the population lived in agricultural communities.[2] Strictly, France is not, as is

---

[2] 9,100,000 out of a working population of 20,500,000 lived in rural communes where over 20 per cent. were engaged in agriculture. 6,500,000 of these 9,000,000 worked in agriculture themselves. A further 1,250,000 lived in rural communes where less than 20 per cent. were employed in agriculture. *Bulletin mensuel de statistique*, October 1952, p. 44.

sometimes claimed, a peasant country—the peasants are not a majority of the population though they are a large and very influential segment of it. But her atomized, small-scale structure promotes political individualism, strong local loyalties, and a political psychology more adapted to resistance than to positive construction. It reinforces the old tendency to *incivisme*, the lack of civic consciousness which makes so many Frenchmen regard the state as an enemy personified in the tax-collector and the recruiting sergeant.

This picture is gradually being changed by the growth of industry, by the importation of a huge immigrant population, and more recently by the recovery of the birth-rate. But the modifications are only regional. There are indeed areas where a comparatively modern industrial structure predominates, and where a genuine proletariat has been formed, without a trace of a peasant or artisan outlook. These regions are growing in size and influence. But they do not yet set the tone for the country's politics, which is still derived predominantly from the more traditional, more backward areas.

2. FRANCE AND BRITAIN: POLITICAL ATTITUDES

DIFFERENCES so deep-rooted explain why few of the political axioms of British politics hold good across the Channel. Even the vocabulary may be most misleading. Words like ' Right ' and ' Left ' have quite different connotations in the two countries. In 19th- and 20th-century France the dominant groups were the bourgeoisie and the peasantry, and they owed their position to the Revolution. It was indeed the heritage of revolution that they were determined to conserve. This was the basic source of the curious contradiction between their words and their deeds—revolutionary language in the political field, conservative actions in the social. Three issues were involved simultaneously: the 18th-century conflict between rationalism and Catholicism, the 19th-century struggle of democracy against authoritarian government, and the 20th-century dispute between employer and employed.) Under the Third Republic the first two in practice merged. On the Continent the terms Right and Left define positions in relation to this political and philosophical struggle, which turns in normal times on the question of church schools, and in crises on the structure of the regime.) The contest over the distribution of the national income provides a new topic of division, which has cut the political Left in two ever since 1848. Thus where Britain had two major political attitudes, France had at least three. The clerical and conservative Right was opposed by a socialist Left, itself, since the rise of the Communist party, internally divided by the deepest fissure of all. But between these two relatively straightforward positions there had to be accommodated the great amorphous mass of the peasantry and small business men, who were social and economic conservatives, but nevertheless ardent Republicans and anti-clericals.

This body of opinion was represented above all by the Radical party, which dominated French politics between 1900 and 1940.

Since Left and Right divided on issues other than those predominant in Britain, it is not surprising that they had a different electoral basis. The equation between industry and the party of the Left, agriculture and the party of the Right is not valid in France. The agrarian Midi is the stronghold of the former, industrial Lorraine votes regularly for the latter. The Socialists first became an important party in the election of 1893: their highest percentage of votes in the provinces was in the agricultural Cher department.[3] In June 1951 the Communist vote exceeded 40 per cent. in three constituencies—one in the Paris suburbs and two in the rural centre, Creuse and Corrèze. The reputation of the Right as more nationalist and more concerned with defence than the Left, though very dubious before 1890 or after 1935, nevertheless has helped to win them the allegiance of the industrial departments on the eastern frontier.

This persistence of the old issues reflects the failure of the industrial workers to impose their own demands on the consciousness of politicians and the public, as the main subject-matter of politics. They have failed partly through sheer lack of numbers, partly because of weakness in organization, which can in turn be traced back to the small scale of French industry and to the individualism of its employees, and partly also because governments are more responsive to the rural vote. The towns divided on class lines and there seemed little prospect of affecting that division by political means: the Church had almost abandoned the urban population as a lost cause. The dominant groups of the Third Republic, the Radicals and their allies, drew their strength from the countryside and small towns, where individualism flourished; they had little following in the urbanized regions, where the economy was changing, the division between proletariat and bourgeoisie was sharpening, and a new and more highly organized type of politics was developing.

The attitude towards government differs as profoundly as political behaviour or political terminology. Habits remain powerful which were formed in an age when politics were a luxury, remote from the realities of day-to-day life. There was no tradition of independent local government to breed an attitude of responsibility. The country's governing personnel was always recruited, far more than in Britain, from the professions and the intellectuals, and far less from business men, farmers, or workers;[4] the more theoretical and unreal character of the issues was both cause and consequence of this situation. For there is a curious blend of idealism and cynicism in the characteristic

---

[3] Bodley, ii, p. 465. Names of departments are shown in Map 1.
[4] Bodley, ii, pp. 157–62. At the turn of the century, more than half the deputies were drawn from the professional classes, while only a fifth were dependent upon agriculture, industry or commerce—the occupations of five-sixths of the electorate.

French attitude to political programmes—an idealism which attaches more importance to the symbolic value of a proposal than to its practical effect, a cynicism which remains unshakably confident that nothing will ever really be done. ' It is well to speak of reforms, but dangerous to put them into practice.' [5] And when, after 1919, the daily life of millions of Frenchmen became more intimately affected by the decisions of politicians, the traditional outlook had become too deeply rooted to be shaken off in a year or a decade.

Moreover, for the reasons discussed above, France is a much less ' integrated ' country than Britain. The internal divisions go deeper, and the feeling of community is less widespread. The Republic one and indivisible was defended with such passion precisely because the centrifugal forces were so strong. French observers frequently deplore the *incivisme* of their fellow-countrymen. But it is important to be clear what is implied by this convenient term. It is not a synonym for bad citizenship; the British or American tendency to undue self-satisfaction may be tempered by recalling the crushing burden of military service, borne by every Frenchman during the decades when conscription was unthinkable in Westminster or in Washington. *Incivisme* is rather an attitude of civic indiscipline—or individualism—in domestic affairs. The traditional French reluctance to pay taxes is only the most obvious example of a general attitude of resistance to power and its holders. Where the instinctive British answer to a governmental demand has been positive, a response of co-operation, the traditional French answer has been negative, a response of hostility.[6] The least agreeable aspect of this outlook is seen in economic matters, where it is reinforced by the characteristic suspicion and tight-fistedness of the peasantry. But the same contrariness protects the individual against oppression, inspires resistance to an occupying enemy, and produces those movements of indignation and protest which arise whenever authority is gravely abused. Alain, the most influential of Radical philosophers, summed up his attitude in the title of one of his books, *Le Citoyen contre les pouvoirs*. Thus, the instability which so appals Anglo-Saxon observers (who greatly exaggerate its real importance) is accepted by democratic Frenchmen as the price which a country with their history and traditions must pay for freedom. Governments can never be trusted and must always be checked; their aims and methods are alike questionable. ' The State is not a referee but a player—and probably a dirty player.' [7]

The constitution of the Fourth Republic is not an important cause of the weakness of French government. Rather it is a symptom; its imperfections of detail matter not in themselves, but because of this absence of a will to govern and to accept government. Nor is it

---
[5] Quoted by André Siegfried, *Tableau des partis en France*, p. 76.
[6] See David Thomson, *Democracy in France* (1st ed.), pp. 14–7.
[7] From a broadcast by Professor D. W. Brogan.

sufficient to complain that the French character is too stupid or too intellectual, too selfish or too utopian, too intransigent or too fond of *combinazioni*, to be capable of managing democratic institutions. The French, like the rest of us, are the prisoners of their past; and the outside observer must endeavour to preserve the attitude of Spinoza: ' Do not laugh, do not weep—try to understand.'

3. THE THIRD REPUBLIC

THE Third Republic was established in 1875 by one vote, in an Assembly with a majority of monarchists who could not agree on a king. It never received the genuine allegiance of its opponents. In the *Ralliement* of the 1890's, the Catholic Church made its peace with the regime. But even afterwards, as the Dreyfus case vividly showed, most Frenchmen of the Right instinctively sympathized with the violent attacks on democracy launched by men like Charles Maurras. Maurras himself lived to become an outspoken apologist for the Vichy regime, and to describe his own sentence of life imprisonment at the liberation as ' the revenge of Dreyfus.'

For though Great Britain has many conservatives (in all parties) who prefer to make progress slowly, it is happily free of real reactionaries. France is not. Men who condemn all that was done in the years following 1789 cannot simply be dismissed as unrepresentative cranks. Fifty years ago an English commentator observed that ' France is the land of political surprises, where lost causes come to life again '. Twenty years ago the most acute of French political writers pointed out that every regime of the past retained its partisans, awaiting the opportunity to reassert their claims to power.[8] New social strata overlaid the old ones but did not destroy them. In 1940 the chance came, and a vast body of opinion showed that it found its true leaders in the men of Vichy—not indeed in the Lavals and Déats, but in the men whose philosophy was summed up in Marshal Pétain's perhaps apocryphal remark, ' France will never be great again until the wolves are howling round the doors of her villages.' [9]

What is at stake in the French political struggle is thus more than certain specific issues of economic or educational, or even of foreign policy. It is the whole framework within which these specific issues should be tackled. To Republicans, the heritage of the Revolution means political freedom, the responsibility of the rulers to the ruled: freedom of opportunity, the chance to rise to the top—and in practice a preference for rulers drawn from the ' under-privileged ' : freedom from clerical domination, freedom to own one's own land. The Right stands for authoritarian government, for the rule of the wealthy and respectable, for clericalism and landlordism. It is understandable

---

[8] Bodley, ii, p. 352. Siegfried, pp. 199–200.
[9] Quoted by J. Galtier-Boissière, *Mon journal pendant l'occupation.*

that for electoral purposes it is essential to look and sound 'Left': it has indeed become almost a recognized rule of French politics that a party adds the word *gauche* to its title at the moment when it contracts an alliance with the Right. Candidates of the Right have been known to disguise themselves under the label of Independent Socialists. Just before the war the most conservative group in the Senate was named the *Gauche républicaine*. Often when a new parliamentary assembly is elected there is a noisy quarrel over the seating arrangements, the party allocated the benches on the right protesting vigorously at this monstrous misrepresentation of its political position—as the R.P.F. protested successfully when the Council of the Republic reassembled in 1948, and unsuccessfully when the second National Assembly met in July 1951.

In the politics of the hustings it was the danger from the Right that played the principal part, but in parliamentary politics the danger from the Left, the Socialist pressure which split the republican majority, became more and more important during the present century. French politics came to focus on these two threats, that from the Right against the Republic, and that from the Left against property. Their tone was therefore overwhelmingly defensive.[10] Moreover, for the historical reasons already discussed, the dominant section of opinion, which feared both threats about equally, was intensely suspicious of the power of the government, and remained so even after capturing it. Two Napoleons had overthrown the Republic, two other generals (MacMahon and Boulanger) had more recently tried to do so; so Alain's ideal minister was Camille Pelletan, minister of Marine in the Combes administration from 1902 to 1905, who systematically disregarded the views of his professional advisers. The results were unfortunate for the navy but, in Alain's view, essential for the regime: the leading intellectual on the Republican side might, indeed, have made his own the slogan of his great enemy Maurras—' *Politique d'abord* '. In 1909 Alain wrote:

> In France there are a great many radical electors, a certain number of radical deputies and a very small number of radical ministers: as for the heads of the civil service, they are all reactionaries. He who properly understands this has the key to our politics.[11]

And this remark was made by the philosopher of the party in power.

Familiarity with office did not change the Radicals' outlook fundamentally. They continued to use their position to weaken the institutions of government, and to thwart the progress of powerful personalities. In 1900 it had been observed that the Republicans

> use all the force of governmental machinery to crush men of parts who seem apt to win popular favour.[12]

---

[10] David Thomson, *Democratic ideal in France and England*, p. 59.
[11] Alain (Émile Chartier), *Éléments d'une doctrine radicale* (4th ed.), p. 25.
[12] Bodley, i, p. 328.

In 1940 this attitude had not altered. The Left, alarmed at having produced Clemenceau in 1917, had made certain that he should have no successor.[13] Promotion went to safe men of the type who had formed the Tiger's cabinet, and whom he had described as 'the geese who saved the Capitol'.[14]

The weakness of government was only partly due to this hostility to strong personalities. It was also the result of many institutional barriers which had been set up in the cabinet's path. The electoral system, as will be shown later, promoted political individualism. The constitution allowed the President, with the consent of the Senate, to dissolve the Chamber : but President MacMahon's dissolution for partisan purposes in 1877 had so discredited this weapon that no successor ever dared make the attempt. Consequently the deputies, knowing they could count on four years before they would have to face the electors again, were free to overthrow ministries with impunity. The working of Parliament was based on committees of specialists, which developed a point of view and a prestige of their own, and whose views the Chamber naturally tended to follow. These might well become nests of hostility to governmental plans, and since the leaders of the committees were almost *ex officio* potential ministers, with an interest in upsetting the government and taking its place, it was very likely that they would in practice behave as critics rather than as allies. Procedural rules left the ministry in a position far weaker than in Britain; it had no control of parliamentary time, the President of the Chamber was far weaker than the Speaker of the House of Commons, and devices like the interpellation seemed to have (and had) been invented for the express purpose of keeping the government powerless to escape from the domination of the deputies. Above all there was the Senate, that powerful and sober second chamber which had been carefully insulated from the dangerous control of universal suffrage, and which stood guard to check any 'hasty' legislation, or any over-presumptuous cabinet, with which the Chamber failed to deal. The governmental system of the Third Republic was indeed

> a machine so well provided with brakes and safety-valves that it comes slowly to a state of immobility.[15]

Yet even the institutional devices were not the main reason for the weakness of French government. That weakness was due in part to the excessive provision of brakes, but even more to the absence of sufficient motive power. It was because there was no majority for action in the country that there was no pressure strong enough to overcome the resistance, which found so many points of advantage in the constitutional framework. This became very apparent at the turn

---

[13] D. W. Brogan, introduction to Alexander Werth, *Twilight of France*, p. xvi.
[14] Quoted J. Hampden Jackson, *Clemenceau and the Third Republic*, p. 170.
[15] Brogan, *loc. cit.*, p. vi.

of the century, when the Radicals and their allies, including most of the Socialists, had an anti-clerical programme to enact. They organized a steering committee, the *Délégation des gauches*, which dominated the Chamber. Since a majority was ready to support its instructions, it could overcome the hostility of committees or interpellators without the least difficulty. The ministry lasted for three years, and wielded an authority as great as that of a British government —because there was for once a real political objective, capable of rallying a real majority. But such a programme had to be political in the narrow sense of the term. The industrial workers were neither numerous nor organized enough to attract similar support for their own demands. The political pattern of the Third Republic was therefore clearly marked: at election times the two wings of the political Left came together to defend the Republic, but once in power they divided over economic and social policy.[16] Reduced to its simplest, indeed over-simplified expression, the peasants would not pay taxes to facilitate reforms from which the industrial workers would benefit. So Chambers, like individual politicians, regularly began their careers with a strong inclination to the Left, and ended them with a strong inclination to the Right—indeed it was made a complaint against the Fourth Republic that this traditional process occurred less smoothly between 1946 and 1951 than had been the case in the past.

The basic reason for the weakness of French government was thus the contentment of the dominant section of opinion. This central block, Centre or even Right in British terminology, but Left in the Continental sense, was wholly negative in outlook, equally opposed to clerical reaction and to socialist experiment, neither wanting nor expecting anything from governmental activity. Its aim indeed was to prevent action, of which it was almost sure to disapprove. Its method of achieving that aim was to keep the government weak and unable to take dangerous steps: and its principal instrument was the Senate, controlled by the moderate wing of the Radical party (older and less subject to electoral pressure than their colleagues in the Chamber) who steadily ejected any ministry which leant too far in the direction of either clericalism or socialism. This situation explains why governments changed so frequently and policies so little: as early as 1875, indeed, Laboulaye had described France as 'a tranquil country with agitated legislators'[17] A fairly self-sufficient, small-scale economy allowed a kind of separation between public and private life to develop. The former had no day-to-day effect on the existence of the ordinary voter, who could judge the behaviour of his deputy by theoretical, doctrinaire standards; the type of question which excited politicians was whether the navy ought to celebrate Good Friday, or

---

[16] See Siegfried, pp. 125–6, for one of many descriptions of this process.
[17] Bodley, i, p. 57. (See Index for brief biographical notes on persons named.)

whether the army should supply guards of honour for civil as well as religious funerals.[18]

The Radicals, as Alain's remark makes clear, suspected all governments because they feared that ministers might fall under the corrupting influence of a reactionary administration. Consequently they were determined to keep the executive strictly subordinate to the legislature, and to overthrow cabinets on the least excuse. The results were paradoxical. Few ministers had time to get to know their departments, or authority to make themselves respected there, so that if a long-term policy were ever developed in a given sector of government, it could only originate from the feared and suspected officials.[19] In its anxiety not to leave a free hand to the executive, Parliament had insisted on taking all decisions itself. But when the financial and economic difficulties of the inter-war years called for measures that were electorally unpopular, no majority for them could be found: the only solution that the deputies could devise was to hand over to the government extensive powers to legislate by decree. Democratic government seemed to mean paralysis, so the capacity for action was restored by suspending democracy.

By the later 'thirties, the system was breaking down. Economic and international crises insistently demanded stronger government. Politics had a real and evident impact on the everyday life of the nation. But the subordination of the executive was too deeply implanted in French political habits to be abandoned, except by the back-door of emergency powers with a time-limit. From February 1930 to February 1934 the country had fourteen ministries. When the Germans entered the Rhineland France had a caretaker government, awaiting a general election, and therefore too timid to call up reservists. When they marched into Austria, France was in the middle of a ministerial crisis. During the Munich episode there was indeed a government, but there was no Parliament; M. Daladier, having been granted his special powers, had sent the Chamber off on holiday, and was able to conduct his policy without being embarrassed by the criticisms of the deputies. ' Defeat did not kill the Third Republic, it merely drew attention to the fact that it was dead '.

---

[18] In May 1951, urgent parliamentary business was delayed by the insistence of the Socialists that, since the Assembly was not to sit on Ascension Day, it must not sit on Labour Day either.

[19] See for example Pierre Maillaud, *France*, p. 39 ; Joseph Barthélemy, *Le Gouvernement de la France*, pp. 142–3 ; Michel Augé-Laribé, *La Politique agricole de la France*, pp. 386–91—referring respectively to foreign, educational, and agricultural policy.

Chapter 2

THE WAR AND ITS AFTERMATH, 1940-1947

THE war shook France out of the economic stagnation and political paralysis which had marked the last years of the Third Republic. Defeat provided the opportunity for a counter-revolution, directed not only against the working-class movement, but also against the democratic regime itself. The Resistance was a revolutionary response to this challenge, and its triumph produced an entirely new political situation. But the new-found national unity was quickly dissipated. The Communist drive for power forced all groups to take sides. During 1945 and 1946 there proceeded simultaneously a national effort at indispensable economic reconstruction, and a bitter political ' cold war ' between the ruling parties, which dominated the contemporaneous attempts to frame a new constitution. When the Communists went out of office in May 1947, the regime gradually returned to normal, and the political practices of the past slowly revived. But to understand the developments of more recent years, the changes in the political scene and in the constitutional structure between 1938 and 1947 must be briefly surveyed.

1. POLITICAL FORCES, 1938-45

BEFORE the second German war the Radicals were politically dominant. Indispensable to every government, they were accustomed to ally with the Socialists at election times, but to drift into coalition with the Right during the course of each parliament's life. The strength of the party lay partly in its representativeness. It appealed to all those who ' wore their hearts on the left and their wallets on the right '. Moreover, it was so loose in its organization and discipline that members with very different opinions could join: the Radicals in the Senate, such as Caillaux, were far more conservative than those in the Chamber, such as the youthful Daladier. Another great asset was the permanent hold on power which its pivotal position gave it; the premiership and ministry of the Interior were generally in its hands. This gave the party the opportunity to train a large number of skilful and experienced politicians, as did on a lower level its extensive hold on local government.

But the Radical party had the defects of its qualities. The body of opinion represented by it was broad but shallow. The attitude of the Radical voters, negative, unconstructive and timid, handicapped the party in a period of crisis. Loose discipline allowed it to attract support from many quarters, but at the expense of diluting its membership so far that it almost ceased to be a party in the British sense, and sank to the status partly of an electioneering machine and partly of a social club. Its hold on power meant that it attracted the professional politician and the less desirable type of hanger-on: few were the political and financial scandals in which Radicals were not involved. And though it had the opportunity to train its young men, it used its chances not to promote strong personalities but to suppress them: the Radicals positively preferred mediocrity to ability.

The Left until 1936 consisted effectively of the Socialist party. Once revolutionary and anti-militarist, the Socialists had in this century settled down to accept the Republic, and were indeed among the most vocal and orthodox defenders of the regime. Until 1936 they refused to take office; when they changed their minds, on becoming the strongest party in the *Front populaire* majority, they were already feeling the breath of competition on their Left. The Communist party, under-represented by the electoral system, leapt at that election from a dozen parliamentary seats to seventy, thanks to its alliance with the Socialists and Radicals. It was now the turn of the Communists to refuse office, offering to the Blum government only the cold comfort of ' support without participation '.

The Right, like the Socialists, were too weak to win an electoral majority. Their position rested, not on votes, but on the sympathies of the influential individuals and groups whose outlook and interests they represented—powerful soldiers like Pétain, powerful bureaucrats like Chiappe, powerful millionaires like Coty, influential writers like Maurras. During the 'thirties the Right became more and more tainted with pro-fascism. Domestically, strong Fascist leagues grew up, of which the *Croix de feu* was the largest but the most moderate. Abroad, the entire Right demanded a policy favourable to Mussolini's Italy and to Franco's cause in Spain, and many of them came to see even the predominance of Nazi Germany as a lesser evil than the rule of a Jewish Socialist prime minister in Paris.

The attractive power of Fascism was not confined to the Right. Its most extreme exponent was the former Communist leader Doriot, and the ' Neo-Socialist ' Déat was hardly less violent. Moreover, the successive Fascist victories sapped the determination and paralysed the will of their opponents. Most Radicals and Right-wing supporters, and fully half the Socialists, feared the consequences of active opposition to Germany: and the Communists, who alone had stood unitedly for resistance at all costs, changed sides when the Nazi-Soviet pact was signed. But long before this, at the time of Munich, anti-Communism had become the main bond between the pacifist forces and the main motive of government policy. And, right up to the moment of defeat, the class war at home was for a large part of the French political world more important than the war against Germany.

The shock of defeat was fatal to the regime. An overwhelming parliamentary majority conferred full powers upon Marshal Pétain as chief of the state—the very name of Republic was abandoned. The Vichy regime was based essentially on the Right-wing sector of opinion, which soon showed that it found there (not, of course, among the German puppets in Paris) the political leadership it really sought. But the Marshal's first cabinet included also two prominent members of the Socialist party, an assistant secretary of the C.G.T. (the trade union federation), and a Radical ex-premier. Conversely, when General de Gaulle issued his appeal on 18 June 1940, individuals of all opinions and of all political origins responded, from the Socialists to the *Croix de feu*[1]; but his support from the Right came from individuals only. In the Resistance inside France, the Communists began to take the lead after 22 June 1941; many Socialists and even more Catholic democrats (hitherto politically unorganized) also participated, along with smaller numbers from other groups.

The Resistance, though directed against a foreign occupier, had all the hallmarks of a revolutionary movement; and at the liberation a revolutionary change was apparent. The old political leadership was repudiated. The Radicals were blamed for the events leading up to the war, for their weakness and lack of responsibility in power, and for their not particularly heroic part under the occupation. Their old Right-wing rivals were still more completely discredited by the Vichy episode. Thus two of the three main groups in the pre-war political scene were under a heavy cloud, while most of the old leaders as individuals, and all of them as a group, had suffered a disastrous loss of prestige. New men rose to the top, ranging—as in any revolution—from inexperienced idealists to more or less scrupulous and patriotic adventurers. But the new movements did not acquire an independent political existence. Three political parties succeeded in canalizing the new enthusiasm.

The Communists earned in votes the reward of their resistance record after 1941, becoming the largest single party, and profited in power from their patient work in the trade unions after 1936, capturing control of the C.G.T. Of equal importance was the sudden emergence of a new party, the *Mouvement républicain populaire*, based on an old tradition of Catholic democracy which had never before found effective political expression, and on a new generation of progressive Christians who had 'found themselves' in the resistance movement. Between these two, the old Socialist leaders hoped to rejuvenate their party, and to make it the link and leader of all the new forces.

In these forgotten years of 1944–45, General de Gaulle was earning distinction at home as the first head of a French government to bring Communists into his administration, and abroad as the chief prota-

---

[1] The Communists denounced him as a hireling of the City of London. See A. Rossi, *Physiologie du parti communiste français*, pp. 86–7, 90–3, 220.

gonist of the middle way between Washington and Moscow—with a suspicion of a preference for the latter. M. Vincent Auriol, later President of the Republic, was General de Gaulle's chief constitutional adviser and agent in dealing with the politicians. The Communists were seeking fusion of their party with the Socialists: the voters of the Right could only find an electoral home with M.R.P.: the General was on intimate terms with Socialists and M.R.P., but sharply divided from the Conservatives[2] and Radicals.

2. POLITICS AND CONSTITUTIONAL REFORM, 1945–47

THE Third Republic effectively came to an end on 10 July 1940, when the Chamber and Senate, sitting together as a National Assembly empowered to revise the constitution, registered the suicide of the regime by voting full powers to Marshal Pétain as chief of the state. The rival government of General de Gaulle established itself at Algiers in 1943. It gradually obtained the recognition of the allied powers, and took control in France in 1944. But until 21 October 1945 its authority was based on no formal or legal title.

On this date the French electorate had three decisions to take. Firstly they had to choose their political representatives. Secondly they had to decide, by referendum, whether the newly elected body should have powers to frame a new constitution. If their answer was negative, the new house would simply become a Chamber of Deputies, a senatorial election would take place according to the pre-war procedure, and the new parliament might or might not proceed to revise the constitution in the manner prescribed in 1875. If the electorate's reply was affirmative, as in fact it was, they had another question to answer. For General de Gaulle's provisional government was unwilling to confer complete power on a single directly elected body, unchecked by any rival institution. It had therefore proposed a scheme to limit the powers of the Constituent Assembly, which must submit its draft constitution to a further referendum within seven months, at which date its authority would expire. The electorate, if it decided to create a Constituent Assembly by its first reply, would also have to accept or reject these proposals of the government.

The first question produced an overwhelming vote of no confidence in the Third Republic. Only the Radicals campaigned in favour of a return to the system of which they had been the principal beneficiaries, and even among their attenuated following, half were not prepared to support them in this. The Assembly was given constituent status by

---

[2] The term Conservative is used to denote the small and shifting right-wing groups such as P.R.L. (*Parti républicain de la liberté*), the Peasant party, the Independent Republicans, and the dissident Gaullists. See below, Chapter 8. Without a capital letter, "conservative" refers to a social and economic outlook, which most Radicals share.

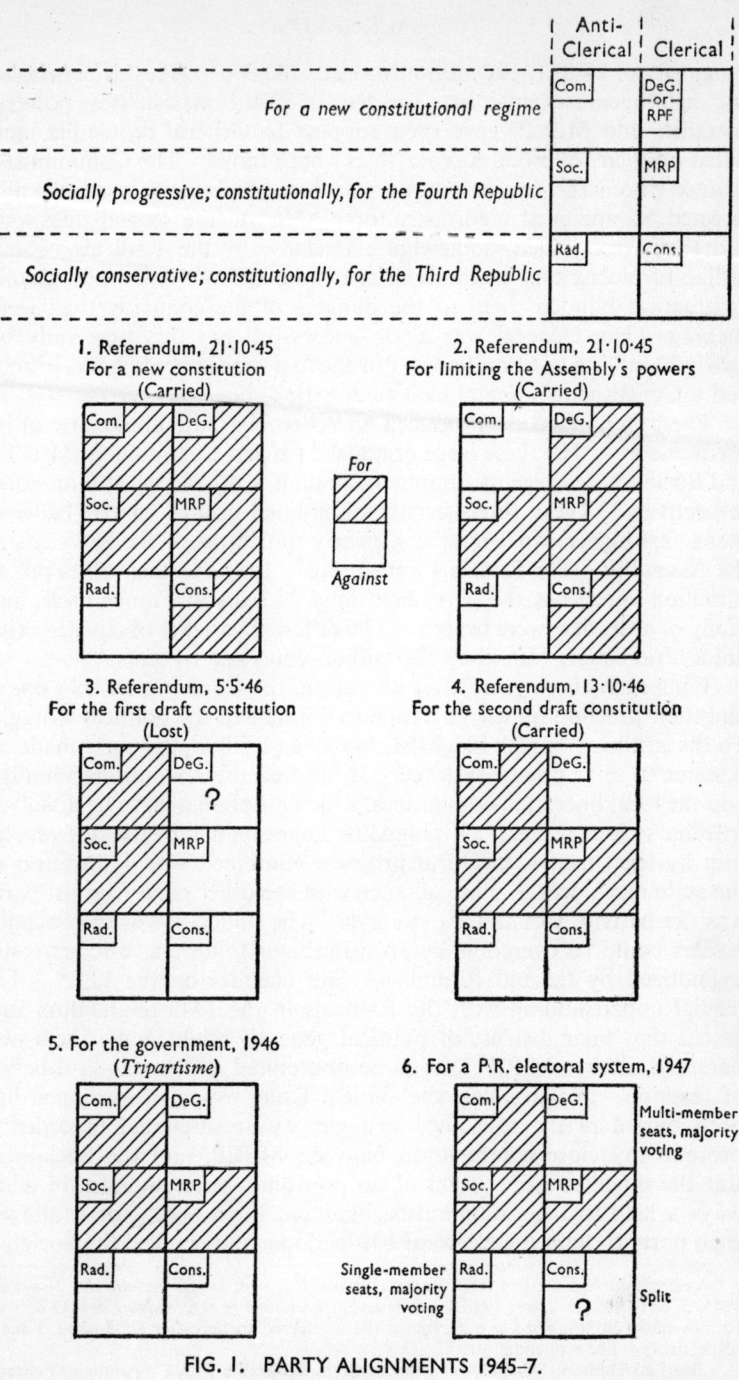

FIG. I. PARTY ALIGNMENTS 1945-7.

a majority of 25 to 1, 18½ million votes to 700,000.[3] But this enormous but heterogeneous majority divided over the Assembly's powers. Socialists and M.R.P. gave their support to General de Gaulle, and called on their followers to vote ' Yes ' both times. The Communists, against whom the restrictions on the Assembly's powers were really directed, campaigned vigorously for a ' No ' to the second question; and they were joined, somewhat illogically, by the Radicals, whose dislike of plebiscitary methods in principle, and of General de Gaulle in practice, blinded them to the dangers of the company they were keeping. The General was again successful, but this time only by nearly 13 million to 6½ million. For the first time in her history, France had a Constituent Assembly with limited powers.

The general election produced an Assembly quite unlike any of its predecessors. The three large organized parties, Communists, M.R.P., and Socialists, emerged triumphant, polling 5, 4¾ and 4½ million votes respectively. These three strictly disciplined groups shared between them, in roughly equal numbers, nearly four-fifths of the 586 seats in the Assembly. The Radicals were routed; they and their allies polled 2 million votes, but the party held only 24 seats in France itself, and many of its leaders were beaten. The different varieties of Conservative did a little better, with about 2½ million votes and 64 seats.

For nearly three years after liberation, the Communists held office, and their pressure on the government dominated the political struggle. To the irritation of men like MM. Marty and Tillon, the party made no attempt to seize power by force. It allowed the revolutionary militia and the local liberation committees, which it dominated, to be dissolved without serious protest. It pinned its hopes on completing the revolution by legal means, electoral progress combined with infiltration of the state machine. A close alliance with the other great Marxist party was the basis of Communist strategy. The reluctance of the Socialist leaders could be overcome by arousing their followers, who were still hypnotized by the old formula of ' no enemies on the Left '. The partial understanding with the Radicals in the 1945 referendum suggested that their distrust of political generals might make them also potential allies. M.R.P. was to be discredited as the standard bearer of reaction; in particular, the clerical issue, which many hoped had been buried in the resistance struggle, was resuscitated in order to prevent any close combination between M.R.P. and the Socialists.[4] But the much-abused system of proportional representation, in many ways a help to the Communists, hindered them here; for it allowed each party to fight the electoral battle alone, and enabled the Socialists

---

[3] Voting figures are taken from Raoul Husson, *Élections et referendums des 21 octobre 1945, 5 mai 1946, et 2 juin 1946*: and Husson, *Élections et referendums des 13 octobre, 10 novembre, 24 novembre et 8 décembre 1946*, referred to hereafter as Husson, i and ii respectively. See Appendix V.

[4] See Léo Hamon, ' Origines et chances de la Troisième Force ', *Politique*, February 1948, pp. 103–5.

to escape being forced into a Marxist coalition which might have alienated them irrevocably from M.R.P.[5]

Immediately after the election, General de Gaulle reconstituted his government, basing it on the support of all the main parties. But a few weeks later, on 20 January 1946, he suddenly resigned, declaring that the task of reconstruction was now complete. His real reason was his exasperation with the quarrels of the parties, and with the need to adapt his policy to their demands. Like some other war leaders, he was more interested and more knowledgeable in military than in economic affairs; reconstruction of the army was his most cherished objective, and it was the interference of party politics in this sphere that precipitated his departure.[6] He considered carrying out a *coup d'état*,[7] but rejected the idea like a good democrat, and even allowed MM. Blum and Vincent Auriol to dissuade him from putting his case to the public in a broadcast address.[8]

General de Gaulle's departure inaugurated a year of *tripartisme*— the rule of a coalition government of the three main parties. Its first head was M. Félix Gouin, the Socialist President of the Constituent Assembly. But the three parties associated in the government (allied would be too strong a word) were unable to reach agreement on the constitutional issue. The Socialists, having failed to arrange a compromise agreeable to both Communists and M.R.P., were obliged to choose. They joined the Communists in voting the draft constitution on 19 April 1946 against the opposition of all the other principal parties, and in campaigning for it in the referendum. Its opponents attacked the draft itself (which conferred virtually unchecked power on a single chamber), the electoral law associated with it, and the controversial preamble, especially the omission of the right to ' freedom of education ' (the guarantee of the Catholic schools). But their hostility was really directed against the sponsors, rather than against the provisions of the draft. They feared that acceptance would constitute a triumph for the Communists, consolidating both their alliance with the Socialists and their domination of that alliance.

The referendum of 5 May 1946 checked the steady Communist advance. For the first time in French history, the electorate answered ' No ' in a plebiscite. The draft constitution was rejected by a majority

---

[5] François Goguel, *France under the Fourth Republic*, pp. 61–2.
[6] The last straw was a large cut in the military budget, moved by the Socialists in order to embarrass the Communist minister responsible, but promptly taken up and carried by the Communists themselves.
[7] He has said so repeatedly: for example at the Vélodrome d'Hiver in February 1950, at a meeting of Gaullist politicians at Levallois-Perret in March 1951, and at the R.P.F. national council at Saint-Maur in July 1952. See *La France sera la France* (a collection of his statements published by the R.P.F. in 1951) pp. 31–3; *Le Monde*, 13 March 1951; *Le Rassemblement*, 11 July 1952.
[8] Gordon Wright, *Reshaping of French Democracy*, p. 131. The fullest account of the General's relations with the parties and with his cabinet is to be found in Chapters IV and V of this work.

of just over one million votes in a poll of 20 million; some Socialists had evidently disregarded the policy of their party and voted with the majority. The Socialists tried to recover the lost ground by a sharp reversal of policy and violent denunciations of the Communists. Nevertheless, in the general election of 2 June they were the principal losers. The Communists gained a little, but M.R.P. gained more. It emerged as the largest party, and its leader, M. Georges Bidault, replaced M. Gouin at the head of the tripartite government. An equally important sign of the shift of power was the replacement as minister of Finance of M. André Philip, a Socialist and a believer in a controlled economy, by M. Robert Schuman, one of the more conservative members of M.R.P.

During the referendum campaign General de Gaulle maintained complete silence; he did not even vote.[9] But after the referendum he emerged from his reserve. On 18 June, in a speech at Bayeux, he denounced the working of the regime, attacked the power of the parties, and expounded his own remedy of strong presidential rule—promptly nicknamed 'the Bayeux constitution'.[10] His open opposition presented a challenge to M.R.P., whose prestige was largely based on its reputation as the *parti de la fidélité* to de Gaulle. But the M.R.P. leaders believed that an unsatisfactory compromise was better than another controversial draft constitution, another rejection by referendum, and another seven months of provisional government. Until a constitution had been adopted there could be no relief from the pressure of elections a few weeks ahead, paralysing government action, and no hope of upsetting the coalition with the Communists. The chairman of M.R.P., M. Maurice Schumann, waged his vigorously anti-Communist election campaign in favour of the constitution under the slogan *Sortir du provisoire pour sortir du tripartisme*.

The Communists, taught by their defeat, and the Socialists alarmed at the idea of alliance with them, made enough last-minute concessions to win over M.R.P. But General de Gaulle, in his second principal speech at Épinal,[11] denounced the new proposals, to the vast embarrassment of the M.R.P. leaders: their paper, *L'Aube*, was driven into complicated verbal contortions to prove that the General's 'Frankly, no!' really meant 'By and large, yes!' The result of the referendum proved how well-founded their fears had been. The constitution was indeed adopted, but by a majority of only 9 million against 8 million. $8\frac{1}{2}$ million electors, just a third of the total, did not trouble to vote. It was very clear that the constitution was accepted not on its merits, but because the alternative was continued provisional government.

The Socialist and Communist parties alone had polled on 2 June

---

[9] *A.P.*, 1946, p. 161.
[10] The full text of the speech is quoted *ibid.*, pp. 534–9. See also *La France sera la France*, pp. 36, 51, 167.
[11] *A.P.*, 1946, p. 245: extracts in *La France sera la France*, pp. 16, 44, 169.

half a million more votes than were given in favour of the constitution on 13 October. Yet, since that date, M.R.P. with its 5½ million voters had changed sides. There was, therefore, a gap of 6 million between the earlier vote for the three parties, and the subsequent vote for the constitution they had formed. General de Gaulle had shown his power. But he was not yet ready himself to re-enter the political arena, and without his sponsorship the Gaullist Union, created by M. René Capitant to defend the ideas of the Bayeux constitution, had little success. The general election of 10 November again gave nearly three-quarters of the seats to the three main parties. M.R.P. lost the half-million votes which they had gained in June, and the Socialist decline continued. The Communists slightly increased their vote, again becoming the strongest party; but their real power diminished, for the Socialist defeat deprived the Marxist parties of their theoretical majority. The groups opposed to *tripartisme* at last adapted their tactics to the electoral system, and divided the constituencies between them; this particularly helped the Radicals, who, with their allies of the R.G.R., won 70 seats. There were 183 Communists, 166 M.R.P., 103 Socialists, and 74 Conservatives. This Assembly was to remain in being until 1951.

The end of *tripartisme* was now near. M.R.P. wanted to demonstrate its anti-Communism to the voters who had deserted it in the referendum; the Communists feared that they were losing their hold on the working class by staying in office. Since neither party would vote for the other's candidate, M. Thorez and M. Bidault in turn failed to secure the absolute majority of the Assembly, which they needed to be elected prime minister. The immediate problem was solved by the formation, on 16 December, of a one-party Socialist government under the veteran M. Léon Blum.

The general public was delighted to find a ministry which knew its own mind: the rival parties were less pleased. In January, the constitution was officially inaugurated by the election as President of the Republic of M. Vincent Auriol, who had succeeded M. Gouin as President of the Assembly a year before. M. Blum resigned, as is customary on the election of a new President, and a new coalition government was formed, under another Socialist, M. Ramadier. The Radical party, after a year in opposition, now returned to office and began its long climb back to power; but its influence was small, and the Ramadier ministry rested on the alliance of Socialists and M.R.P.

The Communists were increasingly uneasy partners. They were opposed to the other parties both on domestic issues, especially wages policy, and on colonial questions: there was a revolt in Madagascar, and the Indo-China war was just beginning. In March, their deputies (other than ministers) abstained in a vote of confidence on this issue, though the party stayed in office in the hope of influencing the government's foreign policy during the Foreign Ministers' conference at

Moscow. By May, France had aligned herself with the west, and a strike at the Renault works warned the Communists that their power in the trade unions was threatened. The whole party, including ministers, voted against the government on wages policy. The ministers refused to resign, and were dismissed from office on 5 May 1947—the most important date in the post-war history of France.

The Fourth Republic had won its 'battle of Prague'. It had taken the risk of admitting Communists into the government, but had, like Italy, escaped the fate of most countries which tried that gamble. The French Socialists had not been enticed into an alliance controlled by their rivals. The Communist party had been kept out of the key ministries, and had not penetrated the governmental machine sufficiently to paralyse it. It was not strong enough to seize power either in free elections or in a revolutionary situation. Its one great asset was its grip on the trade unions: and it was now to be seen whether France could be ruled against the opposition of its largest and best organized party, which commanded the allegiance of the bulk of the industrial working class.

A month earlier, General de Gaulle had re-entered politics. At Strasbourg on 7 April 1947 he appealed to all Frenchmen to rally to his *Rassemblement du peuple français*, a new, non-party movement which was to reform the constitution, combat the 'separatists' (the General's name for the Communist party) and regenerate the national life. His appeal met with a large response in the country. In the autumn the R.P.F. extended its activity to Parliament, setting up an 'inter-group' which all deputies (except Communists) were invited to join, while remaining members of their former parties. But Socialists and M.R.P. forbade their members to adhere, so that the new body consisted of old opponents of *tripartisme*, reinforced by a few M.R.P. dissidents who preferred the leadership of the General to that of the party.

3. SOCIAL CONFLICTS

THE events of 1947 changed the whole character of French politics. In every sphere, domestic, imperial, and international, there were adjustments or even reversals of policy—not necessarily for the better. The working of the regime changed still more sharply. Now that the cohesion of parties was no longer an indispensable means of self-defence against an imminent danger, their rigidity declined. Old individualist habits revived, and profoundly affected political behaviour and constitutional practice.

The creation of the inter-group and the beginning of active Communist opposition both occurred in the autumn of 1947. They opened a new phase of parliamentary life. The problem of the political regime had been dormant, save for occasional stirrings, for fifty years. Now it emerged once more into the forefront of controversy. The drastic solutions, 'people's democracy' leading to Communism, and presidential democracy leading perhaps to authoritarian rule from the Right, both enjoyed massive support in the country. In the Assembly the extreme groups combined in a negative coalition to make government impossible, and afterwards to fight out their own battle over the ruins of the parliamentary republic. Only by the alliance of all the middle parties, loyal to the classic forms of parliamentary rule, could a system of the familiar type be preserved.

Union of the centre groups was indispensable in the interests of the regime, and perhaps of their own survival. But even the constitution itself provoked disagreement between them; Socialists and M.R.P. had created the Fourth Republic, Radicals and many Conservatives still defended the Third. A graver weakness arose from the clash of party ambitions. The middle parties had a common interest in standing together against the oppositions. But this could not suppress their rivalries, or prevent the weaker Radical and Conservative groups, as their parliamentary bargaining position improved, pressing continually for a larger share in power. Nor was this merely a matter of jobs: the majority was deeply and genuinely divided on all questions of policy. If all British governments since the war had required the steady and simultaneous support of both Mr. Aneurin Bevan and Lord Beaverbrook perhaps some degree of instability might have been excused them.

The main cause of division was the economic problem, the way in which the national income was to be distributed. Its most acute aspect was the cost of living issue. In August 1947, it was estimated that the average French town worker spent three-quarters of his wages on food. For many reasons, rationing was much harder to work effectively in France than it was in Britain. Only the best administration can manage a rationing system efficiently and honestly; the British did not invariably stand the strain, and French standards were lower. Moreover, the British problem was very much easier. When half the food supply is brought in through the ports, the administration possesses a means of pressure on the domestic producer. But when nearly all comes from millions of small farmers, the task of extracting it, in the face of their reluctance, has baffled many governments, from Russians during the civil war to allied administrators in Germany.

The difficulties of economic policy in France are nevertheless due also, are perhaps even due primarily, to the reluctance of the ordinary Frenchmen to obey the state in economic matters. The occupation period, when resistance and sabotage were a national duty, reinforced old habits and spread them more widely. But it did not cause them. Resistance to taxation had for a generation made the country unable to raise enough revenue to balance her budget. Since deputies would not risk electoral disaster by voting adequate taxes, governments would not court parliamentary defeat by proposing them. They paid their way by inflation. The monetary problem dominated French politics in the inter-war years, as unemployment dominated British politics. Ultimately, its cause was economic *incivisme*—the determination of the better-off to evade their share of the national burdens. ' France has never found a government that could make Frenchmen as ready to give their money as they were to give their blood.'[12]

The remark that ' France is a land of excessive taxation, fortunately tempered by fraud ' is much older than the last war. But it is no less true of the Fourth Republic than of the Third. In 1948 the ministry of Finance raised £10,000,000 from a check of the tax returns of all Parisians owning American cars; three-quarters of them had been paying no income tax at all.[13] Officials estimate evasion of one tax at 20 per cent., of another at 30 to 50 per cent.[14] Governments have to rely on indirect taxation. The groups which can successfully defraud the treasury, the businessmen and the peasantry, greatly increased their share of the national income just after the war, while wage and salary earners, who could not escape, lost correspondingly. This increasing burden on those least able to bear it was the main cause of the recurring political crises; and it could never be tackled effectively because of the conflicting electoral interests of the centre parties. The one united ministry with a policy was the all-Socialist Blum government of December 1946; the other parties allowed it to survive for a month. Significantly, a public opinion poll found that 62 per cent. considered it the most successful cabinet since liberation,[15] though only 17½ per cent. of the voters supported the Socialist party.

In one form or another the economic problem has been responsible for the fall of most post-war governments. M. Ramadier, in November 1947, was swept out of office by the repercussions of the month's great strikes. M. Schuman's first ministry fell in July 1948 over the military budget, M. Marie's broke up in August over price policy, M. Schuman's second was defeated in September because the Conservatives objected to the appointment of a Socialist minister of Finance. Wages policy split M. Queuille's cabinet in October 1949 and M. Bidault's in February 1950; the latter was finally defeated in June over civil service pay. Throughout 1951 economic policy was in constant dispute within the successive governments; in January 1952 the second Pleven ministry was beaten when it tried to economize on the railways, in February the Faure cabinet was defeated when it proposed increased taxes, in December M. Pinay fell over his proposals to meet the social security

---

[12] *Manchester Guardian*, 6 September 1948.

[13] M. Pleven, *rapporteur* of the Finance committee, to the committee on fiscal reform: *Le Figaro*, 9 December 1948. M. Moch, minister of the Interior, at a Socialist conference: *Bulletin intérieur du parti socialiste* no. 39 (February 1949), p. 69.

[14] *Le Figaro*, 12–13 August 1950. M. Edgar Faure, secretary of the Budget, *J.O.*, 23 May 1950, p. 3814: he quoted an estimate of 3–400 milliards (£300–400 millions) for the total loss through fraud.

[15] *Sondages*, 1947, p. 38. See also Raymond Aron, *Le Grand Schisme*, p. 189.

deficit, and in May 1953 M. Mayer was overthrown on demanding special powers to economize by decree.

These different facets of economic policy all reflect one central theme: the distribution of the national income, and of the burdens and benefits of government expenditure, between wage and salary earners (at all levels) on the one hand, and businessmen and peasants on the other. The clash is partly between rich and poor, but even more between variable and fixed incomes. Small businesses have been growing since the war at a rate which shows better than any other index the advantages of a job in which taxes can be evaded and inflation made a source of profit. Peasants have always held a privileged position owing to their electoral influence.[16] The most passionate Radical and Conservative advocates of a liberal economy are enthusiasts for guaranteed prices and government-controlled markets in the agricultural sector.[17] Estimates differ widely, but all agree that the peasantry pay far less than their share of taxation: one estimate gives them 19 per cent. of the national income and 1·3 per cent. of the taxes paid.[18] The balance of town and country, and the technical inadequacy of France's small-scale industries, are at the root of the long-term economic problem. The bold attempt to remedy these deficiencies through the Monnet plan has entailed real sacrifices; and these have provoked stubborn political resistance, and persistent efforts to shift the burden.

Until 1948 prices rose steadily; either wages rose correspondingly, giving a further twist to the inflationary spiral, or wage stabilization led to strikes and a reinforcement of the Communist party. In 1949 and 1950, however, the heavy investments of the post-war years at length began to produce results. The national income rose, while prices remained stable—until the Korean war destroyed the equilibrium once again. At the same time the post-war governments made a real effort to finance their expenditure by taxes instead of by inflation: the proportion of the national income taken by the government has risen substantially since the war.[19] The ministries of the Fourth Republic may have lasted no longer than those of the Third, but they did try to tackle problems that their predecessors had shelved.

4. THE LINES OF POLITICAL DIVISION

THE economic problem tended to unite the parties which compete for

---
[16] Yet many French peasants and small businessmen are poor. Their excessive number, rather than their individual wealth, constitutes the real burden on the economy. See *Statistiques et études financières, supplément finances françaises* no. 18–1953, pp. 208–9, 215–6: and summaries in *Le Monde*, 6, 7–8 and 9 June 1953, and by Bertrand de Jouvenel in *Manchester Guardian*, 6 and 7 July 1953.

[17] See for example Aron, pp. 215–6; André Siegfried, *A.P.*, 1952, p. xi.

[18] Wright, p. 254. For other estimates see Aron, pp. 220–1: Dorothy Pickles, *French Politics*, pp. 247–8: Goguel, *op. cit.*, p. 191: and *Statistiques et études financières, loc. cit.*, p. 202, and the summaries cited above.

[19] See below, p. 256 n.

working-class votes, the Socialists and Communists, against those with no working-class clientèle, Radicals and Conservatives. M.R.P. at first stood with the parties of the Right in the hope of retaining the vast mass of conservative support which it had acquired at the liberation. But the foundation of the R.P.F. provided a rival centre, which attracted most of M.R.P.'s right-wing supporters. The latter was thus thrown back on the Catholic trade unions, and from 1948 onwards normally aligned itself in economic controversies with the Socialists. A few years later the R.P.F. in turn began to lose these right-wing supporters back to the old-fashioned Conservative groups. From 1950 onwards a tendency developed for the Gaullists to seek working-class votes, and sometimes to vote with the Left in support of working-class claims. But when M. Pinay rallied the conservative forces in 1952, he found widespread support in the R.P.F. ranks.

The economic problem was the most serious, but by no means the only cause of division between the centre parties, whose unity alone could keep a French government in being. Colonial and military questions often produced a similar alignment of forces, with the Socialists and, more hesitantly, many members of M.R.P. advocating conciliation of Indo-Chinese or North African nationalism, while Radicals and Conservatives demanded firm government and the maintenance of white rule. On such issues the Gaullists sided wholeheartedly with the Right. These questions divided the majority roughly on British lines, with a 'Fourth Force' of Conservatives and Radicals finding themselves often more in agreement on policy with the Gaullist opposition than with their 'Third Force' Socialist and M.R.P. partners.

But the relatively simple division into four groups, authoritarian and democratic conservatives, totalitarian and democratic socialists, leaves out of account a historical factor of the utmost importance, the clerical issue. To most foreign observers the problem of the church schools seems a trivial and absurdly inflated dispute. But to many Frenchmen education is as vital an issue as it was to Englishmen half a century ago. It symbolizes the attempt to mould the nation's life, either in a Catholic or in a secular spirit. And even those who feel less strongly, and would prefer a simpler political struggle of the type now familiar in Britain, know that in some regions the question of *laïcité is* still the real dividing line in politics.

No party can ignore the fundamental principles or prejudices of the bulk of its supporters. But this cleavage cuts right across the social and political divisions, splitting the 'Fourth Force' as well as (though less deeply than) the Third, and uniting most Radicals and all Socialists with the Communists, in a common hostility to the claims pressed alike by Conservatives, M.R.P., and R.P.F. This was the weapon used by the Communists, in 1945, to keep Socialists and M.R.P. apart. It destroyed the Schuman government in 1948, and made the Socialists ally with Radicals instead of M.R.P. in the subsequent senatorial elections—provoking a bitterness which gravely weakened the majority up to the 1951 election. Subsequently, it was by exploiting the church schools issue that the R.P.F., by alienating the Socialists from their former partners, finally broke the old majority.

Since politics turn on several different conflicts instead of one major one, no coherent majority can be found—either in the electorate, on behalf of a party, or in Parliament, to maintain a coalition for any length of time. Associates on one issue are bitter opponents on others.[20] M.R.P., for example, has worked with Socialists and Radicals in defending the regime against Communists and Gaullists, the Conservatives generally taking the former side. On matters involving working-class interests, and sometimes on colonial questions, it sympathizes with the Socialists and Communists; the Radicals and Conservatives are hostile, while the R.P.F., which long sided with the latter, became uncertain after the 1951 election. But over church schools, M.R.P. finds its friends (or competitors) among Gaullists and Conservatives, while the Socialists and nearly all the Radicals are associated with the Communists against it. And a situation so complicated puts a high premium on the arts of manœuvre, in which other, temporary combinations can be brought about. Thus tactical considerations often united M.R.P. with the Communists, against all the other parties, in defence of proportional representation; and early in 1952 Socialists and R.P.F. were professing very similar views on the problem of Germany.

The peculiarities of French government are thus caused by the country's history. The battle against the Church and the struggle for political freedom are still political issues in the middle of the twentieth century, and they split public opinion on lines different from those imposed by the contemporary social and economic conflict. This persistence of several major political dividing lines is the basic cause of the instability of government, as the bitterness of the conflicts, and the recent memories of power abused, are the fundamental causes of its weakness. Strong organizations like the Labour or Conservative parties, each seeking to form a homogeneous government and put into practice a coherent policy, are impossible in France. The young and dynamic on each side, impatient with the compromise and weakness of coalition government, are consequently tempted into extremist organizations, which alarm their sympathizers and enrage their opponents. The democratic parties cannot compete effectively because they are at loggerheads over the third issue, the clerical question, which lies between Socialists and M.R.P., preventing the development of a Labour party, and between Radicals and Conservatives, weakening still further the rudimentary links between the political representatives of the bourgeoisie. No French party, therefore, can hope to attract a majority

---

[20] See Figures 1 and 4 (above, p. 15, and below, p. 43).

of voters or of deputies. No French government can be based on a single party, which puts its policy into practice and then submits it to the judgment of the electorate. Every ministry is a coalition. Responsibilities are never clearly apportioned; the government parties devote as much energy to mutual recrimination as to fighting the opposition. The clash of political principles becomes obscured in the complexity of parliamentary manœuvring. The public grows apathetic and cynical; divided ministries, lacking effective support in the country, are too weak to impose necessary sacrifices on any powerful private interest, or organized social group. But these undoubted evils have causes deeper than the structure of political institutions, and tinkering with that framework will not cure them.

Chapter 3

THE SEARCH FOR A MAJORITY, 1947–1953

BETWEEN 1947 and 1953, the orientation of French policy changed slowly but drastically. While they remained in alliance the three ' social ' parties, Communists, Socialists, and M.R.P., had dominated the Assembly and the government. But the departure of the Communists into impotent isolation altered the whole situation. The French proletariat found themselves virtually disfranchised for constructive purposes. Socialists and M.R.P. were not strong enough to govern without Radical and Conservative support, and within the new coalition the struggle to dominate policy was as active as, though less desperate than it had been in the period of *tripartisme*. During the life of the 1946 Assembly a precarious equilibrium was maintained. But in 1951 the isolation of the Communists enabled the conservative groups greatly to improve their parliamentary position, and soon to secure almost complete, though not altogether secure control of power and of policy.

The Radicals and Conservatives, the parties of the Third Republic, were by mid-1953 back in the saddle, and anxious to return, politically economically, to the regime under which they had flourished. The Socialists were in opposition. The new parties, M.R.P. and R.P.F., were increasingly uneasy in office and in opposition respectively; it seemed that they might be again thrown together, as they had been at the outset. Indeed, on the choice and on the fate of these two groups, the extent of the conservative recovery would depend. As the departure of the Communists into isolation had revolutionized politics in 1947, so the emergence of the Gaullists from it might have the same effect six years later.

1. SOCIALIST DISCONTENT

THE tripartite coalition had had great difficulty in holding together. But as long as it did so, governments had no need to worry about their parliamentary strength. The departure of the Communists at once restored the ' problem of the majority ' to the central position which it had occupied during the Third Republic. At that period, the main cause of parliamentary instability was the contradiction between the Radical attitude on political (especially clerical) and on economic questions. Every Chamber began with a period of uncertainty in which the initial left-wing majority, elected on traditional political grounds, fell apart when governments had to deal with financial matters. In the Fourth Republic, the difficulty has been aggravated,

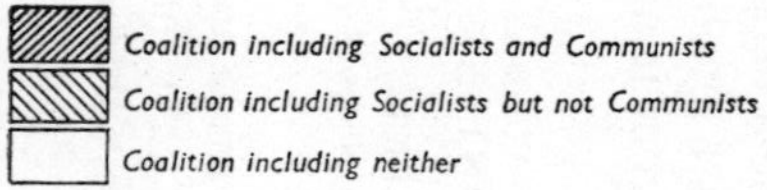

FIG. 2. GOVERNMENTS 1945–53
The Instability of Ministries

Compare with Fig. 3 (The Stability of Ministers) on pp. 30–1.

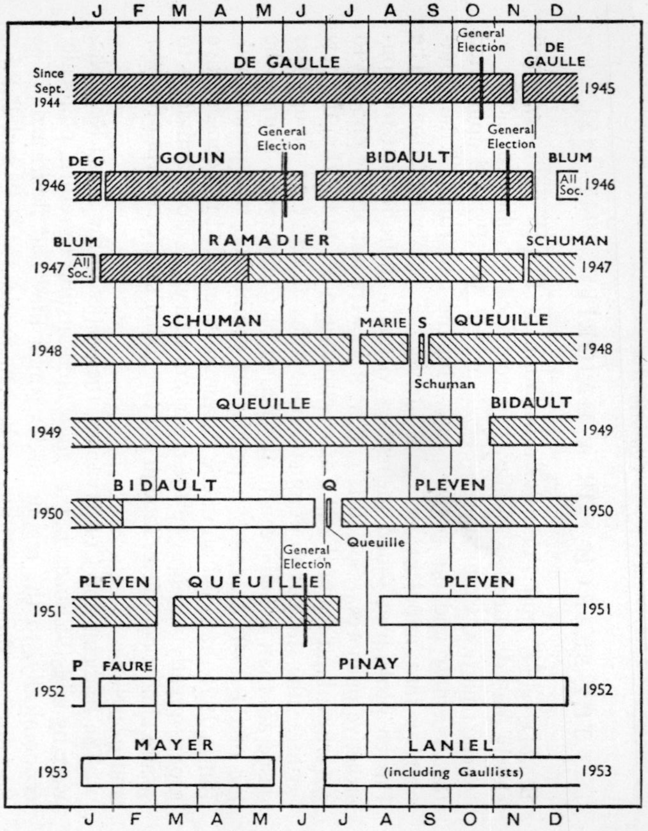

since the extreme groups are much stronger. The 1946 election produced 180 Communists, and the formation of the R.P.F. at first rallied 80 Gaullists. Together they slightly exceeded the combined strength of M.R.P. and the Socialists. The centre combination therefore needed to attract the votes of most Radicals and Conservatives, the least disciplined groups, without alienating the two big parties. But coalitions with no bond except fear of the extremists could hardly produce an effective common policy. Governments were divided and obviously impotent. Electorally, therefore, it became an immense asset to be in opposition. So the self-interested but useful motives which attach men and parties to power were counteracted by powerful pulls in the opposite direction. Deputies were tempted to vote against the government to ensure their own re-election, and parties which had lost ground felt that they could recover it by a spell out of office. The Socialists could not constantly compromise on trade union claims without forfeiting support to the Communists, while M.R.P., unless they could produce results on the schools issue, risked the defection of the Church to General de Gaulle.

These pressures were not remote, but immediate. The French voters went to the polls twelve times in four years: three referendums and three general elections between October 1945 and November 1946, second chamber elections at the end of 1946 and of 1948, municipal elections in spring 1945 and autumn 1947, departmental council elections in autumn 1945 and spring 1949. A new cycle began in 1951. The local campaigns were always fought on a national basis, so that the atmosphere of electioneering was almost permanent. No government, party or politician could plan ahead, for all were preoccupied with averting disaster at an impending election. The compulsion to take short views was irresistible.

Since the general drift was to the Right, the pressure was felt most by the Socialists, who had to sacrifice more and more of their policy to conciliate the growing demands of Radicals and Conservatives who believed the wind was in their sails. Some Socialist leaders urged the party to leave office, and repudiate responsibility for a policy which was not its own: but most feared that this might mean the breakdown of parliamentary government and the triumph of General de Gaulle. The opponents of participation in government replied that continual concessions to their partners for the sake of government unity would both lose votes, and drive non-Communist trade unionists into the arms of the C.G.T. Their fear of unconstitutional industrial action exposed the weakness of the regime; but to point this out is not to prove them wrong.

In practice the Socialist attitude was half-way between the two views. Few upheld unconditional participation in government—after the fall of M. Marie in August 1948, only five Socialist deputies (mainly ex-ministers) at first favoured joining his successor. Those who wished

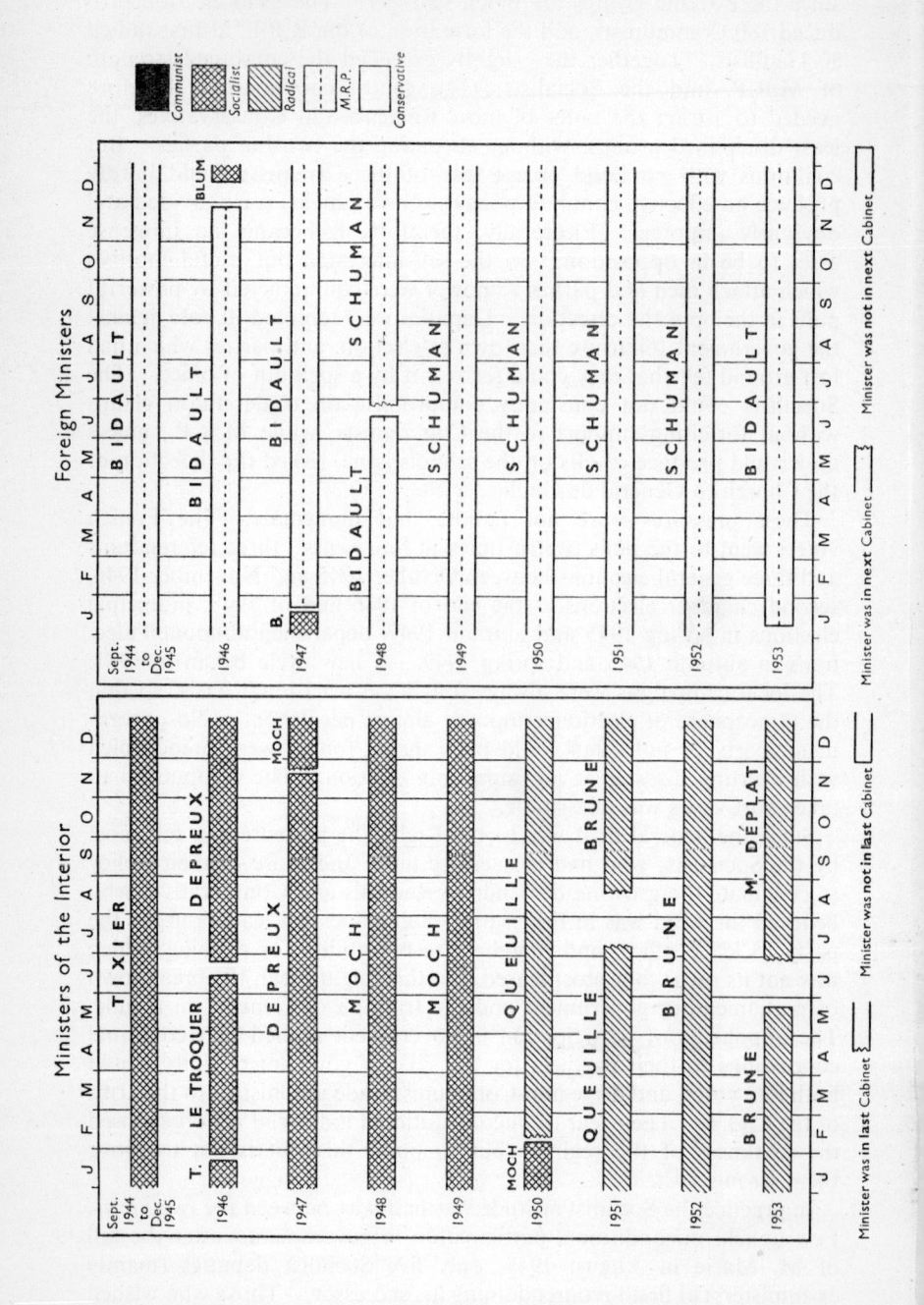

30

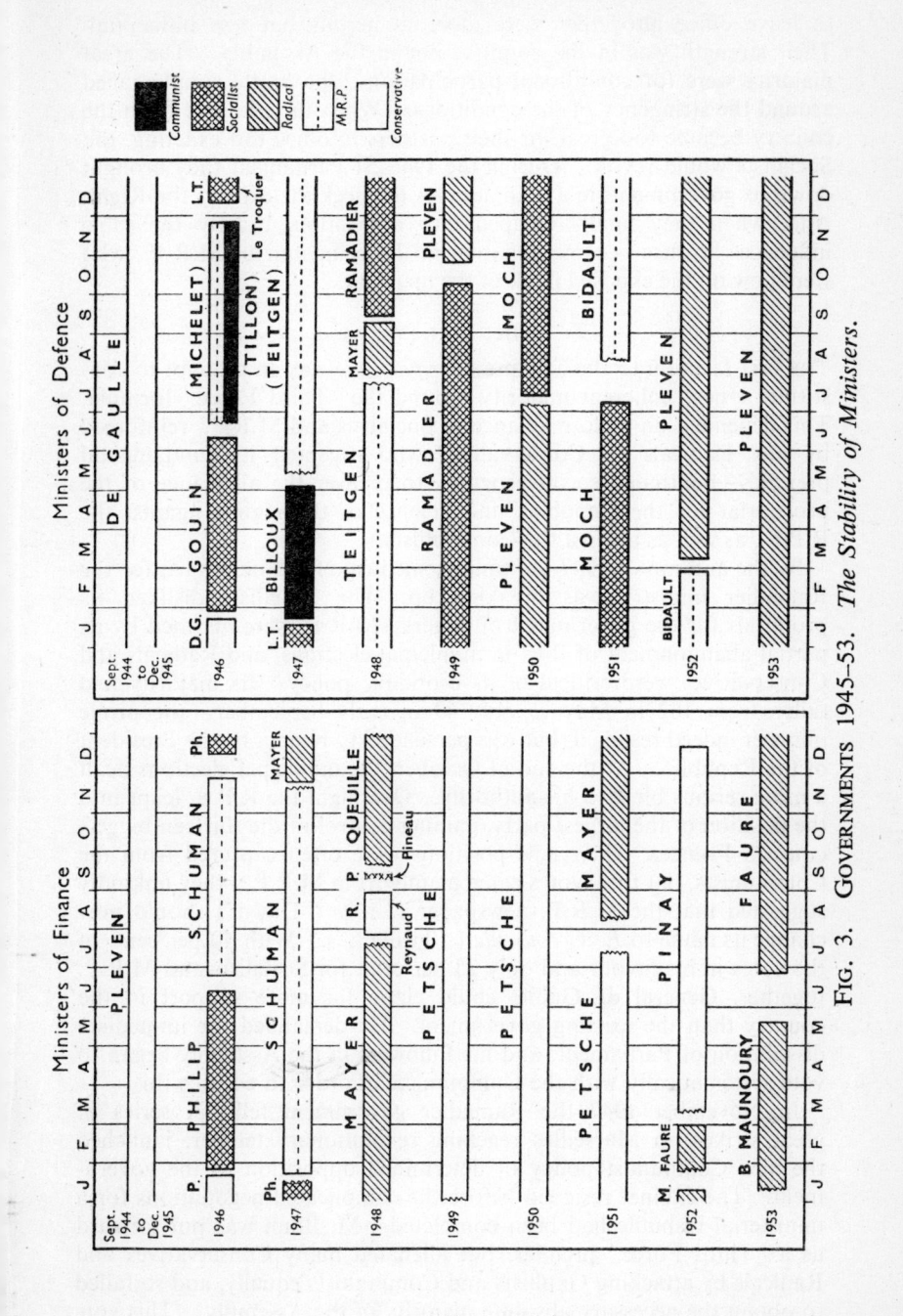

FIG. 3. GOVERNMENTS 1945–53. *The Stability of Ministers.*

to leave office altogether were more numerous but less influential. Their strength was in the country, not in the Assembly. The great majority were for conditional participation: the battle simply raged around the stringency of the conditions. When the pressure from the country became too great, or their partners in office too exacting, the Socialists would revolt. During the 1946–51 Parliament they brought down six governments in a vain attempt to check the drift to the Right. And, when they finally escaped into opposition, exactly the same influences at once became apparent in the behaviour of M.R.P., who were now on the exposed flank of the majority.

2. RADICAL REVIVAL

THE first reaction to the collapse of *tripartisme* was an attempt to constitute a new coherent majority around the 'Third Force' formula. This depended on a close alliance of Socialists and M.R.P., reinforced by any Radicals or Conservatives who accepted its fundamental premises—continued social progress, to recover the allegiance of the proletariat for the Republic, and defence of the regime against the R.P.F., as well as against the Communists.

By the autumn of 1947 the time seemed ripe for a new start, for the Ramadier ministry was breaking up. The Socialists disliked its proposals for the government of Algeria, M.R.P. were alarmed by its partial abandonment of P.R. in municipal elections, and Radicals and Conservatives were critical of its economic policy. Its majority had fallen from 182 in May to only 49 in early September; the prime minister indeed resigned, but was persuaded to remain by the President of the Republic. At the end of October, the municipal elections dealt a more serious blow to his authority. Overnight the R.P.F. leapt into the position of the largest party, gaining control of the thirteen biggest cities in France. Their new positions were often captured from the Communists, but their votes came mainly from M.R.P.; they unkindly suggested that the M.R.P. newspaper *L'Aube* ('Dawn') should now change its name to *Le Crépuscule* ('Twilight'). With 40 per cent. of the votes in his favour and only 25 per cent. for Socialists and M.R.P. together, General de Gaulle could claim far more support in the country than the existing government. He demanded the immediate dissolution of Parliament, and his followers in the Assembly began to vote systematically with the Communists in order to enforce this.

In November 1947 the Ramadier government fell. A series of great strikes, in Marseilles reaching revolutionary temper, launched the new Communist policy of determined opposition to the government. The cabinet resigned before the complicated negotiations for a ministerial reshuffle had been completed. M. Blum was put forward as a 'Third Force' premier, but alienated many Conservatives and Radicals by attacking Gaullists and Communists equally, and so failed to obtain the necessary absolute majority of the Assembly. This vote showed that the 'Third Force' was too weak to govern without support from the old parties, which repudiated its basic ideas. Every future ministry had, therefore, to be based on a temporary and uneasy compromise. Save perhaps for M. Pinay's conservative majority in 1952, every parliamentary combination had a shifting and incoherent character.

The ministerial crisis had been precipitated by the Socialist party secretary, M. Mollet, in order to shift the government to the Left. But the demonstrable need for Radical and Conservative votes brought about, instead, a move to the Right. M. Robert Schuman became prime minister, and was replaced as minister of Finance by M. René Mayer, a Radical with important business and administrative connections. As in December 1946, the leadership of the government passed to a party just repudiated by the electorate.[1] More important than the change of government was the split in the C.G.T. The anti-Communist minority broke away to form a separate federation, the C.G.T.-Force ouvrière, which was nominally politically independent, but in fact friendly towards the Socialist party. There was now some prospect that the combined influence of F.-O. and of the Catholic trade union federation, the C.F.T.C., would provide a counterpoise to Communist control of the working-class movement. Moreover, the internal division and the failure of the strikes greatly weakened the trade union movement as a whole. After the end of 1947 it could neither challenge the government, nor even effectively defend the interests of its members against the employers.

M. Schuman once described his government's life as an obstacle race. An attempt to remove one obstacle, by reconciling the parties of the 'Third Force' with General de Gaulle, was made in March 1948 by the former Gaullist minister M. René Pleven; it was rejected by both sides. The nominal majority split over M. Mayer's stiff 'special levy' at the end of 1947, over devaluation at the beginning of 1948, and over dismissals from the civil service in June 1948. More serious than any of these quarrels was the revival of the clerical issue in May and June, over two questions of mainly symbolic importance, the fate of 28 Catholic schools belonging to the nationalized colliery companies, and the celebrated 'Poinso-Chapuis decree', which opened a possible door to the indirect subsidizing of church schools by local authorities. The schools question was the principal, though not the only cause of the Socialist decision, on 19 July, to bring the government down; a proposal to reduce the military budget (by ½ per cent.) served as a pretext.

Once again a crisis opened by the Left ended in a move towards the Right. The most active conciliator in the late cabinet had been the

---

[1] Aron (pp. 188–9) has suggested that the French preference for weak government produces a permanent tendency for power to revert to the parties in decline, from which there is least to fear. The entry of the R.P.F. into the majority, in January 1953, confirms his thesis.

Radical minister of Justice, M. André Marie. He now became prime minister at the head of a broad coalition in which M. Paul Reynaud, the Conservative leader, was minister of Finance. The Socialists had vetoed the latter's appointment nine months before; now they accepted it reluctantly, only to rebel as soon as M. Reynaud announced his policy. His condition for taking office had been the grant of emergency powers to reorganize by decree the civil service, the taxation system, the nationalized industries, and the social security organization. On securing his powers from Parliament, he promptly raised food prices; the trade unions protested violently, and the Socialists broke up the government.

Significantly, M.R.P. supported the Socialists. In 1947 they had shown their determination to remain politically on the Left, by resisting the appeal of General de Gaulle. This decision had cost them most of their conservative following, and had given greater weight to their working-class *militants*. In 1948 they emerged as a party of the Left in the social and economic sphere too. M. Schuman, narrowly elected to a second premiership, chose as minister of Finance M. Christian Pineau—the only Socialist to hold that office since 1947. His tenure lasted just two days; on 7 September 1948, the cabinet met the Assembly, its conservative supporters rebelled, and it was overthrown by six votes. Three days later M. Henri Queuille, a Radical leader from pre-war days, was elected prime minister.

The significance of the long ministerial crisis of summer 1948 was great, though mostly negative. In terms both of men and of constitutional methods, it seemed (somewhat prematurely) to mark the triumph of the despised Third Republic over the upstart Fourth. In terms of measures, it conclusively demonstrated the impossibility of any clear-cut orientation of policy, whether to the Right or to the Left.

In the period of liberation, new leaders had been called on to replace their discredited seniors. None of the first four candidates for the premiership had held office before the war. But soon the old politicians had to be recalled. Five prime ministers governed France between December 1946 and October 1949, and all of them had been in office by 1940.[2] The Marie administration, with a Radical prime minister and a Conservative minister of Finance, marked an important stage in

---

[2] Of the first four candidates, MM. Gouin and Thorez had been deputies in the Third Republic, General de Gaulle had briefly held office in 1940 as under-secretary for War, and M. Bidault had had no political career at all. Of the next five, MM. Blum, Ramadier, Marie and Queuille were pre-war ministers: M. Schuman had been a deputy since 1919, and took office in 1940 under Marshal Pétain.

Subsequently, a mixture of old and new men came to the fore. Of the nine candidates for the premiership between 1949 and June 1953, five (MM. Bidault, Edgar Faure, René Mayer, Mollet, and Pleven) began their political career in 1944–45; seven (MM. Laniel, Marie, Mendès-France, Moch, Petsche, Queuille, and Reynaud) had been ministers before the war, and one (M. Pinay) had been a deputy.

this revival of the men and forces of the old regime.[3] The reversion was equally apparent in constitutional practice. The Marie cabinet was mostly, and the Queuille cabinet wholly, selected before the respective prime ministers had been chosen by the Assembly. M. Marie developed his predecessor's method of evading the constitution by making matters ' unofficially ' questions of confidence. He defied the spirit of the new regime both by demanding special powers, and by staking the existence of his government on the second chamber's consent to them—an open encouragement to the revival of that body, which was already taking place. The development of the ' Marie constitution ' suggested that the evolution of the Fourth Republic might surprise its founders as much as that of the Third had done in its day.[4]

But this appearance was deceptive, for the political balance had not swung as far as the critics supposed. The events of August and September 1948 defined an equilibrium of forces which was to last for three years. The older leaders and groups regained a share in power, but not a monopoly or even a preponderance. Constitutional behaviour tended towards the habits of the past, without evolving all the way. The successive failures of M. Reynaud and M. Pineau showed that neither a wholeheartedly Conservative policy nor a determinedly Socialist one could command the support of the Assembly. The parties were ' condemned to live together ', doomed to compromise and frustration; and the government was too weak to challenge any of the great organized interests, employers, workers, or peasants.[5]

3. DOCTOR QUEUILLE

M. QUEUILLE proved surprisingly well suited to this difficult situation. He was a characteristic figure of Third Republic politics. A country doctor by origin, he had served in nineteen pre-war cabinets, in a dozen of them as minister of Agriculture. His skill in the despised arts of parliamentary manœuvre was to stand him in good stead. Competent observers gave his ministry three weeks of life; yet it lasted thirteen months, set up a duration record for the Fourth Republic, and reversed the steady drift of opinion away from the parties of the centre.

M. Queuille shared the unheroic view of a pre-war British prime minister—that ' the art of statesmanship is to postpone issues until

---

[3] M. Reynaud was assisted at the ministry of Finance by MM. Laniel and Petsche, so that the three Conservative groups (Republican Independents, P.R.L., and Peasants) were all represented. M. Queuille was at first his own minister of Finance, but soon transferred the post to M. Petsche (who had remained under-secretary); he retained the ministry until 1951. On the constitutional point see below, pp. 178–81.

[4] See Marcel Prélot, ' Ministères éphémères, transformations profondes ', *Politique* No. 37 (September 1948), pp. 720–30.

[5] M. Prélot points out that the Radical recovery meant a victory for the peasants, and that M. Reynaud's policy involved an agreement with the C.G.A. (*Confédération générale de l'agriculture*) and a breach with the trade unions. He adds, ' comme les syndicats de travailleurs avaient éjecté M. Paul Reynaud, les syndicats patronaux avaient exécuté M. Christian Pineau.' (*Loc. cit.*, pp. 729–30.)

they are no longer relevant'. Confronted with a dangerous situation, his first expedient was to lower the political temperature, by deferring for six months the imminent departmental council elections. General de Gaulle protested in angry speeches, hinting at insurrection. But an ugly clash between Gaullists and Communists at Grenoble in September, and a bitter and violent miners' strike in October, frightened the country with the spectre of possible civil war. Opinion rallied to the government, helping it to survive its first difficult months.

In the parliamentary sphere, however, the ministry faced a new obstacle. It had been agreed in 1946 that the upper house, the Council of the Republic, should be wholly re-elected after two years, and that the method of electing it should then be reconsidered. To weaken the Communists, the new law greatly restricted the use of proportional representation (which had made the first Council almost a replica of the Assembly) and reverted to a system like that used to elect the old Senate.[6] M.R.P. suffered nearly as much as the Communists from this change; both fell to a score of members out of a total of 320. Almost half the new senators (a title they forthwith bestowed upon themselves) had sought R.P.F. support at the election. Eventually, indeed, only 58 of them accepted the Gaullist whip, and the R.P.F. could not (as it had hoped) use the new Council to paralyse the entire legislative programme, and so force the government to hold new elections. But the Radical and Conservative senators had little love for the government, and often treated the upper house as a useful opposition weapon; the new 'second thoughts chamber' celebrated its appearance by rejecting the budget.[7]

At the beginning of 1949 the prestige of the government nevertheless stood high. M. Queuille had begun his career in office by enunciating a modest aim: to make it possible for ministerial crises to occur without endangering the regime. But in attaining this desirable objective he undermined his own position by making it easy and safe to overthrow him. Thus he weakened the stability of his government by his very success in improving the security of the political system. Previous ministerial crises had been affairs of desperation, provoked by parties which felt their support slipping away, and their very existence at stake. The impending ones were rather crises of hope, the work of groups or leaders who, gaining ground in the country, felt entitled to exert more influence on policy. In May, M. Reynaud began a vigorous drive to remove the Socialists from office; some even of the M.R.P. leaders (notably M. Bidault) contemplated changing partners, discarding the Socialists and welcoming the R.P.F., but the M.R.P. rank and file firmly vetoed the idea. At the end of July, the Conservatives attacked M. Daniel Mayer, the Socialist minister of Labour, for infringing the wage stabilization policy by granting a holiday bonus to social security

---

[6] See below, pp. 271–2.
[7] See below, pp. 280–1.

employees; the majority fell to three, and only the parliamentary recess saved the government. Before the reassembly in October, the cabinet had broken up. British devaluation had forced France to follow suit, and M. Mayer seized the opportunity to demand a return to free collective bargaining, suspended since before the war. This proposal split the government; attempts at compromise failed, and M. Queuille resigned on 5 October 1949. The crisis which followed was the longest which had occurred since liberation.

The rules of the parliamentary game required that the Socialists, having brought down the last government, should be invited to form the next. President Auriol called on M. Jules Moch, who as minister of the Interior had broken the great strikes, helped devise the new electoral law for the Council of the Republic, and produced several compromise proposals before the Queuille government fell. But M. Moch was too strong a personality to be popular. The bitter hatred of the Communists was indeed an asset to him, but many M.R.P. deputies and some even of his own party were also unfriendly. He was elected prime minister with only one vote to spare, failed to form a government, and had to resign. The same fate befell the next nominee, M. René Mayer. He had a comfortable majority of 158, but was unable to reconcile the demand of his own Radical party that M. Daniel Mayer should leave the ministry of Labour, with the insistence of the Socialists that he should remain there.

It was now M.R.P's turn. The bickerings of the politicians had exasperated the public, and M. Bidault took advantage of this impatience, refusing to confront the Assembly until the parties had accepted his cabinet. This enabled him to form a government, but it did nothing to resolve the conflict. Radical attacks on the budget nearly destroyed his ministry in December, and in February the Socialists resigned over wages policy. Four months later they turned M. Bidault out over the salaries of civil servants—an important nucleus of Socialist voters.

The crisis of June-July 1950 showed that the political balance had changed little in the previous two years. The Socialists were not prepared to give up their new-found freedom without compensation. They helped to elect M. Queuille to the premiership, but refused to join his government, and overthrew him (with the aid of the left wing of M.R.P.) when he formed a conservative cabinet. The Socialist leader, M. Mollet, then drew up a programme including constitutional and electoral reform, to please the Radicals and Conservatives, and a halt to deflation, to satisfy his own party and M.R.P. On this basis the Socialists returned to office; but they were not strong enough to claim the premiership, which fell to the leader of the smallest of the majority parties, M. René Pleven of U.D.S.R.

The approaching general election was now making the coalition very difficult to maintain. Mistrust between the Socialists and M.R.P. had persisted since the former left the Bidault government, and worsened in November, when several M.R.P. deputies voted to impeach M. Moch (now minister of Defence and M. Pleven's principal colleague).[8] Moreover, the conflict over economic policy broke out again, Socialists and M.R.P. advocating subsidies to certain industries, Radicals and Conservatives opposing them. Most serious of all was the division on electoral reform. The Radicals demanded a return to the pre-war double ballot system, to which M.R.P. were bitterly hostile. The Conservatives were divided. The 100 Socialists, who were comparatively indifferent, voted in turn for each solution proposed; but as the 180 Communists voted equally regularly against them, the Assembly negatived them all. For a time the government maintained a precarious neutrality, but at the end of February it at last broke up.

As the Socialists were the party of conciliation on the issue which had now become crucial, M. Mollet was nominated for the premiership. But he failed to obtain an absolute majority, and once again M. Queuille was called on to solve the crisis, which he did by simply reconstituting his predecessor's cabinet. To minimize the ravages of electoral fever, he resolved to hold the elections in June, four months early. Realizing that no electoral reform could pass without the consent of M.R.P., M. Queuille persuaded his Radical friends to give way; and the new law, and the budget, were passed just in time for elections on 17 June.

4. THE NEW ASSEMBLY

THE results showed that the parties which had stood closest to General de Gaulle at the time of liberation, and bore the main responsibility for the creation and working of the regime, had lost ground heavily since the first post-war election in 1945. Of the original $4\frac{3}{4}$ million Socialist voters, $1\frac{3}{4}$ million had deserted. M.R.P. had suffered even more catastrophically, losing half their 5 million followers. The Communists, with 5 million votes, had retained their strength almost unimpaired. Among the opponents of *tripartisme*, the R.G.R. had lost few of their 2 million, or the Conservatives of their $2\frac{1}{2}$ million supporters[9] (the alleged surge of opinion towards these two movements was simply a myth, fostered by the working of the electoral system, but not reflected in the ballots of the electorate). The R.P.F., which had not existed in 1945, now drew 4 million votes from the older parties, and might perhaps have attracted many more but for the intransigence of its tactics.

These figures represent the net results of complex movements of opinion, which were neither continuous in time, nor direct as between parties. By November 1946 the Socialists had already lost a million

---

[8] See below, p. 306.
[9] The figure of $2\frac{1}{2}$ million excludes those voting for Gaullist lists in 1946. If these are regarded as Conservatives, then the latter lost heavily. Goguel, *Fourth Republic*, pp. 90, 102.

votes (half of them to the Communists) while M.R.P. still kept its original strength. To judge by local and senatorial elections, these two parties then both lost votes until 1949, and subsequently began to recover when the cost of living stopped rising. The R.P.F. reached its peak in the municipal elections of October 1947, when it won 6 million votes, or 40 per cent. of the total poll. In the great cities some of these votes were drawn from the working-class parties, but in the country as a whole the bulk of them came from the Right. From M.R.P., the Gaullists acquired conservative-minded electors, bewildered by the discrediting of their old leaders, and desperately seeking a strong bulwark against Communism. In 1945–46 these had been attracted to M.R.P. by the prestige of its novelty, its resistance record, its powerful organization, and the backing of the Church. But by 1947 M.R.P. seemed to have compromised too far with the Communists, and when General de Gaulle stepped in to offer a new source of leadership, these voters flocked to his banner. From the Radicals and Conservatives, most of the R.P.F. gains were of a different kind. Individual candidates of these persuasions accepted the Gaullist label, tacitly reserving the right to return to their original allegiance whenever they chose. After 1949 most of them (especially the Radicals) did so choose, and they took most of their followers back with them. The Radical and Conservative losses to the R.P.F. were thus relatively small, and were compensated by gains from Socialists and M.R.P. respectively.

The 1951 returns showed that the opposition groups, which in 1947 had had nearly twice as many votes as all others combined, no longer commanded a majority of the electorate. The Communists with over 25 per cent. of the votes, and the R.P.F. with over 20 per cent., were still much stronger than any of their rivals singly; but together, the Socialists with nearly 15 per cent., the Conservatives (13 per cent.), M.R.P. (12½ per cent.), and the R.G.R. (11 per cent.) still possessed a narrow majority in the country as a whole. There was also still a clear margin of votes in favour of the social reforms of the liberation (supported by Communists, Socialists, M.R.P., and part of the R.P.F.). On the clerical question the verdict was more dubious, since a section of the R.G.R. was now willing to accept the demands of the Church.[10]

Eighteen months later the leadership of M. Pinay seemed at last to have brought about the Radical and Conservative revival so often prematurely proclaimed by the spokesmen of these groups. But their gains were mainly at the expense of the R.P.F., and represented a transfer of party allegiance by voters who had retained the same basic outlook throughout, rather than a real conquest of new ground. M.R.P. and R.P.F. had both acquired sufficient strength to represent

---

[10] For analyses of these results see Philip Williams, ' The French Elections ', *The Fortnightly*, September 1951: Goguel, *op. cit.*, Part III.

new factors of importance in the political struggle. But neither had held its spectacular initial gains; and on fundamentals the opinions of the electorate in 1953 seemed strikingly similar to those they had professed in the Third Republic.

In the Assembly the changes were greater. The new electoral law (more fully described in Chapter 19) had done its work. It modified the proportional representation system by allowing the parties to form coalitions, and discarded it altogether where any party or coalition won a majority of votes. These provisions were designed to benefit the groups of the old majority. The Radicals, Conservatives and M.R.P. gained most from them, the Socialists (who were frequently left out of the centre combinations) gained least. The R.P.F. could have profited from the new system if it had been willing to contract alliances. But its leaders refused to do so, and in nearly all areas it fought alone, suffering slightly as a result from the operation of the law. The Communists, isolated everywhere, lost heavily from it. Between them the opposition parties had just under half the votes; the old system of 'proportional representation' would have given them a majority of seats, the new law gave them a third.

The new Assembly was well to the Right of its predecessor. There had been many more middle-class candidates than in 1946, and, proportionately, many fewer workers.[11] On the benches of the old majority, about sixty seats had passed from M.R.P. to Radicals and Conservatives. On those of the opposition, eighty Communists had been replaced by Gaullists. The search for a majority therefore had to be resumed in new conditions.

While the six parties were approximately equal, the three strongest were those least able to co-operate in government: the Gaullists, Socialists, and Communists, with 121, 107, and 101 seats respectively. With the Communists in unrelenting opposition, there were five conceivable combinations. The alliance of the four centre parties, which had held together with difficulty in the late parliament and in the election campaign, would still have a comfortable majority if it could be preserved. Without the Socialists, it would have more cohesion but insufficient numbers; a split among either Socialists or R.P.F. would be needed to supply the deficiency. The remaining alternatives all required the Gaullists to abandon their aloof attitude and enter a coalition. They could then choose as partners either Conservatives and M.R.P. (a pro-clerical combination): Conservatives and Radicals (a socially conservative alliance of the former opponents of *tripartisme*): or M.R.P. and Socialists (a socially progressive union of the non-Communist Resistance).

The first government, almost inevitably, was based on the old coalition. But equally inevitably its life was precarious, for all parties

---

[11] *Le Monde*, 17–18 June 1951 : for deputies, see *ibid.*, 6 July 1951.

were calculating the chances of a change of alliances and the establishment of a more homogeneous majority. The Socialists, now that governments could survive without them, were delighted to escape taking responsibility for the policy of others. Some leaders hoped to replace the Socialists with the R.P.F., but on their own terms—above all, the Gaullists must take office without their uncomfortably dominating chief. But to bargain effectively with the R.P.F., these leaders had to keep an alternative open. If the Gaullists could widen the breach between the Socialists and the rest of the majority, their negotiating power would be far greater. This they proceeded to achieve by forcing the clerical issue to the forefront of politics.[12]

The Queuille government had resigned after the elections, in accordance with custom. A Radical, M. René Mayer, was nominated for the premiership, but M.R.P., considering him too anti-clerical, would not vote for him. A Conservative, M. Petsche, then tried, only to fail for lack of Socialist support. At length M. Pleven was elected; the Socialists' satisfaction with his previous government earned him their votes, but not their participation in office. The R.P.F. pressed their advantage. A powerful pressure-group, the Association for Educational Freedom, had enrolled deputies from all the parties favourable to the church schools, and in mid-September its bill (called the *loi Barangé* from the name of its promoter) was passed through Parliament by the combined clerical groups. The government stood neutral, since most Radicals were against the bill; but the old majority was broken, for the Socialists seized the chance to dissociate themselves from their former partners on a matter of principle raised by others.

Nor could the prime minister rely on his nominal supporters. A Socialist bill to tie wage rates by a sliding scale to the cost of living was carried against the government by the Communist and Gaullist oppositions, but also by a ministerial party, M.R.P.[13] While Radicals and Conservatives agreed in attacking M. Schuman's conciliatory policy towards Tunisian nationalism, the right-wing Conservatives of the Peasant group wished to remove the Radical Finance minister, M. René Mayer. The ministry won its solitary triumph in December, when the Schuman plan was easily ratified. But its budgetary proposals proved fatal to it. They called for special powers to reorganize the social services and the nationalized railways. This drove the Socialists into opposition, and the cabinet was defeated at the beginning of January 1952.

It was now clear that no government could long survive against the united opposition of the Socialists and of the Gaullists. M. Edgar Faure, the youngest of the Radical leaders, became prime minister, and tried to regain Socialist support by concessions in European,

---

[12] Compare the Communists' use of the same question in 1945: see above, p. 16.
[13] The Council of the Republic came to the government's aid, and the bill became law in a drastically amended form, only in the middle of 1952.

Tunisian, and budgetary policy, and above all by accepting their sliding scale bill. In consequence he was overthrown at the end of February, when many of the Conservatives and of his own Radical party revolted against increased taxation. To reconstitute the old majority, it was necessary to prove to these rebels that an alternative government of the Right was not available; the nomination of M. Antoine Pinay, the Conservative minister of Works and Transport, was expected to demonstrate this. Certain that he had no chance of election, M.R.P. and the Radicals voted for him in order to earn Conservative support in the future. But to the general astonishment M. Pinay achieved the impossible. Twenty-seven Gaullist deputies, defying their whip, elected him to the premiership by a narrow margin.

M. Pinay attempted to shift the whole direction of economic policy, by rejecting new taxes and relying on loans to balance the budget, and to produce a political readjustment, by bringing part of the R.P.F. into the majority. His government, although almost all its members had served in previous administrations, therefore marked the most important turning point in French politics since the dropping of the Communists. The 'Pinay majority' was based on the R.G.R., the Conservatives, and the conservative wing of the Gaullists, who in July left their former leader in order to support the government. M.R.P. occupied the vulnerable position so familiar to the Socialists. Its leaders sat in the cabinet, but the *militants* opposed it. The M.R.P. deputies were divided in several crucial votes, and in December 1952 their defection brought down the ministry.

But M. Pinay's term of office had altered the whole political situation. By displaying the internal divisions of M.R.P. and R.P.F., he had made new parliamentary combinations possible; finding their electoral support undermined, the Gaullist deputies hastened to enter the majority by supporting M. Pinay's successor, M. René Mayer. M.R.P., though opposed to the Gaullists over foreign policy, could hope to find among them allies against the conservatism of the older parties. But these, especially the Radicals, looked upon the R.P.F. as a victim to be squeezed rather than as a partner to be welcomed. The year 1953 left various political possibilities open; but after the Pinay government, there could be no simple return to the equilibrium of 1947–52.

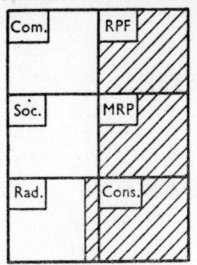

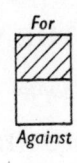

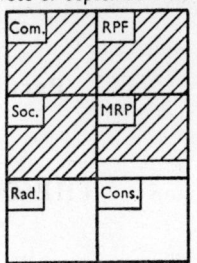

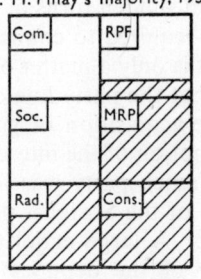

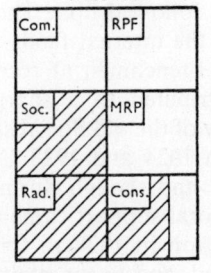

Fig. 4. PARTY ALIGNMENTS, 1951-3.

Part II. THE PARTIES

Chapter 4

THE COMMUNIST PARTY

1. HISTORY

THE French Communist party, like its opposite numbers elsewhere, uses varying tactics to attain its unchanging objectives. Moscow's sharp and sudden turns of policy often embarrass its faithful followers, who are required to contradict themselves overnight. But the embarrassment is only a matter of public relations; the hardened Communist knows that the party line of the moment is merely a means to the true ends, the acquisition of governmental power in his own country and the promotion of the interests of the U.S.S.R.

The French party was founded in December 1920, when the Tours congress of the Socialist party split over affiliation to the Third International. A large majority of the membership (though only a small minority of the deputies) voted for affiliation on Moscow's terms, which included the expulsion of the dissentients and the adoption of the name of Communist party. But the initial success of the movement was not followed up. The repercussions of the struggle for power in Russia, the internal feuds within the party, the resentment of revolutionary Frenchmen at receiving instruction from backward Moscow, all contributed to a sharp decline of the Communist party and a recovery of the old Socialist party and its associates in the trade unions. Between 1924 and 1928 Communist membership fell from 88,000 to 52,000; and though during the same period the party gained votes, its electoral support came largely from traditional voters for the Left. Its decision in 1928 to treat the Socialists as the main enemy to be destroyed, and to maintain its candidates against them on the second ballot, lost the Communists 40 per cent. of their votes between the two ballots. Their membership in the Chamber fell to a dozen.[1]

Nor did the situation improve for some years. The party was divided by bitter personal and political rivalries. M. Thorez, arrested in 1929, believed that he had been betrayed by another member of the central committee, and that his colleagues had seized the opportunity

---

[1] The fullest account of the development of the French Communist party is Gérard Walter, *Histoire du parti communiste français:* it ends in 1940. The point of view is sympathetic to the party. Useful material on the period 1936–45 may be found in Henry W. Ehrmann, *French Labour from Popular Front to Liberation*, in Rossi, and in an article in *Esprit*, no. 80, May 1939, pp. 157–70. On the party organization to-day, see Alain Brayance, *Anatomie du parti communiste français*. The 1928 figures come from Walter, p. 191, and Rossi, p. 331. On the press, see below, pp. 389–91.

to be rid of him by refusing to pay his fine. When he came out of prison a year later, he described the party as weak and declining in numbers, full of mutual suspicion, lacking any sense of reality, and ruled by an arbitrary leadership which demanded from its followers uncritical obedience.[2] The separate Communist trade unions had proved a complete failure. In the 1932 election the party lost 300,000 of its former million votes, and on the second ballot little more than half its remaining supporters continued to vote for it against better-placed candidates of the Left. If the Socialists had replied in kind by maintaining their candidates where a Communist was in the lead, the latter would have lost eight of the ten seats which they retained.[3] In the Chamber and in the provinces (though not in the capital) their political influence was almost negligible. But the party itself was not primarily concerned with immediate electoral success. Expulsions, reorganizations, and changes of line were gradually building it into a compact and thoroughly disciplined movement which was available to forward whatever policy seemed likeliest to bring it to power.

The *Front populaire* gave the Communists their chance. As late as the beginning of 1934 the party line still insisted that social democracy, not Fascism, was the really dangerous enemy of the working-class. In the riots of 6 February 1934, Communist ex-servicemen joined in the Fascist attack on the Chamber of Deputies. But a week later there was a sudden change, and on 12 February Communist and Socialist trade unionists joined in a huge anti-Fascist demonstration in defence of the despised bourgeois Republic. A word from Stalin in commendation of the French rearmament programme put an end to Communist anti-militarism. By the time of the 1936 election the Radical, Socialist and Communist parties had formed a close alliance for the second ballot. The electoral system no longer harmed the Communists so severely, and for the new Chamber they won $1\frac{1}{2}$ million votes, and contributed 70 members to the *Front populaire* majority.

The new line was decided from above, without prior discussion by the rank and file.[4] But it was certainly more popular than the old one, among many party members as well as among voters. An even greater advantage of the change was the certificate of republican respectability bestowed upon the party by its Radical and Socialist partners. MM. Blum and Daladier, by accepting Communist co-operation, seemed to testify that the outstretched hand had really replaced the knife between the teeth. But, though more presentable in public, the Communists had not changed their nature. They refused office in the Blum government, preferring to keep their hands free to exploit domestic discontent, and becoming more and more critical of its foreign policy. Their real sentiments towards their partners of the

---

[2] Maurice Thorez, *Fils du peuple*, pp. 60–1, 69–71.
[3] Walter, pp. 240–1.
[4] See *Esprit, loc. cit.*, p. 167.

Front populaire had not altered at all; when the Vichy regime put the leaders of the pre-war governments on trial, several Communists wrote to Marshal Pétain offering to give evidence for the prosecution. *L'Humanité* protested when Vichy released Socialist leaders from jail, or even when they were treated as political prisoners instead of as ordinary criminals.[5]

The *Front populaire* had come to power at the worst possible moment. As the German menace came more and more to dominate politics, the government drifted further and further to the Right. The Radicals again dominated the ministry by 1938; M. Daladier, three years earlier the chief protagonist among them of the *Front populaire*, became the man of Munich. The Socialists, hopelessly split between pacifists and resisters, went out of office, and saw their political influence disappear. The majority of Conservatives allowed their support for appeasement to turn increasingly into a sympathy for Fascism: the fact that only the Communist party stood solidly for opposition to Germany was enough to discredit the resistance policy with many of the French bourgeoisie. After the general strike of November 1938 the Daladier ministry was primarily an anti-Communist administration.

The signature of the Nazi-Soviet pact led to another complete change of party line. Those who had so recently and so violently denounced every Frenchman who was not prepared for instant war against Germany, turned overnight into demagogic pacifists and anti-patriotic defeatists. Their enemies seized their opportunity: the party and its satellite organizations were suppressed, and the Communist deputies were expelled from the Chamber. But the bewilderment of the public during the 'phoney war', and the anti-working-class policy of the government, enabled the Communists to survive this repression without the serious loss of support which might have been expected. Their defeatist policy continued after the German victory; according to the party line the war was an imperialist one, the main enemy was at home, and the downfall of French imperialism gave the party its opportunity. The leaders hoped that they would be allowed to carry out their revolution with German connivance and the backing of Germany's partner, Russia, just as the men of Vichy hoped to carry out theirs with Italian support and German acquiescence. After the German entry into Paris, the first démarche of the local Communists was not an act of resistance, but an application to the occupation authorities for permission to publish *L'Humanité* legally.

This policy continued until May 1941, when tension between Germany and Russia produced the first signs of change. The outbreak

---

[5] Rossi, pp. 83, 431–2: he quotes the first letter published, that of M. Billoux. Several others were published in *Le Populaire* during the 1951 election campaign by the former president of the high court of justice.

By a curious irony one of the ministers against whom the Communists offered to provide evidence was M. Pierre Cot, to-day their most notable fellow-traveller.

of war between them in June led to another violent reversal. The
'mercenaries of the City of London' became overnight 'our gallant
British allies' and the Gaullists changed with equal suddenness from
traitors to comrades. Now that the safety of the Soviet Union was at
stake, the Communists took the lead in resistance activity, showing a
zeal and a heroism which were easily confused, by non-Communists
and by many of the rank and file of the party itself, with patriotic
enthusiasm for the French cause. But if the coincidence of French
and Russian interests allowed the party to adopt a 'national' policy, it
by no means led to any relaxation in the struggle for power.

The resistance movement itself helped the party by acting as a
character purge: at the same time it assisted penetration into circles
previously inaccessible. In agricultural areas Communist influence in
the *maquis* offered a useful basis for the extension of their hold on the
peasantry.[6] A body like the *Front national*, safely controlled by the
party behind a respectable façade of Marins and Mauriacs, enabled
them to appeal to groups which they could not normally reach: for it
was the Right which was most willing to work with the Communists,
and to take at face value their claim to be patriotic Frenchmen—the
Socialists, having more experience of them, were much more suspicious.[7]
The party's first ministerial posts, bestowed on it by General de Gaulle,
conferred a guarantee of respectability similar to that given by the
Front populaire, and for much the same reasons. Above all, the war
completed the Communist capture of the trade unions. Under the
Front populaire their penetration was already well advanced. In 1940
many of the bitterest anti-Communist union leaders went over to
Vichy, and when they were discredited their remaining colleagues had
neither the numbers nor the organization to compete with the party.

The sharp changes of party policy might have destroyed the Communists' reputation for consistency and cost them some peripheral
support. But they strengthened the cohesion and discipline of the
solid core of *militants*. Those who survived these repeated switches
were reliable followers, available for any purpose for which the leadership wished to use them. The resistance movement gave the party
new advantages. It restored the patriotic reputation briefly acquired
under the *Front populaire* and forfeited in 1939, it allowed them to
approach elements of the population which previously they had been
unable to touch, and it consolidated their hold where it already existed.
Then in 1944 victory over Germany came in sight, and the objective of
internal power became increasingly important. At the liberation the

---

[6] Observers have commented on the fact that Communism penetrated rural France
most successfully where the *maquis* had been most active. Duverger, *Partis politiques*,
p. 350. Goguel, *Esprit*, November 1945, p. 951.
On French peasant Communism see E. M. Earle, ed., *Modern France*, Chap. 13, by
Gordon Wright; and H. W. Ehrmann, *American Political Science Review*, vol. xlvi
(March 1952), pp. 19–43.

[7] Jacques Debû-Bridel, *Les Partis contre de Gaulle*, pp. 36, 52.

Communists did their best to discredit the maximum number of experienced political leaders, to use the purge of collaborationists to rid themselves of potential opponents, and to pay off old scores. In particular, during the brief period of disorder, they murdered several ex-Communists who had left the party in protest against the Nazi-Soviet pact—some of whom, though not all, had since become collaborators.[8] But the liberation gave them another opportunity. It enabled them to use revolutionary violence in some areas and for a short time, but it also gave them their first chance to become a government party, with the added prestige and power of that position, and the possibility of infiltrating a part of the machine of the bourgeois state.[9]

2. ORGANIZATION

IN its organization as in other ways the Communist party is unique. The basic unit of other parties is the section, which groups members living in a given local government area. In the Communist party it is the cell, composed of from three to thirty members who work in the same establishment.[10] The cell meets at least weekly, but when the unit is based on the place of work there is in fact continuous contact between its members. In practice, however, cells based on the workplace are only suitable for those working in large establishments: isolated members, housewives, and those working individually, artisans, peasants and intellectuals, are therefore organized in local cells based on the street, ward or commune, which differ from the sections of other parties only in their smaller size. In the 1920's the introduction of the cell system, which was modelled on that of the Russian party, met with a good deal of resistance from party members;[11] even to-day there appears to be a spontaneous preference for organization by locality, which the leadership must continually combat. The extension of the party's influence beyond the industrial workers at the time of liberation caused a great growth of local cells, and in 1946 there were 28,000 of them compared with only 8,000 workplace cells. But the party leaders struggle continually to encourage the latter. Local cells, like sections, may be better adapted for discussion meetings and electoral activity, but they are less suitable for effective action and agitation on instructions from above; nor can they be easily transformed, as workplace cells can, into underground organizations.[12]

---

[8] Rossi, pp. 444–5 gives details.
[9] See below, pp. 385-7.
[10] Fifteen to twenty is the optimum: on reaching thirty a new cell should be formed. But for lack of a capable secretary this is not always possible; cases of cells numbering sixty (even, very rarely, over a hundred) are known, though frowned on by the party authorities.
[11] Walter, pp. 171 ff.
[12] On the advantages and disadvantages of the cell as a form of organization, and on the preference of the members for organization by locality, see Duverger, *op. cit.*, pp. 45–55. Workplace cells also minimize ' horizontal ' contacts (see below, pp. 49, 52).

The members of the cell elect a secretary, and also a bureau, of which each member is responsible for a particular sphere of party activity. The bureau, like all higher organs in the Communist hierarchy, has a dual function and a dual responsibility. Its functions are both to act and to inform: to carry out the instructions of the leadership, but also to convey to the latter the response which their directives are receiving. Its responsibilities are both upward and downward; the members of the bureau may be dispossessed either by their constituents who elected them, or by the next higher party organ, the section.

The section usually groups all cells in a particular ward or rural commune, though some large factories have their own sections. Each cell is represented through delegates, the cell secretaries and bureau members. There is thus no direct contact at the base with members of other cells: all links are vertical, maintained by way of a higher organ in the hierarchy,[13] and attempts to create horizontal links, which might interfere with the unique chain of command, are frowned on as the gravest of offences against discipline. The delegates meet every six months in a sectional conference, which chooses a committee for day-to-day activities. The sections are grouped into departmental federations,[14] working through a conference of section delegates meeting every six months and electing a federal committee. This committee, in consultation with national leaders, chooses the federal secretary, who must normally have been a party member for at least three years. Again the central direction of the party may, and often does, dismiss and replace the federal officials.

The highest authority in the party is the national congress, composed of delegates elected by the federal conferences (or in conditions of illegality by the federal committees) and meeting in theory every two years: the last two congresses were held at Strasbourg in 1947, and at Gennevilliers in 1950. In alternate years, or more often if necessary, a national conference is convoked, consisting of delegates chosen by the federal committees, which like all other executive bodies are responsible to their superiors as well as to their constituents. The national congress elects a central committee of sixty to eighty members, meeting at least every two months and acting as a consultative assembly of the party.[15] This chooses, at the congress, several other bodies of which three are important: the political bureau of fourteen, meeting weekly and in charge of day-to-day activities: the secretariat of four

---

[13] Brayance, pp. 42–3, 66.

[14] The ports of Calais, Boulogne and Dunkirk are all controlled by a federation extending over the coastal areas of two departments, Nord and Pas-de-Calais. J. Fauvet, *Les Forces politiques en France*, p. 32; Brayance, p. 70. In 1953 four separate federations were set up in Seine. *Le Monde*, 25–26 October 1953.

[15] Despite the rules, the central committee did not meet from December 1952 to June 1953; and the national conference at Gennevilliers in March 1953 was the first meeting of federal delegates since the congress in the same place three years before.

which is the centre of the organization:[16] and a control committee of six which gets little publicity, but which is sometimes said to be the decisive authority, especially in the internal affairs of the party.[17] These elections invariably take place by acclamation. At Gennevilliers in 1950 M. Mauvais, said to be an adherent of M. Marty and the extremist wing, was dropped from the secretariat and replaced by M. Lecœur, from M. Thorez's home department of Pas-de-Calais; and M. Ramette, leader of the Nord party, lost his place on the politburo. Two years later M. Marty, the party's *vieillard terrible*, and M. Tillon, its chief resistance leader, were removed from all their offices, and the former was subsequently expelled. None of these changes aroused any whisper of dissent.

The Communists have always regarded Parliament as a minor field of operations. Before the general election of 1924, the first in which the French party participated, the Communist International laid down that it must apply strictly the rules drawn up at the second congress of the International. The Communist deputy must ' remember that he is not a " legislator " trying to find a common language with other legislators, but a Party agitator sent into enemy territory to carry out the decisions of the Party. He is responsible not to the anonymous mass of electors, but to the Communist Party.' He must make use of his parliamentary immunity to facilitate the illegal as well as the legal work of the party, subordinate his parliamentary to his party work, and introduce ' purely propagandist proposals, drafted not with a view to their adoption but for publicity and agitation', as the party leaders may require. The parliamentary group is under the complete control of the party executive, which must approve its choice of officers, has a representative with a right of veto at all its meetings, and must give instructions in advance on all matters of importance, including the right to choose who shall speak for the party and to approve the text of their speeches. Every Communist candidate must give a written undertaking in advance to resign if called upon to do so by the party.[18]

In practice nearly all the party leaders are deputies: of the 1950 politburo members, M. Mauvais alone had no seat in the Assembly, and he had been a senator. This personal link prevents any clash between parliamentary group and organization, such as distracts the Socialist party : but the attitude of the leaders ensures that the outlook and policy of the *militant* prevail, not those of the ordinary deputy. The Communist members are outside the parliamentary fraternity, the

---

[16] Consisting until 1952 of MM. Thorez, Duclos and Marty, who had all belonged to it for twenty years, and M. Lecœur, who replaced M. Léon Mauvais in 1950. M. Étienne Fajon replaced M. Thorez during the latter's absence in Russia, and M. François Billoux has attended since M. Marty was dropped.

[17] See François Goguel, ' Les Partis politiques en France ', *Encyclopédie politique de la France et du monde*, vol. i, p. 285. Brayance, p. 105. It was the control committee which prepared the accusations against MM. Marty and Tillon in 1952.

[18] Theses of the second world congress, quoted Walter, pp. 143–4.

république des camarades. Their inferior status in the party is emphasized by the requirement that they place at its disposal most of their salaries, above the limit of a skilled worker's wage: this both prevents the development of a ' deputy's outlook ' among them, and helps the party funds—in 1946 this source brought into their central coffers nearly twice as much as ordinary contributions from the members.[19] Other measures are taken to diminish the sense of their own importance so natural and normal in members of legislative bodies: for instance, Communist parliamentarians do not present bills and resolutions on their own account, they take them ready prepared by the party's services. But the low rating given to parliamentary activity results in a low level of membership. The Communist deputies are hard workers. But their educational background often makes them less articulate than other members, and their truculent approach makes mutual understanding very difficult. The successes of their leader, M. Duclos, and of their brilliant fellow-traveller, M. Cot, show that these handicaps can be overcome. But apart from a few procedural specialists, who are extremely assiduous and skilful in manœuvre and obstruction, the rank and file make little impression on the Assembly. Their object, indeed, is not to convert their parliamentary colleagues but to encourage their followers in the country, or to put their Socialist rivals into embarrassing situations.

Thus the characteristics of Communist organization are essentially military. The high command is in theory elected, but in practice it is self-chosen.[20] It retains the right to dismiss and replace subordinate authorities. Its instructions are carried out with discipline and precision by the lower ranks; the basic unit, the cell, is chosen as a weapon adapted to a struggle for absolute power, not mere parliamentary success, and more suitable for permanent agitation (legal or illegal) than for occasional discussion and electioneering. Discussion within the party indeed goes on vigorously: every effort is made to convince doubtful comrades of the correctness of the party line. But this is

---

[19] In the party's 1946 budget levies on salaries of ministers, deputies, senior officials, editors, etc., amounted to 72½ million francs, while the central office share of membership contributions (a quarter of the total) was 38½ million. Roger-A. Priouret, *La République des partis*, p. 177.

In 1950 a *questeur* of the Assembly stated that the party drew 156 million francs a year from its levy on its members of parliament. *J.O.*, 14 June 1950, p. 4789. (M. Schauffler's speech).

[20] It is self-chosen in two ways. The delegates at the national congresses have complete confidence in the leadership, and invariably ratify the single list of names presented to them. In addition, Article 7 of the party's constitution allows the higher authorities in the party to co-opt their own members, and to nominate members of lower committees, when the central committee judges it necessary. Article 26 allows the central committee, in circumstances of which it is the judge, to decide that delegates to the national congress should be chosen not by the federal *conferences* but by the federal *committees*, executive bodies which the central committee itself is entitled to dismiss and replace. The leaders can thus select their own constituents.

At all levels, leaders are effectively (though not nominally) chosen from above and not from below. See Brayance, pp. 50-1, 74, 79, 98-9.

necessary only at the base. At the higher levels more experienced members are chosen, who have a clear appreciation of the real as distinct from the nominal objectives of the party. Discussion in the lower ranks serves two purposes: to inform the leaders of the reception given to their policies by the members, and to bring to light signs of heresy.

If the latter are discovered, the reliable Communists who represent the cell at higher levels, and are responsible to their superiors, ensure that the danger is observed and checked: since there are no direct links between cells, only indirect contacts through delegates to the section above, it is very difficult for dissent in one cell to contaminate another. Attempts by leaders to by-pass the chain of command and make direct contact with the lower levels are considered the worst form of treason. As the isolation of each cell checks any attempt at revolt from below, so the subordination of the parliamentary group reduces the likelihood of its occurring at the top. The party forms a rigid, disciplined hierarchy admirably adapted for arousing mass agitation in periods of legality, and for converting itself into a clandestine organization the moment the necessity arises.

3. CLIENTÈLE

THE great increase in the party's membership was acquired at two periods, that of the *Front populaire*, and that of the liberation. Between 1934 and 1937 the number of adherents rose from 45,000 to 333,000: still below 400,000 in 1944, by 1946 it had passed the 900,000 mark. Three years later it had dropped back to 750,000, and by 1952 it was less than 600,000.[21] Communist membership is about equal to that of all other parties combined—and it demands more of the individual than membership in any other party.

One of the most striking characteristics of the Communists is their emphasis on youth. The leaders have great power in so centralized an organization, and they use it to insist on early promotion; they are fond of pointing out that M. Thorez entered the politburo at twenty-five and M. Benoît Frachon, now leader of the C.G.T., at thirty. The great growth of the party at the time of liberation made it essential to keep control in the hands of experienced and reliable leaders, so that in 1952 the youngest member of the politburo (Lecœur) was aged forty. But the effort to infuse young blood at the top continues, and was a notable feature of the Gennevilliers congress. The average age of the Communist parliamentary group in 1946 was forty, below that of any other important party. At Gennevilliers the average age of the dele-

---

[21] Fauvet, p. 36.   Brayance, pp. 205–7: he estimates that about a sixth are really active. For the 1944 figures and comments on them, see Duverger, *op. cit.*, pp. 111 and 350. *L'Observateur*, 18 June 1953, gives an estimate of 420,000.

gates was no more than thirty-one; two-thirds of them were between twenty-five and thirty-five, and hardly any were over forty-five.[22] Half the members of the politburo in 1952 were men in their forties.

The encouragement of youth by the leadership is reinforced by pressure in favour of the industrial working-class element in the party.[23] In general, petty-bourgeois origins are considered as dangerous for a revolutionary party as middle age. In this respect another campaign was carried on before and during the congress of Gennevilliers: M. Marcel Servin, almost unknown as a deputy but a powerful figure in the party organization, complained early in 1950 that only 44 per cent. of the federal secretaries and only 37 per cent. of the members of federal committees were workers, and that the proportion must be greatly increased.[24] No doubt here too the dilution of working-class influence in the party can be attributed to the great extension of its appeal at the time of liberation. Between 1937 and 1945 party membership in industrial regions rose by only 50 per cent. But in semi-industrial regions it doubled, and in agricultural areas the 1945 figure was three and a half times the 1937 one; party membership as a percentage of population was actually largest in the rural parts of the country.[25]

The electoral strength of the party is impressive. From just under 1½ million votes in 1936, or 15 per cent. of the votes cast, the Communists jumped to 5 million in October 1945, over 26 per cent. of a total doubled by the admission of women. By October 1946 the party had gained another 500,000: in June its advance was most marked in the agricultural departments, in October in the industrial ones. If local elections are any guide this progress was continuing until 1949, or even later in the mining areas. By the general election of 1951, however, the Communist vote had fallen back to 5 million. Nearly half the loss of 450,000 votes occurred in the areas where the Church is strongest and the dominant issue is that of the Catholic schools—in twenty-nine north-western, eastern frontier and Cevennes departments which contain altogether only 27 per cent. of the electorate. This suggests that the damage took place at the fringe rather than at the core of the party's support. But its industrial advance, too, has been checked. The working-class constituencies, the scene of the main

---

[22] *Ibid.*, p. 195. *L'Humanité*, 6 April 1950 (M. Gourdeaux's report). See also Brayance, pp. 70, 214–5. On the Communist *electorate*, cf. Appendix VII.

[23] However, the anti-political tradition among French trade unionists is still strong. When M. Benoît Frachon first took office in the C.G.T. in 1936, he abandoned his place in the politburo, and has never officially returned to it. This, however, was merely a face-saving device. The party claims him as one of its principal official leaders, and though nominally not a member of the politburo, he attends all its meetings.

[24] *Le Monde*, 13 February 1950. Duverger, *op. cit.*, p. 186, quotes corresponding figures for some other party bodies.

[25] *Ibid.*, p. 53. But the subsequent fall in membership appears to have been most severe in agricultural areas.

Communist progress in November 1946, contributed more than their proportionate share of the losses five years later.[26]

The party remains strongest in three separate regions: the northern industrial area lying between Paris and Belgium, the rural departments on the northern and western edge of the *massif central*, and the predominantly agricultural Mediterranean coast, together with part of the hinterland. In the last two areas its power derives not from its claim to be the party of the proletariat, but from its successful annexation of the traditions of 1789. In the south and centre almost all the departments where Communism is strongest have been on the Left since the beginning of the Third Republic: only in the northern industrial area does the party owe its position primarily to a specifically working-class appeal.[27] The influence of Communism on the peasantry is a remarkable phenomenon, not confined to the poor *métayers* of the centre, but extending to prosperous southern farmers and winegrowers, owning their own land and voting to express a political rather than a social choice. In some rural areas Communist leadership in the *maquis* gave the party a foothold which greatly improved its political position, both directly and, through giving its members the opportunity to take over official positions, indirectly.[28] But, interesting and important as peasant communism may be, it should not obscure the crucial fact that, outside Alsace-Lorraine, the great bulk of the industrial working-class votes to-day for the Communist party.[29]

---

[26] There are fifteen highly industrialized departments, in which the percentage of the occupied population employed in industry and transport exceeds 40. (See map in F. Goguel, *Géographie des élections françaises—Cahiers de la Fondation nationale des sciences politiques*, No. 27—p. 133). These fifteen departments include 35 per cent. of the electorate; 45 per cent. of the Communist gains in November 1946, and 51 per cent. of their losses in 1951, occurred in them. The omission of the city of Paris would reduce but not eliminate the discrepancy.

[27] Goguel, *Géographie*, pp. 117 and 105, gives maps showing the distribution of the Communist vote in 1951, and the date at which the Left-wing departments acquired their political colour. See also Fauvet, p. 39. In rural Corrèze, only 1,000 of the 54,000 Communist voters were members of the party: Brayance, p. 69.

[28] See note 6. For example in Haute-Vienne, where one Communist was prefect and another was mayor of Limoges, the party gained greatly in prestige among the peasantry through holding positions which made it appear a ' serious ' instead of a ' wild ' movement. In 1952, the former mayor of Limoges broke with the party as a result of a quarrel arising originally out of differences over tactics in the resistance movement. To judge by subsequent by-elections, his defection made no difference to the party's popular support. (*Le Monde*, 7 October 1952, gives the figures.)

[29] See *Cahiers de la Fondation nationale des sciences politiques*, Nos. 1 and 12. In the former M. Pierre George undertook a detailed study of the Paris suburb of Bourg-la-Reine in the June 1946 election, when census figures were available for comparison. He shows the close correlation between the proportion of wage-earners and the strength of the Marxist parties in the three electoral divisions of the suburb, and the even closer correlation between the proportion of industrial workers and the Communist vote. (Charles Morazé and others, *Études de sociologie électorale*, pp. 67 ff.). In the latter, M. Lavandeyra derives similar conclusions from a study of another Paris suburb, Saint-Maur-des-Fossés, where the Communist share of the industrial workers' vote was higher than in Bourg-la-Reine. In nine of the eleven electoral divisions of the suburb the gap between the two percentages was 1·5 per cent. or less, and in the other two it was below 4. (Pierre George and others, *Études sur la banlieue de Paris*, p. 132.)

4. CHARACTERISTICS

THE assets of the party are numerous.[30] Its organization is superb, and has indeed been described as the finest administration in France.[31] The party keeps a tight hold over its members, claiming to influence not merely their votes but their entire lives. Most of their leisure time is devoted to it. It dominates their whole mental outlook as well as their personal activities. ' There is a communist literature in France which takes care of every reading need of its public, from novels and poems to cook-books and farmers' almanacs. Outside of the communist sphere of influence, nobody reads this body of literature; inside it, nobody reads anything else.'[32] Yet this totalitarianism within a democratic society does not destroy, in France any more than elsewhere, the Communist appeal to the intellectuals, from Picasso to Joliot-Curie. In France this support is of peculiar importance because of the exceptional prestige of the intelligentsia, and it is perhaps on a larger scale because of the strength of the Left-wing tradition—an asset in dealing with intellectuals as in appealing to the peasantry. The Communist appeal is indeed astonishingly wide. It is not only the largest, but also the least regionalized of French parties, with support distributed over the whole country. Outside the ranks of the party itself satellite organizations, from the Tenants' League to the Federation of Ciné-Clubs, spread its influence in a dozen subsidiary fields.[33]

The heart and centre of the party's power, however, lies in its control of the trade unions. Young, active working-class leaders are naturally attracted to an organization which offers full scope to ability, promotion by merit, encouragement for youth, and a vigorous and uncompromising defence of working-class interests, without any of the reservations and inhibitions felt by parties with a sense of government responsibility. In office the Communists allowed no considerations of cabinet solidarity to blunt their attacks on ministers of other parties, and abandoned their own policy of wage restraint as soon as it seemed likely to weaken their position in the trade unions. Out of office, they promoted every popular cause without any regard for consistency, practicability, or budgetary stability.[34] Their whole political activity

---

[30] Rossi, chapters xxvii–xxix, has an excellent discussion of the Communist appeal to different sections of the population.
[31] See Fauvet, p. 21.
[32] Herbert Lüthy, ' Why Five Million Frenchmen Vote Communist,' *Socialist Commentary*, December 1951, p. 289.
[33] Duverger, *op. cit.*, pp. 131–2. Party control of the Tenants' League is incomplete: Brayance, pp. 143–4.
[34] In 1946 and 1947 the search for peasant and shopkeeper votes repeatedly led them to join the extreme Conservatives in attacks on food rationing and economic controls, both in debates in the Assembly and in violent demonstrations in the country. *L'Humanité*, in May 1947, appeared with a banner headline, ' Assez de dirigisme bureaucratique et tracassier '. *A.P.* 1946, p. 191 ; 1947, pp. 97, 139, 245 ; 1948, p. 42.
M. Queuille, then prime minister, estimated the cost of the bills promoted by them just before the 1951 election at 2,000 milliard francs (£2,000 millions). See below, p. 257 n.

is concentrated on a single objective, the acquisition of power; they have no scruples about the methods they use to obtain it, and no concern for specific policies except as means to this one end.

The experiences of 1935–38 and of 1945–47 show how difficult it is to work with the Communists for long.[35] So they are now excluded from the ordinary parliamentary arena, able to intervene for obstructive but not for constructive purposes, falsifying the whole balance by removing most of the weight of the Left from the political and parliamentary scales. Their bitter hostility to the regime drives their opponents together, so that many of their political wounds are self-inflicted: more than one government has been saved from defeat by the fury of the Communist attacks on it. Yet the party no doubt regards these short-run reverses as a small price to pay for the purity, homogeneity and discipline which its intransigence secures it. Every parliamentary demonstration of general hostility to the Communists reinforces among the workers that sense of isolation from the community which is the source of the Communist hold on their imagination.

Outside the Assembly, the main weakness of the party is its inability to use for Moscow's purposes the strength it can command as the defender of working-class interests. Many workers adhere to Communist-controlled trade unions but remain suspicious of the party itself. Thus in the election of administrators for the social security system in April 1947 the C.G.T. candidates polled only half their claimed membership and the C.F.T.C. (Catholic trade union) candidates nearly doubled theirs; there was widespread discrimination against individual Communist leaders.[36] Even so the C.G.T. kept 60 per cent. of the total vote, compared with 26 per cent. for the C.F.T.C. At the end of 1947 the anti-Communist minority left the C.G.T. and set up the *C.G.T-Force ouvrière*, a nominally independent trade union federation which is in fact on friendly terms with the Socialist party; in the 1950 social security elections it took 15 per cent. of the votes from the C.G.T. The Catholic share also dropped by 5 per cent., to the advantage of the minor groups, some of which were sympathetic to F.-O.

The reluctance of the workers to respond is still more marked when active agitation rather than voting is in question. Communist efforts to use their hold on the unions for political purposes have failed lamentably in recent years. The failure of the 1949 general strike when M. Moch was elected to the premiership, the party's inability in 1950 to stop arms arriving from America or troops leaving for Indo-China, the poor response to the anti-Eisenhower campaign in 1951,

---

[35] Yet when their strategy dictates a policy of co-operation, their single-minded devotion can produce results which none of their rivals can match; witness the admirable restraint of the trade unions during the liberation period. ' Les communistes ont récrée pour les leurs la notion de responsabilité que les Français des dernières Républiques ont totalement perdue.' Brayance, p. 13.

[36] *A.P.*, 1947, p. 77. G. de Beaulieu in *Politique*, July 1947, pp. 557 ff.

and the collapse of the protest strikes against M. Duclos' arrest in 1952, all show that the C.G.T. is not available as a weapon of political pressure.

At this point the party's fundamental organizational basis, an asset in so many other ways, becomes itself a weakness. The cell unit is intended to facilitate organized action and agitation, and to help to identify party work with the member's daily life. But this identification itself conceals a danger: the member may concentrate only on those aspects of party work which really concern him intimately. Professional and trade union demands dear to the rank and file may come to bulk much larger in some minds than the political slogans handed down by the leadership. This is the heresy of ' economism '; and it is not confined to the lower levels in the party. Leaders who have to work in the unions and who know the real wishes of their followers naturally resent the dissipation of their strength and credit in futile demonstrations, ordered from outside as part of a long-term strategy remote from day-to-day reality, and often bearing no relation to the interests of the French working class. M. Benoît Frachon himself has been suspected of tendencies to ' economism ', and the turnover among his subordinates (which has affected men as important as M. Marcel Paul, former minister of Industrial Production and recently deposed leader of the electricity workers), reflects the struggle against this deviation as much as the pressure to promote younger men.

Moreover, the party's effective strength has sharply fallen since 1946. Even in votes there seems to be a saturation point for Communism. In the Paris ' red belt ', where they were strongest before 1939, they made hardly any progress in the liberation period,[37] and in 1951 actually polled a lower percentage vote than in 1936. In the trade union sphere the secession of F.-O. has weakened the C.G.T. But the decline of trade union power in general is even more significant. The distribution of votes between unions in 1950 meant less than the fact that a third of those eligible to vote did not do so at all. Political strikes meet with no response, but even strictly professional ones rarely succeed: in 1950, the combined pressure of the unions backed by open governmental and newspaper sympathy proved too weak to overcome the resistance of the Michelin owners at Clermont-Ferrand. A trade union movement too weak and divided to win strikes even with 'neutral' opinion behind it, and reluctant to allow its remaining strength to be dissipated in political adventures, is of very little use to a revolutionary party. Nor do their other assets compensate for this weakness. Their hold on key positions was limited even when the party held office, and such infiltration as they were able to achieve has now been reversed.[38] And, as 1947 showed, the appearance of a Communist

---

[37] Goguel, *Esprit*, November 1945, p. 956; *Fourth Republic*, p. 98.
[38] See below, pp. 385-7.

threat calls into being a reply from the other extreme. In the municipal elections of that October the R.P.F. led the field in all the thirteen largest cities in France, and any serious Communist recovery might well restore that position. Revolutionaries without the support of the towns are unlikely to be successful, at least in France.[39]

This rallying of opinion to the strongest anti-Communist movement at a moment of crisis is no accident. Though endeavouring to extend its appeal to the widest possible range of groups, the party deliberately sets out to draw a sharp line between itself and all its political rivals. ' Nous ne sommes pas un parti comme les autres.' All opponents are confounded together. The Communists thereby risk providing their divided enemies with a bond of union. But they also go far to establish among the masses the impression they most wish to create: that on the one side stands a determined, energetic, youthful movement conscious of the day-to-day problems which beset the ordinary Frenchman and able to offer solutions for them, on the other quarrelling cliques of tired old men interested only in devising a series of cynical bargains to prolong, probably for corrupt purposes, their stay in office. Political disillusionment provides fertile soil for this Communist campaign. After the elections of June 1946 the French Gallup poll found that 58 per cent. of Communist voters declared themselves completely satisfied with their party: among their rivals the highest proportion was 31 per cent., for M.R.P. Only 9 per cent. of Communists were not reasonably satisfied: the corresponding percentages were double for Socialists and M.R.P., and higher still for Radicals and Conservatives.[40]

The difference was not merely statistical. The whole psychology of the French Communist *militant* is very different from that of the ordinary politically minded Frenchman. Party members display none of the individualism which so frustrates the efforts and weakens the force of rival parties. In times of crisis they have shown that they can count on exceptional discipline and devotion for the advancement of their creed. Perhaps more remarkable still, in humdrum matters like running a municipality they have been able to develop among their constituents a quite unusual sense of civic responsibility. Their dynamic qualities, their complete certainty and conviction provide for many an immensely attractive contrast to the doubts and hesitations of their competitors, old-fashioned, unsure of themselves, and internally divided. Yet the Communist achievement in changing the whole mental outlook of their *militants* (for it is nothing less) has been bought

---

[39] For an assessment of Communist strength in 1947, see Vernon Van Dyke, ' the position and prospects of the Communists in France ', *Political Science Quarterly*, March 1948, pp. 45–81.

[40] *Sondages*, 1948, p. 225. In 1952, 62 per cent. of Communist voters professed full confidence in their party ; again M.R.P., with 51 per cent., came second. *Ibid.*, 1952, no. 2, p. 6.

at a high price. Rigid discipline requires complete suspension of the individual judgment. Absolute certainty in the triumph of the cause leads to willingness to accept any crime that serves the party's ends. The Communist party is in fact a state within the state, warring against its legal rival; the qualities of citizenship which it evokes are perverted to destructive and disastrous ends. In the last resort the most important psychological achievement of Communism is to kill the intellectual and pervert the moral integrity which originally inspired its best recruits.

Chapter 5

THE SOCIALIST PARTY

1. HISTORY

THE Socialist party is frequently referred to by the initials of its official title—S.F.I.O., *Section française de l'internationale ouvrière*. It was founded in 1905 by the junction of smaller socialist groups, which had for years been engaged in bitter tactical quarrels. The latest and greatest of these arose out of the Dreyfus case: one wing of the movement, led by Jean Jaurès and supported by most Socialist deputies, advocated an electoral and parliamentary alliance with the Radicals to save the Republic, while others under the leadership of Jules Guesde favoured the orthodox doctrinaire Marxist line of opposition to all bourgeois governments. One Socialist leader, Millerand, had accepted the ministry of Labour in the Waldeck-Rousseau cabinet, and his expulsion from the party became a symbolic issue. In 1904, when the international Socialist congress at Amsterdam passed a resolution calling for his expulsion, Jaurès accepted the decision, and the united party was established a year later. The affair demonstrated at the very beginning two characteristics of French Socialism—its profound internationalism, and its strong suspicion of leaders. The rank and file tend to suspect treason, to fear that members of parliament are too easily tempted by the wiles of the bourgeoisie; the deputies, always impressed with the dangers of the immediate political situation, are convinced that their supporters in the country are impractical doctrinaires, sadly devoid of political sense. The conflict apparent in 1905 has never been fully resolved.

Even before 1914 the Socialist party had long ceased to be revolutionary in anything but words. The energy of the real revolutionaries went into trade union activity, not into party work, and their creed was not communist but syndicalist. The Socialist party ardently defended political democracy and the parliamentary republic, and its leaders—including even Guesde, the prophet of doctrinaire Marxist orthodoxy—took office in the government of national unity in 1914. But as the war went on its opponents grew in strength within the party, and their resentment found eventual expression in the split at Tours, when the Communists took the great majority of the membership with them (though, significantly, only a fifth of the deputies).[1]

---

[1] Membership, Communists 130,000 to 140,000 ; Socialists, 30,000. Walter, p. 50. At the end of 1920 the united party claimed 180,000 members; at the end of 1921 the Socialist fraction had 52,000. Pierre Rimbert, ' L'Avenir du parti socialiste ', *Revue socialiste*, new series no. 54 (February 1952), p. 125. Deputies, 53 Socialists and 13 Communists. Walter, pp. 45, 53.

The old Socialist party had not by 1924 retrieved its electoral position: but it had the advantage of an alliance with the Radicals (the *Cartel des gauches*), and formed the left wing of M. Herriot's parliamentary majority. But Socialists and Radicals differed too deeply over economic policy for their common republican and anti-clerical outlook to form an adequate foundation for a lasting alliance. The Radicals in the last resort preferred to govern (though not to face the electorate) in alliance with the Conservatives rather than with the Socialists. This choice was moreover forced on them by the unwillingness of the Socialist rank and file to permit any compromise ; in 1929 the old quarrel between deputies and *militants* flared up again, when the former decided to take office in a Radical government, but were overruled by the latter.[2] In 1932 the electoral alliance with the Radicals was restored, but again failed to provide a basis for a stable majority. The most moderate Socialist deputies, who resented the *militants*' ban on compromise with the Radicals, resigned to form a separate group led by M. Renaudel; another section, headed by MM. Déat and Marquet, broke off to form the Neo-Socialist party, which fell increasingly under Nazi influence. In 1936 the alliance of the Left parties, reconstituted and extended to include the Communists, won another electoral victory. The Socialist party, the largest group in the new majority, took over the leadership of the government. This first experience of office in peacetime lasted for only two years.

This short-lived victory did not put an end to the dissensions within the party. The desperate and deteriorating international situation caused a serious division, which grew more acute as Nazi power increased. M. Blum and most of the leaders officially opposed appeasement, though somewhat half-heartedly: but at least half the party, led by its general secretary, M. Paul Faure, allowed their traditional and profound pacifist inclinations to lead them into acceptance, first of appeasement, and later of the Vichy regime. In 1940 the Socialists provided nearly half (36 out of 80) of the votes cast against the conferment of full powers on Marshal Pétain: but three-quarters of the Socialist members of parliament were on the other side. M. Paul Faure's chief trade union ally, M. Belin, held office in the first Vichy administration.

During the occupation many Socialists took an active and creditable part in the resistance movement; some resistance organizations were, indeed, like *Libération-Nord*, predominantly controlled by Socialists. Their contribution was perhaps less spectacular than that of the Communists or the Catholics, for the latter had more solid organizations behind them: but on an individual basis the party had nothing to be ashamed of. Its position at the time of liberation seemed to be very strong. Parliamentary democracy and political freedom had

---

[2] See below, p. 65.

recovered their prestige: drastic social reforms were widely recognized to be inevitable and overdue: many of their pre-war rivals had been discredited, and the Socialists seemed to have an obvious rôle to play in reconciling the Communists and Catholics, two groups virtually excluded from power in the Third Republic, which now suddenly appeared to press their claims. 'Humanist' leaders, like M. Blum, hoped to rejuvenate their movement as a French Labour party, emancipated from a Marxist creed which it had long ceased to take seriously, and open to new blood from the resistance organizations, for which the Socialist party could provide the most natural political home. But the opportunity was lost. The rank and file remained attached to the old doctrines, the old prejudices, and the old personnel: they would not grant rapid promotion to newcomers with no record of service to the party. The organization was much too democratic for the leaders to be able to counteract this resistance. Membership indeed increased slightly, though in 1946 it was only 25 per cent. above the peak of ten years before. But the potential new members, and above all the potential new leaders, were mostly diverted to other groups [3] or, more frequently, out of politics altogether. On the other hand, a purge of the members who had supported Pétain, more drastic than in any other party, ensured ideological purity at a considerable sacrifice of practical experience.

The election of October 1945 showed that the Socialists were only the third largest party. They found themselves somewhat in the position of the British Liberals in the 1920's, ground between stronger rivals on either flank. Whether they worked with the Communists against M.R.P., as in their support of the first draft constitution, or with M.R.P. against the Communists as in the subsequent months, they still lost votes on one side or the other. When the Communists went out of office in 1947, the Socialists found themselves virtually the prisoners of a conservative majority. They were too weak to impose a policy of their own: at most they could try, with M.R.P.'s help, to stop the complete dismantling of their post-war reforms. But they dared not repudiate responsibility for policy by going into opposition, for without their parliamentary support no majority could be found; in 1947 and 1948 the resignation of the Socialists would have put General de Gaulle in power. They were consequently obliged to retain office in governments they disliked, alienating most of their followers by continual compromises and the rest by occasional outbursts of frustration and anger. A relatively old and tired leadership had to face a situation difficult enough to deter younger and more vigorous men.

After the second electoral defeat, in June 1946, the division within the party became acute. At the Lyons congress of that year the policy of the old leadership was repudiated and most members of the former

---

[3] The break-up of the Socialist–U.D.S.R. alliance was typical: see below, p. 144.

executive committee lost their seats. M. Daniel Mayer, a protégé of M. Blum, who was supposed to represent the ' humanist ' wing of the party, was replaced as general secretary by M. Guy Mollet, the doctrinaire Marxist mayor of Robespierre's Arras. He succeeded in extending the authority of the executive over the deputies, and tried hard to take the party into opposition. Upon the expulsion of the Communist ministers in May 1947 he nearly persuaded the Socialists to withdraw too, and six months later a speech of his brought down the Ramadier government. But a few years worked a great transformation. M. Mollet, the Marxist, had before long become an advocate of participation in government, while those who opposed this course were led by a group of ex-ministers of whom the chief was M. André Philip, a devout Protestant and undoubted ' humanist '. And this difference, too, was settled by 1951; for when the withdrawal of the Socialists became possible without playing into the hands of the R.P.F., the party gave virtually unanimous approval to that policy. Its internal divisions disappeared as soon as its hands were free.

2. ORGANIZATION

THE organization of the Socialist party is thoroughly democratic. The basic unit is the section, though large sections may create smaller groups within them: the latter, however, are only formed for organizational convenience, and may not undertake public political activities. The section is based on the smaller administrative units of French local government, the ward, canton or commune. Its members meet monthly or fortnightly for business and political discussion. But a great many communes, perhaps two-thirds of the total, have no Socialist section, or one which hardly functions. In each department the sections are combined in a federation, the middle level between the base and the summit. To acquire a right to representation at the national level, a federation must include at least five sections and at least 100 members. The sections comprised within a particular constituency may also form unions for strictly limited electoral purposes.

Both financially and politically, the control of the rank and file over the organization is complete. Financially, the central organization takes only a small fixed sum (16 francs) from each subscription: the minor units fix their own share, and consequently decide the total subscriptions payable—thus in Paris the federation takes 40 francs, and the various sections between 20 and 50. The independence of the smaller units is thus completely safeguarded.[4] Politically, their power is equally unchecked. They elect their own officers, who are respon-

---

[4] Duverger, *Partis*, pp. 79–80 (1950 rates). A sliding scale of subscriptions, varying according to income from 32 to 100 francs a month, has now been adopted. But though local treasurers may collect the full sum from their prosperous members, they rarely pay more than the minimum into headquarters. Report of the 45th National Congress, pp. 15–16. The central office share has however been much increased since 1950.

sible solely to them—there is no analogy to Communist ' centralism '. They also elect their own representatives at higher levels, and may decide how the latter shall vote. Before each annual national congress members of the party (in practice usually, though not necessarily, leaders with a national reputation) draw up motions defining its policy on general or on specific issues. These motions are circulated to the congresses of the departmental federations, which are held a few weeks before the national congress: the authors of the motions travel round also to defend their points of view.[5]

The party constitution (Article 18) now requires all executive committees of the party, at the sectional, federal and national levels, to be chosen by majority vote. But for deliberative bodies, like federal and national congresses, P.R. is laid down in Articles 18 and 21. Each unit has a representation proportionate to its membership. Thus in the national congress each federation has at least one mandate, plus another for every twenty-five members. Nothing prevents wealthy federations, like Pas-de-Calais or Sénégal, buying more party cards than they can dispose of in order to increase their influence in congress.[6] The mandate system slightly under-represents the larger federations, but still leaves them in a very strong position. Thus for the 1952 congress the half-dozen biggest federations had one mandate for every 25 members, the twenty weakest one for every 20 members; the former nevertheless had 1,606 mandates out of 3,937.[7] Yet the congress often pays more attention to speeches from the weaker federations, which are carrying the flag in enemy territory, than to those from strongholds where the Socialists are, at least locally, a ' government party '.

A federation (or a section in a federal congress) may instruct its delegates how to vote on a given motion: if this is withdrawn or combined with another motion, as often happens, the delegates are usually allowed to use their own judgment, but are sometimes required to abstain. If there are differences of opinion within a federation, its mandates are divided proportionately between the opposing groups. The extent of this practice varies greatly from time to time. On 1 March 1952, for example, the national council (*conseil national*)— a kind of emergency congress, to be described shortly—met and debated two opposing motions on general policy and a preliminary amendment. Thirty-five federations voted solidly for the successful motion, 23 voted for the unsuccessful one, and 29 divided their mandates: on the preliminary amendment, however, only seven were

---

[5] The motions are lengthy affairs: the eleven put forward before the 1952 congress averaged about 1,750 words. Six had at least one deputy among their signatories; of the rest, four were signed only, and the fifth partly, by Parisian members. *Bulletin intérieur du parti socialiste*, no. 62 (May 1952), pp. 11–33.

[6] Duverger, *op. cit.*, p. 103.

[7] Report of the 44th National Congress, pp. 219–20, gives the relevant figures for each federation.

disunited. In December 1951, on the question whether the parliamentary group or the executive committee should determine party policy during government crises, a dozen federations split their votes.[8]

Between annual congresses, authority in the party is in the hands of two bodies. The national council meets every three months, or more frequently if convoked (as it often is) by the executive committee at a moment of political crisis: its most celebrated extraordinary meeting in recent years was that of May 1947, when it narrowly decided to allow the party to remain in the Ramadier government despite the departure of the Communists. The national council consists of one delegate from each federation, voting by mandates; the executive committee and representatives of the parliamentary party have the right to attend, but not to vote (though distant federations, like those from Corsica, Algeria, or colonial territories, sometimes give them proxies). The national council is thus in effect a small-scale emergency congress. Its functions correspond to some degree to that of the central committee of the Communist party, though they are less extensive because it meets less frequently. Its composition is, however, altogether different, since it consists of delegates controlled effectively by the rank and file, not of members nominally chosen by acclamation in congress, but in reality co-opted by the party leaders.

The essential authority in the party is the executive committee. For most of its life this body, then known as the permanent administrative committee (C.A.P.), had relatively restricted functions. In particular, the parliamentary group decided its own tactics in normal circumstances, though in a very exceptional case it might be overruled: thus when in 1929 the deputies decided to take office in the government (for the first time while the country was at peace) the C.A.P. summoned an emergency national council which rescinded the decision.[9] The method of election was as important as the restriction of powers. The contest was between opposing lists, nominated by the different wings of the party. These were represented on the committee in proportion to their voting strength at the congress. Between congresses, therefore, the separate wings tried to organize support in each federation, having their own newspapers and sometimes even an extra subscription.[10] The Socialist party of these years often appeared more as a federation of parties than as a united whole.

In an attempt to overcome these liabilities, the constitution and title of the C.A.P. were changed in 1944. Its powers were extended, and its name was changed to *comité directeur* in recognition of the fact. At the same time it was laid down, in the hope of weakening the fissiparous tendencies described, that it should be chosen by majority vote and not by P.R. For this election the delegates vote not by mandates

---

[8] *Ibid.*, pp. 179–80, 174–5.
[9] Duverger, *op. cit.*, p. 224.
[10] *Ibid.*, p. 145.

but as individuals, a method which over-represents the smaller federations.[11] Separate lists are no longer presented, and the candidates compete on an individual basis. The executive committee chooses the officers—the general secretary and two assistants, the treasurer and an assistant, and three bureau members: there is no president at any level in the Socialist party.

It was hoped that majority voting would give greater coherence to the leadership of the party: and indeed in the internal revolution of 1946 the partisans of M. Mollet secured all but 10 of the 31 places, defeating most members of the former executive. But since then the contest has been less clear-cut, and as a rule only about 45 candidates are nominated. Other factors besides the struggle of political factions naturally intervene: some members have a great personal reputation,[12] while others receive the votes of neighbouring federations on grounds of regional sympathy, for the differences between northerners, Parisians, and men of the Midi are no less among Socialists than among other Frenchmen.

One problem common to all French parties is felt by the Socialists more acutely than by any of their rivals. This is the tension between deputies and rank and file. As we have seen, the very formation of the party was marked by a triumph of the intransigent wing, the strict Marxist group who were always ready to suspect the integrity and loyalty of their parliamentary representatives. The tendency of French politicians (not wholly unknown elsewhere) to make a career on the Left and conclude it on the Right, went some way to justify this attitude of mistrust, which found clear expression in the party's statutes. In their original form, no member of parliament might be a member of the C.A.P., nor could a deputy be delegated as a representative of his federation on the national council, though the parliamentary group as a whole might nominate up to 5 per cent. of the members of the latter. To-day the position of the deputies is very much stronger: since 1913 up to ten of them, a third of the total, can be elected to the C.A.P. and its successor the *comité directeur*,[13] and they may also represent their federations on the national council.

---

[11] Each federation is entitled to at least two delegates, with one additional for every 15 mandates (or fraction thereof if greater than seven). This gives the small federations a stronger position in electing the executive committee than in any other decision. In 1952 the six strongest federations, with 40 per cent. of the membership, had only 113 of the 374 delegates. The federations with less than 500 members apiece had the same number of delegates (112), although their aggregate membership was only 16 per cent. of the total. The first group had one delegate for every 354 members; the latter one for every 137. Report of the 44th Congress, pp. 219–20. A proposal to revert to the P.R. system was heavily defeated at the 1953 congress.

[12] It is of course reputation with the *militants* that counts, not reputation with the electorate: the two may differ considerably. Thus in 1951 M. Moch lost his seat on the party executive. Two months later, in the general election, he secured 7,000 personal votes from supporters of other parties than his own. Both in 1950 and in 1951 the party treasurer and the two assistant secretaries, none of whom were deputies, were among the five names at the head of the list.

[13] *Règlement du parti*, Article 31.

This advance of the deputies has not, however, been made without difficulty. Though their personal rights are greater, the struggle for influence between the parliamentarians and the representatives of the *militants* has not diminished. When M. Mollet won his victory in 1946, he and his supporters further increased the powers of the executive committee, which now include control of the party's propaganda, press, *militants*, and representatives on public bodies (*élus*), and execution of congress and national council decisions. It also settles election strategy; in 1951 the local federations were allowed a free hand, except that they might not enter alliances with Gaullists or Communists, and required the executive's permission to form joint lists with other parties. Despite these extensive powers, the deputies, in their long tug-of-war with the executive, acquired by the compromises of 1949 and 1952 a stronger position than they had previously enjoyed.[14]

The executive committee wields authority, not only through its disputed right to decide party policy and tactics, but also through its undoubted powers in matters of discipline. It can dissolve and reconstitute a federation for grave acts of collective indiscipline: the federation of Pyrénées-Orientales suffered this punishment in 1950.[15] Similarly a federation, with the approval of the national executive, may dissolve a recalcitrant section. Individual members are subject to the decisions of conflicts committees, one for each federation and one at the national level. These are nominated in the appropriate annual congresses, and are composed of members of five years' standing (ten years for the national committee), belonging to no other departmental (or national) body: not more than a third of their number may be members of parliament.

Parliamentarians are subject to the control of the executive committee. The penalties which may be imposed are a warning (private or public), a formal censure, suspension from party duties—which deprives the member of the right to be a candidate, to speak or write in the name of the party, to represent it in any capacity, or to hold any party office—and, in the last resort, expulsion: against the two last there is an appeal from the federal to the national conflicts committee. Sanctions naturally depend on the offender's record as well as on the gravity of the offence. Thus on 30 January 1952 the executive censured half a dozen deputies (including four ex-ministers) for indiscipline: one persistent rebel was suspended for three months, which in the case of a deputy involves the loss of his place on parliamentary committees. On 12 March the committee considered the case of the 20 members who had voted against the party line over the European Army. They included the same persistent rebel, who was suspended for a year,

---

[14] See below, pp. 370–2.
[15] See below, p. 354.

three more of the recent offenders, who were suspended for two months, and sixteen others, who were censured.[16]

3. CLIENTÈLE

THE split at Tours had a disastrous effect on Socialist membership, which it reduced from 180,000 in 1920 to 52,000 a year later. With occasional setbacks, numbers climbed slowly back to their former level, which was passed in 1936; a year later the record figure of 285,000 was reached, though 100,000 of these had fallen away by the outbreak of the war. A great new influx at the time of liberation almost doubled the 1939 numbers, and in 1946 the new record of 354,000 was reached. In every subsequent year membership has dropped: 100,000 were lost in 1947–48, and over 70,000 in the following year. At the end of 1952 the number of party cards sold (the basis of the earlier figures) was only 116,000, representing a fully paid-up membership of 83,000.[17] All political parties have suffered a fall in membership since liberation, but in no other case has it been so large. It was serious enough that the 1952 figure was the lowest since 1928. Worse still, this was the sixth successive year that membership had fallen: no previous decline had lasted more than two years. For the first time, also, a general election year saw a reduction instead of the usual increase.

The electoral strength as well as the membership of the party has fallen almost by half since the time of liberation: from $4\frac{1}{2}$ million at the election of October 1945 to $2\frac{3}{4}$ million in June 1951. From 20 per cent. of those voting in 1932, and 19 per cent. in 1936 (before woman suffrage) the Socialist share increased to 23 per cent. in 1945, only to fall back at each subsequent general election to only 14 per cent. six years later.[18] This decline, however, unlike the fall in membership, was not continuous. Of the total loss of $1\frac{3}{4}$ million votes, more than a million deserted the party before November 1946, and the results of subsequent local elections suggest that in 1949 the Socialists, like their M.R.P. allies, began to recover a little of the lost ground.

One of the gravest aspects of the Socialist decline is its effect on the age-structure of the party. Most parties democratically controlled by their rank and file tend to give great weight to length of service as a criterion for promotion; the Socialist party constitution requires five years' membership as a qualification for becoming a delegate to the party congress or national council, for election to the executive committee, for editorship of the party newspaper, or for adoption as a

---

[16] *Bulletin intérieur du parti socialiste*, no. 62 (May 1952), pp. 41–3.
[17] Figures for 1952 from Report of the 45th Congress, pp. 115, 121–2; for earlier years from Rimbert, *loc. cit.*, p. 125; see also Fauvet, p. 87. As usual with French statistics, the authorities are in slight disagreement. Duverger, *op. cit.*, pp. 104 ff., discusses the significance of the figures of changing membership since 1920.
[18] Rimbert, *loc. cit.*, p. 127: see also Fauvet, *loc. cit.*, and Duverger, *loc. cit.*

parliamentary candidate.[19] This does not make it easier to recruit new leaders or to maintain rapid promotion. The numbers of experienced Socialist politicians were thinned by a drastic purge of those who had voted for Marshal Pétain in 1940: nevertheless, many more than half the Socialist candidates in the election of October 1945 had already held elective office in the Third Republic—much the highest proportion of any political group. At the beginning of the 1946 legislature the Socialists had fewer young deputies (aged 35 or less) than any of their rivals. Even among local leaders veterans are preferred: among the members of federal executive committees in 1951, 70 per cent. were more than forty years of age, and 30 per cent. more than fifty. Only in an eighth of the federal committees were the under-forties in a majority.[20]

The consequence has been that the Socialist appeal to youth, and in general to new elements outside its traditional ranks, has proved decidedly ineffective. Before 1939 the proportion of new members to old ones in any given year never fell below 15 per cent.: since 1945 it has regularly been below 4 per cent. The Socialist youth organization (in France as in other countries) has always been looked on with suspicion by the party leadership. In 1947, on account of its long-standing Trotskyist tendencies, it was deprived of its autonomy, and therewith of much of its appeal to youth. In 1953 the organization existed in only 45 of the 90 French departments. Among women, the greater frequency of religious observance weakens the appeal of the anti-clerical parties (less so for the Communists). They play little part in the direction of the Socialist party: in 1951 the 1,800 members of federal committees included only a hundred women. Correspondingly, organizations like the family associations are almost all in clerical or Communist hands.[21]

The Socialists suffer from another weakness even more disturbing to their leaders—the loss of their hold on the working-class. Few of their active members are industrial workers: 249 out of over 1,800 members of its federal committees, or 13 per cent., belonged to this

---

[19] *Règlement du parti*, Article 13. The German Socialist Egon Wertheimer, in his excellent *Portrait of the Labour Party* (Putnam, 1929), describes British socialism as situated in ' an incomprehensibly different world ' from that of the European Marxist parties. On the Continent, he says, it would be quite impossible for an aristocrat and recent convert from Conservatism, like Sir Oswald Mosley, to receive instant acceptance in the working-class movement. The difference persists; when Mr. Percy Cudlipp became editor of the *Daily Herald*, he was not even a member of the Labour party.

Duverger, *op. cit.*, pp. 188–97, discusses the age structure of parties and concludes that parties with a democratic structure tend to prefer older leaders.

[20] On candidates in 1945 see Husson, i, p. xxix. On deputies, Duverger, *op. cit.*, p. 196. On federal committees, Rimbert's second article in *Revue socialiste*, no. 55 (March 1952), p. 292.

[21] On the proportion of new members to old, Duverger, *op. cit.*, p. 112. On the Socialist Youth, Report of the 45th Congress, p. 49 (but compare the 1950 figure of 30.) On women in the federal committees, Rimbert, *loc. cit.*, no. 55, pp. 292–3. On family associations, Fauvet, p. 8.

class in 1950. Exactly half were either civil servants (by themselves over a third of the total) or black-coated workers, while 37 per cent. belonged to other social groups. In the parliamentary sphere the matter is even clearer. Among the Socialist candidates in 1945, 21 were industrial workers: the number of civil servants was ten times as great, the teaching profession alone contributing 140 candidates. Among members elected the proportions were the same: five industrial workers, forty teachers, and ten other civil servants. In November 1946 almost the same number of teachers and civil servants stood as candidates, but the manual workers had increased to 39 (one of them employed in agriculture): only three of the latter, however, were elected, compared with 36 civil servants (all but four of whom were teachers).[22] The 1951 figures were very similar to those of 1946.

At the same time the rank and file of the party is slowly becoming less proletarian. Only nine departments appear among the twenty with the largest membership both in 1919 and in 1952; most of those which dropped out in the intervening years were industrial, most of those which took their place were agricultural. However, the Socialist following among the workers has not been wiped out; the party is still distinctly stronger in industrial than in rural areas, and recently the loss of members has been a little less severe in the former.[23]

A similar picture emerges if votes rather than members are considered. The electoral basis of the party has shifted perceptibly in the last twenty years. In 1932 its vote exceeded 20 per cent. of the electorate in 29 departments; in 1951 it reached 15 per cent. in 23. But of the latter group, seven were newcomers, mostly rural departments where the Radical party had suffered heavy losses. Indeed in taking over old Radical strongholds, the Socialists were tending to become a regional party; 16 of their 23 strongest departments were south of the Loire, most of them far to the south. Their industrial influence had not, however, disappeared: they kept 20 per cent. of the electorate in each of the five Nord and Pas-de-Calais constituencies, the most industrial part of France; and even in Paris, where they were weak, they did much better in the working-class quarters than elsewhere. Nor in 1951 were their losses concentrated in the industrial areas, as those of

---

[22] Husson, vol. i, pp. xix, xxix; vol. ii, pp. xxvii, xxx: the civil servants include those who had retired. For the federal committees, Rimbert, *loc. cit.*, no. 55, p. 297.

[23] For the 1919 figures, Rimbert, *loc. cit.*, no. 54, p. 130. For those of 1952, Report of the 45th Congress, pp. 123–6.

Of the 11 departments which dropped out, four were highly, and three more fairly industrialized (i.e. had respectively over 40 per cent., and between 30 and 40 per cent., of their working population employed in industry and transport). Of the 11 which were added, none were highly, and only four were fairly industrialized.

But in 1952 the 20 strongest Socialist departments still included 11 of the 32 fairly or highly industrial departments, compared with only 5 of the 41 purely rural departments (50 per cent. working in agriculture); and the five strongest Socialist departments were all highly industrial.

Occupational figures from the map in Goguel, *Géographie*, pp. 132–3.

1946 had been. They were not recovering working-class support from the Communists, but they were beginning to check the damage.[24]

The same weakness among the industrial workers is evident in the trade union sphere. *Force ouvrière*, where Socialist influence is strong, is careful to preserve its nominal independence. But it has failed to shake the hold of the Communist-controlled C.G.T., and except among white-collar workers (especially those in government service) it is weaker than its Catholic rival, the C.F.T.C. The Socialist position is however a little better than the numerical weakness of *Force ouvrière* suggests. For, firstly, some independent unions, such as the Paris Metro drivers, often co-operate tactically with *force ouvrière*. Secondly, individual Socialists elected to works committees in their own plants can sometimes build up a strong personal position, since they concern themselves more with genuine grievances and less with political agitation than their Communist rivals. And, thirdly, the influence of the non-Communist unions extends beyond their own membership. They act as a rallying point for many workers who belong to C.G.T. unions, or to none at all, offering them a means of testing whether the C.G.T. calls for strike action really conceal political manœuvres. For the inability of the C.G.T. to get its instructions obeyed, its non-Communist rivals are largely responsible.

4. CHARACTERISTICS

THE weaknesses of the Socialist party are obvious and need no stressing. Over the years since liberation it has left the impression of an ageing, bourgeois party, sadly lacking in dynamic energy, and continually buffeted by the attacks of more powerful rivals. Its shifting geographical and social basis is slowly bringing it to resemble the Radical party of the Third Republic, and as it slips into the Radical skin it seems also to be acquiring Radical habits. A quarter of a century ago freemasonry, hitherto the backbone of Radicalism, began to invade the Socialist party.[25] Among the S.F.I.O. deputies and would-be deputies many are neo-Radicals in spirit—the most distinguished of them is M. Ramadier, chairman of the parliamentary group of freemasons before the war, prime minister in 1947, who twenty years ago left the Socialist party for a time because he believed it should co-operate in office with the Radicals, and who remains the chief advocate of partici-

---

[24] See maps in Goguel, *Géographie*, pp. 76 and 114.
Of the 29 departments where in 1932 the Socialists were strongest, nine were fairly or highly industrialized. By 1951 the Socialist vote had fallen below 15 per cent. of the electorate in two of these nine, and in eleven of the other twenty.
On Paris see F. Goguel, ' Structure sociale et répartition des votes à Paris . . . 1951 ', *Revue française de science politique*, vol. 1, pp. 326 ff.
The 15 highly industrialized departments include rather more than a third of the electorate. In 1951 they contributed just over half the Communist, and just over 30 per cent. of the Socialist losses.

[25] Albert Thibaudet, *Les Idées politiques de la France* (8th ed., 1932), pp. 186–7.

pation in government among the party leaders to-day. With the support of former Radicals the Socialists have acquired something of their temperament, and are indeed in danger of taking over their reputation—that of a party which has lost its soul and deteriorated into an electoral machine, concerned with little but clinging to power at any cost, and interested in persons rather than in policies, in tactics and combinations rather than in principles. Some of the graver scandals of the years since 1945, notably the Algerian wine affair in 1946 and the scandal of the generals in 1950, have involved the entourage of leading Socialist personalities, and this unfortunate fact has not helped the party's reputation.[26]

At the other extreme are the *militants* of the provinces. The charge against them is not one of excessive love of office and power and lack of concern for principle. It is the reverse: a doctrinaire intransigence which fails to realize the necessity for compromise in a system based on party coalitions, and which pays too little or no heed to governmental necessities. At the top the Socialists are a government party, too much so in the view of many. But at the base they are, as they have always been, fundamentally an opposition-minded party: and in the end it is the rank and file which has the last word.

The difference is one of tactics as well as of temperament. For both sides the central problem is one of opposition to communism. The *militants* and the Left, though still regarding themselves as Marxists, are no more disposed to compromise with the Stalinist enemy than the party leaders and the right wing of the party. But one section prefers opposition, with a free hand to advocate Socialist policies and repudiate responsibilities for actions and attitudes which they deplore, while the other relies rather on entering the government to secure practical reforms to benefit their clientèle, or at least to prevent injury to them. The opponents of participation are, however, by no means identical with the working-class section of the party. In France as in Great Britain it is the middle-class Socialists, those who are in a small minority in their own areas, who show the greatest devotion to doctrinaire principle, and the least interest in the responsibilities of power and the practical problems of politics. The large working-class federations like those of Haute-Vienne and Nord generally support the official leadership, while those in which middle-class influence predominates, such as the Rhône federation, are in a state of chronic rebellion: for instance, on the important tactical issue of whether the parliamentary

---

[26] Thus in 1951 the Socialists were described as ' un parti de clientèle . . . de ministres et de députés, de maires et de conseillers-généraux, de préfets et de policiers, véritable coalition d'ambitions et d'intérêts au sein de laquelle survivent, d'une manière étrange, quelques militants ancien style, petits rentiers politiques mangeant mélancoliquement le capital de leurs souvenirs.' Gilles Martinet, ' La gauche non conformiste ', *La Nef*, April–May 1951, p. 55. Cf. below, pp. 306, 327n.

Long before the war, M. Herriot had applied to the Socialist party the sign displayed by a restaurant in his constituency: ' Restaurant ouvrier—cuisine bourgeoise '.

group or the executive committee should decide policy in a governmental crisis, the smaller federations decided the issue in the latter's favour.[27]

French governments since liberation have so often sacrificed working-class interests to those of peasants and businessmen (whether by design or through impotence) that they could hardly have expected to retain the steady support of the Socialist party. Yet when that support has been forfeited the reason has not always been a concern for immediate working-class interests. Besides being an old party the Socialists often give the impression of being an old-fashioned one, giving excessive weight to questions like that of *laïcité*, which for many are dead issues. This is the hidden reef which has wrecked any hope of launching a French Labour party, as so many (led by M. Blum) hoped in the promising atmosphere of the liberation years. Only by combining the Socialists and M.R.P. in one solid organization could the democratic Left hope to carry real weight in coalition politics, and to impose the reforms without which the Communist hold on the French workers cannot be broken. The resistance struggle should have killed the suspicion that a Catholic could not be a good republican. 1945 offered a chance, perhaps slender and certainly fleeting, to build a party which could genuinely bring into the Fourth Republic two groups which had largely been excluded from the Third—the devout Catholics and the industrial workers.

It proved impossible to achieve. The Socialist party is a democratic organization, and the foresight of a few leaders could not prevail against the determination of the *militants* to stand by their old traditions and prejudices. They would accommodate themselves neither to the generation from the resistance movement, which broke away with U.D.S.R. or retired into political disillusionment, nor to the new phenomenon of progressive Catholicism, which found expression in a new party with which the Socialists have learnt to work, but which they have not yet come to trust. For them the shadow of the Vatican, of the reimposition of clerical tyranny on France, still renders M.R.P. intensely suspect. Over the Catholic schools the Socialists will admit no compromise: less than ever now that the decline in their industrial following has left them so largely a civil servants' party. The astonishing proportion of teachers among the Socialist leaders shows why they consider the question of *laïcité* so important. It is a bond between the 'neo-Radical' type of deputy and the most intransigent of the provincial *militants*, for in the countryside it is the question that counts, and the Socialists depend electorally upon the rural schoolteacher as

---

[27] Among the larger federations six (including Pas-de-Calais, Seine, and Seine-et-Oise) voted for the motion giving powers to the executive committee; ten voted against it; one abstained, and one divided fairly evenly. Among the smaller ones 33 were in favour, 22 against, three split, and five abstained. All the colonial votes were cast for the motion. Report of the 44th Congress, p. 144. But see below, pp. 371–2.

much as M.R.P. relies on the *curé*. On the problems of modern industrialism Socialists and M.R.P. have few quarrels, while Socialists and Radicals have little or nothing in common: yet the local elections of 1949 showed clearly that the Socialist *militant* would rather vote Radical than M.R.P. In western departments like Finistère Socialists have even plumped for an anti-clerical Gaullist in preference to a supporter of M.R.P.[28] The 1951 election showed to what an extent the Socialist party has become first and foremost the defender of *laïcité*. There were only eight metropolitan constituencies out of 103 in which its share of the vote did not fall: and in six of these it was fighting alone, without the embarrassment of clerical allies.[29]

The last serious weakness of the Socialist party, and for long the most conspicuous of all, is its tendency to internal division. Internal democracy in the party has gone further than a care for pure efficiency would have dictated. The rank and file are really in control, and the leadership has nothing but its prestige to oppose to them. The departmental federations enjoy a high degree of autonomy; since they play very different electoral rôles (essentially anti-clerical in Brittany and Anjou, primarily anti-Communist in Haute-Vienne, still that of a working-class party in the northern industrial area, etc.) the tactics they prefer are often contradictory. At the top there is the difference of outlook between parliamentarians and executive committee. Compared with their modern rivals if not with their old ones, the Socialists seem individualistic and undisciplined. One would expect a movement of freethinkers to show more signs of waywardness than either Communists or Catholics, but it is not merely an intellectual matter. Nor is it a simple question of organization, though both Communists and M.R.P. are much more centralized parties. These can call upon more intense loyalties, largely because neither is a purely political movement; the one has in the C.G.T., the other in the Catholic Church and its satellite organizations, a more solid and durable social foundation than the Socialist party possesses. Both claim more from their members than electoral support or even political education: both reach out into all the activities of daily life. Movements with an answer to all questions are more positive and more effective at reaching the masses than the individualist, libertarian parties. The liberal attitude of the anti-clerical parties is in some ways more attractive to foreigners with a Protestant background: but it is not an asset to a movement seeking a mass appeal in a country with a Catholic past.

---

[28] Fauvet, p. 95.
[29] Gironde (second constituency), Aveyron, Deux-Sèvres, Haute-Loire, Bouches-du-Rhône (first constituency), Ariège, Pas-de-Calais (first constituency), and Finistère: the order is that of the percentage gain, which in Finistère was nil. Only in Bouches-du-Rhône and Ariège was the party fighting in alliance with M.R.P. The list excludes cases where the apparent gain simply reflects the withdrawal of another party's list (e.g. Vendée).
In the two constituencies where the Socialists did best they nevertheless lost seats, owing to the working of the electoral law (see below, p. 324). But this does not affect the argument advanced here.

Yet it would be unjust to conclude the description here. For the party's weaknesses were largely the result of its exceptionally difficult situation. Men in office in France are always suspect, and are more vulnerable than ever when they possess office without power. But it would be unfair wholly to blame the Socialist ministers for their impotence to obtain the results which would satisfy their supporters. It was not caused by any fear of responsibility: they were at all times willing to take the most difficult posts, but were hardly ever allowed to do so. M. Moch, indeed, took over the ministry of the Interior when it was the most-avoided post in the government, and left it the most sought-after: but the one attempt since 1946 to put a Socialist back at the ministry of Finance proved fatal to the prime minister who attempted it. Nor was their failure the result of any inherent inability to make up their minds or to act with speed, unity, and decision: this was demonstrated once and for all by the one month of all-Socialist government in December 1946. Nor again was it due to inherent factionalism. In the situation in which the party was placed differences and divisions were inevitable. But the return of the Socialists to opposition produced an instantaneous cure, and the quarrelsome and divided congresses of the earlier years were succeeded by almost complete harmony and unanimity at those of 1950, 1951, and 1952 [30]—while the strains which had hitherto afflicted the Socialists were instantly transferred to the party which now formed the exposed flank of the majority, M.R.P.

For the task of defending the interests of the poor by democratic means is an appallingly difficult one in a country where the trade unions are Communist-controlled. It is harder still when the country is not even predominantly an industrial one, so that a large peasant and petty-bourgeois class stands ready to obstruct reforms, however overdue, for which it is reluctant to pay. Yet parliamentary government can never be really stable in France while a quarter of her population, led by the organized force of the trade unions, considers that Western democracy has nothing to offer. Only in 1936 and in 1945–46 was any attempt made to reconcile the industrial workers to the Republic, on both occasions largely under Socialist leadership. That its efforts have largely failed should not deprive the party of the credit for tackling a problem which its rivals have generally obstructed or ignored.

Finally, the S.F.I.O. has the strength of democracy as well as its disadvantages. It is the only political organization in which the rank and file exercise genuine and complete control. It fights out its internal battles in the open, instead of doing so behind closed doors. In return it enjoys a very high degree of loyalty, solidarity and comradeship which are more genuine than the obvious rifts on the surface: its loss

---

[30] The division in 1952, over the rearmament of Germany, was on entirely different lines from those of previous years. Germany was again the main issue in 1953; the critics of the party's general strategy did not press their case.

of only three deputies out of a hundred, between 1946 and 1951, is a tribute to this fact.[31] Where so many of its rivals are either totalitarian conspiracies or co-operative societies of political careerists, a party which sets out to achieve genuine social and political changes within a democratic framework can stand the comparison without excessive shame.

---

[31] Colonial members excluded.

Chapter 6

THE MOUVEMENT RÉPUBLICAIN POPULAIRE [1]

1. HISTORY

THE *Mouvement républicain populaire* represents an old tradition in French thought, which has never hitherto found effective political expression. At least since the time of Lamennais there have been Catholics who were aware of the problems created by the industrial revolution, and Catholics (not always the same ones) who were anxious for reintegration in the French political community, from which under the Third Republic they were at first virtually excluded. In the early years of this century Marc Sangnier's review *Le Sillon* formed for Liberal Catholicism a focus as important as that provided for reactionaries by Maurras and the *Action française:* both these rival movements were condemned by the Vatican at about the same time. Their leaders survived: Sangnier ended his life as honorary president of M.R.P., and on his death was officially honoured by his old political opponents the Socialists: Maurras was sentenced to life imprisonment for collaboration, and just before his death in 1952, he celebrated his compassionate release by demanding the execution of the minister of Justice responsible for the purge.

During the years between the two wars the progressive Catholic tradition was represented by two small groups, the *Parti démocrate populaire* and the *Jeune République*. The former was confined to a few regions, Brittany, Lorraine, and one or two mountainous departments in the south. Political commentators found some difficulty in classifying it either with the Right or with the Left. The *Jeune République*, founded by Sangnier shortly after the suppression of the *Sillon*, was not strictly speaking a party at all, but an extra-parliamentary organization or 'league'. It was less clearly confessional, less electoral, and more progressive than the P.D.P., and in 1936 it officially adhered to the *Front populaire*.

It was not, however, the political organizations which were most important in preparing the way for M.R.P. The real foundation of the movement lay in the great extension after 1918 of the social activities of the Church. One important source was the development of the Catholic trade unions, the C.F.T.C. (*Confédération française des travailleurs chrétiens*): another, the rise of the Catholic youth organizations, *Jeunesse ouvrière chrétienne, Jeunesse agricole chrétienne*, and *Associa-*

---

[1] For a full account of M.R.P. see M. Einaudi and F. Goguel, *Christian Democracy in Italy and France*.

tion catholique de la jeunesse française. Supporters of the various progressive Catholic movements came together to collaborate on M. Francisque Gay's paper *L'Aube;* with contributors from the *Parti démocrate populaire*, the *Jeune République, Action catholique*, and the Christian trade unions, it was a forerunner of the combination which later produced M.R.P. This first common venture occurred only in 1938, but shrewd observers had for years predicted the possibility of such an event. Albert Thibaudet, writing in the 1920's, described Christian socialism as one of the six great French political traditions, and declared that only leadership was needed to create a powerful new movement from the material already assembled.[2]

These developments were crystallized by the war and the resistance movement. The progressive Catholic groups had shown the vigour of their democratic convictions before the outbreak of the war by refusing to compromise with Fascism either at home or abroad, and opposing Mussolini's attack on Abyssinia, Franco's rising in Spain and the capitulation to Hitler at Munich with equal determination. After the defeat their members and leaders could claim a splendid record in the resistance movement, in which M.R.P. ' found itself '. The movement was constituted in 1944 at Lyons, one of the principal centres of Catholic Resistance. Its aims were ambitious. Starting with new men and a clean sheet, it set out to retrieve for the Republic two groups within the nation which were dangerously alienated from it, the Catholics and the working class. It chose to call itself a movement, not a party, in order to emphasize that its purposes were not limited to electoral success, but extended to the promotion of the general principles and doctrines of the Church: it was hoped that in the purified atmosphere of the new regime, the complete regeneration of French political life could be achieved.

In pursuing these ambitious objectives it enjoyed several important advantages. A solid basis in the Catholic youth and social organizations was made still firmer by the powerful support of the clergy; among the parish priests this was generally based on conviction, but many of their superiors had reason to welcome the opportunity of associating themselves with an organization which possessed an impeccable resistance record. This strong backing ensured that it was well adapted to a political situation in which the strength of the Communist party put a premium on effective organization and discipline. The M.R.P. leaders were in no way tainted with responsibility for the despised regime of the inter-war years, for the war itself, or for the Vichy counter-

---

[2] Thibaudet, p. 118: ' Il y a une jeunesse, elle attend un guide; des cadres, ils sont prêts pour un tableau; des hommes, il leur faudrait un homme.'

Among the better-known M.R.P. leaders MM. de Menthon, Letourneau and Colin were active in the A.C.J.F., and the first two, along with MM. Bidault, Teitgen, Robert Schuman, and Lecourt, in the P.D.P., of which M. Raymond Laurent was general secretary: M. Maurice Schumann belonged to the *Jeune République*, MM. Dacon, Bouxom, and Robert Prigent to the J.O.C., etc.

revolution. They enjoyed the great prestige of novelty, an admirable resistance record, and the tacit blessing of the greatest of Catholic resisters, General de Gaulle. Millions of French conservatives, bewildered by the discrediting of their former leaders, were seeking a powerful bulwark against the threat of Communism, and believed they had found it in M.R.P. So it achieved an initial success which astounded its own leaders as much as everyone else: in August 1945 the movement had 100,000 members,[3] in October it secured 4¾ million votes.

But the early triumphs were artificial. Only a minority of M.R.P. voters shared the progressive political and social attitude of the party rank and file; the majority were Conservatives, for whom M.R.P. was the best available barrier against Communism rather than a permanent political home. The attempt to preserve this swollen electoral following caused the M.R.P. leaders and deputies to adopt a more conservative attitude than the membership would have wished, but they did not go far enough to satisfy their voters. During 1946 M.R.P. first acquired new support by leading the opposition to the first draft constitution, then forfeited it again by its reluctant acceptance of the second. To millions of M.R.P. voters this was compromising too far with Communism. There was as yet no electoral alternative for them to turn to: but they were able to express their resentment in the referendum of October 1946, when some two-thirds of the M.R.P. voters, especially in the conservative north, responded to the appeal of General de Gaulle rather than to the instructions of the party. If the General gave the lead, these voters would turn from a party whose aims they had never really shared, to follow a leadership much more attuned to their own ideas.

In April 1947 that lead was given, and the 'lost Conservatives' went over in droves from M.R.P. to the R.P.F. In the municipal elections of that October M.R.P. had only 10 per cent. of the votes, as against 25 per cent. the year before. After that date the decline was halted, and a numerically weaker but more homogeneous movement emerged. M.R.P. deputies still felt the pull of competition from the parties on their Right, but the steady determination of the rank and file to maintain the Socialist alliance continued to check attempts at flirtation with the Gaullists.[4]

2. ORGANIZATION

The organization of M.R.P. is basically similar to that of the Socialist party, but gives a good deal more power to the leadership. The normal basis of sections and departmental federations is maintained: to be

---

[3] Wright, p. 76.
[4] See below, p. 370.

affiliated nationally, a federation must include at least five sections of ten members each, with a total membership of a hundred, and must have been active for six months. It is controlled by an annual congress, an executive committee (*comité directeur fédéral*) and a bureau. The subscription rate, as with the Socialist party, is fixed by the federation: there seems sometimes to be difficulty over the collection of affiliation fees by the centre.[5] In most federations the parliamentary representatives of the movement subscribe part of their salaries to party funds, but this is not obligatory as it is in the Communist and Socialist parties.[6] For local elections candidates are chosen by the federation, but for Parliament, for the departmental councils, and for the municipal council of Paris the confirmation of the national executive committee is required. The method of nomination is left to the federation; for example in Côtes-du-Nord in 1951 the federal congress itself chose the head of the list, but allowed the committee to pick the other candidates, two of whom were deputies up for re-election.[7]

The structure of the organization at the national level is on the familiar model. There is an annual congress, which can be convoked for an exceptional session by the *comité national* or by a quarter of the federations. The *comité national* is a 'little congress', or national council, equivalent to the Socialist *conseil national*. It meets every two months (or oftener if summoned by the executive committee, or by a third of its own members). The executive committee (*commission exécutive*) meets at least fortnightly and elects a bureau which is permanently responsible to it.

The composition of these bodies differs considerably from that of their Socialist counterparts. In the latter party care is taken to safeguard the position of the *militants*. In M.R.P. the pressure is the other way, to preserve the deputies and leaders against too strong an influence from the rank and file. The situation of the early years, with a membership on the Left and an electorate on the Right, may have contributed to this situation: the deputies were well aware that if the *militants* carried the movement too far to the Left they would forfeit most of their support in the country.[8] But with the departure of many of the right-wing voters into the R.P.F. this justification lost some of its force.

In the Socialist party, representation in the national congress is proportionate to membership. In M.R.P. it is based on a sliding scale—one delegate for every 50 members up to a total of 200, for every 100 members between 201 and 5,000, and for every 200 members (or fraction

---

[5] Thus *L'Action fédérale* (a monthly bulletin for local party officials), no. 14 (January 1950), p. 14, warns federations that they must not use the central share of the subscriptions for their own purposes, but must pay it over as soon as possible.
[6] *Ibid.*
[7] *Le Monde*, 16 May 1951.
[8] Duverger, *Partis*, pp. 215–6.

over 100) above this limit. The object was to avoid the domination of the congress by half a dozen powerful federations, as sometimes occurred in the Socialist party. It was feared that this would turn M.R.P. into a regional organization based on the areas where its predecessors had a foothold, and that the consequence would be a weakening of its appeal elsewhere. But a by-product of the system was to strengthen the leadership, for in a new and inexperienced party like M.R.P. there is a tendency for opposition to come mainly from the strong federations, and their influence is reduced by the sliding scale arrangement.[9] In addition to the one vote per delegate cast by the representatives of the federations, every M.R.P. member of parliament, of the Assembly of the French Union, and of the national council has a personal vote.

The position of the leaders and parliamentarians is still more carefully safeguarded in the remaining central institutions of the party. The national council and executive committee include as *ex officio* members the president, honorary presidents, general secretary, and treasurer of the party, the presidents of its parliamentary groups (including that in the Assembly of the French Union), ministers belonging to M.R.P. when the party is in office, and five ex-ministers elected by the parliamentarians when it is not. All these except the ministers are also members of the executive committee's bureau.[10] The M.R.P. deputies and senators elect a third of the current total membership of the national council, which is not fixed; it numbered 187 in 1951.[11] Twelve of these parliamentary representatives are chosen by the national council to serve on the executive committee, which numbers about fifty. The M.R.P. members of the Assembly of the French Union have the same proportionate representation on the national council as their parliamentary colleagues, and two representatives on the executive committee.

The rank and file are represented on the national council through the federations, which are entitled to one delegate for every 1,000 members or fraction thereof. These delegates may not be members of parliament, but their 'alternates' may be. On the executive committee the federations have 18 representatives, who may not be parliamentarians, and are elected by and from the national council. In addition the latter body co-opts 24 *militants* to its own ranks, and elects five to the executive committee. The bureau of the executive consists of the party officials, the chairmen of the three parliamentary groups, and seven

---

[9] *Ibid.*, p. 170. But see below, p. 370n.
[10] The national council includes, besides ministers in office, those who have held office since the last congress: if there are none, five ex-ministers are elected. But the executive committee includes only actual ministers or their elected replacements. These, with the *ex officio* members, may not exceed a quarter of its total membership.

The presidents of the parliamentary groups are included among their representatives enumerated below. The presidents of the three Assemblies themselves, if members of M.R.P., have the same rights as ministers.
[11] Fauvet, p. 193.

members elected by the executive; in 1951 all but one of these were deputies, and most were former ministers.[12]

This complicated structure places the parliamentarians in a very strong position. Their apparently restricted membership is reinforced in several ways. There is separate representation for the members of the Assembly of the French Union, whose outlook is nearer to that of the deputy than to that of the *militant*.[13] The most prominent leaders of the movement sit in their own right, and carry great personal weight. The co-opted *militants* are likely to be chosen among adherents rather than among opponents of the leadership; there is indeed nothing to prevent the choice of members of parliament. And parliamentarians may act as alternate members. This becomes important in a political crisis, when a special meeting of the national council is called: for a distant federation will often ask its deputy to represent it, since he is sure to be available in Paris. Discontent among the rank and file thus rarely finds effective expression, except at national congresses. And the statutes are not easily changed from below. Modifications can only be proposed by the national council, by the executive, or by a quarter of the federations, and they must be voted in the national congress by a two-thirds majority.

Among the M.R.P. *militants* discipline has been well kept: dissensions, such as that caused by the creation of the R.P.F., have affected half the party's voters and many of its deputies, but comparatively few of the active rank and file. These are on the whole less individualist than their Socialist opposite numbers, and more willing to accept the instructions of the leadership. Collective indiscipline is dealt with on the initiative of the executive committee by the national council, though only a specially called national congress can dissolve a recalcitrant federation. Individual rebels are subject to the control of a committee of discipline and arbitration, composed of four members of the national council elected by it (two of whom and two only must be members of parliament) with the general secretary of the party in the chair. When this committee disagrees with the member's local federation the matter is referred to the national council. A parliamentary group may be required by the executive committee to vote unitedly on a particular

---

[12] For the 1951 bureau see *Le Monde*, 20 July 1951.
Of the 24 members co-opted by the national council, twelve represent the specialized organizations of the party (to be discussed below) and two its members on local authorities: these are chosen from lists prepared by their 'constituents'. The other ten are co-opted freely.
The composition of the national council is governed by Articles 32 to 35 of the *Statuts nationaux*, that of the executive committee and its bureau by Articles 43 to 46. Perhaps by an oversight, Article 32 does not include the treasurer as a member of the national council.
[13] But in comparing M.R.P. with the Socialists it must be remembered that members of the Assembly of the French Union can sit on the Socialist executive as representatives of the *militants*. The Socialist *comité directeur* elected in 1951 included five members of that Assembly: if they were counted as parliamentarians the latter would be within one vote of a majority among the Socialists too.

measure, though this now rarely occurs: if a member defies this decision, the case goes to the discipline committee, with an appeal from its decision to the national council. The latter also has a general jurisdiction over internal disputes the solution of which is not otherwise provided for.

Finally the organization of M.R.P. includes one markedly original feature. The doctrines of the party are strongly influenced by corporative ideas: as a Catholic movement it repudiates individualism and seeks to work through a series of specialized organizations. Each federation must establish such specialized organizations (*équipes*) at least for women, youth, workers, peasants, the professions, and managers (*cadres*), as a condition of affiliation to the party. The national council includes twelve representatives of the corresponding national organizations, chosen by itself from lists drawn up by the organizations. Despite the relative obedience to discipline and the powerful sense of solidarity and devotion to a common cause which are so characteristic of M.R.P., these bodies (especially that of the workers) do form the nucleus for the development of a potential opposition within the party.[14]

3. CLIENTÈLE

M.R.P. has suffered like its rivals from the general decline in the strength of parties. Its fortunes have paralleled those of the Socialists. Like them it has been losing members steadily since 1946, falling from 200,000 to less than half that number.[15] Like them also it has lost heavily, but not continuously, in terms of electoral support. At the peak, in the election of June 1946, it had $5\frac{1}{2}$ million voters: within the next five years 3 million of them deserted it. But the first half-million had gone before the end of 1946, and the October referendum showed that a high proportion of the rest were only awaiting the appearance of a satisfactory alternative. It emerged in the shape of the R.P.F. a few months later, and M.R.P. went through a serious crisis. But since the low point of 1947–48 there has been a recovery, in terms of votes at least, and with the assistance of the new electoral law, the movement remains a force to be reckoned with.

Like the Communists, M.R.P. enjoys the advantage of being a young party. As a new organization, it could not make length of membership a criterion for holding office, and the only restriction of this kind is the requirement that delegates to the annual congress must have been members for at least a year (unless they represent newly-formed federations). M.R.P. congresses are dominated by young men in their thirties, though the average age is not quite so low as it is among the Communists.[16] Within the movement itself the voting age is eighteen

---

[14] Thus at the Paris congress in 1953 the workers' *équipes* defeated the platform on the issue of workers' control in industry. *Le Monde*, 24–25 May 1953: see also the Epilogue.
[15] Fauvet, p. 182.
[16] See e.g. *Le Figaro*, 19 May 1950 (on the Nantes congress).

for all purposes. The parliamentary group in 1946 had a proportion of young members (under thirty-six) exceeded only by the Communists.[17] This appeal to youth is extended by M.R.P., which likes to call itself ' the party of the family ', to women also. Its statutes require every federation to elect at least one woman vice-president; and in the 1946 Assembly it elected nine women as deputies, no other party (except the Communists) having more than three.[18]

The social composition of a party with a religious basis is rarely clear-cut or easy to establish. M.R.P., like the old German Centre party, includes employers, workers, and peasants alike. Indeed its parliamentary membership is extraordinarily representative of French politics; in both November 1946 and 1951 the proportion of its candidates drawn from professional, business, peasant and working-class circles respectively was very similar to the national average (slightly larger for peasants, slightly smaller for workers). The same was true of those who were elected. In both these elections, about half the M.R.P. deputies were professional men: among the remainder there were rather more businessmen than peasants or workers.)[19]

The working-class element in the party is more important among its *militants* than among either its deputies or its electors. It accounted for 20 per cent. of the 100,000 adherents in 1950. Twenty-two per cent. were engaged in commerce or industry, 15 per cent. in agriculture, and 8 per cent. in the professions (including students). Civil servants, with whom railwaymen were rather oddly included, made up 10 per cent. of the total, and the rest were retired or unspecified.[20] Among the

---

[17] Duverger, *op. cit.*, p. 196. In 1951 M.R.P. had the highest percentage of all.

[18] The difference was less marked, however, in 1945 and in 1951. Even in November 1946 M.R.P. had more women deputies than other parties not because it had more women candidates (the proportion was much the same among Socialists and Radicals), but because it put more of them at the head of its lists.

[19] Percentage engaged in :

	Professions 1946	Professions 1951	Business 1946	Business 1951	Peasants 1946	Peasants 1951	Workers 1946	Workers 1951
Of all candidates	41	36	15	21	13	16	21	20
Of M.R.P. ,,	43	38	15	20	15	20	18	17
Of all deputies	51	54	12	16	10	13	16	13
Of M.R.P. ,,	49	54	14	14	12	10	12	10

1946 figures taken from Husson, ii, pp. xxvii and xxx. *Cadres* (industrial and commercial) have been counted as businessmen, and artisans as workers ; those of unstated occupation have been omitted. Though M.R.P.'s professional percentage coincides with the national average, this conceals a deficiency among those engaged in teaching, and an excess among other professional occupations. Among candidates there is a similar deficiency of industrial, and excess of black-coated workers.

In November 1946 there were among the M.R.P. deputies (excluding those from overseas) 23 businessmen, 20 peasants, 20 workers, 77 professional men (16 of them teachers) and 18 of no stated occupation (Husson, *loc. cit.*). The official figures for 1951 give 12 businessmen, 8 peasants, 8 workers, and 45 professional men.

[20] Jean Fonteneau, assistant secretary of the party, at the Lyons congress: *M.R.P. à l'action*, no. 115 (May 1951), p. 54.

electorate as a whole, M.R.P. usually maintained a solid basis of support in the industrial areas.[21] Moreover, detailed studies of individual localities show that a substantial section of the working-class, perhaps a third, voted even in 1946 for parties other than the Socialists and Communists; it seems probable that most of these were black-coated workers and that they mostly voted for M.R.P. But no direct correlation could be established. In Paris in 1946, when it had a great deal of unreliable conservative support, M.R.P. did best in the bourgeois quarters. But in 1951 M. Goguel found that it did almost equally well everywhere, and that the few discrepancies could be explained by 'accidental' factors, such as the personality of a deputy, or the presence of large religious communities.[22]

In the country as a whole in 1951, M.R.P. was in danger of becoming a regional party. Of the eighteen departments where it was supported by 15 per cent. of the electorate, seven were in the north-west, and four more on the Franco-German border. Thus, despite its determination to remain a party of the Left, M.R.P. found its most effective support coming from the traditionally conservative areas where the Church had always been strongest. Twenty years earlier, in 1932, the parties of the Right had won the votes of 30 per cent. of the electorate in fifteen of these eighteen departments (reaching 45 per cent. in eight of them). The Radicals had reached 30 per cent. in only four, and the Socialists and Communists combined in only two, Tarn and Drôme.[23] With the decline of M.R.P. over the country as a whole, nearly half its deputies (37 out of 83, overseas members omitted) were elected from the western and north-eastern departments, where its appeal depends on its Catholicism rather than on its progressiveness. This development threatened to revive the tension between deputies and *militants*. For the relatively greater parliamentary influence of these areas of strength inevitably tended to accentuate the clerical character of the party, rather than the social reform side of its activity which was so important to the *militants*.

---

[21] In June 1951 there were 18 departments in which the M.R.P. vote fell below 5 per cent. of the electorate. None of these was among the 15 highly industrialized departments (see above, p. 70n), and only three (Aube, Cher, and Seine-et-Marne) were among the 17 fairly industrialized ones. (Goguel, *Géographie*, comparing pp. 97, 113 and 133.)

In 17 departments industry alone occupied 20 per cent. of the working population. They included 37 per cent. of the national electorate. M.R.P. won 41 per cent. of its total vote in them: only the R.P.F. did better than this, and all the other centre groups fell below their national average in these areas. Goguel, 'Géographie des élections du 17 juin 1951', *Esprit*, September 1951, p. 364.

[22] See the studies of MM. George, Lavandeyra, and Goguel, noted above, pp. 54n, 71n. If the social criteria used by the latter in 1951 are applied to the figures for November 1946, it becomes obvious that M.R.P. then invariably did best in bourgeois arrondissements.

[23] Goguel, *Géographie*, comparing pp. 49, 77 and 113. For the Radical vote in 1932 see W. Pickles, 'The geographical distribution of political opinions in France', *Politica*, 1936, p. 178.

4. CHARACTERISTICS

M.R.P.'s greatest asset is that it is a party with a philosophy and a purpose, not a mere electoral combination. This gives it great internal cohesion, and imbues its *militants* with a strong sense of loyalty and devotion. The June 1946 poll showed 31 per cent. of M.R.P. voters declaring themselves completely satisfied with their party, a higher proportion than any rival except the Communists could claim. It was the more remarkable in that many M.R.P. voters soon proved to be birds of passage, so that the solidarity of the others must have been high indeed.[24]

The doctrinal unity of a Catholic party is not the only basis of M.R.P.'s solid middle layer of *militants*. The structure of the movement is another. For the corporative tendencies of Catholic thought, and the social activities of the Church, provide M.R.P. with a set of ready-made organizations with a special appeal to various categories (youth, women, workers, etc.), which give the party an effective means of approaching the masses. Its leaders do not suffer from the individualist illusion that man's political concerns are mainly contemplative and personal. They realize that his interest in politics is active, collective, and stems from the realities of his daily life; and this appreciation gives them a wider and more resounding appeal than that of the individualist parties. They have indeed managed in this respect to learn usefully from the successes of the Communist party.

M.R.P. has the further advantage of freshness.[25] As a new party it has suffered over a shorter period from the 'contagion of the world's slow stain', and as a party with a mission it has a better chance of resisting future deterioration, than some of its rivals. Was it wholly accidental that when the Paris parliamentary correspondents held a poll to choose the most *aimable* deputy in the 1946 legislature, the first three places went to M.R.P. members?[26] But a public *penchant* for political morality is not without its disadvantages. M.R.P. shares many of the weaknesses as well as the virtues of the Nonconformist conscience in British politics a few decades ago. On the one side there are a real concern for the tone of public life, a political vision not limited to personal careerism, a willingness to allow idealism and imagination to intrude even into foreign affairs, an appreciation of problems outside the usual political categories, such as the grave scourge of alcoholism. On the other there are the illiberality which seeks to

---

[24] *Sondages*, 1948, p. 225.

[25] In the general election of October 1945, 62 per cent. of the M.R.P. candidates had held no previous elective position in national or local government. The proportion in other parties was lower (Communists 56 per cent., Radicals 48 per cent., Socialists 43 per cent.) except among the Conservatives, who were obliged to put forward new men, since most of the old ones were ineligible. For the figures from which these percentages are calculated, see Husson, i, p. xxii.

[26] *Le Monde*, 3 May 1951.

impose the moral standards of a single group on their fellow-citizens, and a tendency to think of political forms as possessing a life of their own independent of the forces which control them; abroad, an exaggeration of what structural changes can do, as in the programme of European integration; at home, a similar exaggeration of the use of legislation, which often only forces social evils underground, or (as in the case of *pastis*) brings the law into contempt because it cannot be enforced.

This description, however, applies much more to the M.R.P. *militants* than to their electors. The difference involves a real danger for the party. For its constitution gives very great power to its parliamentary leadership. Deputies, and especially potential ministers, are always more impressed with the advantage of governmental participation than are the rank and file party members. If the former feel that their re-election depends mainly on pleasing conservative voters rather than progressive *militants*, they may shift party policy further to the Right than the latter are prepared to stand. For among the active members the trade unionist element is numerous and influential: the left wing of M.R.P. is well to the Left of the Socialist party, and might indeed be described as Bevanite. The hold of the leadership on day-to-day policy is hard to shake, but at annual congresses discontent sometimes explodes. So, at Strasbourg in 1949, the *militants* killed M. Bidault's flirtation with the Gaullists, and at Nantes in 1950 the Left opposed the re-election of the general secretary, and obtained 224 votes for their candidate against 341 for the official nominee.[27]

The secession of the left wing would take out of the party comparatively few deputies, but it would remove much of the active membership in the country and nearly all the trade union support; with the departure of just the forces which give M.R.P. its freshness and vitality, the movement as it has hitherto existed would disappear, or lapse into just another clerical conservative group—a kind of Christian Radicalism. But besides this danger the movement faces another. Deputies from different regions have different electoral interests. The working of *scrutin d'arrondissement* in the Third Republic turned the Radical party into a coalition of members whose seats depended on contradictory alliances, and deprived it of any homogeneity of ideas or consistency of policy. With control so largely in the hands of the members of parliament, M.R.P. is in some danger of being reduced to a kind of Christian Radicalism in this respect also.[28]

Real efforts have been made to avoid such a development. Fear that *scrutin d'arrondissement* would threaten the unity of the movement largely accounts for M.R.P.'s bitter and successful opposition to its return. Every effort is made to make the movement's deputies work

---

[27] See below, p. 370.
[28] Duverger, *op. cit.*, p. 216. But for one great difference see below, p. 385n.

and act as a team: perhaps nine-tenths of the parliamentary work of an M.R.P. member takes place on a party rather than an individual basis. On the other hand, strictly disciplined voting has been abandoned, since the coercion of the Left would inevitably lead to the early break-up of the movement. The danger of personal dissensions, in addition to political and regional ones, has on the whole been kept in check by the team spirit which is so strong in the party.[29]

Nevertheless its internal divisions became more apparent after the 1951 election than they had been for five years. As the election approached, many M.R.P. deputies began to show signs of wishing to dissociate themselves from their connection with the anti-clerical Socialists. The attacks on M. Moch in November 1950, and on his subordinate M. Bertaux in February 1951 [30] were only in part due to a disinterested concern for the purity of public life. And the new electoral law made contradictory alliances almost as inevitable as *scrutin d'arrondissement* would have done;[31] only the intransigence of the R.P.F. kept so prominent an M.R.P. leader as M. Robert Schuman from allying with these opponents of the government in which he served. A quarter of the M.R.P. members held their seats by alliance with the Right or even the R.P.F., and in opposition to the Socialists. Moreover, the election halved the party's parliamentary numbers, thereby increasing the relative weight of the regions where it was strongest. As we have seen, the western and north-eastern departments, where the church schools question overshadows every other issue, now supplied nearly half the M.R.P. deputies. With the Gaullists threatening to outbid them for the favour of the Church, M.R.P. was obliged to compete in demanding concessions for the Catholic schools, even at the price of a violent quarrel with the Socialists.[32] This broke the Third Force and made the resumption of effective power by the Conservatives only a matter of time. When it took place, in the Pinay ministry, M.R.P. feared the odium of destroying the government; they were thus placed in the situation so familiar to the Socialists, and so much dreaded

---

[29] See below, pp. 365, 361, 360 respectively.

[30] See below, p. 306, for the attacks on M. Moch.

M. Bertaux had been M. Moch's *chef de cabinet*, and was appointed by the latter as head of the *Sûreté nationale*. He was criticized for alleged slow progress in reforming the security services after the scandal of the generals, because of the escape of certain Communists in the south from an attempt to round them up (one was said, without proof, to have had previous associations with him), and because he was acquainted with a gangster whom he had met in a concentration camp, who was thought to have engineered the theft of the jewels of the Aga Khan's Begum in 1949: one of M. Bertaux's subordinates had charged him with hamstringing the inquiry on this account. He retired after these attacks (which there is no reason to regard as well-founded).

[31] For the new electoral law see below, pp. 322–6.

[32] Later, at the 1953 congress, a left-wing proposal for a *trêve scolaire* in order to restore the Socialist alliance was attacked, as electorally disastrous, by one of the most progressive western members, M. Monteil of Finistère. *Le Monde*, 24–25 May 1953.

by themselves—that of bearing responsibility for a policy which they deplored but were unable to alter.[33]

M.R.P. is the only party which has held office (except for one month) ever since liberation. The party therefore shares the pivotal position in French politics previously occupied by the Radicals. The Catholic democrats have become as indispensable to every majority as the conservative anti-clericals. This change has its drawbacks. For a party concerned with power rather than principles can change sides more easily than a movement acutely conscious of its mission : an organization manipulated by its leadership has a freer hand than one influenced by its rank and file : and an old party, which has traditionally co-operated alternately with Right and Left, finds willing partners much more readily than a new movement which prides itself on the originality of its doctrine and outlook.[34] M.R.P. has yet to acquire the practised skill in manœuvre of the old Radical hands. A party which so publicly displays its conscience may improve the tone of public life or the direction of governmental policy, but it is unlikely to facilitate the smooth working of the political machinery.

---

[33] M. Teitgen's presidential address to the 1953 congress reproduced precisely the old argument of the Socialist leaders; that if M.R.P. went into opposition it would make government impossible, discredit the regime, and play into the hands of the extreme Right. *Ibid.*, 26 May 1953. But see the Epilogue.
[34] See Goguel, *Christian Democracy*, pp. 130–2, 214–24.

Chapter 7

THE RADICAL PARTY

1. HISTORY

THE Radical party, officially the *Parti républicain radical et radical-socialiste*, was established in 1901, and is therefore an older foundation than any of its rivals. Radical politicians had worked together as a group since the early days of the Third Republic, and the official formation of the party did not change the situation very drastically. The organization remained highly localized, not to say rudimentary. Even in the Chamber of Deputies two separate Radical groups, sometimes hostile to one another, survived for ten years after the establishment of the party, and there never was a single official Radical group in the Senate. Yet, in spite of their lack of cohesion, the Radicals dominated French politics during the first forty years of the century, forming the principal component of most governments, and establishing in particular almost a prescriptive right to possess the ministry of the Interior.

The official foundation of the party made relatively little difference to the technique of Radical politics. But it coincided approximately in time with a drastic change in the character of the movement. In the first years of the Republic, before the Boulangist crisis, the centre of Radicalism was in Paris: by 1901 it had shifted to the provinces. The Radicals had in the early days put forward a sweeping programme of constitutional reform (abolition of the Presidency and Senate, election of judges, etc.) and more limited social proposals. But the acquisition of power by the party had changed its outlook; there was no need to crusade for the abolition of a Senate which the Radicals in effect controlled. Increasingly, Radicalism became a conservative force, content to possess the state and no longer eager to reform it.

Socially, too, a corresponding change was taking place. The Radicals were essentially a party of the lower middle class, of school-teachers and shopkeepers, country doctors and small peasant proprietors. Hitherto their hostility to the old governing class had been the most important feature of their political outlook. But the development of an industrial working class led to clashes which showed that their fear of the latter was equally profound. In the Paris suburb of Bobigny the market-gardeners, recent immigrants into a commune which they dominated, were Radicals of the Left, hostile to the conservatism of the older tenant-farming inhabitants: but when in the first decade of the century the industrialization of the commune began, bringing with it strikes and wage demands among the agricultural workers, the market-gardeners of Bobigny swung with astonishing suddenness away from their traditional attitude and into an alliance with their old conservative enemies.[1] In the Chamber the clashes between Clemenceau and Jaurès, notably over the right to strike, foreshadowed the evolution of Radicalism towards the Right.

Clemenceau, however, represented a declining tendency in the Radical tradition. His personal authoritarianism, his willingness to use any means in the service of his passionate patriotism, his scorn for committees and his liking for individual responsibility, derived from an authentic brand of Radicalism which had origins running back to the Jacobins, but which in recent years had been swamped by the rival Radicalism of the election committees.[2] This dominant variety still distrusted every sort of power, governmental or military, ecclesiastical or economic. These provincial lawyers and doctors still claimed to defend the small man against the big, the provinces against Paris, the constituencies against the bureaucracy. Their traditional outlook, vocabulary, and enmities were derived from the Revolution, and bound them to the Left. Much of the effectiveness of Radicalism between 1900 and 1914 came from the recently acquired backing of freemasonry, which gave the party a more solid basis and a greater cohesion than it had at any other time.[3] But in terms of practical present-day politics, rather than the politics of the past, only one issue ranged them firmly with the Left, the clerical question. And when the Radicals won their greatest victory, in separating Church and State, they undermined the foundations of their own strength. The intellectual sterility of Radicalism was a commonplace of political commentators. The separation, by taking much of the bitterness out of the dispute over the position of the Church, damaged the Radical party by weakening its last remaining element of ideological vitality.

The provincial Radicals of the committee type had a limited vision, bounded by the horizon of their constituencies. Too often they conceived of politics as an eternal round of petty local jobbery and intrigue leading to electoral triumph—and more opportunities for local jobbery and intrigue. They were a group singularly ill-fitted for power in wartime. Clemenceau, in the last fling of the old ' proconsular Radicalism ', swept the party aside, and brought two of its chief leaders, Caillaux and Malvy, to trial for defeatism bordering on treason. In 1919 the Radicals did not venture to oppose him electorally, contenting themselves with defeating his presidential candidature in the safe secrecy of the parliamentary ballot a year later. But as soon as they dared they reverted to the old Socialist alliance, and in 1924 the *Cartel des gauches*

---

[1] *Cahiers de la Fondation nationale des sciences politiques*, no. 12: Maurice Agulhon's article in Pierre George and others, *Études sur la banlieue de Paris*.
[2] For the conflict between the two Radicalisms, see Thibaudet, pp. 147–51.
[3] Duverger, *Partis*, pp. 176–7.

came to power. Clemenceau scornfully commented: ' 0 plus 0 plus 0 equals 0 '.[4]

The parliamentary strength of Radicalism was swollen by the electoral system, for the party profited by fighting in some regions as the representative of the Left against reaction, and in others as the standard-bearer of moderation against the revolution. Some Radicals were therefore elected with the help of Socialist votes at the second ballot, others with the help of Conservatives. This successful balancing in the middle of the electoral see-saw increased the numbers of the party in Parliament, at the expense of its cohesion. There was permanent tension between the respective supporters of a Leftward, and those of a Rightward orientation. The former had the sympathy of most *militants* in the country, and predominated at election times. The latter were powerfully reinforced by the Radicals of the Senate, older than their colleagues in the Chamber and less dependent on the electorate; their point of view found most effective expression when the budget and financial matters were discussed. The Radical-Socialist alliance of 1924 fell apart within two years over finance, and those of 1932 and 1936 suffered the same fate (though the latter was exceptional in that the Communists also participated in a combination in which the Radicals were junior partners only).

The Radical party was one for quiet times, ill-suited to the responsibilities of crisis. Most of its leaders and members of parliament moved from support for the Munich policy to voting for Marshal Pétain in 1940. The most representative of the Radical leaders was M. Camille Chautemps. The son of a former Radical minister, he was a prominent freemason, and presided as prime minister over both the outbreak of the Stavisky scandal, and the liquidation of the *Front populaire*. In 1940 he played a decisive part in the cabinet decision to ask for an armistice,[5] and later he became vice-premier in the Vichy government. A few leading Radicals suffered deportation (like MM. Herriot and Daladier) or even death at the hands of the Germans, but the party's contribution to the resistance movement was not impressive.

In the unfamiliar world of 1945 the Radicals found themselves at a grave disadvantage. Their prestige was low: it had suffered through the party's heavy share of responsibility for 1940, and had not subsequently been redeemed. To the new voters in particular their outlook seemed impossibly decadent and outmoded. Changed conditions of political life worked against the Radicals. A party based on distrust of *les pouvoirs*, of every kind of organized authority, could not compete effectively in a regime of disciplined or even ' monolithic ' political units,

---

[4] Thibaudet, p. 143.
[5] By suggesting that to ask on what conditions an armistice would be granted need not imply the inevitable acceptance of whatever conditions were required by the Germans. This was the evasion which saved the face of the hesitant members of the cabinet.

backed by powerful social organizations such as the trade unions or the Catholic Church. The Radicals relied less than any other organized party on the activity of a mass membership, and more on the personal influence of a few local *notables* in each district. But they could no longer depend on these, for though the party itself had characteristically decided not to expel those of its parliamentary representatives who had voted for Marshal Pétain, most of them were none the less made ineligible by law to hold any position in public life. The Radicals avowed their preference for the old constitution, the old electoral law, and the old press at a time when the public condemned the first as ineffective, and the others as demoralizing influences on political life. Women had the vote for the first time, a change which the Radicals had always blocked for fear of the power of the priests. And the shift in public opinion was demonstrated by local elections earlier in 1945, which convinced Radical voters that a vote for their own party would be thrown away, and that to stop the Communists it was necessary to turn elsewhere.[6]

Yet at the same time the Radical leaders were conducting a strange flirtation with the Communists. Its basis was purely negative, a common and deep distrust of General de Gaulle. In the constitutional referendum campaign of October 1945 the two parties advocated opposite answers to the first question (a new constitution) but the same negative answer to the second (limited powers for the constituent assembly). The Communist motive for desiring an assembly with full power was clear enough; in the case of the Radicals their violent objections in principle to the plebiscite added force to their practical distrust of General de Gaulle. Since the campaign centred on the second question, the Radicals and Communists co-operated to the extent of an unofficial non-aggression pact for the general election which was held on the same day.

The 1945 election resulted in a disastrous defeat for the party, most of its leaders being beaten, and only two dozen seats being saved. This experience showed the Radical leaders that they must accommodate their tactics to the new electoral system. This gave a clear advantage to the stronger parties,[7] which was naturally greatest where their smaller competitors multiplied opposing candidatures. In April 1946 a Radical-U.D.S.R. alliance was announced,[8] and in November the Radicals negotiated a pact with P.R.L., the new Conservative party, by which each refrained from contesting a number of departments.[9] Inside a year, the Radicals had switched from friendship with the extreme Left to friendship with the extreme Right. Contradictory

---

[6] See *Cahiers* ... no. 16: M. Duverger and others, *L'Influence des systèmes électoraux sur la vie politique*: F. Goguel's article, pp. 80–1.
[7] See below, p. 316.
[8] For the U.D.S.R. see below, pp. 143–6.
[9] Priouret, p. 106.

alliances in different areas at one election had given way to contradictory alliances over most of the country at successive elections. The Radical vote benefited very little, but the combinations made a considerable difference to the party's parliamentary strength.

The sudden rise of the R.P.F. swept most of the Radicals along with it. Electoral success had, after all, been the party's principal objective; in the local elections of 1947 and the second chamber elections of 1948 most Radical candidates found it expedient to acquire Gaullist support by accepting the R.P.F. label, though the sequel showed that this was in the great majority of cases merely a marriage of convenience. The older leaders, and especially M. Herriot, retained all their suspicions of generals in politics, and in 1951 they at last persuaded the party to forbid its members to hold simultaneous membership in the R.P.F. In the general election of 1951 three-quarters of the Radical deputies won their seats in alliance with the Third Force parties, Socialists and M.R.P.[10]

2. ORGANIZATION

The organization of the Radical party, at first sight similar to the normal pattern, in reality differs in several respects. It possesses most of the usual forms, but the names do not mean the same thing. At the lowest level even the name is different. The basic unit is the committee (*comité*) not the section. Committees existed before the party, as autonomous constituency associations, and the party was formed by their combination. The committees must adhere to a departmental federation, with the usual apparatus of an annual congress and an executive committee (*commission exécutive*).

The committee, territorially, is usually based on the canton. There may, but need not, be an *arrondissement* federation between the local and the departmental level, and a regional federation between the latter and Paris; the South-west, East Central France, Languedoc-Provence-Corsica are among the regions which have such an organization, and M. Daladier's election to the presidency of the latter in May 1950 was a significant stage in his return to the front rank. The federations enjoy the greatest autonomy in choosing their candidates and their electoral tactics; the central organization of the party, though sometimes considered top-heavy, consequently needs smaller resources than those of its rivals.[11]

The composition of the party is its most peculiar feature. Its membership comprises three categories: local organizations (i.e. local committees, departmental and *arrondissement* federations), members of

---

[10] Out of 78 Radical and allied members for French constituencies, 58 were elected in alliance with the Third Force, 3 in alliance with the R.P.F., and 17 in opposition to both.

[11] Daniel Halévy, *La République des comités*, pp. 191–2, compares the finances of the Radical and Socialist parties in 1929, when the budget of the latter was ten times that of the former. Unfortunately the Radical party no longer publishes these figures.

local committees, and newspapers which support the party's doctrines and adhere to a departmental federation. The unexpected inclusion of newspapers has historical causes. In the early years of the Third Republic the departmental press was of immense political importance, the focus of electoral activity and often the decisive influence in the choice of candidates. The early local associations from which the Radical party grew were largely centred on the local paper. Nor did this importance greatly diminish as time went on. Powerful figures in the Radical party, such as the Sarraut brothers, or M. Herriot, owed much of their authority to their control over great journals like *La Dépêche*, of Toulouse, or *Le Progrès*, of Lyons, which exercised wide political influence over a vast area, and formed the nucleus of groups within the party. An odd situation arose, however, when papers adhering to the party changed hands; the growth of chains, like those of Patenôtre and Laval, made it possible for non-members of the Radical party to be represented at its congresses, and to influence its decisions.[12] Later, at the time of liberation, newspapers which had appeared under the occupation were transferred to new ownership; this process had important political effects, especially in weakening the Radicals to the profit of the Communists and Socialists, and its reversal was one of the chief Radical objectives after the war.[13]

There is a second anomaly in the conditions of membership. The party is composed both of organizations, adhering in their own right, and of the individual members of those organizations, joining on a personal basis. The apparent reason for this curious arrangement is connected with the loose provisions governing the composition of the party congress. This consists of all the members of the national council (rank and file delegates plus party members in public office—see below), editors of newspapers belonging to the party, and representatives of the federations—whose voting strength is settled not by statute, but by the national council. But any party member may usually attend on purchase of a special card. Such rank and file supporters have no right to vote, but if their sympathies are strongly with one faction they may be able to influence the atmosphere of the congress, create an artificial 'public opinion', and so affect the delegates' decisions indirectly. These provisions give great importance to the location of the congress, for members from nearby departments naturally find it easier to attend. The outgoing leaders thus always have an initial advantage, since they will arrange for the congress to be held in a city favourable to their point of view. But the openness of the congress also makes it possible for particular leaders or groups to buy up quantities of cards, and pack the meetings with their own supporters.[14]

---

[12] Duverger, *Partis*, p. 177. Goguel, *Encyclopédie*, i, pp. 323–4.
[13] See below, pp. 389–91.
[14] Duverger, *op. cit.*, pp. 60–2, 169–70. Goguel, *loc. cit.* Pierre Frédérix, *État des forces en France*, pp. 131–2, 212–3.

The Radicals, like the other parties, have a 'little congress', or national council. It meets every three months, and is known as the *comité exécutif*. Its functions include the taking of interim decisions between congresses; almost more important, it has the duty of making the arrangements for the next congress, fixing where it shall be held, drawing up the agenda, and naming the *rapporteurs* (whose reports are invariably accepted). It also elects various committees, notably the usual committees on discipline and finance. The national council includes both elected and *ex officio* members. Each federation is entitled to a delegate for every 200 members or fraction thereof. But these representatives of the *militants*, who number about 300, are heavily outnumbered by the *ex officio* members. These are both party leaders (the president and general secretary of each federation, former presidents and general secretaries of the national party, and members of its executive committee) and public men who belong to a local Radical committee: the positions which qualify include membership of either house of Parliament, the Assembly of the French Union, the Economic Council, certain overseas assemblies, and departmental councils. The quorum is 150; the total membership has fallen from 1,800 in 1936 to about 1,200 in 1951. If the quorum is not reached, the executive committee of the national council may refer decisions to another session, to which ' the provincial members shall be summoned ' (*sic*). The arrangement offers evident scope for the Parisians (mostly members of parliament) to dominate the organization in normal times.[15]

The Radical executive committee includes seventy members ; formerly known as the *bureau*, it is now called the *commission exécutive*. Forty, who may not be members of parliament, represent the rank and file; these serve for two years, half of them being elected by the new national council at each annual congress. Twenty-five represent the parliamentary groups, ten each from the Assembly and from the Council of the Republic, and five from the Assembly of the French Union. The rest are officials, the political and administrative presidents of the party, the general secretary and assistant secretaries, and the treasurer: the presidents are elected by the congress, the others by the executive itself. Members of the executive are divided into three categories, vice-presidents (ten *militants* and five parliamentarians), secretaries, and assessors. The executive committee meets every month, and controls the normal working of the party. In governmental crises, however, decisions are in the hands of a joint sitting of the executive and the members of parliament: this combined body was set up shortly

---

[15] *Statuts du parti*, Articles 14, 15, 19b. Duverger, Goguel, *loc. cit.* Before 1914 the departments were represented on the national council according to population, not party membership (two delegates each plus two per 20,000 inhabitants). Between the two wars both bases were used: one delegate for every 100,000 inhabitants or fraction thereof, one for every 200 members or fraction thereof. After 1945 the population category was abolished.

before the first world war in order to associate rank and file representatives with these decisions, which had hitherto been the prerogative of the parliamentarians alone. From the name of the town whose delegate proposed its establishment, the joint body is known as the *Cadillac* committee. There is also a bureau of the executive, meeting every Wednesday evening to take day-to-day decisions. It consists of the officials, the vice-presidents, and the secretaries, but any other member of the executive may attend.

The most notable characteristics of Radical organization are the imprecision of the party's statutes and the looseness of its discipline. The ill-defined arrangements for the party congress and the small quorum on the national council (only an eighth of the total number) make it easy for cliques to manipulate the machine.[16] The members of parliament dominate the organization: their prestige gives them great authority over the other *ex officio* members, but in addition they enjoy the immense advantage of being present in Paris, which the low quorum enables them to exploit to the full. The effective power of the rank and file is correspondingly limited. Very often the officers and the executive committee are elected by acclamation. Even when real differences of opinion manifest themselves, they may merely indicate a division or a struggle for influence among the members of parliament, rather than a genuine rank and file demonstration.

Some critics of the party perhaps underestimate the extent to which the opinion of the *militants* can express itself.[17] Elections are not always carried by acclamation. At the Toulouse congress of 1949 there was a singularly bitter struggle for the presidency between M. Herriot, the leading Radical supporter of the Third Force governments, and M. Daladier, his former pupil, his opponent from the days of the Third Republic, and the only pre-war leader of the party to take the opposition line.[18] The *militants*, anxious to retrieve the positions lost at the time of liberation, mainly followed M. Daladier, whose policy seemed to offer the better hope of electoral success. So furious was the battle that many observers thought the party was disintegrating. But this affair does not go very far to prove that the rank and file exercise real influence

---

[16] The most important decision on party policy in recent years was the ban imposed on ' political bigamy '—i.e. simultaneous membership of both the Radical party and the R.P.F. The national council which took this decision was attended by over two-thirds of the 1,200 members (*Le Monde*, 15 March 1951) and the vote was 543 to 128. At the same meeting, the expulsion of a former vice-president, M. Chambaretaud, and of the secretary of the Young Radicals, M. Bayet, was confirmed by less than a quarter of the membership (271 out of 382 present). *L'Information radicale*, 6th year, no. 61 (March 1951).

[17] Contrast, for instance, the views of Duverger (*op. cit.*, p. 213) on certain pre-war congresses with the judgment of the same events by Thibaudet, pp. 144–7, 188, by Soulier, *L'Instabilité ministérielle sous la Troisième République*, p. 371, or by Siegfried, p. 148.

[18] The struggle between MM. Herriot and Daladier was long ago christened the ' war of the two Édouards '. But in those days it was M. Daladier who was on the Left, supporting the *Front populaire* which M. Herriot disliked. (But cf. below, p. 148n.)

on Radical policy. The old leadership triumphed, by the comfortable majority of 759 to 351.[19] In any case, the conflict was much more a quarrel between two sets of parliamentary leaders than a real 'grass roots' revolt. In 1950 M. Daladier was elected president of the R.G.R.[20] This at once brought the tension to an end, and at the next Radical congress at Deauville, no trace of it remained.

The ease with which the machine can be manipulated involves the party in less danger than might be expected, since the whole organization is so loose. Considering politics as essentially electoral, the Radicals have always allowed their local federations complete tactical autonomy. By the 1951 election, this had been modified by a ban on association with the Communists, imposed four years earlier. But alliances with the R.P.F., though frowned on by the party leaders, were not forbidden, and were occasionally made. There were even Radical federations which regarded electoral combinations as so important that they were willing to choose their candidates to suit their partners.[21]

With some members owing their election to the support of extreme Left votes, and others dependent on the extreme Right, the Radicals have never been able to impose effective parliamentary discipline. In important divisions some members of the party are always to be found on each side, and others among the abstainers. One of the ablest and most prominent Radical deputies, M. Mendès-France, flouts all the party orthodoxies with impunity by advocating stringent economic controls, drastic taxation, a much smaller military budget, and negotiation in Indo-China. *Discipline de vote*, the requirement that all members should vote together on a particular proposition, is virtually never applied.[22]

The looseness of the party was shown again by its relations with the R.P.F. For four years Radicals were permitted to remain simultaneously members of both organizations, in spite of the open hostility to General de Gaulle of M. Herriot and most of the official leaders of the party. But at the end of 1950 the most prominent of the 'political bigamists', M. Chaban-Delmas, mayor of Bordeaux, came to M. Herriot's own city of Lyons to speak on behalf of the R.P.F. candidate in the coming election. Much of the impetus of the Gaullist movement was by this time exhausted, and M. Herriot seized his chance. The affair was referred to the discipline committee, which decided on technical grounds to take no action. M. Herriot promptly resigned the

---

[19] *A.P.*, 1949, pp. 198–9.
[20] See below, p. 147. M. Herriot resigned his honorary presidency four days later.
[21] The Aube Radicals sought an alliance with the R.P.F., were refused, and formed one with the Socialists—substituting a new candidate at the head of their list as a result. *Le Monde*, 31 May 1951. Those of Bordeaux actually nominated two leaders at the same time, one in case negotiations with the R.P.F. proved successful, the other to stand in the event of any understanding with the Conservatives. *Ibid.*, 22 May. (In the end no list was run.)

For the 1951 electoral law, and the importance of alliances, see below, pp. 322–5.
[22] See below, p. 361 n.

presidency of the party (his usual means of pressure) and, after some demonstrations of rank and file support for his point of view, the national council agreed by a large majority to force the ' bigamists ' to choose between their two loyalties.[23]

This decision was justified by a convenient article in the party statutes forbidding members to belong to any other political organization. But the article had remained unused for four years; the party leaders could invoke or ignore it as they pleased. Since 1947 Radicals had been permitted to belong to a rival and hostile party, opposed to ministries supported or even headed by their own leaders. Even in the chaotic days before 1914, when there were two separate Radical groups in the Chamber and none in the Senate, the Radical party had more real unity than this: it at least had ideological common ground in the struggle against clericalism, and force and cohesion through the backing of freemasonry. But the social issue already cut across the clerical one, damaging the unity of the party; as it has grown in importance, and as freemasonry in its division and decline has ceased to provide an effective cement, the Radical party has degenerated more and more into a mere electoral co-operative society.

3. CLIENTÈLE

THE Radical party does not usually publish figures of its membership, and estimates have varied astonishingly: in *Esprit's* 1939 survey of the parties, one contributor suggested 80,000, another 200,000.[24] At the Toulouse congress in 1949, however, M. Daladier broke the usual rule, and stated that the membership was 51,000, a decline of 11,500 since the year before.[25] In votes, the Radicals and their allies remained steady between 1946 and 1951; according to M. Goguel's figures they lost 150,000 votes during that period, retaining almost exactly two million in the latter year. This small drop presumably concealed a larger loss of votes to the R.P.F., compensated by a gain from the Left. Their share of the electorate fell from $8\frac{1}{2}$ to 8 per cent.[26]

In effective political power, however, the Radicals and their friends have been making steady progress ever since liberation. It took them time to adjust themselves to the new and unfavourable electoral conditions, but the defeat of October 1945 was sufficiently severe to provide a strong incentive. Their numbers rose steadily, from 45 metropolitan

---

[23] *A.P.*, 1951, pp. 34, 72. The Vendée federation threatened to leave the party unless ' bigamy ' was forbidden. *Le Monde*, 14 March 1951.
[24] *Esprit*, no. 80 (May 1939), pp. 176, 209.
[25] Fauvet, p. 110.
[26] Goguel, *Fourth Republic*, p. 90. Husson, i, pp. xxxiii–iv; ii, p. xxxii, gives slightly different figures for 1946,

Agreed statistics are impossible to obtain for the Radical and Conservative groups, since alliances and joint lists offer so much scope for individual judgment and differing classifications; in 1946 Gaullist lists presented a particular complication.

deputies in that month to 55 in November 1946 and 78 in 1951; including overseas members, the figures were 59, 70 and 95 respectively.[27]

But the real recovery was not so much in popular support as in the party's renewed grip on power. In the departmental councils, and generally for the Council of the Republic, majority voting was used; and the Radicals could profit, as in the old days, by contradictory alliances in different departments—in some areas with the Socialists, in many with the Conservatives, fairly often with the R.P.F., very occasionally with the Communists. In national politics the revival was still more conspicuous. From the date the new constitution was inaugurated, both houses of Parliament were presided over by adherents of the party which had most vigorously defended the merits of the old one, and in 1951 they acquired the presidency of the Assembly of the French Union also. Since 1947 the Radicals have held at least three of the six principal ministries. They well earned the title *le parti des présidences*.

The Radicals have been described as the party of a bygone age,[28] and their reverence for seniority is very apparent in their constitution as well as in their behaviour. Twenty years ago M. Thibaudet went so far as to maintain that there was no such thing as a young Radical idealist.[29] Yet it is a mistake to consider the party as no more than a collection of greybeards. The younger Radicals are more numerous and important than might be expected. Some of the ablest political newcomers of the liberation period—notably M. René Mayer and M. Edgar Faure—chose to join this party. The great upheaval of the 1939–45 war and its aftermath removed (through age or ineligibility) many of the older leaders, and gave their juniors the opportunity to step into their places. Since rank and file influence is so weak, there was no pressure from the *militants* to check this ascent, as there was in the Socialist party. So in 1946 the Radical parliamentary group, with an average age higher than any other, yet contained a larger percentage of young members than the Conservatives, and twice as many (proportionately) as the Socialists.[30] In 1951 the youngest deputy, M. Maurice Faure, was a Radical.

In social composition the Radical party is essentially middle class. Two-thirds of the R.G.R. deputies (Radicals and their allies) in the 1946 National Assembly were professional men, mainly lawyers and civil servants: the rest, apart from two peasants, were all businessmen or of unstated occupation (i.e. professional politicians). Almost half the 544 candidates were professional men, including nearly a hundred civil servants and more than a hundred lawyers and doctors. A quarter

---

[27] These figures under-estimate the recovery of the Radicals themselves. Among the members elected in 1945, half belonged to U.D.S.R. (see below, pp. 143–6.) which was not yet in partnership with the Radical party. The latter elected 24 members for France proper in 1945, and 68 in 1951.

[28] Fauvet, p. 103. Radical voters tend to be elderly: cf. Appendix VII.

[29] Thibaudet, p. 258.

[30] Duverger, *op. cit.*, pp. 194–6. 'Young' means 35 or under.

were businessmen.[31] In Paris, M. Goguel's maps of the 1951 election show that R.G.R. votes came predominantly from the bourgeois quarters.[32] But in the provinces the party is still essentially a lower middle-class affair, run by the shopkeepers, doctors and lawyers of the small country towns, and in some regions by the better-off peasants and small landowners. In the industrial areas the Radicals and their allies were everywhere weak; in the 17 industrialized departments used in M. Goguel's calculations, their percentage strength was only half the figure reached in the rest of France.[33]

In the election of October 1945 the departments where the Radicals proved to have held their own bore little relation to the areas where they were strongest before the war. Political survival was essentially a personal matter, depending on the presence of a well-known local leader who had retained his right to stand, and even this was not always sufficient to save the seat. By 1951, however, the party had returned approximately to the geographical basis it possessed in the 1930's, though somewhat restricted.[34] The basis of Radical as of Socialist strength was south of the Loire; out of 36 departments where 10 per cent. of the electorate supported the party or its allies, only nine were situated north of the river (three in the east, two in the west, and four in the Paris basin). The south-west was its real stronghold. Eleven out of 21 departments where the R.G.R. vote exceeded 15 per cent. of the

---

[31] Husson, vol. ii, pp. xxx, xxvii, respectively. The 1951 figures were very similar.
Out of 55 deputies representing metropolitan France, 15 were civil servants, 11 were lawyers, and 12 were of other professions; 6 were of unstated occupation, probably professional politicians; 9 were businessmen, and 2 peasants. (In 1951: 7 peasants.)
Of the candidates, 242 were professional men (94 civil servants, 48 lawyers, 55 medical professions. 139 were businessmen, 54 peasants, 66 workers, employees, or artisans (only 22 ouvriers), 53 unstated. In 1951 : 161 business, 79 peasants, 49 workers (10 ouvriers).

[32] *Revue française de science politique*, vol. 1, no. 3, pp. 329–31. The other Parisian studies quoted elsewhere are less useful for the R.G.R., which, at the relevant dates, ran no list in the constituency including Saint-Maur-des-Fossés, and polled only 6 per cent. of the votes in Bourg-la-Reine.

[33] 4·9 per cent. against 9·8 per cent. *Fourth Republic*, p. 113.
The R.G.R. vote exceeded 15 per cent. of the electorate in 21 departments, and was between 10 and 15 per cent. in another 15. In the first group only two, Eure and Haute-Marne, were among the 32 fairly or highly industrialized departments (see above, p. 70n). In the second group only four, Loire-Inférieure, Isère, Rhône, and Seine-et-Oise, were among the 32.
Of the 15 highly industrialized departments, two (Rhône and Seine-et-Oise) had an R.G.R. vote above 10 per cent. Four (Seine, Oise, Seine-Inférieure, and Loire) had between 5 and 10 per cent. In the other nine the R.G.R. polled less than 5 per cent. of the electorate. From Goguel, *Géographie*, comparing pp. 110 and 133.

[34] In the general election of 1932 the Radicals and their associates were supported by over 30 per cent. of the electorate in 37 departments, and by less than 30 per cent. in 52 departments. (Corsica omitted.) W. Pickles, 'The geographical distribution of political opinions in France', *Politica*, 1936, p. 178.
Of the 20 departments where the R.G.R. had over 15 per cent. of the electorate supporting it in 1951 (omitting Corsica), 16 were among its 32 strong departments in 1932, while four (Jura, Alpes-Maritimes, Lot-et-Garonne, Indre) were not. Of the 15 where its 1951 vote was between 10 and 15 per cent., seven were among the 32 best twenty years earlier, and eight were not. In all the four industrial departments with an R.G.R. vote of this size, the party's strength was relatively new.

electorate, were in the quadrilateral south of the Loire and west of a line drawn from Dunkirk to Perpignan.

4. CHARACTERISTICS

THE assets of the Radicals are political in the narrow sense of the word. They have great experience, and show great skill, in playing the game of party politics, and attracting under their umbrella a wide variety of opinions. North of the Loire they can present themselves as a party of the Left, opposing clericalism and reaction; in Paris they are a conservative party; in the south they may win right-wing votes as the last bulwark against the Marxists. They flirt with Communists and Conservatives, Gaullists and Socialists at different dates, in different areas, but with equal facility. The members who have deserted them in recent years have chosen the most widely separated destinations, MM. Pierre Cot and Dreyfus-Schmidt becoming fellow-travellers of the Communists, MM. Michel Debré and Chaban-Delmas taking leading positions in the R.P.F. Both were developing to an extreme genuine strands in the Jacobin tradition, the one its pressure towards the Left, the other the 'proconsular Radicalism' described by Thibaudet. Bonapartism and the Paris Commune alike derived their origin and traditions from the French Revolution.

This inclusiveness of the Radical party strengthens its numbers but weakens its cohesion. It makes it more difficult to pursue a definite and positive policy, but it ensures that the party can always put forward a serious claim to power. Thus over many years the Radicals have acquired great parliamentary and political skill. To ascribe their postwar recovery to their gifts of leadership would convey too flattering an impression; the outlook of their elder statesmen is somewhat timid and negative. Yet the success of M. Queuille, where other parties and leaders of a different type had failed, was an object lesson in the advantages of political experience, and of the old-fashioned ability to manœuvre and to wait. The younger leaders, men like MM. René Mayer and Edgar Faure, are often of a more vigorous and positive cast of mind than their seniors, and the continuing attractive power of the party is shown by the fact that so many of them have remained within it, despite the temptations of the last few years. The flirtation with the Communists attracted only a few; that with the Gaullists proved to be for emergency use only. Most of the 'bigamists' had returned to their original hearth long before sentence was pronounced; most of the remainder, when forced to choose, came down on the same side. M. Giacobbi, the first chairman of the Gaullist 'inter-group' in the Assembly, entered the government in 1950. So also did M. Bourgès-Maunoury, one of the leaders of the 'young Turks' who had made life so difficult for ministers in the previous winter; his ally, M. Gaillard, followed suit a year later. M. Daladier, the most important rebel of all, was never prepared to carry his differences to an extreme: the war of the two Édouards was not fought to make Charles de Gaulle king.

Among the people, as distinct from the politicians, the party retains some of the prestige of its past. For forty years it was, after all, the predominant political group, the party of the average Frenchman or at any rate of the average provincial. The cult of the small man, the fear of *les pouvoirs*, the defence of the ruled against the rulers, the demand for equality, and the suspicion of aristocracies of birth or wealth, are deeply ingrained in French political psychology. The Radical party, the party of the French Revolution, stood for these values and these suspicions. But these are wasting assets, dependent on past recollections and traditions, and slowly coming to appear irrelevant to the present. To a large extent they have been taken over by the Socialist party, which acquired the outlook as well as the electoral following of its old rivals. The Radicals, finding their original supporters attracted away by a party further to the Left, have had to fall back on a rather more prosperous clientèle: thus they now find themselves defending the interests of farm lessors, not those of lessees.[35] At the same time, with the rise of Communism, the social issue which places them on the Right has greatly increased in relative importance compared to the political and clerical issues upon which they were on the Left. Politics, so long a spare-time activity,[36] now affect daily life really and intimately; parties can no longer afford to base their existence on remote intellectual preferences.

These developments have shaken the position of the Radical party. Many years ago Barrès declared that he was torn between Socialists and Conservatives, but could never join the Radicals, since they had no ideal. A Radical elder statesman replied that he was mistaken; the Radical ideal was the separation of Church and State.[37] Many of the younger generation thought that he had proved Barrès's point; however that may be, the separation was achieved in 1905, and since that date the Radical party has been living on its intellectual capital.

In 1930, M. Siegfried believed that its allegiance to the Left constituted its only *raison d'être*, and M. Thibaudet found in *laïcité* the central feature of the Radical outlook.[38] Twenty years later the situation had changed drastically. Some older leaders still looked longingly back to 1924 and the *Cartel des gauches*, and retained the traditional preference for the Socialist alliance and 'no enemies on the Left'. The rural school-teachers, once the backbone of Radical constituency organization, had not all gone Socialist: and no provincial Radical wished to make electoral alliances with the Socialists impossible in future. Conse-

---

[35] Fauvet, pp. 111–2.
[36] Robert de Jouvenel, *La République des camarades*, p. 4: 'La politique y (i.e. in France) est le goût des individus: elle n'y est pas la condition de leur vie.'
[37] Thibaudet, p. 120 ; cf. pp. 47–8.
[38] *Ibid.*, pp. 159–61, 165; Siegfried, p. 160.

quently, most Radical deputies found it prudent to oppose the Barangé bill to subsidize church schools. But their campaign was half-hearted; to-day the Socialists are the real champions of *laïcité*.[39] The 'young Turks' of 1932 were on the Left of the party, those of 1952 were on the Right. M. Daladier, once the protagonist of the *Front populaire* with the Socialists and Communists, tried in 1951 to organize a Fourth Force with the Conservatives.[40] Freedom of manœuvre is still highly prized by the party; but if driven to choose, most of its members would regard the defence of material interests against the danger from the Left as still more important than the expression of an ideological preference which, for many of them, refers to issues and quarrels of the past.

The Radicals are old-fashioned in other respects. As M. Siegfried noted twenty years ago, and as the distribution of their votes still shows so clearly, they represent in the last resort all the most economically backward elements in French life, the small towns, the regions least affected by modern industrial developments, the political traditionalists.[41] Their negative conception of politics, summed up in the slogan *ni réaction ni révolution*, appeals to the most timid and least adaptable sections of the petty-bourgeoisie. The Radicals no longer possess a *mystique* to inspire their followers to a wider and more vigorous outlook, and their leadership is not of a kind to supply the deficiency. They are devoted to *scrutin d'arrondissement*, the electoral system which tends to make the deputy the delegate of his constituency, and to narrow his horizon exclusively to matters directly affecting it. Essentially a defensive party, protecting the citizen against the government, they are inhibited from vigorous action when in office by their own traditions and outlook. They prefer weak and conformist leaders, and avoid or repress dangerously strong personalities.[42]

No political organization could have been less adapted to the difficult

---

[39] An analysis of three significant divisions, that on M. Marie's bill on 4 September 1951, that on M. Barangé's bill on 10 September 1951, and that on Article 6 of the educational budget on 9 November 1952, shows that the Radical attitude to *laïcité* now depends on the member's electoral situation. Deputies sitting for the Paris area, where the party's following is wholly right-wing, those for Algerian constituencies, and those elected in alliance with Gaullists or Conservatives, favoured these pro-clerical measures. Members elected against strong Conservative competition steadily opposed them. Those who temporized nearly all represented departments where the Conservatives were weak, and the Radicals had a good chance of winning their votes in the future.

[40] But see below, p. 148n., and Epilogue.

[41] Siegfried, pp. 159–60, remarks that the Radicals represent all that is most out-of-date in France from the American point of view, and that in the perspective of the future they are the true conservatives.

In the 1947 municipal elections their share of the vote in the villages was twice as great as in the smaller towns, and three times as great as in the larger towns (those of over 9,000 inhabitants). Fauvet, p. 102. In 1951 they did twice as well in the 74 relatively backward departments (where production per head was less than the national average) as in the 26 advanced departments: 10 per cent. of the vote in the former, 5 per cent. in the latter. Goguel, *Géographie*, p. 141; *Fourth Republic*, p. 117. See also Appendix VII.

[42] See Siegfried, pp. 77, 95, 123–4; Halévy, pp. 46, 96–7, 165.

decisions of the 1930's, or to the appalling trials of the German occupation. Before the outbreak of war, the *Esprit* survey remarked that the Radical party, which saw politics entirely in electoral terms, was altogether incapable of functioning in conditions of illegality.[43] In the Resistance movement Radicals played a smaller part than any other group. Their double failure of leadership, both before and during the war, cost the party most of its followers, and went far to discredit it even with those who remained. In the referendum of October 1945 two-thirds of the Radical voters repudiated the political regime under which the party had grown and flourished; and public opinion polls showed the Radicals to be much less satisfied than any other political group with their party's ideas and personalities.[44] In the subsequent years the Radical leaders, manœuvring with their accustomed tactical skill, regained their self-confidence and their hold on power. But the party did not recover its intellectual identity and sense of purpose.

If France is to remain a great power she cannot afford timid political leadership. Her industrial re-equipment demands painful sacrifices, her foreign policy requires clear-cut choices. But the Radical party exists for the specific purpose of protecting its clientèle from painful sacrifices and clear-cut choices. In its devotion to the interests of the most backward sections of the population, the high protectionist and tax-shy peasants and small businessmen, the Radical party constitutes an obstacle to any constructive and vigorous economic policy. In its extreme lack of discipline and liking for contradictory alliances, it contributes greatly to political confusion—even in its own ranks, where congress delegates often applaud with equal enthusiasm speakers who employ a common vocabulary to advocate diametrically opposed policies.[45] Yet despite their defects, indeed because of them, the Radicals perform important functions in French political life.

For though the Radical electors are opposition-minded, the leadership is not. When a party has held power for so long, its chiefs inevitably acquire a tradition and a *sens de l'état*, which are too often lacking in groups without experience of government. And the extreme laxity of Radical discipline permits the prominent men of the party to preach their individual views with complete freedom. In spite of the equivocations which characterize the attitude of the party as a whole, it

---

[43] *Esprit*, no. 80 (May 1939), p. 182.
[44] Only 670,000 voters wished to retain the constitution of the Third Republic; on the same day, the Radicals and their allies polled 2,131,000 votes. In June 1946, only 16 per cent. of Radical voters declared themselves fully satisfied with their party; the average for all electors was 28 per cent. In October 1947 the Radicals were much less pleased than other voters with the municipal candidates they were supporting. In 1952 they and the Conservatives were the only groups most of whose followers had not full confidence in their party. *Sondages*, 1948, pp. 225, 240; 1952, no. 2, p. 6. Cf. Appendix VII.
[45] *Esprit*, loc. cit., p. 177. A.P., 1947, p. 170, shows that this habit survived the liberation. See also for example *Le Monde*, 13 October 1953.

continues to count among its leaders M. Mendès-France, the most rigorous advocate of economic sacrifices and clear priorities abroad, and M. René Mayer, the Finance minister who made the most determined attempt to tax the peasantry. This wide embrace enables the Radicals to call on many men of great intellectual ability; the debate on the European army at their 1952 congress was of remarkable quality. And this tolerance also benefits the whole political life of the country, since it affords a platform from which minority views can be put by men of unquestioned standing.

In addition, the Radical party provides an indispensable element of continuity. Its extreme flexibility, which allows it to switch without embarrassment from one coalition to another as occasion offers, allows inevitable political transitions to occur with the minimum of disturbance. The parochial, unimaginative timorousness of the traditional Radical outlook may be ill-suited to the problems and dangers of the twentieth century. Yet it provides a useful buffer between rival forces which are more active, constructive, and dynamic, but also violent and mutually hostile. In a land with many political extremists, only the rule of the moderates can preserve liberty. 'Perhaps it was a Radical party that Spain lacked in 1936.' [46]

---

[46] *Esprit, loc. cit.*, p. 187; cf. pp. 174, 183, 221. The party has played the same rôle since 1945.

Chapter 8

THE CONSERVATIVE GROUPS

1. HISTORY

IN the political spectrum before 1939, the space to the Right of the Radical party was filled by an amorphous series of shifting, ill-organized groups. All of them could broadly be described as Conservative, though the differences between their brands of Conservatism often cut across the nominal lines of political division. They could be roughly classified into the Centre, which formed part of every normal governmental majority, and the Right, which was considered dangerous by good republicans, and was consequently excluded from power before the 1914 war.

The forces of Conservatism in France have never been able to organize effectively for parliamentary action; and they demonstrated this weakness at the very birth of the Third Republic, which was brought into existence by a predominantly monarchist Assembly which could not agree who should occupy the throne. The electoral following of the Conservatives has been based on the local influence of individual *notables* in those parts of the country where the leadership of the old ruling class remains a political asset. But it proved impossible to impose any form of discipline on these political feudal chiefs. There has never been a Conservative party exercising any real authority over its members in parliament, or supported by a large popular following in the country: mass movements of the Right have always taken the form of frankly anti-parliamentary leagues, such as *Action française*.

During the early years of the Third Republic the entire Right was in opposition to the regime. But during the 1890's it became clear that the royalist and authoritarian cause was lost, and after the Dreyfus affair new political divisions came into prominence. New organizations were founded in each of the first three years of the new century: the *Alliance démocratique*, *Action libérale* and *Fédération républicaine*. They demonstrated the appearance of a new Conservatism, no longer seeking to change the existing form of the state. None of these movements called itself a party, and all were extremely loosely organized. No discipline was imposed on their members of parliament, who could and did belong to more than one group at the same time, the groups being indeed little more than electoral alliances. In the case of the *Alliance démocratique*, which belonged to the Centre rather than the Right, many candidates until 1910 enjoyed both its support and that of the Radical party.

The new Centre and Right accepted the Republic, drawing their strength from those who feared the intentions of the Left in social policy, over the position of the Church, or on matters of national defence. But lingering suspicion of the Right-wing groups kept them for many years in the ranks of the opposition: only in 1897–99 and in 1912–13 did governments risk the cohesion of their majority by accepting the support of openly Right-wing elements. However, the declining importance of the clerical issue and the growth of Socialism gradually shifted the centre of political gravity. The Radicals found it necessary from time to time to accept Conservative support, either at the polls or in Parliament: and though their *militants* in the country still disliked such combinations, these caused much less embarrassment now that open opposition to the Republic had virtually disappeared from the Chamber of Deputies. So it came about that the Conservative groups held or shared power for fourteen of the twenty inter-war years.

Within the ill-organized mass of individualists who represented Conservative opinion, various tendencies could be distinguished. A section of the bourgeoisie, powerful especially in the *Alliance démocratique*, was intensely conservative on social and economic questions, but rather *laïque* in outlook on the clerical issue. Conversely, the small *Parti démocrate populaire* was passionately Catholic, but so progressive in social matters that many observers refused to regard it as a conservative party at all. In this sector of politics, political divisions were moreover based on personalities as much as on policies. M. Flandin, president of the *Alliance démocratique*, M. Reynaud, an unruly individualist from the same group, M. Laval, who committed himself to no organization, M. Marin, ultra-nationalist president of the *Fédération républicaine*, each had a different outlook and a separate following.

The riots of February 1934, which drove from office a Radical government and replaced it with a predominantly Conservative one, gave a great fillip to the development of the anti-parliamentary leagues, and especially to Colonel de la Rocque's ex-servicemen's association, the *Croix de feu*. The result was a reaction to the Left, the electoral victory of the *Front populaire* in 1936, and the dissolution of the leagues, the *Croix de feu* transforming itself into the *Parti social français*. This largest but most moderate of the semi-fascist organizations seemed quite likely to develop into the first genuine party of the parliamentary Right: it had a working structure of committees in the constituencies, and retained a large, though essentially bourgeois, popular following. Though its followers in the Chamber were a mere handful, competent observers believed that if elections had been held in 1940, it would have won a hundred seats.[1]

In 1940, however, it was not a new Chamber but a new regime that was installed. The Vichy government, in its earlier stages, corresponded to the real desires of the great majority of the French Right. Admira-

---

[1] Duverger, *Partis*, p. 393 ; Fauvet, p. 134.

tion for Fascism—though for Mussolini rather than for Hitler—had been steadily growing in Conservative quarters in France, for their acceptance of the Republic had never been whole-hearted, and they had been terrified by the *Front populaire*. Many individual Conservatives, such as M. Marin, were opposed to Vichy, but the great majority accepted this traditionalist, authoritarian regime as their own.

Thus at the time of liberation, a large proportion of the Conservative politicians of the Third Republic found themselves discredited by the consequences of the Vichy policy. Those who remained set about organizing a new party which, it was hoped, would take its place as the fourth great political organization of the Fourth Republic. With no outstanding leader available, the presidency of the new *Parti républicain de la liberté* was conferred on M. Michel Clemenceau, son of the Tiger. But the customary fissiparousness of French Conservatism showed itself from the beginning: several prominent leaders refused to join, were excluded, or dropped out in the early months. The P.R.L. never managed to establish an effective local organization, and it was too much a class party to acquire any popular following. During the 1946-51 legislature it retained a parliamentary group of nearly thirty members, many of whom were at the same time followers of de Gaulle. But it did not survive as a separate group into the 1951 Assembly.

The other main Conservative parliamentary groups of the Fourth Republic are the Republican Independents and the Peasants.[2] The former included nearly all the Conservatives who, in 1946, were for one reason or another not in P.R.L. They were rather more moderate than the latter party, more willing to support and to participate in Third Force governments. The Peasants began as a tiny group of half a dozen members from the poor, intensely Catholic departments of the Cevennes: at the beginning of the 1946 legislature they were allied to M.R.P. During the succeeding five years they steadily recruited members from the other Conservative groups, and by the 1951 election they numbered more than twenty; their political position was between P.R.L. and the Independents, most of them voting with the opposition less frequently than the former, but more often than the latter.

In 1949 the Independents and Peasants set up a joint 'Centre' to co-ordinate their activity, and in the general election of 1951 it was this body which organized the Conservative campaign. A hundred Conservative deputies were returned. More than fifty (including the few remaining P.R.L. members) joined the Independent group. The remaining forty adhered to the Peasant party, which thus became an important element in the majority. In November it split into two equal halves over the issue of participation in the government. The rival groups reunited in June 1952, but split again eighteen months later.

---

[2] The A.R.S. (*Action républicaine et sociale*), a group of dissident Gaullists who turned Conservative in 1952, is discussed below, pp. 136-7.

The various Conservative groups, clearly in opposition in the period of *tripartisme*, had gradually drifted into relationship with the parties of the majority as the centre of gravity shifted towards the Right. In the general election, out of 87 metropolitan Conservative deputies, only 21 were elected in alliance with Gaullists, 33 forming part of combinations in which the Socialists also participated, and the rest winning their seats in opposition to both. The intransigence of General de Gaulle was mainly responsible for this result: for many Conservatives, such as M. Christiaens in the Lille constituency,[3] were anxious to ally with the R.P.F., and were only induced to join with the government parties because of the refusal of the Gaullists to accept their appeals. In the new Assembly the Conservative deputies were divided. Some, represented in the government itself by the leader of the Peasant party, hoped for a complete change of majority and the formation of a government led by the R.P.F. Others, more sympathetic to their old partners, wished to work closely with the Radicals in a ' Fourth Force ' combination, which would act as a counterweight to the Third Force in social and economic policy. But the Fourth Force was as incapable of real cohesion as its rival, and for the same reason: the clerical issue placed its component elements on opposite sides, though it engendered far more bitterness between Socialists and M.R.P. than between Radicals and Conservatives.

2. ORGANIZATION

SINCE individualism is the outstanding characteristic of the French Conservatives, there is little point in attempting to trace in detail an organization which hardly exists. The *Centre national*, established in 1949, is governed by a *comité directeur* of twelve, representing the Independent and Peasant members of the two houses of Parliament, and a general secretary, M. Roger Duchet, Independent senator for Côte d'Or.[4] There are departmental *Centres*, which are really committees of *notables*—local councillors and leaders of the business and agricultural organizations of the district. The *Centre national* played an important part in organizing Conservative electoral activity in 1951, and its endorsement is valuable when several Conservative candidates are in the field.[5] But its role is strictly limited. It can influence the behaviour of the Conservative leaders in a given department, but it cannot make or break a deputy, it does not attempt to impose a uniform policy on its supporters in different parts of the country, and it functions more effectively as a clearing-house for settling the affairs of outgoing

---

[3] *Le Monde*, 8–9 April 1951 ; *A.P.*, 1951, p. 127.
[4] The *comité directeur* in March 1953 consisted of 8 deputies (5 Independents, 3 Peasants) and 4 senators.
[5] This is especially evident in by-elections. In Vosges in April 1952, and in Paris in June and December, the candidate of the *Centre* was well ahead of his numerous Independent rivals.

deputies up for re-election, than as a combative party organization out to stimulate contests in other departments.[6]

Indeed, it might be argued that the main importance of the *Centre* is in influencing on the internal affairs of the Conservative groups. These still revolve around differences of personalities. The *Centre* has never had a president, since it would be difficult to avoid choosing M. Paul Reynaud, and the rivalry between him and M. Duchet has long been as marked as the Herriot-Daladier conflict.[7] Another of the principal candidates for Conservative leadership, M. Flandin, has been under the heavy handicap of being ineligible for public office.[8] Finally the startling rise of the Peasant party has brought a new set of personalities to the front.

The Peasants are the heirs of the *Parti agraire*, a small and somewhat demagogic movement founded between the wars by M. Fleurant-Agricola (until this venture plain M. Fleurant). In its pre-war stronghold in the Cevennes it maintained its position even when the M.R.P. and R.P.F. were at their respective peaks. By 1950 it had organized federations active in half the departments of metropolitan France, and had begun to penetrate many of the remainder.[9] After its success in the 1951 election its leader, M. Antier, who though a minister had fought the election in alliance with the Gaullists, declared publicly that the R.P.F. should be invited to form the next government.[10] He took office as minister of Agriculture in the Pleven administration, but continued to work for a change of majority and a pro-Gaullist government. The *comité directeur* of the party approved of his policy, while the parliamentary group followed his under-secretary, M. Laurens, who on M. Antier's dismissal in November 1951 was invited to fill the vacant place. The Peasant group in the Assembly then split into two equal halves (though the group in the Council of the Republic remained united). In June 1952 unity was restored at the congress of Com-

---

[6] Nevertheless, its announcement concerning the 1952 senatorial elections showed how fully the Independents had adopted the outlook and vocabulary of a party. 'A Paris et en Seine-et-Oise les seules listes patronnées et investies par le centre national sont les listes dites " Union des Indépendants et du R.G.R." Toutes autres listes d'indépendants ou " indépendants français " sont considérées par le centre comme des listes de division.' Quoted *Forces nouvelles*, no. 14 (17 May 1952): cf. *Le Monde*, 9, 11–12, and 14 May 1952, and 21 April 1953.

[7] In December 1950, M. Duchet's resignation was demanded by a meeting of certain Independent members, convoked by M. Reynaud. See *Le Monde*, 14 December 1950 ; *A.P.*, 1950, p. 54.

M. Pinay is closely associated with M. Duchet and M. Flandin, as is M. Laniel with M. Reynaud. Eight of the twelve members of the *comité directeur* of the *Centre* belonged to either the Pinay or the Laniel government; only one belonged to both.

[8] See below, pp. 148, 192n.

[9] Beginning with six active federations (five of them in the Cevennes) and four provisional committees, the party had expanded until at the end of 1950 it had federations working in 45 departments, and committees set up in 17 more. It claimed a membership of 25,000. Fauvet, p. 144.

[10] *A.P.*, 1951, p. 177.

piègne [11]: a new and enlarged *comité directeur* was elected by acclamation, the parliamentarians having almost half the seats, and being further protected by a decision that they should retain the freedom to vote as they chose. The Peasant party is thus not much better disciplined than its Independent allies: and since (as described below) it represents the most backward parts of the country, and the most reactionary elements in politics, it is not very well fitted to provide an effective organization for French Conservatism.

3. CLIENTÈLE

THE various Conservative groups polled almost exactly $2\frac{1}{2}$ million votes at each of the three elections of 1945 and 1946 [12]; since they contested more departments in the first of these elections than in the last, this apparent stability conceals a real, if small, advance. But during the next five years the R.P.F. came on the scene. The traditional Conservatives polled just under 2,300,000 votes in June 1951, 9 per cent. of the total electorate.[13] Their parliamentary strength, however, has grown steadily: from 62 metropolitan deputies in each of the two Constituent Assemblies they advanced to 70 in November 1946, and 87 in 1951. Including overseas members, they had 74 deputies at the beginning of the first legislature of the Fourth Republic, and over eighty at the end, in spite of defections to the R.P.F. The 1951 election brought the number up to 99.

Not unexpectedly, the representatives of the Right were both older and more bourgeois than their rivals. At the beginning of the 1946 legislature their deputies had a higher average age than those of any group except the Radicals, and a smaller proportion of young members than any but the Socialists.[14] Their candidates were overwhelmingly middle class: a quarter were businessmen, a fifth peasants, more than a third professional men. In the Assembly middle class predominance was even greater. No worker, employee or artisan was elected as a Conservative member, and the proportion of these groups among the candidates of the Right was even smaller than among those of the R.G.R.[15] The Conservative votes in Paris vary closely according to the

---

[11] *A.P.*, 1952, pp. 3, 16, 44, 54–5, 58, 78. The conflict between deputies and *militants* soon revived, for M. Antier, having captured (or packed) the party organization, tried to expel M. Laurens. See *Le Monde*, 29–30 and 31 March, 3, 4, and 11 April, and 14 May 1953. The group split again on the old lines at the end of 1953.

[12] Husson, i, pp. xxxiii–iv and ii, p. xxxii, gives the figures as 2,546,000 in October 1945, 2,540,000 in June 1946, and 2,466,000 in November 1946. Goguel brings the last figure up to 3 million (by including the votes cast for all Gaullist candidates, excepting those who were elected to the Assembly and there adhered to the R.G.R.). *Fourth Republic*, p. 90.

[13] *Ibid.*

[14] Duverger, *op. cit.*, pp. 195–6. In 1951 they were on both counts the oldest group.

[15] Husson, ii, pp. xxvii and xxx.

Out of 414 candidates, 147 were professional men (55 lawyers, 43 civil servants), 111 peasants, 76 businessmen, 35 workers, and 45 of unstated occupation. Of 70 deputies

bourgeois character of the *arrondissement* in question, the correlation being even closer than in the case of the R.G.R.[16] Like the Radicals also, though not to the same extent, the Conservatives were weak in the industrialized parts of the country: in the seventeen most industrial departments their percentage vote was only three-quarters of the figure reached elsewhere.[17] The R.P.F., in fact, had made more serious inroads on the strength of the old Right-wing forces in the towns than it had been able to do in the countryside.

Geographically, the Conservative groups before 1939 had dominated above all the West, and the Eastern frontier regions as far as Champagne. Of the fifteen departments where 45 per cent. of the total electorate voted for them in 1932, nine were in the first and four in the second of these two areas: outside them, the Right was strongest in various scattered, often mountainous southern departments, especially in the Cevennes region.

The second German war hardly changed this basic situation. The combined votes of the R.P.F., M.R.P., and minor Conservative groups in 1951 reached 45 per cent. of the total electorate in thirteen of the departments where the Right had attained that figure twenty years before, and only just missed it in the remaining two. They added another eleven departments from the same parts of the country, four eastern, four Cevennes, two Alpine, and one Breton, in all of which the Right had had a strong position in 1932.[18] But the new movements had taken a much higher proportion of the Right-wing vote in the West than they had been able to do elsewhere. Consequently, though the combined forces of the pro-Catholic parties still dominated the same areas as their predecessors, the strength of the old-style Conservatives had shifted. Of the fifteen departments where these groups had the support of 20 per cent. of the electorate in 1951, six were in the Cevennes and only two in the West: five of the remainder were in the East or in Champagne, the other two being Alpine.

The Independents and Peasants fought the 1951 election on common lists, each member subsequently deciding which group to join. Usually Conservatives elected on the same list joined the same group, so that

---

elected for metropolitan France, 35 were professional men (20 lawyers, 4 civil servants), 12 peasants, 15 businessmen, and 8 of unstated occupation. The proportion of businessmen and peasants (40 per cent. of the Conservative deputies) was much higher than that in any other group—M.R.P., with 28 per cent., coming next.

The official figures for the metropolitan Conservative deputies in 1951 gave their occupational composition as: Independents, 25 professional, 5 peasants, 13 businessmen, 2 unstated. Peasants, 11 professional, 18 peasants, 7 businessmen, 2 unstated. *Les Élections législatives du* 17 *juin* 1951 (*Documentation française*, 1953), p. 55. The Peasant split was largely between 'lawyer-peasants' and real peasants, although some of the self-styled agriculturalists have only tenuous connections with the soil.

[16] Goguel, *Revue française de science politique*, loc. cit. ; see also Pierre George, *loc. cit.*
[17] 7·8 per cent. against 10·2 per cent. Goguel, *Fourth Republic*, p. 113.
[18] 30 per cent. of the electorate in all eleven departments, and 37½ per cent. in seven of them. Compare the maps, *ibid.*, p. 344, with those in Goguel, *Géographie*, p. 49.

the division between them was by departments, though occasionally colleagues chose different groups (as in Meuse and Aveyron), while conversely two Conservatives elected in opposition to one another might come together for parliamentary purposes (as in Haute-Saône or Basses-Pyrénées). North of the Loire, three-quarters of the Conservative members joined the Independent group. But along the river and to the south of it, two-thirds of them chose the Peasant party, which predominated in the six Cevennes departments (from which it drew a third of its members), and outnumbered the Independents in the west. Thus the Independents broadly represented the Conservatism of the industrial and up-to-date regions, the Peasants that of the backward rural areas.[19]

4. CHARACTERISTICS

THE peculiar features of parliamentary government in France have been greatly affected by the character of French Conservatism. Since the beginning of the twentieth century there have always been Conservative parliamentary leaders who accepted the Republic and sought to promote their political objectives within the existing structure of the state. But the mass of Conservative opinion, represented in the constituencies by the local *notables*, had never really reconciled itself to the Republic, at bottom regretted the French Revolution itself, and would have liked to reverse it. The Right, indeed, was fundamentally not conservative at all, but reactionary in the strict sense of the word.[20] Its latent and occasionally open hostility to the regime kept the old wounds alive, and confused and falsified the whole political struggle by maintaining on political grounds the hostility between Conservatives and Radicals, who had so much in common on economic and social issues.

André Siegfried, in 1930, at a moment when the Right seemed to have settled down to accept the parliamentary regime, commented that its essential basis lay in those social classes which repudiated the pretensions of universal suffrage and claimed, or at least felt, that their birth or fortunes entitled them to rule the country. Around the landowners,

---

[19] In the economically most advanced departments, where the index of production per head was over 110 (national average 100), 18 Independents and 3 Peasants were returned. The most backward (departmental index under 70) elected 2 Independents and 15 Peasants, and the remainder 27 Independents and 22 Peasants. (For the departments in each category see Goguel, *Géographie*, p. 140.)

[20] 'La réaction est une formation politique (ou une déformation) spéciale à la France . . . une résistance d'abord active, puis devenue passive, contre un régime politique qui est né beaucoup moins de la volonté générale que de la carence, de l'absence et des malheurs des anciens régimes. La troisième République n'est pas apparue en France comme un état de droit, mais comme un état de fait, dans un pays qui n'était pas républicain, qui ne l'avait jamais été, et qui le devint peu à peu . . . par crainte d'un cléricalisme militant.' Thibaudet, pp. 33–4.

the capitalists, and the Church gravitated larger groups socially dependent upon them. Here, in Siegfried's view, lay

" the key to the French political system. It would remain incomprehensible if one failed to see that among us the counter-revolutionary spirit is continually re-created, crystallized as it were, in ever new forms."

In his view the battle between Right and Left was essentially between the political claims of a social hierarchy, and the opposing demand for democratic equality.[21] Twenty years later this distinguished conservative was still lamenting, as one of the gravest weaknesses of French democracy, the lack of ' a great, *intelligent* Conservative party.' [22]

For since 1932 the Right, while retaining the support of large sections of the electorate and indeed benefiting from the more acute fear of Communism, has seen the foundations of its political position undermined. In the middle and later 'thirties its more authoritarian followers seemed to have found in Fascism an acceptable substitute for the monarchy or the empire, now clearly defunct. But Fascism, and the traditional authoritarianism of Vichy, were alike discredited by the war. At the same time it became apparent that nationalism, for forty years one of the most important elements in Conservative psychology in France, had with a very large section of the Right been thrown overboard when it conflicted with their social preferences. The rise of M.R.P. deprived the old-style Conservatives of the support of the Church, on which hitherto they had always been able to count. And the pressure of the Gaullist movement, exerting a compelling attraction on both the voters and the politicians of the Right, deprived the orthodox Conservatives of many of their most alert and active-minded members.

The old-fashioned Right, indeed, had suffered as much as the Radicals from the shock of the war and its consequences—and for much the same reason, that both were survivals from the past, backward-looking in outlook, rather than parties adapted to the modern world. But the influence of the Conservatives had always been less, as that of the Radicals had been greater, than their numbers would suggest. Part of the weakness of the Right was the suspicion of disloyalty to the regime, which often made their political support an embarrassment rather than an asset.[23] Part of it was due to the individualism and lack of discipline which caused so much Conservative energy to be diverted to internal disputes and personal rivalries. Much of it was because the parties of

---

[21] Siegfried, pp. 59, 68–71.
[22] *Le Figaro*, 23 July 1951.
[23] ' Théoriquement un vote de droite vaut un vote de gauche, mais pratiquement ce n'est pas toujours vrai: l'homme de gauche, par le prestige de son origine, bénéficie d'un privilège, et même s'il n'est que la minorité, il lui arrive encore d'imposer ses directions, comme s'il disposait d'actions à vote plural. C'est que la République, par le redressement d'une sorte d'instinct, ne se résigne qu'avec peine aux majorités qui la font dépendre d'hommes n'ayant pas son esprit.' Siegfried, p. 191.

the Right expressed class interests too openly and narrowly to be able to win electoral victories, unless the circumstances were very unusual. And if the first of these weaknesses was diverted after 1947 to the R.P.F., the others remained to damage the old-fashioned Conservatives.

These disadvantages delayed their political recovery, and the direction of government policy did not pass into their hands until 1952. But their real power was greater than the composition of ministries suggested. They enjoyed the sympathies of many senior officials, and the newly and powerfully organized employers wielded considerable influence on the administration. The details of economic policy were often repugnant to business or the peasantry, but its general lines were much more satisfactory to these groups than to the industrial workers.

The Right also acquired another, more surprising asset. By far the most striking success with public opinion of any political leader since liberation was won by a Conservative, M. Pinay. This popularity was not altogether to his credit. To some extent it was cheaply acquired by simply postponing uncomfortable problems to his successors. It also largely reflected the deep (though unjustified) French contempt for politics and politicians, for M. Pinay was welcomed precisely because his personality and background were different from those of the familiar figures of the parliamentary merry-go-round. His sudden rise to fame was thus based in part on the anti-political, anti-parliamentary, unhealthy *incivisme* [24] to which the French Right is always prone. But at the same time this welcome for the little man, the *Français moyen*, owed something to the same not unattractive sentiment on which was founded the popularity of Mr. Attlee in Britain, and of Mr. Truman in America.

Despite the political triumph of M. Pinay, the weaknesses of French Conservatism are even more conspicuous to-day than before the war, since the impact of the new political movements has been greatest among their most alert and enlightened members. This did not become obvious immediately. M.R.P. attracted those Conservatives who were primarily pro-clerical, leaving to P.R.L. those who were principally interested in social and economic policy. But, though representing an extreme section of Right-wing opinion, P.R.L. belonged to the modern world. Its support came mainly from business and the professions, and its leaders had mostly been active in the resistance movement. But its hopes of becoming the great party of the Right were destroyed by the rise of the R.P.F., which exercised its attraction particularly upon this comparatively alert, active-minded, largely urban Conservatism.

Thus the losses due to Gaullist and M.R.P. competition cannot be measured merely in numbers. Those who went over were the least hidebound, the most capable of adjusting their ideas, those who sat for modern and industrial constituencies rather than for backward rural

---

[24] He had the enthusiastic support of the neo-Fascist press.

ones.[25] And later, when the R.P.F. declined, it was Conservatives of this type who remained most faithful to it; those of the more old-fashioned variety, peasants in the countryside and Vichyites in the towns, had joined only because the Gaullist label was an electoral asset, and departed as soon as it became a liability.[26] It was no accident that the Conservative group which had come to the fore by 1951 was not P.R.L. but the Peasant party, which was unquestionably narrower in outlook, more exclusively a pressure-group for a single interest, representative of a more backward section of society, and politically more reactionary [27] than any other group in Parliament. The Independents were slightly more numerous and often considerably more enlightened (no one could describe M. Reynaud as out of touch with reality): but a group of independents, torn with personal and political rivalries, makes an inadequate basis for effective political action. And the trend, represented by the rise of the Peasant party, may be expected to continue. The forces which supported Vichy are steadily regaining ground. In the press, former collaborators show astounding and growing boldness. At elections, the Pétainist vote has become an important factor—in November 1952 the Gaullists in the capital split on the issue of cooperation with the Vichyites in the coming municipal elections, and in March 1953 the Paris Conservatives chose to ally with the Vichyites rather than with the Radicals. The repeal of the ineligibility laws will restore to political life the leaders excluded for their conduct in 1940 and under the occupation. These developments can hardly fail to strengthen the backward-looking, obstructive, and perhaps anti-democratic elements in French Conservatism.

---

[25] In March 1949 21 metropolitan deputies belonged to the two Gaullist groups (see below, p. 125 n.). Sixteen of them represented mainly or fairly industrialized departments (defined as above, p. 70 n.).

[26] See below, pp. 136–7.

[27] When Marshal Pétain's lawyer, M. Isorni, was elected as an avowed Vichyite deputy in 1951, the Independents refused to have him associated with their group, but the Peasants accepted him. M. Laurens, the Peasant leader, was vice-president of Vichy's *Corporation paysanne*—though his rival M. Antier was one of the first resisters.

Chapter 9

THE RASSEMBLEMENT DU PEUPLE FRANÇAIS

1. HISTORY

THE *Rassemblement du peuple français* was created by General de Gaulle's speech at Strasbourg on 7 April 1947. But Gaullism as a political movement was born seven years earlier, when on the anniversary of Waterloo the under-secretary for War in the outgoing French government proclaimed that France had lost a battle, but had not lost the war. With that repudiation of defeat, General de Gaulle set out on what was in fact a revolutionary path. He was entirely alone, without organized backing of any kind. His earlier writings had revealed the extreme, almost ferocious self-confidence and self-sufficiency of his nature: it is hardly surprising that the resounding vindication of his solitary stand in 1940 should have confirmed in his own mind the certainty of his own mission. When Mr. Churchill addressed him as 'the man of destiny', the response was assured, for General de Gaulle had cast himself in that rôle since the age of twelve.[1]

The decision of 1940 and its consequences profoundly influenced the character of the R.P.F. They gave it its structure, the centralized organization which makes it to the greatest possible extent the instrument of its founder's will. They gave it its leadership, for General de Gaulle never fully extended his confidence to any but his earliest collaborators: late comers found little welcome from him. They further gave the movement much of its policy, for the General's own constitutional views, and indeed his whole order of political values, were profoundly marked by the fear of a recurrence of 1940 and the need to devise ways of meeting such a catastrophe in advance.[2] The events of 1940 even bequeathed to the R.P.F. many of its internal problems. For that revolutionary decision placed the General in opposition to the

---

[1] Wright, p. 42.
[2] Cf. his speeches at Bayeux on 18 June 1946 and at Marseilles on 18 June 1948, and his declaration to the press on 17 August 1950:

'A lui (le chef d'État), s'il devait arriver que la patrie fût en péril, le devoir d'être le garant de l'indépendance nationale et des traités conclus par la France.'

'La nation se rappelle comment un régime du même genre, quoique avec des vices moins criants, s'évanouit littéralement quand le malheur contre lequel il n'avait pas su nous défendre, eut forcé les portes de la patrie.'

'La catastrophe, si elle survenait, provoquerait leur effondrement (i.e. des pouvoirs publics) soit qu'ils disparaissent dans le néant, soit qu'ils abdiquent entre les mains des agents de l'envahisseur, soit qu'ils se jettent dans la subordination vis-à-vis de l'étranger. Mais le salut de la patrie est la loi suprême. Il faudrait donc qu'en temps voulu un autre pouvoir parût, moralement capable de prendre en charge l'indépendance et les intérêts de la France. Cela s'est fait déjà! Que le pays en soit sûr: cela se ferait encore.'

A.P., 1946, p. 538 ; 1948, p. 329 ; 1950, p. 296. See also below, p. 161 and n.

great bulk of the French Right, which was loyal to Vichy, and to most of the influential men and classes in the country. Ten years later these men and these classes formed the bulk of the new Gaullist movement: but neither they nor their leader could wholly forget that at a crucial moment in their lives and in the life of their country they had taken opposite sides.

General de Gaulle's prickly intransigence, his self-sufficiency and indeed arrogance, the character of some of his associates, and the determination with which they waged the political struggle at Algiers, provoked acute suspicion of his and their intentions. But the doubts proved unjustified. The General established neither a dictatorship nor the strong presidential regime he himself desired. His government held free and genuine elections only five months after the end of the European war, and allowed the country to make its own constitutional choice. No doubt he influenced the results, by the form of his constitutional proposals, by allowing women to vote (against Radical protests), and by his new electoral law. But all these disputed decisions were honest attempts to find a democratic solution in a revolutionary situation.

Three months after the election, the brief honeymoon between the General and the parties came to an abrupt end. Conciliation and compromise had never been marked features of the prime minister's character, and he soon became exasperated with the task of governing through the medium of three rigid parties, each obsessed by the need to maintain its political position intact. No doubt he made too little allowance for the difficulties of partners who had to combat a totalitarian and demagogic rival on the electoral battlefield. But the position of a nominal head of the state and of the government, unable ever to move a step without first conciliating three strong, mutually suspicious parties, served by a ministry whose solidarity was little more than a mockery, would have disillusioned a more patient and a more humble man.[3] Making no attempt to seize power,[4] General de Gaulle quietly withdrew into private life. He left M.R.P. to bear alone the brunt of opposition to the Socialist-Communist draft constitution, and did not even cast his own vote. Not until that battle was over did he fire his first shot, the Bayeux speech on 18 June, in which he issued his call for a presidential constitution.

These events produced a divorce between the former premier and his late political allies. The Radicals had opposed him throughout, even allying with the Communists in order to do so. The Right neither loved nor trusted him. Certain Socialists had always been suspicious of him. But the breach with M.R.P., between the party of Catholic Resistance and the Catholic leader of Resistance, was more surprising and decisive.

---

[3] See above, p. 17 n., and below, pp. 381–2.
[4] See above, p. 17 and n.

In January the prime minister had felt himself betrayed by his friends when they had failed to resign with him. But, if one individual could retire to his village in silence, a great political party could not do so. M.R.P. had to take responsibilities and earn unpopularity by remaining active and on the stage. Nor dared they retire from office and leave the Socialist lamb in a *tête-à-tête* with the Communist tiger. On the other hand, they could themselves reproach their former leader with his silence at the critical moment of the referendum. And the breach was soon to widen, for in the referendum of October 1946, the *parti de la fidélité* found itself directly opposed by the leader to whom it had proclaimed its faithfulness, and discovered that something like two-thirds of its voters preferred his leadership to that of the movement.

Shortly after the Bayeux speech, M. Capitant, one of the chief Gaullist leaders from Algiers, founded the Gaullist Union to advocate the proposals of the 'Bayeux constitution'. Millions of voters were hostile to *tripartisme*, and disillusioned with M.R.P. as a bulwark against Communism. But though willing to follow the General himself on a specific issue, they were not yet ready to throw over a solid and organized, if unsatisfactory party, and waste their votes on a new, weak group which did not even enjoy the General's personal endorsement. At the November election, the Gaullist Union secured no more than 300,000 votes.[5] But the referendum, not the election, gave the true measure of Gaullist electoral influence.

The creation of the R.P.F. coincided with the political turning-point of the post-war years, the breach between the Communists and their late partners in office. On 7 April General de Gaulle made his speech at Strasbourg, following it up a week later with a public appeal for support. At the beginning of May the Communists went into opposition. The government now faced the task, which many believed impossible, of ruling the country against the hostility of most of the organized workers. In this atmosphere of alarm and tension, the Gaullist appeal had an immense success: the continuing economic difficulties and colonial troubles exasperated the voters, and the great near-revolutionary strikes, at the end of the year, enabled the R.P.F. to appear as the only organization sufficiently determined and dynamic to check the Communist advance. By the end of 1947 the R.P.F. claimed a million members, more than the Communists themselves. And in the municipal elections of October 1947, they (with their allies on coalition lists) secured six million votes, 40 per cent. of the total—far more than M.R.P. and Socialists combined. They had united the Conservative and Radical followings, taken over the disillusioned from M.R.P., and in many places (notably Paris) eaten into the electoral support of the proletarian parties too. General de Gaulle's triumphant return to power seemed only a matter of time.

---

[5] Half a dozen members were elected on its ticket. Most of them joined U.D.S.R.

In the early stages of the movement, the General and his supporters earnestly denied that they intended to construct a new party. The *Rassemblement* was intended, they maintained, to attract Frenchmen belonging to any existing political organization who were loyal to the state (excluding collaborators and Communists). It would form no new parliamentary group, only an ' inter-group ' of deputies who would retain their membership of their former parties. If these came mainly from the R.G.R. and the Conservative groups, this was not the fault of the Gaullists but of the ' Third Force ' parties, for Socialists and M.R.P. both forbade their members to join the inter-group.

But the great expectations of November 1947 were never realized. After the municipal elections, General de Gaulle declared that the results showed that the Assembly was wholly unrepresentative of public opinion and should be dissolved. But this required the assent of the Assembly itself [6]; and the government parties had no intention of committing political suicide—perhaps, indeed, plunging the country into civil war. The inter-group acquired the support of only eighty deputies: the inevitability of the General's triumph was evidently not appreciated at the Palais Bourbon. The R.P.F., though not a new party, began trying to impose voting discipline on its supporters just as if it were one, and came up against the refractory individualism of the French deputy of the Right.[7] In November 1948 it made a great effort to capture control of the upper house, and after the election claimed that 150 of the 320 members belonged to the inter-group there. But this success was not only much smaller than had been hoped, it was itself hollow. It very soon became obvious that many candidates, especially among the Radicals, had welcomed Gaullist support in their campaign but had no intention of accepting Gaullist discipline: and when the R.P.F. formed within the inter-group a separate group of members pledged loyally to obey orders, it recruited only fifty-eight members. The remainder voted with the R.P.F. when so disposed, as they often were on social and economic questions; but they could not be relied upon in a real attempt to turn out the government.

The long Queuille ministry, from September 1948 to October 1949, put an end to the Gaullist hopes of early success. It followed a rapid sequence of ministerial crises naturally exasperating to the public and

---

[6] For the constitutional provisions regarding dissolution, see below, pp. 227–9. In the conditions of 1947 the Assembly could legally be dissolved only with its own consent: to be quite certainly constitutional, a two-thirds majority (the majority required for a constitutional amendment) would have been required. General de Gaulle demonstrated his determination to come to power by unimpeachably legal means when he demanded that the Assembly should dissolve itself by a two-thirds majority vote.

[7] M. Montel, a vice-president of the inter-group, and twelve of its Conservative members resigned in protest against instructions to oppose M. Reynaud's financial programme in the brief Marie government. M. Montel subsequently became leader of the anti-Gaullist wing of P.R.L., as M. Herriot led the anti-Gaullist wing of the Radicals. Both sat for the Lyons constituency; traditionally, ' Paris is the capital of France, but Lyons is the capital of the Republic '.

advantageous to the Gaullists. But at the very beginning of M. Queuille's term of office, the clash at Grenoble, in which two men were killed, alarmed the country with the spectacle of possible civil war. The new ministry secured its respite: prices stopped rising, and at the beginning of 1949 a successful loan was floated: the R.P.F. began to have its own serious internal troubles, with clashes between parliamentarians and *militants*, between clericals and anti-clericals, in just the same way as the parties it despised. There were only two dozen disciplined Gaullists in the Assembly, and when the government was first seriously endangered, in May 1949, the attack came not from the R.P.F. but from the orthodox parliamentary Conservatives, sufficiently self-confident since the recent local elections to play for their own hand. Most of the Radical Gaullists abandoned the movement during this period. When the Queuille ministry finally broke up in October, the crisis lasted a month: yet even this unfortunate spectacle no longer profited the R.P.F.

By 1951 it was evident that the Gaullists would not obtain power by themselves. But they still might, together with the Communists, possess a clear majority in the new Assembly. They could then threaten to make all government impossible, and dictate their own terms. To avoid this result the electoral law was changed, and replaced by one which put a premium on party alliances, and in consequence damaged parties which were too suspect or too intransigent to contract alliances.[8] The first was the case of the Communists, the second that of the Gaullists. The General had learnt his lesson from the Council of the Republic elections, and (probably wisely) refused to swell the ranks of his parliamentary supporters with men whose electoral commitments divided their loyalties.[9] The local R.P.F. branches were allowed to enter into electoral combinations in only a handful of departments: partly as a result, and partly because the movement won rather fewer votes than had been expected (perhaps in consequence of the electoral law), the Gaullists returned only 120 strong, instead of 200 as their optimists had hoped.

At the beginning of the new legislature they scored an important success. By forcing to the front the question of the church schools, they obliged M.R.P. either to oppose them and forfeit the support of the Church, or to follow them and break with the Socialists. When the Barangé bill to subsidize the Catholic schools went through in September 1951, the old majority was broken. It would take little now to drive the Socialists into opposition along with the R.P.F. and the Communists, and those three disciplined groups together held a majority in the Assembly. Two governments fell, one through Socialist

---

[8] See below, pp. 322–5.
[9] Of the eleven R.P.F. deputies who owed their election to alliance with Conservatives, eight revolted before or in July 1952: less than a quarter of the other members of the group did so. See below, p. 137 n.

and the other through Radical defections, and the R.P.F.'s moment seemed to have come. By standing firm it could make its own terms. But the Gaullist manœuvring had unexpected results. The alienation of the Socialists had shifted the centre of gravity of the majority far to the Right. A Conservative, M. Pinay, was therefore put up for the premiership. The old Conservatives in the R.P.F. recognized in him their own man and their own policy, and insisted upon voting for him although he had the misfortune not to be General de Gaulle. In March 1952 he became prime minister at the head of the most Conservative parliamentary majority France had known for twenty years.

In the Gaullist movement months of friction followed. By-elections showed that within a year two-thirds of its voters had deserted it, and that the loss was heaviest in middle-class areas.[10] The persistent rebelliousness of the Conservative wing provoked corresponding indiscipline on the other flank. In divisions the once monolithic group split, in the Radical manner, into three factions (for, against and abstainers), or saved its unity at the price of unanimous abstention. At length the General and his advisers decided to force a decision. New disciplinary rules were imposed in July 1952, and a quarter of the Gaullist deputies resigned to form a new group. With the departure of the most conservative element, the R.P.F. leaders shifted towards the Left. Further right-wing defections followed before the end of the year; and in January 1953 the parliamentary group decided, in defiance of the leadership, to enter the governmental majority by supporting the election of a prime minister, M. René Mayer. In May, heavy Gaullist losses in the municipal elections having convinced the General that he had failed, he announced the withdrawal of the R.P.F. as such from all parliamentary and electoral activity. The deputies, rechristened U.R.A.S. (*Union des républicains et d'action sociale*) were at last free to participate fully in the parliamentary game. Two months later their leaders were in office.

2. ORGANIZATION

THE R.P.F. shares with the Communists a belief in the extreme importance of organization. Its fundamental structure is similar to that of other parties. There are small local units based upon administrative divisions (commune, canton, and arrondissement), federations for each department, and at the national level an annual congress, a national council meeting less frequently, and an executive committee dealing with day-to-day matters. But the differences are emphasized by the

---

[10] The R.P.F. lost two-thirds of its 1951 votes in Loire in May 1952, in north-west Paris in June, in Seine-Inférieure in November, and in southern Paris in December. All parties lose votes in by-elections, especially on the first ballot: but even in percentage terms, the Gaullist share of the vote was halved in each case. But in the proletarian constituency which contains Lille and Roubaix, a strong R.P.F. candidate did comparatively well in a by-election in November.

frequent use of a special vocabulary: Gaullist members are known as *compagnons*, the congress as the *assises nationales*, etc. These differences arise from four features, all of which can be matched by analogies among the other parties, but which taken together give the R.P.F. its peculiar character. These features are an attempt to organize by place of work, which recalls the Communists: a corporative structure, carried further than in the case of M.R.P.: a rivalry between deputies and *militants* which can only be paralleled among the Socialists: and a degree of centralized control unknown outside the Communist party.

The R.P.F. workshop organizations are known as *groupes d'entreprise*. They are officially described as ' counter-cells ', the function of which is to spread Gaullist doctrine within the factory, and to oppose the Communists. But it is realized that these political aims cannot be achieved without some trade union activity being undertaken [11]— although the R.P.F. repudiates any intention of creating a trade union movement of its own.[12] Group meetings are closely regulated: ten minutes must be devoted to a study of the current political situation, twenty to Gaullist doctrine and policy, twenty to factory affairs, etc.[13] The existence of these workshop groups demonstrates the Gaullist desire to learn from their opponents and to profit by adopting a similar structure, better adapted for persistent action and agitation than the local section. But the Gaullist groups cannot really be compared with the Communist cells. For the latter constitute the fundamental feature of Communist organization, whereas the former are merely a parallel structure existing alongside the ordinary local sections based on residence. Above all, the scope for such groups is much less in the R.P.F., which does not have a proletarian following on a scale at all comparable to that of the Communists.

There were at one time departmental and national committees which united the groups on an occupational basis, but these have now been abolished. National organizations survive, however, for various ' social ' and intellectual activities.[14] Both types of professional

---

[11] *L'Action ouvrière* (the official R.P.F. bulletin for *groupes d'entreprise*) special number of May 1951, quoted in the *Dossier du candidat* issued by the R.P.F. for the 1951 election, Part 5, pp. 32, 36–7.

[12] But it had strong influence in the small *Confédération générale des syndicats indépendants*. This movement split in April 1952. The secretary, a former Communist deputy, was accused of wishing to turn it into a satellite of the R.P.F. Among his chief opponents was M. René Belin, former assistant secretary of the C.G.T., who later became minister of Labour under Vichy. *Le Monde*, 10 and 11 April 1952.

In the autumn, *Le Rassemblement* (no. 271, 23–29 October 1952) recorded with satisfaction the secretary's triumph over his opponents. Cf. *J.O.*, 19 February 1954.

[13] *Dossier du candidat*, Part 5, p. 34. Their resolution at the 1952 congress hinted at some resentment against centralized control. See *Le Rassemblement*, no. 274 (13–20 November 1952).

[14] E.g. youth, family, and ex-servicemen's affairs. The latter organization consists of departmental committees and a national council, partly elected by the departmental committees, partly chosen by General de Gaulle himself. At its head is a national delegate who is a member of the executive of the R.P.F. *Dossier*, Part 5, p. 23.

organization are represented throughout the party's structure. They elect half the members of the departmental councils, the other half being chosen on a territorial basis. They are also represented on the national council, where they choose nearly a third of the members, and at annual congresses, where however the number of their delegates has sharply declined in recent years.[15]

This decline reflected the gradual evolution of the R.P.F. as its founder originally conceived it—a broad non-partisan movement appealing to all sections of the population, and especially to the workers —into the party of revived conservatism which it rapidly became. Another consequence of this evolution was the growing strain between the leadership outside Parliament, and the Gaullist sympathizers in the Assembly. All of the latter had been elected under other auspices, and few were ready, after rejecting the discipline of a party, to submit to that of a military leader. The decision to organize 'inter-groups', instead of disciplined parliamentary parties, proved more satisfactory to the politicians than to the General. The former acquired an electorally profitable label without undertaking clear commitments in return, the latter found himself with an impressive paper following on which he could not rely. Attempts to impose voting discipline simply provoked resignations.[16] So at the end of 1948 separate groups of faithful Gaullists were set up in both houses, and were joined in each case by about a third of the inter-group concerned.[17] After the 1951 election the inter-group and its equivocations disappeared from the Assembly.

The parliamentarians also demanded a voice in the policy-making institutions of the movement, from which they had been completely left out. None of them sat on the first national council, and they were specifically excluded from the executive (from which M. Diethelm, one of the very first and chief Gaullist leaders, had to resign on his election to the upper house in 1948). In the summer of 1949 some concessions were made. Members of parliament were given the right to attend meetings of the departmental council in their own constituency, and of the national council; a special liaison committee was set up; and soon afterwards four deputies and three senators were added to the executive committee, bringing its membership up to twenty.[18]

---

[15] At the first *assises*, at Marseilles in April 1948, three-fifths of the 2,000 delegates represented the social and professional element. At Lille, in February 1949, these accounted for about half the total of 3,000. *A.P.*, 1948, pp. 52–3; 1949, p. 27. At Nancy in 1951, and at Paris in 1952, they were heavily outnumbered.

[16] See above, p. 121 n.

[17] The group in the Council of the Republic was called *Action démocratique et républicaine*, and had 58 members. In the Assembly there were two, the main one called *Action démocratique et sociale*, with 18 members at the end of the legislature, and a smaller one, the *Républicains populaires indépendants*, consisting of half a dozen ex-members of M.R.P., affiliated to it. This complication disappeared after the election.

[18] Fauvet, p. 242 n., gives the names of the members of the *conseil de direction* (but omits M. Diethelm, who returned in June 1949).

These concessions were made slowly and grudgingly, and were in part cancelled out by other measures. They were sufficient for the time to satisfy the faithful Gaullists, but not the less devoted sympathizers. In the middle of the negotiations there was a bitter quarrel over electoral discipline, which led to the resignation of the inter-group's chairman, M. Giacobbi.[19] And after the 1951 election trouble flared up again. For a majority of members of the executive won seats in the Assembly, and many of them came to resent the power of external advisers to settle the movement's tactics without regard to the views of the Gaullist deputies. The conflict came to a head in July 1952, when new disciplinary rules were imposed. Thirty rebels resigned: but even the loyal members of the parliamentary group felt that the new rules went much too far.[20] A few months later General de Gaulle, recognizing the dangers of this situation, agreed to measures reducing his immense personal authority, and allowing more representation to rank and file opinion. But the concessions came too late, and in May 1953 the disillusioned leader renounced his parliamentary followers.

The openly authoritarian structure of the R.P.F. is its most distinctive organizational feature. Power is concentrated at headquarters, the *direction*. This consists of the President, who controls it (*assure la direction*, as the official handbook says): and of a secretariat and an executive, chosen by him to assist in this task. The secretariat consists of his personal collaborators; some of its members work in Paris, others in the field as regional delegates. Weekly meetings are held in Paris. The general secretary is named by, and takes his instructions from the President. It was the secretariat which, in July 1952, forced through the new rules of parliamentary discipline.

The executive of the movement has suffered various changes during its short life. It began as the *comité exécutif*, with 12 members, who could not be members of parliament. In 1949 its name was changed to *conseil de direction*, and the number increased to 20, seven of them parliamentarians. By October 1952 there were 29, of whom a majority were deputies or senators, and only two came from outside the political world of Paris.[21]

---

[19] See below, pp. 134–5.

[20] The decisions of July 1952 provided for the representation of the parliamentarians (including the three presidents of the groups in the Assembly, Council of the Republic, and Assembly of the French Union) on the executive: for regular meetings of a liaison committee consisting of the members of the executive and delegates of all the groups, which all parliamentarians might attend: and for occasional meetings of the executive and one of the groups, at the request of either party. But it also required the observance of party discipline on all votes of confidence, censure or investiture, and authorized the groups themselves to insist upon it on other major matters (constitutional, defence, imperial, foreign, or social policy). Most of the deputies favoured the compromise proposals of M. Chupin, which provided for more effective parliamentary representation on the executive, and fuller consultation between executive and group. *Le Monde*, 5 and 11 July 1952. *A.P.*, 1952, pp. 52–4.

[21] Twelve deputies, four senators, and three counsellors of the French Union; four ex-deputies, four Paris leaders (such as M. Malraux), and two provincials.

General de Gaulle had complete control over the executive. Its members were picked by him, though after the 1951 election he was careful to bring in certain prominent leaders of the parliamentary groups. He convoked the weekly meetings, and exercised entire discretion; after the revolt over M. Pinay's investiture, weeks went by before the executive met, and then an unofficial meeting was held to which a leading rebel sympathizer was not invited. But, in November 1952, this personal domination was relaxed, and the parliamentarians and the organization in the country were each permitted to nominate representatives on the executive.[22]

The other national bodies are the annual congress and the national council. The former includes representatives of the departmental councils, the *groupes d'entreprise*, and the social organizations. Their numbers are fixed each year by the national headquarters, in proportion to membership. In theory the congress elects the President, but in a movement created round and dependent upon one man, this has no practical importance at present. The effective work of the congress is done in committee, where active and genuine discussions take place; at the public sessions reports are presented and motions adopted, but without any open clash of views.

The national council (*conseil national*) differs from the corresponding body in other parties both in function and in composition. It is chosen by the congress, and meets twice or three times a year. It includes representatives of the departmental councils, the social groups, and the national headquarters: R.P.F. members of parliament were at first excluded from it, then allowed to participate as observers, and later given formal representation by delegates. The latter change, made at the Nancy congress of 1951, increased the membership from 140 to 230.[23] The normal function of the national council is long-term policy-making, and in it were originally hammered out the two most distinctive items of the R.P.F.'s programme, those for educational allowances (*allocation-éducation*) and association of labour and capital. But it can be used for other purposes; it was an enlarged national council, containing 615 delegates and several hundred more non-voting members, which met at Saint-Maur in July 1952 to consider the new rules of parliamentary discipline, and by adopting them by a huge majority (478 to 56) provoked the split in the Gaullist parliamentary group.

It is in the constituencies that the authoritarian structure of the

---

[22] *Le Monde*, 12 November 1952. *Le Rassemblement*, no. 274 (13–20 November 1952).
[23] Of whom 70 represent the territorial organization and 70 the professional and social organizations (26 of them from the working-class side of the movement); 63 members of parliament (40 deputies, 20 senators, 3 counsellors of the French Union), and 30 chosen by the executive. *A.P.*, 1951, p. 294. The members include prominent Frenchmen of various types, writers and archbishops, generals and film actors, mayors and ambassadors. M. Fauvet listed some of the better known names: *op. cit.*, p. 243 n.

R.P.F. is most evident. There are, indeed, departmental councils, numbering forty or fifty, elected annually by the *compagnons* on a half-territorial, half-corporative basis, meeting every month, and choosing their own chairmen. But these are purely consultative. They control their own finances, and set up committees to study proposals, either of their own or from the leadership, for incorporation in the policy of the party. But they have no powers of decision in political matters.

These powers are invested in a departmental delegate, who is selected by and responsible to the central organization. The council may offer advice to him, but may not communicate direct with headquarters without informing him, and must send its resolutions through him. He is assisted by subordinate delegates for smaller areas, whom he appoints, and by functional delegates (for propaganda, working-class activities, security—*service d'ordre*, youth, etc.) who are appointed by national headquarters on his recommendation.

The departmental delegate performs much the same functions as a federal secretary in other parties; but his status is more like that of a prefect in the official hierarchy. He is responsible to the superiors who appointed him, not to his constituents. Indeed one of his principal tasks is to ensure that the local units in his area conform to national policy. But the practice does not always fit the theory; there are cases of delegates supporting their departmental council against headquarters, like ambassadors who reflect the views of the government to which they are accredited. Thus late in 1951 the delegate in Meurthe-et-Moselle, M. Parisot, resigned his post in sympathy with the departmental council, which promptly elected him as its chairman—and was soon afterwards disaffiliated.[24] To check such developments there are twenty-two regional delegates, who are chosen by and belong to the national secretariat, and are reliable instruments of its policy.

Internal disputes within the movement are settled by the departmental or regional delegate, unless they concern *compagnons* holding an elective position (either in public life, or in the movement itself). These are decided by the executive committee, which has since 1949 been advised by arbitrators selected by and from the national council. But the last word always rests with nominees of the centre, not with representatives of the membership.

This structure enables the national headquarters to keep close control over the local units. Parliamentary candidates are really chosen by the General himself, and local tactics are decided at the national level. The machinery ensures central control, but it also provokes local friction. At every election the R.P.F. suffers a crop of resignations by local leaders affronted at the peremptory instructions conveyed to them from

---

[24] *Le Monde*, 8 and 9 January, 18–19 May 1952; *Le Figaro*, 17–18 May 1952.

above.[25] Too heterogeneous to enjoy a natural unity of purpose, the movement has tried—with indifferent success—to use enforced discipline as a substitute.

An outstanding personality will always make a great impact upon the movement which he leads: the British Conservative party under Sir Winston Churchill is a notable example. That General de Gaulle is such a personality is evident not only from his public achievements, but also from his remarkable success in winning the personal devotion of men of all parties and views who worked with him during the war. That he is an autocrat by temperament is no less obvious from his writings, his speeches, and his private behaviour: thus in November 1952 a dissentient Gaullist deputy, M. Vigier, was summoned by the General, rebuked for his conduct, given five minutes to make his self-criticism, and promptly expelled when he declined to do so.[26] But his impact on the R.P.F. has been so exceptionally powerful because of the circumstances. He is leader, not of an old organization with an established hierarchy and decades of tradition behind it, but of an entirely new movement, constructed according to his own ideas and led by his devoted disciples. The R.P.F. is built round its leader, and may not survive without him.

3. CLIENTÈLE

WITHIN a year of its foundation, the R.P.F. was claiming a million and a half members. By the end of 1950 its strength was estimated at only a third of that figure.[27] Its influence had fallen sharply as the economic situation improved and the Communist danger receded: and the decline was apparent in voting strength as well as in membership. In the 1951 election the R.P.F. came second with $4\frac{1}{4}$ million votes, or 17 per cent. of the electorate; the Communists retained a long lead over it, but no other party reached 3 million votes.[28] From a representation of two dozen in the Assembly, the R.P.F. leapt into first place with a group of 120:[29] for the electoral law, though it had done the Gaullists

---

[25] In November 1948 several local leaders in Grenoble resigned, owing to differences over electoral tactics, and were followed by the departmental delegate for propaganda: *A.P.*, 1948, p. 200, which gives other instances of disaffection. In Aube, in 1951, the propaganda delegate resigned because headquarters would not allow an alliance to be made with the Conservatives. *Le Monde*, 16 June 1951.

In Morbihan, before the 1951 election, a departmental congress of the R.P.F. voted overwhelmingly to contest the election in alliance with other pro-clerical groups. But the regional delegate and General de Gaulle insisted on running a separate list, which was not allowed to ally with the Conservative-M.R.P. coalition. The departmental delegate, the three R.P.F. senators, and even two candidates on the Gaullist list then broke with the R.P.F. and came out for the coalition. *Le Monde*, 23 May 1951. See also below, pp. 134–5.

[26] *A.P.*, 1952, p. 85 (M. Vigier's account).

[27] The first figure was claimed by M. Soustelle at the Marseilles congress: *A.P.*, 1948, p. 52. The second is quoted in Fauvet, p. 227 n.

[28] M. Goguel's figures in *Fourth Republic*, p. 90.

[29] Here, as elsewhere, *apparentés* are counted as members of the group.

some harm, had injured the Communists much more severely, and had robbed them of their position as the largest party. But this result, remarkable as it was for a movement fighting its first general election, was far less than the R.P.F. had reasonably hoped for. Since the municipal elections of October 1947 they had lost 2 million votes, and fallen from 40 to 20 per cent. of the votes cast. Only a small part of the loss was attributable to their appeal being stronger in the towns than in the countryside. For, compared with those municipal elections, the R.P.F. lost half their votes in Seine (i.e. Paris and suburbs), nearly half in Lille and Nantes, 40 per cent. in Rouen, a third in Marseilles, a quarter in Toulouse and Bordeaux. These losses were partly accounted for by the recovery of the government parties, especially M.R.P., from their low ebb of 1947. But in the main they were due to the defection of Radicals and Conservatives, who had crept under the Gaullist umbrella when it was first unfurled, but had since decided that they no longer required to borrow the General's prestige for electoral purposes.

It is generally agreed that the R.P.F. has a greater appeal to the younger generation than any other political movement except the Communists. In the 1946 Assembly all but two of the little group of faithful Gaullists were under fifty years of age.[30] But in the 1951 election the General, anxious to collect a strong parliamentary party, seems to have placed less emphasis upon youth: the average age of the R.P.F. members was almost fifty, though the group included a higher proportion of young men than most of its rivals.[31]

In the social composition of the leadership, M. Fauvet has pointed out the important part played by the 'technocratic' element. In his occupational classification, the largest single group in the 1950 national council was that of the industrialists and engineers, who numbered 33 out of 150: there were also 26 civil servants, 17 doctors, and many lawyers and commercial men.[32] In the 1951 Assembly, 57 out of the 106 metropolitan R.P.F. members were professional men (15 lawyers, 14 civil servants, 10 doctors, 6 generals, etc.), 30 being businessmen or engineers, and 15 agriculturalists.

But, as in other parties, the composition of the mass movement does not necessarily correspond to that of the leadership. The 2,000 or 3,000 delegates to national congresses are by no means predominantly drawn from the intellectual and governing classes: they have been described by M. Malraux as 'the rush-hour crowd' (*la foule du métro à six heures du soir*). Over the country as a whole, and department by department, the R.P.F. draws its support from the traditional strongholds of the Right; but in the big cities its following is much more

---

[30] Ages at the date of election. One of the two was a colonial member.
[31] Seven R.P.F. members aged 35 or less were returned from metropolitan France in 1951, compared with 5 Communists, 5 M.R.P., 3 Radicals, 3 Socialists, 2 Conservatives, and 1 U.D.S.R. *Les Élections législatives*, p. 54.
[32] Fauvet, p. 239 n.

popular than bourgeois, as the detailed results in the Paris region clearly show. Between 1947 and 1951 the middle-class elements, which at first welcomed General de Gaulle as a defence against Communism, sought safer and less adventurous champions among the Conservatives and Radicals: the proletarian quarters gave much better results than the respectable ones.[33]

The R.P.F. has, in fact, appealed on different grounds to town and countryside. In the former it has relied on its novelty, and has taken pains to equip itself with an original programme, particularly in social matters. But in the latter it has struck root only in traditionally Conservative or former Bonapartist strongholds, and familiarity rather than revolution has been its keynote. In 1951 there were 23 departments in which it won the votes of more than 20 per cent. of the total electorate. In 21 of these, the parties of the Right had reached 30 per cent. of the total in 1932; the Radicals had done so in 7; but the Socialists and Communists combined had attained that figure in only one of the 23, Gironde.[34] The Gaullist attraction for voters of the Left is virtually confined to the big cities.

It is, however, precisely in the modern, urban parts of France that the R.P.F. has made the greatest impact. In the 1947 municipal elections its own lists (as distinct from coalition ones) won under 10 per cent. of the votes in the small communes of under 2,500 inhabitants, but over 20 per cent. in the larger ones (and 28 per cent. in towns of over 9,000). The 26 departments of modern economic structure included half the strongholds of the R.P.F.: and, outside the western region, the Gaullist share of the electors reached 20 per cent. only in the industrialized areas.[35]

The Gaullists made virtually no impression on the southern half of

---

[33] M. Goguel's article in *Revue française de science politique*, vol. 1, no. 3, pp. 330, 333. There is confirmatory evidence. Between 1946 and 1947 the combined Communist and Socialist vote in Paris fell by 137,000, which went to the R.P.F. Between 1947 and 1951 those two parties only gained 5,000, so that the R.P.F. kept these Left votes. The 300,000 which it lost, mainly in the richer western quarters, went to the Radicals and Conservatives. (*L'Observateur*, 21 June 1951.) And this loss of over half of its votes in Paris proper compared with a loss of less than a quarter in the working-class *banlieue*. Again, in the north-west Paris by-election of June 1952, the R.P.F. lost least heavily in the most proletarian arrondissement, the 18th, and most heavily in the most bourgeois, the 16th. But in the municipal elections of 1953 the Socialists regained most of the votes they had lost six years before.

I am grateful to Mr. Nicholas Wahl, of Harvard University, for informing me that, in his unpublished study of the R.P.F., he found that its principal support came from non-working-class voters living (because of the housing shortage) in working-class districts.

[34] From Goguel, *Géographie*, comparing the maps on pp. 49, 77, 107. For the Radicals, see W. Pickles in *Politica*, 1936, p. 178.

[35] *A.P.*, 1947, pp. 363–4. The first two figures are taken from the R.P.F.'s statistics. That for the towns of over 9,000 (which are included in the previous figure) is from the ministry of the Interior, but does not differ appreciably from the R.P.F. statistics.

Of the 23 departments where the R.P.F. reached 20 per cent. of the electorate, 11 had an index of production above the national average. Goguel, *Géographie*, maps on pp. 107 and 140. In all the eastern and Parisian departments concerned, except Haute-Saône, at least 30 per cent. were employed in industry and transport. *Ibid.*, p. 133.

the country. Their three zones of strength were the old Conservative west and east, and the Paris basin in between. The western zone continued southwards as far as Bordeaux, and those three coastal departments were the only ones south of the Loire in which the 20 per cent. figure was attained. After the secession of July 1952, 53 of the R.P.F.'s 74 metropolitan deputies came from north of the river.

4. CHARACTERISTICS

ONE important question-mark on the future of French politics is the way the R.P.F. may be expected to develop. Yet of its place in the country's political tradition there is no doubt. It is the current expression of the Bonapartist outlook, deep-rooted in certain regions, which lies fallow for generations, then suddenly bursts forth with explosive violence.[36] The demand for a government with authority, the vigorous nationalism in foreign and imperial matters, the determined and not unsuccessful attempt to attract support from Left as well as Right, are all hallmarks of the movement's character. At the same time, it suffers from the weakness of all such campaigns. The distinctive features which mark them off from ordinary Conservatism, and give them an appeal to circles which the latter cannot touch, at the same time cause orthodox Conservatives to regard them as dangerous adventures into which it is unwise to plunge unless no other course seems open.

The R.P.F. drew its strength from many sources. It acquired millions of votes from disillusioned supporters of M.R.P., who had voted for that party on conservative grounds and felt deceived by its compromise with the Communists. But very few M.R.P. leaders went over, and still fewer *militants*; these indeed proved much less willing than their chiefs to compromise with the Gaullists, even for short-term and tactical purposes.[37]

The Radicals flocked to the R.P.F. banner in 1947, but mostly returned to their former allegiance in 1949. Their defection was caused partly by the easing of the political situation, which made dangerous methods of salvation less attractive, partly by the return of

---

[36] 'Le bonapartisme . . . vise à établir l'autorité dans le cadre de la démocratie: un chef national, plébiscité par tous les Français, qui mate l'anarchie, fait taire les " bavards " des assemblées, voilà cette vigoureuse conception gouvernementale, où l'égalité subsiste mais où l'ordre prime la liberté, où les conquêtes matérielles de 1789 sont à la fois garanties contre un retour de l'ancien régime et contre les menaces de la révolution sociale. Appelez le chef comme vous voudrez, empereur, consul ou président, peu importe, ce ne sera jamais un roi mais toujours un tribun, qui consolide la démocratie sous le signe de l'ordre sociale . . . le bonapartisme persiste comme un état d'esprit latent, en dehors même de toute organisation, et de temps en temps il ressort: ses manifestations sont d'ordre éruptif.' Siegfried, pp. 203–6.

' Si on ne pare pas à temps au danger, ce sera demain le mépris, apres-demain la révolte . . . le Parlement, chez nous, n'a jamais été vraiment populaire, et les vieux brocards césariens traînent toujours au fond des esprits.' Leon Blum, *La Réforme gouvernementale*, p. 22: the work was first published, anonymously, in 1919.

[37] See below, p. 370.

the Radical party to governmental power, and partly by the growing tendency of the R.P.F. to take the clerical side on the issue of education. The marriage had been one of convenience—another instance of the Radical willingness to associate with any partner in the hope of electoral profit, and of the Radical skill in getting the best of the bargain. The most temperamentally conservative party in the country, distrustful of new solutions, anxious above all for a quiet life, existing—in so far as it had a philosophy at all—to defend the citizen against the government, and afraid of strong political leaders (especially if they happened to be generals), was an extraordinary source for Gaullist recruitment. The explanations were temporary: the reaction of property seeking immediate protection against Communism, the need of politicians to retrieve the disaster which had struck their party. A few individuals like M. Chaban-Delmas and M. Michel Debré, standing for the other, 'proconsular' Radical tradition,[38] had joined from a more genuine sympathy and stayed with the movement when the final choice had to be made: the former took his departmental organization with him, while the latter retained the confidence of his local party until the very last moment. But these were exceptions.

The old Conservatives might welcome General de Gaulle's attitude on economic, colonial, or even constitutional matters. On the other hand they distrusted some of his more adventurous associates, and they were bitterly hostile to many of the things his government had done at the time of liberation—to the purge, to the nationalization of industry, to the admission of Communists to office. Most Conservatives had favoured Marshal Pétain in 1940, and the leading apologists for Vichy remained aloof from the R.P.F. and bitterly hostile to it. The rank and file, however, attached less importance to these differences. They voted *en masse* for the new variety of Gaullism, and many of the parliamentary Conservatives thought it wise to follow the trend.

The pressure of these millions of Pétainist votes affected the R.P.F. in its turn. The General and the movement gradually shifted their ground on questions such as the treatment of the imprisoned Marshal, amnesty for those condemned after the war, and revision of the laws making former pro-Pétain politicians ineligible for a political career. In April 1950 Colonel Rémy, a prominent leader both in the Resistance and in the R.P.F., wrote an article advocating rehabilitation for the Marshal, in which he declared that the Vichy shield had been as necessary to the country in 1940 as the Gaullist sword, and that General de Gaulle had himself spoken of the need for two strings to France's bow.[39] The article was disavowed, and Colonel Rémy had to resign from the Gaullist executive; but the phrase itself was not denied, and it was apparent that the General's views had changed considerably from the

---

[38] See above, p. 91.
[39] *A.P.*, 1950, pp. 78–9. Colonel Rémy's article appeared in *Carrefour*, 11 April 1950.

days when he spoke bitterly of *Père la Défaite*. But if the former resistance leader now found himself at the head of many of his war-time opponents, and opposed to most of those who had once supported him, he certainly did not intend to disavow the past. In April 1952, when M. Maurras celebrated his compassionate release from prison by publicly demanding the execution of the minister of Justice who had conducted the purge, the R.P.F. joined with vigour in the indignant protest of the resistance elements in the Assembly. In November, the General's brother denounced the revival of the old supporters of Vichy, and the R.P.F. expelled the president of the Paris city council for accepting Vichyite allies in the coming municipal elections.[40]

The R.P.F. was established in the first place as a movement to revise the constitution (which remains one of its primary purposes). But, instead of a rally comprising members of all parties and working for one essential but limited objective, it became a disciplined movement seeking power, a new party in everything but name. Consequently it found itself obliged to take up its own line on all the major issues of the day. Its solution to the constitutional question is discussed elsewhere.[41] On imperial questions, and on foreign policy generally, it shares the nationalist outlook of the old Right, though sometimes, especially in relation to France's allies, expressing it more vigorously. The hardest problems of policy were found in the two fields which mark the dividing lines between the other parties, the educational and the social.

When the Gaullist movement began to work out its attitude to other than constitutional problems, it seemed plain that it would act as a socially conservative party. But the clerical question appeared likely to divide it from top to bottom. The general secretary, M. Soustelle, and the national propaganda organizer, M. Malraux, were opposed to the General's own clerical tendencies. The education committee at the first national congress failed completely to reach any agreement.[42] In the constituencies, acute friction between the two wings of the movement came to a head in the Melun by-election in June 1949. M. Lespès, an M.R.P. deputy turned Gaullist, was nominated by national headquarters to contest a vacancy on the departmental council. But the local R.P.F. organization was dominated by another deputy and three senators, all Radicals, who disliked the intervention of national headquarters, especially on behalf of a clerical candidate. They put up a nominee of their own, who was elected. The rebellious deputy was promptly expelled, and the senators censured. The inter-group sup-

---

[40] *J.O.*, 13 April 1952, M. Soustelle's speech. *A.P.*, 1952, p. 85. M. Maurras' open letter to the President, in which he called for the trial and execution of M. de Menthon, must be judged in the light of a journalistic career in which he repeatedly incited his disciples to the murder of political opponents.
[41] See below, pp. 161–3.
[42] *A.P.*, 1948, p. 53.

ported its chairman, who resigned in protest against these measures. With the parliamentarians openly quarrelling with the executive, and clericals with anti-clericals, the R.P.F. was at a low ebb.[43]

The Gaullists were helped to solve this problem by the widespread Radical defections of the next few months, which left them with a following predominantly sympathetic to the claims of the Church. Their ingenious solution, the *allocation-éducation* (a subsidy to the parents of school children instead of to the schools themselves) was designed to satisfy the Catholics, while provoking the anti-clericals as little as possible. And when the issue came to a head in September 1951, the R.P.F. polled all but five of its 120 deputies in favour of the Barangé bill.

It was after all upon the social issue that cohesion proved impossible to achieve. The departure of its former casual ' fellow-travellers ' in 1949, when it became clear that the R.P.F. was not going to advance to an early and complete triumph, had simplified matters over education but complicated them on economic issues. For the departing Radicals were socially conservative. Many supporters of P.R.L. and similar groups, moreover, now felt themselves strong enough to enter the electoral struggle without the need for association with the R.P.F. By 1950, therefore, just as the preponderance of supporters of the Catholic schools had become more overwhelming, that of the social and economic conservatives had become less so. The result was soon apparent in policy.[44]

The R.P.F. had always denied that it was merely a new disguise for traditional Conservatism; and when the new Council of the Republic first met in November 1948, and again when the new Assembly met in July 1951, the Gaullist members refused to take the benches assigned to them on the extreme right.[45] Yet their votes seemed to justify the

---

[43] The four members of parliament sent an outspoken letter of protest to General de Gaulle: ' Nous avons trop combattu la féodalité des comités directeurs des partis pour l'accepter du R.P.F., dont les méthodes et les ukases font qu'il cesse d'être un rassemblement pour devenir un parti. . . . A la tête du R.P.F., certains éléments ambitieux, impatients et peu soucieux des traditions républicaines sont en train de compromettre le destin du Rassemblement. . . . ' *A.P.*, 1949, p. 123.

In the Melun election M.R.P., angry with M. Lespès' desertion to the R.P.F., had supported the dissident Gaullists against him in spite of their anti-clerical attitude. But six months later another local by-election in the department was won by a Conservative, supported by R.P.F. and M.R.P., against the opposition of a Radical, backed by the Gaullist dissidents—and by P.R.L. And in the 1951 general election M. Bégouin, the deputy expelled by the R.P.F. over the affair, was elected as a Radical with a prominent local Catholic as his second, while the candidate he had sponsored in the Melun by-election put up an independent list against him. French local political alignments are sometimes complicated.

[44] During 1953 a similar evolution occurred in imperial policy, and it became clear that an important section of the R.P.F. was prepared to conciliate North African and even Indo-Chinese nationalism. The former Sultan of Morocco, at the time of his deposition in August 1953, was represented in Paris by a Gaullist deputy, M. Clostermann; and the Gaullist leader in the cabinet appears to have opposed the deposition. See also *J.O.*, 4 June 1953, p. 2975 (M. Diomède Catroux's speech).

[45] In the upper house the problem was solved by giving the R.P.F. the seats high up at the back of the chamber. But in the Assembly, where there are more violent sittings,

case of their critics. Thus, early in 1950, the R.P.F. joined the Radicals and Conservatives in trying to amend, against the wishes of the trade unions, the bill to restore free collective bargaining. But even at this time its members voted for the proposed wage bonus, disliked by the Conservatives. And *Le Rassemblement* denounced the government as the puppet of the American trusts, with a violence of expression hitherto unknown outside the Communist press.[46]

After the 1951 election the determination of the R.P.F. to dissociate itself from orthodox Conservatism became more and more evident. The General himself, in his first press conference, attacked the employers' organization and its political power.[47] In September 1951 the R.P.F. joined the Socialists, the Communists, and most of M.R.P., against the government, the Radicals, and the Conservatives, in carrying through the Assembly a bill to establish a sliding scale for wages. In March 1952 the Gaullist leaders announced that they would enter no government unless both M.R.P. and the Socialist party were also included.[48]

But many Gaullist deputies were Conservatives at heart, and shared the desire of their colleagues outside the R.P.F. to weaken the Left-wing influence in the government. Twenty-seven of these rebels, defying the party decision to abstain, put and kept M. Pinay in office. The 'radical' wing then revolted in its turn. In April the sliding scale bill, against which successive governments had fought a long delaying action, came back to the Assembly. The prime minister demanded a further postponement. A quarter of the R.P.F. members, the conservatives, voted for him: another quarter, mainly the members for urban constituencies, voted against him [49]: and the remaining half abstained. In July the Gaullist leaders at length decided to reimpose discipline, and twenty-six right-wing dissentients left the R.P.F. The movement had lost most of its Radical adherents in 1949: in 1952 it lost many of its Conservatives. The centre of gravity shifted well to the Left.

The rebels formed a new group, the A.R.S. (*Action républicaine et sociale*), which was joined by earlier dissidents and soon numbered

---

the other parties were unwilling to concede these strategic positions, and combined to vote the R.P.F. into the unpopular seats on the right. The Gaullists argued that the Radical party were now the real right wing, and one ingenious Radical suggested in reply that the authoritarianism which had always been the hallmark of the Right was now best expressed by the Communists. *A.P.*, 1948, p. 221; *Le Monde*, 27 June 1951 : 14, 18, and 19 July 1951.

[46] *Ibid.*, 15–16 January 1950 (the remark is M. Fauvet's).

[47] *Ibid.*, 24–25 June 1951. The General was reported as attacking ' le syndicalisme patronal aussi politisé que l'autre. " On l'a bien vu lors des élections ".'

[48] *Ibid.*, 2–3 March 1952.

[49] Twenty-eight R.P.F. deputies voted against postponement, 59 abstained, and 26 voted for it. Of the 28 who opposed postponement, half represented Seine and Seine-et-Oise. Two-thirds of the R.P.F. members for these departments voted on that side (14 out of 22), compared with one-third of the members for other highly industrialized departments (8 out of 27), and only 6 of the remaining 67 Gaullists.

thirty—a quarter of the original Gaullist group. It included most of the members whose seats depended on Conservative votes, who had themselves previously sat as Conservatives, or who represented the Conservative west: and also most of the lawyers on the R.P.F. benches. It was weakest among the deputies of the great towns—though not, it soon became clear, among Gaullist voters or local leaders there.[50]

On domestic issues the new group worked closely with the Independents and Peasants, both at election times and in the Assembly. It tended to be further to the Right than the former, more sympathetic to urban business interests than the latter, and rather better disciplined than either—as befitted a party led by M. Barrachin, former general secretary of Colonel de la Rocque's *Parti social français*, and by M. Frédéric-Dupont, a leader in the riots of 6 February 1934. Only on foreign affairs, and especially over the European army, did many members of A.R.S. retain a Gaullist rather than a Conservative outlook.

The R.P.F. is now in decline. But it is not yet dead. Faced with an imminent Communist threat, non-Communist opinion in the country would no doubt turn to General de Gaulle. So far, the danger has not been near enough to justify so adventurous a choice: but 1947 showed clearly enough which way middle opinion would go in a crisis. Pending the emergency, the Gaullists could hope to profit from the impatience and frustration which must at times beset any observer of the French political system. Its inefficiency, though less grave than a superficial view would suggest, is real enough to cause dissatisfaction in a country where the parliamentary tradition is somewhat fragile. More serious still is the total failure of democracy in France to find means of appealing to the imagination. The impatient, the enthusiastic and the youthful find the Fourth Republic, as they found the Third, a drab or indeed a sordid regime. Parliamentary manœuvres, political impotence, and administrative scandals offer easy scope for the enemies of the existing system.

The *mystique* of authority and discipline always has its appeal, especially to youth, and the political and social conditions of France

---

[50] 11 R.P.F. deputies had formed a common list with the Conservatives, or had been elected because the Conservatives agreed to an alliance with them instead of with the government parties. (See below, pp. 322–5, for the working of the electoral law). Eight of these 11 members were among the rebels. So were 13 of the 29 members who had sat in the previous Assembly—8 out of 11 who had been P.R.L. candidates in 1946, and 5 out of 18 who had stood under other auspices. 8 of the 16 R.P.F. deputies for the nine departments from Calvados to Vendée (omitting peninsular Brittany) were involved, and so were 8 of the 15 Gaullist lawyers. In general, the deputies with unsafe seats were the most affected. In 16 constituencies the Gaullist deputies were divided between rebels and loyalists, and in only four of them was it the man at the head of the list who rebelled.

In the Paris area (Seine, Seine-et-Oise, and Seine-et-Marne) the dissentients were only 3 out of 22, and in the constituences including Lyons, Marseilles, Lille, Bordeaux, Strasbourg, and St. Étienne, they were only 2 out of 14.

do not diminish its attractiveness. The R.P.F. had a freshness and a dynamic vigour which the older parties lacked. Yet there were disadvantages in these qualities too. Strict discipline may be an asset in a movement with a genuine common outlook. But there were many differences between General de Gaulle and his followers, and the intransigence of the leader, a virtue in a moment of crisis, became a liability in a long political campaign. In the constituencies, the imposition of tactics dictated from headquarters produced constant friction and successive defections; in the Assembly, the R.P.F. soon found itself obliged to behave like its rivals, and to wage the fight on a terrain where skill and experience were on their side.

The R.P.F. clearly shares some of the features of a Fascist movement. Its policy exhibits the characteristic combination: the simultaneous appeal to national revival and to social revolution, and the demand for strong government superseding futile party bickering, and maintaining the dignity and power of the state against the rampant demands of pressure-groups and sectional interests. Its psychology is marked by the cult of authority and the belief that the leader is always right, particularly among its younger and less prosperous adherents. It recruits its leaders from the managerial elements in society, but seeks with success to appeal to a section of the poor, especially to those who are proletarians in economic status but resent and repudiate such a social classification.

Yet France is neither Spain nor Italy—still less Germany. General de Gaulle's record is not that of a Fascist, whether one considers 1940 or 1944–46. His own declarations have lapsed only occasionally from a determination to seek power alone by legal means.[51] The glorification of violence has played no part in R.P.F. propaganda, and the 'shock troops' of the Gaullist movement have been kept firmly in a position of subordination.[52] The nationalism of the R.P.F. has certainly been no more violent than that of the German Social Democratic party: its social programme has been much more tentative and much less demagogic than that of Fascist movements, while at the same time it has attracted far less capitalist support than they enjoyed. 'The balancing, the reconciliation of great pressure-groups by a strong executive' is a potentially dangerous remedy for a weakness which, if not tackled, itself menaces the health and perhaps the survival of French democracy.[53] Minor analogies with Fascist movements, such as the strong Gaullist appeal to former combatants in the Indo-China war, are

---

[51] Both his most criticized speeches, that at Lille on 12 February 1949, and that at Bagatelle on 1 May 1951, were ambiguous warnings rather than defiant threats. *A.P.*, 1949, p. 311; 1951, p. 129.

[52] Fauvet, p. 237.

[53] The quotation is from H. Stuart Hughes on ' Gaullism ' in Earle, ed., *Modern France*, p. 259, where the question ' Is this Fascism? ' is answered with a hesitant affirmative. Aron (*op. cit.*, pp. 225–6) argues powerfully the opposite view.

clearly outweighed by one sharp contrast: several prominent figures in the R.P.F. are Jews.[54]

The R.P.F. could conceivably develop into a Fascist movement, if, for example, it came to power at a moment of acute crisis and was promptly faced with a Communist-led general strike. But if the domestic and international situations remain relatively tolerable, the Gaullists are unlikely to acquire sufficient strength to take power on their own account. After 1952 they could no longer hope to paralyse the normal working of the regime, and so force their way into a position of dominance. The departure of the right wing left a curious *mélange*, held together by little except the personality of the leader. In the late 1930's the last similar movement, Colonel de la Rocque's *Croix de feu*, developed into a respectable parliamentary Conservative organization, the *Parti social français*. The R.P.F. was much less conservative on social matters, but might easily have undergone a similar political transformation. General de Gaulle would not permit such a frustration of his purpose; he preferred division in the Assembly, disaster in the constituencies, and ultimately complete withdrawal from the ordinary political arena. His followers in Parliament, left leaderless by his decision, maintained throughout 1953 the formal cohesion of the party. But every important division displayed the differences within the ranks of the re-named U.R.A.S. Most of its members settled without apparent discomfort into the conservative parliamentary majority; but there were a dozen regular and another twenty occasional dissentients, drawn mainly from the industrial constituencies, from the most active resistance elements, and from the General's personal associates.[55]

---

[54] E.g. M. Gaston Palewski, the General's former *chef de cabinet* and a member of the executive, and his brother—both deputies: M. Moatti, another deputy: M. Henry Torrès, a prominent R.P.F. senator who had once been a Communist: M. Raymond Aron, the well-known journalist, long a member of the *conseil national*.

[55] For a useful review of the R.P.F.'s history see C. Casalegno, ' Grandezza e decadenza del movimento gollista ', *Occidente*, November 1953, pp. 392–410.

Chapter 10

THE MINOR PARTIES

FRANCE possesses a rich crop of minor parties, many of them entirely ephemeral. A few are examined in this chapter: firstly the extreme left-wing groups, revolutionary or neutralist offshoots of larger formations: then a single middle-sized party, U.D.S.R., the uneasy ally of the Radicals: next the R.G.R. (*Rassemblement des gauches républicaines*, the somewhat nebulous organization by which U.D.S.R. and Radicals are linked) and various splinter groups which also belong to it: then a number of small movements of the extreme Right: and finally the separate groups of overseas deputies.

These little parties may be electorally negligible, but they are not wholly without interest and importance. Some, notably those of the neutralist Left, influence the public mind much more than their derisory showing at the polls would suggest. For the intellectuals to whom they appeal help to create the climate of opinion; though their outlook does not decide their neighbours' votes, it may nevertheless affect their attitude to specific political problems. So, from 1900 onwards, the *Action française* exercised an enormous attraction upon the entire Right, though it could hardly elect a single deputy. The protest groups of the Left are much less influential than this, but they do express a disquiet over the treatment of the industrial workers, and especially over foreign policy, which extends far outside their own ranks. Some Radicals and many Socialists are affected by a ' Bevanite ' outlook, which is perhaps strongest of all in M.R.P.; the left wing of that movement is much more extreme than the official Socialist party.

Other groups, lacking the following to constitute a popular movement, or the cohesion to exercise intellectual influence, are able through their strategic position to play a vital parliamentary role. There is always an important place in French assembles for a little group of able men, who have no bitter enmities, whose marginal situation entitles them to a large share of ministerial posts, but whose entry into a government arouses less jealousy among the big parties than extending the power of any one of themselves would provoke. In the Third Republic this part was played by the Republican Socialists, the party of Briand, Painlevé, and Paul-Boncour. In the Fourth, it has fallen especially to U.D.S.R.

Yet other organizations have their origins in the country's history. The list of minor groups is littered with the relics of the past. Some, like the royalists, represent an ancient tradition. A few, such as the *Alliance démocratique*, form the last remnant of once powerful movements, now dead but for the name, and a frustrated politician or two clinging to it—like a National Liberal in Great Britain—in the hope that it can still be used to advantage. Many are mere cliques, formed around a particular leader or group; an example is M. Paul Faure's *Parti socialiste démocratique*, which is drawn from the Socialists who followed Marshal Pétain in 1940.

Not all of these lesser groups look backward for their inspiration. Some are new departures; and though most of these are quite ephemeral, and the rest may appear so, they cannot be entirely neglected. For M.R.P., once the largest party in France, had its forerunners among the petty splinter groups of the Third Republic. An infant movement of the future may again be concealed among the shadowy ghosts of the past.

1. THE EXTREME LEFT

MOST of the minor groups of the extreme Left are combined in the *Union progressiste*, formed in December 1950. Many of them are organizations of 'fellow-travelling' ex-members of the Third Force parties. The *Radicaux et résistants de gauche* (who include M. Pierre Cot, the best known of all the Progressives), unite the left-wing Radicals expelled by their party at the Lyons congress of April 1946, for favouring a Communist alliance and opposing the decision to enter the R.G.R. The *Union des chrétiens progressistes* was established early in 1948. The *Parti socialiste unitaire*, created in September of the same year, comprises the pro-Communist elements in the Socialist party, grouped around the paper *La Bataille socialiste*, who were expelled for opposing the drastic laws for the maintenance of order during the great strikes at the end of 1947. These three bodies established a joint committee in April 1948, which also included members of the *Jeune République*—a movement which before 1939 had had some importance as a forerunner of M.R.P., but had subsequently lost most of its leaders, some having joined M.R.P., like M. Marc Sangnier, and others U.D.S.R., like M. Claudius Petit.

At the end of 1950 this committee was broadened into a more substantial movement, and re-named *Union progressiste*. Its new supporters were 'neutralist' rather than fellow-travelling in outlook, and the 1951 general election showed this distinction to be a real one. The *Union progressiste* had a national organization based on the usual pattern of congress, national council, executive and secretariat, and claimed to have set up departmental and local committees in thirty departments, especially on the west coast, in the centre, and in the south-east.

The Progressives maintained a separate group in the Assembly, the *Union des républicains et résistants*, which in 1950 changed its name to *Union des républicains progressistes*. Most of its members were either left-wing Radicals, who after their expulsion from their old party headed joint lists with the Communists, or members of the *Rassemblement démocratique africain*, a West African nationalist movement with Communist sympathies. A parliamentary group with less than fourteen members has to ally itself with a larger group for committee elections: the Progressives were affiliated (*apparentés*) in this way to the Communist party (except between 1949 and 1951, when they were strong enough to achieve a nominal and temporary independence).

Early in 1950 a new extreme Left group appeared in the Assembly, the *Gauche indépendante*. This included three former M.R.P. deputies who had broken with their party, one of them an abbé, the second a marquis, and the third a professor of medicine who led the parliamentary fight against coca-cola. A couple of other ex-M.R.P. members were also briefly associated with the *Gauche indépendante*, which was affiliated to the Progressive group, before passing into full membership of the latter.[1] This accession helped to compensate for the defection of the R.D.A. In October 1950, after a quarrel among its leaders, that organization broke with the Communists; it began voting with the government in critical divisions, and subsequently became affiliated to U.D.S.R.

In the 1951 election the former deputies of the Progressive group went different ways, the 'fellow-travellers' accepting places on Communist lists, while the 'neutralists' fought on their own. Four of the former held their seats, but all the neutralist deputies were heavily defeated. Eight more neutralist lists appeared, mostly in the Paris area: only one of them in Seine-Inférieure east, reached 2 per cent. of the total.[2]

The *Union progressiste* includes only the extreme Left groups which, though not necessarily complete 'fellow-travellers', are willing to work with the Communists. Opposed to co-operation with the orthodox Communists are two dissident groups, the *Mouvement communiste français* and the *Parti communiste internationaliste*. The former was launched before the election by M. Darius Le Corre, once a Communist deputy, and received somewhat disproportionate attention in the press. M. Le Corre (who was attacked and badly beaten by Communists during

---

[1] For the careers of these two members see below, p. 362 and n.
[2] All the ex-Radical Progressives stood on Communist lists, and two, MM. Cot and Meunier, were re-elected. M. de Chambrun, Christian Progressive son of a railway magnate (described on his 1946 election posters as *fils de cheminot*), and M. d'Astier de la Vigerie, from a family of aristocratic royalists, also saved the seats which they had originally won with Communist support. The former was the only survivor from the Catholic extreme Left; every member associated with the *Gauche indépendante* was defeated—one on a Communist list, the rest as neutralists. Two Socialist members had gone over to the Progressives in 1948: one stood as a neutralist in Paris, the other as second Communist candidate in Allier: both were beaten.

The *Parti socialiste unitaire* had differed from the Communists over the question of Tito, with whom many of its members sympathized. Its general secretary, who had been Socialist deputy for Aisne in 1945, contested that department in 1951 against both Socialists and Communists, winning 6,000 votes out of 220,000.

the election campaign) stood for Seine-et-Oise north, and received 7,000 votes out of 358,000; two months after the election, his movement split.[3] The P.C.I., the Trotskyist party, had contested seventeen constituencies in November 1946, and had deprived the Communists of a few seats, but in 1951 they put up only two lists. In Seine-et-Oise north, where they had had 14,000 supporters in 1946, they gained 5,700 votes to 7,000 for M. Le Corre and 3,700 for a neutralist list: in the north-eastern suburbs of Paris they added 1,000 to their former vote of 4,500, but had only $1\frac{1}{2}$ per cent. of the total. Other independent Communist lists won about 1 per cent. each in western Gironde (Bordeaux), Indre, and Meurthe-et-Moselle. In Paris the movement supported neutralist candidates.

The *Rassemblement démocratique révolutionnaire* was launched in 1948 as an attempt to rally the non-Communist supporters of social revolution both within and outside the Socialist party. It had the backing of the Socialist youth movement and of the left wing of the party, always much nearer to anarchism than to Communism, and it also attracted some sympathy from left-wing Catholics associated with the review *Esprit*, from sections of the Trotskyist P.C.I., and from detached intellectuals such as M. Sartre. But the movement struck no roots, and was internally divided over foreign policy, especially its attitude to America. Most of its leaders soon returned to their original home in the Socialist party.

2. U.D.S.R.

THE *Union démocratique et socialiste de la résistance* is the most important of the minor parties, and the only political group in France which has its roots exclusively in the resistance movement. Its nucleus was in the *Mouvement de libération nationale*, a federation of resistance organizations from both the occupied and the unoccupied zones. M.L.N. split in January 1945, a minority favouring fusion with the Communist-controlled (though not exclusively Communist) *Front national*. In June this element went over, to form the ephemeral *Mouvement unifié de la renaissance française*, of which M. Herriot became president—a symbol of the Communist-Radical alliance, then in its heyday. The anti-Communist majority of M.L.N. opened negotiations with other resistance movements which resulted, also in June 1945, in the formation of U.D.S.R. At that time it was a federal body, controlled by a *comité directeur* on which the constituent movements[4] were separately represented. It was not a political party, but the predominant tendency was favourable to the Socialists, and in several departments, especially in the Paris area, Socialists and U.D.S.R. entered an electoral alliance and formed common lists.

---

[3] *Le Monde*, 15–16 August 1951.
[4] M.L.N., O.C.M., *Libération-Nord, Ceux de la Résistance,* and *Libérer et Fédérer.*

This policy proved a disappointment, both because the Socialist rank and file were suspicious of the newcomers and unwilling to give them good places on the electoral lists, and because Socialist policy, influenced by reluctance to break with the Communists, led that party into courses which U.D.S.R. disliked. The break came with the adoption of the draft constitution in April 1946, which the Socialists supported along with the Communists. Some of the U.D.S.R. deputies elected on common lists with the Socialists went over finally to the larger party, and a few others supported the draft constitution, though remaining in U.D.S.R. But the bulk of the new movement decided to oppose the new constitution, and entered into alliance with the Radicals in a new combination, the R.G.R.[5] In November 1946 U.D.S.R. abandoned its federal structure and decided to organize as a new political party.

The movement has the usual organization of national congresses, sections in the communes, departmental federations, executive committee and bureau. But this is really a façade: U.D.S.R. is essentially a group of leaders, members of parliament, local councillors, and journalists, and has no existence among the electorate as a whole. In certain departments individual deputies have built up a clientèle of their own, but the party depends on their personal position, and not the other way round. There are supposed to be fifty departmental federations in existence, but the ineffectiveness of the organization was bitterly criticized at the Marseilles congress in October 1951, and the general secretary resigned in consequence. As in the Radical party, in the absence of a genuine and active mass membership, the machinery is available for manipulation by the supporters of rival leaders.[6]

U.D.S.R., small and artificial as it is, is situated very close to the centre of gravity of French politics. In its early days it attracted support from the most diverse quarters. One wing of the party was attracted to the Socialists: the first general secretary, M. Leenhardt, an assistant secretary, M. Ribière, and several deputies were later elected to the Assembly as Socialists. But U.D.S.R. was also an important recruiting ground for Gaullists. M. Soustelle, the first general secretary of the R.P.F., M. Malraux, its chief propagandist, and M. Capitant, its first parliamentary leader, were all associated with U.D.S.R. in 1946. Another element came from the *Jeune République*, the progressive and mainly Catholic group which had given many leaders to M.R.P.—to which party this section of U.D.S.R. remained sympathetic.[7] Yet

---

[5] For the R.G.R., see next section.

[6] Personal disputes within the party were deplored by the general secretary in his resignation statement. They were reflected in ' les discussions acharnées et interminables sur la validité du nombre de mandats de telle ou telle fédération d'outre-mer, ou encore le long débat nocturne sur la question de savoir s'il faudrait un délai de présence au parti avant de pouvoir être élu au comité directeur.' *Le Monde*, 21–22 October 1951.

[7] Its leader, M. Claudius Petit, fought the election of 1951 on a joint list with M.R.P. and Conservatives. At the Marseilles congress in October, he vigorously defended M.R.P. and the Barangé law against the attacks of the anti-clerical wing.

despite the attractions of so many other parties, the official links of U.D.S.R. were with the Radical party, with which temperamentally it had least in common: the bond between the most characteristic product of the Third Republic and the most characteristic product of the resistance movement was indeed ' un mariage de raison plus que d'amour '.[8]

Its central position has made U.D.S.R. a useful barometer of the course of French politics. Its birth signalized the failure of the Communists' first bid for power, in which they had hoped to exploit their hold on the resistance movement. Its breach with the Socialists helped to frustrate the second Communist bid, in which they tried to organize a Marxist coalition under their own control; for, by breaking with its Socialist allies, U.D.S.R. played its part in depriving the Communist-Socialist combination of its former parliamentary majority. As a resistance organization, U.D.S.R. might have been expected to support *tripartisme*: instead its defection to the Conservative opposition pointed the way the electorate was to follow in subsequent years. It was the nucleus of the Gaullist movement, and provided many of the principal leaders of the R.P.F.; yet among the groups which allowed double membership, it was the first to realize that this could not be a permanent solution, and that its members must make their choice. In spring 1948 M. Pleven had tried to reconcile the R.P.F. and the government parties[9]; in June 1949 he found himself unable to keep Gaullists and non-Gaullists together within his own party; and by July 1950 he was himself prime minister. The role of his government was not to strengthen the majority on its Right by an understanding with the R.P.F., but to restore it on the Left by bringing back the Socialists after their brief period out of office.

M. Pleven's decision to opt for the Third Force influenced both the character of U.D.S.R., and its relations with its neighbours. It affected the party's character because, with its key position in the centre of politics, in an Assembly where the majority was always precarious, U.D.S.R. was the chief of those marginal formations whose support is so necessary to every French government: it had, for instance, saved M. Schuman's first ministry (by abstention) in February 1948, and destroyed his second in the following September.[10] As we have seen, it was like the small pivotal parties of the Third Republic in being both too well placed to be ignored, and to small to be feared. But, since those days, the introduction of colonial deputies into the Assembly has added a new refinement. For a group in the centre of the political

---

[8] Fauvet, p. 123.
[9] U.D.S.R. had played this rôle before. When General de Gaulle quarrelled with the Communists in November 1945, and with the Socialists early in January 1946, it was U.D.S.R. members who produced the solutions which induced him not to resign.
[10] *A.P.*, 1948, pp. 19, 154. M. Pleven had been a highly conservative minister of Finance in the de Gaulle government, and in 1948–49 U.D.S.R. was almost a Conservative party; see, e.g. *A.P.*, 1949, pp. 58–9, 127, 131.

scene, always in power, has attractions for deputies to whom the sympathy of the administration is electorally important. The departure of the Gaullists in 1949 reduced the U.D.S.R. group in the Assembly from 27 members to 14, 5 of them from overseas constituencies. In the 1951 election only 9 members were returned from metropolitan France, but they were soon reinforced by 14 overseas colleagues.[11]

When U.D.S.R. changed from an opposition to a government party, its relations with its partners were also affected. The Radicals had been steadily extending their influence in the government, and in the summer of 1948 they secured the premiership. But during 1949 M. Pleven and U.D.S.R., though electoral allies of the Radicals in the R.G.R., formed part of the opposition to M. Queuille, the Radical prime minister. This cause of friction disappeared when U.D.S.R. entered the majority, but it was replaced by another. For in May 1950 the R.G.R. elected as its president M. Daladier, leader of the opposition wing of the Radical party. U.D.S.R. contested the regularity of his election, and even considered abandoning the R.G.R. altogether.[12] When M. Pleven became prime minister two months later, it was the Socialist rather than the Radical party which seemed to be his favourite partner, and which was most satisfied by his conduct of affairs.

In the 1951 election the R.G.R. held together as an electoral combination, and fairly successfully discouraged its constituent parties from competing against each other.[13] But when the clerical issue was raised in the following September the allies divided, most Radicals taking the anti-clerical side, while most U.D.S.R. members voted for the Barangé bill. A month later, at the Marseilles congress, the U.D.S.R. organization was captured by the pro-Socialist wing of the party. But this did not affect the essentially governmental attitude of the deputies, who gave as steady support to the Pinay ministry which the Socialists opposed, as to the Faure administration which they favoured.

---

[11] By the beginning of 1952.

[12] The pro-government elements in the R.G.R., now including the majority of both U.D.S.R. and Radicals, maintained that the election had been rushed by the opposition elements, including all the minor parties. *Le Monde*, 7–8 and 9 May 1950: and see below, p. 147.

[13] The electoral law made such arbitration much harder by providing that only national parties, running lists in at least thirty constituencies, could obtain its advantages by participating in coalitions (see below, Ch. 19). This clause helped to multiply lists even where there was no hope of winning a seat.

In 17 of the 103 metropolitan constituencies there were two different lists deriving from R.G.R. parties: but in six cases only were retiring R.G.R. deputies faced with opposition. In eight of the 17 constituencies both rival lists formed part of the same *apparentement* (coalition); here the conflict reduced the chances of winning a seat, but showed no fundamental hostility. In the other nine cases the opposition was complete.

Twelve of the 17 cases found Radicals and U.D.S.R. officially opposing each other. In four of these the latter had less than 1,500 votes, and in two more, less than 3,000. Most of these constituencies, together with Hautes-Pyrénées where a nominal U.D.S.R. list was given four votes, were presumably contested in order to raise the number of U.D.S.R. lists to the required total of thirty.

3. THE R.G.R. AND ITS COMPONENT GROUPS

The *Rassemblement des gauches républicaines* is an alliance of half a dozen political organizations. It includes one major party, the Radicals; one middle-sized group, U.D.S.R.; and four small parties, ghosts from the past, most of them led by politicians whose war-time record had made them ineligible for a political career under the legislation passed at the time of liberation. In the general elections of June and November 1946 and of June 1951, the R.G.R. acted as an electoral clearing house between its component parties, its primary purpose. But in practice it has sometimes been used for another, unavowed object—as a weapon in the internal struggle for control of the Radical party.

The constitution of the R.G.R. is federal, each of the constituent parties being represented in its bureau.[14] This central organization is virtually all that exists of the R.G.R., which makes no general effort to establish local federations with individual membership. But at the centre the over-representation of the minor parties, all of which are hostile to the policy pursued since liberation and anxious to forward a conservative reaction, gives the opposition wing of the Radical party an advantage which they have sometimes been able to use. Their leader, M. Daladier, stood against M. Herriot for the presidency of the party at the Toulouse congress in November 1949. He lost, but six months later minor party votes elected him president of the R.G.R. U.D.S.R. and the pro-government Radicals complained that the election had been rushed, and M. Herriot resigned his honorary presidency of the *Rassemblement*.

With the advent of M. Daladier, attempts were made to extend the scope of the R.G.R.'s activities. In M. Herriot's own Lyons headquarters a bitter struggle developed. The local secretary of the R.G.R., a prominent but rebellious member of the Radical party, had already begun recruiting individual members and establishing his organization as a rival to the Radicals. Just before the election of M. Daladier, M. Herriot pressed unsuccessfully for action against the dissentients. In March 1951 the Radical *comité exécutif* agreed to expel them. But at

---

[14] The R.G.R. bureau has very complete powers to control its activities. Article IX of the statutes lays down that it consists of 20 to 30 members, 11 of whom hold specific posts (vice-president, treasurer, etc.). It must include a representative of each affiliated party, the chairman of the R.G.R. group or inter-group in each house of Parliament, in the Assembly of the French Union, and in the Economic Council, two representatives of women, and two of youth: the last four have to be approved by the bureau itself. According to Article IX it is elected for two years by the congress, and meets monthly: but Article VII states that it is elected for one year, and Article XIII that it meets at least three times a year.

The congress comprises the bureau, all members of R.G.R. groups in the four assemblies, 10 representatives each of the parties, of non-party supporters (these must be approved by the bureau), of women, and of youth, and 200 representatives of the departmental federations, allocated according to membership. But no congress has ever been held (November 1953).

the election in June M. Chambaretaud, the rebel leader, standing as an independent, won enough votes to prevent the government coalition securing an absolute majority.[15] And in the autumn local elections, the minor R.G.R. parties campaigned for the R.P.F.

Just after the general election, M. Daladier sought to strengthen the power and prestige of the R.G.R. in the Assembly, and his own influence within his party, by persuading the bureau of the R.G.R. to propose the creation of a single parliamentary group. The Herriot wing invoked Article 61 of the Radical statutes, which forbids Radical members of parliament to belong to more than one group, (though this had not been used to stop the formation of single R.G.R. groups in the Council of the Republic and the Assembly of the French Union). M. Daladier's scheme failed; separate Radical and U.D.S.R. groups were retained in the Assembly, and he had to content himself with the presidency of an inter-group embracing both.[16]

The small parties belonging to the R.G.R. are the *Alliance démocratique*, the *Parti républicain et social de la réconciliation française*, the *Parti socialiste démocratique*, and the *Parti républicain socialiste*. They are cliques formed around political leaders of the past, rather than movements with genuine roots. The *Alliance démocratique*, once one of the most important Conservative organizations in the country, retained thirty deputies in 1939. But its resistance element left it at the liberation to enter P.R.L., and the remnant comprised little more than the associates of M. Pierre-Étienne Flandin, a former prime minister who held office under Vichy, and was ineligible for election. A number of A.D. members have sat in the Assembly (as Conservatives, not as R.G.R. representatives), and several have held office, notably M. Pinay. Its general secretary headed the Conservative list in Dordogne in 1951, and in the 1952 senatorial elections, a third of the electors in Yonne voted for M. Flandin, in spite of his ineligibility.[17]

The *Réconciliation française* is the remnant of Colonel de la Rocque's *Parti social français,* and was represented in the 1946 Assembly by M. Guy Petit, for parliamentary purposes a member of the Peasant party. In 1951 he was joined by M. de Léotard, elected second on a Radical list in Paris, and *apparenté* to the Radical group. The *Parti*

---

[15] An absolute majority of votes would have secured *all* the seats. See Ch. 19.

[16] Among Conservatives and Radicals electoral and parliamentary behaviour are sometimes only loosely related. The leader of the Peasant party was a minister, but fought the election in alliance with the R.P.F. M. Daladier, the most prominent of the opposition Radicals, formed a coalition with M.R.P. and the Socialists. After the elections, however, both began to conform their conduct to their electoral commitments. The Peasant leader sought with such vigour to bring the Gaullists into office that he procured his own dismissal. M. Daladier moved to the Left, being a very active opponent of the bills to relieve church schools, supporting the sliding scale for wages (with only two others of his party), calling for a renewed alliance with the Socialists, and vigorously criticizing official policy in Indo-China. (And see the Epilogue.)

[17] On M. Flandin see below, p. 192 n. The political position of the A.D. was no less confusing before the war: see below, p. 363.

socialiste démocratique consists of the friends of M. Paul Faure, for twenty years general secretary of the Socialist party, in the late thirties leader of the pacifist opposition to M. Blum within the party, and later a supporter of Marshal Pétain. Most of its leaders were ineligible, though half a dozen former deputies were still entitled to stand for Parliament. The P.S.D. claims to have forty departmental federations, many of them in the south-west, but its membership is under 7,000. The *Républicains socialistes* were before the war a small group of politicians, mostly ex-members of the Socialist party, whose central position and governmental tendencies earned them a large share in almost every ministry.

The minor parties, whose primary interest was the abolition of ineligibility and the return of their leaders to political life, held a joint meeting early in 1951 and affirmed their mutual solidarity, and their hostility to the governments supported by their larger partners, Radicals and U.D.S.R.[18] In the general election the R.G.R. usually gave their members places low on the lists where they had no chance of success. Several members of the A.D. and the R.F. stood as Conservatives. In Paris some effort was made to distribute places evenly: three of the six lists were headed by Radicals, and one each by members of U.D.S.R., R.F., and P.S.D. But only the first four leaders secured election, though one of the Radicals pulled in M. de Léotard (R.F.) as his second.

4. CONSERVATIVE GROUPS

FOUR minor Conservative groups deserve brief mention. Two, the Taxpayers' Defence movement (*Défense des contribuables*) and the *Rassemblement des groupes républicains et indépendants français*, were *ad hoc* bodies created for the 1951 election, products of the provision that only organizations running at least thirty lists might participate in *apparentements*. The others, the Pétainists and the royalists, represent more permanent tendencies in French public life.

The Taxpayers' Defence movement derived its driving force from the P.M.E. organization (*Petites et moyennes entreprises*).[19] Its lists mostly fought in isolation, representing Conservative opposition to the government coalition, and accepted *apparentements* in only seven constituencies (four times with the government parties, once with other Conservative groups, and twice with the R.P.F.). These seven included all the five departments in which its vote exceeded 5 per cent. It elected one deputy, M. Bessac, retiring M.R.P. member for Lot, who had long been in disagreement with his party. He fought in alliance with the government coalition.

The R.G.R.I.F. was a peculiar combination of dissident Radicals

---

[18] *A.P.*, 1951, p. 33.
[19] F. Goguel, *Fourth Republic*, p. 88 ; J. Fauvet, *Le Monde*, 15 June 1951. On the P.M.E. see below, pp. 331–2.

and Socialists in some areas, with extreme Right-wingers in others. It was purely an electoral alliance with no sort of real cohesion. Most of its lists were allied with the government parties, or with Conservative groups. But some fought alone, and in Yonne it was associated with the Socialists. It won 5 per cent. of the votes in ten scattered departments, and elected six members—five Conservatives and a Socialist.[20]

The Pétain group, U.N.I.R. (*Union nationale des indépendants républicains*) ran too few lists to be able to enter *apparentements*. The Marshal's defence counsel was elected in Paris, the French colonists of Oran (Algeria) chose his former *chef de cabinet,* and one of Vichy's ministers of Agriculture won a seat on the same ticket in Calvados (Normandy). U.N.I.R. also gained just over 5 per cent. of the votes in Tarn. Their deputies did not set up a separate parliamentary group, but joined the Peasants or Independents.[21]

French public life is full of paradoxes, but perhaps the most engaging of them all is provided by the character of the royalist movement. The tradition of the old monarchy was reactionary and authoritarian, that of the Orleanist branch was bourgeois and conservative: and in the twentieth century the driving force behind what was left of the monarchist movement came from the passionately nationalist and reactionary *Action française.* But the present pretender to the throne, the Comte de Paris, who unites the claims of both branches of the Bourbon house, has broken with the political tradition of his family. He disavowed the *Action française* in the 1930's, and apart from a single lapse in 1940, when he declared his support for Marshal Pétain, he has since insisted that a restored monarchy can only be constitutional, and must abandon the links with social and economic privilege which have formed the basis for previous monarchies and monarchist movements.

In 1947 he renounced the active leadership of the French monarchists, but his secretariat still issues a monthly bulletin of political commentary. This has faithfully supported the Third Force governments, unpopular as they were with the classes on which the monarchy has in the past relied. It has called for better treatment of the workers, warned against the dangerous attractions of Gaullism, condemned the behaviour of King Leopold of the Belgians as destructive of all that monarchy should stand for, and praised the record of the bitterly criticized 1946–51 Assembly as a great improvement on many of its

---

[20] One of the Conservatives, M. Estèbe, member for western Gironde, was an open supporter of Marshal Pétain: some of the others (who sat for Basses-Pyrénées, Haute-Saône, Loire, and Aisne) had similar sympathies. The Socialist was M. Conte of Pyrénées-Orientales (see below, p. 354); other notable R.G.R.I.F. candidates were M. Chambaretaud, M. Herriot's rival in Lyons (above, p. 148) and M. Houdet, who had been the successful rebel Gaullist candidate in the Melun by-election, which so damaged the R.P.F. in 1949 (above, pp. 134–5).

[21] There was a short-lived Pétainist group of two, which disappeared when the Peasant party split, its members joining the opposition Peasant group.

predecessors.[22] A law of 1886 forbade the pretenders, or their eldest sons, to reside in the country. The Comte de Paris's steadfast moderation, his admirable war record, the insignificance of the monarchist movement, and the prospect that his eleven children would leave him comparatively little time for political agitation, played their parts in bringing about the repeal of this law in June 1950.[23]

After his return, the Comte de Paris commented with distress on the lack of contact between the political leaders and the mass of the people, as a disquieting element in French life. But he followed this observation, a normal charge for a pretender to make, by the unexpected rider that he felt the electorate showed an unreasonable tendency to put the blame on the politicians, whereas in his view most of the fault lay with the *incivisme* of the public.[24] Rarely can a pretender faced with a governmental system against which so much can be, and is, said with widespread acceptance, have defended so consistently the record and the leaders of the other side. Indeed the Comte de Paris and his associates have shown a better sense of the social implications of democracy, and of the political requirements of the Republican tradition, than most of those who use the phrases in their perorations.

5. COLONIAL GROUPS

DEVELOPMENTS in the French Union are not discussed in this work. But colonial representation in Parliament has an impact upon party politics which requires brief mention. The overseas members fall from this point of view into three categories: those who join one of the main French parties: the extreme nationalists, usually associated with the Communist party: and the moderate nationalists, who maintain their independence.

The first category is the largest of the three, although the allegiance of colonial deputies to their chosen group is often somewhat loose. Members representing white electorates, and pro-administration native deputies, usually joined M.R.P. (in 1946), the R.P.F. (in 1951), or the Radical party. Others from native constituencies preferred the Communists, the Socialists, or M.R.P.

The extreme nationalists came from three areas, Algeria, Madagascar,

---

[22] *Le Monde*, 24 April 1950, 2 December 1950, 28 February 1951, 8 June 1951, quotes characteristic extracts.

[23] Both the Comte de Paris and the Bonapartist claimant, Prince Napoleon, had fought in the Foreign Legion: the latter, after escaping from imprisonment by the Germans, also fought with the *maquis* and was severely wounded. In recognition of his services he had already been allowed to return to France. The Comte de Paris's eldest son had also been permitted to study at Bordeaux, so that the repeal only applied to the Bourbon pretender himself. Repeal was opposed by the Communists and (in the upper house) by the Socialists. Members of families which have ever reigned over France are still ineligible for Parliament, under a law of 1884 which many commentators forget, and for the Presidency of the Republic, under Article 44 of the constitution.

[24] In an interview with *Sud-Ouest*, quoted *Le Figaro*, 22 May 1951.

and West Africa.[25] One Algerian nationalist movement, M. Ferhat Abbas's U.D.M.A. (*Union démocratique du manifeste algérien*) returned a dozen members to the second Constituent Assembly, but refused (in protest against the new constitution) to contest the elections of November 1946. A more extreme movement, M. Messali Hadj's M.T.L.D. (*Mouvement du triomphe des libertés démocratiques*) won half a dozen seats at that election. Its deputies usually (though not invariably) voted with the Communists[26]; in 1951 they were eliminated. Madagascar's three native nationalists were arrested and imprisoned in 1947 for instigating rebellion; they nevertheless kept their seats until the 1951 election, when three moderates were returned. The organ of West African nationalism is the R.D.A. (*Rassemblement démocratique africain*). Until 1950 it was affiliated to the small fellow-travelling Progressive group. It then broke away, after a quarrel among its leaders, and its deputies (six in the first National Assembly and three in the second) began voting for the government. In 1952 its members affiliated to U.D.S.R.

The more moderate tendencies are represented by various groups. That of the Algerian Moslems, formed after the elections of November 1946, subsequently broke up: its members drifted away into larger parties. The Overseas Independents (I.O.M.—*Indépendants d'outre-mer*) came together in 1948. Most were native Socialist, M.R.P., or Progressive deputies who had grown dissatisfied; others had been unattached. The group has fifteen members, and has been affiliated for purposes of committee representation to M.R.P. U.D.S.R. is almost a second I.O.M. group.[27] In 1945 one-third, and in 1952 two-thirds of its deputies represented overseas constituencies. But at the first date they were mostly *colons*, and at the second mostly natives; the group's attitude on imperial issues has evolved accordingly.

The impact of the colonial members depends on the general political situation. The mutual hostility between settlers and natives naturally reduces their influence, since the net advantage to be gained from their support is usually nearer fifteen votes than eighty.[28] Yet when the French members are very evenly divided, even fifteen votes may have decisive importance, as the Constituent Assemblies showed.[29] Shaky

---

[25] Tunisia, Morocco, and Indo-China were protected states; their native inhabitants were not French subjects and had no parliamentary representation. But see below, pp. 271 n, 294; and note that Cochin-China was a colony, and could (but never did) elect a deputy.

[26] But in November 1947 they voted for M. Blum as prime minister.

[27] In June 1953 it emphasized this position by laying claim—unsuccessfully—to the Colonial under-secretaryship hitherto normally held by an I.O.M. member.

[28] There were 75 overseas deputies in 1946, 77 in 1949, and 83 in 1951. See below, p. 191 n.

Native voters choose native members. But in 1951 Dr. Aujoulat, Colonial under-secretary and an I.O.M. deputy, transferred from the white constituency in his colony to the native one. Campaigning with the slogan, 'His face may be white, but his heart is as black as a black man's,' he was triumphantly elected. *Le Monde*, 21 June 1951.

[29] See below, p. 167.

governments may modify their policies to retain the support of a wavering section of overseas deputies; thus the electoral law in the African territories was modified by the pressure of the native members in May 1951, and North African policy was changed to satisfy the *colons* in the following November.

In general, however, the chief political effect of overseas representation has been a slight but useful reinforcement of ministerial stability. For while the 'first category' of colonial members naturally divides according to party, and the small second category joins the opposition, the moderate native deputies have normally given reliable support to the majority.[30] In return for their votes, they exact material concessions for their constituencies. In this way the overseas territories obtain from parliamentary representation advantages which are not merely symbolic.

---

[30] They went into opposition when M. Mayer deprived them of the Colonial undersecretaryship in January 1953. They had also policy grievances; cf. the speeches of MM. Aujoulat and Senghor, *J.O.*, 27 May 1953, p. 2862, and 4 June 1953, p. 2974.

Part III. THE CONSTITUTION

Chapter 11

THE CONSTITUTIONAL PROBLEM

1. THE PROBLEM IN THE THIRD REPUBLIC

POLITICAL and institutional factors acted and reacted on one another to produce the governmental instability which was so characteristic a feature of the Third Republic. But, among its complex causes, the most fundamental was the structure of political opinion in the country. The desires of the majority were negative. In matters political they feared the revival of the reactionaries, the return to power of the groups which stood for hierarchy and authority in society, of the landlord, the Church, and later the big capitalist. They feared the power of government, which they considered an independent and dangerous force, likely to corrupt those who wielded it; ministers from the political Left were distrusted almost as much as those of the Right. At the same time, the Left majority in political matters was divided over social and economic questions, most of its followers preferring caution to experiment, and seeking in this sphere also to restrict the power and the demands of the state. There was thus a popular majority opposed to positive government either in its traditional, or in its newer spheres of activity.

The political institutions of the country had been shaped to serve the purposes of this negative majority, and had in turn increased its influence. The electoral system was admirably devised for blocking the most dangerous candidate, whether a political reactionary or a social revolutionary.[1] But its consequences were not merely negative, they were fissiparous as well. For every splinter group or individualist candidate could contest the first ballot for propagandist purposes, without running the risk of presenting the seat to the enemy. And the single member constituency enabled the deputy to entrench himself in his own district and acquire a personal position which was very difficult to shake.

So suspicion of governmental power in the wrong hands, and the clash between the political and the economic fears of the majority, prevented the development of a two-party system in France, and made acceptable an electoral law which encouraged negative politics. This system in turn promoted individualism and party fragmentation, ruling out even the possibility of a few strong parties, and helping to produce

---

[1] See below, pp. 311–12.

the chaotic welter of small groups which occupied the Chamber. From these small groups a majority had somehow to be constituted; its inevitable artificiality, and consequent instability, was the immediate cause of the weakness of French government.

Every majority, it has been said, included within its ranks a minority which would have preferred association with other partners in a new majority. In part, this discontent was caused by clashes of policy. There were always groups in the centre which feared that their more extreme associates were going too far, and were disposed to change alliances in order to check the movement. In part the division was electoral; very few members of the middle-of-the-road groups could hold their seats on centre votes alone, almost all required the support of extremists either of the Right or of the Left, of clericals or of socialists. In consequence, while the various centre parties were ranged along the political spectrum according to the outlook and preference of their members, each group was internally divided according to the particular electoral position of each individual deputy.

These factors of division were not offset by any counteracting factors of cohesion. The foundations of British party discipline were all missing in France. For the reasons given above, the divisions of opinion into two blocs, though obvious in each French constituency taken separately, did not translate itself into parliamentary terms; there was no large group of members sharing a common political outlook. Then the party whip could not be used effectively. The threat of expulsion from the party and the nomination of a rival official candidate held no terrors for a deputy whose following was largely personal and who, if he could distance the intruder on the first ballot, would recover the latter's votes on the second. Consequently this sanction was virtually inoperative. Thirdly, the French government could not wield the threat of dissolution. A general election imposes a substantial fine on members of parliament, even when they run little risk of losing their seats. The prime minister's right to dissolve if he is beaten gives him a powerful means of pressure against rebels in the house, and of appealing to the country on a clear-cut issue which divides his party from his opponents. No such pressure could be used in France. The deputy's re-election depended much less on his party and much more on his personal position; the clash between the opposing groups was not clear-cut; and the right of dissolution was, in practice, denied to the head of the government.

The absence of the dissolution in France was the result, not of constitutional provisions, but of political developments. The constitution of the Third Republic was devised by royalists unable to reach agreement on the person of the monarch—for the advocates of 'strong government' suffered from the group system quite as much as their opponents. But the men of 1875 intended to establish a regime which could readily be transformed into a monarchy when the time was ripe.

They gave to the President of the Republic the right to dissolve the Chamber before the expiration of its legal term, provided he obtained the consent of the Senate. Both the Presidency and the Senate would, it was hoped, be strongholds of conservatism against the menacing power of a Chamber based on universal suffrage, and the dissolution would be their weapon for keeping the latter in check.

Matters in fact developed very differently. In 1877 the first President, the monarchist Marshal MacMahon, dissolved the Chamber for obviously partisan purposes, and tried to use his control of the administration to secure a conservative majority in the new house. In this he failed, and the victorious republicans proceeded to take over effective control of the state. In 1879 MacMahon was forced out of office, and in the same year the republicans gained a majority in the Senate. Before the Third Republic was five years old, the assumptions of its makers had broken down. Presidency and Senate were no longer instruments of political conservatism, and the dissolution power had been discredited. It was never used again.

After 1879 there was a steady tendency to elect only safe and mediocre men to the office of President. Such men would hardly attempt to challenge the authority of the elected house. The Senate passed by gradual degrees into the hands of the parties which predominated in the Chamber. It was consequently not very likely to consent to a dissolution directed against the majority of the latter. In fact, it was not once asked to do so, partly no doubt because it was known that it would refuse. A more important reason still was the reaction of the public to the events of 1877. Henceforward the idea of dissolution was firmly associated in the public mind with the memory of an attempted *coup d'état* against the Republic. Lastly, the events of 1934, the occasion when dissolution of the Chamber was most seriously envisaged, showed that there was another obstacle to overcome, besides a timid President, a hostile Senate, and a suspicious and angry public. The weakness of French government meant that it was chronically short of money, and unable to pass the budget on time. More often than not, a government which wished to dissolve the Chamber would first have had to secure the consent of that body itself to an unusually large grant of money; and it was just such a demand from the Doumergue government, which, acting as a danger-signal, caused the Radical party to bring the ministry down rather than put it in a position to contemplate dissolution seriously.[2]

With no effective means of bringing the life of the Chamber to a premature end, members were secure in their seats for four years. The effect on their psychology was profound. The overthrow of a cabinet held no terrors for them, since their personal position was not adversely affected; indeed, it might be a positive advantage, opening the way to

---

[2] Soulier, pp. 559–60.

the possibility of promotion. This was especially true among the pivotal centre groups, whose marginal position enabled them to raise 'a record crop of ministerial portfolios to the acre'.[3] So the slight shifts of public or parliamentary opinion, which in Britain produce a trimming of governmental policy or at most a cabinet reshuffle, in France lead always to a change of cabinet. But the practical effect is much the same, since as a rule most of the ministers in the old administration pass straight into the new, often retaining their old offices. The change at the top, like the change below which it reflects, is of marginal importance only.

While the electoral system and the absence of any effective power of dissolution were the most important institutional causes of the weakness of French governments, they were not the only ones. The procedure of the Chamber handicapped the administration. Control of parliamentary time was out of its hands, and was jealously preserved by the house itself, acting through a committee (the Presidents' Conference) comprising the chairmen of the political groups and of the standing committees of the Chamber. One procedural weapon above all, the right of interpellation, was particularly dangerous to governments. The interpellation is a short debate, on any subject great or trivial, which is concluded by a vote. The vote may be on a simple motion, 'The House, having heard the minister's explanation, passes to the order of the day'; alternatively, the motion may be qualified (*motivé*) by expressions of confidence in, or disapproval of, the government's attitude.

The interpellation was a weapon which destroyed many ministries and made the reputation of many critics (notably Clemenceau). But, as in so many other instances, the significance of the institution depended upon the political situation. The very existence of such a device, like the determination of the Chamber to retain control of its own programme, reflected a conception of politics which regarded criticism of the ministry as the principal parliamentary duty. It was more important to keep the executive safely subordinate to the representatives of the people than to give it the degree of independence which would enable it to govern effectively. For power, in France, is always suspect.

Again, the danger of the interpellation lay largely in the expectation that the fall of the government was, on the whole, quite as probable as its survival. In these circumstances it was natural for the promoters of interpellations to acquire friends and merit by voting for each other's motions, and for deputies and even ministers in office to decide their course, not in relation to the present cabinet, but by calculations about the probable composition of its successor. Where there was no solidarity in the majority, there could be little in the government either, and

---

[3] Siegfried, p. 169.

each minister acted for himself, or at most for his group, with little consideration for the collective interests of the cabinet as a whole.

Another source of weakness inside the Chamber was the existence of an alternative leadership, provided by the committees. These bodies, elected since 1910 by the proportional representation of parties, specialized on particular aspects of the political scene, the sphere of each corresponding roughly to that of a government department. The parties tended to send the same members to sit year after year, so that the committees established a certain corporate sense. Their chairmen and *rapporteurs* held a special position in the discussion of bills, both in procedure and in prestige; committee work also gave great opportunities for informed criticism of administration. Committee positions were a natural training-ground for potential ministers. Being based on proportional representation, the committees should in theory each have reproduced the government's majority in the house. But that majority was shaky and heterogeneous, and accident might easily concentrate a number of its less reliable members in particular committees. The chances of personality might put dubious friends, or even open opponents, in positions of influence; indeed, committee chairmen and *rapporteurs* had a direct personal interest in attacking the government, since, if it fell, they were obvious candidates for ministerial positions in the next combination. The Finance committee above all was a deadly destroyer of ministers.

A further obstacle to the power of the Chamber, and of the ministry which in theory represented it, lay in the existence and strength of the upper house. In the eyes of the makers of the Third Republic, the Senate was the essential feature of their work, the real guarantee that conservative principles and interests could defend themselves effectively against the menace of universal suffrage. A minimum age of forty prevented the dangerous influence of youth creeping in. The method of election, indirectly through local authorities, provided a barrier against popular pressure which was reinforced by a nine-year term of office and election of only a third of the members at a time. Since the local authorities had themselves been elected at an earlier date, the Senate consisted of old men representing opinions expressed many years before. Above all, the composition of the electoral colleges was weighted very heavily in favour of the countryside and against the great towns. Everything had been done to make the Senate an impregnable bastion of conservatism.

The early discrediting of the parties of the Right, and their internecine quarrels, lost them control of even this position at an early date. Their final touch had been the inclusion of a large body of life senators, a quarter of the total: but when these came to be elected, the Bonapartists and certain royalist supporters of the legitimate line formed an alliance with the republicans against the adherents of the Orleanist princes. The republicans, presented with control of the Senate by the ineptitude of their opponents, forced through a constitutional revision in 1884, which abolished life senatorships, and altered the composition of the electoral colleges in such a way as to increase the influence of the small country towns at the expense of the rural areas, without, however, improving the position of the great cities. By the end of the nineteenth century the Senate and Chamber were both passing from the hands of the moderate republicans into those of the Radicals, and the desire of the latter to abolish the Senate was receding into the background.

The precise constitutional position of the Senate was obscure. It was clear that it had equal rights with the Chamber in legislation, and also (except that it had no right of initiative) in finance. Its members participated along with the deputies, who were twice as numerous, in the National Assembly which both elected the President of the Republic, and revised the constitution. But the responsibility of the government to one house or to both was an issue hotly disputed. Whatever the legal rights of the matter, the practical influence of the upper chamber grew steadily. The sheltered electoral position, frequency of re-election, and long term of its members attracted the ablest politicians to it; since French ministers are permitted to speak in either house, membership of the Senate was in no sense comparable to isolation in an impotent House of Lords. With the ablest and most influential politicians in its ranks, the growth of its power was inevitable, and this in turn further increased its attractiveness to such leaders. But the Senate, again unlike the House of Lords, consisted of practising politicians. Consequently it used its power with much greater skill, being careful never to challenge the Chamber unless it could be sure of victory. It built up its strength by slow degrees. For most of the period of the Third Republic the Senate did not attempt to overturn governments, though it might upset their programme by blocking their bills; characteristically, it preferred not to reject ' ill-considered ' legislation outright, but to bury it in committees for an indefinite length of time. In the last few years, however, it was becoming bolder; between 1875 and 1929 the Senate forced three governments out of office, between 1930 and 1938, four. In practice, as well as theory, the upper house was asserting its power over the executive as well as over legislation.

Yet though these institutional barriers to governmental authority were real enough, they derived their importance from the political situation. During the first years of the century, the separation of Church and State provided a real programme behind which a genuine majority could unite. The Combes ministry controlled the Chamber as effectively as a British government, through the operations of the *Délégation des gauches*. This body, a steering committee of the majority parties, dealt with the interpellation nuisance and the committee danger without difficulty. Interpellations which might threaten the government were simply adjourned *sine die*: the majority, having a motive for unity, held together to vote for the delay proposed by its leaders. Equally effective discipline was applied in committees. The power of the ministry was only broken when its programme had been put into force, and the loyalty of its followers weakened on other grounds.

In the same way, the power of the Finance committee and of the Senate was to a great extent a function of a particular political situation. Electoral necessity attracted the men of the centre towards the Left; at the opening of every legislature there appeared to be a left-wing majority. But as soon as economic and social questions came to the fore, this majority began to disintegrate, and the search for a new combination began. Senate and Finance Committee owed much of their power to their attractiveness to able men, but a good deal also to their key rôles in this recurrent struggle. A pivotal position in the Chamber, and a predominant one in the Senate, was occupied by the moderate Radicals, *laïque* and politically republican, but terrified of social experiment. The upper house, too cautious to risk its prestige by an unsuccessful act of aggression, only moved against a government when it was confident that it expressed the real desires of this crucial group in the Chamber: it acted as a support and an encouragement, an ally to strengthen the political weight of its friends, rather than as a rival institution.

The Finance committee's influence was often exerted in the opposite direction. By a political accident its Radical members in the inter-war period were often to the Left of their party colleagues. Moreover, the opposition groups were able to increase their relative weight by sending their best men to the Finance committee, whereas the ablest members of the government parties were in office. Thus, the Finance committee tended on more than one occasion to focus the opposition of those centre deputies who still preferred the left-wing connection, and who disliked the ' concentration ' governments formed by the drift of the moderate Radicals into association with the Conservatives. In the recurrent manœuvre by which the Radicals and their friends reversed their alliances, the Finance committee acted as a brake, the Senate as a goad.

But the Senate was not invariably a Conservative instrument. It expressed that essentially middle-of-the-road opinion, equally hostile to political reaction (i.e. clericalism) and to social change, which predominated in the country. The four governments it destroyed in the 1930's included two of the Right, led by Tardieu and Laval, as well as two of the Left, led by Blum. The Senate was the balance-wheel of the system, preventing policies or governments moving too far away— in either direction—from the political centre of gravity. It could fulfil this traditional (but rarely achieved) function of a second chamber because its views happened to coincide with those of the dominant section of the electorate. Its power had essentially political rather than institutional roots. Governments were weak, and programmes were hard to carry, not because of the faults of the constitution but because public opinion, or the principal elements in it, preferred weak government and inaction. The pressure of that opinion determined the working of the institutions, and dictated the character of the system.

2. PARTY VIEWS

THE makers of the Fourth Republic thus set themselves an impossible task. They tried to solve by constitutional changes a problem the roots of which were not in the forms of the constitution at all, but in the political divisions of the people. Since the conditions within which they were working had not altered, their reforms could only be conceived within a narrow framework.

The essential constitutional problem was that of the relationship between executive and legislature. French democratic tradition, realized in the Third Republic, had firmly subordinated the former to the latter; for this solution France paid a high price in governmental instability and executive weakness. Among great powers, only two ways have been found of overcoming these disabilities within the assumptions of democracy. One is applied in Great Britain, and rests essentially on strict party discipline, which ensures that the nominal authority of the House of Commons over government is transformed into the real control of the government over the House of Commons. The other operates in the United States, and avoids the necessity of subordinating either legislature or executive by separating the two in constitutional independence, each within its own sphere, neither being able to affect the existence of the other. But these two drastic solutions are not available in France: political factors rule them out of court as answers to the democratic problem. Each arouses disquieting historical memories, and each is sponsored by groups whose democratic good faith is contested by their opponents.

The American solution is advocated by General de Gaulle and his followers. An executive dependent on Parliament cannot, in French conditions, be a stable one: therefore there must be an executive independent of Parliament. This would have other advantages. In a crisis like that of 1940, a President could go into exile as a National Assembly of nine hundred men could not.[4] And there would be nothing but gain in removing power from the feeble, factious and corrupt parties; the General shares the views of the critic who

---

[4] *A.P.*, 1946, p. 163. Article 45 of the constitution prescribes that the ministers can be appointed only after the Assembly has elected the prime minister in the required manner, 'except when a case of *force majeure* prevents the meeting of the National Assembly.' This proviso was introduced in answer to criticisms by General de Gaulle. Jacques Théry, *Le Gouvernement de la IVe république*, p. 117 n. For the General's criticism, see his statement of 27 August 1946 (*La France sera la France*, p. 41). On his views, see also above, p. 118 n.

denounced an earlier regime as 'the shuffling of a greasy and well-marked parliamentary pack'.

The Gaullist constitutional scheme differs in some ways from the American pattern. The President would be chosen by an electoral college, as in the United States; but its members, instead of being themselves directly elected, would comprise the two houses of Parliament, supplemented—or swamped—by representatives of various aspects of the national life: local authorities, intellectual or economic activities, the French Union, etc. The General had much the same purpose as the Founding Fathers. They wished to shelter the Presidency from popular pressure, but were frustrated from the beginning by the rise of parties. His scheme was designed to weaken the parties, but it could not prevent them transferring their attention (as in America) to the preliminary stage, the choice of the electoral college itself. At most, the Gaullist proposals might weight the system in favour of some of the contending groups, and against others.

Again, the powers of the Gaullist President would differ from those of his transatlantic prototype. He would indeed choose and dismiss his ministers, though they would also apparently be responsible to Parliament—a contradiction not resolved in the General's rather sketchy and generalized statements. He would possess important powers not enjoyed by his United States colleague. A bill on which the government suffered parliamentary defeat might be submitted to a referendum by the President; alternatively, in case of political deadlock, he would have the right to dissolve the Assembly.[5] The latter would have no corresponding means of ridding itself of the President, whose position would be overwhelmingly strong. He would combine the security of tenure of the American President with the British prime minister's 'big stick'. He would suffer neither the weakness of the first in dealing with Congress, nor that of the second in having always to watch for shifts in the floating vote. He would enjoy the advantages of both offices, without being subjected to the corresponding checks upon either.[6]

---

[5] The General stated in 1948 that the President would need the consent of ministers to exercise his right of dissolution. Asked what would happen if President and ministers disagreed, he replied: 'Dans ma conception du régime qui convient à la France, il ne peut pas y avoir de désaccord entre le Président de la République et le Conseil des ministres, car le Président de la République serait le chef du pouvoir exécutif, comme il l'était d'ailleurs dans la Constitution de 1875 et parce que c'est lui qui choisirait les ministres.' *La France sera la France*, p. 49. The Gaullists often tend to consider the Parliament as an obstacle to popular government (cf. *ibid.*, p. 50); at their 1952 congress M. Capitant argued that the R.P.F. would restore to the people the rights of which they had been robbed, in the social and economic sphere by capitalism, and in the political by the system of representative parliamentary government. *Le Monde*, 12 November 1952: *Le Rassemblement*, no. 274 (13–20 November 1952).

[6] Jules Ferry, in 1884, warned his countrymen against taking the United States as an example when revising the constitution. 'Dans un pays centralisé comme l'est le nôtre, dans un pays unitaire où l'administration est assez forte, cette indépendance de l'exécutif vis-à-vis du législatif conduirait vite à la domination de l'exécutif sur le législatif.' Quoted Bodley, ii, p. 244 n.

Such a regime is nothing new in French history. Seventeen years before the sudden ascent of the R.P.F., M. Siegfried reminded us that Bonapartism, now expressed in the demand for a republic with real authority, was a latent force of great potency, always liable to explode with eruptive violence.[7] General Bonaparte was only the first and greatest of a long line of military men with political ambitions: for many French republicans, the *Canard Enchaîné* summed up the programme of General de Gaulle in the phrase,

'La France manque de pain? Moi, je serai le Boulanger.'

The democratic credentials of the Communists are far more suspect than those of the R.P.F. The Communist constitutional solution derives from the tradition of the Revolution, from the Convention of 1793 and the Paris Commune. It is the concentration of complete power in the hands of a single Assembly, unchecked by any rival authority, electing the President, controlling the government, supreme over executive, legislature and judiciary alike. But this arrangement, which apparently gives complete power to the Assembly, would in fact centre all effective authority in the government. For a body of six hundred men cannot really rule. The imposition of such a load of responsibility on the legislature would oblige that body to organize itself in order to avoid complete collapse. In the chaos of loose and conflicting parties the single really disciplined and effective block, the Communist party, would dominate through its cohesion, its willingness to follow a definite strategy and accept the instruction of its leaders.

If the Communist party were willing to abide by the rules of the democratic game, this solution would have many advantages. Its power and numbers would oblige its opponents to coalesce into an equally powerful and numerous block as the only means of competing, and France would find herself with a two-party system of the British type. For, paradoxically enough, the Communist constitutional answer (taken at face value) is very much the same as the British : an elected house, possessing virtually complete legal authority, but making its theoretical powers effective by handing them over to a committee of the leaders of the majority. As in Britain, party discipline is the essential element in this solution, without which its operation cannot be understood.

Such a system is only tolerable when there is confidence that the party in power for the time being will use its strength with restraint, and in particular that it will refrain from using it to subvert the democratic system itself. Since no such confidence can be felt with respect to the Communist party, the idea of a two-party system in which it would be one of the protagonists is rightly seen by Frenchmen as the first stage to imminent civil war. Nevertheless many good French republicans, whose democratic intentions are not in doubt, are attracted to a consti-

---

[7] See above, p. 132 n.

tutional solution on the same lines as that of the Communists, but with safeguards to prevent them achieving the predominant position at which they aim. In particular the Socialist party, which draws its intellectual inspiration from the same revolutionary tradition, also favours the single Assembly in its constitutional ideas, and indeed joined with the Communists in supporting the first draft constitution in April 1946. When that proposal was rejected at the May referendum, the parties of the Left found themselves obliged to compromise with M.R.P.: but the October constitution is nevertheless based essentially on Socialist ideas, though some of them have become distorted. Many of its principles, and even some detailed provisions, can be found in M. Blum's early work on governmental reform. Still more are anticipated in the proposals for post-war reconstruction, which M. Vincent Auriol put together under the occupation.[8]

The Socialists considered that the faults of the Third Republic were that it buttressed the power of conservative interests, and that it encouraged a type of politics which centred on personal and parochial squabbles rather than on a fundamental clash of policies. Their answer to the first was to abolish the checks to the Assembly, by eliminating the Senate as an institution with power, and by wiping out altogether the Presidency of the Republic. In answer to the second they proposed to change the electoral system, contending that proportional representation would extend the politician's horizon, weaken local ties, destroy the demoralizing alliances which were essential to success under the second ballot, and elevate the whole tone of public life. Their constitutional programme included various other measures, designed to replace the shifting, incoherent groups of the old regime by powerful parties based on a common ideology.[9]

They hoped to see the mass of scattered petty groups of the old Chamber replaced by a few organized parties, each with its coherent outlook and its disciplined following in and out of Parliament. Since elections would be fought on the clear issues of principle which divided these parties, a definite majority would emerge. This would solve the problem of governmental stability. The Assembly would elect a prime minister, the central figure of the whole constitution as the Socialists envisaged it. He would form a government drawn from and representing the majority which had elected him. Since there would be a community of outlook between majority and government, the security of the latter would be guaranteed. It would not need means of pressure on the Assembly such as the votes of confidence which had been so prodigally employed in the Third Republic. The executive

---

[8] Léon Blum, *La Réforme gouvernementale*, especially pp. 39, 62–3, 150–3, 163, 167–9, 175–9, 218, 222–7.
Vincent Auriol, *Hier . . . Demain*, vol. ii, pp. 21, 23, 31, 33, 38, 51, 142, 197–8, 208, 223, 239–40, 249, 261, 273, 285.
[9] See below, pp. 344–6.

being only a projection of the legislature, the two would normally be in harmony, and the stability of the former would be happily combined with the final authority of the latter.

In the event of a clash, the Assembly must of course have the last word: this was fundamental to French democratic thinking. It could always turn the government out by a vote of no confidence. But to prevent this being done with the light-hearted irresponsibility characteristic of the Third Republic, the Socialists wished the defeat of a government to bring about the automatic dissolution of the Assembly which caused it. In minor matters the Assembly could instruct the government to change its policy, which the latter, unable itself to call for a vote of confidence, would be obliged to do. Such a system would indeed have secured executive stability of a sort, for the cabinet would remain in office as long as the majority of the Assembly wished it to do so. But it would have been stability without authority, for the government would be wholly subordinated to the pressure of its followers and without effective means of putting counter-pressure upon them. The system reflected the traditional French democratic distrust of power and its holders: but whatever its faults it was a logical and complete scheme, and proved in practice to lie nearer than any other to the lowest common denominator of opinion in 1946.

Less need be said of the outlook of the other democratic parties. The Radicals simply wished to retain the Third Republic, or as much of it as they could. The Conservatives were divided about details, but all wished to strengthen the executive and to impose barriers against the unchecked will of a single Assembly. M.R.P. favoured the inclusion in the constitution of provisions reflecting its corporative outlook: the family vote (weighting a man's vote according to the number of his children) was a characteristic example of the type of suggestion proposed by it. But its effective fight on the constitutional issue was waged for the same ends as Conservatives and even Radicals desired—to preserve what checks and balances could be saved, and to maintain some independence for the executive against the legislature. Its attitude was expressed by M. Paul Coste-Floret, the *rapporteur* of the constitution. He declared that in France presidential government would tend to dictatorship (*pouvoir personnel*): an Assembly regime (the arrangement of the Convention of 1793, with all powers in the hands of the legislature) was adapted to revolution: democracy would only work in a compromise system, balanced between parliament and executive.[10]

This distinction has played a crucial part in modern French political thought. The constitutional lawyer regards it as his essential task to determine whether a given constitution corresponds more closely to an ' Assembly regime ' or to a ' parliamentary regime ' (the term used for

---

[10] *J.O.*, 20 August 1946, p. 3185. He summed up: '... le régime présidentiel condamné, le régime d'assemblée écarté, force nous est de revenir au : ... régime parlementaire.'

the balanced system, in which the popular house is checked by a partly independent executive, second chamber, or similar device).[11] Yet perhaps this distinction has been overdrawn, as a result of investigating legal principles too carefully and paying too little attention to political facts. For the prototype of the admired parliamentary regime was the British constitution in the middle of the nineteenth century. Yet that system in practice curiously resembled the Third Republic.[12] Parties were weak, loose, inchoate, and at times numerous. Leaders founded their position on personal followings and skill in manœuvring, rather than on authority over an organized party. Majorities were uncertain, even on the morrow of a general election, since most contests were fought on a personal and local basis rather than over basic political principles. Governments survived or succumbed by tiny majorities, very often in single figures, and marginal groups (like the Peelites) possessed a vast importance and could use it to secure preferential treatment in the distribution of offices. Occasionally a great surge of opinion would sweep through the house, uniting all elements against the administration, as in the course of the Crimean war. The majority in a House of Commons at the beginning of its life might bear little relation to the majority at the end of the same house. Important political issues remained open questions, on which members of the same government might publicly disagree. Every ministry (whether so called or not) was in fact a coalition of minor groups which differed profoundly among themselves. Despite the strength of the Lords, the influence of the Crown, and the reserve power of dissolution, the House of Commons as an institution was at the height of its political power.

For the nominal transfer of authority to the Commons, with the advance of democracy, has weakened and not strengthened it. In the absence of effective rivals, the House of Commons has concentrated in itself more power than it can effectively use. It has found itself obliged to impose tighter discipline, to organize into more rigid blocks, to transfer its newly-extended authority to the government in order to get business done. As it has approximated to the theoretical position of an omnipotent assembly ruling without a rival, it has sunk in practice to an organ for ratifying the decisions of the executive, and a sounding board for the rival parties to appeal to the electorate and to test the latter's reaction: it is no longer an institution with a real independent position of its own, but a link (albeit an essential one) between the genuine powers, government and electorate.

---

[11] An 'Assembly regime' concentrates all power, judicial as well as executive, in the hands of a single sovereign chamber. A 'parliamentary regime,' conceived on the English model, has as its essential hallmarks an irresponsible chief of state, ministers responsible to the legislature, and a right of dissolution in the hands of the executive. All constitutional lawyers consider a second chamber as a normal, and some regard it as a necessary feature of a parliamentary regime. Measures to ensure a judiciary independent of Parliament would also represent a step towards a parliamentary regime.

[12] Cf. the lament in *Economist*, 23 April 1853, quoted *Economist*, 25 April 1953; and Disraeli's speech of 30 August 1848: *Parl. deb.*, 3rd ser., vol. ci, col. 705–6.

If this argument is accepted, the distinction between an Assembly regime and a parliamentary regime seems something of a legal fiction.[13] For the conservative critics who denounced the Third Republic and pointed to nineteenth-century Britain as the example of a true parliamentary regime were misunderstanding the nature of the British system at that date, which was not unlike their own. And those who feared that an Assembly regime must undermine the position of the executive had failed to notice that the power of government had grown steadily in Britain as the bulwarks of the 'parliamentary regime' were shorn away. The concepts were too legalistic: they were based on constitutional forms and not on political realities, for the distinction ignored the really crucial factor, the rise of organized parties.[14]

3. THE CONSTITUTIONAL COMPROMISE

THE constitution of October 1946 was the product of a compromise between the pressure of the Left for a strong single chamber, and the resistance of the Right which sought to introduce checks and balances. M.R.P. generally sided with the Right, and the balance between the two groups was extraordinarily even; several major issues were decided by single-figure majorities, in which a handful of colonial members provided the crucial votes. Disgruntled conservatives bitterly attacked the 'Madagascar constitution' which emerged. The struggle turned on the position of the President of the Republic and of the second chamber, both their powers and the method of electing them: the electoral law, the machinery for constitutional revision, and the independence of the judiciary. But there was firm agreement between the major parties that ministers must be responsible to the Assembly. General de Gaulle's original plans for constituting a provisional government after liberation had not provided for this. But the politicians knew very well that the shape of the provisional regime would greatly influence the structure of the permanent constitution, and they successfully insisted that, even in the period of the Constituent

---

[13] The following description of the Third Republic illustrates the difficulty of making the distinction in practice:

'... On disait parfois que la France pratiquait un gouvernement parlementaire "inauthentique"; non, il était authentique dans sa structure qui comportait tous les éléments du régime parlementaire véritable, mais son jeu avait abouti à une rupture, au détriment de l'Exécutif, de cet équilibre dont la recherche est le but même de cette combinaison constitutionnelle. Dans ses résultats, il inclinait vers le gouvernement d'assemblée...' J. Laferrière, *Manuel de droit constitutionnel*, (2nd ed., 1947) p. 822.

Most authors are reduced to similar admissions of the inapplicability of the theory: see for instance G. Vedel, *Manuel élémentaire de droit constitutionnel*, p. 582, on Britain: M. Prélot, *Précis de droit constitutionnel*, p. 221: M. Duverger, *Manuel de droit constitutionnel et de science politique*, pp. 157, 278—both on the Third Republic. Among the fullest and most realistic discussions of the question in relation to the Fourth Republic is that in Théry, Chapter V.

[14] It is argued below, pp. 231-2, that the strength of British governments does not primarily depend on the right to dissolve the House of Commons.

Assembly, ministers must be responsible to it.[15] Three years later President Auriol, defending the existing constitution against Gaullist criticism, described the responsibility of ministers as the keystone of democracy and the Republic.[16]

Thus the failure of the constitution makers to provide France with a strong and stable executive was almost inevitable. It was not due to their ineptitude but to the refractoriness of the materials with which they had to work. Because fear and suspicion were the dominant political emotions, a democratic constitution meant one in which the administration was kept under firm control. At the very commencement of the Third Republic, one of its leaders, Jules Ferry, uttered two illuminating remarks. One must rank among the least successful of historical prophecies:

> France, delivered from the corruptions of the Empire, has entered into the period of the austere virtues.[17]

But the other, 'What France needs is a weak government', expressed in its briefest form the dominant outlook among French republicans then and since.

As the constitution-makers were unable as well as unwilling to build a fundamentally new structure, they could only try to repair the more glaring faults of the old one. The details of their work show how preoccupied they were with discovering the weaknesses which led up to 1940, and preventing their recurrence. Article 13, which forbids the Assembly to delegate its legislative power, was directed against the practice of decree-laws, by which during the 1930's timid and irresponsible legislatures, unwilling to vote the unpopular measures which they knew to be necessary, empowered the government to legislate by decree and thus freed it from effective parliamentary control. Article 94, which forbids the revision of the constitution at a time when all or any part of mainland France is under enemy occupation, is a still more striking attempt to legislate for 1940. The legal status of the Vichy regime was based on the vote by the National Assembly, on 10 July 1940, of full powers to Marshal Pétain. Its legitimacy was hotly disputed. Article 94 would prevent such a situation arising again.

As general staffs are said to prepare for the last war, the politicians of 1946 prepared for the last constitutional crisis. Given the material with which they had to work, it is hard to see what else they could have done. In 1948 the results of their efforts were summed up, succinctly if not altogether justly, in the phrase 'The Fourth Republic is dead—it has been succeeded by the Third'. The remainder of this book is a commentary, as far as the working of the constitution is concerned, upon that contemptuous verdict.

---

[15] Théry, pp. 15–6. Wright, pp. 82–4.
[16] Speech at Quimper, 31 May 1948: *A.P.*, 1948, p. 333. See also speech at Bordeaux, 14 June 1948.
[17] Bodley, ii, p. 327.

Chapter 12

THE PRESIDENCY AND THE PREMIERSHIP

1. THE POWERS OF THE PRESIDENT

THE royalists who created the Third Republic had designed a constitution which could be transformed into a monarchy as soon as they could agree on who should occupy the throne. Among the bulwarks which they established against the menace of democracy, the office of President of the Republic was one of the most important. But because of its imposing nominal powers, the Presidency was feared and restrained in a number of ways. There was legal restriction: every official act of the President, except his resignation of office,[1] required the countersign of a minister. There was the development of a political convention: after the crisis of 1877 no President ventured to assert his right to dissolve the Chamber if the Senate supported him. There was also the silent but effective method of ensuring that dangerous men were never elected to the office. Professor Brogan has drawn attention to the early stages of the decline of the Presidency in discussing the first four incumbents:

> Thiers had been chosen as the greatest living French statesman, MacMahon as the most honourable French soldier: Grévy had been elected in 1879 because of what he had said in 1848, Carnot was elected in 1887 because of what his grandfather had done in 1793.[2]

The fundamental principle of the constitution, it was remarked just before the election of Carnot, was that the President's job was to hunt rabbits and not bother with the government of the country.[3]

The members of parliament who elected the President established this tradition by a careful avoidance of men of eminence, independence of mind, or even marked ability. Sometimes they made mistakes, and chose an assertive man who had to be removed: Casimir-Périer in 1895, Millerand in 1924 were no more able to defy the politicians than MacMahon had been in 1879. But it was simpler and much less

---

[1] In the Fourth Republic he nominates candidates for the premiership without countersign, since the Assembly has to approve the nomination before it becomes effective. Théry, p. 111: M. H. Fabre, ' L'investiture du Président du Conseil,' *R.D.P.*, 1951, p. 197 n. It is not required for certain of his actions as chairman of the Constitutional Committee (see below p. 176, n. 25), and for some other matters, notably the right of pardon, it is purely formal. Suggestions that it was not needed for actions taken by the President in his capacity of President of the French Union, or in that of head of the High Council of the Magistrature, have been negatived by the precedents set by President Auriol.
[2] Brogan, *Development of Modern France*, p. 198.
[3] J.-J. Weiss in 1885, quoted Théry, p. 29.

trouble to reject the strong or influential men when they stood for election, as Gambetta was beaten by Grévy, Ferry by Carnot, Waldeck-Rousseau by Félix Faure, Clemenceau by Deschanel (who soon afterwards went mad), and Briand by Doumer. Election by secret ballot put a premium on intrigue for this purpose.

The status of the President depended very largely on the means by which he was chosen. In the Second Republic, direct election by the people gave him a personal standing so strong that he was able to overthrow the regime and make himself emperor. In the Third, this danger was avoided by subordinating the President to Parliament. Legal sovereignty was possessed by a joint sitting of Chamber and Senate, the National Assembly. This body had two functions to perform, the revision of the constitution, and the election of the President every seven years.

When the new constitution came to be drafted, the position of the Presidency was one of the principal matters in dispute. The parties of the Left regarded the office as useless if not positively dangerous, and the Socialists proposed to abolish it altogether. Alternatively, they could try to reduce its status by emphasizing its subordination to Parliament. Sovereignty was to be transferred from the joint session of both houses to the lower house alone: to mark this change the title of National Assembly was bestowed on the old Chamber of Deputies. The Left wished the President to be elected by the new National Assembly, as he had formerly been by the old: but they wished to have the election by open ballot, instead of secretly as in the past.

The conservative parties were anxious that the President should retain some independence, and wished to prevent his becoming merely a puppet of the Assembly. They proposed to associate the upper house with his election, as in the Third Republic, and to retain the secret ballot.[4] This would permit members to break party discipline. Under the open ballot, Presidents would be the evident nominees of particular and known parties. Secrecy might render them somewhat less dependent on their sponsors; and at the first election it would greatly improve the prospects of General de Gaulle.[5] The first draft constitution, however, was a left-wing project, and reflected the desire of the Left for a puppet President: he was to be elected by the single chamber, the National Assembly, in an open ballot.[6]

---

[4] Conservatives wished still further to weaken the position of the deputies in the electoral college. M. Ramarony, the spokesman of P.R.L., proposed to add to the members of the two houses an equal number of electors chosen by the departmental councils. *J.O.*, 11 April 1946, p. 1704. The Gaullists favour an even larger non-parliamentary element.

[5] Twenty years earlier the Chamber of Deputies, in making a nominal choice between secret and open balloting, had in reality decided to overthrow the Herriot government: Soulier, p. 175.

[6] On the first three ballots a two-thirds majority was required for election, subsequently three-fifths. (Article 90.)

The first draft was rejected at the referendum of May 1946, and it became clear that the Left must make concessions. The most important of these was their acceptance of a second chamber; on the insistence of M.R.P., its members were given the right to participate in the election of the President as their predecessors the senators had done. But the political significance of their inclusion was much less. The outlook of the Senate had not been the same as that of the Chamber. Indirect election, a longer term, and a high minimum age had made it a far more conservative body, so that the presence of its members in the electoral college had real political importance. In the Fourth Republic this was no longer true. The new second chamber, the Council of the Republic, was at first elected in such a way that its party composition precisely reflected that of the Assembly. Thus the addition of its members did not affect the political balance in the body which chose the President. In 1948, however, the manner of electing the upper house was changed to one much nearer to the method used in the Third Republic, with drastic effects on its party composition. This constitutional victory of the conservatives proved, therefore, more important than it appeared at first sight.[7]

They also scored a second, less important success over the secrecy of the ballot. A compromise was arrived at, by which the method of voting was not mentioned in the constitution itself, but by a gentleman's agreement the first election was to be secret. In the same way the constitution does not decide what majority is required to elect a President; but, on the first occasion, the old rule of an absolute majority of valid votes was maintained. General de Gaulle was not a candidate, and the secret ballot hardly impaired the rigidity of party discipline.[8]

Another struggle occurred over the extent of the President's powers. Under the Third Republic these had appeared to be great, for the President was nominally head of the executive as well as formal chief of the state. But in practice the manner of his election, as a nominee of Parliament, deprived him of independent prestige. The requirement of a ministerial countersign for every action he took, left him entirely without power. He could not command, he could only influence. An adroit President could do something to affect the course of domestic affairs by skill in picking prime ministers, and his advice carried weight in foreign policy by virtue of his status, experience, and long tenure.

---

[7] For the 1946 and 1948 laws on the election of the Council of the Republic, see below, Ch. 17.

Even under the original law, the composition of the two houses would be politically identical only if they were elected at the same time. In the future this would not have been the case. But the first presidential election was the crucial one. The first President of the Fourth Republic would set the precedents, and if General de Gaulle were elected they might be startling.

[8] M. Duverger, *Manuel*, p. 338 (on the rule); Priouret, p. 29 (on the voting).

Presidential elections are now governed by the law of 8 December 1953 (quoted *R.D.P.*, 1953, p. 1028), which provides for secrecy of the ballot and requires an absolute majority for election. See Epilogue.

But there was a very marked difference between the powers which he appeared to wield and those which he in fact exercised.

The makers of the Fourth Republic set out to whittle down the nominal powers and bring them into closer relation with the real ones. The first Constituent Assembly set up a committee to prepare a draft constitution, on which (as in the parent body) the Left had a majority. This committee deprived the President in quick succession of the right to preside over the cabinet, over the new committee on pardons, and over the Council of National Defence. He retained only the right to sign treaties and receive ambassadors, to appoint (in the cabinet) to certain high official posts, to take the chair in the new High Council of the Magistrature, of which he was to appoint a minority of the members, and to initiate the procedure for deciding whether a new law conformed with the constitution.[9]

The first Constituent Assembly restored a few of the lost powers. The President regained his nominal position as commander in chief, was to preside over the Council of National Defence as well as that of the Magistrature, and was to appoint, at a cabinet meeting, some senior officers and officials. He recovered the chairmanship of the cabinet and was to keep its minutes—the first appearance in France of the cabinet secretariat which has proved so important in Great Britain.[10] He could not himself choose potential prime ministers, but was to transmit the names of possible candidates to the President of the National Assembly: the last two duties caused M. Herriot, a staunch adherent of the Third Republic, to describe him as a combined clerk and postman.

The second Constituent Assembly, which drew up the constitution now in force, strengthened the President's position a little further. Certain minor prerogatives envisaged by the original committee, like the right to choose two members of the High Council of the Magistrature, or to set in motion the procedure for deciding on the constitutionality of a law, had been abandoned in the first draft but were restored in the second. The President regained the right to address the Assembly by messages, and to refer bills back to it for a fresh deliberation, which he had had in the Third Republic. Pardons, under the first draft to be granted by the High Council of the Magistrature, were now to be given by the President in that body. The list of appointments made by him in the cabinet was extended to take in all the higher posts, the lower ones being left to the prime minister. Above all the President was again permitted to nominate candidates for the premiership, not merely to transmit names to the President of the Assembly. These changes did not affect the central legal change, that nominal responsibility for the executive government of the country, conferred in 1875 on the President

---

[9] *S.C.C.*, I, pp. 118–27, 129, 142.

[10] These provisions proved of great importance in the unexpected development of the Presidency. See R. Drago, ' L'Article 32 de la Constitution du 27 octobre 1946,' *R.D.P.*, 1953, pp. 157–69.

of the Republic, was now expressly transferred to the prime minister. But since every act of the President still required a ministerial countersign,[11] the difference in practice seemed likely to be small.

2. THE PRESIDENCY IN PRACTICE

THOUGH the constitution makers devoted so much attention to reducing the prerogatives and importance of the Presidency, its influence and activity have in practice greatly increased. The changed status of the head of the state is among the most remarkable constitutional developments of the Fourth Republic. This curiously paradoxical situation, so characteristic of French politics, is due to the vigour and determination of the first incumbent, M. Vincent Auriol. But, by a further and still more characteristic paradox, M. Auriol was himself the principal architect of the constitution—and an advocate of the abolition of the office which he was to fill so successfully.[12]

M. Auriol was an experienced Socialist politician, who had entered the Chamber of Deputies before the first world war. He took office for the first time in the *Front populaire* government of 1936, in which he was minister of Finance. In 1940 he was one of the minority who voted against Marshal Pétain: for a time he was interned by the Vichy authorities. During this period he sketched his proposals, subsequently published, for constitutional reform. It has been said that the constitution of the Fourth Republic owes more to this work than any previous French constitution has owed to a theoretical treatise.[13] In 1943 he was evacuated to Algiers, where he was to become the chief link between General de Gaulle and the politicians, a role he continued to fulfil after the return of the government to France. As President of both Constituent Assemblies, he found himself obliged on occasion to act as unofficial President of the Republic; there was, for instance, no one else to take the initiative in solving ministerial crises. In the interminable conflicts of constitution making, he was the most tireless and unremitting producer of compromise solutions: without his work it is hard to see how either Constituent Assembly could ever have reached any major decisions.[14] It was appropriate that the man most responsible both for the conception and for the delivery of the new constitution should become its first official head.

The President of the Republic is supposed to be the guardian of the

---

[11] See above, p. 169 n., and below, pp. 187–8.
[12] *Hier . . . Demain*, ii, pp. 234–7.
This was much less inconsistent than it might appear, for fear of General de Gaulle had prompted much of the Left's suspicion of the Presidency. Moreover, the inconsistency has many precedents in French history. Jules Grévy, President of the Republic from 1879 to 1887, had formerly advocated a republic without a President. Antonin Dubost, who had wanted to abolish the Senate, was later for many years President of the upper house.
[13] Priouret, p. 45: and see above, p. 164 n.
[14] Wright, pp. 151–216, *passim*.

permanent interests of the state, above the passing changes and quarrels of party politics. In a nationally recognized emergency he is the natural head: thus in 1947 he was the chairman of the committee which, with the support of every party and major religious group, appealed to the peasants to deliver their corn in good time to the hungry towns.[15] Foreign visits, like that to the United States in April 1951, have been used, not for formal courtesies, but for a vigorous public and private presentation of the French case. Nor has M. Auriol regarded his domestic duties as limited to completely non-controversial matters. As guardian of the national interests he presides at cabinet meetings,[16] and he is not always a silent chairman: on occasion he takes the initiative himself, as in January 1950, when he insisted that the government must act against Communist sabotage of the defence programme and the Indo-China war.[17] In March 1952 he intervened in the Tunisian dispute with a personal letter to the Bey, which was both suggested and drafted by him.

The President has a special position over external affairs and national defence. He has effective access to all diplomatic documents (which was not always the case with his predecessors). He takes the chair at meetings of the Defence committee (consisting of the cabinet ministers concerned and certain military chiefs) and of the Council of National Defence (a consultative body which does not in practice meet). The division of ministerial responsibility between the prime minister (under Article 47) and the Defence minister, the frequent changes in both offices, and the constant alterations in the organization of the defence departments, have given to the continuing President of the Republic much more influence in this sphere than had been anticipated.[18]

President Auriol has interpreted defence of the interests of the state to include also defence of the present political regime, the parliamentary republic. At the height of the Gaullist challenge in 1948, the President virtually made himself the effective leader of the Third Force, and during that summer he conducted a sort of oratorical duel with his former chief: in his speech at Quimper on 31 May he denounced the R.P.F.'s agitation for new elections as destructive of political stability, and there and at Bordeaux on 14 June he insisted that the responsibility of ministers to Parliament was the fundamental feature of a republican constitution.[19] The Gaullists attacked this series of speeches as a breach of the tradition that the President of the Republic did not utter controversial opinions:

---

[15] *A.P.*, 1947, p. 104.
[16] The French cabinet meets in two capacities : as the *conseil des ministres*, with the President of the Republic in the chair, and as the *conseil de cabinet*, without the President, for tactical and party political discussions. (It does not follow that the President is without influence in the latter sphere). In recent years *conseils de cabinet* have become comparatively rare: Drago, *loc. cit.*, p. 168.
[17] *A.P.*, 1950, p. 9.
[18] See Marc Suel, ' La défense nationale et la constitution,' *R.D.P.*, 1950, pp. 670, 672: and an article by Georges Marey in *Le Figaro*, 5 December 1950.
[19] *A.P.* 1948, pp. 332–3, for the Quimper speech.

but President Auriol had evidently come round to the view of General de Gaulle, that the President of the Fourth Republic must behave differently from his predecessor of the Third. At Tarbes, on 20 October 1951, the President aroused criticism from the opposite extreme. He expressed his disquiet at the prevalence of profiteering, frauds against the revenue, and the exploitation of the poor by the rich and of the community by the selfish. But he also spoke on foreign policy, denouncing the subversive activities of the Cominform, defending the Atlantic pact policy, criticizing the ' iron curtain ', and advocating international disarmament with effective control. Violently attacked by the Communists for this speech, President Auriol replied with a vigorous defence of his own conception of his office, which he refused to consider as the post of a passive, silent figurehead. There was, he maintained, room for a ' moral magistracy ' with the right to advise, to warn, and to conciliate: impartiality was a very different matter from indifference.[20]

The President's interpretation of his duties as guardian of the permanent interests of the state finds another expression in the great importance he has attached to his post as president of the High Council of the Magistrature. This body was a creation of the liberation period, and the first committee on the draft constitution reached unusual unanimity in assigning its presidency to the head of the state, in his role as a national rather than a political figure. President Auriol has taken the strongest personal interest in its development, which has not always been easy. It has had to face both the immediate resistance of the ministry of Justice, resentful of the power it has lost, and the permanent danger of political pressure in a country where the independence of the judiciary has been incomplete. In this struggle the support of the President of the Republic has been indispensable and firm. Thus in April 1950 he would not allow the cabinet to discuss certain judicial decisions in favour of accused Communists, insisting that these were matters for the High Council of the Magistrature alone. As president of the latter body, however, he intervened personally in October 1948, both with the Council and with the senior judges, to urge them to apply with rigour the laws against speculation in foodstuffs.[21]

The right of pardon, transferred by the first draft constitution from the President to the High Council of the Magistrature, is now exercised by him in the Council. But he is neither bound by its views, nor in practice tied by the need for a ministerial countersign, which in such matters is given automatically—pardons are recognized to be in effect

---

[20] Ibid., 1951, p. 669, for the Tarbes speech: pp. 291-2 for the Communist attack on it and the President's reply, which was delivered to the Foreign Press Association on 15 November. See also Le Monde, 16 November 1951.
[21] On the High Council of the Magistrature, see below, pp. 300-5.
On the 1950 incident, see A.P., 1950, p. 76: Le Monde, 24 April 1950. On that of 1948, ibid., 16 October 1948.

a personal prerogative of the President.[22] In the period of liberation the exercise of this right had great political importance, which accounts for the Communist anxiety to remove it from the President's hands.[23] Subsequently President Auriol employed it extensively to amnesty minor offenders of the occupation period, and especially to correct the startling differences between penalties which were awarded for the same offence in different courts, and in the same court at different dates. He also used this right in one case of major political importance, that of the Malagasy deputies implicated in the rising of 1947.[24] Like General de Gaulle before him, he has taken his duties in this respect very seriously: they have been estimated to occupy a third of the time of the head of the state.

Besides his duties as guardian of the national interest, the President of the Republic performs the function of an arbitrator in the day-to-day working of the political system. On constitutional matters he has special authority, recognized by his position as chairman of the Constitutional Committee.[25] His services are often called upon in constitutional deadlocks, and in this connection he has found a use for a power possessed by his predecessors, but never exercised by them. This is the right to refer a bill back to the Assembly for further consideration, which he is given by Article 36 of the constitution; to be passed into law, the bill must then go through the whole legislative process again.

This right came into effective use during the period of the provisional government. In the Third Republic a government anxious to refer a bill back might have met with opposition from a President of the Republic who was unwilling to link his personal prestige with the policy of the government. This difficulty disappeared in the provisional regime, when the prime minister was himself fulfilling the duties of head of the state. At the same time the absence of any second chamber made it particularly useful to have an alternative means of arranging for the revision of badly drafted bills. The provisional government used this power a dozen times in nine months:[26] and though the left-wing majority in the first Constituent Assembly denied it to the President, it was restored to him in the second, the *rapporteur*, M. Coste-Floret, describing it as ' fundamental '.[27]

President Auriol has used this weapon with caution. Employed too

---

[22] Théry, p. 42.
[23] *S.C.C.*, I, p. 124: M. Fajon's statement.
[24] See below, p. 239 n.
[25] The Constitutional Committee is the body which decides whether or not a law infringes the constitution: on it see below, pp. 289–92. The order convoking it, and the record of its deliberations are signed by the President of the Republic without the countersign of a minister: but the message informing the National Assembly of the committee's decision is formally countersigned. A. Soulier, ' La délibération du Comité Constitutionnel du 18 juin 1948,' *R.D.P.*, 1949, p. 213.
[26] Théry, p. 66.
[27] *J.O.*, 12 September 1946, p. 3701.

frequently, as a mild version of the American President's veto, it might merely drive the Assembly to react by a more determined assertion of its own policy, with consequent damage to the prestige of the Presidency. During the great strikes at the end of 1947, a drastic law for the maintenance of order was passed; the Communists exhausted all the resources of parliamentary obstruction, and at length the C.G.T. (including the anti-Communist minority) appealed to the President to refer it back under Article 36. He declined to do so.[28] The right of reference back was used only eight times during the 1946–51 legislature: once at the request of the Constitutional Committee, to resolve a procedural conflict between the two houses: once as an alternative to reference to the Constitutional Committee, which was not possible under the conditions laid down by the constitution: and on the other occasions as an escape from procedural difficulties—for example in October 1947, when there was a conflict between the law and a treaty over nationality regulations in the frontier districts ceded by Italy, and in August 1948, when two provisions of the new rent law were found to be contradictory, too late for correction in either house. The right was not used in the first two years of the new Assembly. Presidential messages under Article 36 have to be countersigned, but this is recognized to be a formality.[29]

The President acts as a political as well as a constitutional arbiter. In this respect his most important task (which is discussed in the next section) is that of nominating a potential prime minister in a ministerial crisis. But he can also assist by preventing the crisis arising at all. President Auriol's skill as an inventor of compromises, demonstrated during the constitution-making period, has not deserted him. Sometimes, as over the proposed electoral law for the Council of the Republic in May 1948, he has broken a complete deadlock in the cabinet. On other occasions he has avoided a crisis by refusing to accept the resignation of a disillusioned prime minister who had not suffered defeat

---

[28] *A.P.*, 1947, p. 243.
[29] The first two cases are discussed below, p. 291.

For the nationality case, see Théry, p. 67, and Duverger, *Manuel*, p. 339: for the case of the rent law, J. Bruyas, ' L'évolution du Conseil de la République,' *R.D.P.*, 1949, p. 560, and G. Berlia, *ibid.*, 1950, p. 682, note 1: for the countersign, A. Soulier, *ibid.*, 1949, p. 213, and R. Drago, ' L'évolution récente de la notion d'inviolabilité parlementaire,' *ibid.*, 1950, p. 405.

Bills were referred back by the President on 5 September 1947, 28 October 1947, 18 June 1948, 27 August 1948, 27 January 1949, 19 July 1949, 1 August and 13 October 1949 (both these messages dealing with the immunities bill), and 23 January 1951. The last instance was of such minor importance that the ' fresh deliberation ' was delayed for a year, and then took place without debate in the house—a procedure which can be used only if no member objects. (See *J.O.*, 5 February 1952, p. 427.) Two of these eight bills, one on parliamentary immunity, and one dealing with credits for road construction in Algeria, were referred back just before the 1949 summer recess; four years later, the first had just been passed in an amended form, but the second had still not been reconsidered.

The Assembly's Standing Order 22 requires committees to report on such bills within a week: this is evidently not taken very seriously.

in the Assembly.[30] But this has not always proved possible: M. Queuille in October 1949, and M. Pleven in March 1951, refused to withdraw their resignations: both men feared that a formal vote in the Assembly, by publicizing the split in the majority, would merely widen the gulf between the government parties, and make their reunion behind the next cabinet more difficult to achieve. The President's 'moral magistracy' can often fulfil a useful, but never a decisive role: its success depends on recognition that it must be exercised with caution, and that it can only be weakened by attempts to press it too far.

3. CABINET-MAKING [31]

THE President may sometimes play an important part in averting ministerial crises, but his main task is to solve them when they do occur. There are three necessary stages in the formation of a new ministry: the choice of a prime minister, the selection of his colleagues, and the acceptance of the new government by Parliament. In the Third Republic the Chamber of Deputies became involved only at the third stage. The crucial first step was entirely in the hands of the President. It was contended that this situation gave him too much opportunity to forward his personal preferences. If his choice coincided with that of the Chamber, his rôle was superfluous; if not, it was undemocratic.[32] He might pick a minister whom the Chamber would not support, so that the crisis would quickly rebound. He might even deliberately choose a premier unacceptable to the Chamber in order to force a dissolution, as President MacMahon had done in 1877. A less sensational manœuvre was frequently practised. The early days of a ministerial crisis are occupied by party bargaining, and characterized by party intransigence; the crisis only becomes soluble when the country is exasperated, so that more prestige is lost by obstructiveness than by abandoning previous demands. Many Presidents would nominate

---

[30] For the May 1948 case see *Le Figaro*, 27 May 1948.

The President dissuaded M. Ramadier from resigning in September 1947, when his majority fell below fifty on a vote of confidence. When on 30 November 1950 the Assembly voted, by a constitutionally insufficient majority, a Communist motion to impeach M. Moch, the minister of the Interior, M. Pleven submitted his government's resignation out of solidarity with his colleague: the President induced him to withdraw it and seek a new vote of confidence. M. Pleven resigned on 28 February 1951, because one government party (M.R.P.) abstained on a vote of confidence: the President persuaded him to carry on, but the cabinet finally broke up next day. M. Queuille resigned when the Assembly narrowly failed to carry the new electoral law against the opposition of the upper house: but the President successfully urged him to stay in office, and a new bill was brought in and passed.

See M. Flory, 'La liberté de démission du Président du Conseil,' *R.D.P.*, 1951, pp. 815 ff.: and below, pp. 226–7.

[31] For a fuller account of ministerial crises and the President's rôle in them, see Philip Williams, 'Crisis in France: a Political Institution', *Cambridge Journal*, October 1953, pp. 36–50.

[32] M. Pierre Cot, *J.O.*, 17 April 1946, p. 1968.

candidates they disliked in the early stages, keeping their own favourite in reserve for the crucial moment later on. Presidents, whatever their other defects, were always experienced politicians, and by skilful timing they could exercise a great deal of influence, especially in excluding ' dangerous ' men like Gambetta and Clemenceau from their share of power.[33]

During the provisional period before the constitution was adopted, prospective prime ministers were designated by the Assembly itself.[34] Two votes consequently took place, one on an individual, at the first stage, and another on his team, at the third. The first draft constitution maintained this system, leaving to the President only the restricted function of transmitting to the President of the Assembly the names of possible candidates. It was hoped that two objects would be served. Ministries in intimate contact with the Assembly would be chosen, thus ensuring governmental stability: and the hand of the prime minister would be strengthened against that of the mistrusted President, who might well be General de Gaulle.

This solution was proposed by the Left, but opposed by M.R.P. The latter wanted only one vote in the Assembly, taken at the third stage, after the formation of the government, as it had been in the Third Republic; and they threatened to oppose the second draft constitution unless this point[35] were conceded. There was another objection to the earlier plan. An Assembly of six hundred cannot solve a political crisis: the initiative must be taken by some individual.[36] During the provisional regime, this task was in fact performed by M. Vincent Auriol as President of the Assembly, and if the first draft constitution had been accepted, that office would probably have become a shadow presidency, to the satisfaction of the Left. The final compromise satisfied M.R.P. by insisting on only one vote in the Assembly, but pleased the Left by taking it at the first stage and not at the third. The vote on the individual leader and his programme was retained, that on the ministerial team abandoned. This provision appears in Article 45 of the constitution.

At first this solution proved unexpectedly successful. Since M.

---

[33] On the rôle of Presidents in the Third Republic, their personal preferences, and their dislike for strong prime ministers, see Soulier, pp. 275–302. M. Félix Faure's choice of a Radical prime minister in 1895, in order to demonstrate the impracticability of such a government (*ibid.*, p. 294) recalls the efforts of MM. Herriot and Martinaud-Déplat, at the end of 1951, to persuade the President to put in a Conservative-Gaullist coalition in order to show that it could not survive, and thus regain Conservative support for the alliance of the centre parties—efforts which gave M. Pinay his chance.

[34] There were precedents in the election of Cavaignac in 1848, and of Thiers in 1871. The system had been proposed by Grévy in 1848, by Naquet in 1875, and by men so different as M. Blum and M. Henry de Jouvenel in the 1930's. Théry, pp. 95 ff.

[35] Also the secret ballot for presidential elections (above, p. 171).

[36] On the other hand it is arguable that the Assembly will have less confidence in a premier chosen by an external authority than in one picked by itself. See Soulier, pp. 496–7.

Vincent Auriol and not General de Gaulle became President, there was harmony instead of the anticipated conflict between the head of the state and his prime minister. Consequently, the new system strengthened the latter, not against the President, but against his ministerial colleagues. This became clear when, in May 1947, the Communist ministers and their followers tried to bring the Ramadier government down by voting against it on a question of confidence. In the Third Republic, a coalition government would have fallen if the largest of its component parties withdrew its support. But M. Ramadier did not resign. He maintained that under the new constitution the Assembly invested a prime minister, not a government. The vote showed that he personally retained the confidence of the Assembly. The President supported him and, as the Communist ministers would not resign, signed a decree stating that their ' duties . . . had come to an end as a consequence of their vote '.[37] Their places were filled, and the government remained in office. In the following October M. Ramadier reconstructed his administration, calling for the resignation of all his ministers and reducing the number of posts, but without vacating office himself.[38] In February 1950 the departure of the Socialists from the Bidault government produced a situation like that of May 1947, except that the Socialists were more friendly to their late colleagues than the Communists had been; M. Blum indeed went so far as to say that it was the prime minister's republican duty, as well as his constitutional right, to remain in office.[39]

But signs were quickly apparent of a tendency to revert to the custom of the Third Republic. Most prime ministers agreed to a debate on the composition and policy of their cabinet, leading to what was in effect, though not in form, a vote of confidence.[40] So, in practice, there was a return to the position of the provisional regime, with the Assembly

---

[37] The Communist minister of Health, M. Marrane, sat in the Council of the Republic and had therefore not voted on the question of confidence. He was not dismissed, but resigned immediately afterwards.

An alternative weapon available to the government was an individual vote of no confidence in the ministers concerned, under Article 48 of the constitution. Théry, p. 130.

[38] The under-secretary (*secrétaire d'état*) to the prime minister's office did not resign; the new status belonged to the premiership as an office, not to the premier as a person., See A. Sauvageot, 'Le cabinet Ramadier et la pratique constitutionnelle', *Revue politique et parlementaire*, no. 576, March 1948, p. 245.

[39] *Le Populaire*, 4–5 February 1950.

The constitutional doctrine of the Third Republic was expressly contrary to such a procedure. See Léon Bourgeois, *J.O.* (Chambre des Députés), 14 June 1898, p. 1760, quoted Soulier, p. 79 n.

[40] Two, MM. Marie and Queuille, refused a debate, but the refusal itself led to a short discussion and an eventual vote.

The possibility of such a development is implied by Article 45, which provides that ministerial crises occurring within a fortnight of the formation of the government do not count towards making a dissolution of the Assembly possible. See Théry, p. 111. It was explicitly recognized by the *rapporteur-général* of the constitution: *J.O.*, 28 September 1946, p. 4200.

intervening both at the first stage and at the third. In September 1948 the second Schuman government fell at this hurdle. Two days after its formation, it was beaten by six votes: the prime minister had had Conservative support at his investiture, but had forfeited it by making a Socialist minister of Finance.

But in October 1949 M. Bidault became prime minister. The crisis had lasted a month, and two previous premiers, elected by the Assembly, had failed to form governments. The public clearly felt that the deadlock had lasted long enough. When the Communists presented the customary interpellation on the composition of the government, he refused a debate. The Assembly supported him by a show of hands: so easily was this extra-constitutional growth of a second vote cut out. But in the following February, after the departure of the Socialists, M. Bidault did accept a debate on policy, which he survived by a narrow margin with the Socialists abstaining.

The next ministerial crisis occurred in July 1950. M. Queuille formed his second government, and tried to repeat M. Bidault's performance of nine months before. But this time the Assembly refused to postpone the debate. The Socialists had voted for M. Queuille personally, but they disliked his ministers, and the second Queuille government, defeated by 113 votes, shared the fate of the second Schuman government in 1948. The subsequent prime ministers had better fortune. All but one of them called upon the Assembly to refuse a debate on composition and policy, and obtained a favourable vote. Only M. Edgar Faure, in January 1952, followed the earlier practice and agreed to a debate, which enabled him to state his policy on the grave situation in Tunisia.

The partial reversion to the practice of the Third Republic was not confined to this point. Under the new procedure, the prime minister was invested as an individual by an absolute majority of the Assembly, and then selected his colleagues. But before long the parties began to stipulate for guarantees in advance before agreeing to commit themselves to a candidate. Thus it became desirable for the prospective prime minister unofficially to choose his colleagues even before standing for his personal election. The second stage came to precede the first, or at least the formal completion of the first.[41] M. Marie, in July 1948, made known in advance the main lines of his prospective cabinet; but M. Queuille in the following September was the first prime minister to compose his government before confronting the investiture debate.

---

[41] The *rapporteur-général* had anticipated this development too. ' Nous désirons . . . que le président du conseil désigné . . . procède à ses consultations pour savoir quelle sera à peu près la composition du cabinet. Il vient alors devant l'Assemblée nationale et lui indique quels seront le programme et la structure de son cabinet. De cette façon, la physionomie de la première discussion est complètement transformée . . .' (*Ibid.*)

Significantly, both men belonged to the Radical party, which had always been the champion of traditional procedure.

The Queuille government resigned in October 1949. MM. Moch and René Mayer in turn secured the Assembly's investiture as prime minister, without having taken the precaution of forming their governments first. Neither proved able to do so afterwards. These unprecedented circumstances [42] reduced the investiture procedure to a farce. M. Moch had indeed been invested by the narrowest possible margin, one vote more than the required absolute majority. But M. Mayer had had 341 votes in his favour and only the Communists against him. It was clear that the parties did not regard the investiture vote as a serious commitment.

M. Bidault, who was nominated next, went to the investiture debate with his cabinet list in his pocket, and formed his government successfully. When it fell, nine months later, M. Queuille refused to make any promises in advance of the investiture debate. He was elected by a large majority, including the Socialists. But as soon as his cabinet list appeared, they turned against him, and so did the left wing of M.R.P. His majority of 363 against 208 turned overnight into a minority of 221 against 334. In case prospective premiers had still not learnt their lesson, the parties now began to take a hand, the Radicals announcing that they would vote no investiture without first knowing the composition of the proposed government. M. Pleven conformed to their wishes, formed his cabinet before the vote, and was safely installed. The investiture procedure seemed to have become a complete nullity. In November 1950 the Assembly passed by a large majority a resolution in favour of constitutional revision, including a return to the government-forming practice of the Third Republic; the vote was again to be taken at the third stage, on the team, instead of at the first, on the man. But no immediate change was made; [43] and after the 1951

---

[42] There was no direct precedent, but there had been several warnings of such a possibility. One had occurred in the very first post-war ministerial crisis, when General de Gaulle, after being elected almost unanimously by the Assembly, resigned his mandate owing to the exigencies of the Communists. In the first crisis after the inauguration of President Auriol, the late *rapporteur-général* of the constitution himself announced that his party would reserve its attitude towards the government until its full composition was known. (*J.O.*, 21 January 1947, p. 31: see Théry, p. 111 n.) In September 1948 M. Schuman abandoned the attempt to form a government when the Socialists refused to join, but the President induced both to change their minds. The government was formed, though it was at once defeated in the Assembly.

[43] The procedure for revising the constitution will be described below, pp. 287–8. It is set in motion by a resolution setting out the ' objects ' of the revision, and passed by an absolute majority of the Assembly. A bill embodying specific proposals is not brought forward until either the Assembly has repeated its resolution, following a three months delay, or else it has been accepted by the Council of the Republic. (Art. 90.) In this case, both houses voted the resolution, but uncertainty over the majority's intentions with regard to the powers of the upper house led to the shelving of the whole proposal, which did not return to the Assembly as a bill until July 1953. See below, pp. 287–8.

election the constitution showed itself unexpectedly flexible, for the original procedure returned to favour.[44]

The resolution of November 1950 envisaged a further return to pre-war practice, since the government was no longer to require the support of an absolute majority of the Assembly. The original grounds for this constitutional requirement had been reasonable. In the old Chamber snap votes and small attendances were common. The constitution of the Fourth Republic tried to minimize their danger by requiring an absolute majority for several important decisions, including both the investiture of a prime minister and the overthrow of a government. This should provide stability, since the Assembly would only install a government of which it genuinely approved, and would only overturn it if a really significant shift of opinion had taken place. The early working of the rule was satisfactory: most of the prime ministers of 1946 and 1947 obtained far more than the 'constitutional' majority.[45]

But the provision introduced an element of rigidity which, in dangerous situations where governments were hard to form, might make it impossible to elect a prime minister at all. And, if the cabinet were to be voted on as a whole, the difficulty might well be greater still, for experience strongly suggests that it is easier to rally votes in favour of a man than it is to retain them for a government.[46] But even

---

[44] M. Mollet, in March 1951, stood without having formed a government, and was rejected through getting only a relative majority. M. Queuille told the Assembly that he proposed to retain his predecessor's cabinet virtually intact, and succeeded in keeping the government together. But the one change he did make nearly wrecked his government: for when he offered M. Bidault a vice-premiership, the Socialists demanded one for M. Ramadier, and only the insistence of M. Ramadier himself persuaded them to give way. M. René Mayer in July 1951, and M. Petsche in August, stood without forming a cabinet, and failed to secure election.

The first five cabinets formed after the 1951 election were, however, all put together after the investiture of the prime minister. M. Pleven enjoyed the personal goodwill of the Socialists, but might have forfeited their votes if the composition of his government (which inevitably represented a shift to the Right) had been known to them in advance. M. Pinay, before his election, was hardly regarded as a serious candidate. The crisis of New Year 1953 was a curious inversion of that of October 1949 : this time M. Bidault, who again tried to form his ministry before the vote, had to renounce his candidature, while M. Mayer, who again refused to look beyond the investiture debate, made up for his previous failure by successfully forming his cabinet after it.

[45] This majority varies slightly (see below, p. 184, n. 47) but in the two Constituent Assemblies it was about 294, during most of the first National Assembly 311, and during the second 314.

Of the first five prime ministers elected after liberation, M. Bidault had least votes; without Communist support, he polled only 384. The rest all exceeded this figure by at least 100 (de Gaulle 555, Gouin 497, Blum 575, Ramadier 549). But the break up of *tripartisme* changed the whole parliamentary situation. Of the next fifteen prime ministers elected, only five reached M. Bidault's figure (Schuman 412 in November 1947, Pleven 391 in August 1951, Faure 401 in January 1952, R. Mayer 389 in January 1953, Laniel 398 in June 1953) and seven had less than 360 votes. Thus while four of the first five were invested with 200 votes to spare, in seven of the next fifteen cases the margin was below 50, and in only one was it above 100.

[46] From November 1946 (when the first National Assembly was elected) to June 1953, fifteen governments were formed. Eleven received an absolute majority from the

under the terms of the constitution it soon proved difficult. As early as November 1947 M. Blum was prevented from becoming prime minister by this clause, receiving a majority but an insufficient one. In September 1948, M. Schuman was invested with only 11 votes to spare. He resigned when the Socialists refused to join his government, but President Auriol persuaded him to withdraw his resignation on the ground that no one else seemed likely to muster the necessary number of votes. This incident illustrated the possible dangers of the provision, though the President's fears were in fact ill-founded, as M. Queuille's election showed. In October 1949 M. Moch was invested by a margin of only one somewhat dubious vote.[47] Seven subsequent candidates for the premiership have failed through obtaining only a relative majority.[48] For the parties soon realized that, if a fixed number of

---

Assembly, one (Bidault's in October 1949) avoided a vote altogether, two (the second Schuman and second Queuille ministries, in September 1948 and July 1950) were beaten, and only one was given a relative majority. This was the government of M. Pinay in March 1952, which won its vote only by 290 to 101.

On the other hand, every prime minister but one lost votes between his investiture and the appearance of his government. (Blum lost 31, Ramadier 28, Schuman first ministry 90, Marie 22, Schuman second ministry 33—defeated, Queuille first ministry 11, Queuille second ministry 142—defeated, Pleven first ministry 44, Pleven second ministry 1, Faure 5, Pinay 34, R. Mayer 5, Laniel 12). The one exception was the third Queuille government in March 1951, which added 29 to the prime minister's supporters in the investiture vote. Experts are said to estimate that a prospective premier alone, with his *cortège d'espérances*, can expect forty votes more than a prime minister with his colleagues —and his *cortège de déceptions*: G. Berlia, *R.D.P.*, April 1953, p. 440 n.

Completed ministries tend to have more opponents than isolated prospective premiers, as well as fewer supporters. The second Schuman ministry was defeated because over 100 conservative abstainers went into the opposition, and the second Queuille ministry because the Socialist party changed sides altogether. In the 1951 legislature MM. Pleven and Faure retained their own supporters intact, but the Gaullists, who abstained on the investitures, voted against the governments. The case of M. Pinay was peculiar, for while the votes in his favour fell by 30, those against him also dropped by 100, the Socialists abstaining on the ground that the country had shown its desire for a Conservative experiment.

[47] The definition of 'absolute majority' had been much discussed at the time of M. Blum's candidature in November 1947, which was thought likely to succeed or fail by a vote or two. (In fact it failed by 11 votes.) It was decided that all seats not legally vacant must be taken into account. In October 1949 there were three seats vacant out of a nominal 622. That for Cochin-China had never been, and never was filled: the member for Oceania had died during the summer and the by-election had not yet taken place: and another deputy, who resigned the day before M. Moch's investiture, had not yet been replaced. But the three Malagasy deputies, who were in prison under sentence of death for their part in the 1947 revolt, had to be counted in the total. They remained deputies, though unable to vote, until the 1951 election, and were indeed later joined by another member imprisoned for fraud. *J.O.*, 21 November 1947, pp. 5113–4.

At the time of M. Moch's nomination the legal total of the Assembly was thus 619, and the absolute majority 310. M. Moch had 311 votes. But some were open to a good deal of doubt. M. Montel, at Lake Success, was consulted by transatlantic telephone: as after two hours his reply was still inaudible, his vote was cast in M. Moch's favour. So was the proxy vote of M. Temple, in French Congo, who however, subsequently wired his confirmation. No Gaullist votes for M. Moch had been expected; but one was cast, by the member for Réunion, who was visiting his distant constituency.

[48] M. Mollet in March 1951, M. René Mayer in July, and M. Petsche in August of the same year; and MM. Reynaud, Mendès-France, Bidault, and Marie in May and June 1953.

favourable votes is required, abstention is as effective a means of damaging a candidate as open opposition, while it costs less in terms of parliamentary and public goodwill. So the Gaullists abstained in all the first five investiture votes of the 1951 legislature, M.R.P. in the first (on M. René Mayer), and the Socialists in the second (on M. Petsche). The Communists always cast a hostile vote, since their strategy is to emphasize their distinction from all other groups. But for the remaining parties there seems good reason for normally preferring the more courteous and less aggressive course.[49]

The investiture procedure did not fulfil the purposes for which it was intended. It proved impossible to discuss the programme of the government apart from the struggle for office: men and measures were inseparable, and the reversion to the practice of forming the cabinet unofficially in advance destroyed the attempt to isolate the prime minister and his ideas, and to obtain a ' pure ' vote on policy divorced from personal considerations.[50] The effort to strengthen parliamentary control was frustrated, not by reversion but by innovation: the practice of refusing debates on the composition and policy of the ministry actually left the Assembly less powerful than the Chamber had been. And the attempt to weaken the influence of the President of the Republic had so little success that academic observers, like political opponents, doubted whether any of his predecessors had wielded as much personal influence in this sphere as President Auriol.[51]

---

[49] Every candidate hitherto nominated for the premiership has had a relative majority in his favour. By a kind of ' investiture courtesy,' parties vote for a prospective premier in the expectation of reciprocal treatment when their own men come to stand. Opposition is expressed by abstention. The Communists have voted against all investitures since November 1947, and the Socialists against six since March 1952. But they have been virtually alone, except for Conservative and some R.G.R. hostility to Socialist candidates, and Gaullist dislike of M. Queuille.

Courtesy might go further: if a candidate was thought certain to fail, members who hoped he would do so might nevertheless vote for him with an eye to the future. The unusually strong Pinay government of March 1952 came into existence because, to the general astonishment, 27 Gaullist rebels reinforced such a ' courtesy majority ' sufficiently to convert it into a real one.

Because of such practices, the absolute majority rule is less obstructive than it seems. Candidates who now obtain a relative majority might well not do so if such a majority were sufficient to put them in power.

[50] Under the 1953 revision proposals the prime minister and not the cabinet would still appear before the Assembly, thus preserving his new status; but his ministers would be already chosen, so that the personal investiture is in effect abandoned. The absolute majority rule has also been dropped, though only by 309 to 300 (R.G.R., Socialists, and most Conservatives, against M.R.P., R.P.F., A.R.S., and Communists). Had the Gaullist or M.R.P. ministers voted with their parties, it would have been retained. Its defenders argued forcibly that to set up cabinets without authority, to which most deputies were hostile from the start, was no solution to the problem of governmental stability; it might reduce the duration of crises, but would increase their number, and would make ministries even weaker than before. See *J.O.*, 22 July 1953, pp. 3781–5.

[51] M. H. Fabre, ' Un échec constitutionnel: l'investiture du Président du Conseil,' *R.D.P.*, 1951, p. 211. *Carrefour* (Gaullist weekly), 25 July 1951, ' Vincent Ier, Roi de France.'

M. Fabre's article contains the fullest discussion of the whole development of the investiture procedure.

This influence had to be used with care. The prestige of the Presidency is involved in the incumbent's success in choosing potential prime ministers, and defeats like those of M. Blum in November 1947, and of M. Mollet in March 1951 (both members of M. Auriol's own party) do the office no good.[52] As a protection against such incidents the device of *missions d'information* was developed. The President asks a politician to investigate the situation on his behalf, without the reputation of either man being engaged by a formal nomination. The agent may then accept or refuse nomination, according to the result of his enquiries. Until 1953, M. Bidault in October 1949 was the only prospective premier to have accepted formal nomination without any form of preliminary investigation: about half the candidates were given these informal *missions d'information*, and so were three men who did not stand, MM. Lecourt and Marie in September 1948 and M. Mollet in July 1950.[53] The choice of politicians who are not themselves candidates has been attacked as unconstitutional by both Communist and moderate opinion. To the latter it appeared as a step towards a *régime d'assemblée*, and when M. Mollet was chosen, the Radicals announced that they would discuss the situation only with a prime minister designate.

The President's part is not finished when he has picked his nominee. He takes an active and personal share in the inter-party bargaining; thus in July and again in September 1948 he persuaded the Socialists to reverse their decision to stay out of office, and was then able to induce the despondent potential premiers, MM. Marie and Schuman, to continue the efforts they had resolved to abandon. The institutions

---

[52] A. Sauvageot, *loc. cit.*, pp. 247–8.
In October 1949 the President spoke of resigning his office if M. Bidault, like his two predecessors, failed to form a government after his election to the premiership. J. Fauvet, *Le Monde*, 26 October 1949.

[53] In the extreme case, the prospective prime minister may pass through five stages. The first, which may be dispensed with, is the unofficial *mission d'information*. After it, or without it, he is officially invited, and becomes *président du conseil pressenti*. He may undertake further consultations with the parties before the acceptance which converts him into a *président du conseil designé*. An absolute majority of the Assembly makes him *président du conseil*, but he still has to form his government.
In the most straightforward case, a successful *mission d'information* leads directly to nomination, as with M. Ramadier in January 1947, M. Moch in October 1949, and M. Queuille in July 1950. At other times it leads to someone else's nomination. M. Lecourt and M. Marie were invited at a moment when M. Schuman had already been elected but had failed to form a government: their object was to prepare for a resumption of his task by M. Schuman, and they were successful. M. Mollet, who announced in advance that he would not accept nomination, drew up the programme on which the Pleven government was based; in the next crisis he was himself nominated for the premiership. M. Queuille in March 1951, and M. Petsche in the following July, both undertook *missions d'information* which led to the nomination, first of another candidate who failed (respectively M. Mollet and M. René Mayer), and only subsequently of themselves. M. Blum, in November 1947, had held his consultations and been picked as the next prime minister while the Ramadier government was still in office.
M. Schuman in November 1947, M. Marie in July 1948, and M. Bidault in October 1949, accepted nomination without going through the preliminary stage; so did the first five prime ministers elected in the new Assembly.

devised to exclude the influence of President de Gaulle have been strongly marked by the views and personality of President Auriol.

4. THE PREMIERSHIP

THE position of prime minister was the keystone of the constitutional settlement of October 1946. This settlement was based in the main on Socialist constitutional ideas. As long ago as 1919, M. Blum had sketched his proposals for reform. In his view the essential need was the organization of stronger parties, so that an effective government could come into being with the support of a coherent parliamentary majority. The prime minister ought to be the leader of such a majority, uniting the executive and the legislature in pursuit of objectives common to both.[54] But to fulfil such a task, he required much greater power and prestige than he had hitherto possessed, and these could be conferred on his office without waiting for the slow growth of an effective party system. M. Blum wished, in fact, to bring the French system nearer to the British. By strengthening the position of the Assembly against the second chamber, and of the prime minister elected by it against the President of the Republic, the framers of the constitution were consciously pursuing the same objective.[55]

In previous constitutions the title of prime minister has never been mentioned: in that of the Fourth Republic it appears fourteen times.[56] His personal, individual election by the Assembly emphasizes his authority over his colleagues; he alone is chosen by the representatives of the people, while the other ministers are appointed by him (as specified in Article 46) and have no democratic title of their own. His political, legislative, and executive supremacy, demanded by M. Blum in 1919,[57] is asserted in a series of articles. In the Third Republic any minister could make a matter an issue of confidence in the government, and administrations could be destroyed by the rashness of a subordinate.[58] Article 49 of the new constitution reserves this right to the prime minister alone. Hitherto any minister could introduce bills. Article 14 declares that ' The President of the Council of Ministers and members of Parliament have the right to initiate laws '. Subordinate ministers, as such, have not, though they retain effective charge of the legislation of their departments. Article 38 repeats the old provision for ministerial countersigning of the acts of the President of the Republic. But there is a significant change; two ministers must now

---

[54] *La Réforme gouvernementale*, pp. 151–3.
[55] ' Nous avons voulu instituer un véritable chef du gouvernement, un premier ministre au sens anglais du terme.' M. Paul Coste-Floret, *rapporteur-général*, *J.O.*, 5 September 1946, p. 3552.
[56] Articles 14, 38, 40, 45 (twice), 46, 47 (three times), 49, 52 (twice), 54, 55. The council of ministers was mentioned twice in the 1875 constitution, and five times in that of 1946 (Articles 30, 32, 49, 51, 55), while the latter mentions the cabinet four times (Articles 49 twice, 50, and 52). Théry, p. 120.
[57] *Op. cit.*, pp. 62–3.
[58] See below, p. 212.

countersign, which was the normal practice in the past;[59] and the prime minister must be one of them, a legal requirement which was intended as a source of strength, but may rather involve an additional burden and responsibility.[60] Other constitutional provisions and practical reforms establish the executive authority of the prime minister, many of the former transferring to him powers previously vested in the President of the Republic.

The creation of a prime minister's department was regarded by M. Blum as a reform of crucial importance.[61] Before 1914 the head of the government had either to take on an extra ministry, which overburdened him, or to remain without a department, which left him in a weak position as against his colleagues. Between the two wars the position was uncertain, the *office du président du conseil* being alternately created and abolished by successive governments; in 1934 it was restored by M. Flandin, and when M. Blum came into power two years later it was naturally retained and strengthened. Now, a much stronger department exists, to which control of the civil service is attached, and which frequently takes over responsibility for particular problems.[62] Moreover the prime minister's constitutional right to appoint his colleagues gives him full authority to modify the structure of government. After 1920 the creation or merger of ministries required legal action, though this provision was frequently disregarded.[63] Under the Fourth Republic, new departments have frequently been set up, like the ministry of Youth, Arts and Letters in January 1947, or abolished, like the same department in October of the same year. Cabinets have varied in size from thirteen to twenty-six, or from thirteen to forty if under-secretaries are included.[64]

---

[59] Théry, p. 88 n.

[60] In May 1948 the Schuman government was deeply divided over a decree issued by Mme Poinso-Chapuis, M.R.P. minister of Health, which anti-clericals feared might indirectly make it possible to subsidize church schools. The prime minister's prospects of appeasing this quarrel were greatly impaired by the fact that his signature, necessarily, appeared on the decree.

[61] For a different view see Soulier, p. 567; he maintains that the personality of the prime minister has always been the decisive factor, irrespective of the existence of a department. On the position before 1939 see Théry, p. 123.

[62] Food, broadcasting, information, and atomic energy are among the matters which are or have been direct responsibilities of the head of the government. See A. Bertrand, 'La Présidence du Conseil et le Secrétariat-général du Gouvernement,' *R.D.P.*, 1948, pp. 435 ff.

Despite the creation of the new office, prime ministers have often thought it wise to take over a department as well. The ministry of Finance was held by M. Queuille for a few weeks in his first government, by M. Faure, and by M. Pinay: it was always difficult to fill, and M. Faure explained that if it added a burden to the premier's load it also removed one, since he no longer had to spend a large part of his time arguing with the minister of Finance. In his second and third administrations M. Queuille retained the ministry of the Interior, which he had held in the governments preceding them. Similarly, M. Bidault kept the Foreign Office in June 1946, and M. Schuman in September 1948. M. Blum also was his own Foreign minister, and M. Gouin was nominally his own minister of Defence.

[63] Théry, p. 126.

[64] The smallest cabinet was that of M. Ramadier after its reconstruction in October

Article 47 specifies that the prime minister is responsible for ensuring the execution of the laws. In France, where decrees implementing the general provisions of laws have so much importance, this is a significant change. In the Third Republic this responsibility belonged to the President, though the need for a minister's countersign meant that effective power was in the government's hands. The transfer of nominal authority to the prime minister (not to the cabinet as a whole) further emphasizes his pre-eminence. Most official appointments, too, are now, under the same Article, made by the prime minister instead of the President; the most important posts, however, are filled by the cabinet, with the President in the chair.[65] A third paragraph of Article 47 gives the prime minister specific responsibility for defence matters. His powers in this respect may be delegated to the minister of Defence, and usually are, but practice has varied greatly in different circumstances. M. Ramadier kept very close control of his Communist minister of Defence, M. Billoux, whereas some other holders of the office, notably M. Moch in the first Pleven government, have enjoyed an entirely free hand.[66]

The prime minister's position has thus been immensely strengthened, but it is limited by two important qualifications. One of these is constitutional; his great powers are never exercised alone.[67] Those which he discharges under Articles 38 and 47, namely the issue of decrees, appointments to minor posts, and supervision of the country's

---

1947 (though M. Moch, two years later, attempted to form one smaller still). The same Ramadier cabinet began with 26 members, a total not yet exceeded, but it had no under-secretaries. M. Faure, in January 1952, formed a government of 40 members, 26 of them cabinet ministers.

The separate existence of certain departments depends on political, not on administrative factors. Thus Merchant Marine appeared in the first Queuille government, was reduced to an under-secretaryship by M. Bidault, but regained its place as a full ministry in every succeeding administration until that of M. Pinay. Commerce was separated from Industry for a few months of the Ramadier cabinet, in M. Pleven's second government, and in those of MM. Faure and Mayer. Population existed for four months in 1946, to satisfy M.R.P. who had lost the Health ministry to the Communists. Economic Affairs is in a different position, since policy questions as well as party claims are involved in its independence (see below, pp. 391–2). The Post Office is another department which has sometimes been reduced to under-secretaryship status. One new ministry of great importance, that of Associated States (i.e. Indo-China), was created in July 1950, and survived for three years.

[65] The cabinet appoints, among others, members of the *Conseil d'État*, ambassadors, university rectors, prefects, generals, colonial governors, and senior officials (Article 30). Judges are named in the High Council of the Magistrature (Article 84), and ministers by the prime minister (Article 46). For all other appointments the prime minister is responsible under Article 47.

One difference between France and Britain is indicated by the curious fact that the transitory, political prime minister controls the civil service and makes minor appointments, while the President, who represents the permanent interests of the state, has charge of the cabinet secretariat and minutes.

[66] But in 1948, when large powers for the defence of West Africa were delegated to the High Commissioner there, this was attacked as unconstitutional. *A.P.*, 1948, p. 224.

[67] With the nominal and apparently accidental exception of his exclusive right to introduce bills under Article 14. See Théry, pp. 87–8, 132.

defence, require the countersignature of another minister. Those of greater importance, the highest appointments, putting the question of confidence, and dissolving the Assembly, must be settled in a cabinet meeting with the President of the Republic in the chair.[68]

The political qualification is still more important. In the absence of a coherent party system, the constitutional revolution envisaged by M. Blum could not come about. Everything possible in the way of texts has been provided to make the prime minister an effective leader, but the constitutional design has been undermined by the power of the parties.[69] In the period of *tripartisme* his dependence upon them was complete. When that era came to an end, governments found themselves relying on narrow margins in the Assembly, which the defection of even a minor group could destroy. These conditions, so familiar in the Third Republic, produced the same results. The men who rose to the top were the conciliators, the specialists in keeping together a fractious and unruly team. MM. Queuille and Pleven were the most successful of all. The former led the longest ministry of the Fourth Republic by cautious postponement of decisions, the policy stigmatized by his opponents as *immobilisme*. The latter survived by maintaining neutrality on the most burning issues, by allowing proposals he loathed to be carried against him without making them questions of confidence, and by changing his policy on major matters to hold marginal votes.[70] In choosing candidates for the premiership from a given party, the President regularly turned to that member of it who had been the most active mediator in the previous government; these were the credentials of M. Maric in July 1948, of M. Moch in October 1949, and of M. Mollet in March 1951.[71] Such shifts and devices were necessary for survival, and such talents led to political advancement. The strong, positive leader with a programme of his own was at a discount, not at a premium. And the strength of the premiership as an institution could be no greater than the strength of the individuals who filled it.[72]

---

[68] Articles 30, 49 and 51.

[69] See below, Ch. 23.

[70] M. Pleven kept neutrality, allowing none of his ministers to vote, over electoral reform in his first government (see below, pp. 223–4) and over subsidies for church schools in his second. He opposed the bill to establish a sliding scale for wages in September 1951, but when challenged by the R.P.F. to make his opposition a matter of confidence, declined to do so because this would mean his defeat. In the following December he threw over M. Schuman's conciliatory policy in Tunisia, apparently because to lose the votes of the *colons'* friends in the Assembly would have been fatal to his ministry. (*L'Observateur*, 29 November 1951. See also *Le Monde*, 24 November 1951: *Manchester Guardian*, 4, 13, 18, and 19 December 1951, 21 January 1952: Léo Hamon, *Esprit*, 1953, pp. 839–40.)

[71] M. Marie had been the main conciliator in the bitterly divided Schuman government. M. Moch was chosen because he had been the most fertile producer of compromises when the Queuille cabinet was breaking up: but his temperament, which was not that of a conciliator, led to his failure. M. Mollet was responsible for solving the crisis of July 1950, and was himself nominated on the next occasion, March 1951. Soulier, pp. 484–5, 488, 494, discusses the role of the conciliators in the Third Republic.

[72] *Ibid.*, pp. 565–74, for an elaboration of this point.

Chapter 13

THE NATIONAL ASSEMBLY

1. THE DEPUTIES

IN the Third Republic, the National Assembly was the title of the body, composed of deputies and senators sitting together, which elected the President of the Republic, and had the power to revise the constitution. In the Fourth, this title was transferred to the former Chamber of Deputies, to emphasize its new position as the repository of all authority (except in constitutional matters), delegated to it by the sovereign people under Article 3 of the constitution. The three advisory bodies which surround it, the Council of the Republic, Assembly of the French Union, and Economic Council, have a status altogether inferior to that of the Assembly, or indeed to that of the Senate of the Third Republic.

The Assembly consists of 627 members, of whom 544 represent metropolitan France (including Corsica), 30 sit for Algerian constituencies, and the remaining 53 for colonial departments and territories.[1] Its members must be at least 23 years of age, and must have discharged their liability to military service: they may not be on the active list of any of the fighting services, nor hold or have held, within the six months before their election, certain administrative or judicial positions giving them authority within their constituency.[2] Bankruptcy and, for varying periods, certain criminal offences also involve ineligibility for election.[3] Legislation passed at the liberation, but repealed in 1953,

---

[1] On the topics dealt with in the next four chapters, and especially on procedural matters, see D. W. S. Lidderdale, *Parliament of France*. Peter Campbell, 'The French Parliament', *Public Administration*, Winter 1953, brings Mr. Lidderdale's book up to date.

The two Constituent Assemblies had 586 members, of whom 522 sat for metropolitan, 26 for Algerian, and 33 for colonial constituencies: there were also 5 representatives of Tunisia and Morocco. In June 1946 these were increased to 544, 30 and 45, respectively, a total of 619. The representation of the overseas territories was reduced by one when Cochin-China, which had never elected its deputy, became technically independent. But Africa had already been given three more members (for Haute-Volta) in 1947, and a further six were added in 1951.

Of the overseas deputies, ten represent old colonies having the status of departments: Guadeloupe, Martinique and Réunion have three members each, and French Guiana one. Fifteen of the Algerian members, and five of the other African deputies, represent constituencies of French citizens (in effect white colonists).

[2] M. Rastel, elected U.D.S.R. member for Eure-et-Loir in 1951, was unseated because he had been prefect of the department within the six months limit. See Peter Campbell, 'Vérification des pouvoirs in the French National Assembly,' *Political Studies*, vol. I, no. 1 (February 1953), p. 70.

[3] The Assembly may declare deputies who commit such offences after their election to have forfeited their right to sit. But the three Malagasy members convicted of treason, and M. de Récy, convicted of fraud, retained their seats until the end of the legislature (and continued to count as members for the purpose of reckoning the absolute majority), even though they could not vote.

made ineligible those sentenced to ' national indignity ' for collaboration or responsibility for the Vichy regime.[4] Members of families which have reigned over France were made ineligible in 1884.[5]

No person may belong to more than one of the four quasi-parliamentary bodies. A member of one, elected to another, must make his choice within a month. So, in December 1946, a number of deputies retired to the calmer waters of the Council of the Republic, while in 1951, seventeen members of the latter body seized the opportunity to enter the principal Assembly. Similarly, a member who holds a post paid by the state (with the exception of ministers, but including holders of administrative positions in nationalized or state-subsidized businesses) must resign one or the other position. If he loses or resigns his seat, he may return to his official post with full pension rights. If he accepts such a post while a member, he is considered to have automatically resigned.[6]

Each Assembly judges the eligibility and verifies the credentials of its own members. In 1952 a deputy named Ducreux, killed in a car crash, was found to be carrying two identity cards, one in the name under which he had been elected, and the other bearing his real name, under which he was wanted for collaborationist activities during the occupation. This incident led the Assembly to impose stricter requirements over credentials.

When parliaments reserve to themselves the right to settle disputed elections, they generally misuse their power. The Assemblies of the Fourth Republic have been no exception. The Communists tried in June 1946 to unseat two former premiers (MM. Daladier and Reynaud), and in 1951 to contest the election of Marshal Pétain's counsel, M. Isorni, not on grounds of ineligibility or electoral irregularity, but

---

[4] Those sentenced to national indignity remained ineligible even though relieved of the sentence owing to their subsequent conduct. This provision, contained in a law of October 1946, was directed against the former prime minister M. Pierre-Étienne Flandin.

Ineligible persons sometimes contested local elections in defiance of the law, occasionally with startling success. M. Milliès-Lacroix was re-elected mayor of Dax by majorities which increased each time his election was annulled. Before the general election of 1951, prefects were warned that ineligibility applied to candidature, not merely to membership, and that votes cast for ineligibles were spoiled. This discouraged the ineligible leaders who had intended to stand in several constituencies: many of them, like M. Pébellier in Haute-Loire (below, p. 198) persuaded relatives to contest the election in their place. In the senatorial election of May 1952 in Yonne, 307 out of 932 electors voted for M. Flandin despite his ineligibility.

The amnesty law of July 1953 abolished this type of ineligibility.

[5] See above, p. 151, n.

[6] Besides ministers there are excepted the holders of certain professorial chairs, religious appointees in the three departments to which the *lois laïques* do not apply (because they were German from 1871 to 1918), and deputies on government missions, provided that the duration of the mission does not exceed six months. This limit, instituted in 1928 and removed in 1941, was restored in January 1950 by a consolidating bill. But such missions may be renewed by the government at six-monthly intervals up to a total of two years. This provision was introduced by an amending law, to allow M. Naegelen, Governor-General of Algeria, to keep his seat in the Assembly.

simply as political undesirables. The R.P.F. opposed the validation of M. Thorez on equally flimsy grounds. Though these crude attempts failed, some very unsatisfactory decisions have been made. In 1951 several seats in two constituencies depended on a disputed interpretation of the electoral law.[7] In Seine-Inférieure the majority parties voted for the ruling which favoured them against the Gaullists and Communists. But in Bas-Rhin the head of the R.P.F. list, who would have been unseated by a similar decision, was General Kœnig. Unwilling to risk the odium of removing him, the Assembly simply voted for the alternative interpretation, thus in a single hour deciding two identical cases in opposite ways.

Article 23 of the constitution provides that members of parliament shall receive a salary equivalent to that of a certain category of civil servant. The category, which is fixed by the ordinary law, has since 1938 been that of *conseiller d'état*, and the salary in 1953 was about £2,100. Rather less than half is treated as an expense allowance, and is not taxable. Members pay special rates for railway travel, may frank letters written in the precincts of the chamber to which they belong, and may make free telephone calls from there to correspondents in Paris. There is a contributory pension scheme, the amount varying according to length of service, with a maximum of three-quarters of the current salary.[8]

The most important privilege of members is that of immunity from arrest for criminal offences, except with the permission of the chamber to which they belong, or in cases where they are caught in the act (*en flagrant délit*). In the Third Republic this immunity applied only to the period when Parliament was sitting, but Article 22 of the constitution extends it to the whole term of membership, while for speeches and votes given as a member immunity is absolute, under Article 21. The courts, in settling cases of *flagrant délit*, and the Assembly in its decisions, have both shown a marked tendency to lean towards the side of the accused.[9]

---

[7] On this point see Appendix VI; and on the whole topic, Campbell, '*Vérification . . .*" *loc. cit.*, pp. 65–79.

[8] *Le Monde*, 10 January 1950, has an informative article on the financial position of the deputy. Salaries were increased from £1,400 at the beginning of 1952.

To draw a pension, the ex-member must be aged at least fifty-five, and have served in more than one parliament. Members' wives are allowed cheap travel between Paris and the constituency. Since May 1953, deputies also receive a secretarial allowance of £25 a month.

[9] On the Assembly's attitude, see R. Drago, *R.D.P.*, 1949, pp. 350 ff., and 1950, pp. 403 ff. During the life of the 1946–51 Assembly only 15 out of 328 applications to prosecute were granted, and during the first year of the 1951 legislature, none out of 145.

In April 1950 the Brest court refused to try two Communist deputies, arrested for leading a riot in the town, on the ground that the custom of the Third Republic permitted the arrest of members *en flagrant délit* without the permission of the house, but not their prosecution. This interpretation was disavowed by the Assembly. *Le Monde*, 22, 23–24 and 29 April 1950. *A.P.*, 1950, pp. 285–6.

In June 1952 M. Duclos, the Communist parliamentary leader, was arrested *en*

The number of applications for permission to prosecute was far greater in the early years of the Fourth Republic than it had been in the Third, the overwhelming majority of the requests being directed against members of the Communist party.[10] In 1949 an attempt to tackle the problem was made. An Immunity committee was set up on a permanent basis, to replace the *ad hoc* committees previously used, in the hope both of saving time, and of establishing a body of case-law.[11] A bill was proposed to check any repetition of the government's behaviour over the case of three Malagasy deputies, who were prosecuted for treason after the Assembly had consented to raise their immunity so that they could be tried on a non-capital charge. But the bill provoked a conflict between the two houses, and passed only in 1953.[12] Another measure was introduced to reduce the number of prosecutions, many of which were concerned with intended libel suits against newspapers edited by deputies, by requiring such papers to name another person responsible for their legal liabilities: [13] it eventually passed into law in December 1951. The constitutional changes proposed in July 1953 revise Article 22, in particular by suppressing immunity during recesses.

2. ORGANIZATION AND PROCEDURE

ARTICLE 6 of the constitution lays down that the duration of the Assembly's life is fixed by the ordinary law. Under the Third Republic, the life of a Chamber of Deputies was four years. That of a National Assembly is five. Some jurists hold that an ordinary law can alter the duration only of future Assemblies, and that an existing Assembly cannot properly extend or reduce its own term in this way. The subject came to the forefront of politics in October 1947, when General

---

flagrant délit during a Paris riot, and charged with conspiring against the security of the state. The police claimed, *inter alia*, that two carrier pigeons had been found in his car, dead but still warm. M. Duclos alleged that they were his dinner; and a jury consisting of the President of the National Pigeon-Fanciers' Federation, a professor of natural history, and a military communications expert solemnly agreed that they were eating pigeons. M. Duclos was eventually released. The comic incident thus drew attention to an important fact: the independence of French justice.

[10] Between 1902 and 1940, 102 such applications were submitted: from 1945 to June 1949, 115, of which 94 were against Communists. *J.O.*, 22 June 1949, p. 3639 (M. Duclos' speech). In the first two years of the new Assembly, there were 185 against Communists and 11 against others. But only 1 and 6 of them respectively were presented after the end of 1952.

[11] All types of committee were originally formed by nomination in the eleven bureaux into which deputies were divided by lot. This system was abandoned as a means of choosing the permanent committees in 1902. For immunity cases it survived until 1949: with the establishment of a standing Immunity committee, the bureaux' functions were limited to the verification of credentials.

[12] See pp. 177n, 291. On the whole problem see Pickles, pp. 269–70, 293–4; and on the 1953 law, G. Berlia, *R.D.P.*., July 1953, pp. 697–700.

[13] It is said that a Communist paper in Dakar once introduced a new editor with the statement: 'As frequent prosecution for libel has been causing us serious expense, we have entrusted the management of our newspaper to a member of Parliament. It will no longer be possible to sue us for libel without first obtaining the leave of the House.' Quoted *Times*, 11 July 1949.

de Gaulle declared that the victory of the R.P.F. in the municipal elections proved that the Assembly no longer represented the country, and called upon it to dissolve itself. The April draft constitution had specifically provided, in Article 83, that the Assembly might dissolve itself by a two-thirds majority. This clause was dropped in the constitution adopted in October. But as a two-thirds majority of the Assembly alone can pass any constitutional amendment (except one abolishing the Council of the Republic) the legal possibility of dissolution by this means appears not to have been affected. This was the procedure which General de Gaulle urged the Assembly to invoke.

On 12 May 1951 the first National Assembly of the Fourth Republic did in fact vote a premature end to its own life. Its powers were brought to an end on 4 July, its successor having been elected on 17 June, five months ahead of the normal time. The powers of future Assemblies are to expire on 31 May in the fifth year after their election. This bill went through as an ordinary law, though by majorities sufficient to have carried it as a constitutional amendment.[14]

Under the Third Republic, the minimum ordinary session of the Chamber of Deputies was no more than five months in the year. In practice, extraordinary sessions were invariably held, and were indeed necessary to enable the budget to be voted.[15] But the President of the Republic possessed the right, which was exercised in fact by the government of the day, either to adjourn the Chamber for short periods during the session, or to close the session itself. This power of *clôture* was abolished by the constitution of the Fourth Republic. Governments were thought to have shown too much eagerness to rid themselves of the unwelcome attentions of Parliament, and precautions were taken to prevent their doing so in the future.

Under Article 9 of the constitution, Parliament is in principle in permanent session, and it is required to sit in fact for at least eight months of the year (though adjournments of less than ten days count as part of the session). The session begins on the second Tuesday in January, and should end before 31 December, which is also the end of the financial year. The time-honoured practice of stopping the Assembly clocks (by which time is legally reckoned) at five minutes to midnight on 31 December, and prolonging that day's sitting into the first few days of January, is still employed in the Fourth Republic when the voting of budgetary legislation falls behind schedule. Except in 1947 and 1949, brief extraordinary sessions have been held during the first week of January (not always for budgetary purposes).

---

[14] A three-fifths majority in both houses, or a two-thirds majority in the Assembly alone, is sufficient to pass a constitutional amendment without the need for a referendum. The bill in question passed the Assembly by 362 to 219, and the Council by 278 to 35. But the procedure of constitutional amendment would have involved delay, which would have frustrated the whole purpose of the bill. See below, Ch. 18.

[15] Duverger, *Manuel*, p. 326.

The right to adjourn has been taken from the hands of the government and placed in those of the Assembly itself. In the Third Republic the deputies were accustomed to protest vigorously when they were ' sent on holiday ', but their outcries were frequently neither meant nor taken very seriously. With the responsibility entirely in its own hands, however, the Assembly has found it politically very difficult to vote long adjournments. Its sittings have often been prolonged into August, and the summer recess has rarely begun at the time originally arranged. The number of sittings has been much greater than in the Third Republic—often in the neighbourhood of 300 a year.[16] Restoration to the government of the right of *clôture* was among the constitutional reforms proposed in July 1953.[17]

During the recess, the interests of the Assembly are watched over by its elected standing committee, the bureau. The bureau, under Article 12, is entitled to convoke the Assembly if it considers this necessary, and is obliged to do so on the demand either of the prime minister, or of a third of the deputies. This provision was intended to prevent a recurrence of the situation at the time of the Munich crisis, when the Chamber never met. In September 1949, when France followed Britain in devaluing the currency, the Communist party tried to have the Assembly recalled, but were frustrated by the refusal of the Gaullist opposition to support them.[18]

The standing orders of the Assembly recognize the association of members in party groups, through which committees are elected. Although no deputy may belong officially to more than one group, ' inter-groups ' are often formed, combining the deputies of more than one party, and affording extra presidencies and vice-presidencies to impress constituents. These may be the parliamentary expression of alliances in the country, like the inter-group of the R.G.R., or that which the Conservative groups often form. The most important political inter-group of recent years was that set up by the R.P.F. at the

---

[16] 1947: 218 sittings. 1948: 294. 1949: 266. 1950: 343. 1951: 368. 1952: 229. 1953: 230. In the Third Republic, the Chamber usually held about 140 sittings a year.

[17] But the *clôture* is not to be used until the Assembly has sat for seven months (excluding interruptions longer than a week). The session is to begin on the first Tuesday in October; the election of officers and committees in January very often delayed the passing of the budget.

[18] *A.P.*, 1949, p. 159. The Communist motion was lost in the bureau by 15 to 6. Their 180 members, with the Gaullists, could have produced the 207 signatures needed to compel the bureau to recall the Assembly.

During the strikes of August 1953, 211 deputies called for the recall of the Assembly; but the bureau decided (by 10 votes to 8) that four of the letters bore false signatures, and that the demand consequently failed. A second attempt proved successful; but the bureau did not recall the Assembly for three weeks—only a week before it would have met in any case.

By the constitutional revision bill of July 1953 a majority of the deputies (instead of a third) is required to convoke the Assembly. When Parliament at length met, in October, the Socialists threatened to oppose this provision unless the convocation was made automatic and immediate, once the requisite number of demands had been received.

end of 1947. Standing Order 13 expressly forbids the formation of groups devoted to the defence of private, local or professional interests, of a type which flourished greatly in the Third Republic; but the ban can be evaded.[19]

The Chamber itself is semi-circular, and members' benches are arranged by parties, from the Communists on the President's left to the R.P.F. (against their own violent protests) on his right. There are special benches in front for the ministers, and for the representatives of the committees dealing with the topic under discussion. Members very often speak from their places, but long speeches are delivered from the tribune under the President's desk. Eloquence and oratory are still important parliamentary assets in France. Voting usually takes place in the first instance by show of hands, or, if the result seems doubtful, by calling upon Ayes and Noes respectively to rise in their places. But when individual votes are to be recorded, a ballot vote is held: it may be demanded by any deputy.[20] Members place white (Aye) or blue (No) cards which have their name printed on them, in the urns provided by the messengers. Proxy voting is allowed, and the cards of an entire party are frequently kept and inserted by one of its members (known as a *boîtier*). It is by no means unusual for a handful of deputies to record several hundred votes in this way.[21] Until 1952 there was also a procedure, known as *scrutin public à la tribune*, in which deputies could participate only in person. But this form of ballot, which took at least an hour and a half to complete, proved a dangerous weapon of Communist obstruction. From 1947 successive amendments to standing orders made it more and more difficult to demand such a *scrutin public*, and in 1952 the procedure was abolished altogether.[22]

The officers of the Assembly form a bureau of twenty-four members, elected annually, whose duties are to preside over the debates and organize the staffing and services of the Assembly. Article 11 of the constitution requires the bureau to be chosen by proportional representation of parties.[23] It consists of the President, six vice-presidents who relieve the President in the chair, fourteen secretaries, some of whom must always be present to supervise the counting of votes and the drafting of minutes, and three *questeurs* who are responsible for the

---

[19] For party groups and committee elections, see below, pp. 236, 363–5. For private interest groups, see below, pp. 335–7.

[20] For the different forms of voting under the standing orders, and the circumstances under which they may be employed, see Lidderdale, p. 141.

[21] At the end of the debate on reform of the standing orders on 27 March 1952, the two dozen deputies present carried one amendment by 343 to 247, and another by 352 to 236, and passed the proposals as a whole by 378 to 100 with 110 abstentions. *J.O.*, 27 March 1952, pp. 1579–80.

[22] Except for votes on the verification of credentials (S.O.'s 5 and 38).

[23] This provision was dropped in the 1953 revision proposals. The intention was apparently to deprive the Communists of their senior positions in the bureau, though not necessarily to reduce their numbers: see G. Berlia, *R.D.P.*, July 1953, pp. 685–6. For the point of this change, see below, p. 231.

physical, administrative, and financial arrangements of the Assembly.

At the beginning of each session, the first business is the election of the bureau. The first sitting itself is presided over by the oldest deputy, and the six youngest members act as secretaries. Throughout the 1946–51 Assembly, the oldest deputy was the veteran Communist M. Marcel Cachin, whose tenure of this position led to various amendments to standing orders, restricting the rights of the temporary president. After the 1951 election, M. Cachin found himself junior to a new deputy, M. Pébellier, a Conservative retired haberdasher from Le Puy, who had never before in his eighty-five years of life been outside his native town. M. Pébellier contested the election because his son, a former deputy of the Third Republic, had voted for Marshal Pétain in 1940, and was consequently ineligible. The son wrote and the father delivered an introductory speech which, in its praise of the Marshal and condemnation of the ineligibility laws, contrasted oddly with the revolutionary discourses of the previous *doyen d'âge*.

The President of the National Assembly is the second person in the state, and in all but name vice-president of the Republic.[24] He takes over the duties of the President in the event of a casual vacancy, promulgates laws if the President neglects to do so, and must be consulted before the most important decisions, such as the nomination of a prospective prime minister, or the dissolution of the Assembly.[25] In the event of a dissolution, he automatically becomes prime minister for the period of the general election.[26] Within the Assembly itself, his position is less aloof and authoritative than that of the British Speaker, but it is still further removed from the partisanship of his American counterpart. The President, by custom, does not speak or vote, nor does a vice-president at sittings over which he presides. But very occasionally a President has marked his sense of the importance of an issue by leaving the chair to participate in a debate or division. On 30 December 1949, when Radical defections seemed likely to bring down the Bidault government in a vote of confidence on the budget, M. Herriot gave a lead to his party by casting his personal vote in favour of the ministry.

Election to the Presidency does not terminate a career in party politics. It marks elevation to the front rank. Presidents of the Chamber sometimes became Presidents of the Republic, and often became prime ministers. The President of the first Constituent Assembly, M. Gouin, resigned in January 1946 to take General de Gaulle's place at the head of the government. His successor in the

---

[24] See A. Sauvageot, 'Le Président de l'Assemblée Nationale,' *Revue politique et parlementaire*, October 1948, pp. 122 ff. He points out that, in the Third Republic, three Presidents of the Chamber and five Presidents of the Senate were elected direct from those offices to the Presidency of the Republic.

[25] Articles 41, 36, 45 (by implication) and 51 of the constitution respectively.

[26] Article 52. See below, p. 230.

chair, M. Vincent Auriol, became President of the Republic, and was in turn succeeded by M. Herriot, who had during the previous twenty years held both the premiership and the Presidency of the Chamber on more than one occasion.

Another important authority in the Assembly is the Presidents' Conference, which fixes the provisional agenda. This body consists of the President and vice-presidents of the Assembly, the chairmen of its committees, and the chairmen of all political groups of fourteen or more members. The government is entitled to send a representative. It meets weekly, and draws up the order of business for two weeks ahead.[27] But its recommendations are often altered by the Assembly, partly because of unexpected developments (such as the government's demand for a vote of confidence, which halts the debate for a full day), and partly because the majority in the conference may not reflect that in the Assembly.[28]

The French Parliament differs from the British, and from the American Congress, in containing a party hostile to the whole parliamentary system, and with no inhibitions to prevent attempts to wreck it. The Communists have not indeed obstructed systematically like the Irish nationalists, nor filibustered on the scale of Southern senators. But in moments of acute tension they have occasionally provoked violent disorders in the Assembly, especially during the general strike of November 1947, and in March 1950. In the first case, the Communists fought the government's drastic public order bill, both by procedural obstruction and by defiance of the chair; one deputy remained all night in the tribune, surrounded by fellow-members of his party, but in the morning consented to leave. In March 1950, during the debate on the laws against sabotage, fighting broke out on the floor of the house, which had to be cleared by the guards.[29] In each case the Assembly demonstrated the flexibility of its procedure by voting the disputed bills with unusual despatch—though the obstruction did help non-Communist critics, who contended that the proposals were excessively harsh, to obtain substantial concessions from the government. In 1950 it also did a great deal to convince previously hesitant members that Communist parliamentary strength must be reduced by a change in the electoral law.

The milder forms of obstruction are also practised. During the same

---

[27] A standing order passed in October 1950 required the conference to make arrangements three weeks in advance. Experience proved this to be impracticable, and in 1952 two weeks were substituted for three.

[28] See below, pp. 206–7.

[29] See Lidderdale, p. 156 n; *A.P.*, 1950, pp. 51–3.

A few weeks earlier another noisy debate had turned to violence when a member called M. André Marty ' le mutin,' and the Communists, amid the din, thought he had referred to Mme Vermeersch (Mme Thorez) as ' la putain.' *J.O.*, 27 January 1950, p. 623. But the popular impression, that such incidents are everyday occurrences in the French Parliament, is quite unjustified.

debates of March 1950, a Communist deputy spoke for five and a half hours on one sub-amendment, quoting Soviet price statistics in minute detail. In March 1952 the leading Communist opponent of a proposal to change the standing orders contrived to introduce such subjects as the standard of living, the rate of taxation, German rearmament, Soviet foreign policy, the electoral law, and the position of municipal employees. During the subsequent debate it was pointed out that in the first six months of the life of the legislature, the average Communist member had spoken half as much again as the non-Communists, and that four of the six most loquacious deputies belonged to that party.[30]

The inevitable result has been a strengthening of the procedural checks against obstruction. An exasperated majority can bring debate to an end by a closure motion, though French parliamentary tradition does not allow this procedure to be used as a governmental weapon in the House of Commons manner.[31] Other rules have been steadily tightened up. The right to call for *scrutins publics à la tribune*, once a very effective obstructive weapon, was first limited and then eliminated. Interpellations and urgent discussions can now come before the house only on the proposition of the Presidents' Conference. Counting out the house was made less effective by an alteration of the quorum rules (briefly delayed by difficulties over obtaining a quorum). Restrictions were imposed on the use of dilatory motions, such as the previous question. Moreover such motions may be debated by only four speakers—the minister, the representative of the committee concerned, one private member in favour of the proposal, and one against it.

The same restriction also applies to amendments to bills. But, since the President has no power to select amendments for discussion, obstruction could still be carried on by putting down very large numbers of them. Occasionally, as in the case of the bill for the maintenance of order in November 1947, the government has dealt with this by the drastic method of moving the rejection *en bloc* of all amendments. In March 1952 a more permanent attempt to meet this form of obstruction was made by the institution of ' restricted debate '. This can be applied for by the committee dealing with a bill, after an exceptionally full discussion and the submission of a supplementary report. The procedure involves the abandonment of the general discussion (equivalent to the second reading debate in Britain), the limitation of amendments to those which had already been put forward in committee, the restriction of the right to speak on the final vote to one member of each party, and the limitation of all speeches to five minutes.

---

[30] *J.O.*, 3 March 1950, pp. 1859–81 (M. Lamps' speech): 25 March 1952, pp. 1459–60 (M. Ballanger's speech): 27 March 1952, p. 1528 (M. Loustanau-Lacau's speech). The Communists had spoken 75,000 lines, the R.P.F. 42,000, and the other four major groups about 48,000 each. It is arguable that the isolation of the Communists justified their speaking longer than majority members.

[31] Lidderdale, pp. 137–8.

Restricted debate cannot be applied to bills on matters of first-class importance.[32] For these, the most effective method is the 'organization' of a debate, as in the Congress of the United States. This is decided on by the Assembly, on the proposal of the Presidents' Conference, which estimates the total time needed for the debate and then allocates it between the government, the committees concerned, and the various parties, with an allowance for divisions. Though members are not always checked when their party's time is up, this is an invaluable time-saving device. A proposal was made in March 1952 to organize all debates not subject to the 'restricted' procedure, but the Assembly rejected it.[33]

The most effective of all forms of obstruction consists, not in delaying individual debates, but in upsetting the order of business. The government has no control over the Assembly's agenda, unless it is prepared (like M. Queuille in May 1951, or M. Pinay in December 1952) to stake its existence on a demand for priority for its business. But a government which uses its heavy weapons too often is likely to discover that they wear out quickly. The deputies' inveterate habit of postponing uncomfortable subjects, like the budget, in order to debate popular topics, such as higher pensions, is a serious weakness of French parliamentary practice, and a godsend to the obstructionists.[34]

3. FUNCTIONS

THE National Assembly performs the same functions as most other parliaments, and in the first place that of controlling the government. Under Article 45 it elects the prime minister: under Article 48 he and

---

[32] Bills on constitutional, electoral, financial, and certain judicial matters, amnesty bills, treaty ratification bills, laws referred back for reconsideration by the President of the Republic or by the Constitutional Committee, and proposals to revise the standing orders of the Assembly cannot be dealt with by a restricted debate. (S.O. 38 *quater*.) The device was used less than its authors had hoped: only 8 restricted debates were held between March 1952 and July 1953.

[33] For example the debate on family allowances on 9 May 1951 was organized. The Presidents' Conference allotted an hour for voting, and five and a half hours for debate. The Finance committee and the Agriculture committee had 20 minutes each; so did all the other committees together. The only one involved was the Health committee, which opposed the proposed means of financing the increased allowances. The government was given 30 minutes, the Communists 50, M.R.P. 44, the Socialists 29, and the other eight groups 15 each. *J.O.*, 9 May 1951, p. 4903.

In that case time was distributed between the groups in rough proportion to their numbers. But this is not always so. The debate on reform of the standing orders on 27 March 1952 had nine hours allotted to it—two for voting, and seven for debate. As this was considered a matter for the legislature only, the government took no part. The Franchise and Standing Orders Committee had an hour to defend its proposals, and the Communists, the only group wholly opposed to them, 2¼ hours to put their case. The remaining larger groups had times varying from an hour to 15 minutes, and the small ones 5 minutes each. *J.O.*, 27 March 1952, p. 1500.

These arrangements are often only loosely enforced. An extreme case occurred on 11 April 1951, when twelve hours were spent on a debate on civil expenditure, to which the Presidents' Conference had allotted only 2½ hours. *J.O.*, 10 April 1951, p. 3037, to 11 April 1951, p. 3171; *Le Monde*, 13 April 1951.

[34] Compare p. 208 with pp. 241–2.

his ministerial colleagues are individually and collectively responsible to it. Articles 49 and 50 prescribe the procedure for formally voting confidence or censure. For day-to-day purposes, the Assembly's control is exercised by means of questions and interpellations, and above all through the work of its committees.[35]

The legislative authority of the National Assembly is almost complete. Members of the Council of the Republic are permitted to introduce bills, but these must be sent at once to the Assembly, without prior discussion in the upper house. The latter cannot delay any bill desired by a majority of the Assembly for longer than two months, and in many cases the period is much shorter. Financial proposals must be initiated in the Assembly. Many treaties must be ratified by it, under Article 27, and can be denounced only with its consent, under Article 28. (The list is much the same as in the Third Republic, though treaties dealing with international organization have been added.)[36] Bills for the ratification of treaties cannot be amended, but discussion of them can be adjourned by a motion drawing specific attention to the clauses to which objection is taken. Under Article 7, a declaration of war must be voted by the Assembly; the Council of the Republic must have been consulted, though it need not consent. Amendments to the constitution can be passed only by a special procedure. Unless the Assembly votes them by a two-thirds majority they require the consent of the Council of the Republic, and usually also of the electorate by means of a referendum.[37]

The quantity of parliamentary business has increased greatly under the Fourth Republic. Less than 4,000 texts (bills, resolutions, reports, etc.) were presented for parliamentary discussion in the Chamber which expired in 1914, and only 7,000 in the one which ended in 1936. But in the first legislature of the Fourth Republic there were over 12,000, and in the first year of the second legislature, more than 4,000.

---

[35] See above, pp. 178–85, for the election of the prime minister: below, Ch. 14, for votes of confidence and censure, and for interpellations: Ch. 15, for committees. On the whole subject see E. Blamont, ' Les conditions du contrôle parlementaire,' *R.D.P.*, 1950, pp. 387 ff.

Questions may be written or oral; the latter play a much less important part than they do in the House of Commons. Ten are answered every Friday, and others at one sitting in each month. The minister has five minutes to answer, and the questioner the same time to reply to him: no one else may speak. During 1951, 209 oral questions were put down, of which 107 had been answered by the end of the year.

[36] Treaties of peace, commercial treaties, those affecting the finances of the state, or the personal rights and property of Frenchmen abroad, those altering French domestic legislation, and those affecting international organization require ratification by the Assembly. Treaties adding, abandoning, or exchanging territory require both the ratification of the Assembly and the consent of the peoples concerned. Commercial treaties, alone of the categories enumerated, can be denounced without the consent of the Assembly being required.

[37] On the powers of the Council of the Republic, see below, pp.' 273–6: on financial proposals, below, pp. 257–61 : on treaty ratification bills, S.O. 69, and Lidderdale, *op. cit.*, pp. 202–3: on constitutional amendments, below, pp. 287–8.

Between 1938 and 1951 the *Journal officiel*, in which the debates of the old Chamber and new Assembly are recorded, quadrupled in size.[38]

Private members' bills play a much more important part in France than they do in Britain. In the 1947 session they accounted for three-quarters of all the bills introduced, and for one quarter of those passed;[39] the proportions were much the same in the first session of the 1951 legislature. Many French private members' bills deal with subjects of local or individual concern, which in Britain would be treated under the quite different form of procedure used for 'private bills'. As in Britain, most of the private members' bills which reach the statute book are uncontroversial. In the 1947 session, two-thirds of those passed went through under what is virtually an unopposed bills procedure, which involves no debate in the Assembly.[40]

Another important function of the Assembly is electoral. The President of the Republic is elected by the Assembly and the Council of the Republic, sitting together at Versailles, as in the Third Republic he was elected by the Chamber and Senate together. The Assembly also chooses part of the Constitutional Committee, under Article 91, part of the High Council of the Magistrature, under Article 83, and the whole High Court of Justice, under Article 38.[41]

Article 6 of the constitution permits the Assembly to choose, by proportional representation, up to one-sixth of the members of the Council of the Republic. Under the Council's original electoral law, passed in 1946, this right was fully exercised. But when an entirely new electoral law for the upper house was voted in 1948, the Assembly waived its claim, and since that date it has elected only seven members of the Council.[42] The deputies sitting for France proper also choose two-thirds (sixty-eight) of the metropolitan representatives in the Assembly of the French Union. Other powers of the Assembly include that of amnesty, which under Article 19 can be granted only by law: setting up committees of inquiry with extensive powers, to inves-

---

[38] 3,908 texts in 1910–14: 7,279 in 1932–36: 12,388 in 1946–51. Of the latter, 1,500 were government bills (*projets de loi*); 4,800 were private members' bills (*propositions de loi*), 900 of them from senators; 2,300 were private members' motions, and 3,800 were committee reports. The *Journal officiel* recording the debates of the lower house had 2,323 pages in 1938, 10,304 in 1951, 7,084 in 1952 and slightly more in 1953.

[39] Lidderdale, pp. 178–9.

[40] Under this procedure the effective examination of the bill takes place in committee. There is no debate in the Assembly, which simply votes in turn on each clause, and then on the whole bill. In the 1947 session 48 of the 66 private members' bills passed, and 90 of the 207 government bills went through in this way. Any deputy may object to a bill passing through without debate, but in practice, in the 1946–51 legislature, three-quarters of the objections came from the government (which can declare its opposition at an earlier stage). *J.O.*, 25 March 1952, p. 1464 (M. André Mercier's speech). See S.O.'s 36–38, and Lidderdale, pp. 201–2.

On the subject-matter of private members' bills, see below, p. 257 n.

[41] See below, pp. 289, 301, 305.

[42] See below, p. 271 n.

tigate current problems or scandals: [43] and preferring impeachments against ministers or (for treason only) against the President of the Republic.[44]

4. CHARACTERISTICS

IN the period immediately after liberation, parliamentary life in France seemed to have been completely transformed. The three largest parties, all strictly disciplined, worked together in the government, which was always assured of the support of three-quarters of the Assembly, and sometimes of a still larger proportion. But this support depended on the agreement of the three main parties. Government policy was simply the highest common factor of their respective programmes. Once this was settled, party discipline ensured that the Assembly would pass the government's measures as effectively as in Britain. The political problem resolved itself into reaching and maintaining inter-party agreement. Parliamentary debate atrophied. The result of divisions was rigidly determined beforehand, echoing the decisions of the party executives. Members applauded in unison at a signal from their leaders. If an unexpected development occurred, the sitting would be suspended to allow the different parties to meet and negotiate. The Assembly became a place where decisions were registered, not where they were made.[45]

The breach with the Communists in 1947 put an end to this situation. With the revival of a strong opposition, often able to attract voting support from the opposite political extreme against governments of the centre, the paralysing effect of near-unanimity disappeared. The differences between the M.R.P. leaders and their followers, the revival in the country of the ill-disciplined Radicals and Conservatives, and the growth of internal divisions within the main parties under the pressure

---

[43] Such a committee was established on 17 January 1950 to investigate the 'affair of the generals' (see my article in the *Cambridge Journal*, May 1951). It was composed of twelve members, four nominated by each of the committees of Defence, Justice, and the Interior. This procedure was originally, it seems, adopted to keep the Communists off the committee, but second thoughts prevailed, and it was decided to be more prudent to elect one of them as a member.

This committee, like most of its predecessors, was dominated by party politics. The Communist member released confidential documents to *L'Humanité*, the Gaullist chairman and two sympathetic colleagues interviewed an important witness unknown to the rest of the committee, and eventually several members resigned: after their replacement, the committee consisted only of M.R.P. and Socialists (who were constantly at cross-purposes) and the solitary Communist.

On the whole subject, see P. Biays, 'Les commissions d'enquête parlementaires,' *R.D.P.* 1952, pp. 443–86. A committee has since been set up to investigate exchange dealings with Indo-China; and cf. *R.D.P.*, 1953, pp. 1028–9, for a law making their proceedings secret.

[44] On impeachments, see below, pp. 305–6.

[45] The best account of parliamentary life at this period is by Léo Hamon, 'Le régime parlementaire de la IVe République'.... *Politique*, June 1947, to which this section owes much. See also Hamon, 'La fin du régime de quasi-unanimité,' *Politique*, July 1947: Goguel, 'Les partis politiques dans la IVe République', *ibid.*, October 1947: and below, pp. 359–60.

of opposition criticism, all contributed to restore reality to parliamentary sittings. With the major parties working against each other instead of in uneasy harmony, the votes of the minor groups acquired real importance. The familiar Third Republic situation of small, precarious majorities became the rule again. Surprises were once more possible, and after the 1951 election the Assembly frequently took decisions (such as the easy ratification of the Schuman plan, or the election to the premiership of M. Pinay) which were quite contrary to the expectations of the best-informed observers.

Even in the days of *tripartisme* and party domination, the parliamentary regime retained real political importance. It was a gross exaggeration to say that the deputies could quite as well have been replaced by a small group of party delegates, equipped with card votes according to their party's size. For parliamentary life is not confined to the actual sittings of the house. Interest indeed shifted from the Assembly itself to the committees, the party meetings, and the cabinet, where relations between the parties could be discussed without publicity and its attendant friction. But Parliament retained its importance as a means of bringing the criticisms of the electorate to bear on the administration, and as a melting-pot in which different sections of the electorate made contact through their representatives.

In a country as regionally divided as France, the geographical melting-pot is as important as the social. The deputy maintains very close contact with his constituency: he receives on the average about thirty constituents' letters a day, and may devote as much as half his working time to dealing with them.[46] Provincial members usually spend the weekend in their departments, and often the weekend is a long one, from Friday to Tuesday. Parliament has been compared to the barrack-room as an arena where natives of different parts of the country, and indeed of the French Union, meet and mix.[47] To the sophisticated Parisian this means little. But the horizon of the Catholic peasant from Brittany, or of the Socialist schoolteacher from the Midi, is often extremely limited. In the lobby he makes contact, perhaps only for the second time, with ' foreigners ' from other regions, and with ' enemies ' who profess other faiths. He discovers that their personal problems are not unlike his own. He learns the need for compromise between rival groups, rival interests, even rival ideals. The parliamentary lobby makes a real contribution to the unity of the country.

For interchange between different social groups it is less effective. Many of the most valuable contacts occur within the party groups,

---

[46] See two informative articles in *Le Figaro*, 27 and 28 March 1950. France, like other countries, possesses its epistolary lunatics: one Gaullist member receives a weekly letter from an enthusiast who believes that national salvation lies in paying 50 per cent. of all wages in the form of tickets for the *Loterie Nationale*.
[47] Hamon, *loc. cit.*, June 1947, pp. 389–90.

whose membership is more variegated geographically than socially. The rigidity of some parties creates ideological barriers between members who differ in politics. Above all, most deputies are drawn from a restricted range of occupations. Fifty years ago Bodley remarked on the unrepresentative character of the Chamber, pointing out that half its members came from the scanty professional class, and that agriculture, industry and commerce, in which five-sixths of the electorate were employed, provided only a fifth of the deputies. In the 1946 Assembly this disproportion was reduced, but still evident. A majority of members, 281 out of 544, were professional men, and only 204, three-eighths of the total, came from agriculture, trade and industry. Moreover, if the Communists are omitted, since they exclude themselves from the parliamentary *camaraderie*, the disproportion is much more marked. In Bodley's day the lawyers alone outnumbered agriculture, trade and industry together. In 1946, among the 378 non-Communist members, there were still more lawyers than workers and peasants (69 against 62), and more teachers than businessmen (57 against 54). And the 1951 election marked a reaction from the comparatively broadly-based assemblies of the liberation period towards the less representative Chambers of the Third Republic.[48]

The most striking feature of the day-to-day working of the Assembly is the degree of freedom on which it insists in the conduct of its business. No authority is strong enough to exercise effective power within it. The position of the government is far weaker than that of a British ministry, since without a coherent majority at its back, it can never be sure of the support of its nominal followers. This support must be forthcoming at every sitting if the government is to get its business through: and a disgruntled party or group is as likely to rebel on questions of parliamentary priority as on issues of substance. There are moreover some questions, such as the reform of parliamentary procedure, or immunity cases, with which the government is not supposed to concern itself: by custom it does not intervene in the debates on them, and individual ministers do not vote.

The Presidents' Conference is as little able to impose its will as the government. A collection of three dozen committee and party chairmen may well not be representative of the Assembly as a whole. Indeed, since opposition members now often obtain less than their share

---

[48] Bodley, ii, pp. 155–163. Husson, ii, p. xxx. (Overseas members omitted.)
In the Assembly elected in 1951, 56 per cent. of all the deputies were drawn from the professional classes, 15 per cent. from business, 14 per cent. from agriculture, and 13 per cent. from the working class. Each of these proportions was within 1 per cent. of the corresponding figure in the 1936 Chamber. The only important differences in detail were the decline of law, from 21 per cent. to 14 per cent., and the increase of civil servants (including teachers), from 16 per cent. to 22 per cent. 1936 figures quoted in *A Constitution for the Fourth Republic* (Foundation for Foreign Affairs, Washington, 1948, anon.), p. 82. Those for 1951 in *Le Monde*, 6 July 1951. See also F. Goguel, *Esprit*, June 1953, p. 855n.; and *Les Élections législatives*, pp. 55–6.

of committeee chairmanships, the conference is likely to be unrepresentative, exaggerating the real strength of government parties. As a consequence, the Assembly frequently upsets its proposals, wasting a good deal of time in the process. The opposition groups tried in 1952 to secure proportional representation in the conference, but this proposal was defeated: one of the arguments used against it was that the prestige and authority of the conference would be so strengthened by such a reform that it would be difficult for the Assembly to repudiate its conclusions, as the house ought to be in a position to do.[49] While this attitude prevails, attempts to restrict through standing orders the right to change the agenda can be only partially effective.[50]

Even in the course of the individual sittings, the Assembly is unwilling to be restrained. The position of the President is far weaker than that of the Speaker of the House of Commons. He is treated with respect, but not with deference. Members often contest his decisions, for example by continuing to speak when warned that they are out of order. He can warn, but not impose penalties without the sanction of the house. It is almost impossible for him to check irrelevance, the cardinal sin of parliamentary debate in France.[51] The Assembly is as reluctant as the old Chamber to allow him to set binding precedents. It insists on taking all important procedural decisions itself, and since these are settled by a temporary and political majority, their moral authority for the future is limited.[52] M. Blum argued passionately in 1919 for a change in the tradition of chairmanship, and for the establishment of a position of real authority for the President, as the most important need of the French Parliament. His plea is still valid to-day.[53]

Because of its unwillingness to accept the leadership of any authority, the Assembly is in constant danger of falling into chaos. It undertakes

---

[49] *J.O.*, 27 March 1952, pp. 1542–3 (M. Defos du Rau's speech). Earlier in the same sitting, an attempt was made to empower a committee, consisting of the vice-presidents of the Assembly and the standing committee chairmen, to decide the priority of bills in committee. But it received only R.P.F. and Conservative support. (*Ibid.*, pp. 1507–8.)

[50] In 1948, because of the amount of time wasted on these discussions, it was decided that only one member of each party might speak, and only for five minutes; and that a proposal to change the agenda, after the Assembly had accepted it, could be made only by the government, a committee, or 30 members from three different groups (hitherto any fifty members could make such a proposal, so that the Communists could do it when they chose), and must be voted by an absolute majority. From October 1950, proposals to change the agenda by adding an interpellation, a debate on a subject on which the committee's report is not yet available, or an urgent discussion, might not be made at all, and no changes might be made after the agenda had been voted by the Assembly. These restrictions proved unenforceable in practice, partly because of the attempt to settle business too far ahead.

[51] Lidderdale, pp. 151, 155–6.

[52] *Ibid.*, p. 77.

[53] '. . . il ne s'introduit dans le débat que pour ces gestes supérieurs et ces sanctions rituelles. Qu'on entame à la fois quatre discussions différentes, qu'on bouleverse à la dernière minute un ordre du jour, qu'on recommence pour la dixième fois le même discours, qu'on remette en cause sous une autre forme une question déjà tranchée, qu'on

far too many different tasks at the same time, and finds itself obliged to leave many of them, unfinished, to be resumed after long intervals. For example at the beginning of April 1951, with the general election approaching, the Assembly's agenda still included the constitutional revision proposals passed in the previous November: two major bills of which about half the clauses had been passed, and four more which had been begun and then abandoned (mostly during the previous six months, but one of them as far back as December 1949): 140 bills adopted by the committees concerned, but not yet discussed by the Assembly, three-quarters of them opposed measures: and the budget, already three months overdue, the credits for twelve government departments still needing to be voted.[54] The bitterly contentious electoral law for metropolitan France had still to be dealt with on its return from the Council of the Republic, and that for the overseas territories had not yet been begun. But the government had the utmost difficulty in inducing the Assembly to give priority to the measures (budget and electoral law) which had to be passed if a general election were to take place before the summer holidays.

The history of the procedure for urgent discussion is a significant example of the weaknesses of French parliamentary procedure. This method of obtaining priority for a particular bill was used to such an excessive extent that an actual majority of bills went through under it, and it became the normal instead of the exceptional legislative process (with serious repercussions on relations between the two houses).[55] In 1948, therefore, its use was restricted, so that it could not be employed without the consent of the government and of the relevant committee, or of one of them supported by the Assembly itself. This did little to restrict the flow of demands for urgent discussions, and forced the Assembly to waste much time voting on them when the committee and the government disagreed.[56] Consequently, in 1950, a further change required all such requests to be sponsored by the Presidents' Conference, and all the discussions themselves to take place on Fridays. This effectively discouraged the use of the procedure, by

---

égare une controverse dans la plus oiseuse digression, il ne dira rien, il n'a rien à dire, rien ne l'oblige même à écouter. . . . Ce qu'il faut avant tout, à la Chambre, c'est une autre sorte de président, dont la mission propre soit de défendre le temps et le travail de la collectivité délibérante, de la protéger contre la répétition, la digression, le piétinement, contre tout ce qui décourage de l'attention et de l'effort. Non plus un président arbitraire, mais un président conducteur du débat, assumant résolument l'autorité que la Chambre ne demande qu'à lui reconnaître, l'autorité morale de direction, l'autorité de police rationnelle. Qu'on rompe avec la tradition, voilà tout. Il le faut, mais cela suffit.' *La Réforme gouvernementale*, pp. 171–2.

[54] *Le Monde*, 1 April 1951.
[55] See below, p. 275, .
[56] A valid committee vote in favour of urgency needed the support of an absolute majority of members; but a committee which gave no opinion was assumed to have tacitly accepted the demand for urgency. This latter presumption was reversed by the 1950 rules.

making it frequently slower than the normal: there was even an exceptional case of one bill under the urgency procedure appearing on Friday after Friday for no less than six months. In 1952 M.R.P. proposed simply to abolish the whole procedure, but their suggestion was not accepted by the Assembly.[57]

In refusing to accept a minimum of discipline in the conduct of parliamentary business, the deputies stultify themselves. Their attention is constantly distracted to minor matters instead of being concentrated on the main aspects of policy, which in practice frequently escape from their control. When the Assembly recessed in July 1953, it had held no debate on European, North African, or Indo-Chinese affairs for more than a year.[58] Nor, when such debates do take place, do they always give much useful guidance to the government.[59] In domestic policy matters are made still worse by the extraordinary confusion between the respective spheres of parliamentary and of administrative responsibility: the legislature has to decide how many donkeys are to be kept in the national stud, but the currency can be devalued, or the Monnet plan adopted, without reference to Parliament. This absurd situation is, in part, a direct consequence of the inefficiency with which the Assembly insists that its affairs shall be managed.[60]

In 1919 M. Blum delivered a stinging criticism of the state of parliamentary business, on the grounds of bad arrangement of time, unreal debating, speaking for the constituency instead of the audience, and admitted incapacity to carry the necessary legislation.[61] His attack had lost none of its force thirty years later. The need for drastic changes

---

[57] *J.O.*, 27 March 1952, pp. 1575–6. Cf. *ibid.*, 25 March, p. 1461, M. Lecourt's speech: ' Quant à la procédure d'urgence elle est, dans la plupart des cas, le meilleur moyen de retarder le vote d'un texte. C'est une procédure plus lente que les autres.'

[58] It had however discussed the main lines of policy in five investiture debates during the preceding weeks. But these occasions, in which the prospective premier appears without colleagues or staff to answer a confused succession of questions great and trivial, are no substitute for orderly parliamentary discussion.

[59] In its last debate on Tunisia, in June 1952, the Assembly rejected six *ordres du jour* in succession, and it proved impossible to find any majority at all. *A.P.*, 1952, pp. 228–9. But this incoherence was no new fault of the Fourth Republic; as M. Mitterrand reminded the anti-parliamentary critics, in 1881 the Chamber had rejected 23 *ordres du jour* in a debate on the same subject. *J.O.*, 4 June 1953, p. 2952.

[60] Cf. the criticisms of M. Goguel in *Fourth Republic*, pp. 167–9, and in *Esprit*, June 1953, pp. 853–61.

[61] ' Prenons les travaux de la Chambre pendant une semaine quelconque, et nous retrouverons, du plus au moins, les mêmes vices permanents d'organisation et de méthode. Deux ou trois questions engagées à la fois alternent d'une séance à l'autre. Pour chacune, des amendements sans nombre, des orateurs sans fin prolongeant d'interminables discours au milieu de l'apathie universelle, très peu de députés dans la salle, écrivant leur correspondance électorale, lisant ou redigeant un rapport. ... Sous l'effet du moindre incident l'Assemblée passera brusquement de l'indifférence à l'excitation et au tapage. Mais ce vide et cette indifférence ne dégoûtent aucunement les orateurs; bien au contraire, le nombre s'en multiplie. Puisqu'ils ne risquent pas d'être entendus, ils en parlent pour *l'Officiel* et pour leur circonscription. ... Le président est à son fauteuil, le ministre intéressé à son banc; de temps en temps ils lèvent les yeux d'un dossier ou d'un livre pour échanger un regard découragé. ...' *Op. cit.*, pp. 158–9.

With this may be compared M. Lecourt's speech mentioned in note 57.

in parliamentary methods was admitted by all parties, and many political leaders felt that reform of the Assembly's standing orders could do more for the health of French democracy than reform of the constitution itself. More urgent still, however, was the need for the deputies of the majority to accept, in their own interests, enough direction to make the orderly arrangement of business possible. The successive changes of standing orders did something to cope with the various devices of Communist obstruction, usually, and inevitably, by restricting the rights of the individual member. But they could not deal with the root of the trouble while the majority of deputies insisted on preserving the right to change their minds and repudiate their leaders whenever they chose, however disastrous the consequences to the rational conduct of the Assembly's affairs. The real deficiency was one of will, rather than of technical devices, and it was the absence of any common purpose among the parties of the majority which gave the obstructionists the opportunities they used so skilfully.

Chapter 14

THE ASSEMBLY AND THE GOVERNMENT

THE central feature of any democratic constitution is the relationship between executive and legislature. The broad lines of American federal politics are set by the separation of powers, and the details turn largely on the means by which politicians reconcile what the Founding Fathers put asunder. In Great Britain, the House of Commons is nominally omnipotent, but its power is restrained or even nullified by the rigidity of party discipline. In France, the theoretical authority of the legislature over the executive responsible to it is not frustrated in this way. The details of the constitutional settlement therefore retain great importance in the day-to-day working of the system.

1. CONFIDENCE AND CENSURE: THE THEORY

IN the Third Republic, Chamber and government each possessed means of influencing the behaviour of the other. The Chamber controlled the government through its committees, and especially through its detailed examination of the budget. On day-to-day matters it also possessed the powerful and much used weapon of interpellation, the right to call upon a minister for an explanation of his actions. The government's means of influencing the Chamber were less effective. It could treat a particular decision as a matter of confidence: this instrument was frequently used, but it could easily lead to the overthrow instead of to the success of the ministry. In the background was the power to dissolve the Chamber, which the President of the Republic could exercise with the consent of the Senate. But after 1877 the right of dissolution was never used, and the government's position as against the Chamber was in consequence seriously weakened.

The constitution of the Fourth Republic endeavoured to regulate the relations of government and Assembly in Articles 49, 50, and 51. These attempt to restrict and formalize the use of the question of confidence, to ensure that a ministry can be overthrown only when the Assembly has clearly and deliberately turned against it, and to make the executive's power of dissolution depend upon the use by the legislature of its right to upset governments. This experiment has proved the least successful of all the constitutional innovations of the Fourth Republic. It has failed both through a fundamental confusion of purpose, and through inapplicability to the contemporary political situation of France.

Governments in the Third Republic, weak in relation to the Chamber, frequently had to make constant use of the question of confidence in order to get their way at all. It was employed on the most trivial occasions. In 1928 one minister, anxious that a debate on his department's policy should not be deferred, put the question of confidence against its postponement for a single hour, though the prime minister was so little disposed to stake his government's existence on this point that he later agreed to some days' delay.[1] The Chamber was thus encouraged to treat the question of confidence lightly; knowing that the life of a government was certain to be short, deputies were tempted to vote irresponsibly, and increased the turnover of ministries still further by occasionally upsetting one by accident. Thus in 1924 a minister put the vote of confidence on a clause in a pensions bill which he was piloting through the Chamber; a hundred deputies in the Chamber cast the proxy votes of four hundred absent colleagues; the cabinet was defeated by a majority of seven; and the prime minister, who had been attending a parliamentary committee without knowing what was happening in the house, was informed that his government had fallen.[2]

The traditional suspicion of the administration deprived it of the benefit of any doubt. A politician anxious to continue his ministerial career in the future had to retain the goodwill of the Chamber. This would be forfeited at once if he were suspected of attempting to cling to office after the house had turned against him. So the most successful political leaders were those who were careful to resign at the least indication that their parliamentary credit was nearing exhaustion.[3]

The most dangerous weapon in the Chamber's hands was the interpellation. This is a short debate on the actions of a minister, great or trivial, which is initiated by a private member, and answered by the minister responsible. It bears a slight resemblance to the daily adjournment motion in the House of Commons, with the crucial difference that it is closed by a vote, in which the Chamber passes a motion expressing in terms of greater or less warmth its attitude to the government's policy. A politician could, as Clemenceau did, build a parliamentary reputation almost exclusively on the skilful use of this procedure. Half the governments overthrown by the Chamber fell on interpellations: the risk was so well recognized that deputies and even ministers often decided their behaviour more on a calculation of the probable composition of the next ministry than on an assessment of the policy of the threatened one.[4]

The interpellation was a dangerous weapon because it was negative. Begun by the fortuitous initiative of an individual member, it could

---

[1] Jacques Meyer, *La Question de confiance*, pp. 17–9.
[2] Lidderdale, p. 37.
[3] Soulier, pp. 239, 248.
[4] *Ibid.*, pp. 332, 342, 345. His estimates suggest that out of forty ministries defeated in the Chamber between 1879 and 1938, twenty fell on interpellations (Preface, page c).

easily lead to the defeat of the government by an accidental combination of opposites, which agreed in attacking the existing administration, but could not work together to provide a new one. Yet the procedure was an expression, or at most an aggravation, of ministerial instability—not a cause of it. A government with a disciplined majority could always deal with the interpellation nuisance by refusing to debate dangerous motions. The *Délégation des gauches*, the steering committee of the anti-clerical majority at the turn of the century, adopted this method with complete success, since the parties supporting it were willing to obey the recommendations of their leaders.[5] And after 1914 the number of interpellations increased, and the importance of the subjects raised declined, to such an extent as seriously to impair their effectiveness.[6]

The new constitution attempted to enforce a complete break with these traditions. The Socialist leaders, who largely inspired it, had long deplored the behaviour of deputies and governments alike. The use of the question of confidence to coerce the Chamber into accepting the will of the government on trivial points was in their view a distortion of the constitution. But they equally regretted the tendency of the deputies to upset ministries on insignificant issues. Their constitutional doctrine flowed from an entirely different conception of the relationship between legislature and executive. They wanted to see the development of a strong party system like the British. This would transform the political system, so that Chamber and government, instead of constituting two rival powers, would become two complementary instruments of a common purpose. The government would not need to coerce a majority which fully shared its objectives. The majority, whose policy was being put into operation by the executive, would not wish to upset the ministry on trivial points in order to replace it with another one differing only in detail. Majority and government alike would normally survive, as in Britain, from the beginning to the end of the life of the legislature.[7] Only a drastic division of opinion among the supporters of the ministry could cause the overthrow of a government. This should be recorded in a formal motion of censure, by which the Assembly would register its deliberate change of mind. But it would do so at the price of its own dissolution. The threat of an automatic general election would work, as in Britain, to prevent irresponsible voting. The stability of government which France

---

[5] *Ibid.*, pp. 227–8, 237, 244.
[6] E. Blamont, ' Les conditions du contrôle parlementaire ', *R.D.P.*, 1950, pp. 389–90. Fewer interpellations are now discussed: cf. Campbell, *French Parliament*, *loc. cit.* (above, p. 191).
[7] Article 45 of the constitution begins by providing that, at the beginning of each new legislature, the President nominates a prime minister. Not until paragraph 4 does it bow to reality and admit that this must also be done in case of death, resignation, etc., of the prime minister in office. See A. Sauvageot, ' Le cabinet Ramadier et la pratique constitutionnelle ', *Revue politique et parlementaire*, No. 576 (March 1948).

needed would thus be reconciled with the tradition of legislative supremacy which she cherished.[8]

These conceptions, which had been sketched by M. Blum in 1936 and by M. Vincent Auriol under the occupation, inspired the law of 2 November 1945, of which the latter was the principal author. It established the constitutional regime during the provisional period while the new constitution was being drafted. Under this law, defeat on a specific vote of censure necessitated the resignation of the government, but the rejection of a bill or of an estimate did not. No means was provided whereby the ministry could stake its own existence on a vote of confidence. Within two months this omission had led to a head-on clash between the Socialist party and General de Gaulle. For the former proposed a reduction of military credits, to which the prime minister replied that he would treat the vote of the military budget as a matter of confidence. The Socialists protested that his action was unconstitutional. For the moment the quarrel was patched up, but it led directly to General de Gaulle's resignation three weeks later.[9]

The Socialists were trying to apply their constitutional ideas before the political basis for them had been created. Perhaps they were in any event inapplicable. Certainly they had misunderstood the British example from which they drew their inspiration. For M. Blum believed that a British government was unable to demand a vote of confidence from the House of Commons, and could be ejected only on a vote of censure proposed by the opposition.[10] But British governments, despite their coherent majorities and the tradition of executive authority, could not dispense with this weapon. France in 1945 had neither the coherent majority, nor the common purpose shared by majority and government, nor the tradition of invariably accepting the leadership of the government. In these circumstances, to deprive the executive of the right to make an issue a matter of confidence would have left it helpless before the pressure of the legislature, with no guarantee that the pressure would be exercised responsibly. Governmental stability of a sort might be achieved, for ministries would not fall. But they would have to trim their policy to every breeze of legislative feeling. They would retain office only by sacrificing all authority and all chance of carrying out a consistent policy. No government would hold office under conditions so intolerable.

---

[8] For the Socialist theory see Blum, especially pp. 150–3, 219–23: Auriol, vol. ii, pp. 50, 244, 249: Théry, pp. 188 ff.: Wright, pp. 85–9.

[9] On the points discussed in this paragraph see Théry, *loc. cit.*: J. Solal-Celigny, ' La question de confiance sous la IVe République ', *R.D.P.*, 1952, pp. 732–3.

[10] Blum, p. 222. This passage occurs in a section of the book originally written, not in 1919, but as newspaper articles in the 1930's. On 6 April 1936, in the very year in which *La Réforme gouvernementale* was re-issued, Mr. Baldwin's government resoundingly disproved M. Blum's argument by putting the question of confidence in order to compel the House of Commons to disavow its own recent vote in favour of equal pay for men and women teachers.

The Socialists were thus obliged to give way. The April draft constitution included, and the October constitution retained provision for the government to put the question of confidence. But this right, which was a concession to those who wished to give the ministry a means of defending itself against the Assembly, was still surrounded by conditions inspired by those who wished merely to give the Assembly a means of ridding itself of a government which it was no longer prepared to support. Nevertheless, though the exponents of the Socialist doctrine continued from time to time to express their point of view, in practice the vote of confidence has been used exclusively as a governmental weapon.[11]

Articles 49 and 50 endeavoured to make procedure reinforce, instead of undermining, the position of the ministry. The occasions on which its life was at stake were to be limited, defined, and brought to the attention of the deputies and of the country. They were limited by providing that the government need resign only if defeated on a vote of confidence tabled by the prime minister (Article 49), or on a vote of censure by the opposition (Article 50). The government's decision must be deliberate; the prime minister must consult the cabinet before putting the question of confidence. The deputies' vote must also be deliberate; one clear day must elapse between the putting of the question of confidence or censure, and the vote upon it. The vote must be held by public ballot, and the government need resign only if an absolute majority of the Assembly voted against it.

The last provision reflected the desire to ensure that the fall of a ministry should occur only through the deliberate decision of a clear majority of members. The prime minister must be installed by an absolute majority, and might be removed only in the same conditions. But this idea derived from the Socialist conception of the constitution, in which a government was expected to accept the will of the Assembly on minor points. It was in clear contradiction to the idea of the vote of confidence put by the government as a means to get its own policy accepted. The failure of this part of the constitutional experiment came largely from the confusion of purpose expressed in this provision.

This failure had two distinct aspects. Firstly, the machinery itself worked in an unexpected way: secondly, many governments fell without bringing the machinery into operation at all. The vote of confidence procedure had been formalized and surrounded with safeguards

---

[11] In June 1950 M. Lussy, chairman of the Socialist parliamentary group, reiterated his party's view, accusing the prime minister (M. Bidault) of using the question of confidence to deprive the Assembly of its essential prerogatives. *J.O.*, 24 June 1950, p. 5263.

For a non-Socialist statement of the same point of view see the speech of M. Giacobbi (a leading Radical admirer of General de Gaulle): *J.O.*, 16 May 1947, pp. 1656–7 (quoted Meyer, pp. 119, 127).

in order to ensure that the government would use it less prodigally, and the Assembly treat it less lightly, than had been usual in the Third Republic. These hopes did not materialize. The formal vote of confidence soon ceased to be a rare and solemn event, and was used with steadily increasing frequency. By its side there grew up the device of an unofficial question of confidence, by which the government, without employing the constitutional formula, simply warned the Assembly that it would resign if it did not get its way. This practice, which evaded all the constitutional safeguards, completed the return to the procedure of the Third Republic.

Moreover, questions of confidence and censure were not in fact used to record the views of the Assembly on major clashes of principle between government and opposition. The former, which came into operation at the demand of the ministry, was used mainly to coerce recalcitrant sections of the majority, and sometimes as a weapon of one majority party against another. The latter, which was supposed to be the supreme instrument of opposition criticism, has never been effectively employed at all.

In the second place, the attempt to promote government stability by means of constitutional reform failed completely. Article 51 provided that under certain conditions, after two cabinets had been defeated in the way envisaged in the preceding articles, the government might dissolve the Assembly.[12] It was hoped that by linking the fall of governments in this way with the power of dissolution, deputies would be restrained from irresponsibly overthrowing ministries. But governments proved unwilling to stay in office until ejected in due constitutional form. When defeated in the Assembly they resigned, whether or not there was an absolute majority against them. Many were not defeated at all, but fell apart owing to differences between the parties composing them. The conditions required for dissolution of the Assembly were never fulfilled, so that this restraint could not operate to discourage irresponsibility on the part of the members.

2. CONFIDENCE AND CENSURE: THE PRACTICE

THE increasing use of the formal question of confidence is easy to demonstrate. M. Ramadier put it 6 times in ten months of office. M. Schuman demanded 8 in eight months, though the last was never voted on. M. Marie did not use the formal vote of confidence in his one-month premiership, and M. Queuille put it only once, at the very beginning of his year in office. Thus in the first three years of the 1946–51 Assembly the question of confidence was put 15 times. In its remaining twenty months 31 questions of confidence were raised, and in the first two years of the new Assembly 54, though less than half

---

[12] See below, pp. 228–9.

of the latter were voted on.[13] Budgetary matters accounted for 23 of those in the first Assembly, and for 44 of those in the second.[14]

This great number of votes of confidence was made possible by a procedural decision taken in January 1948. The Schuman government wished to oppose forty amendments to the unpopular taxation programme proposed by the minister of Finance, M. René Mayer. To demand their rejection *en bloc* was to court defeat. To accept a day's delay on each of forty votes of confidence would have been disastrous to the government's programme. The amendments were therefore grouped according to the article and subject affected, and the question of confidence was put on each of five groups, all the votes being taken together after a single day's delay. This practice was used on many subsequent occasions; M. Edgar Faure put 20 votes of confidence on one day in February 1952 (but was defeated on the first of them). It gives much greater flexibility; when speed is not the essential consideration, a vote of confidence can be fixed for several days ahead, and further questions of confidence on the same subject arising during the interval can be taken at the same time.[15]

The delay rule was taken from the arrangements in force during the provisional government of 1945-46.[16] When the vote of confidence is put, the debate on that point is brought to a close. The vote cannot

---

[13] M. Bidault used the question of confidence 13 times. Eleven of these votes occurred on the budget, during his first three months of office, and two during the latter five months. On the last he was beaten—the first time a vote of confidence went against the government.

The first Pleven cabinet held 9 votes of confidence in 8 months. All but two of these were on the budget, and were concentrated into ten days (4 on 31 December 1950, and 3 on 8 January 1951). M. Queuille put 9, of which 7 were to obtain parliamentary priority for government business. One was on 18 April 1951, the rest between 28 April and 12 May.

In his second cabinet M. Pleven put 13; the last 9 were on the budget, and he was defeated on the second of them, so that the others were never voted on. M. Faure put 23, including 20 in one day on the budget; on the first of these he was beaten. M. Pinay demanded 17 formal votes of confidence. Ten were on his first budget, in April; 3 were on non-budgetary matters (2 on the sliding scale for wages, in June and July, one on the parliamentary agenda, in December); and 4 were on his second budget. He won the first of these, but resigned a fortnight later, just before the vote on the others. M. Mayer's first vote of confidence was in May, on his demand for special powers; he was defeated.

For full details (up to July 1952) see Solal-Celigny, *loc. cit.*, pp. 721-756. (He omits one vote, that of 1 December 1950). For complaints of the excessive use of the question of confidence in the Third Republic, see Soulier, pp. 114, 233, etc. In 1929-30, M. Tardieu put 60 votes of confidence in thirteen months of office, of which the Chamber was in recess for five. A. Tardieu, *Le Souverain captif*, p. 49. But this was an exceptional number.

[14] Solal-Celigny, *loc. cit.*, p. 733, completed to July, 1953. (And cf. Epilogue.)

[15] M. Queuille did this in trying to secure priority for the budget in May 1951. For the 1948 precedent see C. Colliard, ' La pratique de la question de confiance sous la IVe République ', *R.D.P.*, 1948, p. 230. On the flexible interpretation of the delay provision, see Solal-Celigny, *loc. cit.*, pp. 724-7.

[16] It was then two days and not one. At one time two days were envisaged for a vote of censure, one for a vote of confidence. (Meyer, p. 114.) Similar provisions were included in the Greek and Czech constitutions after the first world war, and had been suggested in France before 1939. Soulier, pp. 245-6.

The 1953 revision proposals substitute '24 hours' for 'one clear day '.

occur until one minute after the midnight of the *following* day: when haste was necessary, this time has often been chosen. Debate takes the form of five-minute ' explanations of one's vote '. The day's grace provides a breathing-space for the deputies to meditate on the dangers of a ministerial crisis (a somewhat theoretical possibility) and for mediators, including the President of the Republic, to work for compromise. The most celebrated success of this kind occurred in March 1947, on the very first vote of confidence under the new regime, when M. Ramadier threatened to resign unless the Communists voted for his Indo-China policy. But he accepted a precarious compromise, patched up by President Auriol during the day's grace, under which the Communist ministers voted with the government, while the rest of their party abstained. Within a few weeks, however, the Communists were out of office.[17]

A year later, in March 1948, the Schuman government was faced with a situation in which delay was to its disadvantage. A Communist proposal had been introduced directed against the taxes imposed so recently, and with so much difficulty, by M. René Mayer. The constitutional delay would mean waiting over a weekend, during which members would visit their constituencies, and it was feared that marginal deputies might be alarmed into voting against the government: as its majority turned out to be no more than 16, the danger was a real one. Moreover, General de Gaulle was to speak at Compiègne on the Sunday, and ministerial supporters did not wish him to be able to claim that his speech had either saved the government, or destroyed it. The formal question of confidence was therefore not put. Instead, the prime minister informed the Assembly that, if it accepted the Communist proposal, the government could no longer remain in office.[18]

M. Schuman used this method in order to evade the delay requirements of the constitution. But there were other circumstances in which it might be preferable to the constitutional formula. In September 1947, desiring to make the coal subsidy a matter of confidence although the cabinet had not been consulted, M. Ramadier warned that if he were defeated he ' would draw the necessary conclusions ' (though later the sitting was suspended to allow the cabinet to meet, and the question of confidence was formally put). Again, if the vote of confidence was really directed against a party in the government, relations might be less strained if the challenge were made implicit, rather than put in the constitutional form. In this way the Socialists

---

[17] *A.P.*, 1947, pp. 39–43.
In December 1949 the delay period enabled the Radical ministers to warn their party that they would resign office if the majority of Radical deputies voted against the government, whatever the result of the vote. *Le Figaro*, 24–25 December 1949. It also saved a government in December 1950 (*A.P.*, 1950, pp. 232–3), and ensured approval of the European army project in February 1952 (Solal-Celigny, *loc. cit.*, p. 729).
[18] *A.P.*, 1948, p. 326.

were induced to give way over civil service pay in July 1947. Over the Algerian government bill in the following month, the Socialist congress had formally objected to the use of the constitutional question of confidence, which would have broken up the government, so that only the unofficial form could be used.[19]

When the existence of the government is not at stake, the deputies are much more inclined to disregard its advice. A popular proposal to which the government objects, without putting the question of confidence, will often attract the almost unanimous support of the Assembly.[20] The unofficial question of confidence does much to check irresponsible voting of this kind, and it has the advantage of appearing less obviously an interference with the liberty of members. But there is a disadvantage also in this relative lack of publicity. For the question of confidence protects the individual deputy as well as the administration. It allows him to explain to critical constituents that he voted against their favourite proposal, not on its merits, but because the fate of the government was at stake as well. The more clearly and publicly this is brought out, the more effective is the vote of confidence in rallying deputies fearful of electoral consequences.[21] Moreover, a government which puts an unofficial question of confidence links its own existence to the specific issue on which the vote is taken, and defeat, even by a relative majority, entails its resignation. But in regulating the formal question of confidence Article 49 deliberately separates the fate of the government from that of the specific issue. If the ministry is defeated by less than an absolute majority, the proposal itself is lost, but the government is entitled, if it chooses, to remain in office, and one government has in fact done so in circumstances of this kind.[22]

---

[19] Colliard, *loc. cit.*, p. 222, on the coal subsidy, pp. 225–6 on the Algerian question. Meyer, p. 152, on the civil service.

[20] There are innumerable examples. In January 1949 the government was defeated on the petrol tax by 180 votes, in July on differential corn prices by 354, and in December on ex-service pensions by a unanimous vote of the Assembly. In May 1950 a railwaymen's bonus proposal was carried against the government by 541 to 27, and a motion on teachers' salaries by 540 to 27. In April 1951 an increase of 30 per cent. in family allowances was passed by 551 to 34, and in May the government's suggested method of financing increases in these allowances for agricultural workers was rejected by 470 to 36.

M. Pinay, beaten on his proposal for a fiscal amnesty, reversed the decision a few days later by making the question one of confidence. Solal-Celigny, *loc. cit.*, p. 727. But when he did not use this weapon, he too suffered massive defeats: cf. *A.P.*, 1952, pp. 74, 80, 83.

[21] Solal-Celigny, *loc. cit.*, pp. 736–7, discusses the advantages of the constitutional question of confidence, and points out that M. Pinay tried at first to avoid its use, but had to resort to it as opposition to his proposals increased.

[22] On 31 January 1950 the Bidault government demanded five votes of confidence on the budget. In four it succeeded, but on one its majority disappeared, the voting being 293 against 293. As a tie counts in French procedure as a negative result, the proposal was lost: but the government remained in office.

Up to the end of 1953 there was no case of a ministry retaining its position after being placed in a minority on a vote of confidence. Three cabinets had resigned after defeat by a relative majority (the two Schuman ministries, in July and September 1948, and the Faure ministry in March 1952).

These different considerations help to explain why some governments have preferred the official, and others the unofficial form of the question of confidence. The latter was used frequently by M. Schuman, and almost exclusively by MM. Marie and Queuille. It became such a recognized institution that in December 1948 the cabinet formally authorized the prime minister to call for an informal vote of confidence on the budget whenever he chose, and in the sitting of 21 December he did so three times. By the end of the Queuille ministry the constitutional procedure seemed to have become inoperative.[23]

But M. Queuille's reluctance to use it was a sign of strength. He was frequently authorized to do so by the cabinet,[24] but preferred to avoid unnecessary flourishes of the big stick, since he was able to get his way without them. M. Bidault, who succeeded him, was in a much weaker position, and needed every available means of defending himself. His budget was severely attacked, and its essential points were saved only by a drastic use of the question of confidence in its constitutional form. MM. Marie and Queuille, moreover, were Radicals, brought up in the traditions of the Third Republic. M. Bidault was a leader of M.R.P., and had no inhibitions about using his constitutional right to stay in office until ejected by an absolute majority of the Assembly. He remained undeterred when his majority fell to 6, to 4, and eventually to 0.[25]

There was a still more specific reason for the differing attitudes of the two men. Two government defeats in due constitutional form would make it possible to dissolve the Assembly and hold a general election. This prospect was most distasteful to the Radical party, which wished to change the electoral law in its own favour before an election took place, but for opposite reasons suited M.R.P., who found the existing electoral law more to its advantage than any likely alternative. Since defeat on a formal vote of confidence would bring a dissolution nearer, it was an ineffective weapon for a Radical prime minister confronted with recalcitrance on the part of M.R.P., but a most useful one for an M.R.P. prime minister to brandish over the heads of rebellious Radicals or Conservatives.[26]

---

[23] On M. Schuman's use of the unofficial vote of confidence, see Colliard, *loc. cit.*, pp. 226–7. On 16 June 1948 the cabinet decided not to put a formal vote of confidence on the ratification of the London agreements on Germany, but nevertheless to resign if defeated. *A.P.*, 1948, p. 95. M. Marie used the same device on the bill conferring special powers on the government to deal with the financial situation. M. Queuille used it on several occasions—notably the budget in December 1948, the petrol rationing scheme in May 1949, and the holiday bonus for social security employees in July. *A.P.*, 1948, pp. 133, 226 : 1949, pp. 325, 129.

The increased use of the formal vote of confidence by subsequent governments made the unofficial form less necessary, but it was revived under MM. Faure and Pinay.

[24] For example, on new taxes in September 1948, and in the aircraft industry debate in June 1949. *A.P.*, 1948, p. 157 : 1949, p. 98.

[25] See above, p. 219, n. 22, and *A.P.*, 1949, p. 223 : 1950, pp. 2–5.

[26] See below, p. 229, for the conditions in which the Assembly may be dissolved.

M. Bidault used the question of confidence eleven times to protect his budget against

In March 1951 M. Queuille was again prime minister. His government was weak, and had only one advantage. Its fall, with an election imminent and the budget several months late, would arouse great resentment against the party responsible, which could be expressed at an election in the immediate future. In these circumstances M. Queuille could make good use of the formal vote of confidence. In his earlier premiership, he had used it only once during the ten months in which the Assembly was sitting. In 1951 he employed it nine times in ten *weeks*.

After the general election, M. Pleven's government survived for several months without raising the question of confidence. But in this case its absence denoted weakness, not strength. To take sides on the Barangé bill for subsidizing church schools would have broken up the government. To put the question of confidence on the sliding scale bill, to which the government declared its hostility, would have been to court defeat; and when taunted by the R.P.F. for refusing to do so, M. Pleven simply declared that he would not play into their hands by producing an insoluble crisis from which they alone could benefit. To put it on the ratification of the Schuman plan meant reducing the impressiveness of the majority, since it obliged the Gaullists to cast a hostile vote: procedural reasons, however, at last obliged the prime minister to resort to it on this issue.[27]

The vote of confidence thus worked in entirely different ways in different political circumstances. M. Pleven changed an unofficial vote of confidence into an official one, over the austerity programme proposed by his minister of Finance, on the advice of the President of the Republic, who wished him to stay in office until defeated in the constitutional way.[28] His successor, M. Edgar Faure, had a motion on the European army withdrawn, after putting the official question of confidence on it, in order to attract support from the Socialist party.[29] An earlier Pleven government was severely shaken, in November 1950, by a debate on Indo-China in which it had a majority of 150 and the word 'confidence' was not mentioned, precisely because the majority had been obtained only at the price of omitting any expression of confidence from the resolution passed by the Assembly.[30] Confidence is a

---

Radical and Conservative opponents. But when he introduced a collective bargaining bill which M.R.P. and the Socialists wished to amend in drastic fashion, he allowed them to do so without putting the question of confidence, although the cabinet had authorized its use (*A.P.*, 1949, p. 203).

[27] *A.P.*, 1951, pp. 321–2. Solal-Celigny, *loc. cit.*, pp. 723, 735. On the procedural point see below, p. 222 n.

[28] *A.P.*, 1951, p. 287 : a remarkable illustration of the new rôle of the President (see Drago, *R.D.P.*, 1953, p. 166).

[29] Solal-Celigny, *loc. cit.*, p. 729.

[30] *A.P.*, 1950, pp. 229, 233. A general debate usually concludes with a motion, frequently lengthy, by which the Assembly, 'expressing its confidence in the government, passes to the order of the day.' Often 'concealing its mistrust of the government' would better express the feelings of the house; and despite the size of the majority, this was the impression conveyed on this occasion.

continuous relationship, which is reaffirmed or denied in every vote or incident. Ministers and deputies cannot be prevented by constitutional rules from drawing the conclusions from the evidence. If the Assembly has the will to keep a government in office, the constitution can prevent it from cutting the ministry's throat in a fit of absent-mindedness. But the paper provisions can never provide a substitute for political determination.[31]

Nor did the constitutional settlement succeed in concentrating attention on the straightforward clash between government and opposition. The arm of the government, the vote of confidence, was used or neglected according to tactical convenience, not as a method of underlining the importance of differences of principle between the ministry and its critics. The arm of the opposition, the vote of censure, was not effectively used at all.

Sometimes the vote of confidence was employed as a simple procedural manœuvre. The constitution required it to be held by public ballot. But until 1952 a public ballot could take one of two forms, the normal, with proxies allowed, or the *scrutin public à la tribune*, in which they were forbidden. The Assembly had decided that this procedure might not be used in cases where the issue was determined by the presence or absence of an absolute majority.[32] More than one government, threatened with a *scrutin public à la tribune* in which it feared defeat, had to demand a vote of confidence for the sole purpose of enabling proxies to be used.[33]

Frequently, the vote of confidence was used by one party supporting the government as a means of coercing another, or of shifting the blame for a ministerial crisis. An attempt to guard against this was made in the clause providing that the prime minister must consult the cabinet before putting the question of confidence. This provision made it difficult for him to use his power to favour one section of his majority against another, and it allowed the influence of the President of the

---

[31] See further comments in the Epilogue.
[32] The Communist demand for a *scrutin public à la tribune*, in order to prevent M. Moch's election as prime minister, was disallowed by the Assembly in October 1949. A similar demand, made to stop the Assembly overriding the Council of the Republic on electoral reform, was also disallowed in April 1951.
[33] Solal-Celigny, *loc. cit.*, pp. 735-6. Cf. *A.P.*, 1952, p. 19.
In May 1951 M. Queuille had been authorized in advance by the cabinet to put the question of confidence whenever necessary to secure the passage of the government's essential bills. Seeing the Communist benches filling up at 5 a.m. in an almost empty house, he correctly guessed that they had arranged to demand a snap vote without proxies, and outmanœuvred them by putting the question of confidence first. *Le Monde*, 2 May 1951. There was a similar incident two days later. *Le Monde*, 4 May.
In December, the Conservatives called for a vote without proxies over the Schuman plan, at a moment when many government supporters had departed to the Council of Europe at Strasbourg (or simply to bed). On this occasion the manœuvre had not been anticipated, and the unfortunate President of the Republic had to be roused from his sleep and driven forty miles into Paris in order to preside at the cabinet meeting which authorized the use of the question of confidence. *Le Monde*, 9-10 December 1951.

Republic, who presides at the cabinet meeting, to be made available to prevent abuse. But it occasionally deprived a prime minister of this means of defending his policy when, through misfortune or inadvertence, he had failed to ask the authorization of the cabinet for using it.[34]

But cabinet discussion could not altogether prevent political manœuvres of this kind, as the first year of the new constitution clearly showed. The first vote of confidence, in March 1947, was intended to force the Communist party to decide whether or not to observe the rules of ministerial solidarity. The second, in May, made it hard for the Socialists, who voted for the ministry, to carry out their previously expressed intention of leaving the cabinet whenever the Communists did so. In July, when the Socialists proposed increases in civil service wages, M.R.P. urged the prime minister to put the question of confidence against them; he was able to induce them to give way without taking this drastic step. Less than a month later the other government parties used the same weapon to make M.R.P. fall into line on the municipal election law. Having made concessions on this, M.R.P. wanted the Socialists threatened with a question of confidence over the Algerian government law, a course which the recent Socialist party congress had specifically condemned in advance. Again the prime minister (the Socialist M. Ramadier) was able to satisfy the other parties of his majority without openly defying his own. Their success on the Algerian question persuaded M.R.P. to vote confidence in the government on 5 September, over the coal subsidy, though they opposed its policy on the point at issue. Conversely, the Communists voted against the coal subsidy, of which they approved, in order to demonstrate their lack of confidence in the government.[35]

In February 1951 a government broke up over the use of the question of confidence. The Pleven ministry had produced a compromise electoral reform bill, which instituted a double ballot system, much disliked by M.R.P. On its introduction the prime minister put the question of confidence, but to appease M.R.P. agreed to accept the Assembly's decision on a private member's amendment in favour of a single ballot. The vote of confidence was passed on 28 February,

---

[34] Thus M. Ramadier was unable to use it in May 1947, and M. Queuille in April 1951. *J.O.*, 16 May 1947, p. 1657: 24 April 1951, p. 3867.

On occasion the sitting has been suspended to enable the cabinet to meet and authorize the prime minister to put the question of confidence, for instance on 16 July 1947 and on 2 September 1947. Once, on 20 February 1948, the requirement of cabinet authorization was simply violated. Colliard, *loc. cit.*, pp. 222–3.

See also Solal-Celigny, *loc. cit.*, pp. 722–3.

[35] On these incidents see Meyer, pp. 152, 158, 161, 165, 175.

In June 1950 M. Bidault put the question of confidence on a point on which the Assembly had already ruled against him (the applicability of the ' law of the maxima ' to a particular proposal to increase expenditure). He was again defeated. But thirty R.G.R. and Overseas Independent members, who had opposed him on the point at issue, voted with the government when the question became one of confidence: conversely, thirty Peasant and P.R.L. deputies switched from abstention to opposition.

most of M.R.P. abstaining. Next day the single ballot amendment was lost, ministers not voting. The Radicals now called for a vote of confidence on the double ballot clause in the bill; their ministers threatened to resign if the premier refused, the M.R.P. ministers to resign if he agreed. The government was bound to break up, and to avoid widening the breach further, M. Pleven submitted his own resignation.[36]

The vote of censure, which was to have been the principal method by which the opposition expressed its hostility to the government, has fulfilled the intentions of its inventors even less than the vote of confidence. It has simply never been taken seriously. No mention of it was included in the 1947 standing orders, and for two years it remained unused. In March 1949 the Gaullist leader, M. Capitant, thinking that the government was delaying discussion of his interpellations on Indo-China, wrote to the President of the Assembly that he proposed to move a motion of censure. On the basis of this letter (for no motion was presented), a short debate was held on 15 March. As in debates on a vote of confidence, only five-minute ' explanations of one's vote ' were allowed, and the motion was heavily defeated.

The attention of the Communists was thus drawn to a procedural device which, surprisingly, had hitherto escaped their notice. Their leader, M. Duclos, promptly introduced a motion of censure of his own. The Assembly dealt with this in a somewhat frivolous mood. When the date for its discussion was debated, a back-bench government supporter called out 'the ninth of November'. This date, eight months distant, was carried amid general hilarity. By 9 November the government which was to be censured had ceased to exist.[37] In March 1950 M. Duclos introduced another censure motion, this time on account of the law against sabotage, but again failed to get it before the house for debate.

On 11 May 1951 the farce of the first Communist motion of censure was re-enacted in a more complex form. The Communists introduced such a motion, the government proposed that it should be debated in October. The Communists countered by calling for the date to be decided by a *scrutin public à la tribune*, which would waste time and might enable them to defeat the government. A ministerial supporter then proposed and carried that this vote itself should be held on 15 July. By that date a new Assembly had been elected. Two days later the Communists put down another vote of censure over family allowances; on this occasion the government demanded successfully that the

---

[36] He originally resigned on 28 February, because of the abstention of the largest government party in the vote of confidence, the majority being only 243 against 216. The President refused to accept the resignation, as he had not been defeated in the Assembly. But on 1 March M. Pleven resigned again, and this time the President gave way, in order to avoid making it more difficult to form the next government.

[37] *A.P.*, 1949, pp. 42–3. *J.O.*, 15 March 1949, p. 1645.

debate should be held on 1 October.[38] The contrast with Britain is curious; a British government, however burdened its time-table, will invariably give time for a motion of censure to be debated, whereas a French one will treat such a motion simply as a troublesome form of interpellation, to be put off if inconvenient until the Greek kalends.

3. THE FALL OF GOVERNMENTS AND THE DISSOLUTION POWER

THE failure of the machinery provided in Articles 49 and 50 was above all due to the way in which ministerial crises occurred. In the early years of the Fourth Republic, governments were not openly defeated in the Assembly by their opponents. They ' rotted from within ' owing to dissensions between the parties nominally composing the majority. Of the ten ministries which held office during the lifetime of the 1946–51 Assembly, the first and last resigned on formal grounds, the Blum government, according to tradition, on the election of a President of the Republic, and the third Queuille cabinet, according to Article 45 of the constitution, after the general election of 1951. Two more were defeated as soon as they met the Assembly—the second Schuman ministry in September 1948, and the second Queuille ministry in July 1950. Three of the remaining six, M. Ramadier's, M. Marie's, and M. Queuille's first cabinets, fell without any vote in the Assembly. A fourth, M. Pleven's first administration, broke up in March 1951 as a result of a vote in which the government was officially neutral. The first Schuman ministry was indeed defeated in the Assembly in July 1948. But the vote was technically not one of confidence.[39] The majority, 297 to 214, was only relative and not absolute. And the fall of the government was due to the defection of one of its component parties, the Socialists, whose ministers left the government benches for

---

[38] *J.O.*, 11 May 1951, p. 5060 : 12 May 1951, p. 5118–22.
In the new Assembly, a Gaullist put down a motion of censure over the price of corn, and a Communist over the government's procedure with its bill for state scholarships. The Left tried to use the first, and the second was intended, to delay the debate on the bill for subsidizing Catholic schools. The first was never discussed, as varying majorities rejected every proposed date; the second was debated on 4 September, caused an extraordinary procedural tangle, and was eventually lost. On 9 November, a Gaullist censure motion (on the rents of the *économiquement faibles*) was discussed and defeated. And a week later two more were introduced, by a Gaullist and a Communist, in order to force a direct vote on the extremely unpopular increase in the petrol tax. They were debated (for half an hour), but since they could not be passed without an absolute majority, the ministers and their supporters countered the tactics of the opposition by refusing to vote, and no vote was cast against either motion. *J.O.*, 4 September 1951, pp. 6855–68: 9 November 1951, pp. 7854–60: 16 November 1951, pp. 8146–9, 8163.
An official Socialist motion of censure on economic policy (*J.O.*, 26 November 1952) was awaiting discussion when the Pinay cabinet fell. No censure motion was put down against M. Mayer.

[39] The question of confidence had been put on a Radical amendment to reduce the military budget, which was withdrawn. The government was defeated on a Socialist amendment having the same object, but to which the question of confidence had not been specifically applied.

those of their party during the debate—the traditional sign of resignation. Only the prime minister's insistence on a vote brought the matter before the Assembly at all.

The remaining government of the legislature was the Bidault cabinet, which fell in June 1950. It was the only one to be overthrown in the manner prescribed by the constitution.[40] It was defeated on a vote of confidence by an absolute majority when the Socialist party abandoned its previous policy of abstention and went over to the opposition. Defeats in the Assembly now became more frequent. In January 1952 the second Pleven ministry fell in exactly the same way. In the following March the Faure government was beaten on a vote of confidence (though by a relative majority only) because the Radicals and Conservatives failed to obey their leaders. In December M. Pinay, faced with defeat owing to the abstention of a government party (M.R.P.), reversed M. Schuman's 1948 precedent by resigning before the vote. In May 1953 M. Mayer was beaten by an absolute majority on a vote of confidence when the R.P.F. turned against him. Thus up to the end of 1949 three ministries fell through internal dissension, and one after a defeat in the Assembly which reflected internal dissension. From the beginning of 1950 to midsummer 1953, only one government (the first Pleven cabinet) broke up, while four succumbed to defeat in the house, and one resigned to avoid certain defeat.[41]

The change was due to two factors. In the first place the Socialist withdrawal left the majority much narrower and more precarious than before. Governments were more likely to be defeated by their opponents, and could less afford the luxury of quarrelling among themselves.[42] Secondly, the President of the Republic was making a determined attempt to change the tendency. When M. Queuille's first

---

[40] Its immediate successor, the second Queuille cabinet, was also defeated by an absolute majority in the following month. But this occurred on its first appearance before the Assembly, and did not count towards a dissolution under Article 51. See below, p. 229.

[41] Altogether eighteen prime ministers retired from office between the general election of October 1945 and midsummer 1953. Five did so for formal reasons: M. Blum in January 1947, on the election of a President, and the others (General de Gaulle in October 1945, M. Gouin in June 1946, M. Bidault in November 1946, and M. Queuille in July 1951) after general elections. Seven were defeated in the Assembly: the two Schuman cabinets and the second Bidault, second Queuille, second Pleven, Faure, and Mayer governments. Six fell without a vote: the de Gaulle, Ramadier, Marie, first Queuille, first Pleven, and Pinay cabinets.

There were in all ninety crises between 1879 and 1938. Three were caused solely by new elections, and seven by the election of a new President of the Republic. Forty were the result of defeat in the Chamber, and only nineteen were due to divisions of various kinds. Other causes were the illness of the premier, the hostility of the Senate, etc. Soulier, preface, pp. c–d. But among the last eleven of these crises, which took place between 1934 and 1938, only four were due to parliamentary defeats—two in the Chamber, and two in the Senate.

[42] The first Pleven cabinet, to which the Socialists had returned, was the only one to 'rot from within' in the later period (though the Socialists themselves had no responsibility for its fall).

cabinet broke up in consequence of devaluation, and the prime minister resigned during the 1949 recess, President Auriol refused the resignation as unconstitutional, and insisted that the cabinet must meet the Assembly. Reminded that he had accepted M. Marie's resignation in similar circumstances a year before, he declared that he had been wrong to do so. He had to give way, nevertheless, when the prime minister warned that a parliamentary debate would widen the split in the majority, and thus make it more difficult to form the next government. In the same way the President failed to keep M. Pleven in office in February 1951. But he succeeded in stopping M. Queuille's resignation in the following May, and in prolonging the life of the second Pleven cabinet until its defeat, in the manner prescribed by the constitution, in January 1952.[43]

The exact manner in which governments fall has great practical importance, since under the new constitution the cabinet's power to dissolve the Assembly depends on it. In the Third Republic, the President of the Republic could dissolve the Chamber with the consent of the Senate.[44] By convention, this power remained unused after 1877. Its absence profoundly affected the nature of the regime. Deputies, certain of their seats for the full term of four years, could overthrow ministries as recklessly as they pleased without fear of immediate, or probably even of ultimate electoral penalties. The Conservative parties shared with many foreign observers the belief that ministerial stability depended upon the restoration to the government, in practice as well as in law, of the power to dissolve the Chamber. But the parties of the Left were intensely suspicious of such proposals, which they saw as manœuvres to make the already dangerous and suspect executive independent of parliamentary control.

The left-wing parties were predominant when the constitution of the Fourth Republic was framed. They were not willing to allow to the government a power of dissolution which it could use as a weapon to coerce the Assembly. The most they would concede was that the dissolution might be used as an emergency exit from a situation of intolerable deadlock, when the Assembly had revealed itself incapable of providing a stable majority. It could be used as a last resort to punish an irresponsible legislature, but must in no way strengthen the mistrusted executive.[45]

---

[43] The President's attitude was consistent with the position he had taken up during the drafting of the constitution, and recalled that of many of his predecessors: see Soulier, pp. 75–6, 98, 131, 171. For the incidents mentioned see *A.P.*, 1949, pp. 169–70, 338 : 1951, pp. 39–40, 287 : *Le Monde*, 29–30 April 1951, 18–19 November 1951; also above, pp. 177–8, 221, 224 n.

[44] See above, p. 156.

[45] ' Nous n'avons pas voulu inscrire dans la Constitution une sorte de menace; nous avons voulu qu'il y eût une espèce de soupape de sûreté pour le cas où l'Assemblée Nationale se révélerait incorrigible et ingouvernable.' M. Pierre Cot, *J.O.*, 10 April 1946, p. 1679.

'. . . nous n'avons pas admis un appel qui supposerait une dualité, une séparation, qui

The basis of their solution was the Socialist scheme of automatic dissolution. The Socialists envisaged a coherent majority working in harmony with the executive. In case of a breach between them, they proposed to punish both sides by putting an end to the existence of ministry and legislature alike. In the official party proposals for constitutional reform, this drastic step was to be taken only after the second ministerial crisis in the course of a legislature. In any event, the dissolution would penalize the Assembly, but not assist the executive, which would perish at the same moment.[46]

But the makers of the constitution were more afraid of frequent and futile general elections than of frequent government crises.[47] The solution adopted in the first draft constitution was a compromise. It provided for a kind of annual ration of crises.[48] If the Assembly threw out two governments in the same session, the prime minister could dissolve, though he must first consult both the cabinet and the President of the Assembly, the latter being in the best position to judge whether the house was really unable to produce a majority for an alternative government. But these provisions only became applicable in the second half of the Assembly's five-year term; during the first two and a half years the legislature could be dissolved only with its own consent.[49] And the government which decreed the dissolution disappeared in doing so. It was succeeded by the representatives of the Assembly itself: the President of the Assembly became prime minister for the period of the general election, and the other ministries were taken over by the chairmen of the corresponding committees of the Assembly.

These provisions were modified in detail in the October constitution. The defeat of the April draft at the referendum had shown the Left that concessions must be made. So the ' close season ' at the beginning of the life of the legislature was reduced from thirty months to eighteen: only after this period has elapsed do the remaining provisions of

---

mettrait le gouvernement dans une position tantôt inférieure, tantôt supérieure à celle du Parlement. Nous n'avons admis le droit de dissolution que dans un seul cas, celui où l'Assemblée n'aurait pas de majorité, où . . . elle ne parviendrait pas à déterminer sa volonté.' M. Paul Ramadier, *J.O.*, 22 August 1946, p. 3246.

[46] Auriol, vol. ii, p. 249. Théry, Ch. IV. M. Blum had favoured a dissolution in the spring of 1931, on the ground that there was no stable majority in the Chamber (which happened to be a right-wing one). *Ibid.*, p. 207: Soulier, p. 549.

[47] ' Il y aurait quelque chose de plus grave que de changer trop souvent de ministère: ce serait de faire appel, à chaque instant, au suffrage universel et de créer ainsi des crises politiques étendues à tout le pays par des élections trop fréquentes.' M. Pierre Cot, *J.O.*, 17 April 1946, p. 1952.

Seven years later this view was reiterated by M. Lecourt, the spokesman of M.R.P., and by M. Cot himself, who quoted the example of the Weimar Republic. *J.O.*, 27 May 1953, pp. 2859, 2868.

[48] ' . . . vous rationnez la future Assemblée quant au nombre des crises ministérielles qu'elle pourra provoquer. Vous donnez à la future Assemblée deux tickets de crise ministérielle par an.' M. René Coty, *J.O.*, 12 April 1946, p. 1770.

[49] The April draft constitution included an article (81) stating that the Assembly could dissolve itself by a two-thirds majority.

Article 51 come into operation. There was controversy over the period within which the two government defeats must occur. The Left, wishing to limit the power of dissolution, thought twelve months too long, and would have preferred six. M.R.P., trying to extend the power, favoured a two-year period. The ultimate compromise was eighteen months. Thus, during the latter three and a half years of the life of an Assembly, two crises occurring within an eighteen-month period entitle the cabinet, after consulting the President of the Assembly, to dissolve. But two important provisos restrict this right. The crises must be brought about in the manner contemplated in Articles 49 and 50—defeat by an absolute majority on a formal vote of confidence or censure. And if they occur within the first fortnight of the government's existence, they are excluded from consideration, under Article 45. The Assembly is not to be penalized for overthrowing ministries either at the beginning of its own life, when the majority has yet to be ascertained, or at the beginning of theirs, since it committed itself only to the prime minister, and not to his colleagues.

These different restrictions prevented Article 51 ever becoming applicable during the life of the 1946–51 Assembly. Four governments were defeated in it. But the fall of M. Schuman's first cabinet in July 1948 was not on a formal vote of confidence.[50] His second ministry in the following September, and M. Queuille's second in July 1950, were both defeated during their first fortnight. Moreover, only the last of these three had an absolute majority against it. The fall of the Bidault cabinet in June 1950 was the only crisis within the meaning of Article 51, which occurred during these five years. Yet during that time ten ministries went out of office.

The parties of the majority recognized that this position was unsatisfactory, and attempted to deal with it in the abortive constitutional reforms proposed in November 1950. But they found themselves as divided as they had been four years earlier. They could agree on one change only: the elimination of the absolute majority clause. This reform would compel the ministry to resign if defeated, even by a relative majority, on a vote of confidence or censure. At first sight it would weaken the government, by making its overthrow easier. But in practice it would more probably strengthen it. Few ministries were actually prepared to retain power until 'constitutionally' defeated.[51] The loss of this protection would be more than compensated by the fact that the change would make dissolution much easier (at least in theory:

---

[50] See above, p. 225, n.39.

[51] And those ministries which did take this stand deprived themselves, by their refusal to threaten resignation, of their only weapon against the Assembly. This made them very weak indeed. For the Assembly could always force them to change their policy by defeating them on specific points, lobby contacts ensuring that the adverse majority would be only relative and would not force them to resign. See Marcel Merle, ' L'instabilité ministérielle ', *R.D.P.*, 1951, p. 412.

in the 1946–51 Assembly the change would have made no difference in fact).[52] M.R.P., however, regarded the absolute majority clause as a useful barrier against 'orange-peel' crises; and, because of its insistence, in the constitutional reform bill of July 1953 the clause was left unchanged.

The constitution makers took pains not only to make dissolution difficult, but also to ensure that it could never be abused. Their precautions are contained in Article 52 of the constitution. This prescribes the maximum and minimum delay permitted between the dissolution of the old Assembly and the election of the new, and lays down that the new legislature meets on the third Tuesday after the election. Manipulations like those attempted in 1877 are thus ruled out.[53] Article 52 also settles the composition of the cabinet holding office during the period of the general election. In Britain, the old cabinet remains as a matter of course. But Frenchmen have less confidence in the impartiality of their administration. The crudities of 1877 are out of the question to-day. But by urging local political leaders to stand or to withdraw, to make or to refuse an alliance, to support one candidate rather than another, the prefects can still exert a useful influence. Doubtless they cannot alter the will of the people; but they can somewhat modify its visible expression in Parliament.

During a normal general election, the old cabinet stays in office, as it always did in the Third Republic. But a dissolution pronounced by the government raises the spectre of 1877. Article 52 therefore provides that in this case the prime minister and the minister of the Interior retire. (The constitution itself thus testifies to the French suspicion that no ordinary politician can be trusted with control of the administration in a critical election.) The prime minister's place is taken by the President of the Assembly, the most reputable and impartial political personality available. He chooses a new minister of the Interior in consultation with the bureau of the Assembly, which is elected by proportional representation under Article 11. He also appoints at least one minister without portfolio from every group not already represented in the government.[54] Thus, by a curious paradox,

---

[52] The second Schuman and second Queuille cabinets fell during their first fortnight. The two defeats which could have counted, those of the first Schuman cabinet in July 1948, and of the Bidault government in June 1950, were more than eighteen months apart.

M. Giacobbi, the minister in charge of the negotiations, would have liked a drastic reform, reducing the initial 'close season' to twelve months, and abolishing the second time limit entirely. Thus when the Assembly had completed its first year, one 'constitutional' crisis would make dissolution possible. But this went much too far for the Socialists. *Le Monde*, 11 November 1950.

[53] The maximum delay is thirty, the minimum twenty days. For the events of 1877 see Soulier, p. 49.

[54] One representative from each group is enough: proportional representation is not required. It therefore seems a little extravagant to claim, as some have done, that a dissolution is unthinkable because it would bring 'the Communists' back to power. But many people do take this objection very seriously, perhaps on account of reactions abroad, perhaps because their constitutional knowledge is imprecise.

France acquires a government of national union at the moment of greatest political controversy.

These arrangements led to a minor incident at the beginning of the 1948 session. M. Herriot was in poor health, and could not have stood the strain of an emergency premiership during an election campaign. In the event of a dissolution he would resign. The constitution does not provide for such a contingency, but the natural alternative premier would be the senior vice-president of the Assembly. This post was occupied by the representative of the largest party, in the spirit of the constitutional requirement that the bureau should be elected by P.R. The largest party was the Communist, and the senior vice-president was its leader M. Duclos: in the event of a dissolution he would become prime minister—and appoint the minister of the Interior.

M. Duclos was therefore moved down to the third vice-presidency, behind a Socialist and a member of M.R.P. The Communists protested that this was unconstitutional, refused to serve on the bureau (though they were nevertheless elected), and appealed to President Auriol to intervene as guardian of the constitution, which he declined to do.[55] The constitutional revision proposed in 1953 dropped the provision for a special dissolution government, the old administration being left in power;[56] and the method of electing the bureau was to be left to the standing orders.[57]

The working of French government would certainly be profoundly, and probably beneficially, affected if the executive recovered effective power to dissolve the Assembly. Yet the difference can easily be overestimated. The dissolution power alone would not transform French politics and politicians into the image of their British counterparts. The two party systems are too far apart to be reconciled by a simple technical device. And excessive importance has been attributed to the technical device itself.

In the middle of the nineteenth century the power of dissolution may have contributed to the strength and stability of British governments. But, though stronger and longer-lived than French administrations, they were often shorter and always far weaker than British ministries to-day. The recent increase in the power of the executive in Britain is due to party discipline, which in turn depends only to a very limited extent on the right to dissolve. For opposition members obey their leader, who could not plunge them into a general election if they rebelled, quite as regularly as ministerial members obey the prime

---

[55] Lidderdale, p. 104 n., for the 1948 incident.
[56] The Radicals opposed this solution in 1946, but subsequently sponsored it. Their views had changed with their return to power.
However, in the event of a dissolution preceded by a vote of *censure*, the President of the Assembly is to become both premier and minister of the Interior. Additional ministers need not be appointed.
[57] See above, p. 197 n.

minister. Most of them, on both sides, usually do so because they want to: the whips guide rather than compel members into the right lobby, to which they turn willingly either from conviction, or from dislike of the other side. Recalcitrants are coerced by the threat of withdrawal of the whip, followed by opposition by an official candidate at the next election. The danger of dissolution remains a factor, but it has ceased to be the main factor, making for the power of the executive in Britain.

Nor would the dissolution power work at all similarly in the two countries. In Britain, where two parties have usually dominated, a general election has involved a straight fight between them, on a relatively clear set of issues, with one emerging as the government and the other as the opposition. In France, it has recently meant a confused struggle between a series of permanent minority groups, each opposed more actively to its immediate political neighbours than to its more remote, and consequently less dangerous rivals.[58] The power of dissolution might indeed operate to simplify the party structure—though this could not occur while proportional representation petrified the parliamentary membership of each group, making it impossible for an election to indicate how the new government should be composed, or what direction its policy should take. But dissolutions might also lead, as in Weimar Germany, to the electorate returning a succession of unintelligible answers, until at length frustration, apathy, and despair led to the complete abandonment of democratic politics.

It is true that in the Third Republic the alignment of the different groups in two great coalitions of Right and Left enabled general elections to produce intelligible verdicts, even with a multi-party system. But even in these conditions the right of dissolution would involve its dangers. As British Liberals discovered repeatedly between the wars, it can operate against a weaker ally of the prime minister's party, as well as against his principal opponents. In France, where the competition for votes is keenest between the parties which are close together in outlook, premiers would always be under temptation. The mutual suspicions and conflicting interests of the majority groups would make cabinet consent difficult to obtain, while their solidarity would be weakened by fear of the prime minister abusing his authority.

Moreover, the irresponsibility of the deputies is not the root cause of governmental instability. It is largely a reflection of the *incivisme* of their voters. The commonest cause of ministerial crises is the conviction, on the part of a party or group of deputies, that some sacrifice demanded from them jeopardizes their whole electoral future. The threat of a dissolution would doubtless be useful to stave off crises of this kind. But it might not be available. The government's demand being unpopular (*ex hypothesi*) a general election would be likely to

---

[58] See below, pp. 356–7.

benefit its opponents.[59] The dissolution weapon would often be unusable precisely when it was needed most.

Above all, the rise of the Communist party has revolutionized the conditions of French politics. Producing a cleavage much more fundamental than the old division between Right and Left, it has made it harder for elections, even on a majority system, to give intelligible and clear results. It has weakened the influence of the groups in the centre and increased the violence of those at the extremes. And it has ensured that any evolution towards political dualism in France would find one of the two sides dominated by the Communist party. The two-party system can work only if both sides have confidence in the democratic *bona fides* of their opponents. This confidence, for historical reasons, has never been genuinely felt in France, and the growth of the Communist party destroyed it entirely. A two-party system would be even more dangerous for French democracy than a multi-party deadlock. If the restoration of the dissolution power would work to simplify the party structure, that consequence might conceivably prove a disaster rather than an advantage.

The advantage to be sought by making dissolution easier is much less grandiose than the revolutionizing of the party system and the establishment of a really coherent majority. It is to influence marginal votes in critical divisions. To achieve this limited purpose, the power needs to be kept in the background; it must neither become obsolete through total disuse, nor be invoked so frequently as to bring about the dangers discussed above. The deputies would no doubt try to tie the hands of ministers, suspected of contemplating dissolution, by exacting pledges or by refusing supplies. But if these difficulties could be overcome, and the weapon of dissolution were applied rarely, cautiously, and for limited objectives, it might usefully assist governments to hold their own in the Assembly, and help somewhat to promote ministerial stability.

---

[59] Cf. the views of MM. Lecourt and Mitterrand, *J.O.*, 27 May 1953, pp. 2859, 2865.

Chapter 15

THE COMMITTEE SYSTEM

1. HISTORY

THE central feature of French parliamentary procedure is the system of standing committees. No bill or resolution may be debated in the house until it has been discussed and reported upon by a committee, an ordeal from which many never emerge. Under Standing Order 29, bills should be reported within three months at most, but this provision is not enforced. The original sponsor loses control of his proposal as soon as it goes to the committee. He may attend for the discussion, but must withdraw when a vote is taken[1]; and if his bill survives, it comes before the Assembly not as he drafted it, but in the form proposed by the report of the committee, which may be entirely different. Nevertheless, in the case of government measures the Assembly may be asked to disavow its committee and base its discussion on the original text.

The work of the committees is not confined to law-making. They are the effective agents by which the Assembly exercises its control over the administrative activities of the departments. For some, such as the Foreign Affairs committee, in whose sphere little legislation takes place, this is the most important function they perform. The Finance committee, to which all departments submit their budgets, effectively oversees the entire field of administration. At times this machinery of close parliamentary control has had the utmost political importance, especially during the first world war, when the Army committees of both Chamber and Senate (for a similar structure exists in both houses) fought a prolonged battle against the military authorities for civilian control and administrative reform.

The Assembly's Standing Order 24 used to set aside, in principle, mornings and all day Wednesday for committee work. But the great increase of business since the days of the Third Republic has compelled the Assembly to sit three times a day, mornings as well as afternoons and evenings, so that clashes between sittings of the committees and of the whole house have been hard to avoid.[2] Each committee has a room of its own, and a civil servant who acts as secretary. Most of them meet about once a week on the average, generally on Wednesdays, but

---

[1] Standing Order 26. For the position of the committees in parliamentary procedure see Lidderdale, Ch. VII.

[2] S.O. 24 was modified in March 1952, when it was provided that Wednesday mornings and afternoons and Thursday mornings should be devoted to committee work, and that the Assembly should not sit at those times. This decision was unanimous, and has been observed.

the Finance committee finds it necessary to meet two or three times a week. While the others appoint a *rapporteur* for each bill or proposal as it is submitted to them, the Finance committee is organized on a more permanent basis, with a *rapporteur-général* (since June 1946 M. Barangé of M.R.P.) and many special *rapporteurs*, each responsible for a specific section of the budget. The representatives of the committees have a special position in the proceedings of the Assembly. Their chairman and *rapporteurs* sit on a special committee bench, have a privileged position in the debates themselves, and play an important part in deciding whether a proposal is to be accepted for discussion as a matter of urgency. The committee chairmen, along with the chairmen of the party groups, form the Presidents' Conference which proposes the Assembly's agenda.

In the early years of the Third Republic committees were set up on an *ad hoc* basis to deal with each bill as it came forward. The parties of the Left waged a long struggle to change the system, and establish 'permanent' bodies which, though subject to re-election by the Chamber, would have a continuing existence and a settled sphere of activity. As far as possible they wished to see a committee checking the work of each government department, on the model of the Finance committee, which had always been permanent in this sense. They also favoured election by proportional representation of parties, making each committee a mirror of the Assembly as a whole, instead of the older method of election by lot. These proposals were resisted by the Right, who remembered the power of the Committee of Public Safety and the other committees of the revolutionary Convention of 1793. They feared that little parliaments closely controlling the activities of each department of government would weaken intolerably the power of the executive as against the legislature, and would represent a long step in the direction of a *régime d'assemblée*.[3]

The Conservative arguments did not prevail. At the turn of the century the Chamber established permanent committees, roughly parallel with the structure of the government, and in 1910 it decided that they should be elected by proportional representation. The Senate followed suit after the first world war. Both principles now seem firmly established in the French parliamentary tradition, yet the warnings of the Right are sometimes echoed in lamentations proceeding from very different political quarters. Many Conservatives still blame the permanent committees for contributing to governmental weakness, and their criticisms have been echoed with vigour by some distinguished Socialist leaders.[4]

The number of standing committees varies slightly from time to time;

---

[3] For the *régime d'assemblée* see above, pp. 165–7.
For the historical development of the committee system see Lidderdale, *loc. cit.*, and R. K. Gooch, *French Parliamentary Committee System*, Ch. III.
[4] Blum, pp. 187 ff. Auriol, pp. 212 ff.

at present it is nineteen.[5] Each committee has 44 members (the number is a relic of the old system of choosing by lot). Since the size of a committee is about one-fourteenth that of the whole Assembly, each party group is entitled to a place on each committee for every fourteen members it can muster. Groups of less than fourteen members, or deputies not belonging to a group, must attach themselves (*s'apparenter*) to a larger group for electoral purposes, as the handful of Progressives are allied to the Communists.[6] The exact number of seats due to each group is worked out according to a fixed formula, though parties may by mutual agreement trade seats in different committees between themselves. No member may sit on more than two committees. Each group nominates its own representatives as it pleases, and the membership of all the committees is usually settled *en bloc* by general consent, the Assembly merely according a formal ratification to the agreed list. But if fifty deputies challenge the list, a vote must be taken. There was a contest over the Overseas committee in 1950, and a threat of one over the Foreign Affairs committee in 1951.

In the Fourth Republic the tendency has been, not to attack the system of committees, but to reinforce their power. Article 15 of the constitution gives the committees formal status in legislative matters.[7] Article 53 enacts the invariable custom of the Third Republic by stating that ministers are entitled to be heard by any committee on their request.[8] The problem of absenteeism had been serious before the war, and attempts to check it by requiring a larger quorum, or insisting on the resignation of members who missed a given number of meetings, remained dead letters in practice. The Fourth Republic has dealt

---

[5] Economic Affairs; Foreign Affairs; Agriculture; Fermented Liquors (*Boissons*) Defence; Education; Family, Population and Health; Finance; Interior; Justice and Legislation; Merchant Shipping and Fisheries; Communications and Tourist Industry; Pensions; Press; Industrial Production; Franchise, Constitution, Standing Orders and Petitions; Overseas Territories; Labour and Social Security. There are also two smaller permanent committees dealing with Accounts and Parliamentary Immunity respectively.

In March 1952 there was an attempt to reduce the number on each committee from 44 to 32, and to abolish three committees (*Boissons*, Industrial Production, and Merchant Shipping). The object was that each deputy should serve on only one, instead of two committees. This proposal was rejected by a large majority. *J.O.*, 27 March 1952, pp. 1502-3.

From time to time special joint committees are set up, sometimes on a permanent footing, to deal with matters of interest to several standing committees—for example, defence expenditure, the nationalized industries, and the affairs of the European Coal and Steel Authority.

[6] At the annual re-election of January 1951, U.D.S.R. was reduced to thirteen members. M. Petsche, Finance minister in the government of M. Pleven, belonged to no group. He attached himself to U.D.S.R. for a week, and then withdrew again. This friendly gesture at the critical moment enabled his prime minister's group to retain its representation on all committees.

[7] 'L'Assemblée Nationale étudie les projets et propositions de loi, dont elle est saisie, dans des commissions, dont elle fixe le nombre, la composition et la compétence.'

[8] In practice they appear often before the Finance committee, about once a month before that on Foreign Affairs, less frequently before that on Defence, and still more rarely before the others.

with the problem by Standing Order 15, which allows committee members to nominate an alternate to attend in their place.

The first committee on the constitution went so far as to approve a proposal that the committees should be allowed themselves to pass laws, which would come before the full Assembly only if a third of its members so demanded. This provision was dropped from the final draft, and indeed both the constitutions of 1946 expressly denied to the Assembly the right to delegate its legislative authority. But ideas of this kind have gained ground, even in quarters previously hostile, as a means of saving parliamentary time. The new device of restricted debate, instituted in March 1952, and the Gaullist attempt in the same debate to introduce question-time in committee, are recent indications of the growing importance attached to committee activities.[9]

2. THE COMMITTEE POINT OF VIEW

THOUGH the formal position of the various committees is the same, they differ greatly in prestige and importance. Some, such as the committees on Merchant Shipping or even Industrial Production, have little interest for the average deputy. Others, like Agriculture or Pensions, are coveted for the presumed electoral advantage of a position on them. The most important committees of all are almost out of the ordinary ' back-bencher's ' reach. All parties try to put their ablest or most promising men on the Finance and Foreign Affairs committees, and, to a lesser degree, on those on Defence, the Interior, and the Franchise.

When the principle of permanence at length became accepted, a natural tendency developed to re-elect the same deputies to a given

---

[9] The original proposal to allow committees to legislate came from the extreme Left, and received the votes of less than half the committee; M.R.P. members abstained. S.C.C., I, p. 112.

Similar schemes were envisaged by M. Fauvet in *Le Monde*, 4 January 1949, and by the general secretary of the Assembly, M. Émile Blamont, in *R.D.P.*, April 1950—an interesting counterpart to the suggestions of Lord (then Sir Gilbert) Campion when he was Clerk of the House of Commons in 1946. Among those who welcomed M. Blamont's suggestion was M. de Menthon, who had expressed the doubts of M.R.P. four years before. (*Le Monde*, 13 July 1951). *Le Monde* itself made somewhat similar proposals in an article on 9 June 1951. During the debate on the Finance bill, M. Edgar Faure, minister of the Budget, suggested that the Assembly ought only to approve large blocks of expenditure, leaving the separate chapters to be voted by its committee. *J.O.*, 18 May 1951, p. 5499. A provision requiring that the Finance committee of the Assembly should consent to the government's decrees reducing expenditure, and that that of the upper house should be consulted over them, was with difficulty kept out of the 1953 Finance act. But the consent of the Finance, Communications, and Reconstruction committees of the Assembly, and consultation of those of the second chamber, were required for adjustments of certain taxes and for the transfer of certain credits, under the 1953 Finance act (Articles 22 and 65) and investment law (Articles 5, 14, and 18), and under M. Laniel's special powers law (Article 11). *J.O.* (*Lois et Décrets*), 8 February 1953, pp. 1237, 1241, 1256–8: 11 July 1953, p. 6145. For a precedent, see below, p. 262 n.

On restricted debate see above, pp. 200–1.
On question time in committee, *J.O.*, 27 March 1952, pp. 1510–1.

committee year after year. Thus the individual members became specialists, knowledgeable and experienced in their subjects, while the committees as a whole developed a certain corporate sense, a common purpose cutting to some extent across party differences. Committee debates were only briefly reported officially, received very little space in the press, and by custom were not referred to in the Chamber.[10] This absence of publicity enabled much of their work to be approached in a comparatively non-partisan spirit.

From the point of view of parliamentary technique, the advantages of this tendency were evident. Legislation was examined carefully and thoroughly in a small committee of experts, instead of being rushed in haste through a large assembly ill-equipped to deal with matters of detail. But for this gain a political price had to be paid. Committees frequently found themselves in conflict with the government. All institutions naturally seek to assert their own power and independence, and permanent, specialist committees were well placed to do so. Their chairmen often retained their posts for years, outlasting many ministers, and establishing an influence in their own spheres that the latter could not hope to rival. Committee chairmen were, and are, obvious potential candidates for ministerial office.[11] *Rapporteurs* hoped to make their names by vigorous criticism. The leaders of the committees had an evident interest in opposing the government[12]: and the greater the prestige and solidarity of their committee, the likelier they were to succeed.

Proportional representation should have limited the danger by ensuring that the government's majority in the house was reflected in each committee. But it did not always do so. Even in Britain, party whips know that the majority is safer in the whole house than it is in the small committees ' upstairs '. Individual absences, or the strong views of members passionately interested in the topic, prevent the committee being an exact microcosm of the house. The same reasons

---

[10] Lidderdale, p. 169. The decisions of the committee, and the votes by which they were reached, may be discussed.

[11] For examples of powerful chairmen, see Joseph Barthélemy, *Essai sur le travail parlementaire et le système des commissions*, pp. 54, 254–5; and for the alternation of chairmen and ministers, *ibid.*, pp. 124–31.

During the 1946–51 legislature, only five committee chairmen became ministers (MM. Louvel, Maroselli, Montel, Pineau, and Roclore). But in the first two years of the next Assembly's life, eight accepted office (MM. Bégouin, Bonnefous, Paul Coste-Floret twice, Edgar Faure, Garet, Montel, Reynaud, and Sourbet) and one declined it (M. Fourcade). Only MM. Louvel and Coste-Floret stepped straight from the chair of a committee into the corresponding ministerial post. But in four other cases the two spheres of influence overlapped; and MM. Barrachin and Ramarony obtained after an interval the offices corresponding to their former committee chairmanships.

[12] ' Les commissaires sont des ministres en expectative qui dressent des embûches aux ministres en fonctions, c'est la guerre au couteau instituée dans les couloirs du Palais-Bourbon et du Luxembourg.' Poincaré, *L'Illustration*, 29 April 1933, quoted Soulier, p. 194 n. But contrast the view of M. Louis Marin that the committees ask only to be ruled: ' elles sont toutes à plat devant tous les ministères.' Quoted Barthélemy, *op. cit.*, p. 60.

apply with far greater force in France. For the French government's majority is probably smaller and certainly less coherent, party discipline is less effective, and the committees are permanent, whereas in Britain most of their members are in fact appointed by the whips for each particular bill. Deputies with an established reputation in their subject have sometimes been re-elected repeatedly by their party to a committee on which they have proceeded steadily to vote against the wishes of most of their party colleagues.[13] Supporters of the parliamentary minority may acquire personal positions of influence in committees. In 1928 a Chamber returned to support Poincaré elected twenty committees, of which thirteen chose their chairmen from among his political opponents. The Communists after 1947 were far more isolated than any party was in 1928, yet a Communist chairman was re-elected as late as 1949: and though no Gaullists or Communists secured committee chairmanships at the beginning of the 1951 legislature, two of the former were elected in 1952 and 1953.[14]

The very fact that the committees consist of specialists gives them an outlook different from that of the lay majority of their colleagues. This is so even when no electoral interest whatever is involved, as is shown by the unanimity of the committee on Parliamentary Immunity over the treatment of the Malagasy deputies in 1949.[15] Or the distinctive view of a committee may be accounted for, in part by the electoral

---

[13] In the 1924 and 1932 legislatures the Radical members of the Finance committee continued to favour alliance with the Socialists when most Radical deputies changed over to support governments much further to the Right.

The Foreign Affairs committee on 20 December 1950 condemned the sending of an ambassador to Madrid, and in April 1951 voted congratulations to the striking Spanish workers. It was well to the Left of the Assembly, since one Socialist, one M.R.P. and one Overseas Independent member tended to vote more often with the Communists than with their original parties, and one Conservative often took a line of his own. Such shifts will be made difficult by the new Standing Order 16, as amended in 1952, which provides that a deputy who leaves his party automatically vacates the committee seats to which the party elected him. But parties may still be split; thus in 1953 most Socialists on the Foreign Affairs committee were *minoritaires*, opposed to the European army (cf. Epilogue, n. 13), and the parliamentary opposition to it centred there.

[14] The last Communist chairman was M. Midol, re-elected by the Communications committee in January 1949, who resigned at once in protest against the defeat of the other Communist chairmen. (*A.P.*, 1949, p. 3). The Finance committee, which has an elaborate structure of sub-committees, and forty posts as special *rapporteur* of a particular section of the budget, did not remove Communists from these positions until 1951.

A Socialist remained chairman of the Finance committee until after the 1951 election (when M. Reynaud was elected) although the party has been excluded from the Finance ministry since 1946. At the end of 1953 the Socialists held six chairmanships, including Interior, Justice, and Foreign Affairs.

A Gaullist, M. Barrachin, was elected chairman of the Franchise committee in 1949, defeating a Communist. While he was acting chairman in the previous year, the advocates of postponing the local elections (a course to which he was strongly opposed) had thought it worth while to get their bill sent to the Interior committee in order to escape his hostility. (*A.P.*, 1948, p. 134: cf. below, p. 248). The R.P.F. held two chairmanships, Defence and Franchise, both in 1952 (in opposition) and in 1953 (when it had entered the majority).

[15] The Assembly had raised the immunity of the three Malagasy deputies to enable them to be tried on non-capital charges: subsequently they were prosecuted for treason. The question was whether an affirmation by the Assembly of its view of this proceeding

interest, but primarily by the personal background of its members. The Labour committee includes 'syndicalistes de toute obédience'[16]; its M.R.P. members in particular represent the trade union wing of their party. In the same way, a Socialist school-teacher like M. Deixonne, whose entire approach to politics is dominated by his passionate defence of *laïcité* against clerical influence in the schools, naturally chooses the Education committee as his sphere of activity. Or the subject may be of electoral concern to every member, and the committee merely a focus for the discontent of voters in general against the government. The perennial demands of the Pensions committee, and the Reconstruction committee's defence of the housing programme, illustrate situations of this kind.[17]

Such examples indicate that intransigence on the part of a committee does not always reflect the special interests of certain types of constituency. Nevertheless, this is one of its most important causes, as M. Blum pointed out in 1919.[18] To-day the committee still provides an institutional façade for the operation of pressure groups. Each of them attracts members whose constituents are particularly interested in the subject with which it deals. So in March 1949 half the members of the Overseas Territories committee sat for colonial seats, half those on the Reconstruction and War Damage committee for Normandy and Brittany, nearly half those on the Merchant Shipping committee for the principal ports. The great industrial and consuming centres, Seine, Nord, Pas-de-Calais, and the Lyons and Marseilles districts, were entitled proportionately to eight seats on each committee. But while on the Agriculture committee they had only a single representative, they had thirteen on the Economic Affairs committee, and fifteen on the committee on Labour and Social Security.[19]

---

before the hearing of their final appeal would constitute an interference by the legislature with the independence of the judiciary. The Immunity committee unanimously opposed this argument. Its view was put by its chairman, M. Henri Teitgen of M.R.P.: the opposing case was argued by a former minister of Justice, M. Pierre-Henri Teitgen, also of M.R.P. and the son of the former. *A.P.*, 1949, p. 120.

[16] *Le Monde*, 21 January 1950.

[17] In July 1950 the Pensions committee came within one vote of defeating the government. In February 1951 it unanimously threw out the ministry of Pensions budget. *A.P.*, 1950, p. 154; *B.C.*, No. 140 (20 February 1951), p. 4486. In January 1953 it defeated M. Mayer's ministry, almost as soon as it met the Assembly, by 424 to 142.

The Reconstruction committee, early in 1952, was reported to be contemplating resigning *en bloc* in protest against a cut in the housing programme. *Le Monde*, 29 February 1952; *B.C.*, No. 23, p. 495, for the official resolution. See also *A.P.*, 1952, pp. 90, 137.

[18] *Op. cit.*, pp. 188–9.

[19] Twenty-two out of 44 members of the Overseas committee were colonial deputies. Algeria, which is controlled by the ministry of the Interior, has thirty members. Proportionately it should have two seats on each committee, but in fact it had none on the Overseas committee, and twelve on that of the Interior. On the Reconstruction committee, five of the war-devastated Norman departments had ten seats instead of two, and six Breton ones eleven instead of three: all but two of the remainder came from France north of the Loire. No member from inland France sat on the Merchant Shipping and Fisheries committee. But the constituencies including Marseilles, Bordeaux, Cherbourg, Le Havre, La Rochelle, Calais-Boulogne, and Algiers had twenty members, their share

Thus, either through the personal outlook or through the electoral interests of their members, the committees normally represent a point of view different from, though not necessarily worse than, that of the non-specialist member. The Labour committee presses in season and out of season the grievances of the town workers;[20] the Agriculture committee concerns itself with the demands of the peasants. (Significantly, these two are, after Finance, the most active of all.) On a controversial matter like the legalization of *pastis* (*apéritifs à base d'alcool*), *rapporteurs* with the same party background were called on to express the very different points of view of the Health committee, which wanted the ban on it continued: of the Agriculture committee, which wanted it authorized, and taxed for the benefit of the peasantry: and of the Finance committee, which would agree to legalize it only if most of the money so raised were diverted to general budgetary purposes.[21]

The pressure-group function of the committees becomes particularly evident as a general election approaches. In a single week of April 1951 the government met with opposition from the Reconstruction committee trying to double the housing appropriations, from the Communications committee which unanimously condemned its proposal to effect drastic economies on the railways by decree, from the Justice and Legislation committee over the requisitioning of buildings, and from half a dozen others protesting against the insufficiency of their credits.[22] In one week of May, the Labour committee demanded the expenditure of £250,000,000 to raise family allowances and provincial wage-scales, the Education committee advocated an allowance for students, the Finance committee condemned the inadequacy of the government's proposals for higher civil service salaries, the Interior committee called for more vigorous action over slums, the Justice committee prevented the abolition of sixty-three under-worked local courts, the Press committee tried to stop economies on the National

---

being three. Six fishing departments in the Breton region had thirteen instead of two (M. Pleven, who sits for Côtes-du-Nord, thought it worth while to serve on this minor committee). Three of the four deputies for Corsica were among the remaining eleven members. The four wine-growing departments of the Midi were entitled to one seat on committees: on the new committee on *Boissons*, elected in May 1949, they had nine.

[20] It voted unanimously for a large increase in provincial wages in February 1949, and in the allowances of the 'economically weak' (mainly elderly non-wage-earners) in July, and for a bonus on wages in the following January. It drastically altered the government's collective bargaining bill in the interests of the trade unions. For several months it fought to raise family allowances (see below, p. 260 n.). In May 1951 it tried again to bring provincial wages up to the Paris level, and in September it began a long struggle to institute a sliding scale for wages, making them vary with the cost of living. Its plans were usually blocked by the Finance committee; but M. Faure in February 1952, and M. Pinay in June and July, had to resort to formal votes of confidence in order to defeat it.

[21] For *pastis* see below, pp. 336–7. For this conflict see *B.C.*, no. 149, 29 April 1951, pp. 4646–7, 4658; *J.O.*, 9 May 1951, pp. 4905–6; *Le Monde*, 11 May 1951.

[22] 'Chaque commission, chaque groupe, agissent comme s'ils étaient "seuls au monde". Le problème de leur choix est résolu indépendamment des autres. . . . La

Film Centre, and the Pensions committee sought approximately to treble certain war pensions.[23] At such a time the system appears at its worst. The great majority of the committees may constitute no grave threat to the stability of government, but they are instruments of pressure on points of secondary importance, and a further weight in the scales on the side of demagogy and against that of responsibility.

3. THE FINANCE COMMITTEE

THE Finance committee enjoys a position of uncontested pre-eminence over its competitors. It alone was from the earliest days of the Third Republic chosen on a permanent, specialist basis, instead of *ad hoc* and as occasion arose. It is one of the few which even strong critics of the system would retain.[24] But even among this little group of front-rank committees, like Foreign Affairs or the Interior, the Finance committee occupies a special position. For the others concern themselves with a single sphere of interest, important as it may be, whereas the Finance committee investigates the budget of every department, and has never been disposed pedantically to limit itself to the financial aspects of policy.

This exceptional situation has made it a rival power to the government. Like a government, it possessed a general view of all the activities of the state, and its members were men of ministerial timber. The ablest opposition leaders and ambitious ' back-benchers ' of the majority parties found their way there.[25] Membership of the Finance committee was and remains a recognized landmark in a parliamentary career. Out of the 31 non-Communist members of the Finance committee elected in December 1946, 17 had obtained office before the end of that parliament, one of them as prime minister, five as ministers of Finance, and four in junior economic and financial posts: on a strictly mathematical basis their share of ministerial jobs would have been only six.[26] This concentration of ability in the Finance committee gives it a permanent bias towards opposition. As the ' committee of successors ', its members have a greater interest than most deputies in overthrowing

---

spécialisation de travail suffirait à expliquer cette incontinence législative.' M. Fauvet in *Le Monde*, 21 April 1951.

For the committee proposals, *J.O.*, 10 April 1951, pp. 3038 (Overseas committee), 3065–7 (Agriculture, Industrial Production, Health), 3069 (Education); 11th, pp. 3089 (Finance), 3133–6 (Justice), 3163 (Overseas), 3168 (Industrial Production), 3181 ff. (Reconstruction, Finance). *B.C.*, no. 148, p. 4634 (Communications).

[23] *J.O.*, 7 May 1951, pp. 4578 (Press), 4760–3 (Justice); 11th, pp. 5026 ff. (Interior), 5079 (Labour); 12th, pp. 5106 (Labour), 5124 (Education); 15th, pp. 5173–4 (Pensions). *B.C.*, no. 152, p. 4726 (Finance).

[24] Blum, p. 187. Auriol, p. 214.

[25] Barthélemy, *op. cit.*, pp. 101, 285–6.

[26] The prime minister in question was M. Pleven; every Finance minister of the legislature was drawn from the committee, except M. Schuman (who had however been chairman of the committee in 1945–6), and M. Queuille (who held the Finance ministry only for a few weeks of his first premiership). In June 1953 five Gaullist ministers were appointed; four of them came from the Finance committee.

governments. Moreover, since the best individuals in the government parties are in office, the ministerial representatives on the Finance committee are frequently of inferior calibre to the opposition members, and when a party is situated midway between government and opposition, its members on the Finance committee tend to be drawn from the hostile wing.[27]

This bias is counteracted by another and opposite one. Having a general and not a particular view of politics, from the budgetary angle, the Finance committee may be an ally of the government as well as a scourge. It resists ministerial attempts to increase taxation, but it also opposes the popular but expensive proposals of specialist committees because they would burden the budget. Indeed, the institutional barriers set up by the Assembly against irresponsible expenditure are wholly dependent for their effectiveness on the attitude of the Finance committee.[28] The position of the latter is therefore a dual one: in some respects it is the most 'governmental' of committees, while at the same time it is the one whose opposition is most dangerous.

In the latter years of the Third Republic the Finance committee of the Senate, owing partly to the great prestige of its chairman M. Caillaux, was a formidable obstacle in the path of governments, especially governments of the Left.[29] Under the Fourth Republic its power has been drastically curtailed by the weakening of the second chamber. But the Finance committee of the Assembly remains a severe critic, and every government suffers from its attentions. M. Ramadier's budgetary proposals were rejected by it in June 1947, though it later reversed its decision. M. René Mayer, Finance minister in the Schuman cabinet, was defeated in the committee on four major issues in three months, though he usually managed to get his way in the Assembly afterwards. In December 1948 the committee unbalanced the Queuille government's budget, and in May 1949 it unanimously rejected M. Petsche's proposed petrol tax: but on both occasions it gave way in the end.

M. Bidault, at the end of 1949, had the hardest struggle of all. The committee threw out the government's budget and substituted its own unbalanced version, then rejected three successive compromise proposals, supported most of the hostile amendments proposed by the upper house, and was only narrowly defeated on the main points of contention by repeated use of the vote of confidence. The fall of the Bidault government in June 1950 was preceded by a long dispute with the Finance committee over civil service salaries. M. Pleven was

---

[27] See above, p. 239 n. 13. A post-war instance is afforded by the attitude of the Radicals on the Finance committee to the Bidault government's budget in December 1949.
[28] See below, p. 258.
[29] Barthélemy, *op. cit.*, pp. 290 ff.: after his book was written, the Finance committee of the Senate was largely responsible for the overthrow of the two Blum governments. Soulier, pp. 184–90, 215.

remarkably successful in dealing with the committee (of which he had been a leading member) in December 1950, but a year later he too was overthrown in the course of a struggle over the budget. Two months later the committee refused even to consider M. Faure's final budgetary proposals, and even M. Pinay could not persuade it to accept the crucial provisions of his budgets.[30]

The Finance committee is thus very frequently hostile to the government. But it does not always get its own way. Sometimes party discipline can be applied to marginal members within the committee itself, so that it reverses its original decision. So on 23 June 1947 the committee approved the budgetary proposals of the Ramadier government, which it had rejected two days before. On 30 June 1948 the military budget was thrown out in the committee by 13 Communist votes to 0, the pro-government members having refused to vote for it: twelve hours later the M.R.P. and Conservative representatives were persuaded to change their minds, and the credits went through by 23 to 13. Similarly in December 1950 the rearmament budget was first drastically cut, and later restored to its initial figure.[31]

The committee members cannot always be expected to swallow their pride and damage their prestige by a public confession of error. If they maintain their position, the government can still hope to beat them in the full Assembly, where party discipline can work on marginal deputies who have no previous vote to live down. A determined government can generally win at this stage, at least if it is willing to put the question of confidence.[32] For the prestige of the committee has declined since the days of the Third Republic. No ministry since liberation has succumbed to a direct attack by the Finance committee, though the five [33] defeated in the Assembly (up to the end of 1953) had all been weakened by quarrels with it.

The first Schuman government was beaten in July 1948 on its military budget, which had previously been rejected by the Finance

---

[30] For the incidents discussed in these two paragraphs see *A.P.*, 1947, pp. 117, 246–50; 1948, pp. 3, 19, 115, 226, 230–1; 1949, pp. 78–81, 86, 214–8, 222–3; 1950, pp. 123–5, 132–3, 258, 262; 1951, pp. 2, 329–31; 1952, pp. 7–8, 30–2, 36, 81–3, 88, 103, 108, 133.

The leader of the opposition on several of these occasions was himself to be a future victim. M. Faure was one of the chief critics of the Mayer levy, M. Petsche led the attack in February 1948, and MM. Gaillard and Bourgès-Maunoury were the principal opponents of the Bidault government in December 1949.

[31] *A.P.*, 1947, p. 117; 1948, p. 115; 1950, p. 262.

In December 1950 the full committee was following the recommendations of a sub-committee (from which Communists were excluded) in its original scaling down of the proposals. The sub-committee members would not reverse their position, and abstained on the second vote.

[32] When M. Bidault's government's budget was upset by the committee in December 1949, the prime minister demanded as a matter of confidence that the Assembly should consider the original bill instead of the committee's text, and successfully put five more votes of confidence to save the essentials of his project. But on four important points on which he refrained from using this weapon, he was beaten.

[33] Excluding the two ministries defeated on their first appearance.

committee. But that body had changed its collective mind; the leading critics of the government came not from it, but from the Defence committee; and the vote was on strict party lines, the opposition majority of Communists, Socialists and Gaullists receiving no support from other members of the committees concerned.[34] The Bidault government fell in June 1950 over a Socialist bill to raise civil service salaries. This was passed by the Finance committee and by the Assembly, but the prime minister claimed that it was out of order: the Socialist chairman of the Finance committee contested this claim: the prime minister called for a vote of confidence and lost. But again the vote was on a party basis. The chairman spoke for his party, not for his committee, and those committee members who defied their groups did so to support the government, not to oppose it.[35] At the beginning of 1952 the committee rejected the Pleven government's budget and replaced it with an unbalanced one. M. Pleven had to demand a vote of confidence to get the original budget, instead of the committee's substitute, discussed by the Assembly. But on this vote he won, though narrowly. His defeat came on a different issue, the reorganization of the railways, and on this the leaders of the committee were on his side.[36]

In the fall of the Faure government two months later, the Finance committee played a more important part. In rejecting the proposed 15 per cent. increase in all taxes the Assembly was following its lead, and its members were clearly more hostile to the government than most of their colleagues.[37] Yet even in this case the assault was not led by the committee's representatives: its chairman, M. Reynaud, was out

---

[34] Token amendments to reduce the military credits were proposed by the Radical chairman of the Defence committee, and by a prominent Conservative member of it, and substantial ones by Communist and Socialist members of the same committee. The first two amendments were withdrawn, the third was defeated, and the government was beaten on the fourth. *A.P.*, 1948, pp. 115–7.

[35] The three P.R.L. and Peasant representatives on the committee all supported the government on the vote of confidence, voting against their groups. So did another Independent member of the committee. *A.P.*, 1950, pp. 123–6; *Le Monde*, 24 and 27 June 1950.

[36] M. Reynaud, the chairman, and M. Barangé, the *rapporteur-général*, both voted for the government. There were no defections among the members of pro-government parties who sat on the committee. *Le Monde*, 9 January 1952, gives the division list by parties. A year later, the committee upset the budget put forward by M. Mayer rather less thoroughly than those of his predecessors; and when he fell in May 1953, the committee members were somewhat more favourable to him than their colleagues.

[37] The parties split between supporters and opponents of the ministry were the R.G.R., Republican Independents, and the moderate wing of the Peasants. But while half their total membership voted for the government, only two of their ten representatives on the Finance committee did so. (Deputies, 89 for, 65 against, 20 abstentions. Finance committee members, 2 for, 6 against, 2 abstentions.) Further, one of the four M.R.P. deputies who voted against the government was a member of the Finance committee.
Within the committee, the chairman and *rapporteur-général* acted not as would-be supplanters of the government, but as advocates of responsibility. Their influence seemed to be weakening as a result; a few weeks earlier, they alone had voted for the increased taxes proposed by the Pleven cabinet, which were rejected by 37 to 2. Similarly

of the country and abstained on the division, while its *rapporteur-général*, M. Barangé, voted for the government. Both in intention and in influence, the Finance committee is less dangerous to the ministry than it used to be; at worst, it may whittle away a government's credit by steady sniping, but it is unlikely to attempt, and still less likely to succeed in a frontal attack.

4. THE COMMITTEE SYSTEM AND THE GOVERNMENT

WITH the specialist committees pressing for exceptional treatment for the interests they represent, and major committees like Finance able, if they wish, to assert a rival claim to parliamentary leadership, the system might appear a severe liability to a harassed government. But this is not necessarily the case. Often the ministry can play one committee off against another. In December 1951 the adverse report of the Defence committee on the treaty ratifying the Schuman plan, and the doubts of the Economic Affairs committee, were offset by the favourable opinions of four of the others, Foreign Affairs, Industrial Production, Labour, and Finance.[38] Specialist committees advocating increased expenditure frequently find the Finance committee blocking their proposals. Conversely, a minister whose budget is slashed by the Finance committee may be able to secure the support of the specialist committee against it, and there are even cases of a minister mobilizing a parliamentary committee to assist him against his colleague the minister of Finance.[39]

An attack which would be damaging in the Assembly can sometimes be staved off by the confidential revelation, in the privacy of a committee session, of facts and arguments which could not be used in

---

M. Mendès-France, the severest critic of successive governments, became as chairman of the Finance committee a staunch ally of the Laniel ministry.

[38] *A.P.*, 1951, p. 319.

When the substance of a measure concerns several committees, it is assigned to one, and the rest present advisory reports. The Assembly itself decides the rare conflicts of jurisdiction.

Over the Schuman plan, the hostility of the Defence committee expressed the ' specialist ' view of a body concerned primarily with the European army project. In the upper house, the greater strength of the right-wing opposition turned the presumption the other way, and here every committee with a specialist outlook opposed the plan, and only the Foreign Affairs committee favoured it.

[39] The Finance committee is constantly helping the government to resist demagogic demands for expenditure: *A.P.*, 1948, p. 18, gives an example.

Conversely, in April 1950 the Economic Affairs and Industrial Production committees assisted the minister of Industrial Production to resist the Finance committee's attempt to switch investment credits from the coal-mining industry to agriculture: the peculiarity of this conflict was that all the main protagonists were members of M.R.P. *J.O.*, 26 April 1950, pp. 2904–8, 2912–5. A few weeks later the same minister was able to call on the Industrial Production committee to support him over credits for employing mining engineers, and on the Press committee over a film festival. *J.O.*, 12 June 1950, pp. 4647, 4673–4; see also pp. 4645, 4664, 4667, 4669.

At the end of May, after the Education committee had unanimously protested against cuts in the education budget (demanded by the Finance ministry on the advice of an

public.⁴⁰ And if the committee cannot be persuaded by argument, it may be defeated by party discipline. This applies to a variable extent at different times, in different parties, and even in different committees. In the heyday of the *Délégation des gauches*, when there was an organized majority and an organized opposition, the ' whip ' was effective in the committees as well as in the Chamber. The Socialists usually, and the Communists always, behave as disciplined parties, even in committee. Even the Radicals, who rarely get all their members to vote together in the Chamber, have occasionally reacted against particularly flagrant individualism on the part of their committee representatives.⁴¹ In the Fourth Republic, the extension of disciplined voting to a higher proportion of members has increased the government's chance of using effective pressure, either in the committees themselves or in the full Assembly.

The tendency to vote on party lines is naturally strongest where matters of general political importance are involved. It is greatest in the committees whose prestige is highest, precisely because they deal with major issues, and which consequently would otherwise be most dangerous for the government. Their solidarity and corporate sense were further reduced after 1945 by the new rule allowing members to send substitutes in their place to committee meetings. This naturally weakened in every committee the feeling of common purpose, and in the Finance committee it introduced a positive element of discord. For when the budget of the Ministry of Agriculture was under discussion, representatives of the Agriculture committee would arrange to be nominated as substitutes, and attend the meeting as Finance committee members, but with a specialist committee outlook. Opportunity was taken in the 1952 reform of the standing orders to check this practice as far as the Finance committee was concerned.⁴²

---

economy committee), the minister of Education expressed his thanks to the Assembly for its valuable support in winning his departmental battle. *J.O.*, 30 May 1950, pp. 4016–7.

And a year later, when cuts were again demanded, the Education ministry declared in an official communiqué: ' La parole est maintenant au Parlement, et en particulier à sa commission des finances. . . . L'Assemblée Nationale doit dire si elle accepte les économies demandées au ministère de l'éducation nationale.' The committee unanimously (and successfully) opposed them. *Le Monde*, 15 March 1951, 21 April 1951; *B.C.*, p. 4650.

[40] Barthélemy, *op. cit.*, p. 56: but since he wrote, the growth of the Communist party has weakened the force of this argument for the system. This difficulty can be met by setting up a large sub-committee including no Communists, as the Defence committee did in March 1953.

[41] In October 1933 some left-wing Radicals on the Finance committee voted for M. Blum's proposal to nationalize armaments manufacture, but reversed their vote in the afternoon, after being reminded that they were present as delegates of their party. *Ibid.*, pp. 107, 145. On M.R.P. and Socialists, see Epilogue, n. 13.

[42] When the Finance committee discusses a budget, a representative of the specialist committee concerned may attend. But it is not at all the same thing to allow members of the other committee, with its outlook and preoccupations, to appear in the role of acting members of the Finance committee itself. The new version of S.O. 15 requires each group to nominate a list of alternates for the Finance committee, numbering at least one,

The unity of these major committees in particular is often quite artificial. The committee of the Interior caused a great deal of trouble to the Ramadier government in August 1947, over the municipal election bill and over the Algerian government bill, and to the Schuman cabinet in the following summer over dismissals from the civil service. But there was no 'committee view' on any of these matters. The only common element in the hostile majority was provided by the Communists, who were joined by M.R.P. over the municipal election issue, by the Socialists and Algerian Moslems over the Algerian question, and by most groups other than M.R.P. over the civil service dismissals. The Finance committee voted against the government in January 1948 because the Socialists opposed devaluation. To buy them off, the government recalled from circulation the 5,000 franc notes (considered the main medium for hoarding); but this measure too was condemned by the committee—for in gaining the Socialists the government had lost the Radicals and Conservatives. The Franchise committee, in December 1950, provided the classic case of a committee wholly without corporate sense. Since it rejected every alternative electoral reform proposal by majorities of differing political composition, the *rapporteur* had to appeal to the Assembly itself to give the committee a lead and provide a starting-point for its discussion—a precise inversion of the normal working and theory of the system. In fact the crucial compromises were evolved, not in the committee, but in informal negotiations between ministers and the party leaders supporting them.[43]

This division and futility did not deter the Franchise committee from registering a unanimous protest when, in the following week, its Gaullist chairman was not invited to the discussions of the pro-government party leaders on electoral reform. But when real political issues are at stake even the committee's sense of its own dignity has to give way. This became apparent in September 1951. The sponsors of the Barangé bill for subsidizing church schools were anxious not to send it to the Education committee, which was thought to favour *laïcité*.[44] They therefore arranged, by a procedural device, that the bill should be sent to the Finance committee, of which M. Barangé himself was *rapporteur-général*. Their opponents tried to counter this by urging the Education committee to claim jurisdiction. But there

---

and at most half its normal quota of members. All replacements for absentees from the group must be drawn from this list. Some continuity of membership is thereby assured.

The Council of the Republic has restricted the use of substitutes in all its committees.

[43] For the Interior committee, *A.P.*, 1947, pp. 147–51; 1948, pp. 79–80, 91–2. For the Finance committee, *ibid.*, pp. 3, 19. For the Franchise committee, *A.P.*, 1950, pp. 256–7; A.S., 'L'élaboration de la loi électorale du 8 mai 1951', *R.D.P.*, 1951, p. 860.

[44] For example in the previous Assembly the anti-clerical groups had successfully insisted that a bill to establish a school medical service should go to the Education committee instead of to the Health committee, which had unanimously claimed it. *J.O.*, 22 June 1950, pp. 5130–4, 5143–4.

proved to be a clerical majority in the Education committee too, even though its prestige was at stake, and it voted to accept the Finance committee's claim.

Where a committee is in fact the institutional expression of a particular interest, it may acquire thereby a greater sense of solidarity. But for this very reason its prestige in the Assembly is less; the more evidently it is a body of specialists, the likelier it is to be disavowed. The minor committees, even the least united of them, may sometimes win victories against the government. But they do so, not through their intrinsic prestige and influence, but because they are in effect acting as the instruments of a political party which the ministry cannot afford to alienate. In 1948 there was a narrow anti-clerical majority in the Assembly, reflected in the Education committee. But it was small enough to be upset if the votes of the Radical and Socialist ministers were transferred to the other side. When the committee got its way against the government over the colliery schools, it owed its success to the refusal of the Socialist ministers to allow their votes to be used in this way. Its further success over the Poinso-Chapuis decree in the following month was again due, not to its own influence, but to the support of the Socialist and Radical parties, and to the weakness of a government which had just been defeated in six committees in a single week.[45]

The Education committee has to deal with an acutely controversial problem, which divides its members as bitterly as any other cross-section of the public. The Labour committee is a much more homogeneous body. The few anti-labour members usually stay away from its meetings,[46] and in the Assembly, deputies are reluctant openly to oppose its demands. But its occasional victories too, as over the collective bargaining law in January 1950, over family allowances early in 1951, and over the sliding scale for wages in 1951-52, have been gained only with great difficulty, and only through the backing of a particular party, usually M.R.P.[47]

For the government itself often has no more unity of outlook and

---

[45] *A.P.*, 1948, pp. 76–83, 92–5, 224.
[46] During the first eleven months of 1949, 10 divisions were recorded in the committee. The Communist, Socialist, and M.R.P. members (as a group) averaged 9 each, the remainder averaged 3. In December, the committee dealt with the bill reintroducing collective bargaining. For this major occasion, the attendance of the minority improved; out of 25 divisions in that month, the two groups averaged 24 and 14 respectively.

During the whole year, no Communist, and only two M.R.P. members missed more than one division. Only three others (a Conservative and two Socialists) had so good a record. One Radical never appeared at all.

[47] For example, the government's proposed compromise over family allowances, in February 1951, was beaten in committee owing to the defection of 6 M.R.P. members, and barely passed the Assembly, where 32 of them rebelled. The sliding scale bill, in September, was voted by all M.R.P. members of the committee, and four-fifths of 'back-bench' M.R.P. deputies, although opposed by a government in which M.R.P. was well represented.

purpose than a committee. In a multi-party system there is no coherent majority. The same groups which clash openly in the Assembly also fight out their differences behind the closed doors of the committee and cabinet rooms. But both committees and cabinets, in theory positive political forces in their own right, are often in fact no more than battlefields in which the contending parties struggle. There is, however, a significant difference between them. In the ministry the moderate parties alone are usually included, whereas in the legislature and its committees the extremists participate, and can use their influence to upset the carefully balanced compromises by which coalitions live.

It is true that the committees do not threaten very seriously the stability of the government. They often defy, but rarely defeat it on an important issue.[48] At most, they may provide the opportunity for a party to demonstrate that it has ceased to support the majority coalition. Yet the fact that a determined government can nearly always persuade the Assembly to disavow a recalcitrant committee is a condemnation, not a justification, of the committee system. The machinery for putting bills into satisfactory shape before they reach the full house is slow-moving, elaborate, and makes heavy demands on the time and energy of deputies. Special interests can use the committees discreetly to obstruct and smother measures they would not dare to oppose in the house. Responsibilities can never be established. And a record like that of the Finance committee in the 1946–51 legislature, repudiating budget after budget only to be itself repudiated by the Assembly it was supposed to represent, shows that this machinery may actually waste instead of save that scarce commodity, parliamentary time.

Yet some variant of the system there must be. Since the deputies will not permit the government to direct the business of the house, an alternative must be found. There is a vast mass of private members' bills to be filtered, and French members of parliament would not put up with the rough and ready methods of selection used by the House of Commons. Government bills too are worse drafted than in Britain, and need more revision, partly because of the absence of a central drafting department, but mainly because the governments themselves are so short-lived and harassed. The suggestions of the deputies are often accepted, and the committees provide information and training which make their criticisms more pertinent and useful than they might otherwise be.[49] Committee work, too, is more constructive, less partisan, and less propagandist than debate in the Assembly, and plays an

---

[48] Barthélemy, *op. cit.*, pp. 53, 233, 334. Soulier, p. 222. Blum, p. 192.

[49] This training is particularly important because the small size of French ministries reduces the opportunity for able young members to obtain administrative experience. See Professor D. W. Brogan's essay in Lord Campion, ed., *Parliament; a Survey* (Allen & Unwin, 1952), pp. 80–3.

The Churchill government began its career in 1951 with 62 ministers in the House of Commons. Only 35 deputies held office in the Laniel ministry: its predecessors had averaged 29.

important part in building up that spirit of *camaraderie* which is a virtue, not a vice, of the parliamentary system. Even the activity of pressure-groups is less dangerous when it is canalized into recognized channels than when it is exerted beneath the surface.

The power of the legislature over the executive is great, yet without the committee system it would be exercised blindly and haphazardly. Ministers whose tenure of office is short are liable to develop into the defenders of the bureaucracy in Parliament, rather than the spokesmen of the man in the street in the counsels of the administration. A method of close control, like that of the committees, is necessary if the representatives of the electorate are to be able effectively to influence the operations of government.[50] But if the committees are to retain their present responsibilities, or even to acquire more, it will be necessary to ensure that the Assembly has more confidence in them than it often shows at present. Some still favour a return to the old system of appointing them *ad hoc*, to deal with a particular bill or group of bills. More probably, the present system will survive with minor changes, and governments will continue to meet with much frustration, though little serious difficulty, at the committees' hands.

---

[50] See L. Hamon, ' Le régime parlementaire de la IVe République, *Politique*, June 1947, pp. 387, 390, 406 ; E. Blamont, ' Les conditions du contrôle parlementaire ', *R.D.P.*, 1950, pp. 388–9, for tributes to the working of the system; and Goguel, *Fourth Republic*, pp. 166–8, and *Esprit*, June 1953, pp. 856–8, 860–1, for criticism of it.

Chapter 16

THE BUDGET

1. THE LEGACY OF THE THIRD REPUBLIC

THE Finance committee is pre-eminent because the power of the purse is decisive in government. The first function of any democratic legislature is the discussion of the budget. In the parliamentary life of the Third Republic this task assumed even greater importance than in Britain. It took up a larger share of parliamentary time, for there was normally less general legislation in France, and in a shorter session the French Parliament examined the budget much more thoroughly than the British. It was also more contentious politically, since resistance to taxation is far stronger across the Channel. But although (or perhaps because) parliamentary control over the budget was much more detailed and effective in France than in Britain, finance was the least satisfactory department of French government.

Weak and timid ministries, knowing that their life would be short, were constantly tempted to postpone their problems to their successors. Those that did not do so were unable to rely on their majorities to vote for increased taxes, detested by the electorate. In the administration, the ministry of Finance lacked the status and prestige of the British Treasury. In the Chamber, individual deputies (unlike their British counterparts) had the right to propose expenditure for the benefit of their electors.[1] Log-rolling (deputies voting for one another's constituency interests) was common; attempts to check it had been frequent since 1900, but not very effective.[2] The Finance committee of the Chamber could and sometimes did re-write the whole budget, interfering in matters of policy as readily as in those of financial technique. The Senate provided a final obstacle, which inevitably caused delay, though on the substance of the budget it sometimes came to the rescue of the government by restoring resources which the Chamber had refused.

The consequences were deplorable. The budget was invariably voted late, and frequently unbalanced. If it was only slightly behind schedule, it was sufficient to stop the clocks in the Chamber.[3] When

---

[1] '. . . des députés trouvaient au cours des longues séances consacrées au budget une occasion de placer leur intervention—souvent la seule de l'année—en faveur des cantonniers, des gardes champêtres ou du corps de sapeurs-pompiers de leur arrondissement.' J. M. Garraud, *Le Figaro*, 11–12 December 1948. Cf. below, p. 328 n. 3.
[2] See W. R. Sharp, *Government of the French Republic*, pp. 169–71; Lidderdale, pp. 220–2.
[3] See above, p. 195.

the delays were more serious than this, monthly bills were passed granting a proportion of the year's expenditure, known as provisional twelfths, which were finally confirmed when the main bill at length went through. This method caused great administrative inconvenience and made serious financial planning or policy almost impossible. Pressure for expenditure, resistance to taxation, unsatisfactory procedure, and genuine economic difficulties combined to encourage steady inflation, which continued over a generation, and left a decisive impress on the political and economic outlook of Frenchmen: it was interrupted by occasional bouts of severe deflation, which helped to produce discontent and political explosions like that of 1936.

In the Fourth Republic a real effort was made to correct these abuses. Governments tried to tackle problems neglected by their predecessors: to make up for the backwardness of French industrial equipment, the result of decades of neglect, and to renounce the old practice of budgetary inflation. This ambitious programme imposed real sacrifices, the harder to bear since the fiscal system was inadequate and unjust. External aid was in effect offset by the ruinous war in Indo-China. The effort demanded brought successive governments much undeserved unpopularity, and led to many ministerial crises. Its success was limited by the vigorous resistance which it provoked.

In procedure, the presentation of the budget is still frequently confusing, and its acceptance usually belated. The Senate no longer restrains the pressure of the Assembly for higher expenditure and lower taxes. The dangerously tempting remedy of conferring special powers on the government has again found favour. On the credit side, the ministry is better armed both against the individual deputies and against the Finance committee, and the audit and accounting system has been greatly strengthened and speeded up. The general picture still seems depressingly similar to that of the Third Republic, but there has been a significant change in the political circumstances. For most governments have demanded sacrifices to continue tasks indispensable for recovery; and they deserve more credit than they have received for facing unpopularity in order to compel their countrymen to confront realities, instead of seeking immediate political advantages by postponing uncomfortable burdens. The instability of governments since 1946 was a healthier sign than the evasions and abdications of the 1930's—when the Chamber upset ministries no less often, but with much less excuse.

2. BUDGETARY PROCEDURE

THE basic principles of French financial procedure are simple. All expenditure and all taxation must be authorized annually by law. In theory they should be included in a single bill, passed before 31 December, since in France the financial and the calendar year coincide;

but this ideal has rarely been achieved in practice. Parliament votes expenditure in detailed items, known as chapters, and transfers (*virements*) between chapters are not permitted. Particular revenues are not, except in a very few cases, earmarked to meet individual items of expenditure.

Article 16 of the new constitution provided that the budget should include only strictly financial matter, and that budgetary procedure was to be regulated by an organic law. Seven years after the passing of the constitution, the organic law had still not been introduced. And in practice the early budgets of the Fourth Republic were dealt with in a fashion much less orderly than those of the Third. The principles that the budget should be voted by 31 December, and that all financial provisions should be included in a single bill, were regularly violated after 1946.

Delays were worse than ever before. The budget for 1947 was held back by the prolonged wrangle over the constitution: no part of it was introduced until the year 1947 itself, and the main bill did not become law until August. Expenditure meanwhile was met by eight provisional twelfths. At the end of 1947, taxes and credits for civil expenditure in 1948 were authorized at the previous year's level. Later legislation dealt with military expenditure and various other items, and this time it was September before the last financial bill was passed. To prevent this lag perpetuating itself from year to year, a special procedure (for which there were precedents in the Third Republic) was adopted for the budget of 1949. Instead of expenditure being authorized by chapters, each separate ministry was given a maximum up to which it might spend. This reduced the number of individual items to be voted on from five thousand to about fifteen,[4] saved a great deal of parliamentary time, and enabled the principal credits to be voted on 3 January 1949, in spite of difficulties with the Council of the Republic. But the subsequent *lois de développement*, which enabled the Assembly to criticize the details of expenditure, were passed only after much of the money had already been spent.

The new procedure was strongly, though unsuccessfully, attacked by the opposition parties. But government supporters too disliked the virtual loss of their right to assail the budget in detail, and the repetition of the exceptional procedure next year, in the *loi de finances* for 1950, produced much less satisfactory results. The new bill both increased taxes, and included broad provisions for expenditure. The opponents

---

[4] The budget of 1949 had 5,000 chapters. That of 1950 had 3,500—compared with 1,000 in the budget of the United States, which was eight times as large. But the civil budgets for 1951 and 1952 were reduced to 2,000 and 1,200: the latter had only 8,000 pages, as against 18,000 two years earlier (and 5,000 in 1938). This great simplification made effective parliamentary control much more practicable.

For precedents for the procedure used in 1948 see Lidderdale, p. 212 n. M. Edgar Faure, minister of the Budget, vigorously defended his department against charges of unnecessary delay and confusion: *J.O.*, 18 May 1951, pp. 5494–5501.

of higher taxation, presented with block figures only, could not choose the points at which to reduce the credits; they could only vote block reductions in the budgets of particular ministries. Eleven votes of confidence were necessary before the budget proposals were finally forced through in February 1950.

The simplified procedure had aroused so much resentment and resistance that it was in danger of becoming a liability instead of an asset. And the later detailed bills made such slow progress through Parliament that the budget debates as a whole took four times as long as they had ever done before the second world war.[5] Only two bills out of nine had been passed by 14 July: the rest had to be rushed through in the following three weeks. The Court of Accounts, in its annual report presented at the end of June, drew attention to the impossibility of real parliamentary control when more than half the expenditure (on some chapters as much as nine-tenths of it) took place on provisional credits, and to the disastrous administrative effects of a system under which, in 1949, the provisions of the budget were divided into twenty laws spread out over most of the year.[6]

For if the ideal of a budget voted by 31 December was remote, that of one contained in a single bill was equally far from reality. ' Extraordinary ' budgets had been known before: after 1918 they had been adopted to finance reconstruction work, the money being raised by loans instead of taxation. Harassed Finance ministers (and all French Finance ministers are harassed) were often accused of diverting normal expenditure to them. Such separate reconstruction budgets were revived in 1947, 1948 and 1949. But in addition the ordinary budget was divided up into several bills in order to save time, since each bill could be sent to the Council of the Republic separately as soon as the Assembly had voted it. There was some reduction in the number of budgetary bills in 1950: the *loi de finances* voted in February of that year authorized civil expenditure, military credits, and taxation, each of which had in previous years been the subject of separate legislation.

When the Assembly failed to authorize new taxation by the beginning of the year, the Treasury might lose a great deal of revenue. Drawing his conclusions from the long struggle over the 1950 budget, M. Pleven resorted to an ingenious manœuvre for that of 1951. He segregated in

---

[5] During 1950 the Assembly spent 112 sittings and 383 hours in discussing the budget, compared with a record of 28 sittings and 93 hours before the war. ' La France est le seul pays démocratique où une discussion budgétaire présente cette ampleur dévorante, et qui empêche l'Assemblée de voter des projets sérieux et indispensables.' M. Faure, *loc. cit.*, p. 5499.
In 1951 the figures were 127 sittings and 336 hours. M. Courant, minister of the Budget: *J.O.* (C.R.), 28 August 1951, p. 2129.
[6] *A.P.*, 1950, pp. 133–4.
Cf. the views of M. Émile Blamont, secretary-general of the Assembly: ' Le budget est maintenant écartelé en dix ou douze lois au vote desquelles le Parlement perd la moitié de l'année et dont la confusion fait horreur aux professeurs de science financière.' *R.D.P.*, 1950, p. 401.

a separate rearmament budget both credits for military expenditure, and the proposed increases in taxation. This he presented to the Assembly before the normal budget, and he thus obtained the vote of his new taxes in good time, before the beginning of January. The rest of the budgetary legislation was passed only with the greatest difficulty in May, just in time to hold a general election before the summer holidays.

For the budget of 1952 M. Pleven, who was again prime minister, reversed his tactics. He was able to pass before the end of 1951 the whole expenditure side (apart from the military credits which, depending in part on American decisions, were generally the last to go through). But this success, which had not been achieved by any government since liberation, turned out to be a disaster instead of a triumph. For the Assembly, having voted the expenditure, balked at meeting the bill: it first overthrew the Pleven cabinet for proposing economies, and then defeated the Faure ministry on its demand for higher taxes. The Treasury had lost a great deal of prospective revenue before M. Pinay was elected prime minister with a programme which renounced new taxation and relied on raising a successful loan. He therefore demanded and received powers to defer or stop, by decree, expenditure already authorized by the Assembly; and his successors resorted to the same expedient, which reduces parliamentary control of expenditure almost to a nullity.[7]

3. THE GOVERNMENT AND ITS CRITICS

THE private member's right to propose expenditure, the power of the Finance committee, and the intervention of the upper house, all present the government with stumbling-blocks in the Fourth Republic as in the Third. Indeed they are even more dangerous, for ministries since liberation have attempted a much harder task than their predecessors. Between 1938 and 1951 the proportion of the national income taken by the state was raised very substantially.[8] Taxes increased by 80 per cent., although state expenditure rose by less than half. The reason for this

---

[7] See F. Goguel, *Esprit*, June 1953, p. 858 n.
The last of the annual budget laws passed in 1947 on August 13; 1948, on September 14; 1949, on April 20; 1950, on April 8; 1951, on May 24. M. Pinay's budget was through (except for military credits) by 12 April 1952, and M. Mayer's by 6 February 1953; but the revenue proved quite inadequate, and M. Mayer's successor had to bring in supplementary legislation (see Epilogue).

[8] Estimates vary widely; the lack of reliable statistics is a matter of frequent complaint (see, for example, the Economic Council's unanimous resolution of 9 March 1950). An article in *Études et conjoncture*, November-December 1951, discusses the difficulty of accurate computation.
With these qualifications, it may be said that estimates for 1938 are usually of the order of 20 to 24 per cent., and for 1950–51, of 32 per cent. (See L. de Tinguy, under-secretary of the Budget, *Revue politique des idées et des institutions*, 30 October 1949, p. 520; Henri Jeancé, *Le Figaro*, 10 November 1948; Georges Bidault, prime minister, *Le Monde*, 1-2 January 1950; Edgar Faure, minister of the Budget, *ibid.*, 3 April 1951.

discrepancy was that 40 per cent. of governmental expenditure in 1938 had been covered by borrowing and inflation: in 1951 only 22 per cent. was met by loans, American aid, and ' other resources '.[9]

The institutional difficulties which face the governments of the Fourth Republic are broadly the same as those confronting their predecessors. But their operation is somewhat different. Thus, in the case of the member's right of financial initiative, the incentive for the individual deputy to propose expenditure of the ' rivers and harbours ' type has diminished since the abolition of *scrutin d'arrondissement*. Much larger constituencies reduce the electoral impact of local services. Voting for lists instead of individuals makes the member's fate depend much more than it did on the general popularity of his party, and less on his personal record as a constituency representative. The competitive demagogy of the parties constitutes a much greater threat to the budget than the whole sum of proposals to benefit particular constituencies.[10]

Members of the two Constituent Assemblies did not possess the right to propose expenditure. The new constitution restored it to the deputies: but the government disposes of three procedural weapons with which to defend itself against their pressure. These are Article 17

Social security contributions included.) Business and Conservative propaganda estimates the increase as far greater. By 1953 the share of the state was being estimated officially at 40, and unofficially at 48 per cent. (M. Mayer, prime minister, *B.C.* no. 56 (18 May 1953), p. 1236; M. Villiers, chairman of the employers' federation, *Le Monde*, 27 March 1953). Cf. M. Pinay's figures: 30 per cent. in 1948, 33 in 1950, 41 in 1952 (*ibid.*, 20 November 1953): *Statistiques*, etc. (*loc. cit.* above, p. 23 n.), pp. 270–1: *Manchester Guardian*, 6 July 1953.

[9] M. Edgar Faure's figures: *Le Monde*, 17 May 1951; the changing value of money is allowed for. M. Pinay and his successors, however, reverted to the traditional habits.

[10] In May 1951 the prime minister estimated that the various bills presented by the Communists alone would cost 2,000 milliard francs (about £2,000 million) to put into effect. (*J.O.*, 11 May 1951, p. 5079; cf. Pickles, p. 96 n.). On the budget for 1953, 1,200 milliards of additional expenditure were proposed within a week. (M. Duchet, minister of Posts, quoted *Le Monde*, 5–6 April 1953. Cf. M. Pinay's estimate during the debate: *J.O.*, 20 December 1952, pp. 6690, 6694, and *A.P.*, 1952, p. 92).

Compare M. Tardieu's experience in the Third Republic: during his thirteen months of office in 1930 (for only eight of which was the Chamber in session) he had to resist private members' demands for expenditure totalling 15 milliard francs (about £1,800 millions). A. Tardieu, *La Profession parlementaire*, pp. 194, 199.

Private members' bills of purely local interest still, however, occupy far too much parliamentary time. See Maurice Guérin, '. . . La réforme des méthodes du travail parlementaire ', *Revue politique et parlementaire*, October 1951, p. 137. The celebrated *bouilleurs de cru* (peasants entitled to distil, free of tax, a little alcohol for their private use) are championed by deputies of every party from the regions concerned. See, for instance, *J.O.*, 18 May 1951, pp. 5512–3; 11 and 12 December 1952, pp. 6198–9, 6230–4. In the first year of the 1951 Assembly, the subjects upon which most parliamentary bills and resolutions were introduced were, in order: budgetary matters; applications for authority to prosecute deputies; bills to protect local groups or products (from wickerwork to seaweed, and from cauliflower-growers to the sandal-makers of Oloron); bills in the interest of the wine industry; demands for compensation for storm or flood; tax exemption proposals ; protests against the closing of local railway lines ; and bills on housing. The miscellaneous category ranged from the organization of a campaign against porpoises to the increase of the clothing allowance of customs officials, and from the regulation of the profession of ju-jitsu instructor to the ' reorganization ' of the music of the *Garde républicaine*. *Le Monde*, 4 October 1952, quoted *Times*, same date. In Britain, by far the most popular single subject of private members' bills is animal welfare.

of the constitution, Standing Orders 48 and 68 of the National Assembly and, frequently, the *loi des maxima* for the year in question.

Article 17 lays down that increased expenditure may not be proposed during debates on the budget or on supplementary credits. The restriction was first introduced into parliamentary procedure in 1900, as a means of reducing log-rolling, which was easy when each deputy was moving his own amendments to the budget, but more difficult when each proposal had to be presented as a separate bill with its own way to make in committee. However, M. Reynaud, who would have preferred to deprive members altogether of the right to propose expenditure, contemptuously described Article 17 as allowing the deputies to play the fool eleven months out of twelve.[11] Its limited effect was further weakened for a time by the working of the urgency procedure, which allowed any fifty members to demand the discussion of a bill as a matter of urgency. The Communists in particular were able in this way to put forward popular proposals, against which the other deputies were unwilling to vote, and have them discussed at the time when the budget was going through, though not technically on a budget debate. This practice was checked by the restrictions on the urgency procedure introduced in 1948.[12]

Standing Order 48 is more comprehensive than Article 17. It allows the government, the Finance committee, or the committee dealing with a non-financial bill, to demand the ' separation ' (*disjonction*) of any amendment increasing expenditure or reducing revenue. *Disjonction* means that the proposal is ruled out of order as an amendment, and transformed into a separate bill. The demand for it is usually made after the amendment has been debated, but it prevents a vote being taken on it. The effect is to give the decisive word to the Finance committee, which can block under the standing orders attempts to increase expenditure or reduce revenue by way of amendments, and can defeat bills which do so by means of an adverse report on them.[13]

---

[11] *J.O.*, 11 September 1946, p. 3652.

[12] See above, p. 208; and Lidderdale, pp. 199–200, 272–3.

Whatever its effect on the total expenditure of money, Article 17 may even have increased the amount of *time* taken up by deputies' proposals: for there is more electoral profit to be gained from a bill than from an amendment, and from two unsuccessful bills than from one. See L. de Tinguy, *loc. cit.*, 15 October 1949, pp. 491–2.

[13] *Disjonction* is automatic if the Finance committee confirms the genuineness of the increase in expenditure or reduction in revenue.

S.O. 68, which enforces the provisions of Article 17 of the constitution, both provides against the introduction of irrelevant matter into the budget, and bans additional articles which do not create or release new resources. *J.O.*, 16 May 1951, pp. 5270–2, illustrates its use.

On the whole topic, see Lidderdale, pp. 221–4; Goguel, *loc. cit.*, p. 858 n., who maintains that the Assembly can in practice obtain increases only by rejecting or postponing the budget of the department criticized, and so forcing the government to bring in a new one; and the argument between MM. Mitterrand and Reynaud, *J.O.*, 27 May 1953, pp. 2847, 2866, 2871. The former contended that the cabinet could always get its own way, the latter that the rules were often evaded, either by the introduction of a bill instead of an amendment, or by voting expenditure with delayed effect (see note 17). Cf. Epilogue.

Expenditure for the year 1949 was first authorized in a bill (the *loi des maxima des dépenses*) fixing ' ceilings ' for each ministry, and was only subsequently allotted in detail. Article 16 of this *loi des maxima* ruled out any proposal increasing expenditure or diminishing revenue, unless it covered the gap by creating additional resources. This clause, repeated in Article 1 of the *loi de finances* for 1950, and in slightly different forms in subsequent years, proved the most general, and consequently the most useful defence of all. When the Communists opposed Article 1 of the 1950 law, M. Petsche, the minister of Finance, claimed that in the previous year it had stopped proposed expenditure amounting to 775 milliard francs, and reductions of revenue of 200 milliard, mostly put forward by the Communists themselves.[14]

But all three weapons are in constant use. Thus on two successive days in December 1949, seven popular proposals from different parties and committees were ruled out of order under Article 17, and six more under S.O. 48. The Communists had consequently to put their numerous amendments in the form of token 1,000-franc reductions; M. Petsche accepted these, congratulating himself on saving a good deal of money by doing so. Again, in May 1951, when the imminence of the general election caused the government to be assailed from all sides with demands for increased expenditure, the standing orders were wielded so vigorously that half the amendments moved to the *loi de finances* (of which 200 had been proposed), and 34 out of 36 additional articles, were ruled out of order without coming to a vote.[15] If no other procedural weapon is available, the prime minister often resorts to the constitutional vote of confidence. Half the votes of confidence demanded in the 1946–51 Assembly, and four-fifths of those called for in 1951–53, were on budgetary matters.[16]

The Finance committee would usually support the government in resisting demagogic proposals: thus just before the 1951 election it frustrated an ingenious (non-Communist) attempt to evade the 1951 *loi des maxima* by voting expenditure to take effect only in 1952.[17] If this line of defence failed, the government could invoke Article 17 or its

---

[14] *J.O.*, 28 December 1949, p. 7493. The ostensible Communist criticism was that the rule enabled members of the majority to acquire merit by popular proposals which they knew would be ruled out of order (*ibid.*, M. Pronteau's speech).
[15] *J.O.*, 26 and 27 December 1949, pp. 7241, 7261, 7298, 7324; *ibid.*, p. 7274. *Le Monde*, 20–21 May 1951.
[16] See above, p. 217.
[17] After one proposal of this kind had been accepted by the committee and the government, the same technique was used for a whole series of popular causes. See *J.O.*, 11 May 1951, p. 5039; 12 May, pp. 5105–6, 5136–42; 15 May, pp. 5176–7. For its frustration, *B.C.*, no. 152, pp. 4731–3; *Le Monde*, 24 May 1951. In the new Assembly it was revived. M. Reynaud said that every annual budget contained a time-bomb, due to explode in twelve months: *loc. cit.*, p. 2847. In reply the Pinay and Mayer governments sought, and the Laniel cabinet obtained powers to limit expenditure in the forthcoming budget to the level of the current year. Cf. Epilogue.

other defences even against the Finance committee.[18] But though the procedural devices were adequate to keep much of the pressure for higher expenditure in check, in the last resort their effectiveness depended on the political situation. To employ them too rigidly might endanger the government's majority. A prudent minister could then still use them to force a compromise. Thus in April 1949 the government proposed to raise war pensions by 14 per cent. The Pensions and Finance committees both voted unanimously for an increase of 16½ per cent. The government invoked Article 17, but subsequently gave way and compromised on 15 per cent.[19] But occasionally even this was impossible, and the ministry had either to abandon its opposition or to risk defeat. In June 1950, M. Bidault's government fell on a vote of confidence when it invoked the *loi des maxima*, which the Finance committee considered inapplicable, against a Socialist bill which would increase civil service salaries.[20]

The Finance committee has shown consistent hostility to the budgets presented by successive governments. The most violent clashes were in December 1949, over the budget for 1950, and early in 1952, when the committee opposed all the successive solutions put forward by the Pleven, Faure and Pinay cabinets.[21] On both occasions it rejected the advice, not only of the ministry, but of its own *rapporteur-général*.

Its hostility was mainly political, caused by the electoral anxieties of its Radical and Conservative members on one set of issues, and (to a lesser extent) of the Socialists on others. But it was also technical. For the administration found difficulty in abandoning the habits it had acquired during the Vichy regime, when it was freed from parliamentary control. The committee's disquiet in part reflected the fact that the

---

[18] Thus it used Article 17 in this way over the reclassification of civil servants, in January 1950, and the *loi des maxima* over their family allowances in the following May. *J.O.*, 31 December 1949, pp. 7652–3; 31 May 1950, p. 4045.

[19] *J.O.*, 13 April 1949, pp. 2384 ff.

In April 1951 the demand for increased family allowances, which the government had blocked for months, at last became irresistible. The government had raised its original offer of a 15 per cent. increase to 20 per cent.; the Labour committee, which had at first demanded 40, came down to 30 per cent. in a successful bid for the support of the Finance committee. A Communist proposal for 50 per cent. was *disjoint*; the government's bill was rejected by 551 to 34: the *loi des maxima* was invoked against the proposal of the committees: and at length the Finance committee's suggested compromise of 25 per cent. was accepted. *J.O.*, 28 April 1951, pp. 4138–48; 30 April 1951, pp. 4329–47; 1 May 1951, pp. 4401–3; especially pp. 4337 and 4342.

[20] *A.P.*, 1950, p. 125. (Technically the bill concerned regrading.)

In April 1949 the minister of Finance withdrew his appeal to the *loi des maxima* against a proposal relating to compensation for requisitioning in Alsace-Lorraine, after bitter protests against its use from M.R.P. and Socialist, as well as Communist and R.P.F. speakers. *J.O.*, 7 April 1949, pp. 2184–7. The *loi des maxima* for 1953 was not voted until the government had agreed not to use it against rehousing proposals. *A.P.*, 1952, p. 90.

[21] See above, pp. 243–4, 245–6.

information supplied to it was always belated and often inadequate.[22] However, its resistance was rarely successful: its authority was much less than in the Third Republic, partly because its members were less experienced and enjoyed less prestige, and partly because party discipline was more effective in the Fourth. Faced with a choice between the government and the Finance committee the Assembly almost invariably followed the former.

A similar development occurred with respect to the second chamber, after the right-wing opposition acquired the majority there in October 1948. In December the Council of the Republic rejected the main expenditure credits for 1949, and drastically amended the *loi de finances:* in January 1950 it re-wrote the entire budget, and subsequently fought a long battle over the distribution of investment funds: on the rearmament budget for 1951 it replaced the taxes proposed by the government with resources which were already earmarked for other purposes. Its amendments on the last occasion were denounced by the *rapporteur-général* of the Assembly's Finance committee as a ' policy of dud cheques ', and by a former chairman of that body as ' lacking in competence and courage '.[23] The Council protested violently against these imputations, but they indicated the failure of its tactics. For the intransigence of the upper house in practice helped the government instead of hindering it, by provoking the Assembly into reaffirming its own solutions. Thus in financial matters the Council of the Republic was in a weaker position than the Senate, its powers having been reduced by the terms of the constitution, and its prestige by the actions of its own majority.[24]

4. DECREE-LAWS AND SPECIAL POWERS

THE unwillingness of the deputies to vote for higher taxes was only equalled by their reluctance to accept reductions in expenditure. Ministers and independent observers were in doleful agreement that the members of parliament wanted abstract economies and concrete expenses, a reduction in the total of state expenditure but increases in the individual items. In the 1950 budget the National Assembly voted substantial economies in gross, to be allocated in detail by an expert committee: the outcry against its proposals led the minister to remark that economies were perhaps even harder to get accepted than taxes.[25]

To overcome similar difficulties there had developed during the interwar years a practice of giving to the government special powers to make

---

[22] ' Le jour où le Parlement sera de nouveau saisi en temps voulu des cahiers détaillés de dépenses les gouvernements retrouveront la confiance qu'ils ont manifestement perdue au sein de la commission.' J. Fauvet, *Le Monde*, 16 December 1949.
[23] *J.O.*, 5 January 1951, pp. 210–1.
[24] See below, pp. 280–1.
[25] M. Faure in *Le Figaro*, 15 December 1950; M. Fauvet in *Le Monde*, 28 December 1949 ; M. Faure in *Le Monde*, 25 April 1950.

unpopular changes by 'decree-laws', which allowed it to impose taxes and to override ordinary legislation. The powers were granted for a limited period, and the decrees needed eventual parliamentary ratification. The original application of this procedure was made in the first world war: special powers were granted but not used in 1924, first employed in peacetime in 1926, and demanded (and usually granted) in every year but one after 1933. Deputies thus acquired the habit of evading their responsibilities, especially financial ones, and passing them on to the government.[26] Ministries became used to freedom from parliamentary control: at the time of Munich the government had special powers, and was able to avoid summoning Parliament at all. Indeed the French Republic in 1938 was almost as moribund as the German in 1930.[27]

The constitution makers tried to check the practice of decree-laws by Article 13 of the constitution, which forbids the National Assembly to delegate its power to vote the laws. But the causes which originally produced the decree-law procedure had increased rather than diminished in force. Special powers in the hands of the government were demanded by M. Mollet, general secretary of the Socialist party, in July 1947, and by M. René Mayer, Finance minister in the Schuman cabinet, a year later. M. Mayer's successor, M. Reynaud (in the Constituent Assembly a solitary supporter of the decree-law procedure) took office only on condition of receiving such powers, which were granted by the law of 17 August 1948. Later governments obtained legislation allowing them both to reduce, and on certain conditions even to increase taxes by decree.[28] Parliament's failure to deal with the bill for reorganizing the nationalized railways, introduced in November 1950, led both M. Queuille's government in April 1951, and M. Pleven's in January 1952, to seek additional powers to achieve this object without further reference to Parliament: but the former came up against the unanimous opposition of the Communications committee of the Assembly, and the latter was overthrown in a vote of confidence on the issue. The Pinay ministry, in April 1952, was given authority to make by decree drastic

---

[26] Special powers were not always used for the purpose for which they were demanded. Thus the Laval government, under powers given it to save the franc, prohibited foreigners from keeping carrier-pigeons. Werth, *Destiny of France*, p. 152.

[27] On the use of these powers in the Third Republic, see M. Sieghart, *Government by decree*; on their parliamentary history, Soulier, pp. 162 ff., 184 ff.; on the contemporary circumstances which favour them, F. Goguel, *loc. cit.*, pp. 853–5.

[28] A *loi de développement des crédits* in August 1950 allowed the reduction of taxes by decree, provided the Finance committees of both houses were consulted, and that of the Assembly gave its consent. *J.O.*, 2 August 1950, pp. 6423–9.

The rearmament budget of 1951 permitted the increase of existing taxes, unless the Assembly voted sufficient economies in time to save 25 milliards; M.R.P. expressed doubts of the constitutionality of the details of this provision. *J.O.*, 31 December 1950, p. 9936.

Under it, the government increased the petrol tax in October 1951—and the Finance committee condemned it for doing so by 40 votes to 1 (M. Reynaud's). *B.C.*, no. 9, 13 November 1951, p. 142.

cuts in the budget;[29] and in the government crises of December 1952, and May and June 1953, the growing demand for special powers played a central part.

These repeated incidents showed that special powers had not lost their attraction for governments. But it was the 'Reynaud' law of 17 August 1948 which came nearest to challenging the constitution. This instructed the government to take steps by the end of the year to reorganize the civil service, the nationalized industries, the social security organization, and the fiscal system. It gave special authority to make budgetary *virements*, etc., for the purpose. The objectives of the reforms were laid down in the most general terms; 'to make (the administration) more efficient and less costly' (Article 1), or to ensure profitability and promote the idea of individual responsibility in the nationalized industries (Article 2). Certain specific matters were excluded: for example, the judicial system could not be touched under the pretext of reorganizing the civil service, nor could industries be denationalized, nor the majority of shares given up by the state, in any mixed company where it had a controlling interest. The law also conferred *permanent* powers to override existing (but not future) legislation on 'matters of a nature to be dealt with by administrative action' in the same fields, these matters being enumerated at length.[30]

In respect of the causes which provoked it, the method of operation, the broad definition of the objects sought, and the juridical status of the measures taken under its authority, this law bore the closest resemblance to the laws which conferred special powers in the Third Republic. The contrasts were only secondary.[31] The bill was therefore attacked by

---

[29] *B.C.*, no. 148, 23 April 1951, p. 4634.
J.O., 7 January 1952, p. 191. The Pleven cabinet sought powers to deal with the social security system as well as the railways, but fell before a vote could be taken on this proposal.
J.O., 8 April 1952, pp. 1987–8, 1994.
Delegated legislation arouses comparatively little suspicion in France, where the legislature has often passed broadly conceived laws, leaving the administration to fill in details. Indeed, under the Fourth Republic, complaints that legislation was becoming much too detailed have come even from the most orthodox parliamentarians: see, for example, M. Herriot's comments in *Le Monde*, 14 July 1951.

[30] The text of the bill as originally introduced is published in *A.P.*, 1948, p. 339, and that of the law as finally passed, *ibid.*, p. 363. For a full discussion see Roger Pinto, 'La loi du 17 août 1948', *R.D.P.*, 1948, pp. 546 ff. The conception of 'matières ayant par leur nature un caractère règlementaire' (Art. 6), which is new to French law, was introduced into the bill on the advice of the *Conseil d'État*. Pinto, *loc. cit.*, pp. 518, 531.

M. Reynaud's attempted use of the powers conferred upon him broke up the government ten days after the passing of the law. The powers remained to succeeding governments, and fear of the use a Socialist Finance minister would make of them caused the overthrow of the second Schuman cabinet at the beginning of September. M. Queuille's policy of letting sleeping dogs lie meant that they were not used very extensively. But the unpopular fiscal reform of 9 December 1948 was brought into force under the powers temporarily conferred by this law; and its permanent provisions were used in October 1950 to remove the social services attached to the nationalized gas and electricity industries (with an annual budget of £1,000,000) from the control of a Communist-dominated committee. See also Epilogue, note 15.

[31] Pinto, *loc. cit.*, pp. 525–9.

the opposition as unconstitutional, the Gaullists, though advocates of a stronger executive, arguing that this should be brought into existence by an open revision of the constitution, not by surreptitious violation of it. This case, though so plausible at first sight, was dubious in law. For the constitution-makers had deliberately refused to introduce rigid provisions ruling out absolutely any recourse to special powers. They had contented themselves with a general formula intended to discourage, but not completely to forbid their use.[32] But by 1953 it was clear that once again political causes had proved stronger than paper provisions, and another attempt to prevent an abuse of the past was breaking down in face of the continued strength of the forces which originally caused the abuse.[33]

5. ACCOUNTING

It cannot be claimed that Parliament has greatly improved its methods of financial control since the war: but on the administrative side there is more to be said for the Fourth Republic. The ministry of Finance has seen a steady increase of its authority, at both the cabinet and the civil service level. The *inspecteurs des finances* are an extremely powerful body with a very strong *esprit de corps*. In the nationalized industries their influence has replaced that of the engineers and technicians, who were preponderant immediately after the liberation: elsewhere, it has even been sufficient to enable men from their ranks, such as M. Couve de Murville and M. Hervé Alphand, to secure high posts in the most powerful rival service, the diplomatic. The laissez-faire policy of this ministry earned it the hostility of the Socialists and M.R.P., who favoured the establishment of a strong ministry of Economic Affairs, and of many members of other parties.[34] But whatever may be thought of its political influence, its growing ascendancy as a department certainly helped to check the administrative abuses which were apparent in the early post-war years.

A further improvement was the recovery of parliamentary control

---

[32] *Ibid.*, pp. 536–40: M. Pinto argues that decree-laws are not laws, juridically speaking, and therefore do not violate the ban on delegating the legislative power of the Assembly. Most jurists, by his own admission, disagree. Théry, p. 165, regards the question as undecided. See Pickles, p. 275 n.; Goguel, *loc. cit.*, p. 854 n.; the advisory opinion of the *Conseil d'État*, printed in *R.D.P.*, 1953, p. 171, and discussed in *Le Monde*, 20 February 1953; and René Chapus, 'La loi . . . du 11 juillet 1953', *R.D.P.*, 1953, pp. 997 ff.

[33] M. Pinay sought powers to reform the fiscal system by decree if the Assembly did not do so, but he fell without obtaining them. Three clauses in M. Mayer's finance bill were attacked as unconstitutional under Article 13: *J.O.*, 27 January 1953, pp. 510–4: *J.O.* (C.R.), 5 February 1953, pp. 599–603. The Mayer government fell in May over its demand for special powers, which were however granted to its successor; they were limited in time, usually to three months, and were also (a novel provision) conferred on the existing cabinet only; but in scope they were very wide, covering the principal spheres of government service and of economic activity. Cf. Chapus, *loc. cit.*, and Epilogue.

[34] See below, pp. 391–2.

The view of a Gaullist administrative expert is expressed by M. Michel Debré: ' L'image de la France est celle d'une entreprise conduite par son caissier.' *La Mort de l'état républicain*, p. 19. The Peasant party is extremely critical of the Finance ministry: cf. *A.P.*, 1952, p. 90.

over most of the 'special Treasury accounts'. These covered a wide variety of forms of expenditure, from making up the deficit on the nationalized railways to running the state lottery. They offered serious facilities for abuse, since Parliament was often called on to pay for unjustified expenditure far too late to be able to exercise any check upon it. For thirty years the special accounts had been a matter of conflict. In the Third Republic, the ministry of Finance preferred to keep them in being as a means of evading the intervention of the deputies. But at the liberation a change of policy took place. Every department was struggling to maintain and extend the autonomy it had won during the years of confusion, and the ministry of Finance came to fear that any coherent financial policy would thus be rendered impossible. So its weight was thrown on the side of parliamentary authority, and with this powerful support success was achieved. The number of special accounts was reduced from 300 in 1946 to 60 in 1950, and these were brought under effective parliamentary control: in the 1950 report of the Court of Accounts these were among the few services not criticized for lax administrative methods.[35]

There were also improvements in the matter of audit. Parliament's first guarantee that money is being spent on the services for which it was appropriated is provided by controllers, from the staff of the ministry of Finance, who are attached (in inadequate numbers) to the other departments for the purpose. They are at the disposal of the Finance committees of both houses, as well as of their own ministry. But the main task of audit is performed by the Court of Accounts, an independent administrative tribunal of very ancient origin, which possesses extensive powers and works with great thoroughness. The final check is the eventual vote by Parliament of the completed accounts for each year.[36]

In the Third Republic, the reports of the Court of Accounts were very complete, but also usually very belated. They were consequently voted in haste and perfunctorily: the laws of accounts for 1918 and 1919 naturally aroused little attention when they went through in 1937.[37] In the Fourth Republic the Court of Accounts set out to change this tradition. In December 1948 it issued a most vigorous report criticizing extravagance and abuses, especially over requisitioning of buildings and the excessive use of cars, in the administration of the preceding years.[38] Opposition propaganda, especially that of the R.P.F., made extensive use of the report, though the ministerial parties could reply

---

[35] On the *comptes spéciaux du trésor* see L. de Tinguy, *loc. cit.*, 15 October 1949, p. 495: J. Blocquaux, *J.O.*, 25 April 1950, pp. 2807–8. The church schools subsidies under the *loi Barangé* are paid in this way.
For a similar tightening up on the revenue side, see *Le Monde*, 12 March 1953.
[36] For a fuller account see Lidderdale, pp. 224–7 ; and Campbell, *French Parliament*, *loc. cit.* (above, p. 191 n.1).
[37] Sharp, p. 297 n.
[38] The ministry of Marine installed a dormitory, showers, a cinema and a gymnasium in a building which it soon afterwards abandoned. The temporary director of recruiting

that the amount involved was at most about 0·2 per cent. of the budget,[39] that the abuses were mainly concentrated in the new ministries and the Service departments, and that irregularities were almost inevitable in view of the huge turnover of staff resulting from the war and the purge. With more effect, though perhaps with less justice, they could also point out that General de Gaulle had been prime minister in the first years after the liberation.

The effect of the incident on the position of the Court of Accounts itself was of greater long-run importance than the contents of its report. The Court had been given constitutional status by Article 18, which authorized the Assembly to call on it for any form of inquiry or research involving the public finances. The standing orders of the Assembly allow committee chairmen and the *rapporteur-général* of the Finance committee to deal directly with it, and this collaboration has proved valuable. The scope of its activity was extended to include much more preparatory work in connection with the budget. Its methods were improved by making more inquiries on the spot, instead of in Paris. Its prestige was enhanced by the new constitutional status,[40] and it attracted more attention than ever before by its outspoken comments on recent events, which obtained immense publicity through being used as political ammunition. The report of December 1948 was followed by 1,400 dismissals or prosecutions, by the establishment of a new committee of budgetary discipline, by the law extending control over the special accounts, and by another giving the Court of Accounts authority to investigate the social security system: a virtual subsidiary, the *Commission de vérification des comptes des entreprises publiques*, deals with the nationalized industries.[41]

In June 1950, another striking report from the Court criticized the chaotic state of legislative procedure on the budget, and the deplorable administrative consequences, condemned as still much too extensive the fiscal operations conducted outside the main budget, and brought to light continued, though less grave irregularities in departmental administration. But defenders of the new regime might fairly claim that the abuses revealed were less significant than the fact of their revelation.[42] The stronger position and speedier working of the Court suggested that in the financial as in many other spheres, the administrative developments of the Fourth Republic were proving more successful than the political.

---

at the ministry of War chose Regency furniture for his office. In the *Sûreté nationale* itself daily travelling allowances were claimed for journeys that were not taken. The Air ministry (held by the Communists, the self-styled *parti de la probité*) had undertaken unexplained requisitioning of wines, spirits, and lingerie.

[39] The estimate of M. Pineau, former chairman of the Finance committee, at a Socialist party conference: *Bulletin intérieur du parti socialiste*, no. 39 (February 1949), p. 43.

[40] Article 10 of the special powers law of 17 August 1948 forbade the use of those powers to weaken the position of the Court of Accounts.

[41] See Lidderdale, p. 227; and Campbell, *loc. cit.*

[42] M. Maurice Schumann, quoted *Le Monde*, 4 January 1949.

Chapter 17

THE COUNCIL OF THE REPUBLIC

1. THE SENATE OF THE THIRD REPUBLIC

THE most important and characteristic institution of the Third Republic was the Senate. It was the chief of the obstacles placed by the cautious founders of the new regime in the way of a future Left-wing majority, and both sides recognized it as such. Every precaution had been taken to make it a thoroughly conservative body. It was elected by delegates of the various local authorities. But their representation was weighted in such a way as greatly to exaggerate, at first the influence of the conservative countryside, and, after the revision of 1884, also that of the small provincial towns, the strongholds of the republican petty bourgeoisie. The great cities were always grossly under-represented.[1]

Moreover, the members of local authorities were often more conservative than their constituents. Many small communities which voted for the Left in national elections would choose a conservative mayor because he was the only individual in the village with enough time and experience to run local affairs. The paradoxical result could be seen in a department like Aisne, which returned seven deputies of the Left and four senators of the Right.[2] In addition, senators were chosen for a nine-year term, a third retiring every three years: as their constituents had themselves been elected to their local posts some time before, the Senate represented not only a public opinion in which the conservative areas and communities had exaggerated influence, but also one which was many years out of date. Lastly, senators had to be at least forty years of age, and the average was much higher (63 in 1921).[3] And in this very sober and dignified body, influence often went with seniority.[4]

---

[1] Thus Marseilles, with 900,000 inhabitants, elected 24 delegates; the rest of the department, with 250,000 inhabitants, had 313. Sharp, p. 67. Lille, with over 300,000 people, carried no more weight than two dozen neighbouring villages with 4,000 inhabitants between them: each elected 24 delegates. A. Cobban, ' The Second Chamber in France ', *Political Quarterly*, October 1948, p. 324.

[2] Étienne Weill-Raynal, ' L'élection du Conseil de la République ', *Revue socialiste*, May 1948, p. 471.

[3] Lord Bryce, *Modern Democracies* (Macmillan, 1921), I, p. 266 n.

[4] Cf. M. Herriot's advice to a new senator: ' In the first year you do not enter the debating Chamber, but in the lobbies you salute the Senators, giving them their title. The second year you take a place in the corner of the debating Chamber. The third year you risk once or twice a " Très bien ". The fourth year you ask to be made a member of a small committee. The fifth year you ask to be charged with a report on a local by-road: in the sixth year this request is granted. The seventh year you risk one speech at the tribune. The eighth year you speak twice. In the ninth year you are beaten at the polls.' Quoted W. L. Middleton, *French Political System*, p. 171.

Nevertheless, the Senate was not simply a French version of the House of Lords. It did not stand openly on one side of the party battle, but squarely in the centre. For though the Senate was conservative in social and economic matters, it was not politically reactionary. By 1914, it had become the instrument of the moderate Radicals, who were opposed with equal vigour to clerical and to socialist tendencies. It indicated its position in 1913 by rejecting proportional representation, which was favoured by Conservatives and Socialists alike, but opposed by the groups between them. It was the decisive influence which maintained the negative policy (*ni réaction ni révolution*) to which the majority of the electorate were really wedded: and this was the secret of its remarkable power.

For the Senate differed from the House of Lords in authority as well as in outlook. Because of the length of the term of office and the tradition of re-electing outgoing members, it tended to attract the ablest politicians—a development which in turn increased the power, and consequently the attractiveness, of the second chamber.[5] The senators, unlike British peers, had all undergone a regular political apprenticeship, and they were elected by the most active politicians in their localities. They therefore had their ears very close to the ground, and they used their influence with much more skill than the Lords. They rarely rejected bills outright: those they disliked were simply buried in committees from which they never emerged.[6] They did not challenge governments fresh from a general election. They knew that majorities of the Left were unstable, since their marginal elements always tended to seek a change of allies when the elections were past and the budget had to be dealt with. At the critical moment, when the moderate Radicals in the Chamber were already contemplating switching over from a *Cartel* to a *Concentration* policy, from working with the Socialists to working with the Conservatives, their more influential friends in the upper house would intervene to stiffen their determination and hasten their decision. The senators thus did not openly defy public opinion, but tried to circumvent it, or waited for it to change. They would bow before a surge of popular feeling like that of 1936, passing without resistance a mass of legislation which they detested, in the justifiable confidence that their revenge would not be long delayed.

In the later years of the Third Republic these tactics steadily increased the effective power of the Senate. Its constitutional position was vague, especially over the crucial question, the degree to which the government was responsible to it as well as to the Chamber. Custom rather than

---

[5] French ministers, it will be remembered, may speak in either house.

[6] Woman suffrage and proportional representation were two of the proposals which the Senate was able to block until the end. It delayed effective provision for the secrecy of the ballot for nine years, income tax for eight, a weekly rest-day in industry for four, pensions for railwaymen for twelve, etc. Sharp, p. 128; J. Barthélemy, *Le Gouvernement de la France*, p. 82.

law was the decisive factor. The Senate was able to eject two governments before 1914, and a third in 1925. Thus, in the fifty-five years from 1875 to 1929 only three ministries had been overthrown by it: but in the last ten years of the Third Republic it disposed of four. It was significant that two of these were too clerical, and the other two too socialist for the liking of the upper house.

Since its political bias was so clearly defined, the Senate's status was naturally a matter of party controversy. In the early years of the regime its abolition had been one of the principal demands of the Radicals, but they urged it with steadily decreasing fervour, and silently abandoned it when the Senate came under Radical control. Antonin Dubost, who wrote a book advocating abolition of the Senate, ended his career as its President, and was succeeded in that august position by Léon Bourgeois, the first prime minister ever thrown out of office by the upper house.[7] But the demand for abolition was taken up by the Socialists, who were always under-represented there, and maintained by them until the fall of the regime.

The old-fashioned, anti-clerical conservatism of the Senate was extremely unpopular at the time of liberation, when Communists, M.R.P. and Socialists held the ascendancy, and the Radical party was discredited. The 25 to 1 vote against a return to the former regime was largely a vote of censure on the Senate. Accordingly, the first draft constitution contained no second chamber at all, though there were two advisory bodies which formed no part of Parliament. But a unicameral solution was going too far to the other extreme for the marginal voter, and the draft was defeated at the referendum of May 1946. In the second Constituent Assembly the battle was fought out between three tendencies. The Radicals and their supporters favoured a virtual return to the old Senate. M.R.P., like General de Gaulle, wanted a broadly corporative chamber, representing professional and colonial interests as well as local authorities. The parties of the Left, Communists and Socialists, would have preferred no second chamber at all; but, recognizing that there must be one if the constitution were to be accepted at the polls, they hoped to keep it feeble and submissive. For the moment the latter opinion prevailed. But while the powers of the new body were laid down in the constitution, the method of composing it was left to an ordinary ' organic ' law,[8] and could be reconsidered in two years' time.

2. COMPOSITION

THE new upper house was to be entitled the Council of the Republic, the change of name emphasizing that it was not a reincarnation of the

---

[7] E. M. Sait, *Government and politics of France*, p. 125.
[8] An organic law is a law on a major matter of governmental organization, such as the method of presenting the budget, the electoral law, etc. Procedurally it is no different from an ordinary law.

Senate. Article 6 of the constitution prescribes five rules governing its composition. It must be elected on a territorial basis (i.e. with no representation of professional or 'corporative' elements) by the local communities, namely the communes and departments (*par les collectivités communales et départementales*)—a vague formula which could be, and has been, interpreted in very different ways. It is chosen by universal *indirect* suffrage. It is renewed by halves (but exceptional provision was made for the first renewal, as described below). Up to a sixth of its members may be elected by the National Assembly, by proportional representation. Its membership must be between 250 and 320.

These meagre requirements were completed, as far as the first Council was concerned, by the excessively complicated law of 27 October 1946. This law fixed the total number of councillors at 315, compared with 314 for the old Senate. They were divided into four categories. The first, numbering 200, was to be elected by the local communities of metropolitan France. Each department had an electoral college, which included its deputies and the members of its departmental council (roughly equivalent to county council), but of which the overwhelming majority was formed by delegates, of whom there were one for every 300 electors on the register. In the whole of France there were about 85,000 of these 'grand electors', compared with some 3,000 departmental councillors, and 544 deputies. The election took place in two stages. At the first, the voters chose directly the grand electors, casting their votes for lists which they could not alter; between these lists the seats were distributed by P.R. At the second stage, the electoral colleges chose the Councillors of the Republic. In 68 departments which had only one councillor apiece, they elected by simple majority vote. In the 22 larger departments, 59 councillors were chosen by P.R. The remaining 73 of these 200 seats were to be allotted to the *parties* in such a way as to bring about P.R. (based on the first-stage voting) over the whole country, and to the individual *candidates* of each party who had, proportionately, polled best in their own areas.

The second category of councillors consisted of 50 members chosen by the National Assembly. Five of these were to represent French residents in the protectorates of Tunisia and Morocco, and three Frenchmen living abroad. The other 42 were to be chosen by P.R. Seven seats were distributed so as to ensure still more accurate nation-wide P.R.: the remaining 35 were divided, by P.R., between the groups in the Assembly itself. The third and fourth categories consisted respectively of 14 members chosen by the local government bodies of Algeria, and of 51 elected by those of French territories overseas. But the complicated P.R. provisions ensured that the party composition of the first Council was almost identical with that of the first National Assembly.

Article 102 required the whole Council to be re-elected within two years, after the election of new local authorities. By that time the political situation had changed completely. The Communists were out of office, and engaged in active opposition to the regime. Gaullism had attracted a great popular following. P.R., which would guarantee a majority of seats to the combined oppositions, had consequently lost favour with the parliamentary majority. The opportunity was therefore taken to revise completely the law composing the Council. The changes showed how very widely the requirements of Article 6 of the constitution could be interpreted.

The new law of 24 September 1948 fixed the term of membership at six years: under the constitution, half (chosen by lot) were to be renewed at a time.[9] The minimum age of 35 was retained, and so were the ineligibility rules, which are those applying to the Assembly. A candidate might not stand in more than one constituency at a time (as he could for the Senate). The numbers were left substantially unchanged, with 246 metropolitan councillors instead of 242, and 74 overseas representatives instead of 73. The new total of 320 was the maximum constitutionally permitted. The method of electing the metropolitan councillors was completely changed. The complicated provisions ensuring nation-wide P.R. were swept away. The National Assembly was no longer to exercise its right to elect a sixth of the Council.[10] All the metropolitan seats were to be distributed among the departments, which were given one seat for the first 154,000 inhabitants, and another for each subsequent 250,000 or fraction thereof.

In the electoral colleges (the second stage of the election) P.R. was to operate only in the 11 largest departments, which, having a population exceeding 654,000, were entitled to four or more seats, and which elected altogether 72 councillors. The remaining 79 departments, with 174 seats in all, elected by majority vote and a double ballot system.[11] At the same time the composition of the electoral colleges themselves was drastically altered. The deputies and departmental councillors remained members of them. But the 85,000 'grand electors', chosen by the citizens, vanished and were replaced by 100,000 representatives of the municipal councillors. Each municipality was represented according to the size of its council, which increases with population, though of course not proportionately. In

---

[9] The members were divided (according to their constituencies listed alphabetically) into two equal groups: the decision as to which half should be renewed first was made by lot. The law provided that the first renewal should be in May 1952, and the second in May 1955.

[10] The National Assembly was to elect only seven members to the new Council, three representing Frenchmen living abroad, three those in Morocco, and one (provisionally) those in Indo-China. The two representing Frenchmen in Tunisia were now to be chosen locally. The Indo-China member was the newcomer, who brought the overseas total up from 73 to 74.

[11] As usual with a double ballot system, for election on the first ballot the support of an absolute majority of those voting, and of at least a quarter of those entitled to vote, was necessary. On the second ballot a simple plurality sufficed.

electing their delegates, the first stage of the whole process, only the councils of the 1,312 communes with more than 3,500 inhabitants used P.R. Those of the remaining 36,000 elected by majority vote, with three ballots.

Thus the former system, which amounted to direct election disguised (by the thin screen of the ' grand electors ') in order to abide by the provisions of the constitution, was succeeded by a method similar in principle to that used for electing the old Senate. The purpose of the change was, as in the Third Republic, to favour the small communities against the large. For since both Communists and R.P.F. were strongest in the great cities, an electoral law which restricted the representation of the latter was bound to work to the advantage of the parties supporting the regime.

The weighting was not as extreme as it had been in the case of the Senate. The urban half of the population, the half which lives in communes of more than 3,500 inhabitants, elects a third of the municipal delegates: two-thirds of them represent the rural half. The countryside, rather than the small town, is most favoured by the distribution. Thus in Oise, a department containing no big city, nearly two-thirds of the delegates are elected by the tiny communes, those with less than 1,000 inhabitants, which include between them less than half the total population.[12] The large cities, though seriously under-represented, are less badly off than they were in senatorial elections. Thus Marseilles, with three-quarters of the population of its department, elected only 7 per cent. of the delegates before the war, while now it chooses 25 per cent. of them. Paris chooses 22½ per cent. of the delegates for the Seine, instead of 14 per cent., although its share of the population of the department has fallen from two-thirds to less than three-fifths. The eleven next largest towns, with 2½ million inhabitants out of a total of 40 million, have increased their number of delegates from 264 to nearly 900 (out of a total, however, of 100,000).[13]

The Council of the Republic elected in 1948 fulfilled the hope that it, like the former Senate, would represent the local authorities of France. Its 320 members included 107 mayors, and 20 chairmen and 124

---

[12] The 1,349 electors include 5 deputies, 35 members of the departmental council, 448 delegates from the communes with over 1,000 inhabitants (total population 210,000), and 861 from the smaller communes (population 199,000). (Figures for numbers and population of communes taken from Weill-Raynal, *loc. cit.*: numbers of delegates adjusted to conform with the provisions of the law.) The small communes had been still more favoured for the Senate.

[13] Pre-war figures from Sharp, p. 67; post-war ones calculated by the author.

See also Jean Bruyas, ' L'évolution du Conseil de la République ', *R.D.P.*, 1949, p. 553, and M. Duverger, 'Conseil de la République ou Chambre d'agriculture? ', *Le Monde*, 22 July 1953. The latter points out that in the most urbanized constituencies the rural minority is represented through P.R., whereas in the countryside the town-dwellers are excluded from influence by the majority system.

members of departmental councils.[14] Like most French political assemblies, it was dominated in occupational terms by the professional classes, to which 60 per cent. of its members belonged; the largest group, the lawyers, of whom there were 56, fell one short of the combined total of agricultural, industrial and trading interests. There were five workers.[15]

3. POWERS

THE makers of the constitution set out to produce the weakest possible second chamber. This design they pursued in two ways: firstly by making the new upper house politically the image of the National Assembly, so that it would be unlikely to challenge the latter, and secondly by severely restricting its powers, so that it would be unable to do so. The first part of this arrangement was included in an ordinary law, and was quickly altered, for the 1948 law produced a Council in which party strengths by no means corresponded to those in the Assembly. The second part survived, since it was included in the constitution, but in some respects its working was unexpected, and severely criticized.

The Council of the Republic is, under Article 5 of the constitution, a part of Parliament. Its members are in the same position as regards immunity, salary, ineligibility, etc., as the deputies; like the Assembly, it judges the validity of their election, and chooses its bureau by P.R. But precautions were taken to prevent its members acquiring the traditions of the former Senate—although, against the wishes of the Left, it was housed, like the Senate, in the Luxembourg Palace. Many means of differentiation were nevertheless found. The precedence as well as the power of the National Assembly was emphasized by conferring on it the title previously borne by the two houses combined, when they met as the repository of national sovereignty to elect a President or to revise the constitution. The President of the Assembly has replaced the President of the former Senate as the second person in the state. The bureau of the Assembly, under Article 11, acts for the two houses when they meet in joint session, whereas in the Third Republic that of the Senate did so. The President of the Republic, under Article 37, may communicate directly with the Assembly, but not with the Council.

Above all, under Article 9, the meetings of the Council depend on those of the Assembly: their sessions (though not necessarily their daily sittings) must exactly coincide. This prevents any demonstration like that of the House of Lords in 1947, when it irritated the Labour government by meeting in the middle of the summer recess to debate

---

[14] From the speech of its President, M. Monnerville, opening the 1950 session. *J.O.* (C.R.) 17 January 1950, p. 20.
[15] *Le Figaro*, 16 November 1948.

the economic situation. More seriously, since the Council cannot deal with bills until they have passed through the Assembly, this provision crowds far too much of its work into the last days of the session. But all these precautions could not prevent frequent appeals to the tradition of the Senate, symbolized in December 1948, when the Radical, Conservative and Gaullist majority of the new Council promptly celebrated their victory by voting themselves the title of 'Senators, members of the Council of the Republic.'

The powers of the Council are strictly limited. Under Article 29 it joins with the Assembly in electing the President of the Republic, about a third of the electors being senators. Under Article 67 it chooses its proportionate share (a third) of the metropolitan members of the Assembly of the French Union, and under Article 91 it has four representatives (out of thirteen) on the Constitutional Committee. Whereas the Senate was the supreme political court of the Third Republic, the Council plays no part at all in nominating the new High Court, nor is it represented on the new High Council of the Magistrature. While it and its committees may discuss the policy of the government, the cabinet is expressly declared by Article 48 not to be responsible to it: this settles a point which in the case of the Senate was legally in dispute. Under Article 7, the Council must be consulted before war is declared: but its consent is not required. In effect the same position obtains under Article 27 with regard to treaties which require parliamentary ratification, and under Article 20 for legislation. It cannot initiate a revision of the constitution, though it can block one (unless the proposal has the approval either of two-thirds of the Assembly, or of the electorate in a referendum). It can also prevent surreptitious revision, by challenging bills which seem to infringe the constitution before the Constitutional Committee, provided the President of the Republic consents.[16]

The legislative powers of the Council are closely restricted. Its members may introduce bills of their own, but under Article 14 these must be sent at once to the National Assembly, without being debated in the Council. Bills which have passed the Assembly fall under Article 20. They are forwarded to the Council, which must deal with them within two months; if it fails to do so, the bill may be promulgated as it was passed by the Assembly.[17] The delaying tactics of the Senate are thus prevented in a way similar to that suggested by M. Blum in 1919.[18] For two types of bill the Council's period for consideration

---

[16] On constitutional revision and the Constitutional Committee, see below, pp. 287–92.

[17] The only occasion when the Assembly has actually demanded the promulgation of a law in these circumstances was in June 1948: the incident is discussed below, p. 291. Yet only half a dozen bills had actually been dealt with by the Council within the very strict limits required by the rules as then interpreted by the Assembly. S. Grumbach, *J.O.* (C.R.) 15 June 1948, p. 1504.

[18] *Op. cit.*, pp. 167–8.

is still more narrowly limited: in the case of the budget it is restricted to the time actually taken in the Assembly, and in the case of bills passed under the urgency procedure to the time laid down for such cases in the Assembly's standing orders.

The latter provision was more important than it appeared to be. For the abuse of the urgency procedure by the National Assembly still further weakened the far from imposing rights of the Council. Intended to be exceptional, this procedure came to be invoked by every deputy as a means of securing priority for his own bills. The administration, which special powers and Vichy had made contemptuous of parliamentary control, often treated the legislature with scant respect. It would carelessly delay introducing urgent bills until unnecessarily late in the day, and then use the lateness as an excuse for invoking the urgency procedure, which prevented thorough examination.[19] Half the bills passed in 1947 went through in this way, which was particularly damaging to the Council of the Republic since it virtually ruled out effective committee examination there.[20] Complaints came to a head in June 1948, when the Assembly left the Council only 33 hours (including two nights) to consider a bill which was by common consent urgent, but which, also by common consent, raised issues requiring careful inquiry. The Council, unanimously except for the Communists, decided to overrun the permitted limits: the Assembly, with the agreement of all parties in it, demanded that the bill should be promulgated under Article 20. The Council protested to the Constitutional Committee against the Assembly's interpretation of the Article, and won its point. Its success led to a relaxation of the rules governing the urgency procedure, allowing the Council a minimum of three days' grace;[21] and the excessive use of the procedure was eventually checked by revision of the standing orders of the Assembly.[22]

If a bill is passed by the Council in the same terms as those voted by the Assembly, it becomes law and is promulgated forthwith. But if the

---

[19] F. G., ' Premier bilan de la constitution ', *Esprit*, September 1947, pp. 345–6: E. Blamont, ' Les conditions du contrôle parlementaire ', *R.D.P.*, 1950, p. 397, who quotes the case of a government bill to establish a public holiday on the first of May. This was introduced and passed on 29 April 1947, and promulgated next day. In the following year it was found necessary to amend this rushed act: but the necessary legislation was again not brought in until 20 April.

[20] F. G., *loc. cit.*: between January and August 1947, 88 bills were passed under the urgency procedure, and 73 normally: the Council amended 39 of the latter, but only 27 of the former. See also Philippe Gerber, ' Les attributions législatives du Conseil de la République, *Politique*, April 1948, pp. 407–9: and above, pp. 208–9.

[21] But in the Assembly the period excludes, in the Council it includes the time spent in committee.

On the whole incident see Lidderdale, pp. 263–4: *A.P.*, 1948, pp. 98, 336: and A. Soulier, ' La délibération du Comité Constitutionnel du 18 juin 1948 ', *R.D.P.*, 1949, pp. 195 ff.

[22] In 1947 half the bills passed (130 out of 267) went through under the urgency procedure. From January to August 1948, inclusive, the proportion was a quarter (59 out of 237). Bruyas, *loc. cit.*, p. 549. For the whole legislature the figures were 208 and 1,314, and for the first year of the new Assembly (to 12 July 1952) 6 and 224.

Council introduces amendments, the Assembly is obliged to consider them. It may accept them in whole or in part,[23] or it may reject them altogether: its decision is final. There is no way by which it can suggest further amendments in order to arrive at a mutually satisfactory compromise—the practice which prevailed in the Third Republic, and was known as the *navette*. The Council's one real protection is contained in the last paragraph of Article 20, which provides that amendments voted in public ballot by an absolute majority of the Council can be overridden in the Assembly only in the same condition. This qualification seemed of minor importance when it was assumed that the political composition of the two houses would be almost identical, but acquired new significance when the law of September 1948 brought into existence a Council with a political majority very different from that in the Assembly.

In the financial sphere there are further restrictions. Article 17 reserves to the deputies the right to initiate expenditure. Senators, therefore, under their own standing orders, may not move amendments to financial bills which would increase expenditure above the maximum proposed in the Assembly by the government or the Finance committee (though, unlike their predecessors in the Third Republic, they may introduce amendments to increase revenue).[24] If senators themselves bring in bills which would increase expenditure or reduce revenue, these cannot be received by the Assembly (under Article 14 of the constitution) and so cannot be discussed at all.

The broad effect of the constitution is thus to establish a second chamber whose views must always be heard by the Assembly, but can always be rejected by it. The Council never has the first word, for it has no right to initiate, and never has the last, for its advice can always be overridden by the Assembly; but its word must always be spoken, and the Assembly must have the opportunity of changing its mind after hearing the opinion of the *chambre de réflexion*.

4. THE SECOND CHAMBER IN PRACTICE

THE first Council of the Republic made no serious attempt to challenge the authority of the National Assembly, of which it was from the party point of view a replica. Yet, within the constitutional limits which it did not try to exceed, its prestige and influence grew steadily. During the first six months the Assembly frequently rejected without discussion suggestions on which the Council had spent a great deal of time and

---

[23] This has been interpreted to mean, not only that the Assembly may accept some of the Council's amendments and reject others, but also that it may adopt a compromise figure between different amounts. See E. Blamont, ' La seconde lecture dans la Constitution de 1946 '. *Revue française de science politique*, July-September 1951, pp. 305–6.
[24] Lidderdale, p. 265.

trouble.[25] But from June 1947 onwards it became a little more accommodating, partly because the Communists were now in opposition, and partly because the Council took steps to explain to the Assembly the reasons for its amendments, either through personal contacts between the two committee *rapporteurs*, or through the good offices of the government. The new approach was indicated by the acceptance of amendments clarifying the Algerian government bill, and of others modifying the municipal election bill.[26]

In November 1947 the Council for the first time played a significant political role. Paradoxically enough, it was the Communists, the bitterest opponents of a strong upper house, who introduced the change by trying, without success, to use the Council to obstruct the government's bills for the maintenance of order during the general strike. Later, in December 1947 and in August 1948, the majority in the Council found opportunities to assert its claims by restoring to the form desired by the government two bills of major importance, M. René Mayer's special tax measure and M. Paul Reynaud's special powers bill, which had been seriously weakened in the Assembly. That body, having successfully shifted the responsibility, accepted the changes.[27]

On many matters less central to the party struggle, the Assembly agreed to almost all the Council's proposals. In September 1948 it even permitted the Council to amend the new law governing its own future composition. In the same month, however, a more significant incident occurred. The Council, in a vote in which few members took part, reversed the Assembly's decision to postpone the departmental council elections—an intervention which threatened to divide the majority and upset the government. Most of those who voted for this change were Communists; and though the manœuvre failed, it showed how the second chamber could be used as a weapon against the parties of the majority. The lesson was not forgotten.[28]

Closely contested decisions of the Council were easily overridden. But those carried by an absolute majority could be reversed only by a similar majority in the Assembly, which was not always easy to find. The Gaullists hoped to use this provision of the constitution to upset the existing constitutional settlement. If they could win control of the Council at the elections of November 1948, they could then claim that the mandate of the Assembly was clearly exhausted, and that it ought

---

[25] For example, on the law of 30 March 1947 dealing with landlord-tenant relationships, a series of changes unanimously rejected in the Council, were unanimously, *and without debate*, reintroduced by the Assembly. Gerber, *loc. cit.*, p. 407.

[26] Bruyas, *loc. cit.*, p. 547.

[27] Bruyas, p. 548; *A.P.*, 1947, pp. 247, 250; 1948, p. 133.

[28] *A.P.*, 1948, pp. 157–60. M. Marie once went so far as to declare that he would treat the rejection of an amendment to M. Reynaud's bill as a matter of confidence (Bruyas, p. 571; *A.P.*, 1948, p. 132; *J.O.* (C.R.), 13 August 1948, p. 2402). But this surprising development, which was clearly contrary to the spirit of the constitution, has not been repeated.

to be dissolved: if necessary, they could use their majority in the Council to force a dissolution by blocking the government's legislative programme. In this aim they narrowly failed.

The new electoral law for the Council of the Republic had two aspects: it favoured the small communities against the big cities, and it generally replaced P.R. by a double ballot majority system. The first change worked against the extreme parties, which were strongest in the great towns, and the second harmed those parties which found it difficult to attract allies. Both considerations injured the Communists, as had been intended: they were reduced to only 16 metropolitan senators, all elected in the 11 departments where P.R. was still retained. M.R.P. had in any case forfeited much popular support to the R.P.F., and was further injured by the second change, since its Socialist and Radical associates tended to combine against it in anti-clerical alliances. Thus Communists and M.R.P., who between them held a majority of the seats in the Assembly, were the victims of the law, electing barely 40 out of the 320 senators. The Socialists, with 60 members, held their own.

The remaining seats were divided between Radicals, Conservatives, and Gaullists, with a great deal of overlapping between them. The R.P.F. claimed to have recruited 150 members to their inter-group, but only 58 joined the separate R.P.F. group, and events were to show that the 'political bigamists' could not be counted on to obey the Gaullist whip. In the first important vote, on budgetary procedure, M. Pierre de Gaulle could muster only 132 supporters (including the 21 Communists) against 154. The government thus retained a margin in the new Council, though it was small and precarious. But the success of Gaullists and Radicals, and the defeat of Communists and M.R.P., meant that on opposition and government benches alike the social and economic conservatives were far stronger in the second chamber than in the first.[29]

The new majority set out to assert itself in three ways: by trying to extend the powers of the Council, by endeavouring to embarrass the government, and by exerting a conservative influence on policy. The Council's main attempt to increase its powers was made in its new standing orders, adopted in June 1949. These made two important changes, one over the right to initiate legislation, which the Council was unable to maintain, the other over criticism of the government, with which it had more success.

The first change provided that bills introduced by senators should be discussed by the relevant committee of the Council before being sent to

---

[29] At the beginning of 1949 the official figures for the various groups in the Council (including *apparentés*) were: Communists 21, Socialists 61, M.R.P. 21, R.G.R. 86, A.D.R. (Gaullists) 58, various Conservatives 72. Thus the *tripartiste* parties, which had won three-quarters of the seats in the Assembly in November 1946, secured less than a third of those in the Council two years later. *J.O.* (*Lois et décrets*) 1949, p. 539.

the Assembly, unless their promoter requested otherwise. The Council claimed that this was not an infringement of Article 14, since the bills would go to the Assembly before any debate in the full Council had taken place. But the proposal produced an immediate reaction in the Assembly, where the defunct *tripartiste* majority was promptly reconstituted. With the Communists, Socialists, and M.R.P. voting together against the Radicals, Conservatives and R.P.F., the Assembly decided by 429 to 150 that it would refuse to receive any bill which had been dealt with in any way by the Council of the Republic. On this point the upper house had to give way.[30]

The second change was concerned with the procedure of 'oral question with debate'. This was very similar to an interpellation in the National Assembly. It too involved a request to a minister to explain his actions, followed by his reply. But two restrictions had been imposed. Oral question with debate could not be initiated by an individual member: substantial backing was necessary (that of a party leader, of a committee, or of thirty senators). And, above all, it was not concluded by a vote. Even so, the parties which wanted a weak second chamber had opposed its introduction.

In June 1949, the new majority swept away both restrictions, transforming the oral question with debate into an interpellation in everything but name. This development provoked indignation in the Assembly, which claimed that since under Article 48 of the constitution the government was not responsible to the Council of the Republic, it followed that the latter was not entitled to debate and vote on governmental policy. M. Herriot, as a Radical, personally favoured a stronger second chamber; but as President of the Assembly, he wrote a letter of protest to the President of the Republic. The latter expressed sympathy for the Assembly's point of view, but regretted that he could not constitutionally intervene, since the Constitutional Committee could function in one direction only, to protect the upper house against the lower. The Council remained unrepentant. It argued that though its legislative powers were restricted, its debating rights were not; and claimed that its duty to give opinions on declarations of war, ratification of treaties, etc., necessarily implied a right to discuss ministerial policy. On this point, in contrast to its failure to extend its legislative influence, it was entirely successful.[31]

---

[30] Lidderdale, pp. 259-60. *J.O.*, 28 June 1949, pp. 3801-9, 3836-7.

[31] Another attempted encroachment, to which the Assembly took exception, was the Council's practice of introducing entirely new material into financial bills by way of amendments. In May 1950, on a bill dealing with the special Treasury accounts, the Assembly's *rapporteur* successfully protested that this was unconstitutional under Article 17, which reserved to the Assembly the right of financial initiative. *J.O.*, 25 April 1950, p. 3957.

Both this practice, and oral questions with debate, were to be banned under the constitutional revision proposed in November 1950, but subsequently allowed to lapse. See the

In the second place, the new majority tried to embarrass the government. There were exceptional cases like that in March 1949, when the Assembly voted only two of the three provisional twelfths requested by the Defence minister, and the Council restored the third. But such incidents were rare. Much more frequently the opposition parties took up an issue on which the majority was divided, and used the Council of the Republic to exacerbate the division, and so to weaken the ministry. This occurred in May 1949 over the price and rationing of petrol—a politically awkward question in many countries. It happened in April 1951 over the electoral law, when the Council voted for *scrutin d'arrondissement* by an enormous majority, 206 to 37: since it was certain that the Assembly would not accept this, the Council's vote nearly killed electoral reform altogether.[32] Above all, it took place every year over the budget, since the opposition parties could always count on Radical and Conservative support in the ever-popular cause of refusing increased taxation.

The new Council of the Republic showed its intentions at once, at the end of 1948, by making drastic changes in the budget for 1949. The opposition first amended the *loi des maxima*, and then rejected it (as amended) by 105 to 0; 207 government supporters abstained rather than support the mutilated measure, while the Gaullists, after re-shaping the bill, voted against their own version. This provoked a public outcry, and the National Assembly restored the original provisions.[33] On the *loi de finances* the right-wing opposition changed their tactics. This time they amended the bill and then supported it, carrying it by 150 to 23 (mainly Communists). But the governmental senators again

---

report of Mme Peyroles (*A.N.*, Doc. no. 11,431, p. 7) and her speech (*J.O.*, 29 November 1950, p. 8267). The suggested restrictions were not revived in 1953.

For oral question with debate, see Lidderdale, pp. 267–9; Bruyas, *loc. cit.*, pp. 568–70; for M. Herriot's letter of 9 July 1949 and President Auriol's reply of 27 July, *A.P.*, 1949, p. 219; and the important article by M. Marcel Plaisant, chairman of the Foreign Affairs committee of the Council: ' Le contrôle de la politique étrangère par le Conseil de la République ', *Revue politique et parlementaire*, March 1950. See also below, p. 290 n.

The Assembly's case rested entirely on the assumption that every interpellation involved the fate of the government. But this was to treat as a dead letter all the careful constitutional provision for questions of confidence. The weakness of the juridical argument, however, emphasized all the more clearly the deputies' jealousy of the upper house, and their scant regard for the ' confidence clauses '.

[32] *A.P.*, 1949, pp. 39, 81; 1951, p. 97. Since M.R.P. was bitterly opposed to *scrutin d'arrondissement*, and M.R.P. and the Communists together held a majority in the Assembly, there was no hope of its passing—unless indeed the Communists made a sudden volte-face and supported it, as at one point they hinted they might do. When the Council rejected the Assembly's bill, the latter mustered only 308 votes to override it—three short of an absolute majority. The government was on the point of resigning, when M. Herriot proposed to refer the bill back to committee. Eventually a new and slightly amended bill was introduced, and an absolute majority was found to override the Council's opposition—strong pressure having been put on the Socialist recalcitrants whose defection had caused the previous failure. *A.P.*, 1951, p. 100, and below, p. 360.

[33] *A.P.*, 1948, pp. 227–8. The Assembly decided, by a majority, to treat the rejection as one all-embracing amendment. Thus the amendments voted by the Council were never examined in the Assembly at all. Hence, in part, the change of tactics over the *loi de finances*. Bruyas, *loc. cit.*, p. 559.

abstained, there was no absolute majority for the new bill, and the Assembly easily restored its original proposals.[34] The prestige of the Council suffered severely from these manœuvres; even greater damage was done to that of the R.P.F., which had based so much of its propaganda on denouncing the parties and their complex and crafty parliamentary intrigues.

A year later some of the senators had learned their lesson. They were furious with M. Bidault, who had included no senator in his ministry, and were most reluctant to vote for his proposed tax increases. These had had so difficult a passage in the Assembly that an absolute majority could clearly not be obtained for them there.[35] Yet 29 Radical senators deliberately abstained on the decisive vote, to ensure that the Council's new unbalanced *loi de finances* should go through with less than an absolute majority; the voting was 158 to 67, three short of the crucial figure. Deadlock was thus avoided. The Finance committee of the Assembly made compromise proposals, the Council's amendments were duly defeated—and the prime minister took an early opportunity to invite the leader of the Radical senators to join his cabinet. The annual unbalancing of the budget by the Council, followed by a governmental success in the Assembly, was repeated in January 1951 with the budget for that year.[36]

The Council's intransigence on budgetary issues was not solely due to the greater strength of the opposition there. It also reflected the stronger representation of the middle-class parties. There were indeed two different majorities in the Council—a narrow one in favour of the government when its existence was at stake, and a much larger one in support of conservative policies at other times. Thus in January 1950 the Council upset the bill for restoring collective bargaining, making it much less favourable to the trade unions. In June of the same year it tried to switch 30 milliard francs (£30 million) of investment funds from the nationalized to the private sector. (In both cases the *tripartiste* majority of Communists, Socialists and M.R.P. revived in the National Assembly to restore the proposals to their former shape.) Even after

---

[34] *J.O.* (C.R.), 31 December 1948, pp. 3826, 3897–8.

[35] Many Radical deputies would not vote for higher taxes, fearing that their senatorial colleagues from the same party and department would reject these, thus acquiring a popularity which would make them more dangerous rivals when the time came to choose Radical candidates for the next parliamentary election. This was a significant contrast with the Third Republic, when it was the senators who feared the competition of the deputies. J. Fauvet, *Le Monde*, 22 December 1949, 1 February 1950; P. Collet, *Ce Matin*, 30 January 1950.

[36] With the advent of a Conservative administration in 1952, the Council for a moment seemed inclined to act as a counter-balancing chamber, moving Left as the Assembly moved Right; at first it amended the budget on two crucial points, to the satisfaction of M.R.P. But it promptly reversed these decisions, and voted M. Pinay's budget by a relative majority (in order to facilitate the ministry's task in the Assembly) and without any major changes. Next year, it made no difficulties over M. Mayer's budget; but though it voted special powers to M. Laniel, it rejected all his proposed tax increases, and had to be overridden by the Assembly.

the election of the new Assembly in 1951, the Council remained the more conservative body of the two, and was able in co-operation with the government to delay and block the sliding scale for wages, which the deputies favoured.[37] Socially and economically the upper house was still, as in the Third Republic, a weapon of the bourgeoisie and the peasantry against the town workers.

The constitution-makers intended to establish a second chamber too weak to impose its own will on the National Assembly, but strong enough to ensure that the latter's decisions should be, not hurried and accidental, but duly considered. They achieved this purpose. The Assembly can no longer be described as ' complacently listening to the echo of its own voice ', nor the Council as possessing little more political importance than the *Académie française*.[38] On the other hand the new second chamber is not a revived Senate, able by skilful obstruction and pressure to dominate the general course of governmental and legislative action. Thus in this respect the makers of the constitution have attained their main objective. Yet their solution of the second chamber problem has nevertheless revealed in practice both technical and political flaws.

Technically, two particular weaknesses have become evident. The first follows from two constitutional provisions taken together: firstly, that the Council cannot initiate legislation, but must wait for the Assembly to send up measures for it to discuss: secondly, that it must begin, end, and interrupt its sessions at the same time as the Assembly does so. The consequence is that its agenda is far too scanty when it assembles, and far too crowded just before it recesses. Instead of a reasonably steady flow of business, the Council has to complain of idleness for most of its time, and of gross overwork for the rest.[39] This is only partly due to lack of consideration on the part of the Assembly; it is to some extent inevitable under the provisions of the constitution. If senators could introduce bills in their own house, or if at least some government bills could start their legislative career there, the work of the Council could be much more efficiently distributed, while that of the Assembly would be considerably lightened.

In the second place, the method of dealing with the Council's amendments under Article 20 has proved too rigid. For while the Assembly may accept or reject them, it cannot introduce new matter of its own.

---

[37] *A.P.*, 1950, pp. 11, 133; 1951, p. 335. It is often illiberal on other matters; thus in May 1951 it prevented the wide increase in the colonial franchise which the Assembly had accepted, and in July 1953 it refused to extend to conscientious objectors the amnesty which it was granting to collaborators.

[38] Duverger, *Manuel*, p. 355; Priouret, p. 263.

[39] The Council ' attend des semaines entières pour être saisi d'un texte sur lequel il puisse valablement discuter, ou se trouve subitement submergé (en fin de session notamment) par les textes qui lui sont transmis.' Mme Peyroles' report on constitutional revision, *loc. cit.*, p. 6; and her speech, *loc. cit.*

This can lead to absurd situations.[40] Various subterfuges have been used to enable compromise proposals to be brought forward, but none is wholly satisfactory. To withdraw the bill and substitute a new one wastes time, to use the President's right to refer bills back for reconsideration cheapens a device which ought to be reserved for matters more important than drafting amendments.[41]

Similar difficulties may arise when the Council amends or rejects a measure by an absolute majority. From 1948 to 1951 the majority in the Council was very different from that in the Assembly. The absolute majority rule, instead of being exceptional, has been frequently invoked: nearly a tenth of all the bills passed in the 1946–51 legislature were amended or rejected in the Council by an absolute majority.[42] In such circumstances, if the Assembly rejects the Council's view by a simple majority only, a situation of complete deadlock is reached. The measure is neither accepted nor rejected. This occurred only six times in the first legislature, but some of these six bills (notably the 1951 electoral law and the 1951 budget) were of first-class importance. Solutions have been found by referring the bill back to the competent committee of the Assembly, or by withdrawing it and substituting a new one; in either case an opportunity is made to introduce changes sufficient to satisfy one or the other house.[43] But the old *navette*, by which the minister negotiated a mutually satisfactory compromise between the houses, was a simpler and more direct solution than the alternative devices which have replaced it; and it would be perfectly possible to restore it, while safeguarding the Assembly's right to the decisive word.

Even minor changes in the constitution, however, are difficult to make. For the position of the second chamber did not cease to be controversial when the constitution was adopted. The first Council of the Republic, by its cautious determination not to overstep the bounds

---

[40] '... on voit les députés s'acharner, avec un pot de colle et de grands ciseaux, sur l'amendement, essayer d'en supprimer certains mots, couper des membres de phrase et recoller le texte en sautant une virgule, un adjectif ou une proposition incidente ... avec la double préoccupation de n'ajouter ni une iota, ni une virgule, car l'article 20 serait violé, et de reconstituer un texte qui n'offense pas tout de même trop la syntaxe. ...' M. Waline, *Les Partis contre la République*, p. 156.

[41] For these subterfuges see Mme Peyroles' report, *loc. cit.*, pp. 7–8; Bruyas, *loc. cit.*, p. 560; G. Berlia, *R.D.P.*, 1950, p. 682, note 1.

[42] During the first legislature the Assembly passed 1,360 bills, of which the Council accepted 774 unchanged, altered or rejected 540 (in 121 cases by an absolute majority), and had not dealt with 46 when Parliament adjourned. Blamont, 'La seconde lecture ...,' *loc. cit.*, pp. 298, 302.

[43] *Ibid.*, p. 309: one influential senator suggested that the reference back to committee of the electoral reform bill would have been a violation of the constitution (though no exception had been taken to it on previous measures), but that there could be no objection to the withdrawal of the bill and substitution of a new one, which was the course actually adopted.

By March 1953, 168 bills had been amended or rejected by an absolute majority. The number of deadlocks remained at six. *R.D.P.*, 1953, p. 437.

set for it, contrived to still some suspicions. Though at first its moderation led to the systematic disregard of its views, within two years it had enforced its own interpretation of the constitution over urgency procedure, made detailed improvements in many bills which the Assembly was glad to accept, given occasional useful support to the government in persuading the Assembly to revise its views, and acquired considerable prestige as a *chambre de réflexion*.

The second Council presented the anomaly of a supposedly sober, second-thoughts chamber in which extremist opinions were in fact more strongly represented than they were in the lower house. It abandoned the caution of its predecessor, and began openly to claim the position, and if possible also the powers of the old Senate. The Assembly reacted into suspicion and hostility. It developed an intense and watchful jealousy on petty points of prestige.[44] When the Council altered or rejected a bill, the Assembly, so far from reconsidering the merits of the issue, often reacted by affirming its original opinion by an increased majority.[45] The Council complained that the Assembly did not attend to its advice.[46] But this advice was not simply given in a disinterested, non-party attempt to improve the detail of bills while accepting their general purposes. It was more frequently designed for evident partisan objects—to exercise a conservative pressure on policy, to assist the opposition and embarrass the government, or to assert the powers of the second chamber. The parties which controlled the Council used it as an instrument against those holding the majority in the Assembly. While there was nothing illegitimate about this, the hostile response of the parties which favoured working-class interests,

---

[44] The law codifying provisions relating to the *pouvoirs publics*, passed on 6 January 1950, provides two examples of this conflict. The Council altered the arrangement of the clauses, so as to deal together with both houses of Parliament, separately with the non-parliamentary Assembly of the French Union and Economic Council. The Assembly rejected this arrangement, expressly because it implied that the Council's position was similar to its own and superior to that of the advisory bodies. Similarly there was a squabble over nomenclature. The Council knew that, in this bill, the Assembly would not let the word ' senator ' be used, so it tried to avoid the word ' deputy ' also: the Assembly insisted upon introducing it. See M. Cadart's article on the law in *R.D.P.*, 1950, pp. 149, 156.

[45] See, for example, *A.P.*, 1949, pp. 1, 81: 1950, pp. 3–4.

M. Fauvet's comment on the dispute over petrol rationing is significant: ' En bref le pouvoir des sénateurs est moins de réfléchir eux-mêmes que de faire réfléchir les députés. Or ce dont on peut leur faire grief, c'est précisément d'agir, ou tout au moins de parler, dans un esprit qui risque d'aboutir à un résultat diamétralement opposé. En brandissant son règlement comme une arme contre l'Assemblée Nationale, le gouvernement et le régime, le Conseil de la République éveille un réflexe de légitime défense chez ceux qu'il veut combattre et abattre. . . . ' *Le Monde*, 4 June 1949. See also *ibid.*, 6 January 1951.

[46] M. Monnerville, at a conference on administrative and political reform early in 1951, referred to the way the deputies ' renvoyaient d'une chiquenaude ' the Council's amendments, and complained ' Nous avons l'impression d'être inutiles sur le plan de la confection des lois: nos efforts sérieux n'aboutissent à rien.' *Le Figaro*, 8 February 1951. Two years later he complained that the Assembly had frequently rejected the Council's amendments without having read them. *J.O.* (C.R.), 16 July 1953, p. 1339.

of the supporters of the ministry, or of the deputies jealous of the prerogatives of their own chamber, was readily predictable.

The Council's campaign thus retarded rather than advanced its cause. Occasional successes, as in its assistance to the government over the sliding scale bill, must be offset against failures such as those over the budgets, the collective bargaining bill, and the electoral law. In trying to bring about by its own strength a *de facto* revision of the constitution, the Council created among the deputies a state of mind in which even proposals for minor reforms became suspect. Limited and technical amendments could not find favour as long as structural revision remained an important issue in the party battle.[47] This became evident in November 1950. For then the parties of the majority did agree both to restore the *navette*, and to allow bills to be sent for prior discussion in the Council by the Assembly's own decision.[48] But these proposals lapsed with the rest of the constitutional revision scheme; and the second chamber problem was the main cause of the delay in reviving it.[49] The tactics of the majority elected in October 1948 go far to explain the reluctance of the Socialists, and especially of M.R.P., to increase the present meagre powers of the upper house.

Members of the Council can nevertheless play a useful political part as individuals. Their parliamentary status gives them the opportunity to acquire influence in their own party, and so indirectly to affect policy.[50] It is true that the leading politicians are never likely to congregate in the Council as they once did in the Senate, and that many prominent senators regard their position as a mere stepping-stone to membership of the Assembly. But not all do so. The Council's ministerial representation is slowly increasing: from an under-secretaryship or two in the early years, it has risen to three or four places in recent governments,

---

[47] Bruyas, *loc. cit.*, p. 574.
[48] Mme Peyroles' report, *loc. cit.*, pp. 6–7; *Le Monde*, 17 November 1950.
[49] The revision proposals of July 1953 would amend Articles 14 and 20. Private members' bills would go first to the house to which their sponsor belongs; but senators would still be unable to propose increases in expenditure or reductions in revenue. The government would be able to introduce its bills in either house, except for certain categories which must start in the Assembly—namely bills to ratify treaties under Article 27, those increasing expenditure or reducing revenue, and budgetary or financial bills. (*R.D.P.*, 1953, p. 687. The last category, according to the *rapporteur*, would include monetary measures, such as devaluation bills).

The new Article 20 would eliminate the absolute majority clause, but would in return restore the *navette*. The Council would still have to decide on a bill within two months of receiving it from the Assembly; but if the two houses differed, the bill would 'shuttle' between them. If no agreement were reached within 100 days, counted from the time when the Council first received the bill for its *second* reading, then the Assembly's last text would pass into law. For the budget, the Council would (as at present) be allowed no longer time than the Assembly had taken; for urgent bills it would have twice as long (instead of the same time) as the Assembly allows itself by its standing orders. (*Ibid.*, p. 688). The Council may well not accept these changes.

[50] In 1953 the Socialist party amended its statutes to put the Socialist senators on a footing of complete equality with the deputies. Report of the 45th Congress, p. 146.

including one front-rank post, the Interior. One important party leader, the Conservative M. Duchet, seems content to remain a member of the upper house.

The eventual influence of the Council of the Republic is thus still quite uncertain. Clearly it is rather stronger than the makers of the constitution intended, but far weaker than the old Senate; and within those wide limits it is likely to remain.

Chapter 18

THE OTHER CONSTITUTIONAL ORGANS

THE essential provisions of the constitution are those which settle the position of the government and of the parliament, and the relationship between them. But the makers of the Fourth Republic also created a series of peripheral institutions. A Constitutional Committee ensures that laws conflicting with the terms of the constitution are submitted to the procedure prescribed for revising that document. Two advisory assemblies function, in the imperial, and in the economic and social spheres respectively. Ordinary justice is administered under the supervision of a new High Council, and political justice is dispensed by a new High Court. One chapter of the constitution deals with the local government structure. A preamble sets forth the principles of political action upon which the regime is supposed to be founded.

1. CONSTITUTIONAL REVISION AND THE CONSTITUTIONAL COMMITTEE

ARTICLE 90 states the procedure by which the constitution may be revised. It looks complicated, but is really quite simple. There are three stages: the adoption of a resolution to revise the constitution, the passing of a revision bill through the ordinary legislative process, and the acceptance of the proposal at a referendum. The complications arise from provisions allowing certain steps to be dispensed with if parliamentary support for the revision is particularly strong.

The preliminary resolution was part of the revision procedure in the Third Republic. Under the law of 1875, both houses had to pass the resolution by an absolute majority. Under the new ruling the resolution has to go through the Assembly, by an absolute majority, on two occasions separated by at least three months: but the second reading may be dispensed with if the Council of the Republic has meanwhile accepted the proposal by an absolute majority.[1]

The resolution must specify the ' object ' of the revision. On the first occasion when the procedure was set in motion, in November 1950, the Franchise committee of the Assembly interpreted this to mean that the articles and even the particular paragraphs to be revised should be specified, but that the terms of the proposed changes should not be indicated. This omission was unsuccessfully challenged in the

---

[1] In the second committee on the constitution M.R.P. proposed that the consent of the upper house should be required, but were defeated by 19 votes to 19. *S.C.C.*, II, p. 100. (In French procedure, a tie counts as a negative vote.)

Assembly by the pro-Communist M. Pierre Cot, who contended that it invalidated the resolution. As a result of the procedure adopted, the intentions of the reformers had to be deduced from the arguments of the *rapporteur*, or discovered from unofficial sources; as it was three years before a bill was introduced, the precise changes then proposed were never published. The Council of the Republic was in a difficult position. It favoured revision, on a much larger scale indeed than that desired by the Assembly, but it had some reason to fear that the latter wished to use the opportunity to reduce some of the powers of the upper house, in particular those which it had claimed in June 1949.[2] The resolution would not be valid if it were amended: the Council had either to accept or to reject it. It therefore voted the proposal, but accompanied its acceptance with a motion of its own demanding a broader revision, and affirming its determination to maintain all its existing rights.[3]

The second stage is the introduction of a bill, which goes through just the same procedure as an ordinary bill: that is to say, a simple majority of the Assembly is sufficient, unless the Council finds an absolute majority to reject or amend the measure, in which case an absolute majority of the Assembly can override the upper house. The final stage is the referendum. But this may be dispensed with if the bill obtains either a three-fifths majority in each house, or a two-thirds majority in the Assembly.[4]

There are three provisos governing the revision procedure. The Assembly cannot, even by a two-thirds majority, abolish the Council of the Republic by its own authority—though there appears to be nothing to prevent it from removing in this way the meagre powers possessed by the upper house.[5] No change at all may be made, or even initiated, while all or any part of France is under foreign occupation. This restriction, contained in Article 94, is an evident attempt to legislate for a new 1940. And, as in the Third Republic, no revision proposal may effect the republican form of the government, under Article 95.

The special procedure for constitutional revision carries a corollary. There must be a check on the Assembly, in order to prevent surreptitious revision through the ordinary process of legislation.[6] General de Gaulle wished this check, like so many other powers, to be exercised by the President of the Republic. The Socialists wanted it to take the form

---

[2] See above, pp. 278–9. For the grounds of the Council's fears, see above, p. 280 n. 31.
[3] *A.P.*, 1951, p. 8.
[4] These proportions presumably refer to numbers voting, not to total membership, since the converse is not specifically stated.
[5] Article 90, paragraph 8. The text runs: ' Aucune revision constitutionnelle relative à l'existence du Conseil de la République ne pourra être réalisée sans l'accord de ce Conseil ou le recours à la procédure du referendum.'
[6] It was the Communist refusal to accept such a check which finally led M.R.P. to oppose the first draft constitution. Wright, pp. 155–6.

of a referendum; but after the defeat of the first draft constitution they agreed to accept the M.R.P. solution, on which the present Article 91 is based. This establishes a Constitutional Committee of thirteen members: the President of the Republic is chairman, and the Presidents of both houses of Parliament sit *ex officio*. The rest are elected at the beginning of each parliamentary session, seven by the Assembly and three by the Council of the Republic, by proportional representation of the parties: they must not be members of the chamber which elects them. In practice the parties usually nominate professors of law sympathetic to their point of view. One of the first M.R.P. representatives was M. Marcel Prélot, once rector of the University of Strasbourg, and later a Gaullist deputy. The choice of the R.G.R. in the Assembly fell upon M. André Siegfried.

Article 92 deals with procedure. The Committee cannot take any action on its own account: the initiative must come from the Council of the Republic, voting by an absolute majority, and requires the assent of the President of the Republic, for the reference to the Committee is made by him and the President of the Council of the Republic, acting jointly. It must take place within the period allowed to the President for promulgating the law—i.e. ten days normally, five in cases where urgency is claimed. The Committee then attempts to reconcile the two houses, a task which is made no easier by the omission from the constitution of any means of arriving at a compromise text. If it fails in this attempt, it decides within five days of the reference to it (two days in cases of urgency) whether or not the law infringes the constitution. If the law is found to be constitutional, it is promulgated forthwith: if not, it returns to the Assembly, and the procedure of Article 90 must be put in motion before it can become law (Article 93). The last paragraph of Article 92, in a vital proviso, limits the competence of the Committee to the first 89 articles of the constitution (i.e. excluding those governing the revision procedure itself), so that it does not extend to the Preamble.

The last-mentioned provision is of great importance. The framers of the constitution had an extensive social programme which they wanted to enact, including the nationalization of a large sector of French industry, and the transfer of much of the press to new ownership. They were aware of the way in which judicial review in the United States had acted as a brake on social legislation there. This consideration led both Socialists and M.R.P. to reject the Conservative proposals for allowing the courts to pass on the constitutionality of laws. It also led the Socialists to press for a narrow interpretation of the conception of constitutionality, since they feared that under a wide one most social and economic legislation would be challenged. M.R.P. disagreed, and found an unexpected supporter in M. Pierre Cot, who wished to be able to attack as unconstitutional laws which restricted public liberties. But M.R.P. gave way to the insistence of the

Socialists.[7] As a result the competence of the Committee was limited to the defence of the institutions of the state. In reality, as the method of setting it in motion shows, its scope was still narrower. The principal author of these provisions, M. Vincent Auriol, himself later described the function of the Committee as the protection of the Council of the Republic against possible encroachment by the Assembly.[8]

The obvious limitations of the Constitutional Committee have drawn upon it some severe and unmerited criticism, especially from those who advocate that French courts, like American ones, should be entitled to decide whether laws are in conformity with the constitution. It has been suggested[9] that the mere existence of the Committee will prevent the courts from making in the future this claim which they have never made in the past. But this argument is without force. Since the Preamble is excluded from the purview of the Committee, that body has no jurisdiction over the constitutionality of a law in terms of fundamental principles, and there is no reason why its creation should affect at all the attitude of the courts to the question. Again, the whole revision procedure has been attacked as subordinating the constitution to a law which conflicts with it, on the ground that, if the National Assembly reaffirms its support for the law, the constitution has to be revised.[10] This simply mis-states the provisions of Article 93, paragraph 2.

With more plausibility, the procedure has been described as window-dressing, which will never operate effectively, either because its initiators have an alleged interest in not setting the machinery in motion,[11] or because the majority of the Committee, being chosen by the Assembly, is assumed to be responsive to its wishes.[12] The first of these arguments lost what weight it had when, in 1948, the new electoral law gave the Council of the Republic a political majority different from that in the Assembly. The second forgets that the Committee will only have to deal with *prima facie* cases strong enough to convince the President of the Republic as well as the senators, and that the eight representatives of the Assembly will be politically divided (since they are elected by P.R.) and will not be committed to their constituents' cause by *esprit de corps* (since they are not themselves deputies). There seems no

---

[7] *S.C.C.*, II, pp. 101–5. At this stage the control envisaged was to be exercised by referendum, not by a special committee.

[8] *Ibid.*, pp. 405–6, for the letter in which M. Auriol put forward the solution eventually adopted. *A.P.*, 1949, p. 335, for his letter to M. Herriot of 27 July 1949 (on which see above, p. 279 & n.). The material phrase is: '... le comité a été institué pour protéger le Conseil de la République contre les empiètements de l'Assemblée, et non pour une protection inverse.'

[9] M. Waline, pp. 120–1. M. Duverger takes a diametrically opposite view (*Manuel*, pp. 374, 377).

[10] L. Rougier, *La France à la recherche d'une constitution*, p. 119.

[11] Waline, *loc. cit.* By 1951 M. Waline had revised his opinion of the Committee's usefulness sufficiently to accept membership of it.

[12] Duverger, *Manuel*, p. 378; Waline, p. 124.

reason why a good case should not win over two of the eight, sufficient to give the senatorial side a majority.

On the one occasion when the Committee was called upon to give a ruling, in June 1948, it belied all the fears of its critics. The case arose on a bill of minor importance, and concerned not the terms of the bill itself, but the provision in the Assembly's standing orders governing urgency procedure, under which the measure had been passed. The Communists could therefore plausibly claim that the Committee had no jurisdiction and was exceeding its powers. The rest of the Council of the Republic nevertheless (and although its party balance was still identical with that in the Assembly) was united in supporting the appeal to the Committee. The latter reached a conclusion wholly in favour of the Council, and the Assembly accepted its verdict. And the President's power to refer the bill back to the Assembly, under Article 36, provided a means to make conciliation effective.[13]

The Council was less fortunate when, in July 1949, it again wished to invoke Article 92. It had objected to a bill on parliamentary immunity, but the Assembly overruled its amendments. The leaders of the Council would have appealed to the Constitutional Committee if they had been able to do so. But the Assembly had adjourned; the Council was obliged under Article 9 to follow its example, and was therefore unable to vote on the proposed appeal.[14] Since the reference to the Committee cannot be made until after a bill has finally been passed by the Assembly, and must come in the short period before promulgation, a serious loophole was accidentally revealed: for the Assembly, by simply adjourning for ten days after voting a bill to which the upper house objected, could always stop Article 92 coming into operation. In this instance the President of the Republic found a way out by referring the bill back to the Assembly under Article 36. If the President took the side of the Assembly against the Council, this solution would not be available: but in that case Article 92 could not have operated either, for it too requires the President's consent.

The Committee can thus play a useful part in settling minor disputes. But an absolute majority of the Council of the Republic is needed to set it in motion, and on important matters the votes of the senators are determined by political rather than by constitutional considerations. When the opposition attacked M. Reynaud's special powers bill of August 1948 as contrary to Article 13 (which forbids the Assembly to delegate its legislative power), the majority parties swallowed their

---

[13] A. Soulier, ' La délibération du Comité Constitutionnel du 18 juin 1948 ', *R.D.P.*, 1949, pp. 195 ff.; and see above, p. 275 and n.
The Committee's decision was unanimous, apart from one abstention. M. Prélot (a member of it) in *Politique*, no. 37 (September 1948), p. 727.

[14] R. Drago, ' L'évolution récente de la notion d'inviolabilité parlementaire ', *R.D.P.*, 1950, p. 404. Article 9 requires the Council to sit at the same times as the Assembly (see above, pp. 273–4).

doubts and defeated the challenge.[15] When the Barangé bill to subsidize church schools had gone through all its stages, in September 1951, its opponents attempted, as a final manœuvre, to appeal to the Constitutional Committee against it on the ground that it violated Article 1: the division was on straightforward party lines, ranging clericals against anti-clericals.[16] Experience suggests that the Committee will be called on to act in two cases only: that envisaged by its inventors, in which the rights of the Council are infringed, and another which they did not contemplate, in which the balance of parties in the two houses differs even more sharply than it did after October 1948.

2. THE INSTITUTIONS OF THE FRENCH UNION

THE first Constituent Assembly produced a very liberal settlement for the French colonial territories, based on complete equality between Frenchmen and natives, and conceding the right of secession by declaring the French Union to depend on free consent. At the referendum of May 1946 this first draft constitution was overwhelmingly approved in the older colonies, where native voters were in the majority, but equally decisively rejected wherever citizenship was restricted to white men. The election of the following month returned a group of deputies representing the French colonists, who were determined to revise these clauses of the constitution; and General de Gaulle's Bayeux speech, warning against the disintegration of the empire, powerfully reinforced their cause.

Under this pressure M.R.P., with enthusiastic Radical and Conservative support, set out to whittle away what the first Constituent Assembly had granted. 'Free consent' disappeared: 'the pious gesture (was) replaced by the *fait accompli*'. The Left had desired federal institutions built up only gradually, on the basis of elected local assemblies which would eventually choose to send representatives to an assembly of the whole union. M.R.P. rejected this solution. It insisted that central institutions must be set up forthwith, before secessionist tendencies could develop: that the structure of government of each territory must be decided in Paris, so that France could decide how much local autonomy might be permitted: and that separate representation must generally be reserved for the white colonists. This policy, though vigorously opposed by the left wing and native deputies,

---

[15] R. Pinto, 'La loi du 17 août 1948 . . .', *R.D.P.*, 1948, pp. 519–20.
[16] *A.P.*, 1951, p. 224; E. Weill-Raynal, *Le Populaire*, 25, 26 and 27 September 1951; J. Lemasurier, 'Difficultés relatives à l'interprétation des Articles 91 et 92 de la Constitution', *R.D.P.*, 1952, pp. 174–86; G. Pernot, 'Le contrôle de la constitutionnalité des lois', *Revue politique des idées et des institutions*, October 1951, pp. 481 ff. Article 1 states: 'La France est une République indivisible, laïque, démocratique et sociale.'
On the proposal to appeal to the Committee, the anti-clericals had 40 fewer supporters than in the final vote on the bill itself.

eventually triumphed owing to the strong pressure of the Bidault government.[17]

The new French Union was endowed with three central institutions, the Presidency, the High Council, and the Assembly. The President of the Republic is *ex officio* President of the French Union : in this capacity, in accordance with a decision of the first meeting of the High Council, he was assisted by a *cabinet* (secretariat) drawn from the associated states, as well as from the French government departments concerned. He also presides over the High Council itself.

The High Council of the Union was not brought into existence until five years after the adoption of the constitution which created it. The main reason for this long delay was the reluctance of Tunisia and Morocco to join a body which they considered might prejudice their nominal independence, and the French unwillingness to advertise this recalcitrant attitude of the North African protectorates. But their reluctance could not be overcome, and when the High Council assembled for the first time at the end of November 1951, only French and Indo-Chinese representatives attended. The Council's position under the constitution was somewhat vague: its composition was described as comprising delegations from the various states concerned, and its function as that of assisting the government in the general conduct of the affairs of the Union. France, under a law of 1949, was represented by seven cabinet ministers, and each of the three Indo-Chinese states sent a delegation led by its prime minister. The High Council spent two days discussing common military, diplomatic and economic problems. It also elaborated its own procedure, agreeing that it should meet at least annually, might be convoked by the President either on his own account or on request of a member state, should deliberate in private, and should reach decisions by 'mutual consent' rather than by voting: these decisions were not to prejudice the fundamental, freely accepted principles of the Union.[18]

The Assembly of the French Union has had a longer and more genuine existence. During the constitutional debates such a body was agreed to be necessary, not only by the supporters of federalism, but also by their opponents of the traditional school, which favoured assimilating the colonies to France. The logical conclusion of this latter course was overseas representation in the French Parliament, where ten Algerian and ten colonial deputies already sat in the Third Republic. But the assimilationists foresaw the growth of pressure for

---

[17] Wright, pp. 179–80, 201–5, 213–5.
[18] *A.P.*, 1951, pp. 303–5, 391. See also R. de Lacharrière, 'La fonction du Haut Conseil de l'Union Française', *Revue juridique et politique de l'U. F.*, 1949, pp. 1–25, and 'La deuxième session du Haut Conseil de l'U.F.', *ibid.*, 1952, pp. 533–547; and *A.P.*, 1952, pp. 282–3. At its second annual session the High Council decided to establish more permanent machinery, utilizing the Paris representatives of the associated states, and extending the President's *cabinet* into a more formal *secrétariat*. The Union is legally formed by the associated states and the Republic (comprising all the rest).

numerical equality of representation, which would ultimately mean that nearly half the members legislating for Brittany and Champagne would be overseas representatives, interested exclusively in the situation in their own territories. France, as M. Herriot warned, would become the colony of her colonies. This prospect was decisively repudiated when the decision was taken to set up a separate Algerian Assembly, instead of doubling the Algerian representation in Paris. The new Assembly of the Union offered a generally acceptable alternative solution. It had the further advantage that Tunisia, Morocco, and Indo-China, which (except Cochin-China) were 'independent' states whose inhabitants could not claim a vote for the French Parliament, could well be represented in the new body.

The new Assembly began with 150 members, half from France and half from the rest—'overseas France'. It could be increased to a maximum of 240 as the associated states chose to send members, the equal division between French and overseas representation always being maintained. Of the original 75 colonial members, 40 came from western and equatorial Africa,[19] and Africa continued to be the main interest of the Assembly even after the entry of Indo-Chinese members. Cambodia and Laos joined in 1948, and Vietnam in 1950; their 27 delegates, with the 27 'balancing' French members, raised the total to 204; Tunisia and Morocco remain aloof. The overseas France representatives are chosen by the local elected assemblies, which under Article 77 of the constitution have been set up in every part of the French Union. Of the metropolitan members, two-thirds are elected by the metropolitan representatives in the National Assembly, and one-third by those in the Council of the Republic, by proportional representation of parties. The Assembly of the French Union meets at Versailles, where its first sitting took place on 10 November 1947.

It is an advisory body and not a part of Parliament, but under Article 70 its members enjoy the privileges and status of members of parliament (immunity, salary, etc.), and many political parties allow their Councillors of the French Union representation on their governing bodies. The Assembly's sessions are convoked and closed by its President under Article 69: he must summon it at the request of half the members. It may not sit during a parliamentary recess. The Assembly has no power, but on certain matters it must be consulted: under Articles 74 and 75, on laws determining or changing the constitution, or altering the status, of an overseas territory: and under Article 72, on decrees applying a metropolitan law to French territory overseas, or putting particular provisions into force in specific terri-

---

[19] Of the rest, 18 represented Algeria, 7 Madagascar, 4 the Indian Ocean territories (Réunion, Comores, Somaliland, French India), 4 the American (Guadeloupe, Martinique, St. Pierre et Miquelon, Guiana) and 2 the Pacific.

tories.[20] The National Assembly is not obliged to consult the Assembly of the French Union before voting a law which applies overseas, but it was expected to do so. The government of the Republic, or that of any associated state, may also submit proposals to the Assembly. The latter may send resolutions of its own to the National Assembly, to the High Council, or to the government.[21]

From the beginning the Assembly of the French Union has felt that the National Assembly paid insufficient attention to its views or indeed to its existence. The deputies' jealousy and suspicion of any potential rival body led them to refuse to concede any powers to the new institution. The history of the Assembly has been punctuated by a series of indignant protests: in 1948, because it was kept insufficiently informed; in 1949, because the government denied its right to inform itself by sending a mission to study the social services in the overseas departments: in 1951, when the National Assembly resolved (without debate!) that Algeria was outside the competence of the Assembly of the Union.[22] In his inaugural speech after the 1951 general election, the new President, M. Albert Sarraut, complained that in its exile at Versailles the Assembly was sadly out of touch with the political life of the country.[23]

The Assembly of the Union draws little public attention, since its decisions cannot affect the existence or policy of the government. Its debates are hardly ever reported. In the Tunisian crisis which opened in December 1951, its voice was not heard. Nor is this lack of publicity, which is due to lack of power, compensated by any reputation for technical excellence. Though committees of the Assembly sometimes perform useful work, as over the complicated labour code for territories overseas, the deputies rarely pay much attention to it. It has been said that even on its best days the atmosphere is that of the Hôtel de Ville, where there can be debate but no decision, since power resides elsewhere.[24] In the general election of 1951 the President of the Assembly of the Union, M. Fourcade, himself set the example of migration to the Palais Bourbon.

The reverse movement also takes place: for though the metropolitan members include a few experts (such as the distinguished colonial

---

[20] For decisions under Articles 74 and 75 the territorial assembly concerned must be consulted as well. These provisions leave open the eventual option between progress towards assimilation, and development into an associated state.

The last-mentioned variety of decree must be issued in cabinet by the President of the Republic. In practice, governmental decrees are far more important in overseas territories than in France proper. They are often modified in accordance with the *avis* of the Assembly.

[21] Pickles, pp. 230–1, discusses the Assembly's activity and legal competence.

[22] *A.P.*, 1948, p. 100. *J.O.* (*A.U.F.*), 7 April 1949, pp. 427–32; 15 February 1951, pp. 126–39.

[23] '. . . somptueux et glacial exil qui nous déporte dans ce palais de Versailles, où nous sommes décidément trop loin des autres Assemblées, du gouvernement, des administrations, de la presse, et de l'homme de la rue.' *J.O.* (*A.U.F.*), 12 July 1951, p. 665; *A.P.*, 1951, p. 185.

[24] Pierre Frédérix, *Le Monde*, 29 August 1951.

historian Professor C. A. Julien), the *camaraderie* of the parliamentary assemblies which choose them ensures the election of many former deputies defeated at the polls. This is not invariably to be deplored: for example, on the peace treaty with Japan, the opposition case was better put in the Assembly of the French Union than in either house of Parliament[25] because of the presence there of M. Gorse, a Socialist specialist on imperial problems, nominated by his party after he had lost his seat at the general election.[26] But this case was not typical, and too frequently the metropolitan councillors of the Union are neither specially interested in, nor specially qualified for their position.

The increase in the number of overseas deputies, from 20 (including Algeria) in the Third Republic to 83 in 1951, has indeed had more effect than the creation of the new Assembly: for these members, two-thirds of whom represent predominantly native electorates, can affect the fate of the government, and therefore exert an influence on policy which cannot be ignored.[27] While the Assembly remains entirely without power, it cannot expect to receive much attention or respect. It needs at least, in its own sphere, the rights enjoyed in general politics by the Council of the Republic—with which indeed the April draft constitution combined it. In a political climate more favourable to a liberal colonial policy, the Assembly of the French Union might then come to play a useful part. So far, it has brought to the dependent territories only symbolical advantages. On paper, indeed, there has been a revolutionary change in the status of the colonies, and the imposing structure of the Union is designed to offer them the opportunity of steady and orderly progress towards self-government. But it is not certain that the ultimate vision is near or clear enough to hold their allegiance during a long period of transition.[28]

---

[25] The burden imposed on conscientious ministers, of having to defend their policy before *six* parliamentary bodies (three committees and three assemblies) is not the least disadvantage of the present structure.

[26] M. André Philip was another unlucky politician appointed to a specialist body (the Economic Council) at the same time. His report to it on the Schuman plan, in the following November, attracted much attention, and again showed that such appointments are not necessarily unjustified. But contrast *A.P.*, 1952, pp. 237–8.

[27] Thus the pressure of the native deputies obtained a great extension of the colonial franchise in the 1951 electoral law. They would have liberalized it much further but for the opposition of the Council of the Republic. *A.P.*, 1951, pp. 121–2, 136. (On this occasion the desire to hold the general election in June gave the Council the chance to use last-minute obstruction effectively.) And see above, pp. 152–3.

[28] See Pickles, Ch. 10 and 11; and Léopold-Sédar Senghor, 'Pour une République fédérale française', *Le Monde*, 4 July 1953.

In June 1953 the King of Cambodia opened a campaign for independence by a spectacular though temporary flight to Siam. In October, a national congress in Vietnam repudiated participation in the French Union (subsequently adding the qualification ' in its present form '; Article 62 of the constitution, which makes the French government responsible for defence policy, was especially disliked. These events provoked violent resentment in France; a Gaullist deputy warned that the Indo-China war was becoming a more disastrous Mexican expedition. On subsequent constitutional developments, see the Epilogue.

3. THE ECONOMIC COUNCIL

THE Economic Council was created under Article 25 of the constitution. Among the four quasi-parliamentary bodies it is the lowest in status: its members are salaried, but do not enjoy the other privileges which Councillors of the French Union share with members of parliament.[29] The National Assembly sends it bills on the subjects within its sphere, and it reports on them before the committees of the Assembly do so. This sphere, under the organic law of 27 October 1946 on the composition and working of the Economic Council, includes all bills on economic or social matters (with the exception of the budget), and also those economic or financial treaties which come before the National Assembly for ratification. The Council must be consulted on decrees or administrative orders applying bills with which it has dealt, and it may be consulted on other decrees.

The government, under Article 25 of the constitution, must submit the national economic plan to it: other bills may be sent by the government, the Assembly, or a committee of the latter, or (if within its sphere) may be examined by the Council on its own initiative: it has normally twenty days (but only two in cases of urgency) to convey its opinion to the National Assembly. Its reports on bills within its sphere are circulated to all deputies before the opening of the general debate: its *rapporteur* has access to the committees of the Assembly, and may speak in the debate itself on the demand of the committee or of the minister. In March 1951 the duties of the Council were extended to include the presentation, twice a year, of a report on the national income, and on means of increasing production, consumption, or exports. The Council has one further function: it may on the request of the parties concerned examine and arbitrate in an economic or social conflict.

The Council originally had 164 members. M.R.P. wanted a corporative chamber, with professional and regional representation. But the parties of the Left had their way, and instituted a body consisting of delegates chosen by the broad, nation-wide organizations. Forty-five represent the trade unions (26 industrial workers, 9 black-coated workers and minor civil servants, 10 technicians and senior staff); 40 are drawn from commerce and industry (10 artisans, 10 from commerce, 6 from nationalized industry, 14 private employers); and 35 from agriculture (of whom 5 represent workers). The remainder include 9 co-operators, 10 economists and scientists (*Pensée française*), 2 victims of war damage, 8 spokesmen of the family associations, and 15 of the overseas territories.

The law of March 1951 increased the membership by five, replacing

---

[29] J. Cadart, ' La loi . . . du 6 janvier 1950 ', *R.D.P.* 1950, pp. 147 ff., discusses the precise differences between the four bodies.

two of the intellectuals by representatives of the new and energetic Middle Classes Committee, and adding others for miscellaneous activities such as the tourist industry. It arranged for the appointment of 'corresponding members' of the Council in each region. And it altered the distribution of the seats given to the major interests, weakening the position of the larger organizations: substantial representation was given to small as distinct from large employers, all but 3 of the 30 C.G.A. seats were taken from that body and given directly to its constituent units, and the strength of the C.G.T. contingent was halved by reducing it to equality with the much smaller rival trade union federations.[30] Only half the individual members of the reconstituted Economic Council had belonged to its predecessor.

An earlier Economic Council had been set up by the Herriot government in 1925. Dominated by senior civil servants, it aroused little interest, and in 1940 it was suppressed by a law of the Vichy government. Its successor at first met with severe criticism.[31] It fell between the two stools of an economic sub-parliament, which M.R.P. wanted, and a consultative committee of trade unionists, desired by the Left. Its discussions were at first often hurried, especially when urgency procedure was in constant use and only two days were allowed for many bills. And its specialist qualifications were disputable. For the full Council represented employers, workers, etc., as such, rather than technicians from a particular type of industry; and the committees, where its most effective work was performed, were on a proportionate basis. So, on the agriculture committee, only a third of the members were agriculturalists, and these all represented a single organization. During the first year, the deputies ignored three-quarters of the reports presented by the Council; no private interests referred their quarrels to it for arbitration; the government sent no decrees to it, and ignored it when modifying the Monnet plan; and when at the end of 1947 the Council was asked to report on a vital issue, that of wages and prices, its specialist delegation became involved in acrimonious disputes between rival and partisan experts.[32]

But though nominally a weaker body even than the Assembly of the French Union, the Economic Council was in reality better placed than its superior in the hierarchy. It reported on bills before the Assembly examined them, so that no question of prestige prevented its reports

---

[30] The representation of the different trade unions was not specified in the law, but left to the government to decide by decree.
For a full formal account of the development of the Council, see Maurice Aubry, *R.D.P.*, 1951, pp. 414–77. For the debate on its origins, Yves Archambeaud, 'Conseil économique et régime démocratique', *Politique*, no. 36 (July–August 1948), pp. 578–91; for its early working, Maurice Byé, 'Le présent et l'avenir du Conseil économique', *ibid.*, pp. 592–610; and for its procedure and recent activities, *R.D.P.*, 1953, pp. 701–18.
[31] René Chavagnes, 'D'un véritable Conseil national économique', *Revue politique et parlementaire*, March 1949, pp. 209–224.
[32] Byé, *loc. cit.*, pp. 592, 594, 598.

being taken seriously.[33] And it was dealing with matters of interest to every Frenchman, so that its work received increasing attention from the press and public. The trade unions soon discovered its value as a sounding board. In April 1949 they used it to present their demand for a return to free collective bargaining. A government bill for this purpose was introduced in the following November, but it was not to the liking of the unions: they were able to obtain a report of the Economic Council in favour of a version much more favourable to them, and in particular to secure the unanimous rejection there of the government's compulsory arbitration proposal, which the National Assembly later defeated in its turn. In February 1951 the Council rejected as inadequate the government's offer of a 15 per cent. increase in family allowances. The unions could not always get their own way: both in July and in November 1949 they failed to carry resolutions calling for a bonus on wages. But even where they had no clear majority they could often obtain a favourable vote on a popular proposal through its opponents preferring to abstain rather than risk the damaging publicity which a negative vote would bring them.[34]

The Economic Council was sometimes criticized for being unduly responsive to political considerations. But in its divisions, the alignment of forces differed so frequently that it was clearly not predetermined on party grounds. Over the collective bargaining bill in November 1949, the combined trade unions carried their report against the opposition of the employers. But in March 1950 the latter joined with the C.G.T. to defeat a profit-sharing proposal supported by the other unions and by the *Pensée française* representatives. In May the C.G.T. and C.G.A., with some sympathy from small employers, combined in unsuccessful opposition to the Franco-Italian customs treaty. In February 1951, in the division on family allowances, the Communist and Catholic trade unions were united against the employers, but the *Force ouvrière* trade unions abstained along with certain agriculturalists, fearing that a large increase in these allowances would prejudice wage claims, and so damage the interests of single workers. And at the beginning of 1949 there was a stormy debate in which the representa-

---

[33] F.G., 'Premier bilan de la constitution', *Esprit*, September 1947, p. 349. M. André Philip's report on the Schuman plan, presented to the Council in November 1951, exercised enormous influence. Yet the present writer was told by a prominent member of the Economic Affairs committee of the Assembly how much he regretted, in a year's service on that body, never having found time to read a single report of the Economic Council. Cf. Pickles, pp. 230-1, for useful statistics.

[34] Thus in June 1949 a resolution opposing the alienation of nationalized aircraft factories, or the dismissal of their workers, and rejecting most of the government's proposals on the subject, was carried by 79 to 0, with 52 abstentions. In December of the same year reductions in the investment programme were condemned by 74 to 4, with 47 abstentions, and a scheme for increasing and reorganizing the family allowances system was voted by 68 to 0, with 51 abstentions (mostly C.G.T. and F-O). *J.O. (A.C.E.)*, 1949, pp. 275-7, 462-3, 419-21.

For the instances mentioned in the text see *A.P.*, 1949, pp. 64, 203; *J.O. (A.C.E.)* 1949, pp. 218-24, 353-4, 408; 1951, pp. 71-2; *B.C.E.*, 26 July 1949.

tives of the distributive trades found themselves under concentrated attack from all their colleagues.[35]

As a collection of natural enemies, the Economic Council cannot be expected often to achieve unanimity. But even this is not unknown. Compulsory arbitration was rejected by 137 votes to 0 in November 1949, and in June 1950 a government proposal to set up a special jurisdiction to deal with economic cartels, distinct from the ordinary courts, was defeated by 105 to 4. Such decisions, though negative, are useful warnings to the government that its plans may be too unpopular to be pressed.[36] Yet too much must not be read into the shifting alliances, or even the unanimity, of the big groups. For the Council is a political body, and its members must work for the interests of their clients. On most issues that arise, some of the largest component bodies are only indirectly interested; and these are always tempted to offer their support to another big group in anticipation of similar favours in the future. Any proposal requiring a sacrifice from one great interest is thus likely to meet widespread hostility.

There are evident dangers in an institution whose members are all appointed to press the particular viewpoint of a given private interest.[37] At most, only a sixth of them represent the consumer. But as a rule, and especially on major issues of foreign policy, the Economic Council has proved remarkably willing to take long-term views. After showing earlier doubts, it gave conditional approval to the Franco-Italian customs treaty in November 1950 by 104 votes to 39, and accepted the Schuman plan a year later by 111 to 15.[38] And whatever its specific decisions, there are advantages in allowing the views and aims of men like M. Gingembre, the leader of the small employers' organization, to be stated and confronted directly and seriously with those of the trade union leaders and the peasant representatives, rather than having them debated through the propagandist refracting medium of a political assembly. The Economic Council is undeniably a forum for pressure groups, but it is one where they are obliged to operate in the open instead of in the dark.

4. THE HIGH COUNCIL OF THE MAGISTRATURE

THE composition of the High Council of the Magistrature (*Conseil supérieur de la magistrature*) is described in Article 83 of the constitution. Its functions are dealt with in Articles 35 and 84. Like so many

---

[35] *J.O.* (*A.C.E.*) 1949, p. 408; 1950, pp. 197, 221; 1951, p. 72; *B.C.E.*, 13 January 1949.

[36] *J.O.* (*A.C.E.*), 1949, p. 408 ; 1950, pp. 236–9; *ibid.*, p. 317, reports the unanimous vote of a housing proposal by 137 members of the Council.

[37] The *Pensée française* representatives, and those of the nationalized industries, sometimes behave almost as government delegates (though one of the members for the coal industry failed to vote for the Schuman plan).

[38] *J.O.* (*A.C.E.*), 1950, pp. 215–21; 1951, p. 269; *A.P.*, 1951, p. 298.

of the new institutions, it is the product of compromise. Conservatives and Radicals were anxious entirely to exclude political influence, by establishing a Council chosen by, and from among, the magistrates themselves. The Communists and their friends denounced the danger of allowing the judicial profession to develop into a close, self-administering corporation, and favoured a Council entirely elected by, and perhaps from among the deputies. Socialists and M.R.P. shared both fears, and imposed a compromise. But on the principle of establishing such a Council there was no disagreement. All parties desired to remove the supervision of the judges from the ministry of Justice, and to allot this task to a new body independent of the executive.[39]

The Council has fourteen members. The President of the Republic and the minister of Justice are *ex officio* chairman and vice-chairman. The remaining twelve sit for six years, and are equally divided between professional and political representatives. Each grade of the hierarchy of judges (*juges de paix*, and members of the courts of first instance, appeal, and Cassation respectively) elects a member: two more are appointed from among the rest of the judicial professions by the President of the Republic. These six are not re-eligible.[40] The six political representatives are chosen by the National Assembly, by a two-thirds majority, and from outside its own ranks.[41]

The inclusion of representatives of the National Assembly was favoured by the majority as a means of introducing an element outside possible professional cliques and jealousies, rather than with the object of representing political opinions as such.[42] This was indicated by the six-year term of office, longer than that of the deputies themselves, to emphasize that the members of the Council were not directly linked with the chamber which elected them. All the parties picked jurists to represent them, rather than politicians[43]: and in 1950, when the Communist nominee offered his resignation on breaking with the party, President Auriol refused it.[44] And a two-thirds majority was preferred to P.R. as a means to ensure that different opinions secured representa-

---

[39] *S.C.C.*, I, pp. 127–132, 615; II, pp. 87–92.
[40] On this point see *R.D.P.*., 1953, pp. 448–69.
[41] One, the Socialist M. Hauriou, is a senator.
The authorities which choose the full members each elect the same number of alternate members, in exactly the same way.
[42] See the views of M. Cot, speaking for that body of opinion which was most insistent on including nominees of the Assembly: *S.C.C.*, I, p. 129; II, pp. 89, 91: and of M. Ramadier, *ibid.*, II, p. 88.
[43] The Socialists originally offered their seat to M. Blum (a lawyer by profession): on his refusal it went to M. Hauriou, who was a professor of law as well as a senator. In 1952, however, their candidate for the seat then vacant was better known as a former deputy than as a barrister.
[44] *Le Monde*, 20 October 1951. Some months after his offer to resign, the Communists published a confidential document from the Council's records; the suspicion that this member had passed it to the party in 1948, while he was still a Communist supporter, cost him his seat on the High Council.

tion.[45] At the first election, in March 1947, the Assembly's Justice committee drew up an agreed list which was accepted without opposition or vote.[46] But the possibilities of deadlock under the two-thirds rule were shown in 1952, when the struggle to annex the seat vacated by the former Communist member lasted over twelve months and thirteen ballots, without a decision being reached.

The Council meets for several hours every Wednesday at 3 p.m., in the cabinet room at the Elysée. It has three duties.[47] The first is to deal with pardons. In the Third Republic these were a personal prerogative of the President; in the Fourth, under Article 35 of the constitution, he exercises this right in the Council of the Magistrature. This means that he is obliged to ask its advice, though he need not take it: in practice he never diverges from it except on the side of clemency. Pardons occupy a great deal of the Council's activity: in its first three years it considered 75,000 cases.[48] President Auriol used the right of pardon on a very large scale to correct the anomalies and injustices of the purge: by April 1949, 27,000 out of the 38,000 who had been imprisoned, and 15,000 of the 40,000 sentenced to 'national indignity', had benefited from a pardon.[49]

The other duties of the Council involve the careers of an important section, but not of the whole body of French magistrates. These are divided into two branches, the judges (*magistrature assise*) and the public prosecutors and State attorneys (the *parquet*, or *magistrature debout*). The two are distinct, although transfers between them occur, and are generally considered to constitute a merit of the system. The High Council of the Magistrature is concerned only with the former. It is both their disciplinary authority, replacing the Court of Cassation, the highest civil court in France, which performed this function under previous regimes: and the body which decides on their promotion, fulfilling in this respect duties which used to belong to the ministry of Justice. Thus the High Council of the Magistrature, an institution with a political element in its composition, has in the first of these spheres been substituted for a branch of the judiciary, and in the second

---

[45] *S.C.C.* I, p. 617 (M. Coste-Floret's remark).

[46] Duverger, *Manuel*, p. 332.

[47] It also has duties in connection with the High Court of Justice, which tries political figures impeached by the Assembly. The examining committee (*commission d'instruction*) of this body consists of six members of parliament chosen by the Assembly, and a president and two assessors named by the High Council of the Magistrature.

[48] Camille Anbert, *Le Monde*, 16 June 1950. Whole groups of cases were, of course, often dealt with together.

[49] Figures published by the *Mouvement national judiciaire*, the organization of the Resistance magistrates, in *Le Monde*, 14 April 1949. They also pointed out that in other occupied countries the purge had been much more extensive: the number of prison sentences had been 50,000 in Belgium, 40,000 in Holland, and 20,000 in Norway, and the number of prosecutions respectively 400,000, 111,000, and 90,000, compared with 120,000 in France. Allowing for differences of population the relative mildness of the French liberation process is evident. Cf. *A.P.*, 1952, pp. 33, 75: official figures showed 10,000 illegal or irregular executions—but 180,000 racial or political deportees who had not returned.

for a section of the executive: in the one case for an entirely non-political, and in the other for a wholly political body.

Disciplinary action against judges is very rarely necessary. But promotion is an everyday matter: during one year, 1949, the Council appointed to a thousand posts.[50] This is the heart of the controversy which has from the beginning surrounded the Council. For French judges are deplorably ill-paid, and therefore excessively dependent on professional advancement. Though they are financially incorruptible, and independent in that they cannot be removed from their posts,[51] yet the extreme importance of promotion provided the loophole through which political influence was able to creep in. In the Third Republic deputies pressed their demands for favours in respect of judicial appointments as in other spheres. And the practising barrister who was a deputy had a notorious advantage, since judges feared to offend friends, colleagues, or potential successors of the minister of Justice.[52] This was indeed the main blot on the French judicial system. To remove it, Article 84 of the constitution of the Fourth Republic transferred the promotion of judges to the High Council of the Magistrature, and required it to ensure (*assurer*) their discipline and independence.[53] Around the exact meaning of this verb an acute struggle for power developed.

The ministry of Justice was far from reconciled to the loss of its former powers. An irresponsible organization in control of the judiciary was contrary to French tradition, especially when the President of the Republic was at the head of it. The ministry took the view that the Council should supervise its activities from an altitude sufficiently remote to deprive it of any effective power. The Council itself, however, desired genuinely to administer the sphere marked out for it, and would indeed have liked to acquire authority over the *parquet* as well. The cabinet took the side of the ministry of Justice, and in April 1948 actually approved a bill settling the status of the Council, which gave to the upstart body even less scope than the minister had been willing

---

[50] Anbert, *loc. cit.* Decisions are made by majority vote; in 1953 the President revealed that, in six years, his candidates had been defeated on three occasions. *Le Monde*, 9 May 1953.

[51] Except for cause shown and after a hearing, in the Third Republic before the Court of Cassation, and in the Fourth before the High Council of the Magistrature. The new constitution gives constitutional force to the requirement that the judges shall not be removed (see below, note 53). Members of the *parquet*, however, may be dismissed from their posts (though not from the profession) at the entire discretion of the minister.

[52] See R. C. K. Ensor, *Courts and Judges in France, Germany and England*, pp. 40–2. For the safeguards introduced to check these abuses, see *ibid.*, Appendix D, and W. R. Sharp, pp. 196–7.

[53] Article 84 runs:

' Le Président de la République nomme, sur présentation du Conseil supérieur de la magistrature, les magistrats, à l'exception de ceux du Parquet.

' Le Conseil supérieur de la magistrature assure, conformément à la loi, la discipline de ces magistrats, leur indépendance et l'administration des tribunaux judiciaires.

' Les magistrats du siège sont inamovibles.'

to concede.⁵⁴ This bill, however, remained buried in the Justice committee of the National Assembly.

A year later the controversy came to the attention of the public. On 16 March 1949 President Auriol, as head of the High Council of the Magistrature, published a communiqué stating that the Council intended to introduce a bill to remove the examining magistrates (*juges d'instruction*) from the supervision of the *parquet*.⁵⁵ Three days later M. Lecourt, minister of Justice and vice-chairman of the High Council, announced that the ministry proposed to deal with the position of these magistrates itself. The cabinet supported the minister, the rest of the Council unanimously reaffirmed its own point of view. But this time it was the Council which found itself baffled by the shortage of parliamentary time. For its plans required legislation, while the ministry could and did circumvent it by administrative action.

Far-reaching reforms have thus proved beyond the Council's scope. Bills promoted by it have been pigeonholed by the ministry.⁵⁶ The minister has successfully insisted that its decisions, when put into force by the President, require his countersign—a formal matter, however, for the countersign would never be withheld. On a humbler level, the Council's independence was circumscribed in many minor ways. Its staff was tiny, its accommodation inadequate and provided by the ministry,⁵⁷ and the latter still prepared the dossiers on which an overworked body must largely rely. The struggle to take justice out of politics was only begun, not concluded, when the High Council of the Magistrature was set up.

An important beginning, nevertheless, has been made. Decisions over promotion may be influenced by the ministry, but the final decision is no longer in its hands. Even the most powerful deputy now finds it very difficult to exercise effective pressure upon judicial appointments. The existence of the Council ensures that overt attempts at political interference will be checked and publicised, as in April 1950, when the Council (supported on this occasion by the minister of Justice, M. René

---

⁵⁴ *Le Monde*, 14 April 1949.
⁵⁵ *Ibid.*, for this incident and its sequel.
The supervision of the *parquet* over the *juges d'instruction*, who look to them for promotion, is justified from the point of view of the latter's investigating functions, but has unfortunate repercussions on their conduct of other duties. It has a good deal to do with one of the worst abuses of the French system of justice, the too frequent practice of keeping suspects in prison for long periods without trial.
⁵⁶ 'Industrieusement, le Conseil supérieur usine des projets de loi. Méthodiquement la chancellerie les enterre. Ou plutôt elle ne les enterre pas: la lenteur administrative s'en charge. Simplement elle ne les déterre pas.' Anbert, *loc. cit.*
⁵⁷ The committees of the High Council met in the library of the ministry of Justice: during the first winter of its existence the members were obliged to work in their overcoats, the ministry having omitted to repair the radiators. *Le Figaro*, 28 October 1949. Subsequently President Auriol offered a building attached to the Élysée for the use of the High Council, but the credits needed to make it ready for use were disallowed on grounds of economy: it was hinted that the ministry of Justice, fearing that if the Council left its premises it would insist on taking the vital dossiers with it, had intervened to secure this result. Anbert, *loc. cit.* The Council now has its own building.

Mayer) protested against the cabinet's threats to take action against certain judges who had given decisions favourable to accused Communists.[58] The Fourth Republic has registered undoubted progress in this sphere, thanks largely to the personal enthusiasm of President Auriol. Imperfections remain; but the preservation of judicial impartiality towards the enemies of the regime, in a country where they are so numerous, is not a negligible sign of the health of French democracy.

5. POLITICAL JUSTICE; LOCAL GOVERNMENT; FUNDAMENTAL RIGHTS

IN the Third Republic, impeachment cases were presented by the Chamber of Deputies, and tried by the Senate. In the Fourth, they are again put forward by the National Assembly, under Article 57 of the constitution. The resolution must be voted in secret, and by an absolute majority of the members, excluding those who will have to try the case. For impeachments are now judged, not by the upper house, but by a new High Court of Justice, which includes many deputies. Article 58 requires this court to be elected by each National Assembly at the beginning of its life: Article 59 reserves details for a separate law. This law was passed in October 1946, at the same time as the constitution itself.

The Court consists of a President, two vice-presidents, and thirty judges, all elected by the Assembly. Twenty of the judges are chosen among the deputies themselves, by proportional representation of parties. The other ten must not be members of the Assembly, though they are often former deputies.[59] They are elected in a secret ballot, and by a two-thirds majority. The President and vice-presidents, who are deputies, are chosen in the same way. The Assembly also elects thirty alternate judges (twenty from its own ranks and ten from elsewhere, in the same conditions as the ordinary members): three prosecutors, who may be members of the Assembly, though at present only the senior of them belongs to it: and six of the nine members of the committee of preliminary inquiry (*commission d'instruction*). These six must be deputies: the remaining three, including the chairman, are named by the High Council of the Magistrature.

The Court judges impeachments brought for treason against the President of the Republic, or for offences in office alleged against ministers. Its deliberations are normally public, but the final decision must be taken in secret, and by an absolute majority. Up to 1952 only two such motions had come before the National Assembly. On 29 March 1950 the Communists moved to impeach three Socialist

---

[58] *Le Monde*, 28 April 1950. And see p. 175, above.
[59] Of the ten elected by the new Assembly on 28 August 1951, five (two Communists, two Gaullists, and one M.R.P.) were deputies defeated in the recent election. The R.P.F. and M.R.P. also chose defeated deputies as alternates.

leaders (MM. Gouin, Moch and Pineau) in connection with the wine import scandals of 1946; the motion was lost. On 30 November 1950 they again attacked M. Moch, this time on account of reputed irregularities in the 'affair of the generals' in 1949. The deputies voted the motion by 235 votes to 203: many members, it was thought, voted it to deal a blow in secret at the government, at the minister, or at his party, rather than because they genuinely believed the Communist charges. The government demanded and obtained a vote of confidence from the Assembly, in a public ballot, and as the majority for the Communist motion was well below the absolute majority needed for impeachment (viz. 286), the incident had no sequel.[60]

The constitutional High Court of Justice just described should not be confused with the exceptional body of the same name, which sat between 1945 and 1949 to try former members of the various Vichy governments and certain high officials of that regime. It too consisted of members of the Assembly, originally chosen by lot from a panel, and later chosen by P.R. One hundred and eight individuals were accused before it, and it delivered 18 sentences of death, and 38 of imprisonment or national indignity. Its prestige was never high.[61]

The constitution contains five articles (85 to 89) dealing with the local government structure of France. These were inserted on the demand of the Left, which wished to extend the powers of the local authorities and to protect them by a constitutional guarantee. But the articles confine themselves to general phrases, as in Article 85, or to declarations of an intention to legislate, as in Articles 86 and 89. Article 87, with its formal institution of elected municipal and departmental councils, whose decisions would be executed by the mayor or president, and Article 88, with its restrictive definition of the rôle of the prefect, might have been interpreted as instituting a new balance of power in local government, with the elected officers playing a much more important part.[62] But in practice the constitutional provisions have not significantly affected the powers of the prefect.

The constitution is preceded by a preamble containing a declaration of principles. These are specifically excluded from the purview of the Constitutional Committee, under paragraph 3 of Article 92. The French courts have always considered themselves incompetent to

---

[60] *A.P.*, 1950, pp. 50, 229–31. Philip Williams, 'L'Affaire des Généraux', *Cambridge Journal*, May 1951.

[61] Duverger, *op. cit.*, pp. 333–5: Maurice Guérin, 'La réforme de la Haute Cour', *Politique*, June 1948, pp. 554–7.

Of those sentenced to death, ten were condemned in absence. Only three of the remainder, Darnand, de Brinon, and Laval, were actually executed.

[62] See, e.g., V. D. Lipman, 'Recent trends in French local administration', *Public Administration*, Spring 1947, pp. 28–38; and B. Chapman, *Introduction to French Local Government*, pp. 72–8.

inquire, in the American manner, whether a given law conforms with the provisions of the constitution. They seem likely to continue to do so.[63] The preamble thus contains simply a profession of intentions, devoid of juridical force. There is no effective mechanism for punishing violations of its principles.

The first committee on the constitution spent nearly a quarter of its working time considering the declaration of rights.[64] The product of these deliberations was among the most vulnerable parts of the first draft constitution, and contributed to the defeat of that document in the referendum of May 1946. Opponents were able to represent it, forcefully if not altogether fairly, as containing threats to the rights of property, the freedom of the press, and the position of the Church in education.[65] The second committee on the constitution therefore abandoned the work of its predecessor, and replaced it with the present much shorter declaration of principles.

British observers usually doubt the value of abstract pronouncements of this kind. But the 1946 document has been subjected to vigorous attack by French critics also. They comment that it reaffirms *en bloc* both the 1789 declaration of rights, which its authors were simultaneously violating,[66] and the ' fundamental principles recognized by the laws of the Republic '—a phrase so ambiguous that competent authorities have interpreted it in precisely opposite ways.[67] It adds various supplementary principles, from the equality of women and the right of asylum to the nationalization of public services and *de facto* monopolies, and the workers' claim to share in the management of business— a pious aspiration which no attempt has been made to realize. Some clauses merely announce an (unfulfilled) intention to legislate, such as that stating that the right to strike is exercised within the framework of the laws which regulate it. Others, such as that proclaiming the solidarity of the nation in bearing burdens resulting from national calamities, are too vaguely drafted to have much practical importance.

---

[63] Rougier, pp. 109, 114–5, quotes some of the pronouncements of the principal courts refusing to pass upon the constitutionality of laws (a renunciation which he deplores). Duverger, *op cit*., pp. 374, 377, believes that under the new constitution the courts may change their practice: but this is not the general view. However, it has been argued that decree-laws, as distinct from ordinary laws, can be challenged in the courts if they infringe the principles laid down in the preamble to the constitution: R. Pinto, ' La loi . . . du 17 août 1948 ', *R.D.P.*, 1948, pp. 526–7. Cf. Pickles, pp. 233–5; and see above, p. 290.

[64] Wright, p. 135.

[65] *Ibid.*, pp. 156–61.

[66] The purge legislation violated the principle of the non-retroactivity of laws, and the nationalization acts often conflicted with the principles of compensation laid down in the declaration. Duverger, *op. cit.*, p. 371: Waline, pp. 125–6. Rougier, Part I, makes a much more sweeping and partisan attack on the whole political development of post-war France, which in his view infringed fundamental principles of justice.

[67] Waline, pp. 126–7, thinks that it refers to the lay character of the state and in particular of education: Duverger, *op. cit.*, p. 371, argues more convincingly that it affirms in a roundabout way the claims of the church schools. Both agree that it is the most obscure phrase in the whole constitution.

One important liberty is wholly absent: freedom of association, deliberately omitted in 1789 by Jacobins who detested *corps intermédiaires*, seems simply to have been forgotten in 1946.

The declaration renounces wars of conquest, announces France's willingness to limit her national sovereignty in the cause of peace,[68] proclaims equality of opportunity throughout the French Union, and expresses the intention of leading France's colonial subject peoples towards democratic self-government.[69] These principles of domestic and external policy represented the state of mind of a particular political majority in 1946. They did not then command universal assent, and their practical importance depended wholly on the extent to which the groups whose views they express retained their political influence. There is no means of enforcing the principles against a legislature which ignores them. French critics recognize that their direct and obvious utility to the citizen is very limited indeed.[70] Yet there is perhaps a case, in a country where the fundamentals of politics are disputed far more bitterly than in Britain, and where its day-to-day practice is far more obviously dominated by compromise, bargaining, and manœuvre, for a solemn and formal statement of the ends which the activity of the politicians, and the democratic regime itself, are ultimately supposed to serve.

---

[68] Paragraph 15. But this limitation must be on a reciprocal basis: in October 1952 M. Herriot attacked the proposed European Defence Community as unconstitutional, on the ground that this condition was not fulfilled. See *A.P.*, 1952, pp. 66–7, 70.

[69] See Epilogue, n. 7.

[70] Most of the examples cited in these two paragraphs have been taken from the comments on the preamble of the two French critics quoted, MM. Duverger and Waline.

PART IV. THE POLITICAL SYSTEM

Chapter 19

THE ELECTORAL LAWS

1. THE THIRD REPUBLIC

THE characteristic institution of the Fourth Republic, the one which best expresses the spirit of the regime, is the electoral system, as the characteristic institution of the Third Republic was the Senate. In the words of Roger-A. Priouret,

> Elect Councillors of the Republic by a majority vote for individuals and you will see them play an effective part. Do the same for the deputies and there will be a majority and perhaps even a government. But change the Constitution without touching the electoral law, give all the prerogatives and independence you wish to the executive and the second chamber, and you will have changed nothing whatever. All power, including the nominally omnipotent Assembly, will derive from the parties.[1]

But the long history of past electoral laws shows that in France (as elsewhere) the public debate over high principles ends with a decision taken on grounds of individual or party advantage. To understand these considerations a brief survey of the main alternative systems is necessary.

Historically, every important change in the political situation has led to an alteration in the electoral system—either an extension of the franchise, a change in the type of constituency, or a new method of attributing seats. Manhood suffrage was instituted in 1848 and remained until 1945, when women obtained the vote from General de Gaulle's provisional government. Constituencies have sometimes been large, based on the department and electing several members, and sometimes small, containing a single arrondissement and electing one. The former prevailed from 1848 to 1852, from 1871 to 1875, from 1885 to 1889, from 1919 to 1927, and since 1945, the latter intermediately. Under *scrutin d'arrondissement* (also called *scrutin uninominal* because the elector votes for one individual) a candidate is elected on the first ballot if he receives an absolute majority of the votes cast.[2] If no candidate fulfils the conditions, a second ballot is held a week later (before 1919 a fortnight later), at which a relative majority secures election as in Britain. Proposals to abolish the second ballot and substitute the British system have always been unpopular in France.

---

[1] *Op. cit.*, p. 260 (written in 1947).
[2] Provided his vote is not less than a quarter of the registered electorate.

While many parties remain, the possibility of a member being elected by a minority of the voters is regarded as intolerable. It is recognized that the British system might force the electorate into two parties, but this remedy is considered worse than the disease. Frenchmen fear that the creation of two homogeneous blocs would, in a nation so deeply divided, lead not to stable democratic government but to civil war; and this fear has naturally become much stronger since it became apparent that one of the two blocs would be dominated by the Communist party. Occasionally proposals have been made to combine the single-member constituency with proportional representation, notably by M. Blum in *Le Populaire* in July 1949, but they have never found acceptance.[3]

Scrutin de liste, on the other hand, has been combined with several methods of apportioning seats. In the law of 1848 the elector had as many votes as there were seats to fill; a simple plurality sufficed to elect a candidate, provided he polled at least 2,000 votes; the last condition was changed in 1849 to an eighth of the electorate, and this system was restored in 1871. In these conditions a second ballot was very unusual. The *scrutin de liste* system of 1885, however, made it much more probable by requiring, like *scrutin d'arrondissement*, an absolute majority of votes for election on the first ballot. In 1919, an absolute majority of votes again secured immediate election; but there was no second ballot, and if no list had an absolute majority, the seats were distributed by proportional representation. In 1945 the majority and individualist elements of the previous law disappeared; votes were cast for a list, not for individuals, and seats were distributed by P.R. In 1951 the system was again changed, as described below.

For nearly the entire life of the Third Republic the electoral system was *scrutin d'arrondissement* with two ballots; thirteen of its sixteen general elections were held on this basis. It tended to produce several moderate and loosely organized parties.[4] At the first ballot few candidates could obtain an absolute majority, so that at this stage there was no fear of splitting the vote and no deterrent to 'splinter parties'; but at the second this fear became as effective as in Britain. Most constituencies then had a straight fight between a candidate of the Right and one of the Left.[5] About a quarter of the seats would have three-

---

[3] M. Blum advocated a mixed system by which three-quarters of the deputies would be chosen under *scrutin d'arrondissement*, the remaining quarter being so divided among the parties as to arrive at proportional representation over the whole country. A system which involved creating two different types of deputy was bound to be unpopular, although a somewhat similar principle had been adopted for the election of the first Council of the Republic in 1946.

[4] See W. L. Middleton, *French Political System*, Ch. 4: Duverger, *Partis*, pp. 270, 351–2, 357, 364, etc.; François Goguel's article in Duverger, ed., *Systèmes électoraux*.

[5] In the general election of 1928, 187 deputies only were elected in the first ballot; a second was necessary in 420 seats (excluding colonies). In 281 constituencies there were only two serious candidates (i.e. with more than 1,000 votes) on the second ballot, in 130 three, and in 9, four: the third candidates were mostly Communists, and well at the bottom. 530 out of 612 constituencies had either a clear majority on the first ballot, or a virtual straight fight on the second. (Middleton, pp. 95–6.)

[*continued on next page*]

cornered contests, and only a handful would have more than three candidates. A party staging propaganda fights all over the country without regard to the parliamentary consequences might upset this pattern, as the Liberals have sometimes done in Britain. But, again as in Britain, the voters might not follow their party's lead. In 1928 and in 1932 the Communists refused to withdraw their candidates on the second ballot, but their supporters withdrew their votes, casting them for the strongest candidate of the Left against clericalism or reaction. Over the whole country nearly half, and in some areas almost all the Communist voters obeyed traditional 'republican discipline' rather than the instructions of the party.[6]

The pre-war system thus encouraged small parties, since every group and individual had the opportunity on the first ballot to spread propaganda and solicit votes without risking the triumph of the enemy. It developed moderate parties because at the second ballot, with only two serious candidates in the field, the one nearest the centre had the best chance of attracting the doubtful voters. M. Duverger points out that in a British constituency the growth of socialism tended to destroy the Liberal party, polarizing its supporters between the extremes; but in France it turned to the profit of the Radicals, who received Conservative votes on the second ballot as a lesser evil than their new rivals.[7] The electoral discipline of the Left sometimes upset this tendency, as in 1936 when Radical voters obediently threw their votes to Communists on the second ballot. But at other times the electors defied their leaders, as in 1928 when 400,000 Radicals turned to the Conservatives instead of the Socialists. Such divisions meant that the system encouraged loose and undisciplined parties. For in the Midi, the stronghold of the Left, Radical and left-centre candidates attracted Conservative support as a lesser evil than their only real rivals, the Socialists; but in the Catholic west they obtained the second ballot votes of Socialists who preferred them to their clerical opponents. The decisive votes were thus on the extremes rather than in the centre: in

---

On the persistence of two electoral blocs, cf. Siegfried, pp. 51–2, 68–72; Duverger, *Partis*, p. 246; Soulier, pp. 401–2, 406–8, 448–9, etc.; Goguel, *La Politique des partis sous la Troisième République*, passim. It has often provoked comparison, incomplete but instructive, between the first ballot and the American primary.

[6] Gérard Walter, pp. 191–2, 240–1. In 1928 194,000 out of 426,000 Communist voters in constituencies affected, deserted on the second ballot; the party retained almost all its votes in Paris, but hardly any in departments like Nièvre, Saône-et-Loire, Creuse, and Sarthe. In 1932 only 55 per cent. remained loyal on the second ballot, compared with 59 per cent. four years before.

[7] Duverger, *op. cit.*, p. 357. The results of the 1928, 1932 and 1936 elections show how the system benefited the moderate parties. Under nation-wide P.R. the Communists would have gained 54, 38, and 21 seats in these three elections respectively. The Socialists would have gained 8, lost 7, and lost 28. The Radicals and their Republican Socialist allies would have lost 36, 46, and 30; the groups to the Right of them would have lost 34, gained 21, and gained 37. These figures are quoted in Soulier, p. 516 n., from the calculations of M. Lachapelle; those for 1932, on which Soulier is inaccurate, are taken from Lachapelle, *Les Régimes électoraux*, p. 164—they are also quoted in Duverger, *Systèmes électoraux*, Table X, p. 64.

1928 less than fifty deputies benefited neither from clerical nor from Socialist votes.[8] They were precisely calculable, since the first ballot made the situation clear to every voter. And they were different in different parts of the country for members belonging nominally to the same party; the incoherence and indiscipline of the centre groups were primarily due to this factor. Where Britain had nominally extreme parties brought nearer together by their common concern to attract the same floating voters, France had theoretically moderate parties pulled apart by their dependence on extremist support at the second ballot.[9]

A large section of French opinion was extremely critical of the electoral system. Its injustice, in that seats were not related to votes, was the obvious target for criticism but not the only one. The system was said to lead to parish-pump politics, since the personal popularity of the member counted for so much, and most deputies took pains to dig themselves in by acquiring positions in local government—during the periods when the departmental councils were sitting, Parliament would go into recess. So much time and energy were spent on performing constituency favours that French politics tended to become merely, in Burke's phrase, 'a confused and scuffling bustle of local agency'. The system also contributed to the negative character of politics. Alliances were formed solely to 'bar the route' to clericalism or to revolution, and such unstable combinations could not form the basis of a coherent parliamentary majority. And it tended to immoral politics: a candidate near to success on the first ballot might win over the marginal votes by purchasing, with political or financial concessions, the withdrawal of an outsider in his favour. French politics were not a grand contest of opposing principles but a somewhat sordid process of bargaining. For this degradation a large section of opinion, on the Right and on the Left, blamed the electoral system.

Much of this criticism was exaggerated. All politics is a process of bargaining. Doctrines cannot be applied exactly as they stand: to be politically effective they must command wide assent, and must therefore be diluted by concessions to other groups. There is nothing discreditable about this process, which occurs in all political systems—in a nominating convention or in a parliamentary party, in competition for the floating vote or in negotiation for forming a coalition cabinet. In a multi-party system like the French, the inevitable bargains might occur either at the electoral or at the parliamentary stage. *Scrutin d'arrondissement* ensured the former, bringing neighbouring parties into electoral alliance with one another instead of separating them. The sequel showed that this had its advantages.

Purely 'mathematical' bargains, such as Conservative-Communist alliances against Socialists, occurred now and then. But the general

---

[8] *A.P.*, 1929, p. 419, quoted Siegfried, p. 179.
[9] See e.g. Soulier, p. 528.

charges of immorality, still more those of bribery, were exaggerated. And the system had other assets. It ensured genuine and close (perhaps too close) contact between deputy and electors. It enabled the voters to choose, within limits, the men they preferred rather than those the bosses imposed. In France at any rate the greatest defect of *scrutin de liste*, in all its forms, is a psychological one: that it promotes disaffection with politics by weakening the link between member and constituent. *Scrutin d'arrondissement* also allowed the electorate, by the play of second ballot combinations, to make a real political choice when they wished to do so. Immediately after a general election there was little doubt about the nature and extent of the majority, though much about its duration. But for the heterogeneity of majorities the electoral system was not primarily to blame; there was no homogeneous majority among the voters. It was precisely because of this inconvenient fact that most Frenchmen preferred the type of electoral system described. That system was itself the result of the division of opinion which it helped to perpetuate.

2 THE P.R. EXPERIMENT

THE critics nearly all favoured proportional representation, and many of them saw in it the cure for all France's political ills. They claimed that it would ensure political justice, broaden the horizons of deputies by freeing them from parish-pump preoccupations (*la politique du clocher*), and make possible the formation of a real majority. Opponents feared that in each respect the loss would outweigh the gain. Mathematical justice would strengthen extreme groups, involve voting for a party instead of an individual, and transfer power to the machines. The decline of parish-pump politics would mean the destruction of the link between voter and deputy. An organized instead of a chaotic Chamber would spell the end of parliamentary freedom and the rise of rigid, monolithic blocs, voting as units. Parliamentary debate would atrophy. There might be fewer crises, but those that occurred would be harder than ever to solve.

The validity of these arguments depended largely on the details of the system. Many of them concerned the wider debate about P.R. rather than local French circumstances. The principle of P.R. is perfectly compatible with voting for individuals instead of lists, as in the Irish system of the single transferable vote. Such a system, which combines a high degree of justice between parties with a free choice by the voter, would solve many of France's problems; but it is not known or studied on the Continent, where P.R. is taken to imply voting for lists.[10] But these may be more or less rigid. Incomplete lists, con-

---

[10] M. Duverger gives it one passing mention (*Partis*, p. 422); and M. Lachapelle devotes two pages to it. In the long discussions of electoral reform in France during 1950 and 1951, the only mention of it which I observed was by M. Cadart, who had made a special study of the British electoral system.

taining fewer candidates than there are seats to fill, may or may not be permitted: if they are not, small parties may find it difficult, and independents impossible to stand at all. The voter may or may not be given the right to alter the lists drawn up by the parties; if not, the member will be completely dependent on the party organization which drew up the list. Even if alterations are permitted the dependence will not be greatly reduced, since few voters will exercise their privilege. The alterations allowed may take a simple form, the preferential vote; the elector has one vote, which he must cast for a list, but on the chosen list he may move names up or down, or scratch them out. Or the more complicated device of *panachage* may be used; under it, the voter may distribute his choices over several lists, each choice counting as a fraction of a vote. He can do this either by voting for a particular list, but eliminating one or more candidates and substituting others from different lists, or else by writing out a list of his own. This minimizes the power of the party as far as is possible under a list system.

The second important detail is the size of constituency chosen. In the simplest case, the whole country is considered as one constituency. Seats are first allotted to lists obtaining the necessary quotient on a local basis, but the votes remaining are then pooled, and seats are allotted to bring each party up to its proportionate national share. Such a system gives greater power to reward or punish to the party machine, which can virtually guarantee election by giving a candidate a place high on the national list, from which the 'supplementary' members are taken. But it also gives the most perfect accuracy of representation. If the whole country forms in effect one six-hundred-member constituency, then in theory a minority of one six-hundredth should be able to obtain a seat—though in practice there are usually special provisions to prevent it doing so. But with smaller constituencies, only substantial minorities can get representation—in a five-member constituency a minority of one-sixth, in a three-member constituency one of one-fourth

The supporters of proportional representation first came within sight of success in 1919. But the Senate was a stronghold of the conservative wing of the Radical party, which profited most from the centripetal tendencies of the second ballot. It forced on the Chamber a hybrid compromise, in which P.R. applied only if no list won a clear majority of votes.[11] The effect was to give a great impetus to organization and discipline, from which the Right gained in 1919, and the Left in 1924. In 1927 *scrutin d'arrondissement* was restored. By 1945, however, that system was discredited, like the Third Republic itself, among all sections of opinion excepting its Radical beneficiaries. In October 1945 the first Constituent Assembly was elected under a system devised by the

---

[11] By a curious irony a similar struggle had been going on in Britain a few months before. But here the positions were reversed; the House of Lords proposed P.R. instead of the alternative vote—a system identical in principle with the second ballot—which the Commons favoured. Cf. D. E. Butler, *The Electoral System in Britain* (O.U.P., 1953), p. 11.

provisional government. This provided for P.R. and election by party lists, now an almost unanimous demand.[12] But there was to be no national pooling of votes, to which General de Gaulle was strongly opposed, and the countryside was over-represented—a discrepancy corrected in 1946.

The first Constituent Assembly was overwhelmingly favourable to the principle of P.R., which was accepted in the committee on the constitution by 38 votes to 3, only R.G.R. members opposing it.[13] Over the details, the three main parties combined to vote a new electoral law against Radical and Conservative opposition. It included a national pool, from which however small parties were excluded, and it forbade *panachage* and the preferential vote. This law lapsed when the draft constitution was rejected by the electorate in May, and in the second Constituent Assembly the alliance of the three parties broke up. M.R.P. decided to oppose the national pool, while many Socialists were coming to favour *panachage*. By threatening to let the latter be passed, M.R.P. induced the Communists to abandon the national pool, and on 30 September 1946 a combination of these two parties defeated both *panachage* and the national pool.

This heterogenous alliance was thus responsible for the main lines of the law of 5 October 1946.[14] Under this law the department was to form the constituency, though the seven largest departments were split up. Most constituencies returned three, four, or five members. P.R. operated, as in 1945, only within the constituency. Lists were drawn up by the parties, and had to contain as many names as there were seats to fill; there was no *panachage*, and only a theoretical provision for the preferential vote.[15]

General de Gaulle's electoral law thus operated almost unchanged for the first three post-war elections. Its effect on the development of

---

[12] The new system had practical as well as theoretical advantages. It guaranteed to each party the possibility of continued manœuvre in an Assembly which no single group could dominate; in particular, it reduced the risk of a Communist-controlled parliamentary majority. Goguel, *Fourth Republic*, pp. 61–2.

[13] *S.C.C.*, I, p. 47. One Conservative was absent, and there were three declared opponents of P.R. on the committee—M. Pierre Cot, at this time still representing the Radicals, his party colleague M. Marie, and M. Capitant of U.D.S.R. (*ibid.*, pp. 211–2). The other U.D.S.R. representative and all the Conservatives present must, therefore, have voted with the three main parties in favour of P.R.

[14] *A.P.*, 1946, pp. 72–5, 226–8. The Communist-M.R.P. alliance was reconstituted in August 1947 over the law for the municipal elections.

[15] Seine formed six constituencies, and Nord three. Five other departments formed two each. Of the 102 constituencies in France proper, 48 returned four or five members and 13 returned three. Four had two members each, 20 had six or seven, and 17 had more.

The preferential vote was ineffective because unaltered ballots were assumed to represent positive votes for the initial order. Therefore, the preferential vote only operated legally if half the ballots cast for a particular list had been altered; and it would only operate effectively if half had been altered in the same way. In practice the provision was a dead letter. Out of 19 million ballot papers only 364,000 were altered—1·9 per cent. of the valid votes. The highest percentage altered in any constituency was 6·9. Husson, ii, p. xxix. See Appendix VI. 1951 percentages: national, 7 (1,313,000): peak constituency, 17: two peak lists, 47 and 23. *Les Élections lègislatives*, from pp. 48–54.

the Fourth Republic was decisive. It distributed seats between the parties, more fairly indeed than *scrutin d'arrondissement* had done, but still with a substantial bias. The old system had told in favour of the parties of the centre. The new one helped those of the Left—not because they were the Left, but because they were now the strongest groups, and the system favoured size as such. In each of the three elections, Socialists, Communists and M.R.P. between them won about three-quarters of the parliamentary seats. But the effect of the law on the structure and cohesion of parties was even more important than its effect on their numbers.

The law favoured the larger parties for two reasons. In the first place the 'highest average' system of allotting seats was adopted instead of the 'highest remainder' system; the former works to the advantage of large, the latter of small parties (see Appendix VI). In the second place most of the constituencies were relatively small, so that a substantial vote (about a sixth of the total) was needed to secure election. In October 1945 the three main parties had a seat for every 34,000 votes, the Radicals (with only half as much support), one for every 61,000. In June 1946 the situation was much the same; it took less than 37,000 votes to elect a Communist, Socialist, or M.R.P. member, but 59,000 to elect a Radical. Put another way, only 3 per cent. of Communist and M.R.P. votes failed to contribute to the election of a member, while the Socialists wasted $5\frac{1}{2}$ per cent. of their votes in this way, the Conservatives 19 per cent., and the Radicals nearly 47 per cent. Before the November election, however, the Radicals and Conservatives entered into a tacit alliance, withdrawing their lists in each other's favour in a number of departments, which enabled them substantially to reduce the gap.[16]

By favouring the larger parties P.R. actually reduced the number of groups represented in Parliament. This is less strange than it seems. The previous system, the second ballot, tended even more strongly than P.R. to favour a multiplicity of parties. Besides, the reduction was due to the imperfection of the P.R. system adopted—pooling the votes only within the restricted area of the department. This led electors to vote for a large party so as not to waste their vote, whereas in the old days, it was argued by supporters of *scrutin d'arrondissement*, they could vote as they chose—arguments just the reverse of those employed in Britain. Most important of all was a reason not connected with the electoral

---

[16] Husson, i, pp. xxxiii–v; ii, pp. xxxii–iii, 253. In November 'wasted votes' formed less than 2 per cent. of the Communist total, 3 per cent. of that of M.R.P., between 9 and 11 per cent. for Conservatives and Socialists, 27 per cent. for the R.G.R., and 47 per cent. for Gaullists.

The figures of votes per seat were: M.R.P. 32,000, Communists 33,000, Socialists 38,000, Radicals 43,000, Conservatives 35,000.

The R.G.R. put up lists in twenty-one fewer departments than in June (*A.P.*, 1946, p. 580). For the pact between them and the Conservatives see Priouret, p. 106 n.

system. The great growth of the Communist party frightened voters into seeking an electoral bulwark against this danger. Even without a new electoral law it would have driven voters towards the stronger parties, and imposed more organization on them.

3. PARTY VIEWS

During the life of the first National Assembly, proportional representation became more and more unpopular. This development owed something to its effects on general political behaviour: to dislike of the discipline imposed on the elector, who had to vote for a list rather than a man, and on the deputy, who found it less easy than before to defy his party. But the main reason for the discrediting of P.R. was much more specific. It was the growing fear, as the 1951 election approached, that the electoral law of 1946 would produce an assembly in which there simply was no possible majority at all.

A majority had been hard enough to find in the previous legislature. With 180 Communists and 25 Gaullists in permanent opposition, more than three-quarters of the remaining 400 members had to vote together if a government were to be maintained in office. The groups which supported the parliamentary regime had to preserve almost complete solidarity. The defection of the Socialist party, with its 100 members, could bring a government down: but if too many concessions were made to the Socialists, there was a risk of alienating most of the 150 Radicals and Conservatives, with equally fatal results.

If the margin had been precarious in the old legislature, it seemed likely to disappear altogether in the new one, for the rise of the R.P.F. had deprived the forces of the centre of much of the popular support they had enjoyed in 1946. The ministry of the Interior estimated that the Communists might lose votes, but would keep the same number of seats, and that the Gaullists would return 150 strong: for the divisions among the parties of the centre would make the two oppositions the strongest single groups, and thus confer upon them the advantage which the 'big three' had had in 1946.[17] Electoral reform was therefore an important problem in the background of politics from the moment when the tripartite coalition broke up. For some years it was kept in the background by the determined opposition of M.R.P. But as the election approached, the M.R.P. leaders were driven to realize that, by taking the responsibility for producing an 'ungovernable

---

[17] These predictions were published (disapprovingly) by the Gaullist weekly *Carrefour*, 6 February 1951, and attributed to M. Giacobbi, the minister responsible for electoral reform. For the 544 metropolitan seats they gave: 159 Communists, 146 Gaullists, 82 Socialists, 68 Conservatives, 64 R.G.R., 25 M.R.P. The ministry's estimate of the result of the 1951 election (*Le Figaro*, 8 June 1951) proved astonishingly accurate (120 R.P.F., 110 Communists, 100 Conservatives, 95 Socialists, 90 R.G.R., 90 M.R.P. In four cases this was within 4 of the actual figure, and in the other two within 12).

assembly ', they might forfeit even more support than they would lose by a change in the electoral law.

The most passionate advocates of electoral reform were the Radicals. They desired, in this as in other matters, to return to the great days of the Third Republic, when they sat in the middle of the political see-saw, and gained both ways from the operation of the second ballot: when the personal standing of the deputy counted for more than his policy, and if he ensured that the country by-roads of his constituency were kept in good repair, they could become his highways to political success: when a hatred and fear of *les pouvoirs*, dictatorial, ecclesiastical, or military, had bred an attitude of equal hostility to all forms of organized power, including the political or trade union organizations of the masses. The Radical policy was clear—a return to *scrutin d'arrondissement*—and they were buoyed up by a firm conviction that this was what the electorate wanted.[18]

The Radical party was little more than a coalition of *notables*, and had no common objective wider than electoral success. Its ranks were full of well-known personalities, who had over the years acquired strong personal followings in their constituencies. It had never been disturbed by the wayward behaviour of its deputies, who, once elected, voted on opposite sides under the contradictory pressures of their various electoral situations. The older and more individualist parties shared the Radical approach to the problem of electoral reform, and for the same reasons: most Conservatives favoured *scrutin d'arrondissement*, and there was a strong and growing current of opinion in its favour in the Socialist party. But to the newer groups, which had causes to fight for and set store upon discipline, it was the worst possible answer to the problem.

The opposition to electoral reform was led by M.R.P. It is reasonable to credit this party of fervent if somewhat inexperienced moralists with a genuine concern for electoral justice, and a real distaste for the 'sordid bargains' which so often accompanied *scrutin d'arrondissement*.[19] But these were not the only reasons for their attitude. M.R.P. was a new party, drawing its electoral support not from the local ties of prominent personalities, but from *militants* who adhered to a set of political principles, and had a common background and training in the popular movements sponsored by the Church. These active Catholics transferred to politics the discipline learned in religious organization,

---

[18] They may well have been wrong. A poll taken in October 1950 by the French Institute of Public Opinion showed 22 per cent. favouring a double ballot system, 16 per cent. for a single ballot majority system, 25 per cent. for P.R., and 37 per cent. with no opinion. Jean Pouillon, ' Les sondages et la science politique,' *Revue française de science politique*, vol. 1, no. 1 (January 1952), p. 99.

[19] Their own rapid rise to power on the basis of votes given them not from fundamental agreement, but in order to ' bar the route ' to Communism, never seems to have struck M.R.P. as presenting any analogy with the sordid process of acquiring second ballot support.

just as naturally as the free-thinking Radicals tended to political individualism.[20]

M.R.P. opposed the second ballot as vigorously as the single-member constituency. For the purpose of the second ballot was to facilitate alliances: and M.R.P. found alliances difficult to make. Both Radicals and Socialists preferred to maintain their traditional anti-clerical combination, rather than to admit this upstart and suspect movement as an associate—as the second chamber elections of October and November 1948 all too clearly showed. These were conducted on a majority system, and proved disastrous for M.R.P. Rejected by the partners they desired, M.R.P. in many areas seemed inevitably thrown back on a combination with the R.P.F., which most of their *militants* detested. Thus *scrutin d'arrondissement* was abhorrent to M.R.P. in many ways. It would decimate their parliamentary strength—one estimate was that it would reduce them to thirty seats.[21] It would force them into political combinations they disliked. And, since these combinations would differ in different areas, it would wreck the unity of the movement. Radical individualists might accept this consequence with equanimity. But for M.R.P. it would spell the end of all their high hopes of acting as a (sadly needed) regenerating leaven in French public life.

The other relatively new and disciplined parties shared M.R.P.'s dislike for *scrutin d'arrondissement*. The Communists, before 1940, were the main victims of the second ballot system, with its tendency to favour the parties of the centre. Subsequently, they suffered even more than M.R.P. from the reluctance of others to associate with them. They also preferred a system which enforced discipline on their voters and deputies, protecting them from the dangers of association with, or support from, electors of other parties. They were therefore determined supporters of P.R., bitterly criticizing the laws of 1945 and 1946 because they did not go far enough in that direction, but in 1951 preferring the retention of incomplete P.R. to the abandonment of the principle.

The Gaullists were a new and an organized movement. They had had no opportunity to build up strong local positions, and they did not wish to allow their discipline to be undermined by allowing their members to become electorally dependent upon other groups. Their official policy was *scrutin de liste* and a double ballot majority system. In 1947, when the Marseilles congress adopted this programme, the R.P.F. was a potential majority party. It could reasonably hope to run ahead of other anti-Communist groups on the first ballot, and to attract their votes in the second. But in 1948 the Gaullist impetus became exhausted. When it ceased to be a potential majority party,

---

[20] F. Goguel, *Encyclopédie*, vol. i, p. 354.
[21] *L'Observateur*, 8 February 1951.

and reverted to the position of an important minority, the R.P.F.'s outlook changed. Its expectations under a majority system were much less promising than before: as the leading anti-Communist group it had hoped to attract the votes of others, but once it lost that position it risked the defection of its own supporters. For it, as for other isolated minority groups, P.R. was now the best guarantee of fair representation in the new Assembly.

The Gaullist deputies, whose personal and local positions were established, might continue to press the popular cause of electoral reform. But the General's advisers, who could make sure of their places on a party list but who lacked local roots, came to prefer the security of P.R. to the chances of a majority system.[22] In September 1948, for the first time, the Gaullists declared that dissolution of the Assembly was essential even without electoral reform. General de Gaulle stated that *scrutin de liste majoritaire*, and P.R., were the only honest electoral systems.[23] Opponents concluded that the real Gaullist aim was to keep P.R., but shift the responsibility for doing so on to M.R.P.[24]

The attitude of the Socialist party changed even more sharply. In the Third Republic they had always been under-represented, and traditionally they were determined supporters of proportional representation. But they were an old party, strong in well-known personalities, and a decentralized party, with a very high degree of internal freedom. From the beginning a large section wished to modify the rigidities of P.R. by instituting *panachage* and the preferential vote. And after 1946, the Socialist attitude to P.R. itself began to change. It became evident that the new electoral system had improved neither the quality of candidates nor the tone of public life; that it made political alliances more difficult to arrange, and sowed hostility between neighbouring parties; above all that, while doing nothing significant to help the Socialist party (which had little to gain or lose from a change of electoral system), it ensured that their Communist arch-enemies would retain a parliamentary group nearly 200 strong.

The balance of opinion within the Socialist party gradually but decisively shifted. In the areas where the party was weak, P.R. retained support. But where the Socialists were strong, the necessity for a change came to be accepted. More indifferent than any other group to the nature of the system adopted, the Socialists were willing to accept

---

[22] *Le Figaro*, 18 May 1950. The deputies had all won their seats as adherents of groups other than the R.P.F., and a majority system of election would make it easier for them to retain their old contacts.

[23] *A.P.*, 1948, p. 176: 1950, p. 54: he ridiculed the idea that France could be saved by changing the electoral system.

[24] P. H. Teitgen, *J.O.*, 21 December 1950, p. 9443. P.R. would ensure the return of 180 Communists to the next Assembly, which would naturally put the R.P.F. in a very strong bargaining position.

any compromise in order to get reform through. In the Assembly they voted in successive divisions for a double and then for a single ballot, and they agreed to the hybrid system eventually adopted. But in the Council of the Republic, their group (elected by a majority system and representing the party's areas of strength) came out decisively for a return to *scrutin d'arrondissement*.

Internal differences were by no means confined to the Socialists. Every group contained a minority of recalcitrant members whose personal interests differed from those of their party. There were M.R.P. deputies, low on their lists and with little hope of re-election in a large constituency, who had cultivated one corner of their department on the off-chance that *scrutin d'arrondissement* might be voted at the last moment. There were anti-Gaullist Radicals in the big cities, too few to hope for survival under any system except P.R.[25] There were Conservative and U.D.S.R. members who, like M.R.P., opposed a double ballot system, fearing that the extreme parties would lead on the first round (because of the divisions of their opponents) and would polarize the centre vote on the second.

These were not the only complications. Groups had their second preferences as well as their favourite proposals. Thus Communists and M.R.P. agreed in advocating P.R., but differed violently in their second choices. M.R.P., anxious to avoid a double ballot at all costs, favoured a one-ballot scheme with provision for party alliances. For the Communists this was the worst possible solution, since they had no allies: the least undesirable alternative for them was probably *scrutin d'arrondissement*, under which they could at any rate hold their local strongholds. Conversely, some Radicals, if they despaired of obtaining *scrutin d'arrondissement*, were (as in 1945) prepared to adopt complete nation-wide P.R., under which a weak, thinly-spread party would do better than under the law of 1946, with its departmental pooling. Amid all these cross-currents electoral reform had a very difficult passage. Every party in the majority was determined to drive a hard bargain; but none dared take the responsibility for a final breakdown of the negotiations.

4. THE ELECTORAL LAW OF 1951

THE parties of the majority thus agreed on a single objective only—the need to reduce the strength of the Communists without relinquishing the spoils to the R.P.F.[26] There was a prolonged and bitter struggle between M.R.P. and many of the Peasants, who insisted on a single ballot, and the Radicals and the majority of Conservatives, who

---

[25] F. Goguel, ' Sur la réforme électorale,' *Esprit*, January 1950, pp. 160–1.
[26] The normal party motives for wishing to weaken an adversary were powerfully reinforced in the spring of 1950, when the Communist deputies tried to paralyse by violence the working of the Assembly. *A.P.*, 1950, p. 54. And see above, p. 199.

demanded a two-ballot system. The Socialists voted for each in turn, while the Communists opposed both. On 21 February 1951 a series of negative majorities, in which the 180 Communists formed the only constant factor, rejected eight successive proposals. The battle lasted six months, brought down a government, and provoked a conflict between the houses. It was complicated by the willingness of many deputies to obstruct the reform in order to prevent a summer election, and by the desire of the native members to enforce a liberal change in the overseas electoral law against the opposition of the Council of the Republic. But on 7 May the patience of the prime minister was rewarded, and the bill was passed by a majority sufficient to over-ride the recalcitrant upper house.[27]

The new law amended, instead of simply superseding, that of 1946. It retained the same constituencies,[28] and kept the system of party lists, which must still contain as many names as there were seats to fill. *Panachage* was incorporated, and the preferential vote was retained. By-elections, unknown since 1945, were restored; when they occur, the whole department polls, on a double ballot basis. The distribution of seats was still, in theory, determined by P.R. But the whole working of the system was changed by the two essential new provisions, the institution of *apparentement*, and the absolute majority rule.

Everywhere except in the Paris area,[29] lists may combine in an alliance, or *apparentement*.[30] Their votes are then counted together, as if they had been cast for a single list. And any list or *apparentement*

---

[27] The government's bill had been heavily defeated in the Council of the Republic. To pass against the opposition of the senators, an absolute majority in the Assembly was needed on second reading. On 27 April the deputies again voted the bill, but by only 308 to 270—three votes short of the crucial absolute majority. The deadlock was resolved by the introduction of a new bill, differing from the old one only in one petty detail. On the whole subject, see R. G. Neumann, ' The struggle for electoral reform in France ', *American Political Science Review*, September 1951, pp. 741–55.

[28] Except that Gironde was split in two.

[29] P.R. was retained in Seine and Seine-et-Oise. But the method of allotting seats was changed from the ' highest average ' to the ' highest remainder ' system (see Appendix VI) in order to benefit the weaker parties, namely (in Paris) the centre. This provision, the most partisan and least defensible point in the law, transferred nine seats from the extreme to the centre parties.

[30] But only ' national ' parties might participate in *apparentements*. These were defined as organizations running lists in at least thirty constituencies. Only eleven bodies qualified under this provision, some of which, such as the R.G.R.I.F. (see above, pp. 149–50) were invented for the purpose.

The clause tended to multiply hopeless candidatures by forcing minor parties to present bogus lists in order to acquire ' national ' status. ' On a vu dans la nuit de dimanche à lundi accourir dans les préfectures les émissaires de groupements " nationaux " en mal de candidats. Les textes leur faisaient en effet obligation d'être présents dans trente départements au moins et d'y présenter des listes complètes. On mobilisa en hâte les femmes, les amis et les amis d'amis. Quatre groupements succombèrent néanmoins à la tâche. . . .' J. Fauvet, *Le Monde*, 30 May 1951.

Some of the groups which survived the ordeal did so by means of bogus lists. Thus the U.D.S.R. list in Hautes-Pyrénées received only four votes. In Lozère the two U.D.S.R. candidates, a husband and wife, had only one vote between them—the husband's, it was alleged. The R.G.R.I.F. went still further: ten of its thirty-six lists issued no literature

which wins an absolute majority of votes takes *all* the seats.[31] If no party or combination wins a majority of votes, P.R. continues to apply: and P.R. also governs the distribution of seats between the different lists making up an *apparentement*. The result of this system was to enable the government parties, by combination, to obtain the advantages of size which in 1945–46 went to the *tripartiste* parties, and in 1951 would, without *apparentement*, have gone to the two oppositions. Electors anxious not to waste their votes would, under P.R., have been tempted to give them to the Communists or R.P.F. rather than to a weak middle party. But by allowing the middle parties to combine, and giving them a chance of winning an absolute majority, the authors of the law hoped to attract those citizens who meant to ' vote usefully '. Government speakers could and did argue with force that a vote for the R.P.F. was a vote for the Communists.

The system was bitterly criticized in Parliament and in the press, and not only by its victims.[32] Much of the attack against P.R. had really been directed against having to vote for a list instead of a man; and from this point of view the new law made matters even worse. P.R. was alleged to have made the elector a mere puppet in the hands of the party manager: *apparentement*, it was argued, prevented him even choosing his own party. His vote might help to elect an opponent: Catholics supporting an M.R.P. candidate might find their ballots putting in an anti-clerical Radical or Socialist. This was clearly dishonest, and would probably prove ineffective as well, since potential supporters would be deterred by this risk. Thus a large *apparentement*, even if it were achieved, might actually lose votes instead of gaining them. And even if the system worked, the electorate would certainly regard it as rigged in the interests of the *syndicat des sortants*.

Many of these criticisms proved justified. The voter's choice was still fettered, and the introduction of *panachage* did not improve the situation.[33] Anomalies became apparent long before the casting of the

---

and conducted no campaign. Many of its candidates were obvious men of straw, the nominees of more serious candidates, whose election depended on the R.G.R.I.F. being recognized as a national movement entitled to make *apparentements*. One of these, who successfully contested Haute-Saône, had his secretary stand as R.G.R.I.F. candidate in another constituency, while his mayoral assistant and his chauffeur formed the R.G.R.I.F. list in a third. Another, M. Chambaretaud, did better still; one Lyons friend of his stood in Réunion, while the friend's wife was put up for Guadeloupe, on the other side of the world—and neither moved outside their home town. *J.O.*, 23 August 1951, pp. 6468–73 (speeches of MM. Mutter, Coudert, and Dagain).

[31] This rule recalls the electoral law which prevailed from 1919 to 1927: a list which had an absolute majority of votes won all the seats, while P.R. applied if no list had a clear majority.

[32] Thus M. Rémy Roure called it the least honest electoral law in French history, and M. Herriot described it as inept and monstrous. *Le Monde*, 26 April 1951, 20–21 May 1951.

[33] Several thousand *panachage* votes were cast for M. Moch on personal grounds. They raised the average of his list enough to elect three Socialists instead of two—which was far from fulfilling the intentions of the voters concerned. See Appendix VI.

vote. In a district like Lille, M.R.P. leaders had to hope that the Socialists would show themselves sufficiently intransigent in their anti-clericalism to poll their full vote, while the Socialists counted on a similarly extreme attitude on the part of their clerical partners. Where a Socialist, like M. Ramadier in Aveyron, was excluded from an alliance of the conservative centre parties, his only hope of saving his seat lay in a Gaullist campaign sufficiently vigorous to rob the *apparentement* of the absolute majority. All over the country, Communists and R.P.F. had a similar interest in one another's success.

When the votes came to be counted, some remarkable results were announced. In Hérault, fewer than 39,000 Socialists elected three representatives, while 69,000 Communists had none. In the Lille district, 107,000 Socialists had five members and 106,000 Communists none, while 84,000 M.R.P. voters had four, and 94,000 Gaullists none. In terms of gains or losses since 1946, the anomalies were even more striking. For victory or defeat depended on a party's capacity to attract allies, rather than on its own strength. So, in two of the three departments where they did best, the Communists lost seats. The two most successful Socialists in the country were both beaten. The Radical Air minister, M. Maroselli, increased his poll by 4,000, but lost his seat to an independent Conservative, allied to the R.P.F., whose vote was less than half his own.

Dishonest or not, the new law achieved the results its authors had desired. Pessimists had warned that disgusted voters would refuse to go to the polls: but there was no evidence that this actually occurred.[34] They had predicted that the government parties would rarely unite, and that P.R. would continue to operate over four-fifths of the country.[35] But in fact 53 *apparentements* including Socialists, M.R.P. and Radicals were formed, and 36 of them included Conservatives in addition. In 31 constituencies the governmental parties won an absolute majority of votes, and so secured all the seats.[36] In metropolitan France as a whole, the Communists won 71 fewer seats than they would have had under P.R., and the R.P.F. 26 fewer. Among the parties which profited by

---

[34] General de Gaulle was the most distinguished exponent of this theory. Had it been true, the proportion of non-voters should have shown an increase since 1946: in fact it was 2 per cent. less. In the dozen constituencies where no *apparentements* at all were made, and the old system consequently remained in force, there were as many abstentions as there were elsewhere. The proportion was indeed smaller in the Paris area, to which the new system did not apply; but this had been so in 1946, when Paris had the same system as the rest of the country. And the increased number of spoiled papers (from 360,000 to 540,000) was probably accounted for by the complications of *panachage*.
[35] *J.O.*, 26 April 1951, p. 4040 (M. Daladier's speech).
[36] There were 40 constituencies in which a list or *apparentement* won an absolute majority. In 31 of them the victorious coalition included the Socialists, in 7 the Gaullists, and in 2 it excluded both. Of the 31, 25 were in the old republican zone along and south of the Loire. (In two cases, the Conservatives were in the *apparentement*, but the Radicals were in opposition: these are not counted among the 53 mentioned in the text.) See map 5 for the regional distribution both of *apparentements* and of absolute majorities.

the system, the Socialists gained least, since in many departments (especially in the west) they were not admitted to the centre alliance. They had only 16 more seats than the old law would have given them, compared with an extra 30 for M.R.P., 27 for the R.G.R., and 24 for the Conservatives.[37] But such arithmetical computations under-estimate the real gains of the moderate parties, for the desire to 'vote usefully' undoubtedly attracted additional supporters to the *apparentements*. The new law thus helped the allied parties in the polling-booths, and not only at the count.

As a practical device, the electoral law of 1951 thus proved a success. Nor was it much more unjust than other electoral systems. In June 1946, under P.R., the Communists had elected a member for every 26,000 votes, the Radicals one for every 59,000. In June 1951, under the new law, the Radicals won a seat for every 28,000, and the Communists one for every 52,000. It was not clear why P.R. should be regarded as the embodiment of mathematical justice, and the *apparentement* system as a monster of political iniquity. And, if the proportion of votes 'wasted' under the new law was twice as high under P.R., it was still only half as great as it had been in the days of *scrutin d'arrondissement*.[38]

Even on grounds of principle, there was more to be said for the system than most commentators, French or British, were willing to admit. The former had indeed every right to demand that their country should adopt a just electoral law whatever the political consequences. But it was surprising to find supporters of the British electoral system professing themselves shocked by Frenchmen who regarded a working majority (in French terms!) as more important than abstract justice. Under the old law, it might have proved altogether impossible to form a government: at best the R.P.F. would have been able to dictate its own terms. For P.R. would have given 172 seats to the Communists and 143 to the Gaullists—a total of 315, a clear though tiny majority of the 627 members.[39] The two extreme groups, with a little less than half the votes, would have held more than half the seats. The 1946 law would thus have gratuitously endangered a regime which, for all its faults, was preferred by all Frenchmen to the dominance of their extreme opponents, and by most of them to either of the alternatives offered.

The case can be put on more positive grounds. The *apparentement*

---

[37] These figures are based on my own calculations. Mr. Peter Campbell's (*Revue française de science politique*, vol. 1, no. 4, October 1951, pp. 498–502) differ slightly, owing to uncertainty about the precise allegiance of some members elected on coalition lists, different treatment of overseas seats, etc.

[38] There were 24 per cent. of wasted votes in 1951, compared with 45 per cent. in 1932, 44 per cent. in 1936, and between 9 and 13 per cent. in the three P.R. elections. *Le Monde*, 26 June 1951.

[39] In fact the opposition parties would have done better than this, since the electoral law certainly attracted votes away from them and towards the *apparentements*, on the principle of 'voting usefully.'

allowed the elector to express two separate choices, which corresponded to real political priorities. Over most of the country the combination of the middle parties registered the preference of most voters for the parliamentary regime against either presidential rule or 'people's democracy': within this framework, the moderate voter could then exercise his second option, for the economic, social or religious tendency which he preferred. But in those areas where politics revolved around a single issue, that question became the basis upon which alliances were made. In the west, where the problem of the church schools was of over-riding importance, the Catholic voter could opt first for the clerical *apparentement* which united M.R.P. and R.P.F., and secondly, within it, for the parliamentary or for the authoritarian solution to the country's problems.

The system certainly handicapped parties which were unable to make alliances. But there are advantages in weakening the influence of doctrinally intransigent groups, which, if they cannot form coalitions in the country, are likely to find difficulty in joining or even in supporting governments in the Assembly. A more damaging criticism is that the voter had no means of controlling the use made of his vote, since the *apparentements* were settled by the party machines. This certainly expressed the complaint of a great many voters: and any arrangement which weakens the sense of civic responsibility in a country where *incivisme* is already so widespread, deserves to be scrutinized with suspicion. Yet is it so certain that this pressure on the voter is destructive of his sense of responsibility? His desire for a party free of trammels is a utopian demand, a piece of wishful thinking rather than a serious political preference. To make the parliamentary system work at all, parties must compromise with one another in the Assembly: an electoral law which compels the electors to face this fact is not *therefore* less honest than one which encourages their illusion that their party can behave as if it were in a political vacuum. The frustrated Socialist will not like having to choose between an intransigent Communist party which outrages his principles, and a temporizing Socialist one which is for ever compromising them. Yet in real life this is the choice before him. No doubt he prefers his *militant's* dream world, in which no consequences follow the overthrow of a government and no difficulties restrain the realization, overnight, of the paper programme of the party. But there is something to be said for a mechanism which compels him to look the distasteful facts in the face, and the most cogent criticism of the system is that the compulsion is still not strong enough.[40]

---

[40] See Goguel, *Fourth Republic*, pp. 76–8, 161–4. M. Goguel favours *scrutin de liste*, and a majority system with two ballots. To win, the centre parties would have to form joint lists and fight a common campaign; this would create a basis in the country for their co-operation in the Assembly. But to prohibit contradictory alliances in different areas would be extremely difficult, either as a parliamentary or as an administrative operation; and the system without this clause might damage party discipline as gravely as *scrutin d'arrondissement* did. Nevertheless it would be well worth trying.

Chapter 20

PRESSURE GROUPS

WHERE governmental authority and party discipline are weak, pressure politics flourish. One of the commonest political illusions is the belief that the removal of the party whip would free the politician to search according to the dictates of his conscience for that nebulous ideal, the general interest. In the real world, party discipline often constrains the member, but it protects him too. It helps to screen him against the demands of influential groups which claim to control marginal votes in his constituency. And it greatly reduces the danger of parliamentary corruption, since it is easier to enforce responsibilities upon a party than upon an individual.

Political morality is low where authority is diffused. Responsibility in France is not enforced by a coherent opposition upon a government with undisputed power. Instead, it is dissipated among several hundred professional politicians, each sufficiently influential to attract temptation, but sufficiently obscure to have little fear of the consequences. In the Third Republic, a chain of intermediaries of diminishing honesty sometimes linked the politician (often without his knowledge) with the crook. Frequently it originated in the minister's *cabinet*, the little group of half a dozen personal or political friends whom each minister brings into office with him to serve as a buffer against both his official advisers, and the outer world.[1] The scandals of the Fourth Republic have concerned the entourage of ministers, rather than politicians themselves.

Public opinion, always cynical about the profession of politics, naturally fastens upon these spectacular incidents. Yet in the weakness of government in France the recurrent scandals (always exaggerated and often invented) are of less real importance than the power of pressure-groups, for which the public is itself at least as responsible as the politicians.

---

[1] The fate of M. Félix Gouin, prime minister in 1946, shows that this useful institution has its dangers. He unwisely chose his *cabinet* from his Marseilles supporters constituency: some of them took much too active an interest in the importation of wine from Algeria, and though he himself was not directly involved in the scandal, it put an end to his ministerial career. Roger Peyré, the *éminence grise* of the 'affair of the generals,' also appears to have had relations with members of ministerial *cabinets* rather than with the politicians themselves.

The quality of *cabinets* naturally varies at least as much as that of the politicians who choose them; and some leaders, notably Laval, have been well served by *chefs de cabinet* much more reputable than themselves. Abuses of the kind mentioned find much more scope under the American spoils system, and occur (as the Lynskey tribunal showed) where neither of these devices exist. Whatever its dangers, an institution of the *cabinet* type is indispensable if the changing ministers are to keep any effective control over their permanent advisers. It is an essential safeguard against rule by the bureaucracy.

1. THE GREAT INTERESTS[2]

FRENCH politics have always provided a happy hunting-ground for the activities of these bodies. In the Third Republic the laxity of party discipline, and the nature of the electoral system, made individual deputies very susceptible to the exhortations or threats of sectional organizations in their localities,[3] and to the demands of their constituents for favours from the administration. Weak governments could not stand up to the pressure of powerful economic interests. The governor of the (private) Bank of France, in his memoirs, congratulated himself on having forced the Herriot cabinet out of office in July 1926. Nine years later his successors, in the course of their victorious conflict with the Flandin cabinet, issued a communiqué of astounding arrogance which shows where, in their view, the real power in France resided.[4] On the other side the electoral influence of the civil service trade unions, the ex-servicemen's associations, the organizations of shopkeepers or of wheat-farmers, could be used to counteract the financial power of business and the banks.[5] Short-lived, timid and unstable ministries were buffeted helplessly between the conflicting interests.

The new electoral laws of the Fourth Republic did not change the fundamental features of the situation, but they did affect the type and nature of the influences to which the deputy was subjected. Parties were rather more disciplined than before (in 1945–47, much more so). The abolition of *scrutin d'arrondissement*, and the adoption of the

---

[2] The June 1953 number of *Esprit* is devoted to an analysis of the relationship between political and economic power in France.

[3] Before the 1914 war Robert de Jouvenel wrote with his usual ironic exaggeration:
' Un immense marchandage alors s'établit :
—Vote pour mes postiers, je voterai pour tes bouilleurs de cru.
—Vote Clermont-Ferrand port de mer, et je voterai le canal de la Garonne au Rhin.'
La République des camarades, p. 81.
Twenty years later M. Joseph Barthélemy commented in the same spirit:
' S'il s'agit du privilège des bouilleurs, par exemple, l'entente est parfaite entre les représentants des départements qui font bouillir, communistes, socialistes, radicaux, modérés, conservateurs, royalistes. Un Poincariste fervent me disait qu'il n'aurait pas hésité à renverser Poincaré s'il s'était agi du privilège des bouilleurs. Tout député de Normandie vote pour la pomme, tout député de l'Hérault vote pour le vin. J'ai voté pendant huit ans pour le blé et pour l'eau-de-vie de l'Armagnac.' *Essai sur le travail parlementaire et le système des commissions*, p. 86.

[4] M. Émile Moreau, *Revue des deux mondes*, 1 March 1937, quoted Soulier, p. 378 n. (During the 1930's M. Moreau was actively involved in royalist politics.) Cf. Pierre Frédérix, pp. 106–7.
A. Werth, *Destiny of France*, p. 343, quotes the communiqué of 1935, which stated in part:
'... (the government's economic measures) deserve a good mark in view of the difficulties of the situation. This good mark has been given to M. Flandin in the form of credit facilities. These credit facilities may not prove sufficient. He will ask for more credit. Our reply will then depend on whether we are satisfied with the actions of the government during the first respite we have given it as a reward for its present determination to defend the currency.'

[5] Soulier, pp. 158–9, 378–82.

department as the constituency, weakened parish-pump politics by making it electorally unprofitable. Formerly the deputy, concentrating all his efforts on a limited area, could feel that to some extent its development was directly due to his activities, and could acquire popularity as a result of them. Now that those efforts had to be spread over a whole department, their effect was diluted. The member could no longer take the same pride in them, nor expect the same gratitude for them.[6]

But the decline of parish-pump politics did not reduce the pressure, it merely shifted its incidence—from village affairs to departmental or regional ones, from the individual politician to his party, from petty local groups to organizations operating on a national scale. Such bodies range from relatively minor economic interests, such as the road hauliers (whose power is not unknown outside France) or the beetroot growers, to wider movements which appeal to the whole electoral followings of several different parties, and can reasonably claim to represent causes rather than interests.[7]

Among these major 'corporations' are the Catholic Church, the school-teachers and civil servants, and the trade unions. They are strong enough to use political parties as their instruments. For the parties of the Fourth Republic, though more highly organized than their predecessors, have no more hope than the latter of forming a majority government ; and this fact has a profound effect upon their conduct.

A potential majority party dare not identify itself too exclusively with a single interest, for fear of losing the floating vote. But under a system of perpetual coalition, responsibility can always be shifted. A permanent minority party comes to depend on the loyalty of a particular group, whose support it dare not alienate. And the floating vote for which it competes has to be attracted away, not from its fundamental enemies at the far end of the political spectrum, but from the neighbour parties who appeal to the same clientèle. In the clerical west, M.R.P., Conservatives, and R.P.F. are in bitter rivalry for the support of the Church. The Socialists in the industrial areas cling to their remnant of trade union support, of which the Communists seek to deprive them, while in the countryside their organization becomes more and more dependent upon the village school-teachers.

The Church, at the time of liberation, worked mainly through M.R.P. But the formation of the R.P.F. soon gave it an alternative political champion, while P.R.L. also began to bid for clerical support. Since the national electorate did not contain a pro-clerical majority, the Church's pressure was mainly applied at the municipal and departmental level: the problem of church schools is essentially a regional

---

[6] But constituency activities still occupy an important part of the deputy's attention: see below, pp. 349–50.
[7] Thibaudet, pp. 181–2, points out that though no French party can make an effective appeal on the basis of interests alone, if the interests are sufficiently wide they can become the foundation for an ideology.

one.[8] But the 1951 electoral law changed the situation. Directed against the Communists, it split the anti-clerical forces, and offered the Church the chance to win a parliamentary majority. A Committee for Educational Freedom (*Comité d'action pour la liberté scolaire*) sprang into activity in the western departments. It tried with only limited success to persuade all the pro-Catholic parties to form *apparentements* against the anti-clericals. It also waged a more effective campaign to obtain binding pledges from candidates everywhere. 298 of the new deputies gave them—the whole of M.R.P., all but five of the Gaullists, all but two Independents and Peasants, and even a dozen R.G.R. members seeking support on their Right.

These deputies were organized in the *Association parlementaire pour la liberté de l'enseignement*, which required its members to give their support only to a government which accepted the Association's programme. With the aid of some overseas deputies, it was able to mobilize a comfortable majority behind M. Barangé's bill to subsidize the church schools, which in September 1951 broke up the political alliance which had governed the country for the preceding four years. But the A.P.L.E. had the wisdom not to overplay its hand, and after this spectacular triumph it receded into the background of politics.

On the other side, the campaign against the Barangé bill was managed by a *Comité national de défense laïque*, which united various organizations of the educational profession, parents' associations, etc. It had some influence on the Radical party, which had once depended heavily on the rural school-teachers for its electoral organization, and more still on the Socialists, to whom between the wars most of the teachers had transferred their support. These parties are particularly responsive to the material as well as to the ideological demands of the educational profession; but others too can often be enlisted in their defence. So in May 1950 the teachers were able to secure the unanimous support of the Education committee of the Assembly in resisting economy cuts.[9] In defending their standard of living, the teachers make common cause with other civil servants, who collectively form the most important nucleus of Socialist voters, and can count on whole-hearted support from the party in which they play so large a part. But even the most economy-minded political groups are chary of challenging them directly. In February 1948 there was pressure from all sides of the Assembly for concessions to different classes of civil servants. And in June 1950 the entire Finance committee supported their claims for re-grading and salary increases, with the solitary exception of the prime

---

[8] There are twelve departments in which more than 30 per cent. of elementary school children are taught in church schools: eight of these are in the north-west (Brittany and Anjou), and four in the Cevennes. There are twenty-one in which more than half the secondary school children are in church schools: eleven are contiguous departments in the north-west, and three more are in the Cevennes. *Le Monde*, 8 August 1951.

[9] See above, p. 246, n. 39.

minister's party, M.R.P.—which is not, however, as a rule hostile to civil servants' demands.[10]

The trade unions in general are active and vigorous political lobbyists. Their principal instrument is the Labour committee of the Assembly, which is full of their sympathisers.[11] The committee's criticisms of the government's collective bargaining bill in January 1950, and especially its opposition to compulsory arbitration, largely reflected the demands of the various trade union federations, whose views were sponsored by their respective allies, the Communists, the Socialists, and M.R.P.[12] A year later, the same committee put forward proposals for increasing family allowances, which had been suggested to it by an unofficial action committee representing the main trade unions and family associations.[13] In January 1952 it was the lobbying of the Socialist railwaymen's union against the Pleven government's reorganization plans, which led the Socialist party to vote against them and so brought down the ministry.[14]

The great economic interests of the country have surprisingly little parliamentary influence. Open association with big business is unpopular with the electorate, and is shunned even by many of the Conservatives. The *patronat* has closer links with the higher administration than with most politicians.[15] The Bank of France, though nationalized since 1936, retains considerable independence: in February 1952 its governor, M. Baumgartner, replying to the prime minister's request for credits, put the government and the citizenry in their respective places with a regal hauteur which his private predecessors would have warmly applauded.[16]

Small business is a very different matter. The tone of economic life, which is set by the little family firm, still influences profoundly even the large-scale businesses and industries. The survival of the small man is considered an important object of policy; politicians are as responsive to his demands as they are frigid towards his big competitor. The *Petites et moyennes entreprises*, under their active leader M. Gingembre, indeed form an important electoral force in a country where the small

---

[10] *A.P.*, 1948, p. 18: 1950, p. 123.
[11] See above, pp. 240, 241n.
[12] *J.O.*, 4 January 1950, especially pp. 120–2 (speeches of MM. Cayeux, Gazier, and Croizat; and of the *rapporteur*). But could compulsory arbitration have succeeded if the unions were hostile?
[13] *Le Monde*, 8 February 1951: these bodies again intervened in April, when the government tried once again to postpone action. *Ibid.*, 27 April 1951.
[14] 'Pendant le débat sur les lois-cadres—qui visaient le S.N.C.F.—des délégations de cheminots se tenaient en permanence au Palais-Bourbon et la pression, cette fois, n'était pas vaine puisque le cabinet Pleven en est mort.' Roger-A. Priouret, *La Vie française*, 22 February 1952. See also *Times*, 8 January 1952: *Manchester Guardian*, 8 and 9 January 1952.
This was a government too weak to resist pressure from either side, as the settlers' influence on its North African policy had recently indicated. See above, p. 190n.
[15] The ministry of Finance was indeed held from November 1947 to January 1952 (apart from five months) by MM. René Mayer and Petsche, two of the very few political leaders with experience in ' big business.' (But see note 50 below).
[16] *Le Monde*, 2–3 March 1952.

shopkeeper vote alone has been estimated at 2½ million.[17] Though the Radicals and the groups further to the Right are naturally the most susceptible to their influence, Socialists and Communists do not disdain to bid for their support.[18] In the *tripartiste* period the P.M.E. worked mainly through direct action or the threat of it—demonstrations (sometimes violent) in 1947, to demand the end of rationing and economic controls, closing of shops and threats of tax strikes in 1948 to protest against increases in taxation. But as the balance of power shifted, they came to turn their attention to politics. In November 1949 they attracted several other business and middle-class bodies into a *Front économique* to co-ordinate the opposition to M. Bidault's budget. In the 1951 election this body, in which the P.M.E. provided the driving force, inspired the Taxpayers' Defence lists, which tried to organize an opposition Conservatism untainted by association with the Government parties. This attempt failed; but a hundred deputies pledged themselves during the campaign to join a parliamentary inter-group to forward the policy of the *Front économique*.[19]

Among all these major interests the most important is that of the peasantry. Agriculture, forestry and fishing employed 36 per cent. of the working population in 1950. Yet in 1935 it was said, with some exaggeration, that the clamour of one postal workers' union sounded louder to the government than that of the huge but divided agricultural interest.[20] In the period of liberation a serious attempt to organize the whole peasantry was made by the young Socialist minister of Agriculture, M. Tanguy-Prigent. His attempt to attach them to the Left, through the medium of the new *Confédération générale de l'agriculture* (C.G.A.), had no permanent results. The predominant influence within the Confederation passed to the more specialized groups of which it was composed, especially to the *Fédération nationale des syndicats d'exploitants agricoles* (F.N.S.E.A.); most of these were politically sympathetic to the Conservative parties.[21] This development was officially recognized in 1951, when in the reconstituted Economic Council the C.G.A.'s representation was reduced from 30 to 3, 15 being

---

[17] *Manchester Guardian*, 20 May 1950.
On the persistent influence of the small or family firm and its methods and mentality, see David S. Landes, ' French business and the businessman,' in E. M. Earle, ed., *Modern France*, Ch. 19: also John E. Sawyer, *ibid.*, pp. 306–10.
[18] Both tried, just before the 1951 election, to obtain more money for state loans to small and medium businesses. *J.O.*, 6 May 1951, pp. 4708–10, 4726.
[19] *A.P.*, 1947, pp. 97, 172, 226–7: 1948, pp. 9, 166; 1949, p. 205. Above, p. 149 : *Le Monde*, 22–23 July 1951.
[20] Frédérix, p. 36.
[21] See P. Marabuto, *Les Partis politiques et les mouvements sociaux*, pp. 349–59: Gordon Wright, ' Communists and Peasantry in France,' in Earle, *op. cit.*, pp. 226–31: and Wright, ' Agrarian syndicalism in postwar France ', *American Political Science Review*, vol. 47, no. 2 (June 1953), pp. 402–16. In the general election of 1951, there were 17 departments in which the president of the local F.N.S.E.A. stood as a Conservative candidate, and five more in which one of the other officials did so. *Le Figaro*, 31 May 1951. Cf. Epilogue, note 6.

transferred to the F.N.S.E.A., and 12 to the other affiliated organizations. Of the 87 officials of agricultural associations elected to parliament in 1951, 41 were Conservatives, and only 13 belonged to the parties of the Left.[22]

There are many cleavages in French life, but that between town and country is peculiar in its political effects. No party tries to appeal both for Catholic and for anti-clerical votes. Political groups look either to the workers or to the middle class, but few of them set out to cultivate both at once, and those that do make the attempt risk their own cohesion in the process, as the R.P.F. discovered in 1952. But everyone tries to attract the peasant vote. Other major interests limit their appeal to a certain sector of the political spectrum; but agriculture possesses an ' invisible party ' [23] whose members sit on all the benches from the Gaullists' to the Communists'.[24] Equally, members of very different groups combine to oppose its pretentions. Representatives of the urban bourgeoisie are, at least in private, quite as critical of peasant backwardness and privilege as any trade unionist; and in 1950 an extreme Conservative deputy for Paris attacked a proposed increase in rural family allowances on the ground that the peasants contributed far less than the urban middle classes. [25]

The distribution of investment resources provides one fertile source of conflict, which comes up for decision every year. In the early years of the Monnet plan, the basic industries which had been nationalized received 70 per cent. of the investments which had been allotted to them: but private industry and commerce had to content itself with 37 per cent., and agriculture with only 17 per cent.[26] So in April 1950 a campaign was launched to divert to agriculture some of the investment resources which the government proposed to devote to the coal industry. This demand was initiated by the agrarian wing of M.R.P., and supported by the conservative parties and by the Finance committee of the Assembly; it was successfully resisted by the minister concerned, also a member of M.R.P., with the backing of the urban minority of his party, of the Socialists and Communists, and of the Economic Affairs committee (on which the industrial departments are over-represented).[27]

Sometimes the conflict of town and country has a direct effect on

---

[22] C.G.A. figures published in *Combat*, 21 June 1951. There were 7 Communists, 6 Socialists, 8 M.R.P., 8 Radicals, 41 Independents and Peasants, 13 Gaullists, and 2 others.

[23] The expression is M. Fauvet's. *Le Monde*, 1–2 January 1950.

[24] For instances of Communist opposition to taxation of the peasantry, see *ibid.*: also *J.O.*, 30 December 1949, pp. 7599, 7614, 7619–21: 10 May 1951, pp. 4989–98: 16 May 1951, pp. 5246, 5273.

[25] *J.O.*, 29 July 1950, pp. 6208–9 (M. Betolaud's speech): see also *J.O.*, 16 May 1951, pp. 5278–9 (M. Hugues' speech—the protest of a Radical deputy for Alpes-Maritimes, the department which includes the Riviera, against making urban consumers pay for the family allowances of agricultural workers).

[26] *Le Monde*, 10 May 1950.

[27] *J.O.*, 26 April 1950, pp. 2904–8, 2912–5, 2921–2. See above, p. 246 n.

the course of general politics. The fall of the Marie government, in August 1948, was brought about by its acceptance of the C.G.A.'s demands for higher agricultural prices, which cost it the confidence of the trade unions and so led to the defection of the Socialists and M.R.P.[28] In March 1951 M. Mollet, standing for election to the premiership, failed to secure the required number of votes because the Peasant party, and twenty M.R.P. members for agrarian departments, refused to support him owing to dislike of his proposed agricultural policy. Nor was the Peasant party's hostility confined to Socialists like M. Mollet. M. René Mayer, minister of Finance in the Pleven government, belonged to the conservative wing of the Radical party: but the Peasants regarded him as lukewarm towards the interests of agriculture. Their suspicion of him almost destroyed that government in November 1951, and helped to bring down his own cabinet eighteen months later.

Even upon the apparently remote constitutional debate, the repercussions of the clash of urban and rural interests are profound. The pressure for a return to the Third Republic comes particularly strongly from the countryside. For the old Senate was an active defender of agriculture; and *scrutin d'arrondissement* was the chosen electoral system especially of the peasantry, since it was they above all who regarded the deputy as essentially a bestower of local favours, rather than a protagonist of political causes. In the Fourth Republic leaders of the rural community have demanded a reversion to the old electoral law, and a revival of the old second chamber, for the explicit purpose of increasing the political power of the peasantry.[29]

From time to time regional divisions emerge into parliamentary discussion, cutting across political, religious, and social conflict. In 1950 a bill to permit the teaching of local languages in the schools provoked bitter dispute between the Basque and Breton sympathizers with regional autonomy, and the defenders of the Republic one and indivisible. Three years later the trial of thirteen Alsatian conscripts, participants in the S.S. massacre at Oradour-sur-Glane in 1944, led to an unhappy conflict between Alsatians and Limousins. Indeed, among the permanent subjects of dispute, the church schools issue itself is essentially regional, while important economic pressure-groups, such

---

[28] *A.P.*, 1948, pp. 141–2.

[29] 'Pendant toute la Troisième République, le Sénat a été, par essence même, le protecteur désigné de l'agriculture.' Henri Peyret, 'Les groupements professionnels et le Parlement,' *La Nef*, April-May 1951, p. 113. Cf. M. Duverger, 'Conseil de la République ou Chambre d'agriculture', *Le Monde*, 22 July 1953.

M. Dulin, chairman of the Agriculture committee of the Council of the Republic, told a peasant audience in 1950 that a return to *scrutin d'arrondissement* ' permettra . . . à l'agriculture d'obtenir dans les Assemblées la grande place qu'elle mérite,' and a year later urged the F.N.S.E.A. to press for the restoration of the powers of the former Senate; M. Blondelle, president of the F.N.S.E.A., called for political action by the peasantry to make the upper house once again a powerful protector of agrarian interests. *Le Monde*, 28 February 1950, 3 March 1951, 13 April 1951.

as the producers of wine or of beetroots, are often geographically concentrated.[30]

2. THE LESSER GROUPS

MAJOR interests like the trade unions, the C.G.A., or the Catholic Church, act directly upon parties rather than upon individual deputies. They are bound to exert great political influence under any system, and their power is perhaps even greater in the Fourth Republic than it was in the Third. But more characteristic of the old Chamber of Deputies was the fantastic proliferation of parliamentary groups for advocating quite petty specialized interests. They ranged from a group to defend the concierges of Paris to a group for the protection of commercial travellers.[31] The abolition of *scrutin d'arrondissement* did a good deal to reduce the electoral power of these lesser interests. But the Assembly tried to go further, and (in Standing Order 13) to ban completely the formation of private interest groups of this kind.[32]

The success of this attempt was not complete; a really determined interest could evade it by setting up a so-called ' study-group ', like that established in December 1949 for the ' study ' of questions connected with alcohol. This included more than a hundred deputies belonging to all parties from Conservatives to Communists, and had as vice-presidents the chairmen of the Assembly's committees on Finance, Agriculture, Industrial Production, and Fermented Liquors. One of its professed objects was to examine, at the time of the budget, the incidence of taxation on the various interests concerned with alcohol—and it has been estimated that the livelihood of four million Frenchmen depends on its production or distribution in one form or another.[33]

The alcohol interest is at the centre of a characteristic conflict of pressure-groups. By the Béziers agreement of 1922, the market for alcohol for drinking purposes was reserved to the wine-growers, while industrial alcohol was to be produced by the beetroot-growers of the north. The state guaranteed to purchase the alcohol they produced, up to a limit subsequently removed: any surplus above market requirements was compulsorily mixed with petrol and used as motor-fuel.

The Monnet plan envisaged a large increase in beetroot production,

---

[30] On the language issue see M. Dauzat's articles in *Le Monde*, 15 and 29 March, 26 April, and 17 May 1950; and M. Duhamel's in *Le Figaro*, 29–30 April, 5 May, and 12 May 1950. On Oradour, *J.O.*, 19 February 1953.

[31] Barthélemy, pp. 83 ff., gives the fullest description of these groups. He maintains that with few exceptions their influence was negligible, and that their main function was to confer the title of ' Monsieur le président ' on a large number of deputies. (Robert de Jouvenel, p. 72 n., even mentions a (perhaps mythical) group of members dissatisfied with their prefects.)

[32] ' Est interdite la constitution, au sein de l'Assemblée, de groupes dits " de défense d'intérêts particuliers, locaux ou professionnels." '

[33] For the alcohol ' study group ' see *Le Monde*, 5 December 1949. The estimate of 4 million is taken from *Le Figaro*, 15 August 1950. *La Réforme* ,3 January 1953, puts the figure as high as 6 million.

in order to raise the supply of sugar. But since distilleries proved easier and more profitable to establish than refineries, the extra beetroot production, which doubled in three years, was diverted to alcohol instead of to sugar, and began to cause a serious budgetary problem. The Treasury tried to keep down the guaranteed price for beetroot: in December 1949 the minister of Agriculture shook the government by resigning in protest. Two months later the cabinet agreed to reduce the price, in order to force growers out of production. But this provoked a vigorous counter-attack by the peasants, supported by deputies of every party from Communists to Conservatives.[34] In the summer of 1950 they obliged the government to revert for a time to the pre-war practice of employing surplus alcohol as motor-fuel.

This increases the price and worsens the quality in comparison with petrol, and is therefore disliked by motorists and road hauliers (themselves a powerful pressure-group) as well as by the (largely American) petrol interests.[35] It imposes a heavy charge on the budget, since the state pays the growers much more than twice as much as it receives from the petrol companies; in 1952 the chairman of the Health committee, a Paris deputy, pointed out that the alcohol subsidy cost more than half the amount M. Pinay was saving by his cuts in the sorely needed housing programme.[36] There are other reasons for doubting the policy of encouraging alcohol production. Alcoholic diseases are much more prevalent in France than anywhere else in the world. Their direct cost to the state is estimated at £150 millions a year.[37] Though strategic reasons are sometimes invoked to justify the subsidy, it is hardly surprising that a Gaullist weekly once entitled an attack on pressure-groups ' La betterave gouverne la France.' [38]

A subsidiary battle rages around the legalization of *pastis*—the apéritif already mentioned, which was made illegal under the Vichy regime (with its cult of the family) on account of its effect on health. M.R.P. maintained the ban after the war on the same grounds. But it was never effectively enforced, and the Radicals in particular waged a long campaign to remove it. They proposed that *pastis* should again be legalized and taxed; the proceeds might be used to lower taxation on

---

[34] *J.O.*, 31 March 1950, pp. 2724–54: 1 April 1950, pp. 2767–80.

[35] On this point cf. the speech of M. Blondelle, president of the F.N.S.E.A., to seventy parliamentary supporters of the alcohol interest, whose chairman was the brother of the minister of Agriculture. *Le Monde*, 21 May 1953.

[36] *J.O.*, 30 October 1952, p. 4587 (M. Cayeux's speech).

[37] *Le Monde*, 28 October 1952, quoting an estimate in the medical press.

[38] *Carrefour*, 16 August 1950. But this did not prevent Gaullist members sitting for beetroot-growing departments defending with vigour the interests of their clients: see *J.O.*, 16 May 1951, pp. 5247–9.

On the alcohol problem see R. Maspetiol, ' L'agriculture et la garantie des prix', *Revue politique et parlementaire*, March 1950, pp. 250–2; also *Le Monde*, 18 February 1950 and 6 April 1952; *Le Figaro*, 23 August 1950; *Le Monde*, 19 May 1953; A. Sauvy, *L'Observateur*, 21 May 1953; G. Malignac, *Esprit*, June 1953, pp. 903–8; and the report of the *Comité central d'enquête sur le coût et le rendem nt des services publics*, in March 1952.

the wine industry, for ex-servicemen's pensions, for compensation for agricultural disasters, or to raise family allowances for agricultural workers. Just before the 1951 election their campaign was at length successful.[39]

In the country the pressure-groups are more effectively organized than they used to be, but in Parliament itself the new standing order has at least restricted their numbers: there are less than twenty, compared with hundreds in the Third Republic. They can provide technical knowledge and information, and sometimes exert considerable influence. When great forest fires devastated the Landes in the middle of 1949, the 'study group' on the forestry industry led the pressure for compensation to the stricken department, and in July 1950 the Assembly, which found no time to discuss Korea, devoted several sittings to debating agricultural calamities.[40]

The principal purpose of these groups is to exert pressure at the time of the budget. They are naturally most effective when the government is weakest; consequently their most conspicuous period of activity was in December 1949 and January 1950, when M. Bidault's majority fell to single figures on most of the main clauses of his budget. The 'study groups' concerned with alcohol and with tobacco-growing had an effective parliamentary organization. Supported by constituents' telegrams and letters urging members to refuse confidence to the Government, they were able to secure some concessions. But the road hauliers were less experienced, and overplayed their hand. They urged their case with extreme vigour: so strong was the pressure that even in the Socialist party, where discipline is strict, a member was given permission to abstain on this clause. But their threats exasperated the deputies. The Socialist in question in the end voted against them. Their demands were not conceded, the government was not beaten, and the arrogance of their behaviour provoked bitter protests in the Assembly and in the press.[41]

---

[39] *A.P.*, 1948, p. 157: 1949, pp. 78, 86: 1950, p. 155. *J.O.*, 2 January 1950, pp. 13–4; 24 July 1950, pp. 5868 ff.; 26 July 1950, pp. 6008 ff. Cf. above, p. 241.
Members for rural departments were reluctant, just before an election, to oppose a proposed increase in allowances for agricultural workers merely because they disliked the way it was to be financed. On 9 May 1951 the urban M.R.P. members, though supported by only half of their rural colleagues, won a temporary success thanks to the Communists, who feared that the reintroduction of *pastis* might injure the wine-growers, among whom they are strong. *J.O.*, 9 May 1951, p. 4906: for the division list see *ibid.*, pp. 4946–7. But a week later the Communists changed their minds, and the supporters of *pastis* triumphed.
[40] *Le Monde*, 23 November 1949. *A.P.*, 1950, p. 155. The election of a prime minister offers another opportunity to the pressure-groups: cf. the questions put to M. Mendès-France by MM. Hénault and Babet (*J.O.*, 3 and 4 June 1953, pp. 2913, 2958). The former spoke for cider-growers, the latter for the *intergroupe des départements d'outre-mer*.
[41] *A.P.*, 1949, p. 217; 1950, p. 2. *Le Monde*, especially 4 January 1950. The tobacco planters were wise enough to persuade the chairman of the Finance committee, among others, to plead their case. *J.O.*, 2 January 1950, p. 6. Notable protests were made in the Assembly by M. Henri Teitgen (*J.O.*, 3 January 1950, p. 26) and in the press by M. Rémy Roure (*Le Monde*, 30 December 1949). The latter wrote: '... les groupes et les

In subsequent years pressure-groups kept much more in the background. In 1951 the chairman of the road hauliers' federation decided that he could best serve his cause by entering Parliament himself. It was a significant indication that there were limits to what external pressure could achieve, even when the government was at its weakest. Too vociferous an agitation might over-reach itself, and provoke the hostility of the deputies and of the public.

3. METHODS AND CONSEQUENCES

FRANCE possesses, of course, no monopoly of pressure-groups. No French party is as closely tied to an economic interest as the German Free Democrats or the Australian Country party; no French organization is anything like as potent or as sinister as America's China lobby. Yet the weaknesses of the French governmental system perhaps make the activities of pressure-groups especially dangerous there. For, at any rate in domestic politics, the sense of social solidarity is low in France. Political feuds are often waged with a violence unknown in Great Britain. Economic battles are fought with more bitterness and less disposition to compromise. The state is regarded, more frequently and by more people, as an enemy to be frustrated and resisted. There is not, as in the United States, a stable executive enjoying sufficient independence and authority to provide effective national leadership. Alarm at the dissipation of authority and weakness of government in face of powerful sectional interests was the factor bringing to the R.P.F. some of its best recruits; many observers, who oppose the Gaullists' remedy, accept much of their diagnosis and share much of their apprehension.

The revolutionary tradition, the citizen's ultimate duty of insurrection, are part of the French national heritage. Plots and armed resistance to the state are common events in French history, have recurred in peace time in the present generation, and remain as disquieting if remote possibilities in the background of normal political life. Men are accustomed to use means more vigorous than simple persuasion to defend what they conceive to be their rights. In the years after the liberation, too many of them found that a harassed and divided government listened only to those whom it could not ignore. The lesson that the strike was the only means to attract attention was

---

partis ont montré leur faiblesse et leur impuissance devant les forces extérieures au Parlement: les syndicats et les associations de toute sorte. . . . Nous avions parlé un jour d'un autre État qui se substitue à l'État. En réalité il s'agit d'une multitude de petits États, opposés le plus souvent les uns aux autres, parfois puissants et parfois médiocres mais qui dans leur ensemble dominent les formations politiques. De là le caractère sordide de divers marchandages qui se sont produits au cours de ces séances budgétaires . . .'

See also the vigorous protest of M. Queuille, then premier, against the activity of the road hauliers on a previous occasion, in May 1949. *A.P.*, 1949, pp. 327–9.

learned too well, and was not forgotten. Nor was direct action confined to the traditionally revolutionary industrial workers. It became a weapon used by many who would not employ it in Britain. The customs officials were among the most successful exponents of go-slow tactics. During six months of 1951, not a particularly stormy period, prolonged or token strikes were called by the most diverse social groups: butchers and bakers, university students and their examiners (separately!), mayors and milk producers and bank clerks.

The refusal to pay taxes is another weapon often contemplated, though rarely used. In 1950 the bishop of Luzon, speaking for his brother bishops in western France, publicly urged the faithful to ' postpone ' the payment of their taxes until their just grievances over the schools question were remedied. Through the influence of M.R.P., exerted in still higher Roman Catholic circles, the bishop was disavowed, and a potentially ugly crisis averted.[42] In the Midi, the ' Marcellin-Albert committee ' issues fairly frequent calls for administrative and tax strikes to draw attention to the perennial grievances of the wine industry.[43] These are generally ineffective. Yet the *vignerons* have not always refused to follow their intransigent leaders. Fifty years ago, similar protests and demands were the prelude to the great revolt of the Midi in 1907, under the leader from whom the committee takes its name; a third of the local authorities resigned, administrative activity came to an end, soldiers mutinied, and there were clashes between the troops and the peasantry. A few years later the wine-growers of Aube and of Marne resorted to arson, sacked shops, and clashed with the army, the former to obtain the coveted label of ' Champagne ' for their wine, the latter to refuse it to them.[44]

Nor can these demonstrations be written off as confined to small and especially irresponsible or excitable groups. National organizations resort to the same tactics. The C.G.A. has used the threat of a peasant strike to exert pressure on the government over taxation, over prices, and over import policy. In 1949 corn growers withheld supplies from the market in an attempt to raise prices (fixed by the government): not surprisingly, the threat of a 40 per cent. increase in the price of bread produced an outbreak of strikes among the urban workers. Milk producers resorted to a go-slow strike in 1950.[45] The butchers and wholesalers of the meat trade caused particular difficulty to successive governments. The small businessmen of the P.M.E., who had demonstrated so violently against *dirigisme* in the first post-war years, called a

---

[42] *A.P.*, 1950, p. 78. *Le Monde*, 25 April, 3 May, 19 May, and 22 July 1950.

[43] The village of Cazilhac, near Carcassonne, tried to achieve the same object by staging a voters' strike on election day, 1951. *Le Figaro*, 18 June 1951. In August 1953 all the roads in four departments were barricaded by protesting wine-growers, headed by their mayors and deputies; and the local bee-keepers, with their hives, were summoned to protect the barricades against the police.

[44] M. Augé-Laribé, pp. 189–94.

[45] *A.P.*, 1948, p. 9: 1949, pp. 31, 49, 65, 87, 162: 1950, p. 191.

shopkeepers' strike against new taxes at the beginning of 1948, and threatened a general tax strike against further increases at the end of the year.[46] Such threats and pressures contain a large element of bluff. Frequently the organizers find that their followers disobey their calls to direct action. Yet, despite the qualifications, French public men of all views are deeply and justifiably disturbed by the self-centred determination with which their countrymen pursue their own legitimate but limited private interests. One well-known journalist recalled the old fear that ministers were becoming merely the ambassadors of a declining state, France, to other expanding states, composed of the pressure-groups.[47] Another remarked bitterly that ' Private interests, local interests, foreign interests, all pass across the parliamentary kaleidoscope—all save the affirmation, more necessary than ever, of the common interest of Frenchmen.' [48] M. Lacoste, a Socialist ex-minister with a trade union background, expressed his alarm at the implications of the overthrow of a government, in January 1952, by a trade union lobby.[49] M. Pinay, a Conservative businessman, repeatedly warned the interests supporting his ministry that their own rapacity could endanger the policy which they favoured.[50] Very similar warnings were uttered by men as different as the royalist pretender, and the President of the Republic.[51]

The clamorous insistence of the various groups, interests and regions on their sectional aims sets up a combination of pressures which members of parliament find hard to resist. Governments have little room to manœuvre. For the consequent weakness, frustration and

---

[46] *A.P.*, 1946, pp. 19–20, 260–1: 1948, pp. 82, 185: 1951, p. 228. *Le Monde*, 13, 15, 19, 22, 23–24, and 27 September 1951, 13 and 26 October 1951, 22 April 1952, 7 July 1952, etc. (butchers). *A.P.*, 1948, pp. 9, 166 (P.M.E.).

[47] Rémy Roure, *Le Monde*, 22 September 1951 (' Les nouveaux féodaux '): also 23 October 1951. Cf. Aron, p. 193: M. Prélot, *Politique*, September 1948, p. 730.

[48] Roger-A. Priouret, *loc. cit.*

[49] *Le Monde*, 9 January 1952.

[50] For example in his weekend speeches at Beaune, Strasbourg, Lille, and Aix-les-Bains: *Le Monde*, 8–9, 10, 17, and 24 June 1951. M. Pinay's successor, M. René Mayer, remarked that as a basis for policy, ' C.N.P.F. + C.G.A. + C.G.V. + P.M.E.' was as unsatisfactory a formula as ' F.O. + C.F.T.C. + C.G.C. − C.G.T.' *Ibid.*, 2 January 1953.

[51] The Comte de Paris's monthly bulletin wrote of the country being bled white by economic feudalists; the President spoke of the need ' défendre la souveraineté nationale contre les assauts de ces féodalités d'intérêts, corporatives ou technocratiques, . . . qui . . . tendent à se substituer au gouvernement et font peser sur le Parlement des pressions aussi impudentes que scandaleuses . . . il y a aujourd'hui trop d'États dans l'État . . . ' (speech at Pau). Leaders who were not Socialists fully shared these apprehensions. Thus General de Gaulle attacked ' les féodaux de l'argent et de la presse '; M. Mayer, the Radical premier, declared that the Assembly was becoming a ' Chambre des corporations où les organisations économiques, syndicales, professionnelles se reflètent directement '; M. Guy Petit, a Peasant party minister, denounced the growing demagogy of these corporations; M. Teitgen, president of M.R.P., alleged that the Assembly was filled with ' les mandataires des betteraviers, ceux des bouilleurs de cru, les mandataires des petites entreprises et ceux des grandes entreprises '; M. Reynaud, Republican Independent

lack of policy the politicians are blamed. The reputation of their profession does not stand high in France. Yet it is arguable that Frenchmen enjoy better political leadership than they deserve. Weak as they are, governments and parties sometimes show remarkable courage in defying the demands of sectional interests, as M. Schuman's coal and steel plan shows. That they often give way to these pressures may be deplorable, but it is hardly surprising. But the responsibility should be put where it belongs. The ordinary citizen should not be allowed to compound for his own deficiencies by damning those of the rulers whom he chooses and influences.

The country's tragedy lies in the divided loyalties of its people. Its weakness lies in their *incivisme*,[52] in a concentration on their private interests which is sometimes carried to excess. These are not diseases which can be cured by adopting the British electoral system or the American separation of powers. The short cuts to governmental stability and national unity offer palliatives, which may operate usefully on a small scale, but leave the central problem untouched.

---

candidate for the premiership, warned that the ' congrégations économiques . . . pèsent sur (l'État) ou le paralysent jusque dans cette enceinte ': M. Claudius Petit, a U.D.S.R. ex-minister, 'déplore les maux d'un pays où chacun vit replié sur lui-même et cherche à bâtir son confort personnel sans se préoccuper du malheur des autres.' Respectively, *Le Monde*, 27 July 1951, 30 June 1953, and 8, 10–11, 17–18, and 26 May 1953; *J.O.*, 27 May 1953, p. 2850; *Le Monde*, 8–9 November 1953.

[52] See above, p. 5, for the significance of this word.

Chapter 21

THE PARTIES AND ELECTIONS

THE Fourth Republic was the product of a half-completed revolution. The Resistance and the liberation led, not only to the ejection of the Germans, but also to sweeping domestic changes in France. Old élites were thoroughly discredited, and political power passed to new men, new parties and new classes. These newcomers meant to carry out a drastic programme of national reconstruction. But their intentions were only in part fulfilled. Their unity was destroyed by the Communist drive for complete power, which prevented the resistance movement from achieving its objectives. Energy which might have gone into constructive reform had to be diverted into self-defence against the Communist danger.

The makers of the Fourth Republic succeeded, without violence, in the proverbially difficult feat of stopping a revolution in mid-career. If their work suffers from many imperfections, the circumstances of its creation need to be taken into account. The political leaders of the past, sober, experienced, unimaginative, and timid, had mostly been swept by the war into oblivion or disgrace. They had been replaced by a turbulent group of new men, heroes of the war and the Resistance, revolutionary adventurers, fishers in troubled waters, many of them with generous purposes and sweeping plans, but few of them with much political experience. In their midst, an aggressive, unscrupulous, and rigidly disciplined party manœuvred for power. With control of the trade unions, whose co-operation was indispensable for reconstruction, with a foothold in central and local administration, with the prestige born of its triumphs and sacrifices in a cause both patriotic and revolutionary, the Communist party could entertain high hopes of success. Facing a chaotic aggregation of individualists like the deputies of the Third Republic, it could hardly have failed. It could only be held in check by equally rigid organization and discipline on the part of its opponents.

So arose this extraordinary interlude of the years 1945 to 1947, the domestic cold war of the monolithic parties, from which the decision emerged that Paris was not to go the way of Prague. When that crucial victory had been won, and the immediate peril was past, voters and politicians alike thankfully threw off their fetters and resumed many of their old individualistic practices. But the return to the past was incomplete. The Fourth Republic settled into political habits midway between the individualist fluidity of the pre-war era and the disciplined rigidity of the liberation years. This evolution affected alike the electoral position of the deputy, his parliamentary life and behaviour, and the working of the governmental machine.

1. PARTY PREDOMINANCE, 1945–47

IN the Third Republic, the loose organization of parties was often criticized: in the early years of the Fourth, their rigidity came under even more vigorous attack. The new, disciplined parties were said to distort the whole political process. The electorate, it was argued, no longer chose their representatives; they had members foisted on them by the party machines. The Assembly no longer took decisions, it merely registered the pressure of external, irresponsible organizations on the deputies, who voted not according to their conscience, but as they were told. The parties shared out ministerial posts among themselves, and treated the State as a conquered province, to be divided and despoiled: ministries became party fiefs. The government was paralysed by internal conflict; the opposition was concealed within the ministry itself, and neither could perform its function properly. The cabinet was reduced to the position of a diet, in which each section enjoyed a right of veto.[1] Responsibility, the critics alleged, disappeared along with ministerial solidarity. Few decisions could ever be taken, and those derived from the secret bargaining of a few party bosses, often altogether unknown to the electorate. Weimar Germany had had a similar regime, in which the power of party machines was enormous, and that of the electorate negligible; it had been christened the *Parteienstaat*, or party-controlled state. The critics of party domination frequently referred to the Weimar Republic; indeed, many descriptions of it could be applied almost unchanged to France between 1945 and 1947.[2]

The predominance of these rigid and powerful party organizations produced a political situation altogether unprecedented in France. But the new 'mass democracy' was not without defenders. These maintained that the chaos and indiscipline of the pre-war period had themselves distorted the wishes of the electorate, and prevented their translation into action. The Fourth Republic, they claimed, substituted organized for unorganized, and therefore effective for ineffective democracy. The critics replied that the will of the people and that of their representatives might not coincide for long (and the referendums of May and October 1946, and the municipal elections of October 1947 went far to prove their point). But the new regime made only ineffective provisions for dissolution and referendum, and

---

[1] But see below, pp. 381–2.
[2] E.g.: A. J. P. Taylor, *Course of German History* (Hamilton, 1945), p. 195; Geoffrey Scheele, *The Weimar Republic* (Faber, 1945), pp. 124–7; R. T. Clark, *Fall of the German Republic* (Allen and Unwin, 1935), pp. 129–33; Edmond Vermeil, *L'Allemagne contemporaine* (Félix Alcan, 1925), pp. 63–4; the preface to Hesnard, *Les Partis politiques en Allemagne* (Ed. G. Crès, 1923), pp. vii–viii.

no provision at all for by-elections. Consequently, it normally prevented this divorce from becoming apparent, and always stopped it from influencing those in power. The critics therefore denied that the Fourth Republic was a democracy to which organization had restored the capacity for effective action. They maintained on the contrary that it was an oligarchy, composed of mutually hostile elements and therefore even less capable of action than its individualist predecessor, and secret in operation and therefore even less subject to public control. Such an oligarchy was particularly vulnerable to criticism in a country where the predominant democratic tradition was passionately attached to the Republic, one and indivisible, and violently hostile to *corps intermédiaires*.[3]

The increased power of the parties was deliberately willed by most of the makers of the new constitution. They believed that politics before 1939 had been excessively concerned with the interplay of personal and local rivalries, which had confused issues, weakened loyalties, and made it difficult to enforce responsibility. If political life could be organized around the struggle between disciplined national parties expressing different ideologies, the electorate would be given a clear choice, the parliamentary situation would be immensely simplified, and politicians could be held accountable for their actions or for their failures to act. The constitution makers may be criticized for being too academic, too hopeful, or insufficiently experienced. But their objects were admirable, and in the atmosphere of 1945 their outlook was viewed more favourably than the cynical realism of many of their opponents.

All the electoral legislation of the reconstruction period was marked by this determination to promote the growth of strong parties as the only means to honest and stable government.[4] In the de Gaulle government's *ordonnance* of August 1945 the party was to draw up its list of candidates, which the elector could not modify in any way. Incomplete lists were prohibited, making it harder for independents to stand. In the first Constituent Assembly, the original draft permitted only lists representing parties or organizations which were contesting at least ten constituencies, thus eliminating independent candidatures altogether—though this provision was dropped after criticism in the Assembly. The law of 5 October 1946 theoretically introduced the preferential vote, but it did nothing to weaken the effective power of the party. In the campaign itself the small groups were at a disadvantage, though not to the same extent as in Britain. Expenses were paid by the State; lists which obtained less than 3 per cent. of the votes forfeited a

---

[3] Such criticisms form the main basis for General de Gaulle's attack on the regime, and are naturally echoed in the works of his supporters, notably Debré, Debû-Bridel, and, from a more academic standpoint, Waline. See also such non-Gaullist works as Priouret; Théry, pp. 140–5; and Pascal Arrighi, *Le Statut des partis politiques*.
[4] For the provisions discussed in this paragraph see Arrighi, pp. 37–46.

deposit of 20,000 francs.[5] Broadcasting facilities (very much less than in Britain) also depended on the extent of the party's campaign.

The larger parties gained too in the distribution of seats. In the system adopted they were helped by the absence of a national pool. In that projected by the first Constituent Assembly, a national pool was to be instituted, but only parties which obtained 5 per cent. of the national vote, and presented lists in at least twenty departments, might participate in it. In theory, therefore, a party might obtain nearly a million votes without having a single member elected—indeed, the seats it would have had from the national pool would go to its opponents. The 'national seats' would be allotted to parties so as to ensure P.R. on a national scale; as between individuals, two-thirds were to go to the most successful candidates not already elected on a territorial basis, and one-third to persons directly nominated by the parties—the national lists of the Weimar Republic, which made the party leaders irremovable. A similar principle was adopted for the first Council of the Republic, except that in the final stage the supplementary members were chosen by the Assembly, not by the parties directly. The conception that parliamentary seats were the property of a party, not of an individual, was illustrated even more clearly by the case of by-elections. For the Assembly these did not occur: a vacancy was simply filled by the next person on the list of the former member. For the Council of the Republic the same rule applied; and when the original list was exhausted, vacancies were to be filled by the party which had held the seat.[6]

The conception was pressed to an even greater extreme. All bodies exercising power, even the High Council of the Magistrature, were to reflect proportionately the composition of the Assembly. The first Constitutional Committee further extended its attention to the political parties. Socialists and M.R.P. introduced a far-reaching *statut des partis*. In return for legal recognition the parties were to pledge themselves to maintain the fundamental liberties and the rights of man, to repudiate the one-party state, to adopt a democratic internal constitution, and to accept the inspection of their organization and finances by a new authority, representative of the parties but independent of the executive. Electors were to be obliged to vote, and deputies standing on a party's list would be required to join its parliamentary group. The party would have the right to revoke the member's mandate if he resigned from it or broke its discipline.

---

[5] Law No. 46–2151 of 5 October 1946, Articles 29 and 30. The effect was actually to encourage freak candidates, since the publicity was cheap at the price of so small a deposit. Paper, printing, and postage were paid for all lists, petrol and bill-posting only for those which obtained 3 per cent. of the votes. (The limit was raised to 5 per cent. in 1951.)

[6] Law No. 47–615 of 5 April 1947, Articles 2 and 3. Thus in May 1947 the M.R.P. federation of Bas-Rhin was able to nominate one of its defeated candidates for the Assembly to a seat in the upper house. Husson, vol. ii, p. 164.

Socialists and M.R.P. were the only protagonists of the party statute. The Radicals and Conservatives, believing that the party organizations were already far too strong, naturally opposed a measure intended to reinforce their power and cohesion, and to make them semi-constitutional bodies. And by a curious irony it was thanks to the Communists that the individualist point of view finally triumphed. Sure of their own internal discipline, the Communists did not wish to see that of their rivals reinforced. Nothing could be less welcome to them than an inspectorate entitled to investigate their financial resources and the extent to which their organization was democratically controlled. But they could hardly admit this objection publicly. So they left the task of opposition to such fellow-travelling allies as M. Pierre Cot, who could carry greater conviction when they denounced the encroachments of the state, defended freedom of association, and appealed to the opinion of the western democracies. As a concession to the Communists, the majority dropped the party statute from the committee's draft constitution, and the Assembly never had an opportunity of voting on it.[7]

2. ELECTIONEERING

Since 1947 the dominance of the organized parties has greatly weakened. In part this is due to the change in the electoral laws. Whereas the first Council of the Republic was elected in 1946 under a system based on P.R. and giving great power to the party, the second was chosen in 1948 under a new law, with individualism and the majority system clearly in the ascendant. And though party lists were retained in the electoral law for the National Assembly in 1951, yet the incentive to vote for large parties, which had been such an important consequence of the 1946 law, was destroyed by the introduction of *apparentement*.[8]

Nevertheless, too much should not be made of the legal changes. The chief cause of the greater power of parties at the time of liberation was the shift of opinion away from the individualist political groups and towards the organized ones, and the new laws were as much a consequence as a cause of this. The subsequent partial reversal of this tendency was in turn the main cause of the weakening of party domination after 1947. The electoral system was only a secondary factor. Even in the days of *scrutin d'arrondissement* the Communists were the most strictly disciplined party in Parliament and in the country; even under P.R. the Radicals were reluctant to impose discipline on their members and recalcitrant in accepting it.

Nor did the changes in the electoral system effect an absolute reversal

---

[7] For the *statut des partis* see *S.C.C.*, I, pp. 55–66; Arrighi, pp. 38–47; Debû-Bridel, pp. 105–7; Wright, pp. 120–3.
[8] See above, pp. 316, 323.

of the old electoral habits. It had always been maintained that *scrutin d'arrondissement* was largely responsible for the character of French politics, in which the deputy, in the provinces at least, was an important figure with great local prestige, to whom the voter turned to obtain redress for every grievance against the administration.[9] The system was praised or blamed for linking the member much more closely to his constituency than to his party. But experience since 1945 has shown that these characteristics, though not unaffected by the change of the electoral law, were much too deep-rooted to be wiped out altogether by a factor of this kind.

It was argued at first that voting for party lists instead of individuals would eliminate personality from electioneering. The names in the lower places on a party list, where the chance of success is negligible, arouse comparatively little interest—though even these decorative positions can be turned to electoral advantage. But the prestige lost by the candidates who cannot win, accrues to the head of the list. At least one leader of each party in every constituency now plays his personal rôle on a far larger stage than under the previous regime, and becomes a personality known throughout his department. A group like U.D.S.R. is indeed little more than a coterie of locally prominent politicians with personal followings in their own areas; and in 1945 even the Radicals survived as an electoral force, not where they had been strongest before the war, but where a well-known local leader had retained his reputation and his right to stand.[10]

A political leader can become more eminent without becoming more popular. In the 1951 election *panachage* was allowed, i.e. an elector who disliked one of his party's candidates could scratch out that name and vote instead for someone on a different party list. This provision benefited some ministers, such as MM. Pleven and Moch, who received thousands of votes from admirers outside their own parties. But others, like M. Bidault, or M. Claudius Petit (responsible for housing), and opposition leaders like MM. Thorez and Pierre de Gaulle, found their names crossed off many of the ballot-papers cast for their lists.[11]

In a particular constituency the behaviour of the deputy, or the arrival of a strong competitor, may make an immense difference to the result. In Hautes-Pyrénées, a highly conservative department, the M.R.P. deputy was a devout marquis, who headed the poll in 1946. Right-wing disillusionment with M.R.P. was bound to reduce his following in 1951. But when he himself went over to the extreme Left, and departed to stand in Paris, defeat was turned into catastrophe. The party lost seven-eighths of its votes, nearly all of them going to a

---

[9] For a brief but illuminating account of an election meeting under *scrutin d'arrondissement*, see Werth, *Destiny of France*, pp. 249–50.
[10] Goguel, *Géographie*, p. 94.
[11] MM. Bidault and Petit had formed a joint list with their Conservative cabinet colleague M. Pinay; their names may have been deleted by his supporters.

strong new Conservative candidate, M. Fourcade, president of the Assembly of the French Union. Next door in Gers the Radicals nominated M. Abel Gardey, formerly a leading senatorial opponent of the *Front populaire*, who increased their poll at the expense of all the other parties. Sometimes a member's personal position is so strong that he can carry his organization with them even against his party. Thus the M.R.P. federation of Charente went into the R.P.F. with its member, while those of the neighbouring departments, Haute-Vienne and Dordogne, approved the left-wing indiscipline of their deputies.[12] M. Chaban-Delmas, mayor of Bordeaux, took almost the whole Gironde Radical party with him when he went over to General de Gaulle.

But most members who quarrelled with their party suffered for it.[13] Twenty-two former M.R.P. deputies stood under other labels in 1951, but only eight were returned, four as Gaullists and four as Conservatives. Those who turned Gaullist were relatively successful. But those who stood as independents, whether of the right or of the left, usually did worse than the official M.R.P. candidate. Other parties had even less trouble with their rebels. Three ex-Socialist deputies stood again; all were beaten. So were two of the three Conservative members who had quarrelled with their local parties.[14]

Independent candidatures were difficult to organize, since the law did not allow incomplete lists to be presented. Nevertheless, a good many independents stood, and though very few were successful, some were at least picturesque. In Allier five members of one family ran a list which they called *Concentration républicaine*, which obtained 6,000 votes. In Bordeaux a well-known local yachtsman stood as a 'Motorists' defence' candidate. He founded his campaign on *panachage*, urging everyone to strike out two names on the list they chose, and *panache* in favour of his; thus no one would be worse off and he would win two seats. He managed to convince 1,500 voters (or their equivalent in fractions). Mr. Gordon Wright's lament [15] for the disappearance of individualists like the *Mécontent national* candidate has proved premature. In 1951 a list of *Mécontents, antipartis et indépendants nationaux* in north-eastern Paris gained 4,500 votes.

---

[12] *A.P.*, 1947, p. 215; *Le Monde*, 30 September 1948; *A.P.*, 1950, p. 153; *Le Monde*, 26 June 1953. In Amiens (Somme), where the M.R.P. deputy had turned Conservative and the Radical member went Gaullist, each kept his own former voters in 1951. I am most grateful to M. Jean Blondel for showing me his unpublished study which proves this point. On the Dordogne member, see Epilogue, n. 12.

[13] In all 31 members, after breaking with their parties, stood again for their former constituencies in 1951; 17 of them had belonged to M.R.P. Of the 8 who had turned Gaullist, 6 were elected; of 13 who had acquired the backing of another party, 7 were returned; but of the 10 independents, only one (M. Bessac, in Lot) saved his seat.

[14] The three Conservatives were Colonel Félix in Loire-Inférieure, and Canon Kir in Côte d'Or, who stood as 'independent' Independents; and M. Marin, member for Nancy since 1905, who allied himself with M.R.P. Only Kir held his seat.

[15] *Op. cit.*, p. 92.

Voting for party lists, then, has by no means eliminated personal factors and individual initiatives from the electoral scene, but it has done something to limit their scope. Even this is doubtful where the local factors are concerned. These are of least importance in the large towns and in the urbanized departments, but even here they cannot be wholly neglected: the deputy for the first Nord constituency must be active in well-doing on behalf of Dunkirk port. It is not the large towns, however, which dominate French politics; and in the countryside defence of the interests of his constituency and region remains the first duty of the member. The price of wine is still the principal election issue in Hérault, and it was no accident that it was a deputy from that department who led the opposition both to the authorization of *pastis* (aperitifs which, as has been mentioned, were made illegal during the war) and to the invasion of coca-cola.[16] The power of the agricultural interest has even grown as a result of the adoption of large constituencies, for outside Paris almost every deputy has some rural constituents. On the other hand, members for predominantly agricultural departments will often need to pay attention to a minority of industrial workers, who before the war might have been confined to a single *arrondissement*. To some extent, therefore, the clash of local interests has been softened by the larger constituencies, and the intensity of their differences diluted—at least in its parliamentary expression.

The burden of constituency duties has not been lightened by the change. Some politicians even believe that the provincial deputy is the slave of his electors to a greater extent. He has a far larger area to cover, and may well be obliged to spend every weekend, instead of only occasional ones, in his department. Even so, his personal acquaintance with his constituents is inevitably slighter, while the burden of their demands upon him may be even greater. Local councillors are as active as ever in using the member of parliament to put pressure on the administration over purely local affairs. The unfortunate deputy receives both complaints coming from his party's supporters in the department, and also those directed against ministries held by his party.[17] When M. Lecourt was minister of Justice he had in nine months 11,700 requests from deputies for pardons, promotions, etc.,

---

[16] The big constituencies may actually have increased the influence of the main local interests. For if two or three members from a department take up a popular grievance or a demagogic proposal, the pressure on the rest to follow suit is far greater than it was under *scrutin d'arrondissement*. Thus on Tuesday, 5 June 1951, a Radical deputy for Hérault wrote to the prime minister about the state of the wine industry. On Wednesday his Independent rival followed his example. On Thursday an M.R.P. member wrote to the minister of Agriculture, and by Friday M. Moch (who represents the department as a Socialist) had brought the question before the cabinet. *Le Figaro*, 11 June 1951; *Le Monde*, 21 May 1951, also describes the election campaign in this district.
On the importance of constituency interests see also above, p. 257 and n.

[17] Waline, p. 84, quotes the letter of Mme. Viénot, Socialist deputy for Ardennes, who resigned in 1947 because of the physical pressure of the work under the new conditions.

for constituents and friends—an average of one per member per fortnight.[18]

An international reputation will not procure forgiveness for a deputy who neglects his constituency. M. de Menthon, in Haute-Savoie, profited from the popularity of his second, the president of the departmental council, who answered letters;[19] but his Council of Europe colleague M. André Philip was badly beaten at Lyons. M. Naegelen, who held his seat for Bas-Rhin during his three years as Governor-General of Algeria, found it wise to migrate before the 1951 election to the distant Basses-Alpes. When 800 Communist constituents of M. Thorez struck his name off their ballot-papers they were probably only demanding the replacement of the revered leader in his Soviet sanatorium by a live deputy in their Paris suburb.

Changes of constituency are quite usual, especially when a member breaks with his party. Two ex-M.R.P. members moved to Paris for the 1951 election. Another, rejected by his local federation at Belfort, carried the party's colours without success in Allier. Even without such a breach, changes occasionally occur. The R.P.F. in particular, though they denounced the parties for imposing candidates on the electorate, were highly authoritarian in such matters; their generals especially were often ' parachuted ' into departments where they were quite unknown. Strasbourg, the birthplace of the R.P.F., has had unusually bad luck with its Gaullist leaders: the last, General Kœnig in 1951, was the only one of the 45 candidates for the department who could not speak Alsatian—which handicapped his campaign considerably.[20] But the other parties were more concerned to find local men. Just half the deputies elected in November 1946 were born in the department for which they sat.[21]

The list system is not without its electoral uses. In most departments

---

[18] *Le Figaro*, 27 and 28 March 1950 (which quotes M. Lecourt's estimate); and Priouret, p. 20, describing the pressure at the post office at Versailles to obtain the special stamps issued to commemorate President Auriol's election: ' Les philatélistes constituent une clientèle électorale peu nombreuse dont les exigences sont rares mais impératives.' In 1946 the Communist minister of Industrial Production, M. Marcel Paul, was accused by the Socialists of lavish distribution of benefits to his constituency, Haute-Vienne. In 1951 M. Béchard, high commissioner in West Africa, former and future Socialist deputy for Gard, was accused of favouring a firm at Alès in granting contracts. The charges may have been quite unfounded, but they show that such activities are still regarded as electorally profitable.

[19] *Le Monde*, 16 June 1951.

[20] *Ibid.*, 4 June. ' Le général Kœnig a contre lui d'être l'envoyé de la direction centrale. Il vient ici après M. Clostermann, qui sans doute ne fut pas assez présent dans un pays où l'on ne se cache pas d'être demeuré arrondissementier, où l'on demande " un député en chair et en os ", " un député de chez nous ". Aussi bien le candidat du R.P.F. assiste-t-il aux réunions plutôt qu'il n'y participe vraiment. . . . une tête de liste qui reste presque toujours muette.'

On the other hand in Alpes-Maritimes the Gaullist leader, another general, belonged to an old local family, and it was his second, an aircraft manufacturer, and allegedly a large contributor to party funds, but ' un peu dépaysé ', who had to be kept as quiet as possible.

[21] Overseas members excluded. In 1951 the percentage was 53.

only one or two candidates on each list have any chance of election, but the remainder can still perform a useful service by ' strengthening the ticket '. A leading local personality who does not desire election may be brought in to add prestige. Thus the retiring Socialist deputy for Yonne in 1951 agreed to remain on his successor's list in the second place. M. Landry, Radical senator for Corsica, was fourth on a list which derived much of its influence from his patronage. The list's appeal may be broadened by the inclusion of a woman, a peasant leader (universally sought after) or a local personality powerful in circles not accessible to the head of the list. Thus the Radical deputy for Seine-et-Marne persuaded a leading local Catholic to stand as his second, the honorary president of the agricultural *syndicat* of the department third, and two ex-Gaullist mayors fourth and fifth. On the other hand a list headed by two Jews has been regarded as a tactical impossibility even in a party as devoid of racial prejudice as the Socialists.

A coalition like the R.G.R. can satisfy all its groups: thus its list in Indre-et-Loire consisted of three Radicals, a U.D.S.R. member, and a Paul Faure Socialist. Sometimes a party finds it convenient to appease internal discontent by giving a place on the list to representatives of its different wings. But more often the pressure of the local *militants*, or the desire to make a definite impact on the electorate, produces a fairly homogeneous list. M.R.P., for instance, usually presented left-wing candidates in the Seine, but preferred conservative ones in a rural department like Basses-Pyrénées. Again, the list can be constructed to satisfy local sentiment. In Haut-Rhin the Radical, Socialist, and M.R.P. (but not R.P.F.) lists all gave one of their top two places to a citizen of Colmar, and the other to a resident of the rival town of Mulhouse.

3. THE NEW ELECTORAL SYSTEM

THE greatest immediate effect of the change of electoral system was upon the relations of the deputy with his party. But even without P.R. the extreme independence of the pre-war member could hardly have survived intact. The elections of 1945 and 1946 produced a great turnover of political personnel, bringing in new men without the strong personal followings and local machines possessed by their predecessors. The latter were mostly ineligible, since the great majority of parliamentarians had voted for Marshal Pétain in 1940: even among the minority, many were rejected in the new mood of public opinion. The rise of the disciplined parties to a dominant position in the Assembly was alone enough to alter the whole tone of politics. Still, the new electoral law had its importance: at the lowest estimate it provided a convenient mechanism by which the party organization could assert its power. In many constituencies the head of the list of a major party was almost sure of election, while his followers had very little chance.

Much of the energy of the ambitious politician had therefore to be devoted to placating, not the mass of the party voters, but the relatively restricted group of *militants*, who dominate the organization and draw up the list. Some have even considered the local party secretary as the keeper of the deputy's conscience. But there was a certain amount of exaggeration about this picture. In 1945-46, indeed, a great many departmental secretaries were themselves elected to the Assembly, especially in the Socialist party, where the *militants*' influence is greatest. But their successors were naturally less influential men. In the 1951 Assembly only two of the 85 M.R.P. deputies had been secretaries of their local federation when elected, and even among the Socialists, only four senators out of 61 had had this advantage. The secretary's diminishing power to promote his own candidature suggested that his influence over the deputy was also in decline.

The power of the party was at first wielded very vigorously. In the two elections of 1946 the threat not to re-adopt a recalcitrant deputy, or to ensure his defeat by giving him a worse place on the list, was fairly often put into effect. This was not simply caused by an attempt to enforce rigid discipline for its own sake. The liberation, like other revolutions, had thrown up many heroes, some adventurers, and a few scoundrels; and many of the members elected in 1945 had been chosen on grounds other than political capacity. During the following months some of these men found themselves, and others were found by their parties, to be unsuited to parliamentary life. Again, a member working hard for the party in Paris might find his local position weakened by a rival who spent less time in parliamentary and more in constituency activities. As many as 41 deputies were re-adopted, but in a lower place on the list;[22] and though 16 of them saved their seats for the moment, down-grading at one election was very often only the prelude to disappearance at the next.[23]

By 1951 discipline had relaxed, and such drastic weapons were less in use. Political disputes accounted for perhaps one or two of the

---

[22] Thirty-one in June, ten in November. Of the members who retired from Parliament in 1946, without an electoral contest, over two-thirds went in June—although the Assembly elected then had a life legally limited to 7 months, while that chosen in November could last 5 years. This suggests that many of these retirements were caused by political difficulties rather than by age and health. Among Socialists and M.R.P., where the *militants* were strongest, this was certainly so: a third of their members who retired in 1946 stood again for Parliament later.

[23] The figures for members down-graded omit cases where the member had changed his party or where the party had entered a coalition, which were fairly numerous. They also omit members who had moved up on retirement of a leader, but dropped back again on his subsequent return (common among the Communists). But they include cases where a deputy was left in his original position instead of moving up to fill a vacancy above, and an outsider was promoted above his head.

In 1946 there were 16 M.R.P., 9 Socialists, 6 Communists, and 10 others so treated. In 1951 the corresponding figures were three, four (including the Yonne member mentioned on p. 351), thirteen, and four. Of the members for the more urbanized departments about one in five, and of the others about one in eleven, suffered down-grading in one or the other election.

Socialists, and half a dozen of the M.R.P. members who did not stand again. Only eleven non-Communist deputies were re-adopted in worse positions, compared with 35 five years before, and only three of them were beaten. On the other hand the Communist party, which in 1946 had preferred familiar candidates because it was eager to elect the largest possible parliamentary group, was by 1951 giving more weight to political reliability than to numbers.

Scrutin de liste reinforces the Communist party's strict control over its deputies. One or two were even required to resign their seats during the course of the legislature—notably M. Pierre Hervé, the ablest of the younger Communist intellectuals, and M. Marcel Paul, the former minister of Industrial Production. In 1951 three men and five women did not stand again. One of them had been responsible for the embarrassing application to the Germans in 1940 for permission to publish *L'Humanité* under the occupation; and as none was over 51, while their average age was only 43, it seems likely that politics rather than health were responsible in other cases. In 1946 only six of the 41 deputies down-graded had been Communists; in 1951 the proportion had risen to 13 out of 24—and nine of the thirteen were beaten. In Lyons, both the outgoing deputies were displaced, one by a local trade union leader, and the other by M. Pierre Cot, whose former seat was unsafe.

It is significant that most of these cases concerned large urbanized constituencies where the power of the party organization outweighs the personal prestige of the individual member. Here the deputy has to be relatively careful, and to beware of offending his federation too deeply. An M.R.P. member of parliament, for example, might abstain with impunity on a minor issue like the peace treaty with Japan: but in the unlikely event of his wishing to do so on a cherished party principle like aid to church schools, to follow his inclinations would destroy his career. The rural member is in a stronger position, since personality counts for so much more in the countryside. Getting rid of the deputy probably involves losing the seat. The local federation is therefore unlikely to use its powers, and the main restraint on the member is the possibility of expulsion by the national headquarters, which must always be concerned to check infractions of discipline and to maintain the homogeneity of the party. Such considerations hardly affect deputies belonging to a loose party like the Radicals, most of whom are virtually local bosses whom no one is in a position to discipline.

Internal party struggles often revolve around the pressure of the younger generation to remove and replace their elders. There is nothing new about this conflict, which is not limited to any particular country, political outlook, or electoral system. In 1919 it had a good deal to do with some Socialist secessions to the Communist party, and in 1945 the drive to expel those Socialist deputies and senators who had voted for Marshal Pétain five years earlier owed some though not all of its force to the obvious fact that this would give greater opportunities to their juniors. But *scrutin de liste* does mean the concentration of all parliamentary opportunities in a department in the top place or two on the party list, so that the struggle for these is often bitter. Some recent disputes of this kind, though it would be a gross exaggeration to regard them as typical of the normal course of French politics, throw an illuminating light on some of its aspects.

In 1950 M. Noguères, the veteran Socialist deputy for Pyrénées-Orientales, quarrelled with the young secretary of his local party over control of the local newspaper—a political weapon of immense importance in rural France. The secretary, M. Conte, was a local man (unlike the deputy), was mayor of his home town, and was forty years younger than his leader, on whose list he had been third in June 1946, and second in November. The Socialists on the departmental council supported M. Noguères, its president; the party organization backed the secretary, and was disaffiliated by S.F.I.O. headquarters in Paris. At the election next year, M. Conte stood independently. The official Socialist candidate was a sitting senator for the department, into whose place in the upper house M. Noguères was to step. The competing Socialist lists were allied with one another,[24] and with Radicals and M.R.P., against the extreme parties. To complete the confusion, the R.P.F. nominated another former Socialist, while the Communist campaign was fought on the themes of private property, dear wine and tomatoes, and no imports from Spain. The three seats went to the Communist, far ahead of all rivals with 38,000 votes, to M. Conte with 17,000, and to the Radical who was just behind. The orthodox Socialist, with 10,000, was barely ahead of the R.P.F. M. Conte had evidently won many non-Socialist votes ; but in the Assembly he allied himself to the S.F.I.O. group, and was soon re-admitted to the party.

Similar disputes occur from time to time in all parties. In Meurthe-et-Moselle the grand old man of French Conservatism, M. Marin, was displaced after 46 years in Parliament by his second, who was barely half his age. In Gironde, where M. Chaban-Delmas took the Radical organization over to the R.P.F., his chief local opponents were a Third Republic senator, elected to the Constituent Assembly in June 1946, whom he had displaced five months later, and his own colleague M. Dupuy, who was his junior on the party list but much his senior in age.[25] Indeed, this quarrel of the generations has even affected the Communist party, in the affair of M. Prot. This popular local veteran had sat for Somme since 1936. The younger *militants*, led by his active but junior fellow-deputy, tried to force him into retirement.

---

[24] For the 1951 electoral law see above, Ch. 19.
[25] M. Dupuy, whose strength lay in the rural half of this huge department, persuaded the Assembly to split it into two constituencies. But the local Radical congress, meeting in the absence of his supporters, was persuaded not to renominate him. *Le Monde*, 22 May 1951, 2 June 1951.

In April 1949 M. Prot suddenly resigned from the party and began making embarrassing accusations against its local leaders, accusing them of responsibility for an unexplained armed robbery in 1944, and of burning down the party headquarters to destroy evidence. But, to prove that he had no quarrel with the party over policy, he sent his parliamentary proxy to M. Thorez. There was a party inquiry, M. Prot's interesting speeches stopped, and eventually the dispute was settled; censures were distributed all round, but M. Prot and his younger rival both kept their positions for the 1951 election.

This case shows, and others confirm, that party discipline has limits even among the Communists. At least two locally popular deputies, whose removal by the party was predicted, were re-adopted in the end—though one had a son who was a captain in Indo-China. On the other hand, M. Renaud-Jean, who built up in the inter-war years the strong Communist position among the peasantry, and was chairman of the parliamentary group in 1936, has never been forgiven for his disapproval of the Nazi-Soviet pact. Although he did not leave the party, he has been in disgrace with it ever since; though the Communists of his own department of Lot-et-Garonne wished to re-adopt him both in 1945 and in 1951, they were not allowed to do so.[26]

The deterioration in the position of the individual deputy is, then, by no means as striking as many commentators have maintained. The power of the party has declined since 1945–46, when the system allowed the voter no effective choice whatever between persons, and when the whole tone of politics was set by the ' battle of the monoliths '. In the countryside in particular—and the thoroughly urbanized departments return barely a quarter of the deputies—the member has a good chance of building up, by assiduous personal activity and attention to local interests, a position difficult to shake. Among individualist groups like the Radicals, it is the deputy who bosses the organization. A member belonging to a more solid party, unless it is extremely strong in the area, could probably not take enough votes from it to secure his election against the organization. But it would often be easy for him to hold at least a third of his former supporters—quite enough to deprive the party of the seat, and therefore to make it very reluctant to act against him. The reaction of public opinion against monolithic parties has consequently made it very rare for a deputy to be deprived of his position, except in the Communist party where discipline has other foundations.[27]

---

[26] For the *affaire Prot* see *Le Monde*, 28 and 29 April, 14 and 21 May, 14 June 1949: *L'Humanité*, 9 September, *Le Figaro*, 7 and 11 September 1949. For the other two members, MM. Rigal and Dassonville, *Le Figaro*, 30 May 1951, and *Le Monde*, 7 June 1951. For M. Renaud-Jean, Rossi, p. 446, and Gordon Wright's chapter in E. M. Earle, ed., *Modern France*, pp. 224–5; cf. pp. 54 n., 353, on the electoral strength of Communist leaders.

[27] But the size of constituencies makes them expensive to contest, and this does somewhat undermine the member's independence. Rank and file deputies, the ' parliamentary proletariat ', cannot always afford the cost of electioneering. This helps to explain their

But this does not mean that the French politician can nowadays ignore the views of the *militants* and concentrate on wooing the floating vote. No doubt he, like his British colleague, does his best to acquire a personal reputation by non-political services to constituents of all opinions. But his essential job is to represent the outlook and interests of a relatively restricted social and ideological clientèle. Nor does he counteract this narrowness much when he tries to extend his support. For the floating vote in France is not one group in the centre, but a series of grouplets scattered along the political spectrum between the main parties. The Socialist and the Conservative never appeal to the same voters. The former may try to woo Radicals from their allegiance by stressing the anti-clerical appeal and playing down collectivist ideas: in this case he must beware of appearing lukewarm to his own supporters. In other regions he may attempt to outbid the Communists, thereby probably acquiring merit among his own *militants* but risking some loss of votes on his other flank. The aim of the Conservative in the west will be to prove that he is a better defender of property than his Gaullist rival, and a more vigorous protagonist of aid to the church schools than the M.R.P. Elsewhere the pattern may be different. In Nord the religious issue is subordinate and the social issue predominant: M.R.P. competes with the Socialists rather than with the Conservatives, as in Paris Radicals clash with the Conservatives rather than with the Socialists. But nowhere is there a central pool of uncertain votes from which every party seeks to draw. There is only a series of separate pools in which rival parties compete by stressing their claims to be the most active in forwarding particular group interests or sectional ideologies. The attraction of both parties towards a common mean, which is the political function of the floating vote in Britain, is not performed at all in France.

Thus the criticism of party dictatorship, exaggerated as it often is, does draw attention to a real change in the situation, and especially in the relationships between the parties. The abolition of *scrutin d'arrondissement* clarified the electoral contest by slightly reducing the import-

---

dislike of the dissolution: cf. G. Berlia, *R.D.P.*, 1953, pp. 431–2. But instead of subordinating them to their party, it may subject them to the influence of wealthy pressure groups: cf. M. Lecourt's speech, *J.O.*, 27 May 1953, pp. 2859–60.

The sources of electoral and party funds are as obscure in France as they are elsewhere. But occasionally some hints are dropped. Thus M. Boutemy had to resign from the Mayer government, ostensibly because he was a former Vichy prefect, but also because he had more recently been the distributor of electoral subsidies for the French employers' organization, the C.N.P.F.; it was alleged (without contradiction) that in 1951 the Radicals had had £500 for every deputy, and £1,000 for every ex-minister from this source. (*J.O.*, 22 January 1953, p. 578, and 17 February 1953, p. 1067: speeches of M. Pronteau). A few months later evidence of a different kind came to light. A leading Gaullist, M. Diethelm, told a parliamentary committee of inquiry that his dealings in Indo-Chinese piastres had been for his party's benefit and not his own; the officials of the R.P.F., summoned at his suggestion, found reasons for refusing to testify. (*Le Monde*, 1, 22, 23, 30, and 31 October 1953). The R.P.F. may not have been alone in carrying on transactions of this kind.

ance of personal and parochial factors. But the introduction of P.R. obscured the struggle, for it eliminated the second ballot with its simplifying effect, which reduced the whole battle to a straight fight between Right and Left. Parties, except perhaps for the R.P.F. after 1947, could not hope to win votes from their bitter opponents at the other end of the political spectrum. So they concentrated on attacking their neighbours, who were competing for the same clientèle.[28] This *régime des frères ennemis* meant that the bitterest blows of the campaign were exchanged between groups which would have to co-operate in the Assembly if a government were to be formed at all. The alliances, which characterized the pre-war system, were now impossible. Each party fought in isolation from the others, and in hostility particularly to its friends.

The new electoral system therefore brought parliamentary confusion with it. In the days of *scrutin d'arrondissement*, and to an even greater extent under the *scrutin de liste* system of 1919–27, when the election results were announced there was no doubt who had won. The majority might be loose and incoherent, but it was almost always unmistakable. Under P.R., however, with several parties fighting quite independently, the election results in no way decided the composition of the new government. Several majorities were possible, and there were no electoral alliances to indicate which was to be preferred— only bargaining among the parties could decide.[29] The rôle of the electorate was no longer to participate in choosing a government, it was to make fractional alterations to the bargaining power of each group—alterations which could rarely, and then only by accident, influence the result.

The new electoral law of 1951 made little difference in this respect. It did encourage alliances between parties: but these could differ from one department to another, so that they might pull deputies of the same party in opposite directions, and they involved no commitment at all to united action by the allies. They were effective negatively, against the advocates of drastic change, but did nothing to produce positive co-operation between the moderate groups. Majorities in the Fourth Republic remained as unstable as they had been in the Third. A shift of alliances could still produce a complete reversal of policies in the course of a single parliament. One such change had occurred in 1947 under P.R.; and in 1952 the advent of the Pinay government showed that the bond of *apparentement* was too frail to hold the associates together for long.

---

[28] It is sufficient to recall the bitter opposition between Communists and Socialists in the period of *tripartisme*, notably in the election of June 1946, and between M.R.P. and the Conservatives in the clerical departments of the west. The R.P.F. to some extent drew their votes from all quarters; but in 1947 they directed their main attack on M.R.P., and in the 1951 campaign Gaullists and Conservatives very largely concentrated their fire on each other.

[29] See Duverger, *Partis*, p. 430.

But the new electoral laws did make the system less flexible. Since the parties were more rigid, shifts of alliances were harder to bring about. Formerly, political changes had involved brief crises while the balance of petty groups was slightly adjusted. But now they often meant long interregnum periods, in which the great parties sparred for advantage. There was no compensation for this additional friction: the contestants usually ended up much as they had started, since no alternative combination was open to them. For this frustrating situation, *scrutin de liste* bore only a part of the blame. The principal difficulty was the growth in the electoral, and consequently in the parliamentary strength of the ' untouchable ' party or parties, which, in M. Queuille's phrase, condemned the remaining groups to live together.

Chapter 22

THE PARTIES AND PARLIAMENT

1. THE MEMBER

In the National Assembly a corresponding evolution has taken place. The drastic transformation of parliamentary habits which occurred between 1945 and 1947 has been succeeded by a gradual revival of earlier practices. But the reversion has been incomplete. The parliamentary parties remain better disciplined than they were in the Chamber of Deputies; they play a larger part in the arrangement of business and in the life of their members; and they have to pay more attention to the demands of the party organization outside the Palais Bourbon.

In the two Constituent Assemblies half the seats were held by the Communist and Socialist parties. These, even in the Third Republic, had always applied *discipline de vote*—the rule that deputies who voted against party decisions, or even abstained without permission, laid themselves open to sanctions. The sanctions ranged from censure to expulsion, with intermediate stages such as suspension from editorship of the party newspaper, or membership of parliamentary committees. But the real force holding these groups together was ideological loyalty. If this were lost, *scrutin d'arrondissement* left the party little hold over its members. They owed their election as much to their personal position as to party support, and—as the Neo-Socialist defection showed—fear of losing their seats was not enough to keep them loyal. But the introduction of P.R. enabled the party to deprive a deputy of his seat simply by moving him down the list, at least as long as the public voted for parties rather than individuals. Thus the two disciplined groups of the old Chamber had become both more numerous, and more powerful as against their members. They were joined by a third, M.R.P., which also aspired to become a monolithic party: even if this had not been its desire, M.R.P. would have been driven to concentrate its power in the same way in order to retain its influence within the *tripartiste* coalition.

With three rigid blocks, which in agreement could invariably impose their wishes and in discord could paralyse government and Assembly alike, parliamentary debate inevitably atrophied. In the words of M. Théry, ' The National Assembly of 1947 bears much more resemblance to a diplomatic congress than to its predecessor the Chamber of Deputies '. Interest shifted away from the Palais Bourbon where decisions were formally registered, to the party meetings where they were really made. Divisions were no longer affected by the course of debate, which was indeed often suspended to allow the party groups to meet separately.[1] There were complaints of the absence of striking personalities. This was not because the politicians of the post-war years were inferior to those before the war in ability or integrity (the reverse was often the case), but because the structure of the new parties discouraged the rise of leaders. This was a matter of spirit as well as of organization. The newcomers had objectives wider than the electoral or careerist success which was so often the limit of Radical ambition. Consequently, they were more willing to perform useful but inconspicuous service to their cause, and less determined to obtain the limelight for themselves.[2]

The period of complete party domination did not last very long. It was destroyed by the break-up of the original majority. From 1945 to 1947 the three great parties, when agreed, commanded the overwhelming support of the Assembly. But the collapse of *tripartisme* threw governments back into the situation so familiar to their predecessors, in which they depended for a fragile and reluctant majority on the decisions of a few small, ill-disciplined marginal groups or even individuals. For example M. Schuman's first government was saved in February 1948 by the abstention of M. Pleven and the two dozen members of U.D.S.R., while his second was destroyed in September by their hostility.

At about the same time party discipline began to relax a little, and voting became less rigid. In August 1948 nearly twenty M.R.P. deputies refused to support the conservative economic policy of M. Paul Reynaud, the dominating figure in the short-lived André Marie cabinet. Thereafter M.R.P. was rarely without its handful of dissentients, and sometimes disagreement went so deep that a free vote had to be allowed, as in the division which overthrew the second Queuille government in July 1950. Socialist discipline is rarely infringed.[3] But after five years it too began to crack. Fifteen members rebelled over the new electoral law at the end of April 1951, though after a sharp warning from the party executive all but one came round ten days later. On 19 February 1952 there was a more serious incident, when twenty deputies, led by MM. Jules Moch and Daniel Mayer, defied a party decision over the European army. Most of them had the backing of their local federations, and only mild sanctions were imposed.

Despite such exceptional cases the degree of party discipline, though

---

[1] See Théry, pp. 140–1; Siegfried's introduction to *A.P.*, 1946, pp. vii–viii; Waline, pp. 63–7, etc. For recent instances see *A.P.*, 1952, pp. 19, 32, 82, 93.

Such suspensions occasionally occurred in the Chamber of Deputies: see, e.g., Joseph Barthélemy, *Essai*, p. 98; Soulier, p. 364. But these were rare cases, whereas in the liberation period they were normal.

[2] Priouret, pp. 81–3 (referring to M.R.P.).

[3] In December 1946, however, 25 Socialist deputies failed to vote for M. Thorez when he stood for election to the premiership. *A.P.*, 1946, pp. 281–2. A free vote for Socialist deputies must be authorized by the party executive.

poor by British standards or by those of the Constituent Assemblies, remains a good deal higher than before the war. By the time of the 1951 election *discipline de vote* was little more than a memory in M.R.P., yet comparatively few of its members were willing to vote against a party decision. The Gaullists, at first a factor of division within the other groups, proved disciplined enough when they formed their own. And though the well-organized parties lost their own former monolithic character, they did compel their competitors to stiffen their ranks. By 1951 a commentator could speak of even the Independents ' abandoning the outworn conception of individual independence, and gradually substituting that of collective independence '.[4] A recent analysis of the 672 divisions which occurred during the life of the Pinay government,[5] when the cohesion of some groups was under exceptional strain, shows that discipline was much better than is usually supposed. It was rigid on the Left, good among Independents and Peasants, and weakest in the centre (M.R.P., U.D.S.R., and Radicals [6]) and among both wings of the Gaullists. But most groups voted solidly, without a single dissentient *or abstainer*, in at least two-thirds of these divisions: the only exceptions were the Radicals (63 per cent.) and M.R.P. (57 per cent.). Every group polled 95 per cent. of its members in at least seven-eighths of all the divisions. In the Council of the Republic, discipline was less effective,[7] perhaps because routine divisions there are fewer. For in France, unlike Britain, discipline is worse on major than on minor matters. When questions of little public interest are debated, proxy voting allows the deputies to stay away, and the whips to cast their votes. The member who looks to his constituents rather than to his party will be moved to revolt only when the former are genuinely aroused. Thus when the fate of the Pinay cabinet was at stake, discipline was a good deal worse than the figures quoted would suggest.[8]

Certainly the pressure of party orthodoxy has not turned French politicians into mere party hacks. Some members, elected at the

---

[4] Yves Florenne, *Le Monde*, 26 May 1951. See above, p. 111, n. 6.

[5] Peter Campbell, ' Discipline and loyalty in the French Parliament ', *Political Studies*, vol. 1, no. 3 (September 1953), pp. 247–57. His figures would be still more striking if he had excluded overseas members, who are much more wayward than their metropolitan colleagues.

[6] In 1951 the Radicals for once imposed *discipline de vote*, for postponement of the bill to assist the church schools. Even so, ministers were exempted. And seven members who voted against the party line remained unpunished. *Le Monde*, 7 September 1951.

[7] Only 5 groups out of 11 voted solidly in two-thirds of the divisions, and only 3 polled 95 per cent. of their members in seven-eighths of the divisions. And the former included the Socialists, whose unanimity was broken in 33 per cent. of divisions in the Council, but in only 1 per cent. in the Assembly.

[8] Soulier, pp. 454–76, analyses by parties a number of critical votes in the 1920's, which may be compared with the post-war divisions recorded in Appendix IV.

The R.P.F. and M.R.P. parliamentary groups reacted to the breakdown of their discipline by restoring *discipline de vote*, the former for M. Mayer's investiture in January 1953, the latter for M. Laniel's in June. In each case this reflected a recent successful revolt by the rank and file against the leaders; in neither case was it maintained.

liberation when personal heroism in the resistance was a qualification more important than political experience, underwent dramatic changes of mind. The 1946 legislature saw two exceptional cases of deputies who boxed the entire political compass: both were elected as members of M.R.P., went over to General de Gaulle when he formed the R.P.F., became disillusioned with it, and drifted by gradual stages from the extreme Right to the extreme Left: the end of the legislature found them both associated with the Communist party. But they had not carried their voters with them in this progress, and neither survived the general election.[9]

The political breach between the monolithic parties, the growing importance of the minor groups, and the tendency for discipline to become less rigid, have all helped to restore flexibility and life to the parliamentary scene. Very often the outcome of a critical division is uncertain until the last minute, depending on a handful of votes. Party decisions are more important than in the old Chamber, but much less so than in the Constituent Assemblies, if only because it is no longer certain that all members will obey.[10] The suspension of sittings to enable the parties to make up their minds is still fairly common, but this is due at least in part to the fact that the Assembly sits much longer than the Chamber did—often in the morning, afternoon and evening of the same day—so that there is little other opportunity for the parties to meet.

The changes since 1947 did something to weaken the grip of the parties, but little to promote the rise of strong leaders. No doubt the original desire of the new parties to regenerate the political life of France soon lost its initial fervour. But a party based on the support of *militants* in the country is inevitably more concerned with general policies and less with personal advancement than one which is merely an electoral coalition of prominent personalities. Outside the big parties, too, political success went above all—as in the Third Republic— to the talented conciliator. The head of a numerically unimportant group such as M. Pleven's, or a leader of a larger party whose reputation, like M. Queuille's, depended on having no enemies, were strong contenders for the premiership. But the happy position of the man without enemies is rarely associated with a taste for positive and

---

[9] One of the two members, M. Lécrivain-Servoz, deputy for Rhône, moved from the R.P.F. to the *Overseas* Independent group. The other, M. Charles Serre of Oran, became a Conservative: both passed through a small group allied to the Radicals, and both by 1950 were associated with the *Gauche indépendante*. (See above, p. 142.) They then went over to M. Pierre Cot's group of Progressives, allied to the Communists. M. Lécrivain-Servoz contested his old constituency as an independent, while M. Serre stood on a Communist list in Dordogne; both were beaten.

[10] M. Fauvet recorded another consequence: '. . . depuis que les groupes, notamment au centre, sont moins cohérents, que les conversions individuelles sont moins difficiles et les "intérêts" sont mieux organisés, les gouvernements se font et se défont moins en séance qu'en coulisse.' *Le Monde*, 28 December 1949.

vigorous action. The men of strong personality and convictions, such as M. Reynaud, M. Moch, and M. Mendès-France, might enjoy great prestige, but were usually much too unpopular, even in their own parties, to rise right to the top. So M. François Mauriac headed his valedictory article on the legislature ' *L'Assemblée sans visages* ', and went so far as to lament that the scandals of the last five years had been so insignificant, and to hope that the leaders of the next parliament would combine with the party struggle ' a hidden contest of private passions '.[11]

2. THE GROUP

THE political units in the Assembly are not called parties, but groups. Strictly speaking they have no necessary connection with parties at all. In the case of organized parties like the Communists, Socialists or M.R.P., the group is merely the expression of the party on the parliamentary plane. On the other hand the party organization associated with a group like U.D.S.R. is little more than the projection of the parliamentary group into the outer world—the deputies and would-be deputies who form, in the current phrase, the general staff of an army without troops. The Radical party allowed its deputies to belong to two different groups until 1910, and has never organized a single group of senators. And on the Right there was often no connection whatever between the associations which a politician established in the country and on the electoral plane, and the group which he joined in Parliament. In 1928 the *Alliance démocratique* claimed the support of 110 deputies, who were divided between no less than six parliamentary groups, ranging from the far Right to the moderate Left.[12] There were parties without groups and groups without parties, and except on the Left the groups in the Chamber and those in the Senate were quite different.

The political structure of the groups has slowly become more straightforward, especially since 1945. But their procedural importance has increased more rapidly than their ideological coherence. At the beginning of the Third Republic groups were regarded with suspicion: the ruling theory still held that a deputy represented the country as a whole, not a geographical, political or social segment of it—uniting Burke's dislike of local pressures with the Jacobin detestation of *corps intermédiaires*. For ten years, indeed, the groups were not allowed to meet within the premises of the Chamber, or to use its services to send out notices of meetings: and even forty years later the President of the Chamber would not allow members to speak in the name of their group. But life outstripped theory. Almost from the beginning the President of the Republic found it necessary, in holding his conversations in

---

[11] *Le Figaro*, 24 April 1951.
[12] Middleton, p. 128.

order to form cabinets, to consult the chairman of the unofficial groups as well as the holders of official positions in the Chambers. The rise of organized parties, the Socialists and the Radicals, increased the practical importance and power of some at least of the groups.

In 1910 the first great step forward was taken. The agitation for P.R. in the country triumphed in the parliamentary sphere, and the committees of the Chamber, hitherto chosen by lot, became politically representative. This change gave the groups a formal status laid down in the Chamber's standing orders. It also obliged them to organize. Members now had to declare to which group they wished to adhere, and might no longer join more than one. This did help to provide a more solid political basis; but in the succeeding years, the groups contrived to acquire great continuity while remaining extremely incoherent.

This looseness was possible because their purpose, in theory and often also in practice, was purely electoral. In 1930 a member whose group did not re-elect him to the Finance committee formed a new group with the sole object of regaining his place (which he did). But the continuity was no less remarkable. It affected even the group of members who would not join a group, which existed only for the committee elections. This extraordinary collection, ranging from dissident Communists to intransigent royalists, for many years returned to the Foreign Affairs committee the distinguished Conservative M. Mandel, in the first war Clemenceau's secretary, and in the second the most capable and determined opponent of capitulation.[13]

In 1932 the Chamber passed a resolution requiring every group to submit a political declaration signed by all its members—a rather futile attempt to enforce upon the groups a minimum of internal unity.[14] But their powers grew if their cohesion did not. They selected the committees, they settled by agreement the distribution of the seats in the Chamber, and the chairmen of the larger groups (14 members at least) formed part of the Presidents' Conference, which drew up the provisional agenda of the house.

After 1945 the rights of the groups were further expanded to the detriment of those of the individual deputy, and especially of the independent, though the proposal to compel all members to join a group was not pressed. The groups are now mentioned in eighteen of the standing orders of the Assembly, and in three articles of the constitution itself.[15] A parliamentary initiative has come to be con-

---

[13] Barthélemy, *op. cit.*, pp. 92, 94, 101.

[14] Barthélemy (p. 93) quotes an apocryphal (or perhaps typical) example: ' Ni Réaction ni Révolution. Ni Rome ni Moscou. Le Progrès dans l'Ordre, la Paix dans la dignité. La Main Tendue, mais la Porte gardée. La déflation budgétaire dans le progrès social. La répression de la fraude fiscale sans inquisition ni vexation. La réduction du nombre des fonctionnaires dans le respect des droits acquis.'

[15] The constitution requires the Assembly to elect its bureau by proportional representation of the groups, the cabinet in case of a dissolution of the Assembly to contain

sidered, even formally, as a party act rather than a personal one: if the proposer of an interpellation is absent, he may be replaced by another member of his group.[16] The authority of the Presidents' Conference has been extended by making the agenda, as proposed by it, more difficult to alter. An open ballot without proxies could, from 1947 to 1952 when the procedure was abolished, be demanded only once in the same debate by any single group. Debates themselves can be ' organized ', and in some circumstances the right to speak is restricted to one member of each group. Thus where forty years ago the spokesmen of groups as such were not permitted to address the house, to-day there are many occasions when no one else may do so. The growth of their power could hardly find clearer expression.

At the same time, the activities of members of parliament have come to centre more and more upon their group. Members subscribe sums, varying from £3 to £9 a month according to party, to the work of their group.[17] In return they receive services, from ordinary secretarial assistance to the provision of standard replies to importunate pressure-groups. In M.R.P., members of both houses form joint committees known as *ateliers*, each of which deals with a particular aspect of policy. The Socialists have study groups on separate problems, in which deputies, senators, and *militants* work together; and in each of the official committees of the Assembly, one Socialist member is responsible for the work of the party.

Even loose parties like the Radicals meet far more frequently than they did in the Third Republic. The deputy can perhaps exert his most effective influence in these private party meetings, where matters can be argued seriously and not demagogically, and party interests can be taken frankly into account, instead of being treated with the prudish

---

representatives of all groups, and the Assembly's representatives on the Constitutional Committee to be chosen by P.R. of the groups (Articles 11, 52 and 91 respectively). The *Règlement de l'Assemblée Nationale* (1952) mentions the groups in Articles 9 and 10 (the bureau), 12 and 13 (groups), 15 and 16 (committees), 19 (elections by the Assembly), 34 (Presidents' Conference), 38 *ter*, 39, 39 *bis* (organized and restricted debates), 66 *bis* (urgent debates), 79, 82, and 83 (voting procedure), 90 and 92 (interpellations), and 114 (seating). See also Arrighi, pp. 14–19, and Lidderdale, pp. 115–6, 141, 144, and 238.

[16] Article 92. Cf. M. Francisque Gay's view of the function of a committee *rapporteur*, during the period of strict discipline:—'. . . celui de nos amis qui a reçu mission, au nom du groupe du M.R.P., de présenter à la commission un rapport, de le défendre, qui a exposé la position du M.R.P., qui a fait triompher, sur la plupart des points, les vues de notre groupe, celui-là a toute la confiance et a droit à tous les remerciements du groupe du M.R.P.' *J.O.*, 11 August 1947, p. 4233.

[17] *Le Figaro*, 28 March 1950. The Communists pay most of their salaries to the party (above, p. 51). M.R.P. and the Socialists apply the same principle in a much milder form. In 1952 the Socialist member of parliament had to place a tenth of his salary at the disposal of the party. This came to 9,000 francs (£9) a month, of which £3 went to the central funds of the party, £2 10s. to the local federation, and £3 10s. to the group. About a fifth of the party's income for 1952, and an eighth of its estimated income for 1953, was derived from this source. Report of 44th Congress, p. 163; of 45th Congress, pp. 16, 19. For M.R.P. see above, p. 80.

reticence inevitable in public debate. Before this restricted audience, the member may really change votes, and perhaps affect the decision of Parliament.

3. THE EXTERNAL ORGANIZATION

CRITICS of the party-dominated state disliked the subordination of the deputy to his group. But the control of the group itself by the party organization outside aroused even greater indignation. It was regarded in theory as derogatory to the dignity of Parliament, and in practice as making the country more difficult to govern, since the deputies are less doctrinaire and intransigent than the men who control the external organizations of the parties. In July 1950 M. Bidault, whose majority was disintegrating, tried to pull it together by consulting four party leaders: only one of the four was a member of parliament.[18] Such an incident seemed to the critics to expose a transfer of power out of the hands of the sovereign Assembly which was as politically dangerous as it was constitutionally deplorable.

This influence of party organizations on national politics is not wholly new. Soulier, writing in 1938, could claim that ministers were really delegates of their parties and groups, and list several occasions when governments were brought down by external intervention.[19] The Radicals have of late been vociferously critical of the power of the parties; yet one Radical congress broke up the Poincaré cabinet in November 1928, another sealed the fate of M. Doumergue in October 1934, and the party executive committee overthrew M. Laval in January 1936. The policy of the Radicals in a ministerial crisis is settled by the *Cadillac* committee, which consists of the deputies and the executive committee sitting together; but as the former outnumbered the latter by two to one before the 1951 election and by three to one after it, and are likely to attend the committee far more regularly, effective control is nowadays firmly in the hands of the parliamentarians.

In general, however, the growth of better organized parties has meant some shift of influence away from the Assembly. This is most complete in the case of the Communist party, where the subordination of the parliamentary group is unquestioned. Party members may be assigned the post of deputy like any other form of duty, must abandon it when instructed, and must obey orders while they remain. On 29 September 1948, for example, M. Duclos read to the Assembly the text of a statement by the party secretariat authorizing the parliamen-

---

[18] The four were M. Mitterrand, chairman of the parliamentary group of U.D.S.R. (which has no strength in the country), the two assistant secretaries of the Socialist party, and the administrative chairman of the Radical party, M. Martinaud-Déplat (who was later elected to the 1951 Assembly). *A.P.*, 1950, p. 124.
[19] Soulier, p. 356. See also pp. 324, 356–73.

tary group to change its tactics and vote for immediate local elections.[20] External control is least important among the Conservatives, though this does not imply that individual deputies have an entirely free hand— it was a Conservative minister whose resignation was conveyed to the prime minister by the chairman of his group.[21] The Radical organization is not quite as rudimentary as that of the Conservatives, but is usually under the control of the parliamentarians. It is among the remaining three groups, R.P.F., M.R.P., and above all Socialists, that authority has been most divided, and friction most acute.

The friction is caused by an inevitable difference of outlook between the member of parliament and the *militant* in the country. The political enthusiasts do not necessarily or even often hold the same views as the mass of party supporters. The grotesque disproportion in their numbers demonstrates the point. In 1951 there were 74,000 M.R.P. voters in Haut-Rhin, yet the local M.R.P. federation had recently lost its right to representation at congresses because its membership fell below a hundred.[22] M. Duverger has shown that in general, and not merely in France, the membership and the electoral strength of parties rise and fall at different times and speeds, and seem to respond to different political causes, so that the active members can hardly be said to reflect the same outlook as the ordinary voters.[23]

The deputies and the executive committees consequently react to different impulses and considerations. The former have to consider the repercussions of opening or prolonging a ministerial crisis on the situation in the Assembly, where a change of majority may be the result, on the floating voter who may be alienated, on foreign opinion which may become doubtful of the country's stability, on the international situation,[24] and even sometimes, as in 1947–48, on the security of the regime itself. The party executives are neither concerned with these possibilities, nor responsible for the consequences if they are neglected. Their job is to see that the enthusiasm and loyalty of the faithful are not dissipated by a too accommodating spirit of compromise in the

---

[20] *A.P.*, 1948, pp. 159 and 347.
[21] M. Ribeyre in December 1949; see below, p. 383.
[22] Fauvet, p. 182.
[23] Duverger, *Partis*, pp. 101–112. The public opinion poll figures quoted (p. 58 and n.) make one doubt whether the deputies reflect the views of their electors, even at the time of casting their votes, at all effectively. The exception in the case of the Communist party is only apparent; no statistics are needed to show that the peasant voting for the party furthest to the Left, and the active party propagandist, have very different aims. The gap between Communist *militants* and voters appears with every political strike.
[24] It is true that when a change of government is in the air the deputies pay practically no attention to foreign opinion and little to the international situation. (M. Siegfried testified to this indifference twenty years ago—*Tableau des partis*, p. 28—and again quite recently—*A.P.*, 1951, p. xi.) So the Press invariably scolds the politicians for choosing this most inconvenient of all moments for leaving France without a government. If this argument had always been accepted, could France ever have reshuffled her cabinet since 1947? One doubts whether the general public, or even the journalistic critics themselves, would have tolerated quite so much stability and responsibility.

leadership, to ensure that the positive demands of the party are pressed with vigour even at inconvenient moments, and to prevent any unceremonious treatment of its 'sacred cows'. If their intransigence provokes a political crisis, they do not have to solve it. They can behave, at any rate for a time, as if the party were operating in a political vacuum: they acquire the popularity and the votes at congresses, while the parliamentarians have the ungrateful task of whittling down the party promises in order to reach that agreement with other groups, without which no government could ever be formed at all.

The conflict of attitudes is based on causes so deep-rooted that it has affected even the Communists. From the days of the de Gaulle government there were signs of a division within the party between the advocates of participation in office led by M. Thorez, and their opponents inspired by M. Marty. The difference became more acute after M. Thorez's bid for the premiership failed in December 1946, and in succeeding months the pressure of the *militants* grew as they met more and more severe competition from rivals within the trade unions. In April 1947 the party failed to stop the outbreak of a great strike at the Renault works, the traditional starting-point for movements of industrial unrest, and the leaders decided that they could preserve their influence in the unions only by abandoning wage restraint and supporting strikes. At the beginning of May they came out of the government.[25]

The most individualist of parties, like the most centralized of them, has suffered from the same division between leaders and rank and file. The tension and bitterness of the Radical congress at Toulouse in November 1949 has rarely been equalled in an assembly of any party. M. Herriot and the ' third force ' leadership of elder statesmen were fighting to retain their authority against M. Daladier, at the head of the ' young Turks ' and the local bosses who saw in vigorous opposition to the government the royal road to electoral triumph. The revived ' war of the two Édouards ' was fought so furiously that the disintegration of the party appeared imminent, and the protagonists themselves were shocked into patching up a truce.[26]

In the R.P.F. the same conflict took a slightly different form. ' Outside dictation ' was in a sense the *raison d'être* of the movement, founded as it was on the personal prestige of General de Gaulle. But the R.P.F. parliamentarians had in practice no more liking for military discipline in politics than their non-Communist colleagues. In a movement so essentially authoritarian in structure, the struggle was, however, not between the deputies and the representatives of the rank and file, but between the members of parliament and the General's personal advisers.

---

[25] See, e.g., Priouret, pp. 15, 200–5; Marabuto, p. 170; Aron, pp. 191–2. On the general point see below, p. 382 and n.
[26] *A.P.*, 1949, p. 198; Fauvet, pp. 105–6.

In August 1948, only a few months after the formation of the 'intergroup' of Gaullist members, the vice-chairman and twelve others resigned because they resented being ordered to vote against M. Reynaud's financial policy. Thus the measure which caused a breakdown of discipline on the left wing of M.R.P.[27] also attracted several Conservative Gaullists back to the ranks of government supporters—a distant precursor of the achievement of M. Pinay in 1952. A year later the quarrel between the parliamentarians and the 'back-room boys' was still very much alive: the chairman of the 'inter-group' resigned as a result of it, and was given a unanimous vote of confidence by his colleagues. The Pinay episode finally displayed the depth of the division. The doubtless apocryphal dialogue between the General and one of his rebellious followers ('But for me you wouldn't be in Parliament '—' On the contrary, but for you I would be in the Cabinet') summed up the situation in pungent, though too crude terms.[28]

Ambition was of course not the only motive which caused the difference of outlook. The ex-Conservative Gaullist knew that most of his electors would be unable to understand why he should oppose the policy he and they had always advocated, merely because it was presented by a prime minister other than General de Gaulle. The true Gaullist believes that no real reform is possible without changing the constitutional structure, and that the R.P.F. must admit no compromise which allows that essential task to be postponed. But this attitude found little response among most of the movement's voters in the country. Their loyalty was to a conservative policy, and they supported the R.P.F. as an expression of conservatism, not for its own sake. Since the creators of the Rally were far from being simple conservatives, tension between them and their parliamentary representatives was to be expected.

In M.R.P. and the Socialist party the issue was rather different. Here again the parliamentarians gave more weight and the others less to short-term and tactical considerations. But the structure of the three movements differed considerably. The R.P.F. was authoritarian and centralized, always struggling to impose discipline on members many of whom had taken its label for reasons of electoral convenience rather than of conviction. The Socialists are an intensely democratic and highly decentralized party, in which control is completely in the hands of the active rank and file: they have less trouble with parliamentary discipline than their rivals, but more with the conflict between deputies and *militants*. M.R.P. possess a more highly centralized structure than other parties, apart from the Communists and Gaullists, and perhaps a greater sense of common purpose than any except the former. This has enabled the leadership to retain its control fairly effectively,

---

[27] See above, p. 360; and cf. p. 121 n.
[28] Cf. *A.P.*, 1952, pp. 10, 94; above, p. 123; Appendix VII on the R.P.F. voter.

but not to avoid clashes with the representatives of the rank and file.

The constitution of M.R.P. is in two respects more favourable to the leadership than that of the Socialist party.[29] Firstly, the deputies and ministers are strongly represented on the committees which exercise day-to-day control. Secondly, representation at congresses is arranged to weaken the relative power of the larger and most combative federations: the consequence if not the intention has been to improve the position of the leadership.[30] But the latter is by no means automatically victorious. When M. Bidault, in a speech at Cherbourg on 15 May 1949, put out feelers for an understanding with the R.P.F., he was firmly disavowed by the party congress at Strasbourg ten days later. In the following September a Socialist demand for the restoration of free collective bargaining in industry was opposed by the M.R.P. ministers, but supported in outspoken, indeed violent terms by the national council. In 1950, at the Nantes congress, a left-wing candidate for the secretaryship won 40 per cent. of the votes.[31]

The tension between leaders and rank and file, and between deputies and *militants*, is thus a weakness from which all parties suffer to some degree. But it has been most acute among the Socialists. This was partly due to their structure: unlike the Radicals they are a real party, voting as a disciplined unit, but they are more effectively controlled by their rank and file than M.R.P. More important than the structural difference, however, was the political situation between 1947 and 1951. The Socialists were too weak to check the steady drift away from their own policies, yet they could not escape responsibility by going into opposition. They were forced into more and more unsatisfactory compromises which inevitably disheartened and demoralized their followers, and left the impression that they were willing to sacrifice any principle to retain office, even without power. At every crisis they were sharply divided, some fearing that to go into opposition would make government impossible, discredit the regime, lose votes on the Right, and play into the hands of the R.P.F.; others contending that to take responsibility for the policies of others would discourage the rank and file, lose votes on the Left, and strengthen the electoral and trade union position of the Communists. Both dangers were real, and it was wholly natural that the parliamentarians and the national executive members should give different weight to their relative seriousness.

The balance of power within the party swayed back and forth between the two sides as the political situation changed. The electoral disappointments of October 1945 and June 1946 produced an internal revolution. At the congress in August 1946, most of the old executive

---

[29] See above, pp. 80–2.
[30] See above, p. 81. But the big federations are not always in opposition; the strong working-class federation of Nord supported the Pinay government in 1952.
[31] *A.P.*, 1949, pp. 82–3, 159; 1950, pp. 99–100.

committee were defeated, and the left wing took control, replacing M. Daniel Mayer by M. Guy Mollet as general secretary. After a further electoral setback in November, the party decided that its ministers should only remain in the government as long as the Communists did so too. The withdrawal of the latter six months later produced a classic case of ' outside dictation '. M. Ramadier won his legal vote of confidence from the Assembly, but then had to solicit another from the national council of his own party, and only narrowly defeated the opposition of M. Mollet. Constitutionalists expressed shocked surprise at M. Blum's tactless remark in a newspaper article, that the national council would decide ' in full sovereignty '.

The Socialist *militants* on the new executive were unable to enforce their policy on the government, but they were strong enough to bring down three ministries between November 1947 and August 1948. By the following year, positions had changed; M. Mollet was now advocating participation in government, while the opposing wing was led by the ex-ministers. Weekly meetings between the Socialist leaders in the ministry, in Parliament, and in the executive committee helped to ease the tension.[32] But in September 1949 the conflict was resumed. M. Daniel Mayer, now minister of Labour, broke up the cabinet by demanding an immediate return to free collective bargaining. The ensuing crisis lasted for a month, the Radical *Cadillac* committee demanding, and the Socialist executive refusing the removal of M. Mayer; the problem was solved only by a revolt of the Socialist deputies against their executive.

At the extraordinary party congress in December, the parliamentarians won another victory. Decisions on tactics in a ministerial crisis were transferred from the executive itself to a special committee of 46—the 31 members of the executive, reinforced by 9 deputies and 6 senators chosen by their respective groups. These 15 members of parliament, reinforcing the 10 who already sat on the executive, formed a clear majority of the committee of 46. It was the first time the Socialist party had ever set up a policy-making body in which parliamentarians held the majority. The powers of the new committee were renewed in May 1950 and again in May 1951.

For two years it seemed that the conflict was settled—partly thanks to the new body, but partly also to the party's withdrawal from the government in February 1950, which at once restored internal harmony; when the Socialists resumed office in July, they did so on fairly satisfactory terms. But after the 1951 election the quarrel revived, for in December of that year the national council abolished the committee of 46, and restored full control of tactics in ministerial crises to the executive committee. The chairman and vice-chairmen of the parliamentary group treated this as a vote of no confidence in the

---

[32] Jules Moch, in *Bulletin intérieur du parti socialiste*, no. 39 (February 1949), p. 61.

deputies, and resigned their posts in protest; not until April 1952 was a complicated compromise arranged.[33]

Jurists, and members of individualist parties, naturally attack the power of the party organization as dangerous to parliamentary sovereignty, as in the case of M. Ramadier's ' vote of confidence ' after the ejection of the Communists, or to governmental stability, as in the long crisis of October 1949. Indignant Socialist deputies, after the resurgence of the executive committee in December 1951, referred to it as a ' politburo '.[34] But these criticisms, though understandable, are somewhat exaggerated. The executive is sometimes more responsible than the parliamentary group. In February 1951 it showed more concern for budgetary stability than the deputies,[35] and in February 1952 it twice intervened to try to save the Faure government, over the European army and again over the budget. Nor is the pressure of the external committees, even when they are more intransigent than their parliamentary colleagues, the only or even the main cause of party friction. The committees provide a channel for bringing rank and file views insistently to the attention of the deputy. But in any case it is the member's job to listen to those views. The ordinary voter may feel somewhat differently from the *militant*, but equally certainly he feels very differently from the deputy: the distortion is perhaps not much greater in one case than in the other. The deputies of the ill-organized groups, Radicals and Conservatives, accept instructions from no party executive, but they are subject to the direct pressure of their voters; and they certainly show no greater sense of responsibility than their colleagues in the disciplined parties.

The fact is that the parliamentary groups reflect the same influences as the party committees. The difference is not one of black and white but of shades of grey. The conflicts are not between solid, united bodies but between majorities, each supported by a substantial minority of the rival authority. Over the Poinso-Chapuis decree in the summer of 1948, the deputies as well as the *militants* began by displaying extreme intransigence, while the *militants* no less than the deputies yielded to persuasion in the end. Four years later, it was the deputies who first, by a majority, decided to go into opposition to the Pleven ministry.[36] *Scrutin de liste* gives slightly more power to the *militants*

---

[33] The executive's own decision is discussed at a joint meeting with the parliamentary group. This combined body (in which the deputies at present outnumber the others by five to one) can either confirm the executive's decision, or reject it by a three-fifths majority; if it rejects by a smaller majority, the decision passes to a specially summoned national council.

For the internal evolution of the Socialist party, see *A.P.*, 1946, pp. 208–9; 1947, pp. 93–4, 153; 1948, pp. 113–4; 1949, pp. 124–5, 159, 169–71, 178–80, 213–4; 1950, pp. 5–6, 27–8, 31, 101, 146–50; 1951, pp. 130–1, 178, 324.

[34] *A.P.*, 1951, p. 324.
[35] *Le Monde*, 16 February 1951.
[36] *A.P.*, 1952, p. 8. When the Socialist executive also decided to oppose the Pleven government rather than to abstain, the majority included 7 deputies and 12 *militants*,

and the organization. But the institutional faults only aggravate a little the fundamental trouble, namely that, if the voters take short or partisan views, their representatives have to do the same.

And it is too often forgotten that the *militants* too have a case. Compromise in politics, especially in French politics, is admittedly necessary. But the professional politician slips too easily into a state of mind which regards compromise as a virtue in itself. Members of parliament easily lose touch with their electors: living a more comfortable existence, they soon come to forget what the life of the ordinary man is like. Indeed they may never have known: in the 1946 legislature only three of the Socialist and eight of the M.R.P. deputies had been industrial workers. Perhaps French politicians, in the closed world of the Palais Bourbon, lose touch more easily than others. Robert de Jouvenel long ago wrote that ' there is less difference between two deputies of whom one is a revolutionary and the other is not, than between two revolutionaries of whom one is a deputy and the other is not.' [37] Time and again French political leaders have begun their careers on the extreme Left and, as their age and fortune increased, have gone over to a respectable or disreputable conservatism. Millerand, Briand and Laval are only the best known examples. L-O. Frossard, the first general secretary of the French Communist party, resigned from it at the end of 1922 because he refused to abandon freemasonry; in 1940 he held office in Marshal Pétain's first cabinet. It is not all loss if politicians are sometimes reminded that they owe their power to the faith and idealism of millions of simple and naive people. These may cherish hopes that can never be realized, but there is a limit to the amount of frustration that they are prepared to stand.

---

while the minority consisted of three from each group. A few days later two deputies and two *militants* were unwilling to vote for M. Faure as prime minister, but at the other extreme two *militants* and one deputy would not have objected to taking office under him. At the end of February two of each group were opposed to the government over the European army, while a majority of both groups supported the decision to vote for the budget. Only at the beginning of March was there a clear difference of opinion, 11 out of 16 *militants* wishing to vote against the investiture of M. Pinay, while 7 out of 10 deputies would have preferred abstention.

Nor is disagreement any more apparent on matters of parliamentary discipline. In January 5 *militants* and 2 deputies declined to censure a group of rebellious deputies, and in March three of the former and one of the latter adopted a similar attitude.

Bulletin intérieur du parti socialiste, No. 59 (February 1952), p. 19, and No. 62 (May 1952), pp. 41–3.

[37] *La République des camarades*, p. 17. It has ceased to be true since the advent of the Communist party.

Chapter 23

THE PARTIES AND THE GOVERNMENT

THE greater strength of parties perhaps affected the working of government even more than it modified electoral tactics or parliamentary practice. Democracy in France has always meant the rule of coalitions; the diversity of issues, and the consequent multiplicity of political groups, made that inevitable. Permanent coalition bred a set of habits which required some adjustment when parties became more highly organized.

If the continuity of policy was endangered by the frequent dislocation of the governing coalition, it was safeguarded by the similarity between one administration and the next. The same men and the same parties retained responsibility for particular offices over long periods: a change of government in France meant no more than a cabinet reshuffle in Britain. The dangers of ministerial instability, though real, were thus often exaggerated outside France; those of dissension within the cabinet, arising from its lack of common purpose, were comparatively neglected. But for these too there were mitigating factors. The long experience of coalition politics made bargaining and compromise second nature to French politicians. Certain groups participated in every administration, and specialized in the arts of political brokerage. Their own cohesion and sense of principle might suffer, but they performed an invaluable service in providing a stable nucleus of governmental solidarity and continuity, round which others could cluster. And every group which accepted the regime had to recognize the need for constant mutual accommodation.

These practices and habits of mind did not disappear when, in 1945, there came a sudden change from a chamber containing many small weak groups, to one dominated by a few strong and rigid parties. But their operation and their relative importance altered. The problem of the majority, which haunted every ministry of the Third Republic, was thereby solved; that of cohesion within the administration was enormously aggravated. In particular, the determined efforts of the Communists to establish complete control over the ministries they held, compelled their rivals to follow their example. Their ejection in 1947 eased matters in this respect. But when governments became once again dependent for their majorities on small, weak, and ill-disciplined groups, the system regained its old instability as well as its old flexibility. Nor did the governing coalitions escape from serious internal conflicts, for they now had to embrace more widely divergent opinions than those of the Third Republic, and to deal with more immediate and acute problems.

The Fourth Republic, in the governmental sphere also, has settled down to a state midway between that of the previous regime and that of the liberation period. Parties are fewer than before the war, and have better control over their members. The responsibility for making, maintaining, or breaking cabinets is therefore more easily located: negotiations are more open, and the political concessions exchanged are more obvious. Support once granted cannot be wantonly withdrawn without a danger of public discredit. Conversely, since support is given or withheld in larger blocks than before, adjustments are more sudden and less smooth. Just because responsibilities are more clearly apparent, every ministerial crisis is preceded and accompanied by elaborate manœuvres to confuse the issue and shift the blame, which may assist individual parties, but certainly tend to discredit the regime. The small, ill-disciplined groups, whose only apparent principle of action was to participate in each successive government, are now much weaker than they were, and the parties with firmer principles and wider objectives are somewhat stronger. This decline of the 'king's friends', is a welcome sign of health in public life. But in the day-to-day practice of government a price has to be paid for it.

1. CABINETS PASS, MINISTERS REMAIN

WHERE no party ever possesses a clear parliamentary majority, the formation of a government inevitably depends upon a process of bargaining between various minority groups. Since every French ministry is a coalition, and changes of government are so frequent, foreign observers receive an impression of chaos. They often suppose that almost every deputy holds office sooner or later, that every government department changes the main lines of its policy every six months on the appointment of a new minister from a different party, and that political continuity is altogether unknown.

This impression is false. The politicians occupying the principal offices in France change places more often than their opposite numbers in Britain, but they are hardly more numerous. There are sixteen ministries which usually entitle their holders to sit in the French cabinet. From January 1946, when party politics were resumed in France with the resignation of General de Gaulle, these posts were held (up to December 1952) by 66 different persons: omitting the six cabinets which had a life of less than six weeks (and therefore hardly had time to affect administration) the number falls to 58.[1] Britain

---

[1] The sixteen posts (with their British equivalents chosen, in cases of possible doubt) are: Premier, Agriculture, Defence, Education, Finance, Foreign, Health, Industry (Board of Trade), Interior, Justice, Labour, Overseas France (Colonies), Pensions, Post Office, Reconstruction and Town Planning (Town Planning, and its various successors), Works and Transport (Transport). Associated States (i.e. Indo-China) has been omitted, as it was not created until 1950; its inclusion, with Commonwealth Relations as its equivalent, would bring the British total to 62 without affecting the French figures.

(over)

returned to normal party politics a little earlier, when in May 1945 the wartime coalition broke up, and was succeeded by the Churchill caretaker government. Under that administration and its Labour and Conservative successors, up to December 1952, the sixteen corresponding departments were in the hands of 56 ministers.[2] Thus the number of individuals needed to staff sixteen French cabinets is hardly greater than that required to run the equivalent offices in Britain during a single swing and return of the political pendulum. And as there are about twice as many posts in a British government as there are in a French one, the British M.P. actually has a much better chance of office than the French deputy—indeed, this is one minor factor helping to provide British governments with their more solid parliamentary basis.

The sixty-odd French ministers admittedly belonged to several parties, the 56 British ones to two only.[3] But even this consideration does not justify the popular picture of kaleidoscopic change. For offices are distributed between the allied groups on grounds which alter comparatively slowly, and a new minister often comes from the same party as his predecessor. Between May 1945 and December 1952, every British government department twice underwent the major upheaval of a change of government. In France, from January 1946 to December 1952, ten cabinets held office for longer than six weeks, and five parties or groups of parties (Communists, Socialists, M.R.P., R.G.R., and Conservatives) participated in them. But the disturbance to administrative continuity was much less than these facts would suggest. For in Britain, in 1945 and in 1951, there was a change of party and of policy in every government department. In France, responsibility for the Interior and for Indo-China changed only once, and for foreign policy it remained in one party's hands throughout. Five departments had two changes, as in Britain; five had three; only four had more.[4] And changes usually meant less disturbance than in Britain, since the new ministers formed part of a coalition which differed little from its predecessor, and had to temper their reforming zeal accordingly.

The distribution of offices between parties also presents certain consistent features. Seen over a period of years, the long-term shift

---

The formation of M. Laniel's government brought the first French figure up to 73, and the second to 66.

[2] The object of starting with the caretaker government is not to make the comparison more striking, but to allow for the changes made by time in the ruling personnel of *both* parties.

[3] By French standards four, for Nationals and National Liberals would rank as distinct parties.

[4] Omitting the all-Socialist cabinet of December 1946, there were five short-lived ministries in this period: one lasted six weeks, two lasted four, and the other two survived only two days. If they are counted, 7 ministries had three changes, 3 had four or five, 3 had more, and 4 had less.

M. Mayer, in January 1953, practically confined his changes to reversing those made by his predecessor.

of political power is registered clearly; seen at a given moment, the assignment of particular offices to particular parties seems to follow a rough pattern, recognizable although, perhaps, not wholly deliberate.

Six ministerial positions stand out as clearly more important than the rest; three policy-making offices—the premiership, the Foreign ministry and the ministry of Finance—and three power centres, Defence, Justice and the Interior. Each of the five departments has been the stepping-stone to a post-war premiership, and each (except Justice) has been held since liberation both by an ex-premier and by a prime minister in office.[5] Since the breakdown of *tripartisme* the parties of the Third Republic, above all the Radicals, have recovered from their discredit at the time of liberation, and regained most of these six vital positions. The Gouin and Bidault governments included no Conservative or R.G.R. members. M. Ramadier brought these groups back to office in January 1947, but gave them only the least important of the six main posts, the ministry of Justice. In the Schuman cabinet at the end of the year they added a second, Finance. In July 1948 they acquired a third by providing the prime minister, M. André Marie. When the Socialists withdrew in February 1950, a fourth passed into the hands of the former opposition; the return of a Radical, M. Queuille, to the ministry of the Interior symbolized their revival. From March 1952 they held five out of the six.[6]

Among the six principal posts, the Quai d'Orsay was the safe preserve of M.R.P. Only for one month since 1944 did the Foreign Office pass out of their hands—during the all-Socialist government of December 1946, when it was taken by M. Blum himself. With this short break French foreign policy has been conducted since the liberation by only two men, MM. Bidault and Schuman. Thus the country's foreign policy has, with one brief exception, been controlled by fewer men and fewer parties than that of Great Britain in the corresponding period. When M. Schuman was at length dislodged, at the end of 1952, it was M. Bidault who took his place.

On the other hand M.R.P. has never held the ministry of the Interior, which remained firmly in anti-clerical hands. The Socialists controlled

---

[5] But Justice has provided three prime ministers, more than any other office, and is traditionally the senior French department. The Communists certainly regard it as a key position, for they usually tried to obtain it in the countries where they held office in 1944–45.
Only one department, apart from these five, has provided a direct stepping-stone to the premiership. This is Public Works and Transport, which was M. Pinay's ministry before his elevation (and was also held for a couple of days by M. Queuille before his first premiership). No prime minister in office has held a post other than the main five, and only two ex-premiers have done so: M. Reynaud was for two days minister of Associated States, and M. Marie became minister of Education in 1951.

[6] Ministries lasting less than six weeks have again been ignored in this survey. The R.G.R. temporarily lost the ministry of Justice during 1949, and exchanged the premiership for the Defence ministry in 1950.

it until they left office in February 1950, when the Radicals reasserted their traditional claim to the office. The ministry of Justice, an important position during the purge which followed liberation, was at that time a responsibility of M.R.P. But the Radicals demanded it as their price for entering the cabinet in January 1947, and retained it, except for a few months in 1949, for six years. The premiership and the ministry of Finance are political barometers. The former has not been held by the Socialists since 1947, nor by M.R.P. (except for eight months) since 1948. The latter is a still more accurate index of the rightward shift of politics. It passed from the Socialists to M.R.P. in 1946, and to the Radicals in 1947. An attempt to reverse the process and to put a Socialist back at Finance upset the second Schuman government in September 1948. At the beginning of 1949 a Conservative, M. Petsche, began his long tenure of the post, which lasted until the 1951 election; it then alternated between the Radicals and the Conservatives.

The sixth key position, the ministry of Defence, was the main bargaining counter in the distribution of offices. After the 1945 election its disposition caused a political crisis. The Communists were the largest party, and in return for not pressing their claim to the premiership they demanded one of the three ministries of the Interior, Defence or Foreign Affairs. Neither General de Gaulle nor the other parties would agree. Eventually the General himself became titular minister of Defence, the department being divided into two subordinate ministries of Armaments, held by a Communist, and Armed Forces (dealing with personnel) held by M.R.P. The same Communist demand prevented M. Blum forming a coalition government after the election of November 1946. During the first four months of the Ramadier government a Communist minister, M. Billoux, was at last installed in the Defence ministry, but with such restricted powers that effective control remained with the prime minister. Even after the departure of the Communists, the ministry was still treated as a bargaining counter. It was always given to a potential premier, who was hardly ever drawn from the prime minister's own party.[7]

The Communists and Socialists each controlled a fairly coherent group of offices in the tripartite government. The former held the departments dealing with post-war reconstruction and with working-class claims: Industrial Production, Labour, Reconstruction and Town Planning, Pensions, and sometimes Health: they also shared in the control of the Defence ministry. The first two of these offices always went to parties with trade union connections. The Communists held both posts when they were in office. The Socialists then took them

---

[7] Only in the Schuman and Marie cabinets, from November 1947 to August 1948, did the minister of Defence belong to the prime minister's party. (Radicals and U.D.S.R. counted separately.)

over, and when they too resigned in 1950, these offices passed to M.R.P.[8] The latter party was particularly concerned with the problems of the family, and ever since 1946 has sought to control the ministry of Health.[9] The other former Communist ministries were used to satisfy the minor parties who took office after the Communists had left. Reconstruction was at first in the hands of a Republican Independent, and Pensions of U.D.S.R. In the middle of 1948 these offices were exchanged, M. Claudius Petit holding the former for four years, and the latter being shared by four different types of Conservative.

The Socialists, who enjoy the support of most of the *fonctionnaires*, held under *tripartisme* four departments dealing with large numbers of state employees—the Interior, Education, the Post Office, and Works and Transport. The Radicals, who retain some of their traditional support in these quarters, took over Education from them in July 1948, and the Interior and Post Office in February 1950; Works and Transport went to a Conservative, M. Pinay.[10]

In addition to the *fonctionnaire* departments, the Socialists originally had Finance, and also both Colonies and Agriculture, two ministries which tended to go to the pivotal party in the coalition. Colonial affairs were so contentious that only a compromise policy could hold the government together, and such a policy was best applied by the party in the centre of the majority. So in 1947, after the Communists went out of office, the ministry of Overseas France passed from the Socialists to M.R.P. Before the election of 1951 it was held for a year by U.D.S.R., and afterwards usually by a Conservative. Indo-China had a separate minister (for Associated States) from 1950 to 1953; M. Letourneau of M.R.P. held the post throughout.[11]

Agriculture was a highly coveted department, owing to its alleged electoral importance. Its original Socialist holder became a liability when the government needed Conservative support in order to survive. In November 1947 it was given to M.R.P., which kept it until the 1951 election. But in the new Assembly the Peasant party, now forty strong and an important element in the majority, successfully asserted a claim to provide both the minister and the under-secretary. A few months later the two men found themselves opposed to one another. M. Antier, the minister and leader of the party, who had fought the election in alliance with the R.P.F., attempted to overthrow his own

---

[8] A ministry of Commerce was separated from that of Industrial Production for some time in 1947, when it went to M.R.P.; in 1952, when it was held in turn by M.R.P. and U.D.S.R. ministers; and in 1953, when it was given to the Peasant party.

[9] It temporarily reverted to the Communists later in 1946 (M.R.P. taking instead an ephemeral ministry of Population) and went to the Conservatives from 1951 to 1953.

[10] During most of 1946 M.R.P. held the Post Office. Between July 1950 and July 1951 the Socialists recovered Education. The Radicals lost the Post Office to the Conservatives in 1951, but gained Works and Transport from them in 1952–53.

[11] It was however originally created for M. Paul Reynaud. And cf. Epilogue.

government. His party split, and his under-secretary succeeded him both in the leadership and in the government.

After the 1951 election M.R.P. was the only one of the three original partners still holding office. It had exchanged its former association with Socialists and Communists for one with Conservatives and R.G.R. A different distribution of ministries emerged, especially after the first Conservative prime minister was elected in March 1952. M.R.P. kept its peculiar responsibility for external affairs. It had occupied the Foreign ministry throughout, Associated States since that office was set up, and usually either Defence or Colonies. But it was reluctant to keep its economic offices. In the Pleven, Faure, Mayer, and Laniel cabinets it held Industrial Production, Labour, and usually either Commerce or Economic Affairs. Under M. Pinay it renounced all but the first, refusing even under-secretaryships in economic posts.[12]

The R.G.R. held three or more of the six chief positions, Justice, the Interior and Defence; under M. Mayer it had five of them. It added '*fonctionnaire*' ministries like Education and sometimes Works; and minor posts created for purposes of *dosage*, such as Armaments or Merchant Marine. The other second-rank ministries were all in the hands of the Conservatives, who made up in the number of their offices what they lacked in authority.[13]

French government is, then, by no means as chaotic as it appears to be. There are many changes of prime minister, but great continuity of cabinet personnel. The real instability is concentrated in a very few offices: the premiership, the ministry of Finance which was the most sensitive to shifts in the majority, that of Defence and one or two minor posts, which have been treated as bargaining counters. Most departments are held for fairly long periods by the same party, and often by the same individual. And as all French ministries are coalitions, no party can apply its policy without regard to others. A minister from a new party usually makes less difference in France than in Britain; changes of direction are not so abrupt. Of 16 premiers elected from 1947 to 1953, 12 came from the previous cabinet, and 10 joined the following one. These factors should be remembered in mitigation of the instability which is so frequently derided and so rarely understood.[14]

---

[12] Labour went to a Conservative (an ex-member of M.R.P. who sat for Somme, a fairly industrialized department). The other two ministries were abolished.

[13] In the Laniel cabinet the Conservatives held fewer but more important posts; they relinquished Reconstruction and Posts to the Gaullists, but took Justice and the premiership from the Radicals.

[14] For a somewhat similar analysis of the stability of French political personnel see Peter Campbell, *Parliamentary Affairs*, vol. IV, no. 3 (Summer 1951). His argument is based on the degree of continuity between successive cabinets, and on the extent to which all have been based on a nucleus of about twenty political leaders, serving regularly.

2. DEALS AND DEVICES

THE period of party predominance affected the working of government, as well as the life of the deputy and the character of the Assembly. When the restraining influence and prestige of General de Gaulle were removed, the disunity of the cabinet became evident. The ministry seemed no more than an aggregation of representatives of three powerful, disciplined and intensely suspicious parties. In January 1946 the three reluctant partners regulated their mutual relations, and settled the composition and policy of the next administration, in an astonishing written treaty.

> The delegates of the M.R.P., of the Socialist party, and of the Communist party met on 23 January, 1946.
> They proceeded to a broad examination of the situation, and reached agreement in stating that, given the development of the ministerial crisis, the formation of a government in which responsibilities are equally divided, under the leadership of the President of the National Constituent Assembly, appeared to them as the solution which would best meet their common preoccupations.

The document went on to condemn mutual recriminations between the parties, to insist that all of them must support the decisions of the government, to outline a programme for the new ministry, and to ' mandate their representatives in the government to have these proposals included in the ministerial declaration '.[15]

This agreement formally proclaimed the application of the principle of proportional representation to the cabinet itself. In the past certain parties had acquired a kind of prescriptive right to particular posts: the Radicals had long regarded the ministries of the Interior and Education as almost their private property. But post-war practice went a long step further towards the ' horizontal separation of powers '. Parties staked out claims, not to individual ministries, but to the control of a whole sector of the national life. Each acquired certain offices by bargaining with its rivals, chose which of its members should hold these posts, and treated them as a group co-ordinated by the party leader. The cabinet seemed merely a diet, in which the plenipotentiaries of the real powers, the parties, conducted their negotiations. The prime minister declined into a broker among mutually hostile forces, a buffer rather than a leader.

The circumstances of this period were, of course, exceptional. The dominant feature of politics at every level, electoral, parliamentary, and governmental, was the Communist pressure to achieve power, and the determination of their rivals to frustrate them. Rigid discipline and bitter partisanship were the inevitable fruits of this situation. Yet one wonders whether the disintegration of government, even at this time,

---

[15] Text in *A.P.*, 1946, pp. 530–1.

was quite as complete as is usually alleged. All parties were concerned with the problems of national reconstruction; and for many months even the Communists courageously risked their popularity in the trade unions by vigorously opposing demands for wage increases. It is hard for men to assume together heavy common tasks and responsibilities, and still to retain to the full their mutual bitterness.[16] The impression of disunity and disorder may even have been partly fostered by the party leaders, as a convenient means of staving off impracticable or embarrassing demands from their own followers.

However this may be, the withdrawal of the Communists removed the most acute cause of internal friction. Subsequent cabinets were far from being harmonious, but their dissensions had a less paralysing effect. Governmental leadership became possible, though it could not be very vigorous. In particular, the prime minister acquired greater strength. Under *tripartisme* he had had small share in forming his own government. In M. Gouin's ministry, each party had its share of offices allotted in the inter-party bargaining, and was then invited to put forward nominees for them. In January 1947, the newly-elected President of the Republic discussed with the party secretaries and the chairmen of the parliamentary groups both the distribution of offices and the choice of individual ministers; when M. Ramadier was picked as prime minister, his hands were thus tied. But even the weakest of the later prime ministers has at least been able to do his own bargaining.

The extent of his success naturally varies with the political situation. A Socialist veto kept M. Paul Reynaud from the ministry of Finance in November 1947, but did not do so in July 1948; and by October 1949 the Radicals were strong enough to veto a Socialist leader.[17] Some parties insisted on nominating their own ministers; the Communists always did this, even under General de Gaulle, and the Socialists usually, although the second Bidault and first Pleven governments included Socialist ministers chosen personally by the premiers concerned. M.R.P., partly for internal party reasons, generally preferred that the prime minister should choose, but sometimes laid down negative or positive conditions; thus they would accept no economic or financial post under M. Pinay, nor join him at all unless

---

[16] M. Raymond Aron believes that Moscow feared so much the attractions of power and responsibility for the Communist leaders, that it welcomed their ejection from office. *Le Grand Schisme*, p. 198: cf. p. 193. See also M. Ramadier's tribute to M. Thorez as a loyal ministerial colleague: *J.O.*, 16 May 1947, pp. 1651–2.

[17] The minister in question, M. Daniel Mayer, eventually settled the question by ' asking to be relieved by the S.F.I.O. of his mandate as minister of Labour '. The party executive agreed, and picked Dr. Segelle instead, but forgot to inform their nominee: when at 2 a.m. the cabinet met to take the oath, they had a long wait before the new minister of Labour could be fetched from his bed in the outer suburbs.

For the Gouin cabinet see Duverger, *Manuel*, p. 310. For the conference preceding M. Ramadier's nomination, *A.P.*, 1947, p. 4. For M. Daniel Mayer's request to be relieved, *ibid.*, 1949, p. 180.

M. Schuman remained Foreign minister.[18] Even the most individualist parties keep a veto on the acceptance or retention of office by their members; the Radicals warned M. Mendès-France not to accept the ministry of Finance in the Gouin cabinet, U.D.S.R. would not let M. Mitterrand become minister of the Interior in September 1948, and in July 1949 P.R.L. ejected two ministers for refusing to resign office. In December of that year, the Peasant party leader conveyed to the prime minister the undated letter of resignation which the group had exacted from one of its members as a condition of allowing him to take a minor post two months before; the unfortunate man emphasized the involuntary character of his departure by voting for the government, and against his party, in subsequent votes of confidence.[19]

Here again there has been a great change since 1947. With the Socialists out of office, strict party nomination of ministers is now rare. Yet it is not quite unknown. For under-secretaryships the prime minister himself may, like M. Pinay, prefer it; where prestige seems at stake, a party may impose rigid conditions, as M.R.P. did over M. Schuman in March 1952; and for the principal offices a prudent premier will naturally, as in any parliamentary system, inquire in each party about the influence and popularity of its potential ministers, and the strength they can bring to his government.

Party decisions are as decisive in destroying governments as in creating them. But sometimes a party is willing neither to accept a bargain negotiated by its ministers, nor to disavow them completely and take the blame for bringing down the ministry. In such cases curious compromises occur. So in March 1947 the Communist party authorized its ministers to vote for a question of confidence on Indo-China, while the rank and file of its deputies abstained. The Socialists used the same device over devaluation in January 1948, and over the amnesty law on 5 December 1950.[20] Again, all the ministers may abstain, leaving the decision to the private members. This is the normal custom on matters (such as the raising of a deputy's parliamentary immunity) which are considered questions for the Assembly alone. But the method is occasionally adopted for political reasons. It was used by M. Schuman to keep his government together over the colliery schools dispute, in May 1948 [21]; and M. Pleven also resorted to it, in his first ministry over electoral reform, and in his second over M. Barangé's private member's bill to subsidize Catholic schools.[22]

[18] *A.P.*, 1952, p. 26. But in January 1953 they had to abandon M. Schuman. Cf. Philip Williams, ' Crisis in France ', *Cambridge Journal*, October 1953, pp. 40, 49.

[19] See *A.P.*, 1946, pp. 11, 15–16 (Mendès-France); 1948, p. 152 (Mitterrand); 1949, pp. 80, 130, 213, 217, and 1950, p. 5 (Conservatives). Cf. p. 367 above.

[20] The R.P.F. used it over the European army in November 1953.

[21] The issue was whether or not 28 Catholic schools, belonging to the recently nationalized colliery companies, should be brought under the state system.

[22] M. Pinay and his ministers abstained in 110 divisions, 16 per cent. of those occurring in their term of office. Campbell, ' Discipline and loyalty in the French Parliament', *loc. cit.*, p. 251.

The abstention of ministers is roughly the equivalent of a free vote in Britain. A genuine free vote, with ministers casting ballots on both sides, is much rarer. A coalition cabinet cannot advertise its dissensions, even on minor questions, for minor questions are very easily given symbolic importance. However, even this is not absolutely unknown: one occurred in September 1951, on a motion to postpone debate on M. Barangé's bill. Once or twice ministers have even voted against the government and stayed in office; so two U.D.S.R. members of the Queuille administration, on 23 September 1948, voted with their party against deferring the departmental council elections.[23] In January 1951, when the first Pleven government decided to send an ambassador to Madrid, it specifically authorized the Socialist ministers to abstain if an interpellation was moved. It is even said that divided cabinets sometimes reach agreement of a sort by ' horse-trading ' one concession against another; there was an alleged instance of this in March 1949.[24]

3. SHARING THE SPOILS

THE critics of *tripartisme* feared that party conflict was destroying the state, and depriving the government of both dignity and efficiency. They were even more dismayed by the way the antagonists parcelled out the administration among themselves, each treating its own sector as an area to be exploited for its private purposes. So clearly were ministries regarded as party preserves that in the absence of a minister his duties were usually performed by a colleague of his own political outlook, rather than by one from a department with similar functions.[25] Appointments were made with party interests in view. A competent observer, though one hostile to the parties in power, wrote in 1948 (with a little exaggeration):

> The result is that to-day, in any given department, if one knows the political outlook of the minister who has held office longest since 1944, one almost certainly knows also the party loyalty of most of the senior officials of the ministry—even of the technical services.[26]

[23] In 1952 two Radical ministers expressed their dissent on a matter involving *laïcité*. *A.P.*, 1952, p. 83; *Le Monde*, 11 and 12 November 1952.

[24] For the colliery schools question see *A.P.*, 1948, pp. 76–7, for the U.D.S.R. ministers *ibid.*, p. 160, for the ' horse-trading ' incident, *ibid.*, 1949, pp. 38–9. As an exuberant journalist put it, ' " Si vous cédez sur les écoles libres, je vous abandonne un cuirassé." " Si le décret Poinso-Chapuis entre en application, on pourra renoncer à construire un porte-avions." Telles étaient les propositions qu'on entendit formuler dans les couloirs de la Chambre.' *Le Figaro*, 6 March 1949.

For the permission to the Socialists to abstain over the ambassador to Spain, *Le Monde*, 11 January 1951. For the vote on postponing the church schools debate, *A.P.*, 1951, p. 220.

[25] So in February 1950 and again in April 1951 M. Schuman's place was taken by the minister of Health, also of M.R.P. (an ex-under-secretary for Foreign Affairs). In May 1951 the Radical minister of Justice deputized in the Assembly for his colleagues, the Radical ministers of the Budget and the Post Office. (But in the following November, the Conservative minister of the Budget acted for the Radical minister of Finance, and the Radical minister of Armaments for the M.R.P. minister of Defence.)

[26] Waline, p. 69.

Some defence for these developments could be made. The occupation record of many civil servants made their removal inevitable. Active resistance leaders and workers had a claim to greater influence in public life, and since normal methods of recruiting government servants could not serve in this emergency period, there was a strong case for making new appointments from their ranks. But many resistance movements had political connections, like those of *Libération-Nord* with the Socialist party, so that the entry of their members into the public service might involve some unintentional party ' colonization '. Again, the senior positions in the administration had long been the preserve of a rather narrow social class with strong political connections. But their links were with the groups which were discredited at the liberation, and they included few supporters of the two largest parties, Communists and M.R.P. These could claim that their conscious colonization was merely the counterpart of the less conscious but no less effective monopoly enjoyed for years by their opponents.

Even admitting all this, before 1947 party influence in the administration, the behaviour of the parties as states within the state, was a real danger. The Communists set the pace. The social security system was controlled by councils elected by its beneficiaries, and the trade unions were represented on the boards of nationalized industries; this gave the party a foothold in both these sectors. With the economic and social ministries in their hands, they acquired a dominant influence in the public sector from coal to atomic energy.[27] The other parties were compelled to compete. The Socialists, with the advantage of having more sympathizers in the public service than their rivals, were particularly active: the ministry of the Interior was their principal preserve.[28]

---

[27] Communist infiltration went furthest in the coal and aircraft industries. M. Marcel Paul, who as minister of Industrial Production was responsible for the former, increased the number of *directions* in the ministry from the pre-war figure of three to nineteen (*Revue politique et parlementaire*, January 1950, p. 92) and appointed a personal *cabinet* of ten times the normal size.

He obtained control of the coal industry for the party in an ingenious way. The board consisted of six representatives each of the workers, of the consumers, and of the state. All six workers' members were Communists; and so, among the state representatives, were those nominated by Communist ministers. One vote from the consumers' section was needed to give the party a majority. The nationalized railways could choose one of the consumers' members; and without informing either the railways board, or M. Moch, the minister of Transport (who would normally have made the appointment in consultation), M. Marcel Paul simply proceeded to nominate the Communist secretary of the railwaymen's union, who was a workers' member of the railway board. Jules Moch, *Confrontations* (Gallimard, 1952), p. 240n. Cf. Pickles, pp. 83n, 251–2.

In the aircraft industry, under M. Tillon (subsequently found to be a deviationist), advertisements for jobs were placed only in newspapers which supported the Communist party. In one factory ten senior officials were dismissed, seven of the newcomers being known party members. Adolf Sturmthal, ' Structure of nationalized enterprises in France ', *Political Science Quarterly*, September 1952, p. 374.

[28] M.R.P. has never held this ministry; and in 1951 it had no prefect and few subprefects in its ranks. R. G. Neumann, ' The struggle for electoral reform ', *loc. cit.* (above, p. 322, n. 27), p. 744n.

In overseas appointments there was some excuse for political pressure, for policy was made by its application on the spot, and the desire to influence policy was legitimate enough. But once installed in their positions, the nominees of the parties often used them to provide places for their political friends, and they always relied on their party connections for political support at home. So the Radical high commissioner in Indo-China early in 1948 enlisted his party to protest against the conduct of the M.R.P. minister of Overseas France, who was dealing directly with Bao Dai. The Algerian settlers demanded the removal of the governor-general of Algeria; the Radicals backed them, but the Socialists refused to agree—until it was decided to appoint a Socialist cabinet minister to the vacant place. As late as 1950 the replacement of the resident-general in Tunisia was described by a Socialist spokesman as an act of aggression against his party.[29]

Colonization was most dangerous in the security services. French democrats have always been suspicious of soldiers, policemen and secret funds. During the ten years before the war, the attitude of Marshal Pétain and General Weygand, of Admiral Darlan and M. Chiappe did nothing to lessen their deep-rooted distrust. A postwar purge was inevitable and proper, though it carried obvious dangers of abuse. But the conflict was not simply between resisters and collaborators. For the Gaullist secret service and its chief ' Colonel Passy ', were believed by many of the Free French during the war to be quite as much concerned with internal political power as with the struggle against Germany, and to employ much the same moral standards in both campaigns. That these suspicions were not confined to the Left is apparent from the outspoken memoirs of the old-fashioned Conservative General Giraud, General de Gaulle's unsuccessful rival at Algiers.[30]

In this as in other spheres colonization was of two types—the frankly totalitarian attempts of the Communists to accumulate positions which would be of service in a revolutionary situation, and the less thorough efforts of their rivals to keep pace, and to extend their sphere of influence for use in the day-to-day political struggle. Conscious of the danger of the former type, the other parties kept Communists out of the ministerial posts where they could affect the personnel of the security services (except for the Air Force, where a Communist minister in the de Gaulle government conducted a drastic purge in 1944). But locally the party used to the full the positions it acquired at the liberation. When M. Moch took over the ministry of the Interior in November 1947, he found that many of the republican guards (*Compagnies*

---

[29] *A.P.*, 1948, pp. 19–20 : 1950, pp. 90, 101.
[30] General H. Giraud, *Un seul but, la Victoire*, pp. 124–5, 238–9, 283–6, etc. He describes the B.C.R.A. (the Gaullist secret service) as having ' un seul but, le Pouvoir ' (p. 124), and declares: ' Le B.C.R.A. aurait pu aussi bien s'appeler Gestapo que Guépéou. Mêmes méthodes, mêmes résultats.' (p. 284).

républicaines de securité) were unreliable. In eleven of the 65 companies more than 80 per cent. of the members were Communists, and these had to be dissolved and reconstituted. This was the work of a single Communist regional commissioner and a single prefect in the last months of the war.[31]

The struggles of the other parties to extend their influence involved less danger to the security of the state, but perhaps no less damage to the morale of the public service. The 'scandal of the generals' in 1950 revealed the extent to which, in the abnormal circumstances of the post-war years, certain police and military officials had developed the habit of attaching their fortunes to particular parties, and the extraordinary credulity which some of them showed in choosing the most dubious intermediaries as channels for the exercise of backstairs political influence.[32] The chief of the general staff, writing privately to his confidant, urged the latter to press his political friends to make a certain general assistant director of military personnel; he described his candidate as ' a good republican whom, therefore, M.R.P. want to get out of the way ' by sending him out of Paris to a local command.[33] Some months later, when the M.R.P. prime minister had been replaced by a Radical and the M.R.P. minister of Defence by a Socialist, the desired appointment was made—and the new minister came under attack from M.R.P. members, who alleged that he was favouring freemasons.[34]

The scandal of the generals also threw a disturbing light on the working of the secret service. Every department was attempting to build up its own intelligence organization, and all were working at cross-purposes, arresting and intimidating each other's informers, as much for purposes of domestic politics as in the pursuit of their proper ends. Often they appeared credulous, usually unscrupulous, invariably enmeshed in a web of political intrigue. The counter-espionage services of the ministry of the Interior seemed to be trying to hush up a scandal which might involve the Socialist party, to which their minister belonged: they had at least the excuse that the affair might involve national interests as well. The rival service attached to the prime minister's office behaved even more curiously. This organization was the lineal successor of General de Gaulle's intelligence service, which had been so suspect during the war. When the General left office, Colonel Passy left with him, and a Socialist deputy was appointed to reorganize the service. But this unfortunate man appeared virtually isolated in his own organization. Its effective chief was his second in command, who wanted to have two of the leading Socialist ministers shot, and was alleged to be bribing and intimidating witnesses to obtain

---

[31] Jules Moch, *Bulletin intérieur du parti socialiste*, No. 39 (February 1949), p. 67.
[32] See my article on the affair in *Cambridge Journal*, May 1951.
[33] *Le Monde*, 18 February 1950. ' Republican ' in this context means anti-clerical.
[34] *J.O.*, 3 March 1949 (M. Monteil's speech, p. 1204: M. Ramadier's reply, p. 1214).

evidence against them and their party. These sensational revelations led to the fusion of the rival services under a new head.

The dangers of colonization were great, but they were always limited by the mutual suspicions of its practitioners. When M. Thorez, as minister responsible for the civil service, tried to concentrate promotions in the hands of his department, he was prevented by the opposition of the other parties.[35] The ministry of Defence has never been monopolized by a single party, its holders always being excluded from the subordinate posts (Armaments and Armed Forces under some governments, Navy, War, and Air under others) which are given to their rivals. In January 1947 M. Ramadier actually proposed to give every minister an under-secretary from a different party to check colonization, though the plan was not put into effect.[36] Similarly, colonial and diplomatic appointments have been shared out on a principle of proportional representation: thus on 21 January 1948 the cabinet appointed a Socialist junior minister as high commissioner in West Africa, an M.R.P. deputy to Madagascar, and a Radical official to Equatorial Africa.[37]

Moreover, the rigidity of the system was tempered by a natural reluctance to lose the services of distinguished public servants whose merits the electorate have failed to appreciate—or by that intimate fellow-feeling among (non-Communist) politicians which forty years ago led Robert de Jouvenel to write *La République des camarades*. Victims of electoral ingratitude may receive their consolation prizes from their own party, as an M.R.P. ex-minister became commissioner for German affairs soon after losing his seat in the upper house. But even opponents may sympathize with colleagues suffering from a misfortune which might happen to anyone: though the Socialists went out of office after the 1951 election, their defeated leaders all found new public employment within a few weeks.[38] Nor is this always reprehensible. Politics are not necessarily healthier when the livelihood of the practitioners and their families is wholly dependent on electoral success. And sometimes appointments of this kind are (like many of those quoted) justified on the strictest criterion of merit.

Colonization is no longer a serious danger; it was a temporary phenomenon of the period just after liberation.[39] It has now virtually

---

[35] See P.-C. D., 'Pour un plan Monnet administratif', *Revue politique et parlementaire*, no. 579 (June 1948).
[36] *A.P.*, 1947, p. 9.
[37] *Ibid.*, 1948, p. 8.
[38] M. Philip was appointed to the Economic Council (representing *Pensée française*), M. Ramadier to the I.L.O., and M. Guyon to the chairmanship of the *commission des alcools*. The Socialist deputies elected M. Gorse to the Assembly of the French Union.
[39] Even then, critics exaggerated the extent to which ministries were simply fields for party exploitation. M. Debû-Bridel's description of the Socialists as 'comfortably installed' at the Food ministry in 1946 (*Partis contre de Gaulle*, p. 115) shows a lack of humour as well as of objectivity.
In 1953 there were complaints of political interference in the nationalized industries: see *J.O.*, 19 May 1953, p. 2761, and 3 June 1953, p. 2923 (M. Gazier's speeches).

disappeared. In the early years entry into the civil service had to be on an *ad hoc* basis; regular procedure could not be applied, collaborators had to be purged and resisters admitted, the claims of London and Algiers, of those who had stayed at their posts and those who had left for the *maquis*, had somehow to be reconciled. Above all the pressure of the Communists meant that their rivals must compete or perish. But the situation soon changed. Normal procedure was restored in recruitment, and indeed vastly improved: the guarantees of entry by merit are now complete.[40] The system of personal *cabinets*, whatever its disadvantages, at least ensures that the minister can choose personal collaborators sympathetic to him and to his policy, and diminishes the temptation to make promotions on a party basis.[41] The removal of the Communists from office made it less necessary for their rivals to counter-colonize in self-defence. There were many officials, originally appointed on political grounds, who kept their places but chose, or indeed were obliged, to allow their party connections to lapse; and some conscientious ministers who made a deliberate effort to undo the damage which had been done.

4. COLLECTIVE IRRESPONSIBILITY

THE practice of allotting ministries or groups of ministries to the same party over a period of years was indispensable to the whole process of colonization. But to abandon this habit and divide posts up haphazard, or to change the parties in control so frequently that none of them could obtain a real grip, would have brought other disadvantages with it. Departments dealing with cognate subjects but controlled by different parties were only too liable to conflict rather than to co-operate. And in single ministries of great importance in party warfare, a change of minister might occasionally mean a violent reversal of policy, laws hitherto ignored being suddenly put into effect with vigour, others recently employed lapsing into disuse.

The press law of May 1946 provides an extreme example.[42] At the time of liberation the old newspapers, many of which in Paris at least had been notoriously corrupt, were suspended on the ground that they had appeared under German censorship; their presses were transferred provisionally to new Resistance papers. The party political consequences were drastic. In 1939 Radical and Conservative journals had a combined circulation of five million, Socialist and Communist ones of 1,300,000. In 1944 these figures had been exactly reversed: in addition there was an M.R.P. party press with 1,300,000 readers, while the 'non-party' newspapers, most of which had been conservative in

---

[40] In 1953 a few candidates, alleged to be Communists, were excluded from the entrance examination for the *École nationale d'administration*. See *J.O.*, 13 November 1953.
[41] See above, p. 327 and n.
[42] See Jean Mottin, *Histoire politique de la presse 1944–1949*.

outlook, now included many left-wing Resistance organs like *Combat*. The provincial press has always had very great political influence in France, and indeed the Radical party organization was largely based on newspapers; this immense transfer of political power did a good deal to cripple the Radicals in the elections of 1945 and 1946, and to promote the extension of rural Communism.

The Left wished to perpetuate this state of affairs, the older parties to reverse it. The press law of May 1946 was drafted by the Socialist minister of Information in the Gouin cabinet, and voted by Socialists, Communists, most of M.R.P., and a few U.D.S.R. resistance leaders, against bitter Radical and Conservative opposition. It provided for the permanent transfer of the plant and offices of papers which had appeared under the occupation to a government-controlled holding company, which would lease them to new successors; those which had not collaborated would receive some (quite inadequate) compensation. Its authors hoped that the new law would both improve the moral climate of French journalism (for which there was plenty of room) and consolidate the new balance of power in the press world. Their success depended on the vigour with which the law was applied.

The Gouin cabinet went out of office just before the measure was promulgated. But outgoing French ministers remain in charge of current affairs until their successors take over. For a few days in June 1946, therefore, as well as for the one month of the one-party Blum cabinet in December, Socialists were in control of the ministry of Information. In between, it was held for six months by M.R.P. When M. Ramadier invited the Radicals to take office in January 1947, they attached such importance to preventing the press law going into effect that they demanded the ministries of Justice and Information, the crucial departments for that purpose, as the price of their acceptance; they obtained the former for themselves and the latter for U.D.S.R. M.R.P. regained Information along with the premiership at the end of the year; both passed to the R.G.R. in July 1948. The question remained a political stumbling-block, and in October 1949 M.R.P. and Socialists in turn refused to join any government in which these two offices were in the hands of the same party.

The working of the law depended on the party allegiance of the minister concerned. Between June 1946 and December 1948, when its application ceased, 136 newspapers condemned for collaboration had their presses transferred by decree. The two Socialist ministers transferred an average of over twenty a month, compared with less than four a month while ministers of other parties were in office. The contrast was still more startling in respect of papers which had not been condemned. Sixty of these were transferred during the period, more than two-thirds of them (including most of the biggest) by the two Socialists. Under them the rate of transfer of such papers was nearly one a day, under M.R.P. ministers one a month, and under R.G.R.

ministers one in four months. In the later years, those who wished to wreck the law were assisted by the restrictive interpretation put upon it by some, though not all, of the local courts. Yet the legal considerations involved hardly modify the impression that, by and large, the application of the press law of 1946 was governed by party purposes.[43]

But this was exceptional. The party conflict was often mitigated or complicated by other considerations. One great sector of affairs was largely taken out of party politics at the start by the general acceptance of the Monnet plan, by the Communists as well as other parties; M. Monnet remained head of the *Commissariat général du plan* from 1947 to 1952, when he was appointed to the European Coal and Steel Authority. Nor did politicians always prefer the policy of the party to the advice of the civil servants. The minister of Labour differed with the minister of Transport over the dismissal of railwaymen in May 1949, and with the minister in charge of the civil service over wages policy in September, although all three men were Socialists. The minister of Agriculture resigned over the guaranteed price for beetroot in December 1949 after a clash with the secretary for Economic Affairs, a fellow-member of M.R.P. The unfortunate deputy, who in February 1950 signed a motion to grant cheap fares to students in Paris, and was then appointed minister of Transport and had to reject it, symbolized a struggle in which the influence of officialdom was very frequently on the winning side.

French government departments are extremely particularist. When ministries dealing with cognate problems are in the hands of politicians of different views, the clash of parties often merely invigorates a corresponding struggle between the administrations themselves. For example, the ministry of Finance is dominated by the immensely capable and closely knit corps of *inspecteurs des finances*. In some ways the élite of the French civil service, they are hostile both to 'planners' of the Left and to small-farm and small-firm pressure-groups.[44] In pressing for their own economic policy they had the full support of their political chiefs. In the de Gaulle administration the minister of Finance was the orthodox M. Pleven. After six months under the Socialist M. Philip it passed to M. Schuman, one of the most conservative of the M.R.P. leaders. From the end of 1947 onwards it was in Radical or Conservative hands.

Pitted against it was the ministry of Economic Affairs. The holder of that office in the de Gaulle government was M. Mendès-France, a

---

[43] Party newspapers have suffered severely in recent years. *L'Aube*, the M.R.P. daily, ceased publication in 1951; the Socialist *Le Populaire* barely maintains a precarious existence; the Communist evening paper in Paris has disappeared, as have four of the fifteen Communist provincial dailies, and the circulation of *L'Humanité* has fallen very heavily.
[44] Cf. Charles Brindillac, *Esprit*, June 1953, pp. 862ff.; and above, p. 264. Many of them leave government service for private industry in mid-career.

highly unorthodox Radical, who tried to persuade the prime minister to initiate a policy of austerity, limited commitments, currency reform and a controlled economy, rather than to pursue business confidence as the ministry of Finance desired. M. Pleven won this battle as his successors won almost all the others. But M. Mendès-France and M. Philip, who took his place in the next cabinet, had staffed the ministry of Economic Affairs with their own sympathizers. For six years the department waged its losing struggle. The outlook of its officials was so well known that only Socialists and left-wing members of M.R.P. occupied the minister's chair. The first Radical was installed in 1952; until that date, when the individualist parties were in the ascendant, they tried to suppress the separate identity of the department rather than to control it. They were no more able to change the attitude of the ministry than were the collectivist parties to recover for it any effective political influence.

As a result of conflicts of this kind it was remarked that problems concerning a single ministry, such as transport, were usually dealt with far more successfully than those where several departments were involved, such as price policy. The political consequences were even more serious than the administrative. No party felt any obligation to support ministers belonging to its rivals. The treaty of January 1946, on which the Gouin cabinet was founded, insisted that all parties represented in the government must accept the principle of collective responsibility and defend its actions. But this proviso proved a dead letter. A Socialist minister denounced the Communist vice-premier as a deserter, while the Communists attacked the M.R.P. minister of Economic Affairs for authorizing price increases, and M.R.P. accused the Communist minister of Industrial Production of incompetence and of electoral corruption.

Even the departure of the Communists did not eliminate these internal feuds, though it reduced their temperature. In February 1948, over the Poinso-Chapuis decree, the Socialist minister of Education accused his prime minister of violating the constitution; in May 1949, in a meeting of Conservative deputies, two junior Conservative ministers (MM. Pinay and Moreau) led the attack on the new taxes proposed by the minister of Finance, a Conservative from a different party group; and later M. Moreau even expressed his sympathy for the parliamentary critics of his own department, the Air ministry, whose real target was the Socialist minister of Defence.

If Conservative ministers often took time to abandon the habits of opposition, their Socialist colleagues felt no very enthusiastic loyalty to a government and a policy which most of them tolerated only as a lesser evil. Trade union demands might weigh more with them than cabinet solidarity; for example, when *Force ouvrière* called a general strike in December 1949, the prime minister broadcast an appeal to workers to disobey the order, but his Socialist ministers attended the party executive which called on their followers to support the union. In April 1951 a Radical minister stated that a third of the national income was going to the state; he was promptly and publicly attacked by Socialist and M.R.P. colleagues for misleading the public by counting social security benefits as state expenditure.[45]

The inevitable consequence of such conduct is intense mutual suspicion between the nominally allied parties. This was underlined by a characteristic incident in October 1949, when M. Moch was trying to form a government. He offered the economic ministries to M.R.P., who laid down the condition that all parties in the government should publicly assume responsibility for their economic policy. The Radicals flatly refused, claiming that in voting for M. Moch as prime minister they had committed themselves to the proposals contained in his investiture speech, but to nothing more. Very reluctantly M.R.P. gave way; significantly, the minority which opposed doing so was led by the prospective ministers for these departments, who knew what treatment they might expect from their colleagues.[46] But when in addition the Radicals demanded to be given the ministry of Information, M.R.P. finally drew the line at taking sole responsibility for policies which other ministers intended to attack with official resources at their disposal. In the end the mutual suspicions of these two parties made it impossible for M. Moch to form a government at all.

Such open propaganda battles between fellow-members of the same cabinet are comparatively rare. But they are only unusually acute symptoms of an endemic disease—the contradiction between the attitude adopted by parties in Parliament, where they vote for the government, and in the country where they attack it. This is nothing new in French politics. Formerly, indeed, it usually took a less extreme form; in 1924 and in 1932 the Socialists kept Radical ministries in office, but refused to join them, so as to retain a free hand for propaganda purposes. Earlier in 1932, Radical representatives were sitting both in a mainly Conservative government and in the *Délégation des gauches*, the co-ordinating committee of the opposition. But this was immediately before a general election, when the party was preparing

---

[45] For these and similar inter-party clashes see Gordon Wright, p. 222; Priouret, p. 225; Debû-Bridel, pp. 117, 252; *A.P.*, 1946, p. 214; 1948, pp. 78, 92–3; 1949, pp. 77, 97, 170, 200, 337 (quoting M. Daniel Mayer's significant letter of resignation); *Le Monde*, 3, 10, and 17 May 1951.

At the Socialist congress of 1950 M. Moch, out of office for the first time since 1945, criticized the expenditure of only ' cent milliards pour les écoles, mille milliards pour les logements, ce qui nous a coûté notre aviation en cinq ans pour ne disposer d'aucun avion.' *Le Monde*, 29 May 1950. (The Air ministry is one of the few offices never held by a Socialist.)

In 1953 M. Pleven, a senior minister in a conservative government, urged his party to work for the formation of a left-centre majority. *Le Monde*, 27 October 1953.

[46] The minority also included Mme Poinso-Chapuis, whose ministerial career terminated with her celebrated decree in 1948. It is not only Socialists who see more clearly the advantages of the party refusing office when they are themselves unlikely to receive it.

a change of alliances. In the Fourth Republic respect for collective responsibility has clearly diminished: parties no longer feel much compunction about joining a cabinet and then attacking it. M.R.P., the party which can never escape office, has always pressed for a ' pact of the majority '—a common programme to which all the ministerial parties would be committed. But their partners have never been willing to abandon the equivocation which allows them to combine the advantages of opposition with those of office.[47]

The growth of the extreme parties has made it harder to find a majority in the Assembly, and in consequence has widened the gap between parliamentary and electoral politics. Parties find their parliamentary support indispensable to the government; but they cannot dictate policy, since the support of others is equally essential. They may keep the ministry in office in order to avoid the odium of causing a crisis, or the danger of a worse alternative, but they will not lose votes in the country by defending a distasteful policy. All the gradations from keeping the government in by abstention, through voting for it without joining it, to joining it while criticizing it, are frequently practised and constantly discussed.[48] The quarrel between deputies and *militants* is only another aspect of this gap. In Paris the deputy is conscious of the dangers of upsetting the government; in his constituency he becomes aware of the electoral advantages of opposing it. During the six years from October 1945 to June 1951 the Socialist party was out of office for only five months. But in an exceptional department like Haute-Loire, where there were no outgoing Socialist deputies, the party's candidate was able to campaign under an opposition banner, and adopted the slogan of the anti-government parties, ' Don't vote for the old gang '.[49]

Trying to combine the advantages of both government and opposition is not peculiar to France. Cynics might indeed say that it is the formula which every politician is seeking. Under coalition governments the line between the two is always blurred; responsibility is hard to define and easy to evade. Countries where the division of public opinion or the nature of the political system make coalition government inevitable, can hardly hope to escape from this species of political confusion. M. Duverger indeed bases on it a fundamental distinction of character between parties which are in a position to aspire to the sole responsi-

---

[47] But M.R.P. itself showed the same detachment towards M. Pinay, and so did the R.P.F. towards M. Laniel. And cf above, pp. 383–4 and notes.

[48] When M. Thorez was nominated for the premiership by the Communist party, a meeting of the Socialist parliamentary group was called to discuss tactics. After several speakers had agreed that it was essential to vote for Thorez but that it would be a catastrophe for the party and the country if he were elected, a very junior deputy ventured to ask whether, in this case, it might not be possible to abstain. Thereupon two of the older leaders turned to him and remarked simultaneously, ' Jeune homme, vous ne savez *rien* de la politique.'

[49] *Le Figaro*, 17 June 1951.

bility for government, and those which are not.[50] Responsibility can only be driven home to parties which govern alone. These are compelled to be realistic since their faults may be exposed by the test of practice. Others are tempted into demagogy since they can never be exposed—there is always the excuse of the exigencies of coalition and compromise. But if the argument of the early chapters is accepted, strong and stable democratic government, as understood in Britain, is an unattainable objective in France. It is necessary to make the best of a system involving permanent coalitions, with their consequences in irresponsibility. There is no point in blaming the Fourth Republic as such for faults which are much older and lie much deeper—which depend indeed not on constitutions at all, but on a structure of opinion which can only be changed over a period of many years.

---

[50] *Partis*, pp. 315-9.

Chapter 24

CONCLUSION

It is the fundamental argument of this work that the difficulties of French government are due to historical and social, rather than to constitutional or temperamental factors. The cleavages of the past are almost as important politically as the conflicts of the present. The consequent diversity of issues and alignments creates numerous parties. But these are the effect, and not the cause, of the absence of a majority in the electorate for any single point of view.

Old issues persist in the politics of other countries besides France. Wherever Catholicism remained powerful after the Reformation, clericalism remains to-day a political dividing line, and the framework of the state is often still a matter of controversy. In America, where group conflicts are fought out within the two-party system, historical factors are still of the utmost political importance. The persistence of the old dividing lines is a normal rather than a peculiar feature of politics in most countries. But they have exceptional importance in France. For there the industrial revolution began before the political revolution against authoritarianism was complete. No basic agreement had been reached about the objectives of political action, or the fundamental purpose of the state. The continuing philosophic clash found violent expression at the time of the Dreyfus case, in Charles Maurras's formulation of the authoritarian position. Marianne, to some the symbol of republican virtue, was represented by others as *la gueuse*.

Thus two distinct revolutions were at work at the same time. Industrialism vastly increased the stakes of the political game before the rules for the tenure and transfer of power had been agreed. A society already deeply divided was confronted with new problems and conflicts, which made control of the state far more important. For industrial civilization gave rise to demands for governmental intervention to protect the producer against ruinous domestic or foreign competition, the capitalist against the claims of labour, the worker against the pressure of his employer. Further, the French industrial revolution was itself localized, incomplete and stunted. The rural and small-town economy, the old, largely self-sufficient order of peasants and artisans, survived in most of the country, and retained disproportionate political influence.

The American observer who commented that industrial France never repealed its corn laws, was echoing the distinguished French historian who remarked that, if Britain in the 1840's had been a land of artisans and peasants, the Anti-Corn-Law League would have failed, and the Chartists would have succeeded.[1] Universal suffrage came to stay in France in 1848, the year when Chartism collapsed in Britain. And French industrial development was hampered, not only by lack of the raw materials necessary if she were to rival Britain or Germany, but also by political factors. Most French voters wanted power and wealth to be diffused. They resisted the progress of capitalism—speed and standardization, mass production and large-scale organization, plenty and instability—in a word, Americanization. But the twentieth century is ill-suited for experiments in distributism. Through her thwarted economic development, France acquired most of the social problems of industrialism, without its compensating material benefits.[2] Nor did the proletariat become strong enough to compel governments to attend to its grievances. Two distinct types of politics came to operate side by side; the modern politics of class struggle in the progressive industrial areas, the traditional politics of ideological conflict in the economically backward regions. Parties had to shape their attitudes to the needs and demands of both.[3]

Outside the few departments where agriculture has been modernized and mechanized, the main upholders of traditional political behaviour are the peasants—even when this behaviour takes the form of a traditional revolt against the forces of feudalism. Around them congregates a huge petty bourgeoisie, in small-scale industry, in the professions, and above all in commerce. The ' tertiary sector ' of the economy, distribution and servicing as opposed to direct production and manufacture, is enormous in France. And this reflects economic backwardness, not progress. The gap between the French standard of living and that of the British or Americans is largest by far in this overcrowded part of the economy,[4] which represents the traditional outlet for those seeking a precarious and unreal economic independence, and is still increasing rapidly.

The political system is loaded in favour of these old-fashioned social and economic forces. The small bourgeoisie made the Republic, and endowed it with institutions designed to weaken their enemies on Right and Left alike. The second chamber and the electoral system, in both

---

[1] John E. Sawyer, ' Strains in the social structure ', in E. M. Earle, ed., *Modern France*, p. 306. E. Halévy, *The Age of Peel and Cobden* (Benn, 1947), p. 32.

[2] John E. Sawyer, *loc. cit.*, p. 309,

[3] This analysis has no pretensions to originality. For similar views on some or all points, see Siegfried, pp. 33–7, 45–8, 56, 232–4; Goguel, *Fourth Republic*, pp. 141–6; Earle, Chs. IV, XVII, XIX; Middleton, Ch. I; Thomson, *Democracy in France* (2nd ed.), pp. 231–2; Maillaud, Chs. VI and VII; Léo Hamon, *Esprit*, June 1953, pp. 841–5.

A post-war example of the resistance to modernization is provided by Louis Chevallier's interesting book, *Les Paysans* (Ed. Denoël, 1947), pp. 141–56, 169–79. For a case of rapid transition from traditional to modern politics, see above, pp. 90–1.

[4] John E. Sawyer, *loc. cit.*, p. 307. See also Aron, p. 245; Pickles, p. 67; articles on ' The real crisis in France ', *Manchester Guardian*, 3, 4, 10 and 17 December 1951; and *statistiques*, etc. (see above, p. 23), pp. 206–9,—quoted *Le Monde*, 7–8 June 1953.

the Third and Fourth Republics, were devices to buttress the position of 'static France.' The modern areas breed extremists, anxious to establish a strong state under their own control, and liable to drive the country into violent conflict for the possession of power. The easiest way to restrain these dangerous forces is to limit their political weight, and to exaggerate that of the safe, unadventurous, moderate, and easy-going groups which predominate in 'static France'. The consequence is that the country's political and economic centres of gravity no longer coincide. Most electors in 'modern France', where the country's international power and economic future are decided, repudiate a political system which is kept in being by the inertia of their cousins in 'static France'. Economic power becomes divorced from political responsibility, and the country's equilibrium is permanently unstable.

2.

THE history and social structure of France have thus combined to produce the present political circumstances. The persistence of the religious cleavage, especially in 'static France', and the recollection of comparatively recent revolutions in the modernized regions, keep alive anti-democratic attitudes on the Right. The isolation of the industrial proletariat, too weak to enforce even its most reasonable demands, works together with the revolutionary tradition in the rural areas to provide the basis for a mass Communist party. Between them these two dangerous forces preserve, through hope or through fear, the latent authoritarianism of a large part of the electorate, and leave to their democratic rivals only a small and precarious margin of votes and of confidence.

Despite these formidable difficulties, the French democratic tradition retains its vigour. That the system often functions inefficiently is hardly surprising. Far more significant is the persistence of the liberal democratic outlook, and its revival, with renewed fervour, after the most severe defeats. Fifty years ago that acute observer J. E. C. Bodley could argue that France was wholly unsuited to parliamentary government, and must shortly fall prey to military dictatorship. The outcome of the Dreyfus case disproved his thesis; and half a century later the democratic tradition was winning new successes, acquiring for the first time the wholehearted allegiance of a large and devoted section of the Catholic electorate.

Nor is the governmental system itself as insecure or as ineffective as is usually supposed. Its weaknesses are grave enough, and no one doubts their seriousness—least of all Frenchmen, who are their own severest critics. No attempt has been made in this work to conceal them or to gloss them over. Weak and short-lived administrations may have to adjust their politics in order to win or hold indispensable marginal votes. Politicians devote much of their energy to seeking favours from the bureaucracy for the benefit of their constituents, and to acting as local ambassadors in Paris rather than as advocates of a course of political action. Permanent coalition makes politics an affair of perpetual and obvious bargaining, pressure, and manœuvre, in which principles seem at a discount, cynicism flourishes, and sectional interests exercise dangerous influence. Prompt and clear decisions on difficult questions are hard to arrive at, for agreement can often be reached only by shelving the troublesome problem.

Yet a sense of proportion is needed. These deficiencies are not at all peculiar to France. If marginal votes weigh heavily in the calculations of a French prime minister, British politicians watch their Gallup polls and their by-elections with anxious eagerness to discover how to woo the floating voter. Americans concentrate with equal attention on the electoral votes of the key states. Neither British governments, for all their stability, nor American administrations, for all their independence of Congress, are immune from the temptation to play safe and to follow the line of least resistance.

The instability of government is much less dangerous than it appears, since there is so little difference between successive ministries. And the recurrent *crises* (best translated ' reshuffles ') play an important part in the working of the system. They provide opportunities for changing men, bringing in new blood or attracting new parties into the majority. More important, they permit the same men to change direction; the government adjusts its outlook to the shifting mood of public opinion. Above all, they provide the means by which solutions are found to the more intractable problems of policy. They bring pressure to bear on a recalcitrant group by demonstrating to the country where the responsibility for deadlock lies; and in this way they make it possible for difficult and distasteful decisions to be taken.[5]

The French deputy is partly a constituency ambassador, but less obviously than the United States congressman, whose career depends on the loyalty of a single state or district. And the British M.P. finds that the growing functions of the state compel him to spend more and more of his time in similar activities. Nor is this wholly to be deplored. If democratic government is to hold the respect and allegiance of the citizen, the rigidity and inhumanity of bureaucratic decisions must be tempered by effective machinery to correct abuses. ' It is the function of the minister to tell the civil servants what the public will not stand '— and it is the function of the member of parliament to see that the minister does his job. In France, with its highly centralized and

---

[5] See Williams, ' Crisis in France ' (*loc. cit.*, pp. 47–50); and for a severe but illuminating criticism, Edgar Faure, *Le Monde*, 27 March 1953. As he remarks, ' La crise n'est plus la sanction d'une politique. C'est l'excuse d'une concession . . . une sorte de *méthode de gouvernement à secousses*.' (Italics in original).

bureaucratic administration, writers like Alain have always, and rightly, stressed this aspect of the democratic politician's task.

The services rendered by the member to the constituent strengthen the latter's confidence in the political system. For most men react much more readily to personal contacts than to general ideas. Their confidence in their representative helps them to feel that they are citizens and not mere *administrés*. By acquiring the trust of his followers, the member obtains the authority which enables him to explain to them why a particular demand of their party or pressure-group cannot be conceded, why a distasteful policy is necessary, or a disappointing compromise inevitable. The member himself benefits. He can establish a personal position enabling him to differ from his party. For the French insist firmly upon a measure of individualism in politics—and if they pay a heavy price for their preference, the means used to ensure party discipline in Britain or America have their drawbacks too.

The stronger the deputy's personal standing, the more effectively he can negotiate on behalf of his constituents with the representatives of other regions, groups, and schools of thought. For the very purpose of politics is the adjustment of conflicting aims and interests with the minimum of tension and friction. If bargaining and pressure play an important part in French politics, this is equally true of other political regimes. It is a merit of the French system that it exposes the reality, instead of concealing it. For in Britain, the effective bargaining is done behind closed doors in Abbey House, Transport House and Downing Street, and the arrangements reached there are very hard to challenge. No French party has matched the performance of the British Labour party in 1949, in demanding the nationalization of industrial insurance and then abandoning it at the behest of the insurance agents and of the Co-operative movement. No French prime minister has indulged in such blatant political interference with administration as Mr. Churchill over the question of London fares in 1952. Money talks in French politics, but no more loudly than elsewhere. There has been no French equivalent of the ' Mr. Cube ' advertising campaign against sugar nationalization, and there are no French constituencies in the admitted gift of a single trade union.

In America, the bargains emerge after trials of strength between departments of the same administration, between the administration and Congress, and between the federal government and the states. Inter-departmental conflicts frequently occur in France, but they never attain the ferocity of battles between American Service departments. No French pressure group works on the scale, or with the ruthlessness, of the China lobby. If the French parliamentary system is weighted in favour of certain sections and areas, so is the American; the arrangement of congressional representation, the operation of the seniority rule for committee chairmanships, the obstructive power of the South in the Democratic party, and the institution of filibustering, all work in favour of the rural areas and the less enlightened forces in American political life.

A two-party system has many advantages. When the parties are at all disciplined, it imposes responsibilities firmly upon the one holding the majority. It enables more citizens to identify themselves to some extent with their rulers, to feel that the government is 'us' rather than 'them'. But it also conceals from the public view a great part of the political process. Tendencies which in France become the basis for separate political groups, would in Britain or America form factions within the two great parties. Their negotiations and arrangements would be kept as far as possible—more successfully in Britain than in America—from the public eye. But in France the bargains have to be struck openly, at election times or on the floor of the house. The British M.P. can shift his responsibility to his party leaders, who know that the electorate will judge them on broad and general grounds, or on immediate grievances, and that the minor errors of the past will be forgotten in a few weeks. The French deputy bears more personal responsibility for his votes, since discipline is not so strict; and his party is more likely to suffer for its sins, since its supporters can desert it without having to go right to the opposite extreme. This situation leaves the French politician less protected against demagogic pressure. On the other hand, it means that many more decisions are made in the open, that many more points of view are expressed and freely argued, and that the educative function of democracy is to that extent more effectively performed.

The clarity of political discussion loses in one respect, but gains in another. Over particular issues it suffers, through the complexity of the parliamentary and governmental situation; a vast amount of energy is spent in manœuvring to conceal or to shift responsibilities. But understanding of the political process is assisted. Every French democrat must learn that honest men can hold widely divergent views; that the competing social groups have their legitimate but conflicting interests, which it is the useful task of politicians to reconcile; that political bargaining is not shameful or dishonourable, but desirable and necessary.

The politician's task of adjusting conflicting claims is indispensable to society, but it rarely earns him much gratitude. In all countries, the 'fretful constituent' tends to clamour for incompatibles, and to malign his political representative when they are not all forthcoming. France is no exception. A multi-party system makes it hard for any given body of opinion to feel a sense of responsibility for the country's government. And the popular base of the regime has been narrowed by circumstances: the unrepresentative social composition of the political class, and the virtual exclusion from political influence of great sections of the people—devout Catholics during much of the Third

Republic, Communists in the Fourth. It is perhaps natural enough that the profession of politics is not highly regarded, and that its practitioners are rarely held in great esteem.[6]

Yet the French voter's distrust for his leaders is hardly justified. Frequently he receives better political leadership than he deserves. The politicians of the Fourth Republic have shown resilience and determination in their efforts to reform the political and social abuses of the old regime—frustrated though they have often been by the inertia of the older parties, and the excesses of the extreme ones. The majority leaders have shown notable courage in going ahead of public opinion with far-reaching projects for economic reconstruction and European integration. They can hardly be charged with failing to provide imaginative leadership (indeed, they are more vulnerable to criticism for going further than their voters were prepared to follow). With more courage and imagination than many of their predecessors, they have shown no less skill in defeating the Communists, and gradually absorbing the Gaullists. If governments in the Fourth Republic have been as short-lived and as divided as those of the Third, the causes for this state of affairs do the former much more credit. The rising birth-rate, the belated effort to make up for past industrial neglect, the cost of rearmament and of the Indo-China war, have imposed on the present generation burdens which were bound to provoke strong political resistance.

3.

AMONG the most criticized achievements of the post-war leaders was the new constitution which they framed. Based on a series of compromises between opposing forces, their creation lacked any fundamental guiding principle or logical unity. After a few years' trial, few could be found to defend it. Yet its main lines were imposed upon its makers rather than chosen freely by them.

The fundamental difficulty is the absence of a potential majority in the electorate. A parliamentary majority therefore has to be created by artificial means, and its composite nature always makes it unstable. If parliamentary government in France is consequently doomed to weakness and frustration, it is tempting to prefer the other classic pattern of democratic governments, presidential rule on the American model. Among reformers who take this view, many would further argue that the deputies are too independent of their electors,

---

[6] For the unrepresentativeness of the politicians, see above, p. 58 and n.
An indication of their unpopularity was given by a public opinion poll in 1946. Fifty-seven per cent. believed that the current scandals involved important political figures, and only 10 per cent. did not (the rest replied ' don't know '). Fifty per cent. thought the scandals had been brought to light for electoral reasons, and 22 per cent. thought otherwise; only 5 per cent. believed that the really guilty would be punished. *Sondages*, 8 November 1946, p. 266. And see Appendix VII on both points.

and that genuine democracy requires the introduction of institutions like the referendum. But the difficulties are caused less by the system than by the voters and politicians who operate it, and by the historical traditions and associations to which they respond. Constitutional changes would not get rid of these influences. Presidential government or the referendum in France would prove very different from the corresponding institutions in America or in Switzerland.

In the abstract it may well be absurd to identify a presidential constitution with authoritarian rule, and " direct democracy ' with Bonapartist plebiscites. But if enough people behave as if a referendum were a plebiscite, it will become one. If the advocates of a reinforced and independent executive depend upon the groups which have always loathed democracy, then the political system which they favour will be warped unrecognizably by the forces which sustain it. Indeed, the presumed advantage of the presidential system is that an electoral majority is believed to be more easily assembled than a parliamentary one. But to obtain the electoral majority, the voter's whole political approach must be changed; and the inevitable tendency will be to seek this result by employing the one active tradition available for the purpose, the plebiscitary appeal on behalf of a strong national leader. However excellent the democratic intentions of those who favour presidential rule, they could succeed only by exploiting the authoritarian strain in the French political tradition.

A democratic constitution in France must therefore be parliamentary and not presidential. This necessity left the constitution-makers with little room to manœuvre. Inevitably, they concentrated on remedying the faults of the past. Experience has proved some of their ideas ineffective. They corrected some abuses at the cost of creating worse difficulties—as in their withdrawal from the government of the power to close parliamentary sessions. They tried with only limited success to check other practices, such as decree-laws, which were produced by forces too strong for paper prohibitions to withstand. Some of the new institutions, such as the vote of confidence procedure, postulated changes in political conditions which did not take place, and consequently failed in the event to fulfil the intentions of their inventors. By and large, the customs and habits of the Third Republic persisted, and the new constitution worked very similarly to the old.

Yet the attempt to change the system of government was not simply a failure. Some real advances were made, through political as well as legal or institutional developments. The greater effectiveness of the Presidency was the work of its first incumbent, and was by no means intended by the men who had drafted the constitution. The decline of the upper house was indeed enforced by the terms of the new text; but even without those provisions the power of the Senate would have been undermined in 1945 by its extreme unpopularity, and even with them, the Council of the Republic has recovered influence as public opinion has altered. The increased power of the parties has changed the operation of the political system alike at the electoral, at the parliamentary, and at the governmental levels. This was in part due to an institutional change, the new electoral law. But the rise of the Communists obliged their rivals to stiffen their discipline in order to compete. And, more fundamentally, the increasing 'collectivization' of life, and particularly the growth of trade unions, of Catholic associations, of peasant and middle-class organizations, had its inevitable repercussions in the sphere of politics.

One development, as important as any of the strictly constitutional changes, has passed almost unnoticed. At the time of liberation France carried through a silent administrative revolution, which warrants far more attention than it has received. For the constitutional changes were made by a process of compromise, applied almost arithmetically to a series of separate decisions, and lacking any basic coherence. The administrative reforms were the work of specialists, convinced of what needed to be done in spheres with which they were familiar. The central direction of policy was reinforced by the establishment of a cabinet secretariat and the strengthening of the prime minister's office. Civil service recruitment was revolutionized by the creation of a national administrative college. Legislative technique was improved (for governmental projects) by extending the competence in that sphere of the *Conseil d'État*. The Monnet plan organization and other newly created agencies provided the machinery for effective economic planning. In finance, the scope and authority of the Court of Accounts were extended by the constitution, and its prestige was enhanced by its practical working. In local administration the creation of the I.G.A.M.E. or 'super-prefects' (*inspecteurs généraux de l'administration en mission extraordinaire*) fulfilled a double function; in time of civil emergency it ensured that the forces of the state could be deployed efficiently and under civilian control; in normal periods it provided useful machinery for encouraging co-operation between the prefects of neighbouring departments. In the sphere of justice, the new High Council of the Magistrature, set up by the constitution itself and therefore composed according to a politically determined formula, has yet marked an important step forward in the process of freeing justice from political influence.[7]

But the improvements in the machinery of government only throw still more into relief the problem of the political authority which is to control them. A reinforcement of the power of the government will

---

[7] Some of these developments were discussed in articles in *Public Administration*, 1950–51, especially Professor René Cassin's 'Recent reforms in the government and administration of France' (autumn 1950, pp. 179–88). See also R. S. Abbott and R. Sicard in *American Political Science Review*, June 1950 (on the I.G.A.M.E.); A. Bertrand, 'La présidence du conseil et le secrétariat du gouvernement', *R.D.P.*, 1948, pp. 435 ff.; and Chapman, pp. 119–23.

be difficult to achieve, and it is probably not the life-and-death matter it is often supposed to be (and has been supposed to be for sixty years). Yet it is desirable for many reasons. Firstly, ministerial instability does not really promote genuine parliamentary control. On the contrary, it renders the ministers impotent, and therefore ineffective as representatives of the deputies' will, leaving the bureaucracy as the principal source of policy-making—as M. Monnet's part in shaping French economic and foreign policy makes evident.[8] In the second place, the weakness of government gives too much opportunity to pressure-groups or influential private interests to deflect the course of political action in their own interests. Such pressure is, within limits, legitimate and necessary; but if governmental authority is too weak, the limits are likely to be overstepped. Thirdly, the country still stands urgently in need of a costly programme of economic development. Politically, the alienation from the regime of a quarter of the population, including many of the most energetic, imaginative and devoted citizens, is a grave weakness; the first step in attacking the problem is to carry out a long overdue redistribution of incomes, social reforms, and above all, a large-scale housing programme. But both the economic and the social requirements demand sacrifices which only a strong administration can impose successfully, or distribute equitably. Fourthly, the weakness of the political regime is a liability alike to the action and to the reputation of France in her dealings with the rest of the world.

Various minor improvements might be made in the constitutional machinery. But significant change requires the encouragement of more genuine and more stable parliamentary majorities. If groups are to sacrifice parts of their own programme for this purpose, they need the backing of their electors. Consequently the most important of constitutional reforms is a change in the electoral law to encourage stronger, more coherent, and more lasting coalitions. P.R., as practised after the war, was the worst of systems from this point of view, since it emphasized the isolation of groups which would later have to co-operate in Parliament and in government. *Scrutin d'arrondissement* made the future allies compete at the first stage of the campaign, though they came together on a negative basis in the end. The *apparentement* system used in 1951 allowed allied parties to obtain the mathematical benefits of co-operation without in any way abandoning their separate positions. But such an abandonment is ultimately essential, and if it is to be possible in Parliament, it must be founded on similar co-operation in

---

[8] M. Edgar Faure points out (*loc. cit.*) that ministers always hope to survive into the next cabinet and so ' se sentent davantage solidaires de leurs bureaux respectifs que du collège gouvernementale dans son ensemble '; M. Lecourt agrees (*Le Monde*, 8 April 1953); both he and M. Reynaud complain that ' l'administratif et le corporatif sont maîtres' (*J.O.*, 21 May 1953, p. 2819; 27 May, p. 2849); M. Robert Schuman asserts that when as Foreign minister he was responsible for Morocco and Tunisia, policy there was in fact made by the residents-general in defiance of Paris (*La Nef*, March 1953, pp. 7–9; and see the Epilogue).

the country. The experiment of *scrutin de liste majoritaire* is at least worth trying; and, with an electoral system that gave some hope of positive results, the advantages of conferring on the cabinet the power to dissolve Parliament would be greater, and the dangers less. Dissolution would probably not have the far-reaching results which some claim for it, and if they did occur they might be unfortunate; but the threat of it, by influencing hesitant deputies in critical divisions, might have a limited but useful effect.

It is important to keep governments in office for longer periods. But to reassert their authority while they hold office is even more necessary —rather, the two are but different aspects of the same problem. Governments are short-lived because they are weak, so that everyone speculates on the succession; and weak because, their expectation of life being brief, they are always tempted to avoid dangerous and unpopular choices, and to postpone decisions. Greater stability would make for greater responsibility. Firmer leadership and a clearer policy would increase the government's standing in the country, and consequently—as M. Pinay has shown—its chance of survival.

If a changed electoral system gave greater coherence and an increased sense of common purpose to the groups composing the majority, this problem would already be half solved. The other necessary institutional changes lie less in the strictly constitutional field than in that of parliamentary procedure. To make absolute majorities no longer necessary might make the system work a little more smoothly. But the main need is to bestow greater authority on the government, in the arrangement of parliamentary business, and on the President, in the conduct of debate. These changes, and especially the second, require an alteration of attitude much more than a modification of the rules. Such a new approach might render unnecessary drastic solutions like that of the Gaullists (dividing the Assembly into half a dozen sections, each with substantial legislative powers) or the older and more likely solution of a reversion to the decree-laws of the Third Republic. Without the change of attitude, the procedural reforms would lose most of their usefulness. The basic difficulties are political, not institutional in character.[9]

Because of these underlying factors, democratic governments in France are always likely to enjoy less authority than those in Britain or in the United States. The oscillations of politics are more violent, and sometimes go to greater extremes, than in the other great democracies. Authoritarian rule has been recent enough, and the anti-democratic outlook is still sufficiently widespread, to make resistance to power a

---

[9] M. Faure (*loc. cit*) warns against concentrating on institutional reform: ' En y cherchant des remèdes illusoires on n'y trouve souvent que des alibis commodes . . . C'est affaire non pas seulement de " bonne volonté " mais de volonté '. Cf. the views of MM. Lecourt, Mitterrand, and Mendès-France: *J.O.*, 27 May 1953, p. 2860; 4 June 1953, pp. 2866, 2963–4.

fundamental political reaction among French democrats, to many of whom, indeed, it is the very meaning of democracy itself.

This instinctive mistrust of authority expresses itself in various ways. In the economic sphere it produces that *incivisme* which creates so many difficulties for governments and for reformers. But in other spheres of domestic politics its consequences are more fortunate. It ensures that oppression and injustice never pass unopposed. In day-to-day affairs, the system of administrative justice gives the French citizen better protection against abuse of power by public authorities than the British or American enjoys.[10] In major matters, the ordinary Frenchmen's firm sense of justice and of human dignity have been repeatedly demonstrated, from the upheaval of the Dreyfus case to the treatment of the Jews by their fellow-citizens under the Nazi occupation.

The values and outlook of the liberal democratic tradition are firmly rooted in France. The instinctive suspicion of men in power, despite its dangers, is a safeguard of the liberty of the subject, and a far healthier attitude than that of automatic obedience. The French voter belies his superficial contempt for politics by the extent to which he uses his civic rights—the proportion going to the polls is almost as high as in Britain, and far higher than in the United States. Magistrates remain honest and independent of the executive—on a far lower salary scale than their British confrères. Racial tolerance is in many respects more general and more widespread than it is across the Atlantic, or even across the Channel.

French democracy faces much more immediate external and internal dangers than either Britain or the United States. The barrier of the sea may have lost its military value to-day; it has not lost its psychological importance. The strength of the French Communist party presents a challenge which confronts none of the other traditional democracies. Yet the French have preserved their sense of proportion. The democratic decencies survive: freedom of speech, of assembly, and of organization; impartial judicial treatment even for those whom most Frenchmen regard as public enemies; fair elections. In spite of the difficulties arising from the heritage of the past, the ordinary Frenchman clings with remarkable determination and fidelity to the democratic ideal.

---

[10] Unfortunately this cannot be said of personal liberties. Accused persons can still be detained for long periods without trial.

EPILOGUE

BY 1952 the political pendulum had swung far to the Right; left-wing gains at the municipal elections of April 1953 made the parties speculate on its impending return movement. Thus the year was filled with rumours of political *regroupement*, based on the return of the Socialists to a new left-centre majority. But such possibilities were confused by the question of the European army, which provoked complete opposition between M.R.P. and R.P.F., provided a potential link between the Communists and other parties, and divided the remaining groups from top to bottom.

In January M. René Mayer acquired precarious Gaullist support for his new cabinet by sacrificing M. Schuman and by equivocation on the European question. His fall in May, beaten by an absolute majority in a vote of confidence on his demand for special powers, left the next ministry so defeated free to dissolve the Assembly; perhaps in consequence, the crisis thus opened was the longest on record. But its results were not proportionate to its duration. The R.P.F. deputies (rechristened U.R.A.S.) were conceded their demand for office in return for their support, and the special powers refused to M. Mayer were granted to his successor. In giving hesitant members the excuse needed to convince their electors that such a measure was necessary, the normal function of a crisis in the French system was characteristically fulfilled, and governmental instability contributed somewhat to remedy governmental weakness.[1] But the importance of this crisis lay elsewhere. For the first time the basic choices before the country were brought into open parliamentary discussion.

For this President Auriol was largely responsible. In sending first for MM. Reynaud and Mendès-France, he gave a public platform to the two leaders who had most conspicuously stood aloof from office for its own sake, refusing to join cabinets which lacked either the power or the will to act. Both men ran true to form. M. Reynaud announced that if elected he would not form his ministry until the constitution had been revised and the government granted an unrestricted right to dissolve the Assembly; M. Mendès-France, in a heroic attempt to substitute the British party system for the French, declared that he would choose his ministers without regard to party claims, and would require them to promise not to join the next cabinet.[2] His appeal for a clear-cut choice of priorities, and for sacrifices

---

[1] See Philip Williams, ' Crisis in France: a Political Institution,' *Cambridge Journal*, October 1953, pp. 48–50.

[2] Compare M. Edgar Faure's appeal for new prime ministers to be chosen from the opposition, and against reshuffling the old cabinet in every crisis (*Le Monde*, 27 March

all round, brought a remarkable public response which, in the Assembly, found expression in a revolt of the younger and rank and file deputies against their leaders. This brought him the support of the Socialists, of most M.R.P. back-benchers, of many U.R.A.S. and a few Conservatives; his own Radical party voted solidly for him (in some cases only because he seemed unlikely to succeed).[3] When he failed, the next nominee, M. Bidault, followed his predecessors in refusing to hold the usual consultations with party leaders, and affirmed that he would use to the full his constitutional powers; he was beaten by the narrowest of nicely calculated margins. M. Marie then tried, as in 1948, to reconcile opposites; but his masterly equivocations, and his deliberate appeal to men of tried experience (in contrast to M. Mendès-France's call to youth) exasperated those who hoped for change. M.R.P. hostility defeated him in the vote, and subsequently deterred M. Pinay from standing at all. But the blame for the prolonged crisis was now falling mainly on M.R.P., and when M. Laniel was nominated the party thought it prudent to support him.

The new cabinet differed from its predecessor in including both U.R.A.S. members, and friends of M. Mendès-France such as MM. Faure and Mitterrand, and in excluding the Conservatives closest to M. Pinay.[4] It was utterly divided on every question, and the sequel was to show that measures changed less than men. It had four main preoccupations: constitutional, social, imperial, and European. The constitutional revision bill, voted by the Assembly in July, was introduced in committee in the upper house only in February 1954.[5] The social problem was brought to a head by the government's use of the special powers which it was at once granted. The economy decrees, drafted in August, attacked many vested interests; but those affecting workers and state-employees became known first, and these groups foresaw—in the light of experience—that they would once

---

1953); and M. Teitgen's denunciation of powerless ministries based on the lowest common denominator of the Assembly (*J. O.*, 18 June 1953, p. 3103). Contrast the acceptance of office by both men in the Laniel government.

When M. Mitterrand resigned in September 1953 over the choice of a new resident at Tunis, his was the first individual resignation on a matter of national policy since that of M. Mendès-France in 1945.

[3] The Socialist deputies voted to support him, overruling MM. Mollet and Lussy; M. Pleven was almost his only opponent in U.D.S.R.; he had 25 U.R.A.S. votes, and would have had another dozen but for the unauthorized disclosure that General de Gaulle favoured abstention; the hostile vote of the Progressive deputies provoked some resignations in the country. Out of 31 M.R.P. members who had held office or were chairmen of committees, only 12 voted for him; but 40 of the remaining 58 did so, and his few supporters among the leaders included the chairman of the parliamentary group and the secretary of the party, whose positions kept them in touch with rank and file views.

[4] M. Pinay and his intimate friends did not vote for M. Laniel's financial bill in July.

[5] For its terms see above, pp. 185n., 194, 196 and n., 197n., 217n., 230, 231 and n., 285n.

A reform of parliamentary procedure was under discussion in January; the proposals included fewer and shorter sittings, many fewer night sittings, simpler voting methods, more restricted debates, and the passing of more uncontroversial bills without debate.

again bear the burdens which others evaded. Their wrath provoked a spontaneous strike movement, on a scale unknown since 1936, and remarkable for the absence of organization at the top and of violence below—in marked contrast to the Communist-led strikes of 1947 and 1948. M.R.P. pressure obtained some concessions; almost equally widespread discontent soon became evident in the countryside.[6]

The year saw sensational developments in the imperial sphere also. M. Mendès-France's candidature had given emphatic expression to the universal weariness with the Indo-China war, and to the widespread uneasiness about events in North Africa; and the new cabinet dropped both the minister for Associated States and the resident at Tunis. This mood of the public was further strengthened in June, when the King of Cambodia fled to Siam, and in October, when the Vietnam national congress resolved that free Vietnam would not remain within the French Union in its present form. On the French side the notes of 3 July, the treaty with Laos, and the declarations of President Auriol and of M. Dejean indicated that a new doctrine of the Union's constitutional status was slowly evolving.[7] But the ill-success of 'association' in satisfying nationalist aspirations in the Far East had stiffened the opponents of concession in North Africa. In August the deposition of the Sultan of Morocco, the leader and symbol of local nationalism, caused dissension in the cabinet, and exemplified M. Schuman's recent criticisms of proconsular autonomy [8]; there were indeed serious observers who feared that some influential bureaucratic, military, and even ministerial opponents of a new policy, whose most indiscreet spokesman was Marshal Juin, might in certain circumstances endanger the parliamentary regime itself.[9]

By January 1954 the widespread discontent had not yet been har-

---

[6] In the Assembly this turned rural members against the government and split the Peasant party. In the C.G.A. it brought to a head the long quarrel between the old left-wing leaders and the conservative F.N.S.E.A.; the former, excluded from all influence in their own confederation, set about organizing the poor peasants of Central France against the rich northerners who dominated the F.N.S.E.A.

The government did attempt to tackle such vocal pressure-groups as the beetroot-growers and the *bouilleurs de cru;* but it gave way to the wine-growers in August and to the *bouilleurs* at the end of the year.

[7] On developments in Indo-China see above, p. 296 n. The notes of 3 July offered to negotiate new treaties with the three associated states, and a diplomat, M. Dejean, was appointed high commissioner for the purpose. Article 2 of the Laos treaty (the only one concluded in 1953) described the French Union as ' une association de peuples indépendants et souverains, libres et égaux en droits et en devoirs, où tous les associés mettent en commun leurs moyens pour garantir la défense de l'Union.' President Auriol repeated the formula in opening the third session of the High Council a month later, and in January M. Dejean specifically stated that the Union was to be based on the liberal conception of the preamble to the constitution, and not on the centralizing tendencies of its text. *Le Monde,* 25–26 October 1953; 29–30 November 1953; 19 January 1954.

[8] For M. Schuman's views see above, p. 405 n.; for the demand of MM. Faure and Mitterrand to have their protest recorded in the cabinet minutes, see Pierre Corval, *Terre Humaine,* September-October 1953, p. 24.

[9] Cf. M. Fauvet (*ibid.,* p. 107): ' La démocratie est de nouveau à défendre sur le plan politique.' North Africa, first liberated in the war, now pointed the way to authoritarianism: ' S'il n'est pris garde, la France suivra bientôt.'

nessed, and the Assembly 'reinvested' M. Laniel by an absolute majority.[10] He owed his survival to the absence of an alternative, Right and Left being equally divided on the European issue. The official party leaders, MM. Mollet, Teitgen, and Pleven, favoured a revived Third Force which would conduct a progressive social policy at home, and 'construct Europe' abroad. But the Mendès-France investiture had shown that these leaders might not be followed, and opinion subsequently moved in a different direction. In the Radical party there emerged indeed an active opposition to M. Laniel, which sought to restore the old links with the Socialists. But this opposition was anti-clerical, and was led by M. Daladier, largely composed of the section which had followed him in the past,[11] and almost though not quite identical with the 'anti-European' wing of the party. Among the Socialists, the anti-European tendency came almost to command a majority of the deputies. And the left wing of U.R.A.S., varying in numbers from ten to thirty, might well rally to an anti-European combination of the Left.

Meanwhile M.R.P. was moving rapidly Rightwards. In the summer crisis, half its members had opposed M. Reynaud, three-fifths had voted for M. Mendès-France, and almost all had repudiated M. Marie. But with the formation of the Laniel cabinet the moment of revolt passed. Two M.R.P. leaders took responsibility for the *coup* in Morocco; M.R.P. deputies opposed convoking Parliament during the strikes, and voted against the Socialist motion when the house reassembled; the party steadily supported Conservative candidates for the Presidency of the Republic, and in January expelled a persistent rebel of the Left, M. André Denis.[12] In this hardening of anti-European opinion on the Left, and in the drift of the most pro-European party to the Right, the Communists saw an opportunity. From December

---

[10] Traditionally the cabinet resigns when a new President is installed; but he may ask it to resume office. Some argued that under the new constitution the prime minister required a new mandate from the Assembly. In fact M. Laniel offered his resignation early in January: President Auriol refused it after consulting M. Coty: and the government summoned a special session in which its policy was approved by 319 votes to 249.

[11] In 1949–50 the Right attacked M. Bidault and the Socialists supported him; in 1953 M. Laniel, a Conservative, faced Socialist opposition. But nine Radical deputies gave steady support to *both* governments, and eight opposed both, as against four who were for Bidault and against Laniel, and six for Laniel and against Bidault. Thus the split was between pro- and anti-government wings, rather than between Right and Left as such. Similarly among the few Conservative votes cast for M. Mendès-France, a severe critic of successive cabinets, were those of M. Antier and six of his 'extreme Right,' anti-governmental Peasants.

[12] He was expelled for opposing the European army in joint activities with non-members of M.R.P.; his local federation appealed to the national council, which voted for expulsion by 71 to 30; all members of his local executive resigned in protest, and the workers' *équipe* protested against the decision. He and several sympathizers joined the *Jeune République*.

For comments on the evolution of M.R.P., see two articles in *Le Monde*, 9 and 10–11 January 1954, and François Mauriac, 'Une faillite spirituelle,' *Terre Humaine, loc. cit.*, pp. 6–10.

1953 they offered their votes in the Assembly to anti-European candidates. Older sympathies and aversions played a still greater part. During the presidential election at Versailles, some procedural votes seemed to bring the *Front populaire* to life again, with Radicals, Socialists, and Communists on their feet cheering together. When M. Herriot retired in January, the Socialist M. Le Troquer was elected President of the Assembly against the strongly 'European' M. Pflimlin by an absolute majority which included nearly 120 Radicals and U.R.A.S. as well as the Socialists and Communists; and several new committee chairmen owed their elevation to Communist votes.[13] The possibility of a prime minister being chosen in the same way was no longer outside practical politics. Thus by February 1954 any future regrouping of the Left seemed quite as likely to be 'against Europe' as to be for it; meanwhile the foreign policy quarrel prevented both the potential left-centre majority from emerging, and the existing conservative one from using the power which it still enjoyed.

A number of new constitutional developments deserve attention, in addition to those in the French Union and to the constitutional reform bill itself.[14] These concerned financial procedure, votes of confidence, and the Presidency.

In finance, interest centres on the new moves in the perennial contest between cabinet and Assembly. By the law of 11 July 1953 M. Laniel at last acquired the coveted special powers.[15] Against a government better equipped than any of its predecessors to resist parliamentary pressure, the Assembly disposed of one effective weapon only; it could simply refuse to consider the budget of a given depart-

---

[13] The annual re-election of the committees showed the relative strength of personal and political factors. The pro-European Socialist leaders did not venture to replace the party's representatives on the Foreign Affairs and Defence committees, where 'anti-Europeans' were 5 to 3 and 5 to 2 respectively. M.R.P. removed 3 of their 4 'anti-European' *minoritaires* (counting M. Denis) from their places on these committees. The Republican Independents however chose 3 'Europeans' out of 4; one displaced member, M. Bardoux, regained his committee seat by joining the new Peasant party.

[14] See above, notes 5 and 7.

[15] Article 5 defined matters appropriate for administrative action under the Reynaud law of 1948 to include, *inter alia*, promotion and retirement in state employment and the running of nationalized industries; in so far as the additional powers contravened restrictive provisions of the 1948 law, they were to terminate on the fall of the existing cabinet or, at latest, at the end of 1953. Article 6 checked the costly private members' bills (against which Article 17 of the constitution cannot operate) by empowering the government until 1 October 1953, to limit, suspend, or defer until 1955 the financial application of any legislative provision to increase public expenditure. Article 7 allowed the existing cabinet, until 1 October, to pass decrees on most aspects of social and economic life; these would go into force at once, though they must be laid before the Assembly by 31 December and ratified by it; they might modify or abrogate existing (but not future) legislation, but could not interfere with ' matières réservées à la loi, soit en vertu des dispositions de la Constitution soit par la tradition constitutionnelle républicaine dont les principes ont été réaffirmés dans le préambule de la Constitution, ni à la protection des biens et des libertés publiques ' (cf. *R.D.P.*, 1953, pp. 982–4). Any economies realized under this article would go to finance a new investment fund.

ment, and so force the ministry to bring in a new one. This device was used repeatedly during December 1953, especially with the Education budget; after rejecting it three times the Assembly obtained substantial concessions. Despite such difficulties M. Laniel passed by 4 January almost the entire budget for 1954.[16]

The ' official ' vote of confidence was used twice in 1953; M. Mayer was beaten on his demand for special powers in May, and M. Laniel carried a somewhat equivocal motion on the European army (which very nearly broke up his cabinet) at the end of November. If defeated by an absolute majority, he could have dissolved; but the growing feeling that new elections offered the only hope of an escape from the political deadlock weakened this threat. The unofficial question of confidence was used during the finance debates, though its force too was limited by the assumption that the cabinet must in any case resign after the presidential election. More important and interesting was a development which occurred during the two ministerial crises. In January M. Mayer pledged himself not to put the question of confidence over the European army—an expedient which earned him the Gaullist vote and some scathing criticism.[17] M. Reynaud's refusal to repeat this pledge was attacked amid general applause by M. Cot, who protested that so grave a decision ought not to be taken under the shadow of dissolution; M. Mendès-France met this criticism by a promise not to dissolve if beaten in a vote of confidence on this question.[18] Such renunciations, exacted from would-be premiers as a condition of their election, provide a means by which the meagre powers of the government may be still further whittled away in the future.

President Auriol's handling of his last crisis damaged his parliamentary prestige. After the first ritual offer of the premiership to a Socialist and a Gaullist had been declined, he appealed to these two parties not to make the formation of a government impossible—a form of pressure which they resented. Some supporters of M. Mendès-France regarded his early nomination as an attempt to wreck his chances; and M.R.P. were bitterly critical of the choice of a second Conservative when M. Pinay failed. However unjustified, these complaints helped later to rule out any chance of the President being re-elected by consent—though indeed his widespread popularity in the country had from the beginning made such a development unlikely.[19]

The conventional rules for presidential elections—personal voting,

---

[16] Provisional twelfths were needed only for the Defence and Education budgets; exceptionally, they were calculated on the figures for the coming, not for the past year. Defence expenditure, depending in part on American decisions, is usually voted last.

[17] See Edgar Faure, *Le Monde*, 27 March 1953. For unofficial votes of confidence, see R. Chapus, *R.D.P.*, 1953, p. 976.

[18] *J. O.*, 27 May 1953, pp. 2867, 2870; 3 June 1953, pp. 2910–1.

[19] See above, pp. 169–70. For the circumstances of this crisis see Philip Williams, ' A Real Crisis in France,' *The Fortnightly*, August 1953.

secret ballot, absolute majority—were passed into law in December 1953, despite fears that an absolute majority would be hard to find. The fears were justified. The contest of wills between M. Laniel, with his novel theory that as prime minister he had a quasi-constitutional right to be elected President, and the Radicals who would not vote Conservative and privately hoped for a Radical *arbitrage*, prolonged the election to 13 ballots where in the past two had always sufficed.[20] The new President, M. Coty, was a highly respected Conservative senator of seasoned, Third Republican presidential timber; Gaullists and M.R.P. voted solidly for him; and with his election it seemed that the ideals conceived in the Resistance, and so hopefully voiced at the liberation, had been peacefully laid to rest.

---

[20] The 1924 convention of the American Democratic party took 103 ballots to choose a presidential candidate (who required a two-thirds majority). The French *Congrès du Parlement* represents not one party but a dozen.

On the development of the Presidency see articles in *Le Monde*, 23 and 24 October, and 9, 10, 11, and 12 December 1953; M. Dansette claimed (24 October) that President Auriol had during his term been the most important political personality in the country, unlike any of his predecessors since Thiers.

MAPS

NOTES

1. Communist strength (Map 4) was greatest in the traditionally left-wing regions (Map 2), and not in the industrial areas (Map 1).

2. Gaullist strength (Map 3) was greatest in the northern right-wing regions (Map 2), but not in the southern countryside.

3. In the right-wing, pro-clerical areas coalitions were either for or against the claims of the Church; broad combinations, including both Socialists and Catholics, rarely occurred outside traditionally left-wing regions (Maps 2 and 5).

ACKNOWLEDGMENTS

For permission to use maps as a basis for ours we are indebted to the following:

Presses Universitaires de France for Map 1, from *L'Espace économique français;* Librairie Armand Colin for Maps 3 and 4, from *Géographie des élections françaises* (*Cahier des sciences politiques No.* 27) by François Goguel; Mr. W. Pickles for Map 2, from *Politica*, 1936.

DISTRIBUTION OF INDUSTRY, 1946

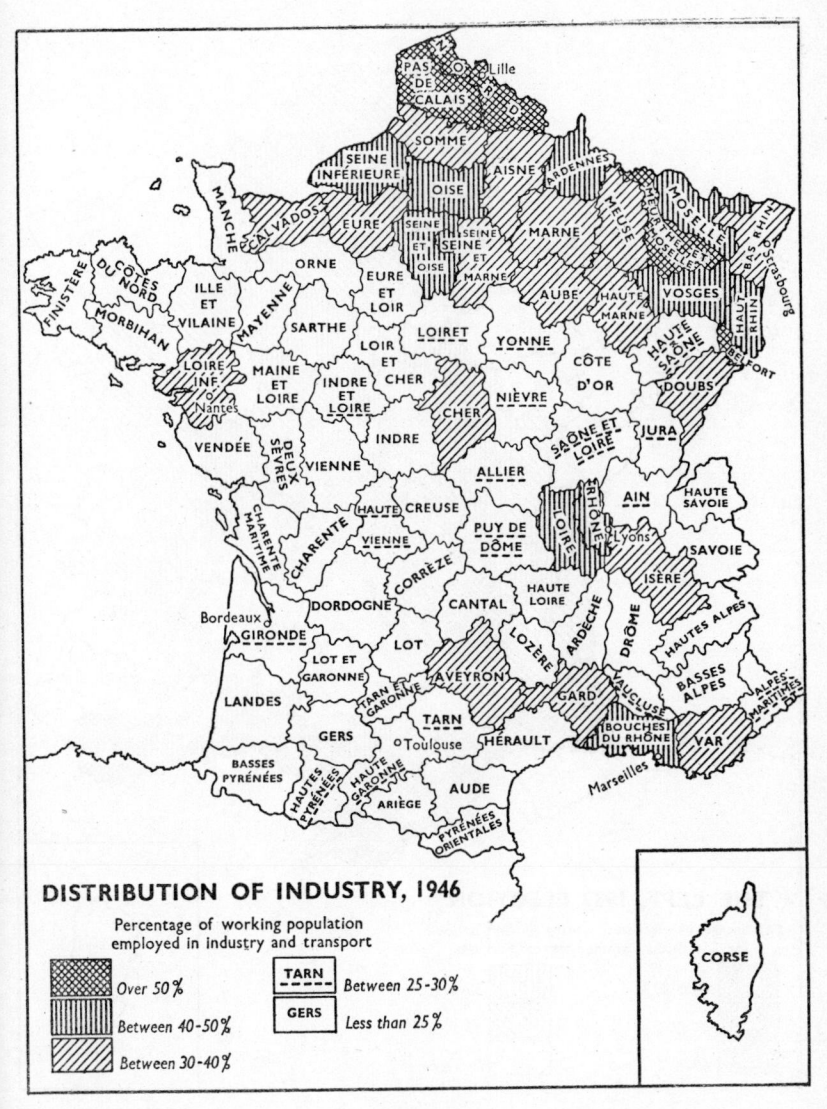

Percentage of working population employed in industry and transport

- Over 50%
- Between 40-50%
- Between 30-40%
- Between 25-30%
- Less than 25%

MAP 1.

THE LEFT, 1932 ELECTION

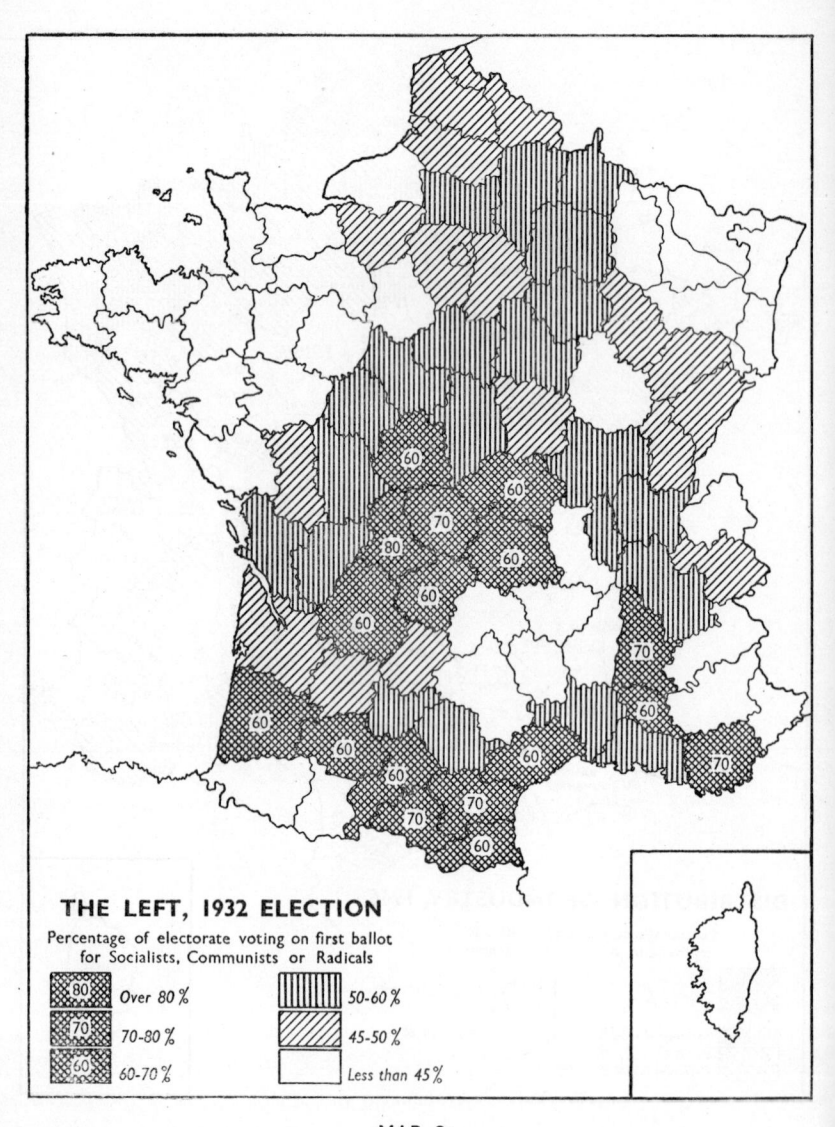

Percentage of electorate voting on first ballot for Socialists, Communists or Radicals

- 80 Over 80%
- 70 70-80%
- 60 60-70%
- 50-60%
- 45-50%
- Less than 45%

MAP 2.

R.P.F. STRENGTH, 1951 ELECTION

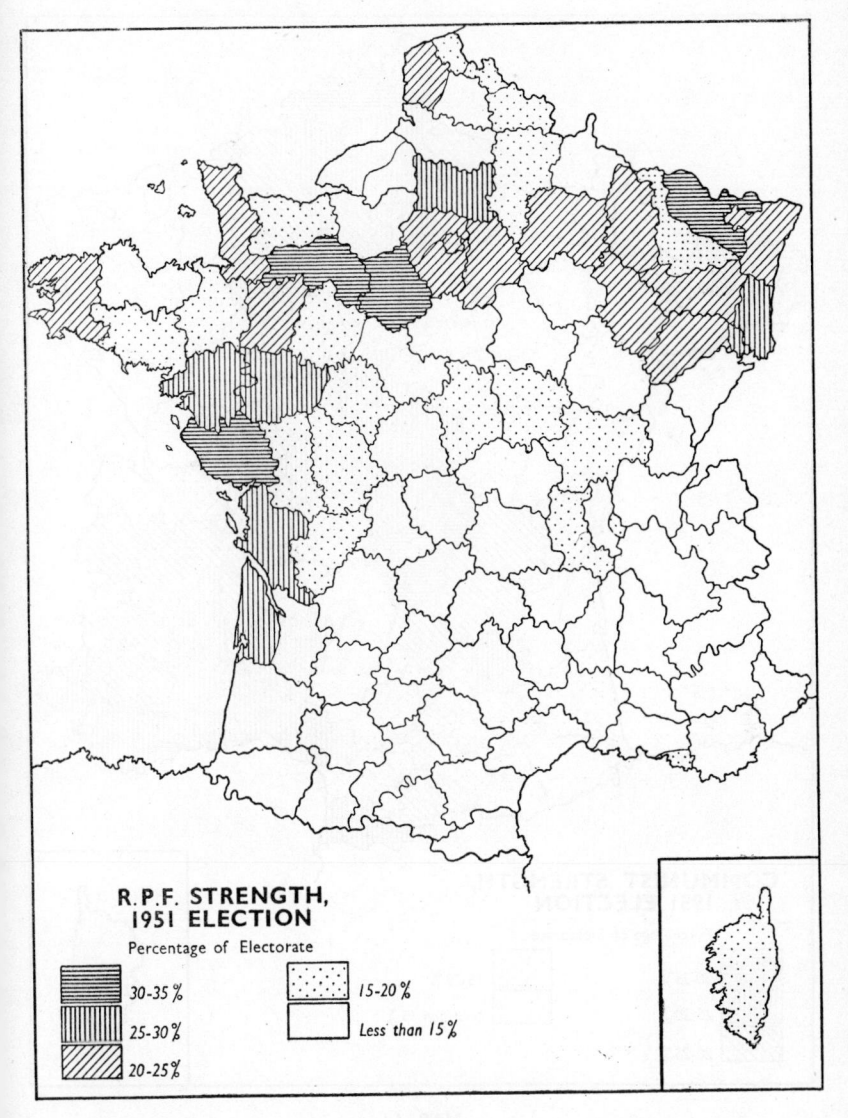

Percentage of Electorate

- 30-35%
- 25-30%
- 20-25%
- 15-20%
- Less than 15%

MAP 3.

COMMUNIST STRENGTH, 1951 ELECTION

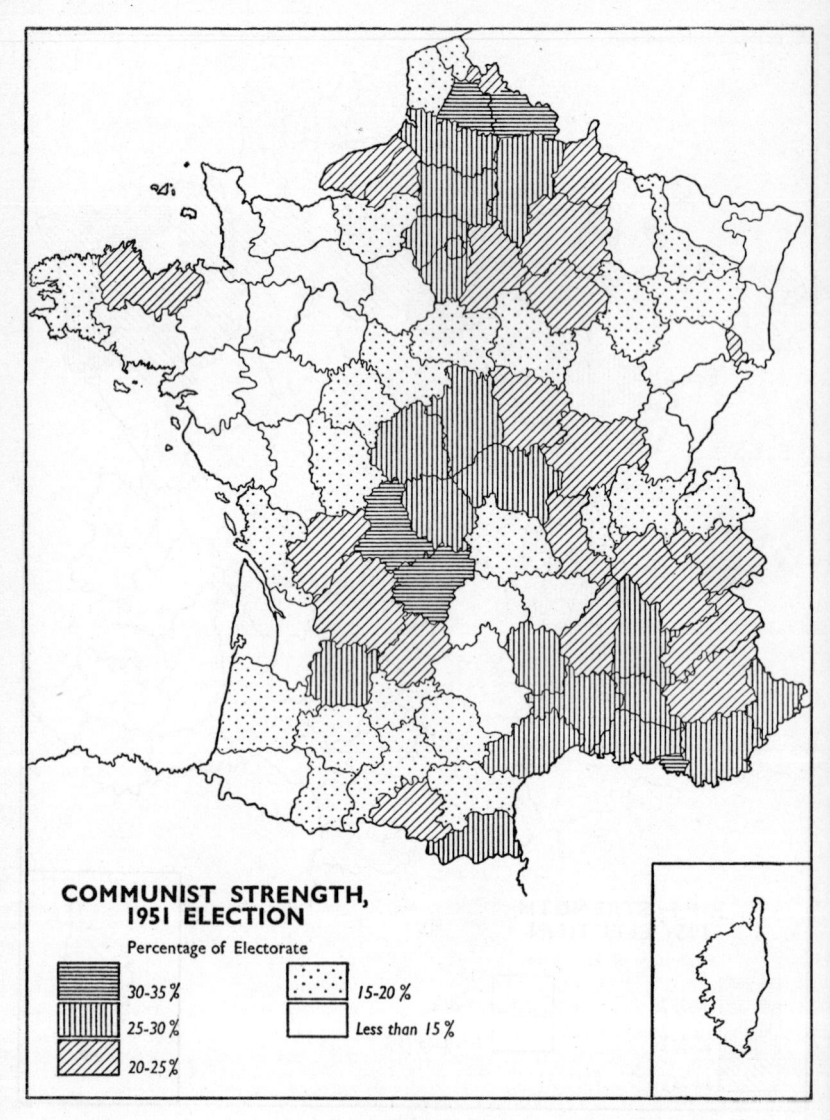

Percentage of Electorate

- 30-35%
- 25-30%
- 20-25%
- 15-20%
- Less than 15%

MAP 4.

ELECTORAL COALITIONS, 1951

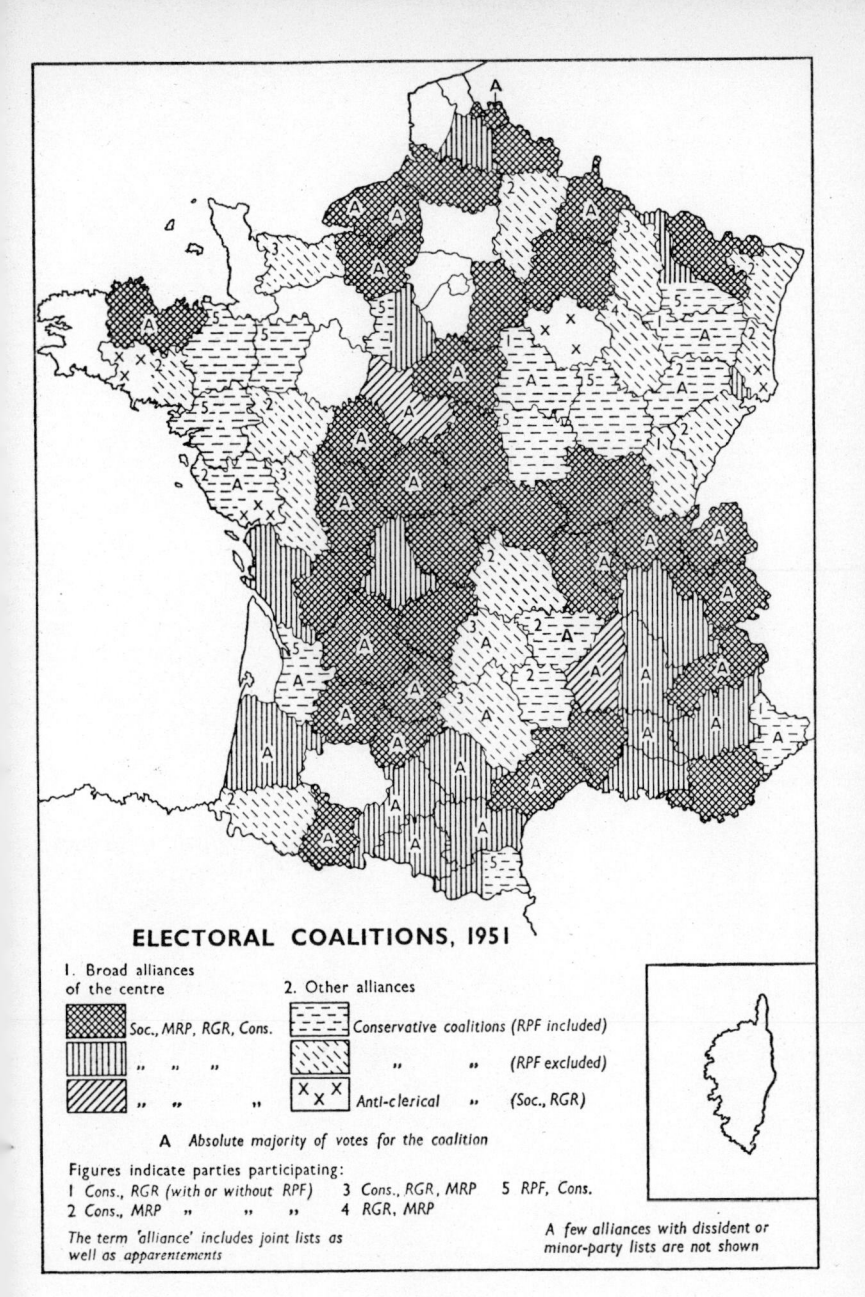

1. Broad alliances of the centre
   - Soc., MRP, RGR, Cons.
   - ,, ,, ,, ,,
   - ,, ,, ,, ,,

2. Other alliances
   - Conservative coalitions (RPF included)
   - ,, ,, (RPF excluded)
   - Anti-clerical ,, (Soc., RGR)

A Absolute majority of votes for the coalition

Figures indicate parties participating:
1 Cons., RGR (with or without RPF)   3 Cons., RGR, MRP   5 RPF, Cons.
2 Cons., MRP   ,,   ,,   ,,   4 RGR, MRP

The term 'alliance' includes joint lists as well as apparentements

A few alliances with dissident or minor-party lists are not shown

MAP 5.

APPENDIX I

CONSTITUTION OF THE FRENCH REPUBLIC[1]

PREAMBLE

ON the morrow of the victory gained by the free peoples over the regimes which have attempted to subjugate and degrade the human person, the French people proclaims anew that every human being, without distinction of race, religion or creed, possesses inalienable and sacred rights. It solemnly reaffirms the rights and freedoms of man and citizen as set forth in the Declaration of Rights of 1789, and the fundamental principles recognized by the laws of the Republic.

In addition, it proclaims as particularly necessary in our time, the following political, economic and social principles:

The law guarantees to women, in all spheres, rights equal to those of men.

Any man, persecuted by reason of his action in favour of freedom, has right of asylum on the territories of the Republic.

It is the duty of all to work, and the right of all to obtain employment. None shall be allowed to suffer wrong in his work or employment, by reason of his origin, his opinions or beliefs.

Every man may protect his rights and interests by trade union action, and belong to the union of his choice.

The right to strike is recognized within the framework of the laws which govern it.

Each worker participates, through his delegates, in the collective settlement of working conditions as well as in the management of enterprises.

Any property, and undertaking, which possesses or acquires the character of a public service or of a monopoly must come under collective ownership.

The nation guarantees, for the individual and for the family, the conditions necessary to their development.

It guarantees to all, especially to children, mothers, and elderly workers, the safeguarding of their health, material security, rest, and leisure. Every human being, who is unable to work on account of his age, of his physical or mental condition, or of the economic situation, is entitled to obtain from the community the appropriate means of existence.

The nation proclaims the solidarity and equality of all Frenchmen in respect of the burdens imposed by national disasters.

The nation guarantees the equal access of children and of adults to education, to professional training, and to general culture. It is the duty of the State to organize free and secular public education at all levels.

The French Republic, faithful to its traditions, conforms to the rules of

---

[1] Translation issued by the French Embassy in London. Articles 96 to 106, which form Chapter XII (Transitional Provisions), have been omitted. The last eight paragraphs of the Preamble are omitted in the Embassy text, and have been translated by the author. A few obvious errors and omissions have been indicated by a footnote where they affect the sense, and rectified directly where they do not.

public international law. It will undertake no war for the object of conquest and will never employ its forces against the liberty of any people.

On condition of reciprocity, France will accept those limitations of her sovereignty which are necessary for the organization and defence of peace.

France, together with the overseas peoples, forms a Union founded upon equality of rights and of duties, without distinction of race or of religion.

The French Union is composed of nations and peoples who pool or coordinate their resources and their efforts to develop their respective civilizations, to increase their well-being, and to ensure their security.

Faithful to her traditional mission, France proposes to lead the peoples of whom she has assumed charge to a state of freedom in which they administer themselves and conduct their own affairs democratically; rejecting any form of colonial rule based upon arbitrary power, she guarantees to all equal access to the public service, and the individual or collective exercise of the rights and liberties proclaimed or confirmed above.

THE INSTITUTIONS OF THE REPUBLIC

CHAPTER 1

SOVEREIGNTY

Article 1. France is a Republic, indivisible, laic, democratic and social.

Article 2. The national emblem is the tricolour flag, blue, white, red, in three vertical strips of equal size.

The National Anthem is the Marseillaise.

The motto of the Republic is: ' Liberty, Equality, Fraternity '.

Its principle is: Government of the people, for the people, and by the people.

Article 3. National sovereignty belongs to the French people.

No section of the people, nor any individual may assume the exercise thereof.

In constitutional matters, it is exercised by the people, through its representatives and by way of referendum.[2]

In all other matters, it is exercised by the people, through its deputies to the National Assembly, elected by universal suffrage equal, direct and secret.

Article 4. Within the conditions laid down by law, all French citizens and nationals of both sexes, who have attained their majority, and enjoy civil and political rights, are electors.

CHAPTER 2

PARLIAMENT

Article 5. Parliament consists of the National Assembly, and of the Council of the Republic.

Article 6. The length of the mandate of each Assembly, its mode of

---

[2] *Par le vote de ses représentants et par le referendum.*

election, the conditions of eligibility, and those governing ineligibility and incompatibility are fixed by law.

However, both Chambers are elected on a territorial basis, the National Assembly by direct universal suffrage, the Council of the Republic by communal and departmental collectivities, by means of indirect universal suffrage. The Council of the Republic is renewable by halves. Nevertheless, the National Assembly can itself, by proportional representation, elect councillors the number of which may not exceed a sixth of the total number of the members of the Council of the Republic.

The number of the members of the Council of the Republic may not be lower than 250, nor may it exceed 320.

Article 7. War cannot be declared without a vote of the National Assembly and the previous advice of the Council of the Republic.

Article 8. Each of the two Chambers is the arbiter of the eligibility of its members and of the validity of their election; they alone can accept their resignation.[3]

Article 9. The National Assembly meets in annual session, in full exercise of its rights, on the second Tuesday in January.

The total length of interruptions of the session cannot exceed four months. Adjournments of meetings lasting more than ten days are considered as interruptions of the session.

The Council of the Republic sits at the same time as the National Assembly.

Article 10. The meetings of the two Chambers are public. Verbatim reports of debates and parliamentary documents are published in the *Journal Officiel*.

Both Chambers may withdraw into secret session.

Article 11. Both Chambers elect their *bureaux* each year at the beginning of the session on a basis of proportional representation of the parties.

When the two Chambers assemble to elect the President of the Republic, their *bureau* is that of the National Assembly.

Article 12. When the Assembly is not sitting, the *bureau*, controlling the acts of the Cabinet, can convene Parliament; it must do so at the request of a third of the deputies or of the President of the Council of Ministers.

Article 13. The National Assembly alone has the right to legislate. It cannot delegate this right.

Article 14. The President of the Council of Ministers and the members of Parliament have the right to initiate laws.

Drafts and projects of laws[4] elaborated by members of the National Assembly are laid before the latter's *bureau*.

Projects of laws[5] elaborated by members of the Council are laid before the latter's *bureau*, and transmitted, without debate, to the *bureau* of the National Assembly. They cannot be received should they entail a decrease in income or an increase in expenditure.

Article 15. The National Assembly examines the projects and proposals,[4] which are submitted to it, through committees of which it fixes the number, the composition and the powers.

---

[3] Embassy text reads '. . . the latter resignation'.
[4] *Projets et propositions de loi*, i.e. government and private members' bills.
[5] *Propositions de loi*.

Article 16.   The draft budget is submitted to the National Assembly.
The draft may contain only strictly financial provisions.
An organic law shall fix the mode of presentation of the budget.
Article 17.   The deputies to the National Assembly have the right to initiate expenditure.
However, no proposal entailing an increase in the expenditure forecast, or additional expenditure may be submitted during the discussion of the budget, of anticipated and supplementary credits.[6]
Article 18.   The National Assembly settles the nation's accounts.
In this matter, it is assisted by the *Cour des Comptes.*
The National Assembly can entrust the *Cour des Comptes* with the carrying out of any investigation or inquiry relating to the expenditure and income of the State, or to the management of the Treasury.
Article 19.   Amnesty can only be granted by a law.
Article 20.   The Council of the Republic examines and gives its opinion upon the projects and proposals of laws[4] voted after a first reading by the National Assembly.
It gives its opinion at the latest two months after the law has been transmitted by the National Assembly. When the budget is under discussion, this time limit may, if necessary, be shortened, so as not to exceed the time used by the National Assembly for its examination and its vote. When the National Assembly has decided upon a rapid procedure, the Council of the Republic gives its opinion in the same time limit as that laid down for the debates of the National Assembly in the latter's rules. The time limits mentioned here are not applied during interruptions of the session. They may be lengthened by decision of the National Assembly.
If the opinion of the Council of the Republic is favourable, or if it has not been given within the time limits set forth in the above paragraph, the law is passed as voted by the National Assembly.
If the opinion of the Council is not favourable, the project or proposal [4] is given a second reading by the National Assembly. It decides finally, and in all sovereignty, upon the amendments proposed by the Council of the Republic, accepting or rejecting them, in whole or in part. In the case of the total or partial rejection of these amendments, the vote following the second reading of the bill, is carried out by public ballot, at an absolute majority of the members of the National Assembly, when the vote on the whole has been taken in the same conditions by the Council of the Republic.
Article 21.   No member of Parliament can be prosecuted, sought out, arrested, detained or judged by reason of opinions expressed or votes cast by him in the exercise of his functions.
Article 22.   No member of Parliament, during the term of his mandate, can be prosecuted or arrested on criminal grounds without the authorization of the Chamber, of which he is a member, except in cases of flagrant offence.[7] The detention or prosecution of a member of Parliament is suspended if the Chamber to which he belongs so demands.
Article 23.   Members of Parliament receive an indemnity, fixed in relation to the remuneration of a category of civil servants.

---

[6] *Crédits prévisionnels et supplémentaires.*
[7] . . . *sauf le cas de flagrant délit,* i.e. unless caught in the act.

Article 24. No one can belong both to the National Assembly and to the Council of the Republic.

Members of Parliament can belong neither to the Economic Council, nor to the Assembly of the French Union.

CHAPTER 3

THE ECONOMIC COUNCIL

Article 25. The Economic Council, whose statute is fixed by law, examines, in an advisory capacity, the projects and proposals of laws [4] which are within its province. These projects are submitted to it by the National Assembly before the latter debates them.

In addition, the Economic Council can be consulted by the Council of Ministers. It must be consulted on the establishment of a national economic plan, the object of which is the full employment of men and the rational use of material resources.

CHAPTER 4

DIPLOMATIC TREATIES

Article 26. Diplomatic treaties regularly ratified and published have force of law, even in cases where they might be contrary to certain internal French laws, without any other legislative measures being necessary for their implementation, than those which would have been necessary to ensure their ratification.

Article 27. Treaties relating to international organization, peace treaties, commercial treaties and treaties which commit the finances of the State, those which concern the personal status and the property rights of French citizens abroad: those which affect internal French laws, and those which carry with them the cession, exchange or acquisition of territory, are final only after having been ratified by a law.

No cession, exchange or acquisition of territory is valid without the consent of the population concerned.

Article 28. Diplomatic treaties which have been ratified and published having priority over internal laws, can be neither abrogated, nor amended, nor suspended without a regular denunciation, notified through diplomatic channels. When it is one of the treaties covered by Article 27, its denunciation must be authorized by the National Assembly, an exception being made in the case of commercial treaties.

CHAPTER 5

THE PRESIDENT OF THE REPUBLIC

Article 29. The President of the Republic is elected by Parliament. He is elected for seven years. He is re-eligible once only.

Article 30. The President of the Republic appoints, in Council of Ministers,[8] the Grand Chancellor of the Legion of Honour, ambassadors and envoys extraordinary, the members of the Higher Council and the Committee of National Defence, rectors of Universities, prefects, the directors of the civil service, generals, and the representatives of the government in overseas territories.

Article 31. The President of the Republic is kept informed of international negotiations. He signs and ratifies treaties.

The President of the Republic accredits ambassadors and envoys extraordinary to foreign powers; ambassadors and envoys extraordinary are accredited to him.

Article 32. The President of the Republic presides over the Council of Ministers.

He has prepared and preserves minutes of the meetings.

Article 33. The President of the Republic presides over, with the same powers, the Higher Council and the Committee of National Defence, and assumes the title of Head of the Armies.

Article 34. The President of the Republic presides over the Supreme Council of Justice.

Article 35. The President of the Republic exercises the right of reprieve in the Supreme Council of Justice.

Article 36. The President of the Republic promulgates laws within ten days of their transmission to the government after their final adoption. This time limit is reduced to five days in cases of urgency declared by the National Assembly.

Within the time limit fixed for its promulgation, the President of the Republic can, by a motivated message stating his grounds, ask the two Chambers for another debate, which cannot be refused.

Failing the promulgation of laws by the President of the Republic within the time limits prescribed by this Constitution, the promulgation is carried out by the President of the National Assembly.

Article 37. The President of the Republic communicates with the Parliament by means of messages to the National Assembly.

Article 38. All the acts of the President of the Republic must be countersigned by the President of the Council of Ministers and by a Minister.

Article 39. Not more than thirty days and not less than fifteen days before the expiry of the powers of the President of the Republic, Parliament[9] proceeds to elect a new President.

Article 40. If, in application of the preceding article, the election has to take place during a period when the National Assembly is dissolved in conformity with Article 51, the powers of the President of the Republic are extended until the election of the new President. Parliament proceeds to elect this new President within ten days of the election of the new National Assembly.

In this case, the appointment of the President of the Council of Ministers takes place within the fifteen days following the election of the new President of the Republic.

Article 41. In case of prevention, duly recognized by a vote of Parliament, in case the Presidency is vacated by death, resignation or any other reason,

---

[8] Insert ' members of the *Conseil d'État* ' (omitted in Embassy text).
[9] Embassy text wrongly reads ' the National Assembly '.

the President of the National Assembly assumes temporarily the function of the President of the Republic. He himself is replaced by a Vice-President.

The new President of the Republic is elected within ten days, except in cases where the provisions of the preceding article apply.

Article 42. The President of the Republic is responsible only in cases of high treason. He can be accused by the National Assembly and sent before the High Court of Justice in the conditions set forth in Article 57 hereunder.

Article 43. The duties of the President of the Republic are incompatible with any other public function.

Article 44. Members of families which have reigned over France are ineligible for the Presidency of the Republic.

CHAPTER 6

THE COUNCIL OF MINISTERS

Article 45. At the beginning of each legislature, the President of the Republic, after the usual consultations, appoints the President of the Council.

The latter submits to the National Assembly the programme and the policy of the Cabinet which he intends to constitute.

The President of the Council and the Ministers can be appointed only after the President of the Council has been granted the confidence of the Assembly by public vote and an absolute majority of the deputies, except when a case of *force majeure* prevents the meeting of the National Assembly.

The same applies during the course of a legislature, if the post is vacated by death, resignation or any other reason, except in cases stated in Article 52 below.

Article 51 does not apply in the case of a Cabinet crisis occurring within fifteen days of the appointment of the Ministers.

Article 46. The President of the Council and the Ministers chosen by him are appointed by a decree of the President of the Republic.

Article 47. The President of the Council of Ministers ensures the carrying out of laws.

He makes appointments to all civilian and military posts, excepting those mentioned in Articles 30, 46 and 84.

The President of the Council controls the armed forces and co-ordinates the work of national defence.

The acts of the President of the Council of Ministers mentioned in the present article are countersigned by the Ministers concerned.

Article 48. The Ministers are collectively responsible to the National Assembly for the general policy of the Cabinet, and individually for their personal actions.

They are not responsible before the Council of the Republic.

Article 49. The question of confidence cannot be raised except after a discussion by the Council of Ministers; it can be raised only by the President of the Council.

A vote on the question of confidence can take place only one clear day after the question has been put to the Assembly. It must be a public vote.

Confidence cannot be refused to the Cabinet except by an absolute majority of the deputies to the Assembly.

This refusal entails the collective resignation of the Cabinet.

Article 50. A vote of censure by the National Assembly entails the collective resignation of the Cabinet.

Such a vote can take place only one clear day after the motion has been tabled. It must be a public vote.

A vote of censure can be adopted only by an absolute majority of the deputies to the Assembly.

Article 51. If, during a period of eighteen months, two Cabinet crises occur under the conditions set forth in Articles 49 and 50, the dissolution of the National Assembly may be decided upon by the Council of Ministers, after consultation with the President of the Assembly. The dissolution will be pronounced, in conformity with this decision, by a decree of the President of the Republic.

The provisions of the above paragraph are applicable only at the end of the first eighteen months of the legislature.

Article 52. In case of dissolution, the Cabinet, with the exception of the President of the Council and of the Minister of the Interior, remains in office to attend to current affairs.

The President of the Republic appoints the President of the National Assembly as President of the Council. The latter appoints the new Minister of the Interior in agreement with the *bureau* of the National Assembly. He appoints as Ministers of State members of political groups not represented in the government.

General elections take place at least twenty days, and thirty days at most, after the dissolution.

The National Assembly in full exercise of its rights assembles on the third Thursday following its election.

Article 53. The Ministers have access to both Chambers and to their committees.

They must be heard when they so request.

They may be assisted in debates before the Chambers by commissioners appointed by decree.

Article 54. The President of the Council of Ministers may delegate his powers to a Minister.

Article 55. If the Presidency of the Council of Ministers is vacated by death or by any other cause, the Council of Ministers charges one of its members to assume provisionally the Presidency of the Council.

CHAPTER 7

THE RESPONSIBILITY OF MINISTERS UNDER THE PENAL CODE

Article 56. Ministers are responsible under the penal code for the crimes and offences committed by them in the exercise of their functions.

Article 57. Ministers can be accused by the National Assembly and sent before the High Court of Justice.

The National Assembly decides by secret vote and by an absolute majority of its members, with the exception of those who might be called upon to take part in the prosecution, the instruction or the judgment of the case.

Article 58. The High Court of Justice is elected by the National Assembly at the beginning of each legislature.

Article 59. The organization of the High Court of Justice and the procedure adopted are fixed by a special law.

CHAPTER 8

THE FRENCH UNION

Section I

Principles

Article 60. The French Union consists, on the one hand, of the French Republic, which comprises Metropolitan France, the overseas *départements* and territories, and on the other hand, of the associated territories and States.

Article 61. The position of the States associated with the French Union is settled for each of them by the act which defines their relations with France.

Article 62. The members of the French Union pool all the means at their disposal, to guarantee the protection of the whole of the Union. The government of the Republic assumes the co-ordination of these means and the control of the policy apt to prepare and ensure this protection.

Section II

Organization

Article 63. The central organisms of the French Union are: the Presidency, the High Council and the Assembly.

Article 64. The President of the French Republic is the President of the French Union, of which he represents the permanent interests.

Article 65. The High Council of the French Union is composed—under the presidency of the President of the Union—of a delegation of the French Government and of the representation which each of the associated States has the power of accrediting to the President of the Union.

Its function is to assist the government in the general management of the Union.

Article 66. The Assembly of the French Union consists half of members representing Metropolitan France, and half of members representing the overseas *départements* and territories and the associated States.

An organic law will determine in which conditions the different sections of the population can be represented.

Article 67. The members of the Assembly of the Union are elected by the territorial assemblies as far as the overseas *départements* and territories are concerned; they are elected, as far as Metropolitan France is concerned, two-thirds by members of the National Assembly representing the mother country and one-third by the members of the Council of the Republic representing the mother country.

Article 68. The associated States can designate delegates to the Assembly of the Union within limits and conditions defined by a law and an internal act of each State.

Article 69. The President of the French Union convenes the Assembly of the French Union and closes its sessions. He must convene it when so requested by half its members.

The Assembly of the French Union cannot sit during the interruption of the sessions of Parliament.

Article 70. The rules of Articles 8, 10, 21, 22 and 23 are applicable to the Assembly of the French Union in the same conditions as in the case of the Council of the Republic.

Article 71. The Assembly of the French Union deliberates upon the projects or proposals [4] which are submitted to it, for advice, by the National Assembly, or the government of the French Republic, or the governments of the associated States.

The Assembly is qualified to pronounce itself on motions submitted by one of its members, and, if it decides to consider them, to charge its *bureau* to transmit them to the National Assembly. It can make proposals to the French government and High Council of the French Union.

To be receivable, the motions mentioned in the preceding paragraph must relate to legislation concerning overseas territories.

Article 72. In overseas territories, legislative power belongs to Parliament, in matters of criminal law, the organization of public freedoms and political and administrative organization.

In all other matters, French law is applicable in overseas territories only under special provisions, or if it has been extended by decree to overseas territories after consultation of the Assembly of the Union.

In addition, by derogation from Article 13, special provisions for each territory can be decreed in Council of Ministers[10] by the President of the Republic after previous consultation of the Assembly of the Union.

Section III

OVERSEAS DEPARTMENTS AND TERRITORIES

Article 73. The legislative system of the overseas *départements* is the same as that of the metropolitan *départements*, excepting in certain cases defined by law.

Article 74. The overseas territories are endowed with a special statute, taking into account their particular interests within the framework of the general interests of the Republic.

This statute and the internal organization of each overseas territory or of each group of territories are determined by the law after consultation with the Assembly of the French Union and of the territorial Assemblies.

Article 75. The respective statutes of the members of the Republic and of the French Union are liable to evolve.

Statutory amendments and the passage from one category to another within the framework set forth in Article 60, can only be brought about by a law voted by Parliament, following consultation of the territorial Assemblies and of the Assembly of the Union.

Article 76. The representative of the government in each territory or

---

[10] Embassy text omits ' of Ministers '.

group of territories is the trustee of the powers of the Republic. He is the head of the administration of the territory.

He is responsible for his action before the government.

Article 77. An elected Assembly is instituted in each territory. The electoral procedure, the composition and the powers of this Assembly are fixed by law.

Article 78. In groups of territories, the management of common interests is entrusted to an Assembly consisting of members elected by the territorial Assemblies. Its composition and its powers are fixed by law.

Article 79. The overseas territories elect representatives to the National Assembly and to the Council of the Republic in conditions fixed by law.

Article 80. All nationals of overseas territories are citizens, on the same basis as French nationals of the mother country or of overseas territories. Special laws shall determine the conditions in which they will exercise their rights as citizens.

Article 81. All French citizens and nationals of the French Union are citizens of the French Union, a title which ensures for them the enjoyment of the rights and freedoms guaranteed by the Preamble to the present Constitution.

Article 82. Citizens who do not enjoy French civilian status preserve their personal status so long as they do not renounce it.

This status cannot, in any case, constitute a ground for refusing or restricting the rights and liberties attached to French citizenship.

CHAPTER 9

THE SUPREME COUNCIL OF JUSTICE

Article 83. The Supreme Council of Justice (Conseil Supérieur de la Magistrature) is composed of fourteen members:

The President of the Republic, Chairman;

The Keeper of the Seals, Minister of Justice, Vice-Chairman;

Six persons elected for six years by the National Assembly, by a two-thirds majority, outside its members, six deputy-members being elected in the same conditions;

Six persons designated as follows:

Four members of the magistrature elected for six years, representing each category of the magistrature, in the conditions laid down by law, four deputies being elected in the same conditions;

Two members appointed for six years by the President of the Republic outside Parliament and the magistrature, but within the judicial profession, two deputies being appointed in the same conditions;

The decisions of the Supreme Council of Justice are made by a majority vote. When votes are equally divided, that of the President prevails.

Article 84. The President of the Republic appoints the magistrates, with the exception of the public prosecutors, upon presentation by the Supreme Council of Justice.[11]

---

[11] Embassy text wrongly omits comma after ' prosecutors '.

The Supreme Council of Justice ensures, in accordance with the law, the discipline of these magistrates, their independence and the administration of the tribunals.

These magistrates are irremovable.[12]

CHAPTER 10
TERRITORIAL COLLECTIVITIES

Article 85. The French Republic, one and indivisible, recognizes the existence of territorial collectivities.

These collectivities are the communes and *départements,* the overseas territories.

Article 86. The framework, the scope, the eventual regrouping and organization of the communes and *départements,* and territories overseas, are fixed by law.

Article 87. The territorial collectivities are administered freely by councils elected by universal suffrage.

The carrying out of the decisions of these councils is ensured by their mayor or their president.

Article 88. The co-ordination of the activity of civil servants, the representation of the national interest and the administrative control of the territorial collectivities are assured, on the departmental level, by government delegates appointed by the Council of Ministers.

Article 89. Organic laws shall extend departmental and communal freedoms; they may[13] provide for certain large towns, administrative rules and structures different from those of small communes, and include special provisions for certain *départements;* they shall fix the conditions of implementation of Articles 85 to 88 above.

Laws shall also fix the conditions in which shall function the local departments of the central administration, in order to bring the administration and the administered closer together.

CHAPTER 11
THE REVISION OF THE CONSTITUTION

Article 90. A revision may take place in the following ways:

Such a revision must be decided upon by a resolution adopted by an absolute majority of the members of the National Assembly.

The resolution makes clear the object of the revision.

It is submitted, after a minimum delay of three months, for a second reading, in the same conditions as for the first, unless the Council of the Republic, informed by the National Assembly, has adopted the same resolution by an absolute majority.

After this second reading, the National Assembly elaborates a draft bill for the amendment of the Constitution. This draft is submitted to Parliament and voted by a majority and in the manner laid down for an ordinary law.

---

[12] *Les magistrats du siège,* mistranslated in Embassy text as ' The magistrates '. See above, pp. 302-3.

[13] Embassy text wrongly reads ' shall '.

It is submitted to a referendum, unless it has been adopted at a second reading by the National Assembly, by a two-thirds majority, or has been voted by a three-fifths majority of both Chambers.

The bill is promulgated by the President of the Republic as constitutional law, within eight days of its adoption.

No constitutional amendment concerning the existence of the Council of the Republic may be effected without the agreement of this Council or without recourse to a referendum.[14]

Article 91. The Constitutional Committee is presided over by the President of the Republic.

It comprises the President of the National Assembly, the President of the Council of the Republic, seven members elected by the National Assembly at the beginning of each annual session, by proportional representation of the political groups, and chosen outside the ranks of its members, and three members elected in the same conditions by the Council of the Republic.

The Constitutional Committee sees whether the laws voted by the National Assembly entail a revision of the Constitution.

Article 92. Within the delay of promulgation of the law, the Committee is informed, by a joint request from the President of the Republic and the President of the Council of the Republic, the Council having reached a decision by a majority of its component members.

The Committee examines the law, endeavours to bring about an agreement between the National Assembly and the Council of the Republic, and if it does not succeed, it reaches a decision within five days of its intervention.[15] In cases of urgency, this delay is brought down to two days.

It is empowered to decide only on matters relating to the possibility of revision of Chapters 1 to 10 of the present Constitution.

Article 93. Any law which, in the opinion of the Committee, implies a revision of the Constitution, is returned to the National Assembly for another reading.

If Parliament confirms its first decision, the law cannot be promulgated before the Constitution has been revised in the manner set forth in Article 90.

If the law is considered to be in conformity with the provisions of Chapters 1 to 10 of the present Constitution, it is promulgated within the time limit fixed by Article 86, the latter being lengthened by the delays provided for in Article 92 above.

Article 94. If the whole of Metropolitan France or part of it be occupied by foreign troops, no procedure of revision may be initiated or pursued.

Article 95. The republican form of government cannot be the object of a proposed revision.

---

[14] Embassy text wrongly omits 'existence of the'. See above, p. 288n.
[15] . . . *cinq jours de sa saisine*, i.e. five days of being *called upon* to act.

APPENDIX II

THE PREMIERS

Premier and Party (a)		Investiture Vote	Date Ministry formed	resigned (b)	Ministers: Com.	Soc.	MRP	RGR	Cons.	Total (c)
1. De Gaulle	N.P.	—	10. 9.44	13.11.45	2	4	3	3	1	22

GENERAL ELECTION, 21 OCTOBER 1945

2. De Gaulle	N.P.	555	21.11.45	22. 1.46	5	5	5	1	1	22
3. Gouin	Soc.	497	26. 1.46	11. 6.46	6	7	6	—	—	20

GENERAL ELECTION, 2 JUNE 1946

| 4. Bidault | M.R.P. | 384 | 23. 6.46 | 28.11.46 | 7 | 6 | 8 | 1 | — | 23 |

GENERAL ELECTION, 10 NOVEMBER 1946

(Thorez	Com.	259	4.12.46)							
(Bidault	M.R.P.	240	5.12.46)							
5. Blum	Soc.	575	16.12.46	16. 1.47	—	17	—	—	—	17
6. Ramadier	Soc.	549	22. 1.47		5	9	5	5	2	26
			9. 5.47	22.10.47	—	11	6	5	2	24
7. Ramadier	Soc.	(d)	22.10.47	19.11.47	—	6	3	2	1	12
(Blum	Soc.	300	21.11.47)							
8. Schuman	M.R.P.	412	24.11.47	19. 7.48	—	5	6	3	1	15
9. Marie	Rad.	352	26. 7.48	28. 8.48	—	6	6	5	2	19
10. Schuman	M.R.P.	322	5. 9.48	7. 9.48	—	4	6	4	1	15
11. Queuille	Rad.	351	11. 9.48	6.10.49	—	5	5	4	1	15
Moch	Soc.	311	(13.10.49)							
R. Mayer	Rad.	341	(20.10.49)							
12. Bidault	M.R.P.	367	29.10.49		—	5	6	5	2	18
			7. 2.50	24. 6.50	—	—	8	7	3	18
13. Queuille	Rad.	363	2. 7.50	4. 7.50	—	—	9	9	3	21
14. Pleven	U.D.S.R.	373	12. 7.50	28. 2.51	—	5	6	8	3	22
(Mollet	Soc.	286	6. 3.51)							
15. Queuille	Rad.	359	10. 3.51	10. 7.51	—	5	7	7	3	22

GENERAL ELECTION, 17 JUNE 1951

(R. Mayer	Rad.	241	24. 7.51)							
(Petsche	Cons.	281	2. 8.51)							
16. Pleven	U.D.S.R.	391	10. 8.51	7. 1.52	—	—	7	9	7	23
17. Faure	Rad.	401	20. 1.52	29. 2.52	—	—	8	11	7	26
18. Pinay	Cons.	324	8. 3.52	23.12.52	—	—	4	7	6	17
19. R. Mayer	Rad.	389	8. 1.53	21. 5.53	—	—	6	9	8	23
(Reynaud	Cons.	276	28. 5.53)							
(Mendès-France	Rad.	301	5. 6.53)							
(Bidault	M.R.P.	313	11. 6.53)							
(Marie	Rad.	272	19. 6.53)							
20. Laniel	Cons.	398	27. 6.53		—	—	5	6	8	22(e)

(a) Unsuccessful candidates shown in brackets.
(b) Date of investiture shown in brackets when no government was formed.
(c) Non-party ministers sat in the first four cabinets (9, 5, 1, and 1 respectively).
(d) All ministers resigned except the premier, who did not seek a new investiture. Treated in the text as a separate ministry.
(e) Included three Gaullists.

APPENDIX IV

THE OPPOSITION

PRINCIPAL VOTES IN THE ASSEMBLY, 1945–53

Date	P.M.	Subject	Gov.	Opp.	Abst.	Com.	Soc.	M.R.P.	Rad.	U.D.S.R.	Cons.	R.I.	Peas.	P.R.L.	A.R.	I.O.M.	Others
1945 13 Nov.	De Gaulle	Investiture	555	0	87	1	3	3	—	—	1	—	—	1	—	—	—
1946 23 Jan.	Gouin	"	497	55	—	161	—	—	—	—	62[24]	20[13]	7[1]	35[35]	—	—	—
19 June	Bidault	"	384	0	161	—	—	—	—	—	—	—	—	—	—	—	—
	National Assembly: Party Strengths																24
4 Dec.	Thorez	Investiture	259	2	351	182	102	166	43	26	74	29	7	38	—	—	21
5 "	Bidault	"	240	24	350	1	25[2]	165	42	26	73	29	6	38	—	—	17
1947 12 "	Blum	"	575	8	33	—	101	1	41[12]	26[12]	6	6	—	—	—	—	6
14 Jan.	Ramadier	"	549	0	66	—	2	2	4	5	22[2]	10[2]	—	12[2]	—	—	7
4 May	"	Wages policy	360	186	63	—	1	1	2	1	54	6	1	38	—	—	11[3]
21 Nov.	Schuman	Investiture (C)	360	277	33	—	1	—	3	3	49	16[2]	7	31	—	—	6
22 "	"	"	412	184	18	183[83]	1	3	24[13]	21[19]	77[1]	16[10]	9[2]	35[34]	17[15]	—	7
1948 5 Jan.	"	Mayer levy	307	274	24	182[82]	1	—	2	2	7	6	—	1	—	—	11[3]
19 July	Marie	Military budget (C)	214	295	95	183[83]	—	1	10[6]	18[12]	77[2]	17[12]	10[10]	34[34]	16[6]	—	2[2]
24 "	Schuman	Investiture	352	190	61	183[83]	100[100]	9[1]	12[1]	15[13]	67	6	12	34	18	—	2[2]
31 Aug.	"	Composition of cabinet	322	185	100	183[83]	—	—	5	13	30[6]	3	—	15	12[2]	—	9[1]
7 Sep.	Queuille	"	289	295	24	183[83]	—	—	12	21	61	10	9	32[32]	11	7[2]	15
10 "		Investiture	351	196	61	181[81]	—	3	5	22[2]	79[3]	20[11]	9	17[2]	18[17]	7	11
										16[6]	39[3]	9	1		12[7]	5	8[3]
1949 26 July	"	Atlantic pact	395	189	22	182[82]	1	2[2]	4	R.P.F.	41	—	—	1	U.D.I.	—	8
29 "	"	Wage bonus	289	286	16	182[82]	1	14[3]	12[8]	11[11]	66[52]	20[12]	13[11]	30[28]	2[1]	13	54
13 Oct.	Moch	Investiture	311	223	70	182[82]	—	13[1]	11[1]	—	24[84]	13[1]	12[5]	28[9]	3[3]	2[2]	55
20 "	R. Mayer	"	341	183	75	181[81]	—	—	5	—	23[23]	5	—	28	3	—	7
27 "	Bidault	"	367	183	55	181[81]	—	13[1]	9[1]	3[2]	20	—	—	18	—	—	3[1]
1950 24 Dec.	"	Budget (C)	303	297	12	181[81]	—	3	23[10]	—	23	21[20]	15[15]	30[30]	4[4]	—	7[4]
7 Feb.	"	Composition of cabinet	230	186	194	181[81]	98	—	11[1]	3[3]	22[2]	14	17	29	—	—	7
24 June	"	Loi des maxima (C)	195	352	24	181[81]	98[98]	—	13[8]	—	60	6[5]	9[2]	26[20]	2	2[2]	6[4]
30 "	Queuille	Investiture	363	208	39	181[81]	—	14[2]	3[1]	2	49[34]	4	5	13[1]	—	2[1]	11[9]
4 July	"	Composition of cabinet	221	334	60	181[81]	—	44[10]	4[1]	4	17[1]	6[6]	1	11[8]	2[1]	—	11[8]
11 "	Pleven	Investiture	373	185	54	182[82]	—	1	3	—	19[2]	4	15	16	1	3[2]	13[8]
1951 8 Jan.	"	Rearmament budget	333	181	92	175[75]	—	—	10	10[9]	20	5	9[3]	25	2[1]	1	13[3]
28 Feb.	Queuille	One-ballot electoral law (C)(N)	[262]	295	54]	177[76]	—	21[1]	37[34]	3	53[1]	11	15	20[17]	—	1[1]	16[12]
6 Mar.	Mollet	Investiture	286	259	68	177[76]	1	—	17[6]	—	50[9]	21[8]	9[3]	27[27]	5[1]	—	9[1]
9 "	Queuille	"	359	205	49	177[77]	—	—	4	5[4]	77[6]	22[12]	23[3]	25[1]	—	1	9[5]
27 Apr.	"	Electoral law (C)	308	270	34	177[77]	16[10]	7[1]	42	3	33[1]	4	4	21[20]	—	10	18[11]
	End of National Assembly: Party Strengths						99	144	18[13]	13	29[27]	6[5]	2[1]	27	—	12	25
						177			46		82	25	23		7		

438

Date	New National Assembly: Party Strengths			103	107	86	75	16	121	96	R.I. 53	Peas. 43	P.U.S.	A.R.S.	9	13
1951	24 July	R. Mayer	Investiture	(N)	241	105	272	103[03]	106	—	12	—	120	79[1]	36	42[1]	—	—	2[1]
	2 Aug.	Petsche	,,		281	101	241	101[01]	—	—	10	2	118[1]	—	1	1	—	—	1
	8 ,,	Pleven	,,		391	102	130	101[01]	—	—	55[46]	—	—	—	—	1	—	—	2
	10 Sep.	,,	Loi Barangé (Church schools)		[313	255	45[1]	101[01]	—	70[81]	3[1]	2[2]	114[14]	4	2	—	—	10[10]	11[7]
	20 ,,	,,	Sliding scale for wages: Gov. opposed		191	402	17	101[01]	—	—	3[1]	—	116[16]	25[21]	9[8]	1	—	—	—
	11 Dec.	,,	'Schuman Plan'		376	240	6	101[01]	1	1	12[9]	1	117[17]	28[3]	5[1]	2	—	1	—
1952	7 Jan.	,,	Economies on railways	(C)	243	341	40	101[01]	106[06]	15[4]	—	—	117	2	—	1	15[13]	—	1[1]
	17 ,,	Faure	Investiture		401	101	120	101[01]	20[20]	7[8]	11[10]	1[1]	114[13]	38[6]	13[12]	3[2]	23	1	1[1]
	19 Feb.	,,	Tax increases	(C)	327	287	7	101[01]	—	14[4]	35[28]	2[1]	115[15]	71[59]	38	10	—	1	1[1]
	27 ,,	,,	Investiture	(C)	283	309	30	101[01]	—	4	—	—	85	—	—	—	22[21]	—	—
	6 Mar.	Pinay	Investiture	(C)	324	206	89	100[00]	106[06]	64[1]	5[1]	2	80[2]	—	—	3[3]	23	—	—
	8 Apr.	,,	Amnesty for tax frauds	(C)	259	210	147	99[9]	106[06]	36[8]	—	—	80[4]	—	—	11	—	—	—
	3 June	,,	Sliding scale for wages	(C)	295	253	69	101[01]	106[06]	16	1	3	84[8]	6[2]	1	24[17]	—	—	3[1]
	9 Dec.	,,	Budget		300	291	28	101[01]	104[04]	—	5	—	21	—	5	6	2	—	2[1]
1953	7 Jan.	R. Mayer	Investiture		389	205	24	100[00]	104[04]	15	7[4]	5	76[7]	20	11[6]	—	4	12[12]	—
	21 May	,,	Special powers: economies	(C)	244	328	48	100[00]	105[05]	49[14]	28[13]	8[3]	41[1]	53[25]	3	—	18[13]	1	3[2]
	28 ,,	Reynaud	Investiture		276	235	109	100[00]	105[05]	—	—	—	—	10	—	—	—	—	—
	5 June	Mendès-France	,,		301	119	202	100[00]	105[05]	35[2]	6	4	55[2]	117[14]	50	36[14]	31	—	4[1]
	11 ,,	Bidault	,,		313	228	81	100[00]	105[05]	73	47[18]	13	16[1]	25[3]	14	9[3]	2	—	3[1]
	19 ,,	Marie	,,		272	209	136	100[00]	105[05]	1	18	4	35[1]	4[2]	1	2[2]	1	5	1[1]
	26 ,,	Laniel	,,		398	206	18	100[00]	104[04]	5	—	2	16[1]	—	—	7[2]	5[1]	—	1[1]
	10 July	,,	Special powers: finance		314	267	34	100[00]	105[05]	7[2]	22[0]	2[2]	29[21]	20[3]	8	1	—	15[15]	3[1]
	23 ,,	,,	Constitutional revision		468	127	16	100[00]	4[4]	23[4]	—	6	—	4	3	—	—	15[15]	1[1]
	9 Oct.	,,	Social policy		299	242	75	99[9]	105[05]	5[3]	27[5]	11[5]	30[7]	6[2]	—	6[2]	—	14[14]	2[1]
	27 Nov.	,,	European army	(C)	275	244	103	100[00]	105[05]	—	31[20]	13[3]	65[5]	20[5]	9[3]	3	8[3]	6	2[2]
	Dec. 1953: Party strengths							100	165	88	75	26	79	136	55	47	34	15	3

(a) Formal votes of confidence are marked (C). Votes in which government was neutral are marked (N).
(b) A French division list contains several categories: For; Against; Abstained; Did not vote; Unable to vote; Leave of absence; Presiding officer. The 'abstentions' column includes also those who 'Did not vote'. When the government was neutral, the votes for and against the *proposal* are shown; in Col. II ministers are counted among the abstainers, but they are omitted from the detail by parties in Col. III.
(c) The large figures show the combined total of negative votes, abstainers, and 'Did not vote'. The small raised figures show the negative votes only.
Parties given are, in order: Communists, Socialists, M.R.P., Radicals, U.D.S.R., Conservatives (all groups combined), Conservative groups individually (*Republican Independents, Peasants, P.R.L.*) and others. Those added later are: *Action républicaine* (dissident M.R.P.); I.O.M. (Indépendants d' Outre-Mer); R.P.F.; *U.D.I.* (mainly the non-Gaullist wing of *Action républicaine*); *P.U.S.* (the opposition wing of the Peasants); and *A.R.S.* (the government wing of the R.P.F.).

APPENDIX V

THE VERDICT OF THE ELECTORATE

(All votes in thousands.)

Warning note.
French election statistics are most unsatisfactory. The variety of political opinions in the constituencies, the complexity and impermanence of their alliances, their imperfect correspondence with the groups in the Assembly, and the loose allegiance of the deputy to his group, make drastic simplification indispensable, and accurate classification very difficult. The official figures published by the ministry of the Interior are not necessarily the most useful.

1. *Three referendums* (*France and overseas*)

	Yes	No	Total Electorate
21 October 1945:			
for a Constituent Assembly	18,585	699	25,718
for the proposals of the government, restricting its powers and duration	12,795	6,449	25,718
5 May 1946:			
for the first draft constitution	9,454	10,585	25,829
13 October 1946:			
for the second draft constitution	9,297	8,165	26,312

(From Husson, *Élections et referendums*; reproduced in *A.P.*, 1944–45, p. 492, and *A.P.*, 1946, pp. 577, 579.)

2. *Four general elections* (*France only*)

Date	Com.	Soc.	M.R.P.	R.G.R.	Cons.	R.P.F.	Others	Total votes	Abstentions	Electorate
21.10.45	5,005	4,561	4,780	2,131	2,546		165	19,190	4,965	24,623
2. 6.46	5,154	4,188	5,589	2,295	2,540		115	19,881	4,482	24,697
10.11.46	5,431	3,434	4,989	2,136	3,073		155	19,218	5,505	25,083
17. 6.51	4,934	2,784	2,454	1,980	2,295	4,266	239	18,952	4,861	24,522

(From Goguel, *Esprit*, February 1947, p. 238, and *France under the Fourth Republic*, p. 90. These figures reproduce those of M. Husson for the first two elections, but differ for the third: in November 1946 M. Husson's classification was: Com. (including Trotskyist) 5,489, Soc. 3,432, M.R.P. 5,058, R.G.R. 2,381, Cons. 2,466, Gaullist 313, Others 64.

There is a discrepancy between the total electorate, and the figures of voters and abstainers combined, which is caused by spoiled papers in all four elections, and increased in 1951 by the operation of *panachage*.)

3. Four Assemblies (*France and overseas*)

Date	Com.	Soc.	M.R.P.	Rad.	U.D.S.R.	Cons.	R.P.F.	Others	Total seats
21.10.45	161	150	150	28	29	64		4	586
2. 6.46	153	129	169	32	21	67		15	586
10.11.46	183	105	167	43	27	71		22	618
17. 6.51	101	107	96	76	19	98	120	10	627

(From the official lists of parliamentary groups. The first three are taken from Wright, *Reshaping of French Democracy*, p. 262, (published in Great Britain by Messrs. Methuen & Co., Ltd., and in America by Harcourt, Brace & Co., Inc.), and refer to dates a few months after the elections concerned. Those for 1951 are from the first official list, modified by two subsequent elections and by the Assembly's decision in the disputed contest in Seine-Inférieure.)

APPENDIX VI
THE DETAILED WORKING OF THE ELECTORAL LAWS
1. *The distribution of seats*

Under the form of P.R. used between 1945 and 1951, votes were cast for a party list, not for an individual candidate. The seats were distributed on the principle of the ' highest average '. This meant that they were allotted in turn, by calculating the *average vote per seat* each list would have, if the seat in question were given to it. The list with the highest average, so defined, got the seat. The final arrangement was such that any change, by transferring a member from one list to another, would have brought the new average of the ' gaining ' list below that of the ' losing ' one.

In the four-member department of Corrèze, in November 1946, the votes were distributed in this way:

| Communists | . | . | 52,864 | Radicals | . | . | 26,082 |
| M.R.P. | . | . | 29,978 | Socialists | . | . | 23,615 |

Total: 132,539

On the first round, the ' average ' for each list was its actual vote divided by one (the number of seats which each list would have if the seat in question were given it). This first seat therefore went to the largest list, the Communist. In subsequent rounds the Communist vote had to be divided by two, since the next seat allotted to it would bring its total up to two. This gave it an average of 26,432. M.R.P.'s average was now the highest, being still the same as its initial vote—i.e. 29,978. It therefore got the second seat distributed, and *ipso facto* its divisor became two, and its average became 14,989. The next seat went to the Communists, since their average was slightly higher than that of their nearest rivals, the Radicals. For the last round, the Communist average became 52,864 divided by three, i.e. 17,621; that of M.R.P. was still 14,989; the Radicals and Socialists, having no member, still had a divisor of one, and an average equal to their total vote. The Radical average was thus the highest, and they got the last seat. Result: Communists 2, M.R.P. 1, Radicals 1, Socialists 0.

But the ' highest average ' is not the only method of calculating under P.R. The alternative is the ' highest remainder ' system. With this, a quotient is obtained by dividing the number of seats into the total vote: in the above case it would have been 132,539 divided by four, i.e. 33,135. A list whose poll reached the quotient—as the Communists did in this instance—would get a seat. But for the seats remaining, its claim would depend not on its *average* (i.e. 52,864 divided by two, or 26,432), but on its *remainder*, i.e. its poll minus the quotient: 52,864 minus 33,135, or 19,729. Each of the other lists exceeded that figure, and the three remaining seats would therefore go to them: all four lists, therefore, would have one seat each.

It is evident that the ' highest remainder ' system benefits the weaker parties; for the strong ones can never get more seats than those which they obtain on a quotient basis, plus one. For the 1951 election the centre groups, having a majority in the old Assembly, therefore adopted this system for the Paris area (departments of Seine and Seine-et-Oise), where the Communists and Gaullists were strongest. It was also used for three overseas departments, Guadeloupe, Martinique, and Réunion. The fourth, Guyane, with one member only, elected by a majority system with one ballot—the only constituency to apply the British electoral system.

2. *Apparentement*

The second important change made in 1951 was the introduction of *apparentement*. The 'highest average' system being the form of P.R. most favourable to large parties, the object of *apparentement* was to utilize this advantage on behalf of parties which could form alliances, by allowing an alliance to count *as one* as against rivals in the distribution of seats.

The figures for Marne in 1951 were:

Allied lists		Isolated lists	
M.R.P.	36,702	Communists	47,200
Socialists	18,607	R.P.F.	45,931
Radicals	16,659	Independents	4,051
Independents	3,907		

Total of *allied* lists: 77,875.

With the 1946 system the five seats would have gone, in order, to the Communists, R.P.F., M.R.P., Communists, and R.P.F. But under that of 1951 the three isolated lists were confronted, not with four weak opponents, but with a single combination with a vote of 77,875. The five seats therefore went to: allies, Communists, R.P.F., allies, allies. The three seats won by the allies were then distributed among themselves on the 'highest average' rule, which gave two to M.R.P. and one to the Socialists. ('Highest remainder', applied to the whole election with the allied lists counting together, would have given two seats to the Communists and one each to R.P.F., M.R.P., and Socialists. If the allied lists had been counted separately, it would have given one seat to each of the five strongest lists).

Finally, the 1951 law enacted that any list or alliance which won an absolute majority of votes, took *all* the seats. Altogether the centre parties won 97 more seats than the 1946 system would have given them: 51 of these gains were due to the absolute majority rule, 9 to the change in Paris, and 37 to the effect of *apparentement*, in enabling the united vote of a coalition to win more seats than the component parties could have done separately.

3. *Preferential vote and panachage*[1]

The seats have to be conferred on persons as well as on parties. In 1946, the lists drawn up by the parties could be altered only in one way. The 'preferential vote' allowed the elector to delete a candidate he disliked, and to move up one whom he favoured. But this was rendered quite ineffective (see text, p. 315 n.) by the provision that the preferential votes for a given

---

[1] In 1951 7 per cent. of all voters altered their ballot-papers in the ways described. The percentages by parties were: R.G.R.I.F. 15: Conservatives 11: R.G.R. 11: M.R.P. 9: Socialists 7: R.P.F. 6: Communists 1·8.

list were not even to be counted, unless at least half the ballots cast for it had been modified in some way. This rule was based on the assumption that unaltered ballots represented positive votes for the original list. Nor was this altogether unreasonable. Without such an assumption, the 800 Communist voters who in 1951 struck M. Thorez's name off their ballots would have deprived him of his seat, without the remaining 99 per cent. of Communist supporters in the constituency being able to affect the issue. But, justified or not, the rule made the preferential vote worthless.

In 1951 the original lists could also be changed by *panachage*. This allowed the voter to transfer a fraction of his vote from the list he had chosen to a candidate on a different list. It gave the elector a freer hand, and weakened the grip of the party organization. But at the same time it contradicted the principle of P.R.—that the vote should be for opinions not persons—and so led to some extraordinary results.

In Hérault, the votes were cast as follows:

Allied lists		Isolated lists	
Socialists . .	39,028	Communists . .	69,433
Conservatives .	25,827	R.P.F. . . .	21,256
Radicals . .	23,596	Independents . .	10,301
M.R.P. . . .	20,766		

The four allied lists had an absolute majority of votes, and therefore took all the six seats. On the 'highest average' system, the Socialists won three, and the other coalition lists one each. The final Socialist average was thus 13,009, just ahead of their nearest rivals, the Conservatives, who with an extra seat would have had an average of 12,913. Three hundred fewer votes would thus have cost the Socialists one of their seats.

The local Socialist leader was M. Jules Moch, who had received no less than 7,000 *panachage* votes from non-Socialist admirers. Each of these had thereby transferred a sixth of his vote to the Socialist list, and the result was to raise its average by more than a thousand. These extra votes did not help M. Moch, who was safely at the head of his list anyway; but they did help his party colleagues, electing two of them instead of one.

An ingenious correspondent, quoted in *Le Monde* of 14 June 1951, showed that the consequences of *panachage* could in theory be stranger still. It *could* happen under the 1951 electoral law that one candidate was elected with no votes at all, while another with 100,000 was beaten. The imaginary constituency has 100,000 voters, 3 seats, and 4 lists competing. List B receives 40,000 votes, list C 35,000, list D 25,000, list A none. But *all* the voters *panache* in favour of the second A candidate, at the expense of one of their own list. Here is the result:

Armand	0	Bertrand	40,000	Charles	35,000	Désiré	25,000
Albert	100,000	Bernard	0	Casimir	0	Denis	0
André	0	Baptiste	40,000	Claude	35,000	Daniel	25,000
Average 33,333·3		26,666·6		23,333·3		16,666·6	
Seats 1		1		1		0	

But since no ballots have been cast for list A, half of *its* ballots have not been altered. So the order remains unchanged, and it is Armand, and not Albert, who is elected.

This absurd example illustrates a point which had practical importance. Suppose that, among the recalcitrant electors of lists B, C, and D, only half had transferred their votes to Albert, the rest simply deleting the candidate they disliked without substituting another. In that event, the total number of valid ballot-papers (*bulletins valables*) would still be 100,000. But list A's vote would be only 50,000, and its average 16,666. The total of *suffrages de liste* (the sum of the averages) would be reduced accordingly, to 83,333. Now if lists A and B had been allied, the combination would have had 26,666 plus 16,666, i.e. 43,333 votes. The second method of calculating the *total* would make this an absolute majority, and would entitle the allies to all the seats; the first would not. In two constituencies, Bas-Rhin and Seine-Inférieure, the absolute majority—and the disposition of eight parliamentary seats—did actually depend on this highly technical point. The sovereign Assembly was unwilling to invalidate General Kœnig, or to risk discontent in the difficult province of Alsace; so it chose the first interpretation for Bas-Rhin, and the second for Seine-Inférieure.

4. *By-elections*

Lastly, the 1951 electoral law made new provision for by-elections. Under the P.R. system, by-elections had not taken place; when a member died or retired, he was simply replaced by the next candidate on his list. By the 1951 law, when a vacancy occurs the entire constituency is polled, on a double-ballot basis—an absolute majority required for election on the first, a relative majority on the second ballot. A fortnight elapses between the two votes. These rules give by-elections great publicity, since scores or even hundreds of thousands of people vote; and they make their results very uncertain, since the party holding the seat on a P.R. or *apparentement* basis is very likely to lose it under this quite different arrangement.

APPENDIX VII

COMPOSITION AND OUTLOOK OF THE PARTIES

I AM indebted for the use of these figures to the *Institut français d'opinion publique*. They are taken from its poll of February and March 1952, *before* the Pinay government and the decline of the R.P.F., and were published in *Sondages*, 1952, no. 3. They show the percentage of voters for each party who belong to the category, or give the answer indicated on the left; in some cases only the highest and/or lowest percentages were stated; 'don't knows' are omitted. The *Institut* has kindly supplied certain corrections to the published figures (The smaller the category, the less reliable the figures.)

	Total	Com.	Soc.	MRP	RGR	Cons	RPF
Percentage of electors, 1951 election	100	20	11	10	8	9	17
1. Composition							
Age: over 50	37	23	37	34	65	45	37
35 to 49	29	35	33	35	24	25	25
18 to 34	34	42	30	31	11	30	38
Sex: men	48	61	59	47	64	47	47
women	52	39	41	53	36	53	53
Occupation: ouvriers industriels	19	44	25	15	10	10	18
,, agricoles	7	10	9	3	5	4	4
fonctionnaires	5	4	9	3	5	6	2
employés	7	6	4	11	1	3	7
industriels et cadres	5	1	4	3	4	10	7
commerçants	4	3	3	5	7	7	7
cultivateurs exploitants	16	5	9	20	31	35	18
professions libérales	1	1	1	2	1	1	1
rentiers et retraités	6	3	7	6	14	8	4
femmes sans profession	30	22	28	30	19	15	32
total salariés (first 4 categories)	38	64	47	32	21	23	31
total profit-makers (next 3 categories)	25	9	16	28	42	52	32
total peasants (cultiv. exp. plus ouv. agr.)	23	15	18	23	36	39	22
Wealth: own a propriété	39	18	32	44	57	58	47
,, car	23	11	21	21	30	43	33
have a domestic servant	13	3	5	15	20	31	17
Size of town: over 100,000	24	20	16	19	23	29	22
20–100,000	17	22	18	14	11	11	22
5–20,000	11	10	16	14	6	5	11
under 5,000	48	48	50	53	60	55	45

	Com.	Soc.	MRP	RGR	Cons	RPF
2. *Confidence in own party*						
**Full confidence in it	†62	48	51	37	31	45
Not ,, ,, ,,	20	33	35	50	55	42
(P) Full ,, ,, in (most frequently named leader)*	47	27	35	45	1	68
,, ,, in (next most frequently named leader)*	47	12	34	21	1	12
Have ever: sold papers, stuck *affiches*	31	8	8	7	5	7
tried to recruit supporters	51	32	35	28	29	42
given money	55	32	23	20	17	15
attended meetings	70	42	35	42	33	37
(P) Have never voted for any other party	68	71	74	59	36	36
(P) No party whatever is deserving of interest	16	26	25	24	38	28
Own party *only* ,, ,, ,, ,,	60	19	12	11	2	28
Several parties are ,, ,, ,,	18	35	46	42	39	29
All parties ,, ,, ,, ,,	—	—	3	1	1	1
3. *General political outlook*						
Favour progress by means of revolution	†41	6	—	1	1	9
,, ,, ,, ,, reform	50	91	95	92	94	85
(P) Own party should in some circumstances take power by force	40	2	3	1	13	26
,, ,, ,, never do so	40	71	79	80	70	52
Some party/parties should be banned	43	31	45	39	70	77
Worst enemy of parl. regime:						
Communists	3	37	49	48	47	55
R.P.F.	46	24	11	10	6	8
(P)**Own party is not intransigent enough	29	33	26	31	30	28
,, ,, just right	42	33	40	38	39	34
,, ,, too intransigent	13	7	13	8	14	29
Don't know	16	27	21	23	17	9
(P)**Own party more useful in office than in opposition	41	61	85	82	77	54
(P)**Most of the ministers are honest men	12	46	52	47	36	23
A minority of ,, ,, ,, ,,	41	39	35	32	33	55
None of them ,, ,, ,,	36	2	1	1	11	8
**What do you regard as most important about your party? (Q1)						
Doctrine	†44	32	34	29	25	13
Programme	25	26	22	25	31	20
Leadership	10	7	11	20	14	35
Cohesion	5	4	3	3	6	5
(P) Spirit	3	12	18	4	14	12
**What attracted you to your party? (Q2)						
travailler pour la paix	32	28	27	18	17	23
façonner l'avenir de la France	4	7	13	11	24	33
défendre des intérêts légitimes	28	24	22	27	30	11
programme, lutte contre capital	39					
personnalité de son chef						18
contre le regime, contre partis						15
esprit de tolérance				38		
entourage, famille, relations		15		12		

	Com.	Soc.	MRP	RGR	Cons	RPF
4. *Attitude to current problems*						
What are the most important problems?						
vie chère	32	43	23	13	31	25
instabilité politique . . .			41	37	60	62
injustice sociale . . .	17	23				
guerre, armements, Indo-Chine .	46			16		
(P) France should try to stay neutral in a general war	†74	78	75	76	67	63
(P)**Rearmament reduces risk of war .	4	26	53	42	59	60
,, increases ,, ,, .	83	29	14	22	12	17
(P) Presence of U.S. troops reduces risk .	2	21	39	54	56	38
,, ,, ,, increases ,, .	82	11	14	13	6	13
,, ,, ,, makes no difference .	11	50	27	20	22	37

* These leaders were: *first*, MM. Thorez, Mollet, Bidault, Herriot and de Gaulle: *second*, MM. Duclos, Moch, Schuman, Queuille, and Soustelle. The difference between the two figures may suggest whether the voter gives his confidence to a man or to a team.

** On these questions the Socialists showed the highest proportion of ' don't know ' answers. On most of the others ' don't knows ' were not specified.

† On these questions peasant Communists gave much more ' revolutionary ' answers than other Communists. On other questions this distinction was not made.

(P) These questions were put to those interviewed in the provinces, but not in Paris.

(Q1) Categories asked in the question.

(Q2) Replies spontaneous.

NOTES TO INDEX

Important page references are set in **bold** type.

Entries starred * indicate that the person or institution is not named in the text.

Proper names are indexed according to the French practice, i.e. Bas-Rhin under R, Mendès-France under M.

When used in a biographical note, the abbreviations *M.P.*, *P.M.*, *Pres.*, and *s* normally indicate date of *first* election or appointment to these offices (see below).

Where a biographical note is given, members have sat since 1945 for their present constituencies unless otherwise indicated.

The following sources have been quoted throughout:

    L'Année politique   *Le Figaro*
    Le Monde   *Le Journal officiel*
        Revue du droit public

Abbreviations

A.F.U.	Assembly of French Union	org.	organization
amb.	ambassador	P.	Party
cap.	capital	Peas.	Peasant
comm.	commissioner	Pres.	President
Com.	Communist	P.M.	Prime Minister
Cons.	Conservative	Rad.	Radical
C.A.	Constituent Assembly	rapp.-g.	rapporteur-général
C.R.	Council of the Republic	rep.	representation, -ive
dém.	démocratique	Rep.	Republic, -an
d.	deputy	resp.	responsibility
disc.	discipline	R.I.	Republican Independent
E.C.	Economic Council	s.	senator, -ial
elec.	electoral	s. d'a.	scrutin d'arrondissement
fin.	finance	s.d.l.	scrutin de liste
H.C.F.U.	High Council of French Union	sec.-gen.	secretary-general
H.C.M.	High Council of the Magistrature	Soc.	Socialist
		T.U.	Trade Union
M.	Minister, Ministry	u.-sec.	under-secretary (*secrétaire d'état*)
M.P.	Member of Parliament		
N.A.	National Assembly	v. of c.	vote of confidence

P.P.F.   449   29

INDEX

ABBAS, *see* Ferhat.
Abbey House, 400
Abbott, R. S., 404n.
absenteeism
 from constituency, 350
 from Parl., 184n., 197 and n., 212, 222 and n.
abstention
 elec., 324, 407
 parl., 145, 185, 224n., 360, 394 and n.
 of Ms., 383 and n., 384
 of everyone else, 383n.
Abyssinia, 78
Académie française, 282
acclamation, election by
 among Coms., 50
 rare departure from, in M.R.P., 87, 370
 among Peas., 112
 among Rads., 97
acclamation instead of election, in R.P.F., 126–7
Accounts
 Court of, 255, **265–6 and n.**, 404
 special Treasury, 265 and n.
 system of parl., 253, 265–7
Action démocratique et républicaine (R.P.F. in C.R.), 125 and n.
Action fédérale, L' (M.R.P. organ), 80nn.
Action française, 107, 140, 150
Action libérale, 107
Action ouvrière, L' (R.P.F. organ), 124n.
Action républicaine et sociale (A.R.S., dissident Gaullists), 14n., 42, 109n., 125 and n., **136–7 and n.**
administration, power of, *see* bureaucracy.
 abuses in, *see* scandals.
 organization of, *see* civil service.
 reforms in, 404
administrative strikes, 339
Africa
 and A.F.U., 293
 Equatorial, 294, 388
 North, policy in
 influence of *colons*, 153, 190 and n., 331n., 386
 N.A. and, 209 and n., 410 and n.
 party views, 24, 41–2, 135n., 181
 West, 142, 152, 189n., 294, 350n., 388
African territories, 153, 191n.
Aga Khan, the Begum, 88n.
agriculture, *see* food policy, peasantry.
Agriculture c'tee
 of N.A., 201n., 237, 240–1, 242n.22, 335
 of C.R., 334n.

agriculture, Confédération générale de l' (C.G.A.), 35n., 332–5, 340n., 410n.
 and E.C., 297–9
 and investment, 346n.
 strike threat by, 339
Agriculture, M. of
 departmental disputes, 336, 391
 holders, 35, 111, 150, 336, 379–80
 and parties, 379–80
 pressure on, 349n.
Agulhon, Maurice, 91n.
aid, external, 253, 256, 257
Air, M. of
 admin. abuses in, 266n.38
 attacks on, 392, 393n.
 Com. colonization in, 385n., 386
 holders, 324
 and parties, 393n.
aircraft industry, 299n., 385n.
Aisne, dept. (cap. Laon), 142n., 150n., 267
Aix-les-Bains, 340n.
Alain (pseud. of Émile Chartier, 1868–1951), 5, 7 and n., 10, 400
alcohol interest, 335, 337, *and see pastis*.
alcoholism, 336
alcools, Commission des, 388n.
Alès, 350n.
algebra, political, 340n.
Algeria
 and A.F.U., 295
 election of 1951 in, 150
 govt. of
 1947 law, 32, 219 and n., 223, 248, 277
 bill of 1949, 177n.
 governor-general of, 192n., 350, 386
 parl. rep. of, 191 and n., 293–4 and n., 296
 and C.R., 270
 parties of
 Cons., 150
 moderates (pro-admin.), 152
 nationalists, 151–2
 Radicals, 104n.
 Socialists, 65
 settlers, influence of, 386 *and see colons*.
Algerian Assembly, 294
Algerian wine scandals, 72, 306, 327 and n.
Algiers
 de Gaulle govt. at, 14, 119, 120, 173, 386, 389
 c'tee rep. of, 240n.
Alliance démocratique, 140, 148, 363

INDEX

alliances
  party attitudes to
    de Gaulle's dislike of, 122 and n., 129 and n.
    M.R.P. finds difficult, 89, 319
    Rads. will accept any, 94, 98, 104, 133
    Rads. (specific), 103, 146
    Socs., 67
  confusion of, in local elections, 135n.
  under *s. d'a., q.v.*
  in 1945–6
    Rad.
      and Com., 143
      and P.R.L., 93, 316n.
      and U.D.S.R., 93
    Soc.
      not with Com., 16–17
      and U.D.S.R., 143
  in 1951
    Cons., 110, 149
    Rad., 94, 98, 104n.
    R.G.R., 146
    R.P.F., 137n.
    R.P.F., refusal of, 122, 129n.
    Socs., 67, 150, 354
  post-1951
    Cons., 117, 137
    Rad., 148
    R.P.F., 117
    attempted regrouping, 1953…408–12
  and see apparentement, elec. system.
Allier, dept. (cap. Moulins), 142n., 348, 350
allocation-éducation, 127n., 135
Alpes, Basses-, dept. (cap. Digne), 350
Alpes-Maritimes, dept. (cap. Nice), 101n., 333n., 350n.
Alphand, Hervé (b. 1907, French rep. at N.A.T.O.), 264
Alps, region of, 113
Alsace, Alsatians, 54, 260n., 334, 350 and n., 445
alternates
  in c'tees, 237, 247 and n.
  Ministers, 384 and n.
ambassadors, 189n., 384
amendments, constitutional, *see* constitution, revision of.
America, *see* U.S.A.
American Political Science Review, 47n., 322n., 332n., 385n., 404n.
Americanization, resistance to, 397 and n.
Amiens, 348n.
amnesty
  in const., 203
  fiscal, 219n., App. IV
  for collaborators, 133, 192n., 282n., 385
Amsterdam, 60
anarchism, 143

Anbert, Camille, 302–4nn.
Anjou, 74, 330n.
anti-clericalism and *laïcité*
  as pervading cleavage, 356, 396, 398
  and army appointments, 387
  cabinet split on, 384n.
  in const., 292 and n., 307n.
  and electoral law, 311, 319, 323, 330
  and M. of Interior, 377, 385n.
  parl. c'tees and, 248 and n., 249
  Senate and, 159, 268–9
  parties and :—
    Alliance dém., 108
    M.R.P., 278
    Rads., 103, **104 and n.**, 159, 411
    Socs., **73–4**, 240
  Défense laïque and, 330
  lois laïques, 192n.,
  and see Church schools.
anti-Europeans, 411–2
Antier, Paul (b. 1905, M.P. 1936, Peasant d. H-Loire)
  and Resistance, 117n.
  as party leader, 148n., 383*
  and party split, 111, 112n., 379–80
  for Mendès-France, 411n.
  as M., App. III
apathy, parl., 209n., *and see* absenteeism.
apparentement
  electoral, **322–6, 443**
    consequences of, 346, 357, 405
    qualifying lists, 150, 322n.
  parl., and groups, 129n., 142, 236
  specific, 125n., 142, 148, 152
appointments
  religious, 192n.
  anti-religious, 387
  overseas, *q.v.*
arbitration
  compulsory, 299, 300, 331 and n., *and see* wages.
  E.C.'s power of, 297
Archambeaud, Yves, 298n.
Ardennes, dept. (cap. Mézières), 349n.
Ariège, dept. (cap. Foix), 74n.
Armagnac. 328n.
Armaments, M. of, 378, 384n.
armaments, nationalization of, 247n.
Armed Forces, M. of, 378
armistice (1940), 92
Army
  power of, 2, 398
  in politics, 7, 16, 130, 350 and n., 386–7, 410 and n.
  and anti-clericalism, 10, 387
  appointments, 189n., 387
  civilian control of, 234
  de Gaulle and, 17
  and see Budget, military; European army; Scandals.

29—2

INDEX

Aron, Raymond, 139n.
  on pol., 22n., 23n., 33n., 138n., 340n., 368n., 382n.
  on econ., 23n., 397n.
Arras, 63
Arrighi, Pascal, 344nn., 346n., 365n.15
artisans, 396 and n., 397
Assemblies, Constituent
  absolute majority in, 183n.
  c'tee chairmen in, 242n.
  and const., 172, 176, 269, 292, 315 and n.
  electoral system for, 314–5
  and parties
    composition, 16, 18, 152, 359
    discipline, 343, 359, 362, 374
  powers, 14–16, 167–8, 257, *and see* Const. (provisional regime).
  Presidents of, 17, 19, 173, 179, 198–9, 381
Assembly, Algerian, 294
Assembly of French Union (A.F.U.), **293–6**
  status
    in draft const., 296
    in Bayeux const., 162
    compared with E.C., 191, 284n., 298
  members of
    election by N.A., 203, 388n.
    election by C.R., 274
    rep. in party counsels, 81, 96, 127n., 147n., 148, 294
  President of, 100, 295
Assembly, National, of 1875;...6, 107
Assembly, National, of 3rd Rep.
  status and powers, 191, 203
  in 1940...14, 161, 168
Assembly, National, of 4th Rep., Chapters 12(3), 13, 14; *also*
  sovereign status of, 191, 273
  and C.R., 273–6, 282–3, 291
  and A.F.U., 295–6
  and E.C., 297, 298 and n.
  elections by
    general, 203
    to C.R., 270, 271 and n., 345
    to A.F.U., 294, 295–6
    to Const. C'tee, 289
    to H.C.M., 301
  groups in
    party, *see* party.
    pressure-, 330, 332, 335–7 and *q.v.*
  and see Parliament; President of N.A.
Assembly, National, of 1946–51
  absolute majority in, 183n.
  Comte de Paris on, 150–1
  and C.R., 275–81, 284–5 and nn.
  dissolution proposed by de Gaulle, 121 and n., 194–5
  party composition, 19
  term of, 194–5

Assembly, National, elected 17 June 1951
  absolute majority in, 183n.
  party composition, 40
  President of, 412
  R.P.F. in, 138
  seating in (of R.P.F.), 7, 135 and n.
  special session of, 411n.
Assembly regime, **163–7**
  alleged steps towards, 186, 235
assimilation, 293–4
Associated States, 293–5 and nn., 410n.
Associated States, M. of, 189n., 375–7 and nn., 379–80
Association catholique de la jeunesse française, 77, 78n.
Association parlementaire pour la liberté de l'enseignement, 41, 330
assurer, meaning of, 303
Astier de la Vigerie, Emmanuel d' (b. 1900, M.P. 1945, Prog. d. Ille-et-Vilaine), 142n.
Atlantic Pact, 175, App. IV
atomic energy, 188n., 385
Attlee, Rt. Hon. C. R., 116
Aube, dept. (cap. Troyes), 85n., 98n., 129n., 339
Aube, L' (M.R.P. organ), 18, 32, 78, 391n.
Aubry, Maurice, 298n.
auditing, 265
Augé-Laribé, Michel, 10n., 339n.
Aujoulat, Louis (b. 1910, M.P. 1945, I.O.M. d. Cameroun III), 152n., 153n.
Auriol, Vincent (b. 1884, M.P. 1914, Soc. d. H.-Garonne 1945–6, Pres. C.A. 1946, Pres. Rep. 1947–54)
  career, 173, App. III
  as Pres. C.A., 173, 199
    in const.-making, 173, 214, 227n., 290 and n.
    in crises, 179
  const. ideas
    in book, 164 and n., 173 and n., 214 and n., 228n., 235n., 242n.
  as Pres. Rep., 17, 168, 173, 279, 280n.31, 290 and n.
  and de Gaulle, 14, 17, 168, 173, 174–5
  elected President, 19, 119
  activity as President, **173–8**, 180, **185–7**, 413, 414n.; *also*
    cabinet-making, 37, 382, 407, 413
    and countersign, 169n.
    and H.C.M., 301–5 and nn.
    presiding in cabinet, 222n.
    reference back, 291
    refusals to act, 231, 279, 280n.31
    refusal of P.M.'s resignation, 32, 218, 224n., 226–7 and n.
    contemplates own resignation, 186n.

INDEX 453

Auriol, Vincent (*cont'd*)
quoted
on pressure-groups, 340 and n.
on French Union, 410n.
mentioned, 37, 182, 350n.
austerity, 168n., 392
Australian Country Party, 338
Austria, German entry into, 10
authoritarianism
as tradition
monarchist, 150
Bonapartist, 403 and *q.v.*
as cause of alarm
in 3rd Rep., 2, 6–7, 10, 154, 169–70
in 4th Rep., 2, 161, 164, 230, 396, 398, 406
of Clemenceau, 91
Coms. accused of, 136n.
in R.P.F., 126–9, 135n., 350
and see Democracy.
authority
cynicism about, 4–5, 26
distrust of, 5, 7–8, 10, 33n., 318, 338, 407
distrust of, in N.A., 206–8
mystique of, 137
and see incivisme; opposition-mindedness.
average, highest, 316, 442, 445
Aveyron, dept. (cap. Rodez), 74n., 114, 324

BABET, Raphaël (R.P.F. and U.D.S.R. d. Réunion), 184n.*, 337n.
Bacon, Paul (b. 1907, M.P. 1945, M.R.P. d. Seine IV), 78n., App. III
Bagatelle, 138n.
Baldwin, Stanley (Earl), 35 *, 214n.
Ballanger, Robert (Com. d.), 200n.
ballot
elec., double, **309–12,** 357
party views on, 38, 223–4, 319, 321–2
for C.R., 271 and n., 278
for by-elections, 322, 445
and see electoral system (*s. d'a.*)
elec., secret, Senate delays, 268n.
parl., *see* parl. procedure (voting).
Bank of France, 328, 331
bankruptcy of deputies, 191
Bao Dai, Emperor, 386
Barangé, Charles (b. 1897, M.P. 1945, M.R.P. d. Maine-et-Loire, *rapp.-g.* since June 1946)
and Finance c'tee, 235, 245nn., 246, 248, 260*, 261*
and Barangé bill, 248
and see Church schools.
Bardoux, Jacques (b. 1874, M.P. (s.) 1938, Peas. and R.I. d. Puy-de-Dôme), 412n.

Barrachin, Edmond (b. 1900, M.P. 1934, P.R.L., R.P.F. and A.R.S. d. Seine V), 137, 238n., 239n., 248*, 369*, App. III
Barrès, Maurice (1862–1923, M.P. 1889–93, novelist), 103
Barthélemy, Joseph (1874–1945, M.P. 1919–28, M. of Justice 1941–3)
on c'tees, 238nn., 242n., 243n., 247nn., 250n.
on constituency interests, 328n.
on officials and policy, 10n.
on parl. groups, 335n., 364nn.
on procedure, 360n.
on Senate, 243n., 268n.
Basques, 334
Bataille socialiste, La, 141
Baumgartner, Wilfrid, 331
Bayet, René, 97n.
Bayeux, de Gaulle's speech at, 118n., 119, 292, *and see* Constitution (of Bayeux).
Beaulieu, Georges de, 56n.
Beaune, 340n.
Beaverbrook, Rt. Hon. Viscount, 21
Béchard, Paul (b. 1899, M.P. 1945, Soc. d. Gard 1945–8, 1951– ; u.-sec. 1947–8, High Comm. W. Africa 1948–51), 180n.*, 189n.*, 350n., 388*
bee-keepers, 339n.
beetroot-growers, 335–6, 340n., 391, 410n., *and see* Blondelle.
Bégouin, Lucien (Rad. d. Seine-et-Marne), 134, 135n., 238n., 351*
Belfort, Territoire de (cap. Belfort), 350
Belgians, King Leopold of the, 150
Belgium, 54, 302n.
Belin, René (b. 1898, M. of Labour 1940–1), 13*, 61, 124n.
Berlia, Georges, quoted, 177n., 184n., 194n., 197n., 283n., 356n.
Bertaux, Pierre (s. Soudan I, 1953), 88 and n.
Bertrand, André, 188n., 404n.
Bessac, Abel (b. 1912, M.P. 1945, M.R.P., Cons. and ind. d. Lot), 149, 348n.
Betolaud, Robert (b. 1901, M.P. 1946, P.R.L. and R.I. d. Seine II to 1951), 333n., 383*, App. III
Bevan, Rt. Hon. A., 21
Bevanite outlook, in M.R.P., 87, 140
Béziers agreement, 335
Biays, P., 204n.
Bidault, Georges (b. 1899, M.P. 1945, M.R.P. d. Loire, ex-pres. of M.R.P.), Apps. II, III, IV
pre-war career, 34n., 78n.
stands for P.M. 1946; 19
1952; 183n.
1953; 184n., 409

454 INDEX

Bidault, Georges (*cont'd*)
as P.M.
election, 1946, 183n.
consultations, 186n., 409
choosing cabinet, **37**, 182
meeting N.A., **181**
use of v. of c., 215n., 217n., 219n., 220 and n., 223n., 244n.
and parties, 366, 392*
as Foreign M., 188n., 377
and N. Africa, 411*
as vice-P.M., 183n.
standing with own party, App. VII
with electorate, 347 and n.
relations with R.P.F., **36**, 370
quoted, 256n.
Bidault cabinet, June–November 1946
formed, membership, 18, 189n.64*, 377
and French Union, **293**
fall, 226n.
Bidault cabinet, October 1949–June 1950
formed, membership, 37, 184n.46, 186n., 189n.64, 382
budget attacked, 37, 198, 332, **337**, 411n, App. IV and Fin. c'tee, 243n., 244nn., **260**
and C.R., 281
reconstruction when Socs. resign, 22, 37, **180**, App. IV
fall, 22, 37, 226 and n., 229, 230n., 243, **245**, 260
bigamy, political, 94, 97n., 98–9, 102, 278, *and see* marriage.
Billoux, Francois (b. 1903, M.P. 1936, Com. d. Bouches-du-Rhône I), 46n., 50n., 378, App. III
bills
amendments to
by C.R., 275–6, 279n., 283 and n.
disjonction of, 258 and n.
grouping of, 217
used for obstruction, 200
and C'tees, 234–5, 248 and n., 250–1
drafting of, 250
and E.C., 297–9
introduction of
in const., 187
by senators, 202, 274, 278–9 and n., 282, 285 and n.
by private members, 203 and n., *and see below*.
priority for, 207n., 208
private members',
numbers of, 203 and n.
cost of, 55n., 257 and n., 412n.
subjects of, **257n.**
senators', *see above*.
promulgation of, 198, 274 and n., 275, 291
reference back of
by President, 176, 177 and n., 201n., 283, 291
to c'tee, 283 and n.

bills (*cont'd*)
unopposed, 203 and n., 409n.
birthrate, *see* population.
Blamont, Émile, sec.-gen. of N.A.
on procedure, 202n., 213n., 237n., 275n.
on c'tees, 237n., 251n.
on budget, 255n.
on C.R., 276n., 283n.
Blocquaux, Jean, (M.R.P. d.), 265n., 279n.*
Blondel, Jean, 348n.
Blondelle, René (b. 1907, founded first beetroot-growers assoc. in Aisne 1929; ex-Pres. F.N.S.E.A.), 334n., 336n.
Blum, Léon (1872–1950, M.P. 1919, P.M. 1936)
cabinets, pre-war, 160, 173, 243n.
and admin., 188
and Coms., 12, 45
career, App. II, III, IV
pre-war, 34
as P.M., 19, 183n., 188n., 377
stands for P.M. 1947: 32, 152n., 184 and n.47, 186 and n.
offered H.C.M. seat, 301n.
political position
pre-war, 45, 61, 149, 247n.
at liberation, 62–3, 73
and de Gaulle, 17
on Ramadier govt., 371
and 2nd Bidault govt., 180
views
on const., 164 and n., 179n., 180, 187 and nn., 188, 190, 214 and nn., 228n., 274n.
on c'tees, 235n., 240 and n., 242n., 250n.
on elec. system, 310 and n.
on parl. reform, 207 and n. 53, 209 and n.
on Bonapartism, 132n.
Blum cabinet, December 1946–January 1947
formed, membership, 19, 33, 184n.46, 377, **378**
popularity, **22** and n.
and press law, 390
fall, 22, 225, 226n.
Bobigny, 90–1
Bodley, J. E. C.
on const., 162n., 398
on occupations of M.Ps., 4n., 206n.
on French politics, 1n., 4n., 6n., 7n., 9n., 168n.
Boissière, J. Galtier-, 6n.
Boissons c'tee of N.A., 236n., 241n.19, 335
boîtiers, 197, 409n.*
Bonapartism
Emperor, 163
pretender, 151n.

INDEX

Bonapartism (*cont'd*)
  plebiscites, 403
  and R.P.F., 102, 131, 132 and n., 163
Boncour, *see* Paul-Boncour
Bonnefous, Édouard (b. 1907, M.P. 1946, U.D.S.R. d. Seine-et-Oise II), 238n., App. III
Bordeaux, 150n., 168n., 174, 240n.
  in 1951 election, 98n., 130, 143, 348
  mayor of, 61*, 98, 348
  R.P.F. and, 132, 137n.
  and see Gironde.
Bouches-du-Rhône, dept. (two constituencies, I Marseilles, *q.v.*: II the remainder)
  1951 election in, 74n.
  rep. in 2nd chamber, 267n.*, 272
bouilleurs de cru, 257n., 328n., 340n., 410n.
Boulanger, General Georges-Ernest (1837–91, M.P. 1888), 7, 163
Boulangist crisis, 90
Boulogne, 49n., 240n.
Bourbon family, 150, 151n.
Bourg-la-Reine, 54n., 101n.
Bourgès-Maunoury, Maurice (b. 1914, M.P. 1946, u.-sec. 1950, Rad. d. H-Garonne), 102, 244n., App. III
Bourgeois, Léon (1851–1925, M.P. 1888, P.M. 1895, s. 1905, Pres. Sen. 1920–3), 180n., 269
Boutemy, André (b. 1905, prefect of Loire 1943, regional prefect at Lyons 1944, M.P. (s.) 1952, Cons. s. Seine-et-Marne 1952–), 356n., App. III
Bouxom, Fernand, (M.R.P. d.), 78n.
Brayance, Alain, 44n., 49–56nn.
Brest, 193n.
Briand, Aristide (1862–1932, M.P. 1902, P.M. 1909, stood Pres. Rep., 1932), 140, 170, 373
Bridel, *see* Debû-Bridel
Brindillac, Charles, 391n.
Brinon, Fernand de (Vichy rep. with German occup. authorities, executed 1947), 306n.
Britain, French Com. and, 1940–1...47
Britain, comparisons with
  general, 1–3
  attitude to authority, 4–5
  attitude to democracy, 406–7
  attitude to taxation, 252
  standard of living, 398
  admin., 21, 189n., 250n., 252
  electoral system, 309, 314n., 316, 325
  parl.
    regime and Ass. regime, 163, 166 and n., 211
    c'tees, 239
    disorder and obstruction, 199, 200
    interpellations, 212
    and premiership, 187 and n.

Britain, comparisons with
  parl. (*cont'd*)
    private members bills, 203
    and expenditure, 252
    second chambers, 268, 273–9
    Speaker and Pres. of N.A., 198, 207
    votes of confidence and censure, 214 and n., 225
  parties
    divisions between, 3–4, 21
    discipline in, **155**, 159, 161–3, 166–7, 213–4, 231–2, 356, 361, 400–1
    and dissolution, 213, **231-2**
    and floating vote, 312, **356**, 399
    minor, injured by electoral system, 62, 310–1
    'relic,' 141
  pol. system
    bargaining and pressure-groups, 400
    constituency interests, 399
    leftism (Bevanites), 87
    marginal votes, 399
    non-voters, 407
    religion and education, 1, 24, 86
    scandals, 327n.
Brittany, Bretons
  clerical question, 74, 77, 113, 137n., **330n.**
  c'tee rep., 240 and n.
  regionalism, 334
  mentioned, 205, 294
broadcasting, 188n., 345
Brogan, Prof. D. W., 5n., 8nn., 169 and n., 250n.
Brune, Charles (b. 1891, M.P. (s.) 1946, Rad. s. Eure-et-Loir, Pres. R.G.R. in C.R.), 281*, App. III
Bruyas, Jean, 177n., 272n., 275n., 277n., 280nn. 31 and 33, 283n., 285n.
Bryce, Lord, 267n.
budget, procedure for, chapter 16 and *also*:
  in Finance c'tee, 235, 250
  and Chamber and N.A., 195, 196n., 201, 211, 217 and n.
  and C.R., 274–5, 285
  not sent to E.C., 297
  and pressure-groups, 337
  and see initiative, financial; taxation (*below*).
budgets, annual, for 1947–54, **254–6**, 259–62 *and also*:
  for 1947: 244
  1949: 220 and n., 280 and n.
  1950: 37, 198, 219n., 244nn., 281, App. IV
  1951: 38, 208, 217n, 221, 281, 283
  1952: 41–2, 217n., 245nn.
  1953: 217n., 245n., 281n.
  1954: 412–3 and n.

budgets, departmental
  and N.A., 208, 247 and n., 412–3
  education, 246n., 413 and n.
  military
    for 1946: 17n., 214
    1948: 33, 225n., 244–5
    1950: 244 and n.
    1951: 261, 262n., App. IV
    1952: 256
    1954: 413n.
  pensions, 240n.
  reconstruction, 255n.
Budget, Ms. of the, 237n., 254–6nn., 384n.
budgetary policy
  economies, 261, 330, 409, 413, App. IV
  investment, *q.v.*
  loans, financing by, 42, 255–7
  loi de finances, 254, 255, 259, 261, 280
  taxation
    fiscal amnesty, 219n., App. IV
    fiscal reform, 263n., 264n.
    increase of, in 4th Rep., 253, 256–7 and n.
    increase of, checked by Pinay, 42
    and nat. income, 256, 393
    and parl. control, 255, 262 and n.
  taxation, resistance to and evasion of, 5, 21–3, 175, 252
    by C.R., 280, 281 and n.
    by Fin. c'tee, 243, 245 and n.
    by P.M.E., 149, 332
    by Rads., 105, 280
    Queuille's (1948), 220n.
    Faure's (1952), 21, 42, 245 and n., 256, App. IV
    Mayer levy, *q.v.*
    Bidault budget, *q.v.*
Bulletin des commissions, 240–1nn., 247n.39, 257–8, 259n., 262–3nn.
Bulletin du Conseil Économique, 299–300nn.
Bulletin intérieur du parti socialiste, 22n., 64n., 68n., 266n., 371n., 373n.36, 387n.
Bulletin mensuel de statistique, 2n.
bureaux of N.A. and C.R., *see* Parliament.
Bureau central de renseignements et d'action (B.C.R.A.), 386n., 387–8
bureaucracy, influence of
  cabinet as defence against, 327n.
  electoral (suspected), 230
  Ms. and, 251, 399
  on policy, 2, 10 and n., 391, 405 and n., 410
  Rad. distrust of, 7, 10, 91
  and see civil servants; Finance, M. of; scandals (admin.).
Burke, Edmund, 312, 363
business as pressure-group, 328, 331 *and see* C.N.P.F., P.M.E.
Butler, Dr. D. E., 314n.

by-elections
  abolished 1945–6, 344, 345
  restored 1951, 322, 445
  local, 1949, 134, 135n.
  parl., 1952, 123 and n.
Byé, Maurice, 298nn.

CABINET
  composition of
    caretaker (for dissolution), 230–1 and n., 364n.
    caretaker (in Britain), 376 and n.
    depts. rep. in, 375
    depts, rivalries of, 391–2
    formation, **178–87**, 188 and n., 381–3, 409
    senators in, 281, 285, App. III
    size, 188 and n., 250n., 376
  in const., 187n.
  functions
    appointments, 172, 189 and n., 190
    and v. of c., 223 and n.
  working
    meetings and title, 174 and n.
    minutes, 410n.
    secretariat, 172 and n., 189n., 404 and n.
    solidarity, lack of, 205, 343, 374, **381–5, 392–5**, 405n.
    and v. of c., 223–4
  resignation, *see* Presidency.
  checks upon, 8–10, **157–61**, 165, 250–1, 260–1
cabinet, of H.C.F.U., 293 and n.
cabinets, ministeriel, 327 and n., 385n., 389
Cachin, Marcel (b. 1869, M.P. 1914, s. 1935, Com. d. Seine II), 198
Cadart, Jacques, 284n., 297n., 313n.
Cadillac c'tee of Rad. P., 97, 366, 371
Cahiers . . ., *see* Fondation nationale des sciences politiques.
Caillaux, Joseph (1863–1944, M.P. 1898, P.M. 1911, s. 1924, chairman Fin. c'tee of Sen. 1932), 11, 91, 243
Calais, 49n., 240n.
Calvados, dept. (cap. Caen), 137n., 150
Cambodia, 294
  King of, 296n., 410
Cambridge Journal, 178n., 204n., 306n., 383n., 387n., 399n., 408n.
Campbell, Peter
  on Ms., 325n., 380n., 383n.
  on Parl., 191nn., 193n., 265n., 266n., 383n.
  on party discipline, 361n.
Campion, Lord, 237n., 250n.
Canard enchaîné, Le, 163
candidatures, **346–51**
  bogus, 322n.30
  of civil servants, 192
  freak, 345nn., 348

INDEX 457

candidatures (*cont'd*)
  independent, 135 and n., 314, 348, 354, 364
  local, 135 and n., 350–1
  and see constituency interests; elections; regional differences.
Capitant, René (b. 1901, M.P. 1945, U.D.S.R. and R.P.F. d., B-Rhin 1945-6, Seine II 1946-51)
  and Gaullist Union, 19, 120
  as M., App. III
  as party leader, 144, 162n., 224
  against P.R., 315n.
Carcassonne, 339n.
Carnot, Sadi (1837–94, Pres. Rep. 1887-94), 169, 170
Carrefour (pro-R.P.F. journal), 133n., 185n, 317n., 336 and n.
Cartel des gauches, *see* gauches.
Cartels and E.C., 300
Casalegno, C., 139n.
Casimir-Périer, Jean (1847–1907, M.P. 1876, P.M. 1893, Pres. Chamber 1894, Pres. Rep. 1894-5), 169
Cassin, René, 404n.
Catholics, *see* Church.
Catroux, Diomède (b. 1916, M.P. 1951, R.P.F. d. Maine-et-Loire), 135n.
Cavaignac, General Louis-Eugène (1802–57, M.P. 1848, *chef du pouv. exéc.* June 1848, stood for Pres. Rep. December 1848), 179n.
Cayeux, Jean (M.R.P. d.), 331n., 336 and n., 365n.*
Cazilhac, 339n.
Celigny, *see* Solal-Celigny.
Ce Matin, 281n.
censure, vote of
  in ' Soc. const.', 213
  in provisional regime, 214
  in const., 215, 222, **224–5 and n.**
  in revision proposals, 229, 231n.
centralization, 2, 230, 306 and n., 399–400, 404n.
  dangers of, *see* dissolution.
  dangers of relaxing, 387
Centre national des Indépendants et Paysans, **109, 110–1**
Ceux de la Résistance, 143n.
Cevennes, 53, 109, 111 and n., 113, 114, 330n.
Chaban-Delmas, General Jacques (b. 1915, M.P. 1946, mayor of Bordeaux, chairman U.R.A.S. parl. group, Rad. and R.P.F. d. Gironde I), 98, 102, 133, 348, 354
Chambaretaud, Léon, 97n., 147–8, 150n., 323n.30
Chamber of Deputies, **154–60, 211–3**
  President of, 8, 198 and n., 363
  in electing Pres. Rep., 203
  term of, 194
  end of, 1940...14

Chamber of Deputies (*cont'd*)
  class composition of, 206 and n.
  Coms. expelled, 1940...4–6
  party discipline in, 359
  tendency to drift to Right, 9, 160
  and see Parliament.
Chamber of Deputies (building) attacked, 6 February 1934...45
Chambrun, Gilbert de (Prog. d. Lozère), 142n.
Champagne, 113, 294, 339
champagne, 339
Chapman, Brian, 306n., 404n.
Chapuis, *see* Poinso-Chapuis.
Chapus, René, 264nn.
Charente, dept. (cap. Angoulême), 348
Chartier, Émile, *see* Alain.
Chartism, 397
chauffeur as candidate, 322n.
Chautemps, Camille (b. 1885, M.P. 1919, P.M. 1930, s. 1934, vice-P.M. 1940), 13*, 92
Chavagnes, René (b. 1883, d. 1924, Rep. Soc.), 298n.
Cher, dept. (cap. Bourges), 4, 85n.
Cherbourg, 240n., 370
Chevallier, Louis, 397n.
Chiappe, Jean (1878–1940, prefect of police 1927–34, pres. Paris munic. council 1935 and 1940, killed flying to Syria as High Comm.), 12, 386
China lobby, 338, 400
Christiaens, Louis (R.I. d. Nord II), 110
Chupin, Alfred (b. 1916, M.P. 1951, ex-mayor Brest, R.P.F. and U.D.S.R. d. Finistère), 126n.
Church, political position of
  and democracy, 1, 3, 6, 154, 398
  and 4th Force, 110
  left-wing Catholics, 73, 143
  lois laïques, 192n.
  and M.R.P., 74, 77–8, 318, 329
  as pressure-group, 329, 335
  and R.P.F., 329
  and schools, *see next entry*.
  and social security, 77, 404
  and symbolic issues, 9–10 and n.
  and towns, 4
Church schools question
  and const., 17, 188n., 292 and n., 307 and n.
  pol. consequences
    divides M.R.P. and Socs., 16 and n. 17, 24–5, 41 and n., 240
    rivalry of M.R.P. and R.P.F., 28, 326, 356
  R.P.F. policy, 135
  as regional problem, 329, 334
  instances
    colliery schools, 1948...33, 249, 383–4 and nn.
    Poinso-Chapuis decree, 1948...33, 188n., 249, 372, 383–4 and n., 392

Church schools question
  instances (cont'd)
    Barangé law, 1951
      and const., 292 and n.
      M.R.P. and, 122, 353
      Rads. and, 41, 104 and n., 146, 148n.
      R.P.F. and, 122, 135
      Socs. and, 41, 122
      U.D.S.R. and, 144n., 146
      passing of, 41, 225n., 248–9, **330**, 383, 384 and n., App. IV
      political consequences of, 122, 190n., 221
      admin. of, 265n.
  tax strike threatened over, 339
Churchill, Rt. Hon. Sir W. S., 118, 129, 400
Churchill cabinets
  1945...376
  1951...250n.
cider-growers, 328n., 337
cine-clubs, 55n.
City of London, 13n, 47
civil servants
  conditions
    recruitment, 389 and n., 404
    pay, 22, 37, 219, 223, 241, 243, 245, 260, 330–1
    allowances, 260n., 265n.38
    reclassification, 260nn.
    promotion, 388, 389, 412n.
    dismissals, 33, 248
    retirement, 412n.
  and politics
    and E.C., 298
    and parties, 331, 378
    and candidatures, 192
    as pressure-group, 328–9
    strikes, 359, 409–10
civil servants, senior
  appointments, 172, 189n., 389 and n., 404
  colonization by parties, 374, **384–9**
  influence on policy, *see* bureaucracy.
civil service
  reform proposed, 34, 263
  Ministerial resp. for, 188, 189n.
  and see bureaucracy; cabinets.
Clark, R. T., 343n.
classes, social
  in C.R., 281, 282, 284
  in E.C., 297
  in electioneering, 333, 356
  in parl., 206 and n., 333
  and see each party.
Claudius-Petit, *see* Petit.
Clemenceau, Georges (1841–1929, M.P. 1876, s. 1902, P.M. 1906 and 1917, chairman Sen. army c'tee, stood Pres. Rep. 1920)
  as critic, 157, 212, 234*
  as M., 8, 91–2, 179, 364
  as pres. aspirant, 170

Clemenceau, Michel (son of above, b. 1873, P.R.L. d. Seine-et-Marne 1945–51, pres. P.R.L.), 109
Clermont-Ferrand, 57, 328n.
clocks, stopping of, in N.A., 195, 252
Clostermann, Pierre (b. 1921, M.P. 1946, U.D.S.R. and R.P.F. d. B-Rhin, R.P.F. d. Marne; aviator), 135n., 350n.
closure of debate, 200
clôture of sessions, 10, 195, 196, 403
coal industry
  Com. infiltration, 385 and n.
  investment, 246n.
  rep. on E.C., 300n.
  strike in, 36
  subsidy for, 218, 223
Cobban, Dr. Alfred, 267n.
Coca-cola, 142, 349
Cochin-China, 152n., 184n., 191n., 294
Colin, André (b. 1910, M.P. 1945, M.R.P. d. Finistère, sec.-gen. M.R.P.), 78n., 87, 409n.*, App. III
collaborators
  amnesty, 282n.
  Ducreux, 192
  ex-Com., 48
  and see purge.
collective bargaining, *see* wages.
Collet, P., 281n.
Colliard, C.A., 217n., 219n., 223n.
colliery schools, 33, 249, 383–4 and nn.
Colmar, 351
colonial
  assimilation policy, 293–4
  appointments; Cs. R.; deputies; elec. law; franchise; govs.; M.Ps.; Ministry, *see* overseas ditto.
  nationalism, *q.v.*
  self-government, *q.v.*
  and see French Union.
' colonization,' 57, 374, 384–9
colons, 152–3, 190 and n., 292, 331n., 386, 410
Combat (Resistance org. and organ) 333n., 390
Combes cabinet, 7, 159
Cominform, 175
Comité d'action pour la liberté scolaire, 330
Comité national de défense laïque, 330
Commerce, M. of
  status, 189n.64
  and parties, 379n., 380 and n.
Commissariat général au plan, 391, 404*
Commission de vérification des comptes des entreprises publiques, 266
Committees of the N.A., Chapter 15
  membership
    alternates, 247 and n.
    chairmen
      chance of office of, 238 and n.
      and Court of Accounts, 266

INDEX

Committees of the N.A.
  membership
    chairmen (*cont'd*)
      and parties, 207, 239 and n., 409n.
      and Pres. Conf., 157, 199, 206–7, 235
    election, 194n., 196, 235
    rapporteurs, q.v.
  in debate
    allotment of time, 201 and n.
    and bills referred back, 177n.
    c'tee bench, 197, 235
    procedural privileges, 200–1, 207nn., 235
    question-time in, 237 and n.
    and restricted debate, 200
    and unopposed bills, 203 and n.
    and urgency procedure, 208 and n.
  political
    conflicts of jurisdiction, 248–9 and n.
    and c'tees of C.R., 277
    discipline in, 239, 244, 247–9 and nn., 412n.
    and govt., 8, 9, 158, 203, 296n. and Chapter 15
  of enquiry, 203–4 and n.
  mentioned, 208
  and see C.R.; Senate; each committee separately.
Committees of C.R., 248n.42
Commune of 1871, 102, 163
Communications c'tee of N.A., 237n., 239n., 241, 242n.22, 262
Communist International, 44, 50
Communist party, Chapter 4, App. VII
  history
    in 3rd Rep., 12, 44–6, 311 and n.
    and Nazi-Soviet pact, 12, 46, 48, 355
    and occupation, 46, 61, 353
    in Resistance, 13, 46–7
    at liberation, 1945–7...11, 13–20, 48
    and de Gaulle, 13 and n., 16, 119
    ejected from office, 19–20
    1947–53...36–41
  clientèle
    numbers, 52
    class and geog. basis, 53–4, 446
    and see trade unions.
    and intelligentsia, 55
    and peasantry, 4, 47n., **54 and n.**, 55n., 332n., 333n., 337n., 355, 390, 398, **448n**
    and youth, 52
  discipline
    of deputies, 50, 346, 350, 361 and n. 368
    of leaders, 49, 52
    of *militants*, 58–9
    of trade unions, 57–8

Communist party
  discipline (*cont'd*)
    of voters, 311n., 319, 346, 359, 443n
    defiance of, successful, 354–5
      unsuccessful, 50 and n., 54n.
  militants, loyalty of, 74
  org., 49–52, 55, 57
  funds, 51 and n., 365
  in Parl.
    bills, cost of, 55n., 257n.
    and c'tee chairmen, 239n., 412
    in C.R., 272, 278
    and convoking N.A., 196 and n.
    and deputies' immunity, 193–4 and n.
    and deputies' salaries, 51 and n., 365
    group, 50, 239 and n., 253, 366, 381
    and impeachments, 306, *and see* Moch.
    obstruction in N.A., 177, 197, 199, 200
    in C.R., 277
    and vote of censure, 224
  and participation in govt., etc., 19–20, 50, 145, 180, **368, 378–9, 382 and n.** 447
  breaches of confidence, 204n., 246–7, 301n.
  infiltration, 57, 374, **385–7**, 389
    checks against, 378, 386–9 and nn.
  making system unworkable, 145, 180, 233, 410
  policy
    clerical, 25, 53
    colonial, 151–2, 174, 218
    const.
      in 1945–6...16–19
      and dissolution, 230 and n., 231
      and elec. law, 25, 38, 40, 45, 315, **319**, 321–2, 325
      and H.C.M., 301 and n.
      and legislation by c'tees, 237
    econ., 55n., 332 and n., 368, 392
    foreign and defence, 13, 17n., 46, 245, 408, 411
    T.U. and social, 47, 56, 263n., 368, 382
  and rivals
    general, 24–5
    Cons., 47, 55n., 312
    Fascism, 45–6
    M.R.P., 62, 72, 119, 315
    Progs., 142, 236
    Rads., 14, 45–6, 92–3, 98, 143, 412
    R.P.F., 36, 57–8, 121, 122, 124, 131, 357 and n.
    Socs., **44–6**, 47, 62, 67, 72, 356–7, 394n, 412
    Auriol, 175
    Comte de Paris, 151n.
  and illegality, 48, 50, 58

Communist party (*cont'd*)
  and scandals, 266n.38, 350n., 354–5, 392
  ex-Communists
    in 3rd Rep., 12, 48, 139n., 373
    in 4th Rep., 50 and n., 54n., 142
  violence used against, 48, 142–3
Communist party statutes, 51n.
Comores, 294n.
Compagnies républicaines de sécurité (C.R.S.), 386–7
compensation
  in const., 307n.
  in press law, 390
Compiègne, 111–2, 218
comptes spéciaux du trésor, 265 and n.
compulsory arbitration, *see* arbitration; wages.
Concentration républicaine, 348
concierges, 335
conciliators, pol. importance of, 33–4, 190 and n., 362–3, 383
Confédération française des travailleurs chrétiens (C.F.T.C.), *see* trade unions
Confédération générale de l'agriculture (C.G.A.), *see* agriculture.
Confédération générale des cadres, 340n.
Confédération générale des syndicats indépendants (C.G.S.I.), 124n
Confédération générale du travail (C.G.T.), *see* trade unions.
confidence
  breaches of, *see* Communist party.
  votes of, Chapter 14, 403
    in 3rd Rep., 164-5, 187, 212
    in 4th Rep.
      on budget, 198, 244n., 255, 259
      against c'tees, 241 and n., 244 and n., 245
      only P.M. may put, 187
      by individual P.Ms.
        Bidault, 198
        Laniel, 413
        Marie (in C.R.), 35, 277n.
        Mayer, 408, 413
        Pleven, 178n., 262
        Ramadier, 19, 178n., 180, 371, 372, 383
      and see individual P.Ms.
      pledges on use of, 413
      unofficial, 35, 180, 216, 218–20 and n., 413
      and individual ministers, 180n., 202
      and see majority, absolute.
Congo, French, 184n.
Congrès du Parlement, 414n.
Congress of the United States, 201
conscience
  of M.R.P., publicly displayed, 89
  Nonconformist, 86
conscientious objectors, 282n.
conscription, 5, 191
Conseil d'État, 189n., 193, 404, 407*

Conseil national du patronat français (C.N.P.F.), 136*, 340, 356n.
Conservatism, French, character of, *see* Reaction.
Conservatives, Chapter 8, App. VII
  defined, 14n.
  history
    in 3rd Rep., 158–9
    under Vichy, 116, 133
    at liberation, 1945–7...13, 109
    and de Gaulle, 14, 119
    1947–53...32–3, 36–42
  clientèle, 109, 110 and n., 112, 446
  discipline
    of deputies, 361 and n., 383
    of voters, 443n.
  militants and deputies, 112n.
  org., 110–2
  in Parl, 14n., 196, 412n.
  and participation in govt., 109, 204, 379–80 and n., 383, 447
  policy
    agric., 23, 111, 332
    clerical, 25
    colonial, 24, 41
    const., 165
      and dissolution, 220
      and elec. system, 37–8, 40, 315 and n., 318, 320–2, 325
      and H.C.M., 301
      and *statut des partis*, 346
    econ., 23, 32, 37, 42, 116
    T.U. and social, 136
  and rivals
    general, 24–5
    and Com., 47, 55n., 312
    and M.R.P., 24, 79, 114, 380, 382
    and Rad., 98, 100, 104, 108, 112–3, 114, 356
    and R.P.F., 7, 100, 111, 115, 117, 121, 136–7, 351 and n.
    and Soc., 110, 356
  and F.N.S.E.A., 332–3
  ex-Conservatives, 122n., 137, 348 and n., 383, 412n.
  and see Action républicaine et sociale; Peasant party; Republican Independents.
constituencies, size of, 314, 315 and n., 349, *and see* elec. systems (*s.d.l.*)
constituency interests and deputy
  in 3rd Rep., 313, 318, 334
  log-rolling, 252 and n., 328 and n
  member's contact
    closeness of, 205, 339n., 349–50
    local men preferred, 350–1
    in R.P.F., 125, 129, 135 and n., 137, 350 and n., 351
  senators' competition, 281n.
  urban-rural difference, 205, 334, 349, 353, 355

INDEX 461

constituency interests and deputy (*cont'd*)
  member's function
    as bestower of favours, 334, 349–50 and n.
    effect of elec. system, 104, 257, 312, 313, **328–9**, 334, 347 and n., **349**
  member's influence on constituents, 219, 347, 399–400
  member's importance to his party, 347–8, 353, 355 and n.
  parl. melting-pot, 205
Constituent Assemblies, *see* Assemblies.
Constitutions, French, Chapter 11; p. 1
Constitution, 1945–6 provisional regime for, **14–20**
  elec. law, 315 ff., 344
    woman suffrage, 309
  finance and private members, 257
  ministerial resp., **167–8**, 176
    govt. and N.A., **213–5**
  premiership, **179–80**
  Pres. Rep., 173, 176
  and de Gaulle, 119
  discontent with, 19
Constitution, April 1946 draft
  and crises, 228
  and dissolution, 195
  and elec. law, 315, 345
  and preamble, 17, 307
  and presidency, 170–2
  and ' second chamber,' 269, 296
  and vs. of c., 215, 217 and n.
  party views on, 17–18, 79, 119–20, 144
Constitution of 4th Rep., Chapter 11, *and see especially*
  C.R., 269–70, 273
  French Union, 292
  govt. and N.A., 228–9
  Presidency, 170–2
  principles, fundamental, 307–8
  referendum, 18–9
  Preamble, *q.v.*
  Article 1...292 and n.
    3...191
    5...273
    6...203, 270, 271
    7...202, 274
    9...195, 273, 291 and n.
    11...197, 230, 273, 365n.15
    12...196
    13...168, 262–4 and n., 291
    14...187 and n., 189n., 274, 276, 279, 285n.
    15...236
    16...254
    17...**257–60**, 276, 279n., 412n.
    18...266
    19...203
    20...**274, 275, 276**, 282, 285n.
    21...193
    22...193–4
    23...193

Constitution of 4th Rep.
  Article 25...297
    27...202, 274, 285n.
    28...202
    29...274
    30...187n., 189n., 190n.
    32...172n., 187n.
    35...300, 302
    36...176, 177, 198n., 291
    37...273
    38...187 and n., 189, 203
    40...187n.
    41...198n.
    44...151n.
    45...161n., **179, 180n.**, 187n., 198n., 201, 213n., 225, 229
    46...187 and n., 189n.
    47...174, 187n., 189 and n.
    48...180n., 201–2, 274, 279
    49...187 and n., 190n., 202, 211, **215**, 229
    50...187n., 202, 211, **215**, 229
    51...190n., 198n., 211, 216, **228-9**
    52...187n., 198n., **230–1**, 365n.15
    53...236
    55...187n.
    57–59...305
    62...296n.
    67...274
    69...294
    72...294
    74...294, 295n.
    75...294, 295n.
    77...294
    83...203, 300
    84...189n., 300, 303 and n.
    85–89...306
    90...182n., **287**, 288n., 289
    91...203, 274, **289**, 292n., 365n.15
    92...**289**, 291, 292n., 306
    93...289, 290
    94...168, 288
    95...288
    102...270–1
Constitution, April 1946 draft, Article 83...195, 228n.
Const. of Bayeux, 18–19, 119, 120, **161–3***, 369
Const., Madagascar, 167
Const., Soc. conception, 228–9
Constitutional C'tee, 169n., 176 and n., 177, 201n., 203, **289**, 365n.
Constitutional revision
  3rd Rep., 1884...267
    1940...14
    1945 (possible), 14
  procedure, 182n., 195 and n., 202, **287–9**

Constitutional revision (*cont'd*)
C.R. and, 274
Const. C'tee and, 289-92
proposals
1950 and 1953...182n., **287-8**
Reynaud, 1953...408
resolution of November 1950...37, 182n., 208
and C.R., 280n.31, 283-5
formation of govts., 182-3
v. of c.: no abs. maj., 229
bill of July 1953...409, App. IV
bureau, 197n., 231
caretaker govt., 231 and n.
clôture, 196 and n.
convocation of N.A., 196n.
and C.R., 285n.
and formation of govt, 185n.
immunity, 194
v. of c.
keeps abs. maj., 230
delay, 217n.
constitutionality of laws, 289-90
consumers, on E.C., 300
Conte, Arthur (b. 1920, M.P. 1951, Soc. d. Pyrénées-O.), 150n., 354
Convention of 1793...163, 165
convocation of N.A., 196 and n.
co-operators, on E.C., 297
Corn Laws, 396-7
Corporation paysanne, 117n.
corporatism
of pressure-groups, 340n.
of M.R.P., 83, 86, 165, 269
of R.P.F., 124
and E.C., 297
corps intermédiaires, 308, 344, 363
Corrèze, dept. (cap. Tulle), 4, 54n., 442
Corsica (Corse dept., cap. Ajaccio), 65, 94, 241n.19, 351
mentioned, 101n., 191
cortèges d'espérances — et de déceptions, 184
Corval, Pierre, 410n.
Coste-Floret, Paul (b. 1911, M.P. 1945, M.R.P. d. Hérault)
as *rapp.-g.* of const., 165 and n., 176, 180n.*, 181n.*, 182n.*, 187n., 302n.
as c'tee chairman and M., 238n., App. III
Cot, Pierre (b. 1895, M.P. 1928, Rad. and Prog. d. Savoie 1945-51, Prog. d. Rhône I since 1951, *rapp.-g.* of draft const.)
constituencies, 353
on const. revision, 288, 289, 413
on elec. and party system, 315, 346
as parliamentarian, 51
pol. position, 46n., 102, 141, 142n.
quoted
on dissolution, 227n., 228n., 413

Cot, Pierre
quoted (*cont'd*)
on H.C.M., 301n.
on Pres. and P.M., 178n.
Côte d'Or, dept. (cap. Dijon), 110
Côtes-du-Nord, dept. (cap. St. Brieuc), 80, 241n.19
Coty, François (1874-1934, s. 1923-4, millionaire perfume manufacturer, founder of *Solidarité française*), 12
Coty, René (b. 1882, M.P. 1923, s. 1935, voted for Pétain 1940 but refused office, R.I. d. and s. Seine-Inférieure, Pres. Rep. 1954), 228n., 411n., 414, App. III
Coudert, Lucien, (Rad. d.), 323n.30
Council of Europe, 222, 350
Council of Ministers, *see* cabinet.
Council of National Defence, 172
Council of the Republic, Chapter 17, 397-8, 403-4; *see also*:
status, 191, 288 and n., 291
and A.F.U., 294, 296
c'tees of, rules for, 248, 279
elec. law for, 1946...309, 345 and n.
functions
in revising const., 182n.
in declaring war, 202
in electing Pres. Rep., 203
seating, 1948...7
members
bills introduced by, *see* bills.
migration to and from N.A., 192
part elected by N.A., 203, **270, 271 and n.,** 345
rep. in party orgs., 96, 148
and see Parliament, members of.
and parties
disc. worse in, 361
R.P.F. and, 121, 122
strengths, 1948...36
and policy
budgets, 254, 255, 261
elec. reform, 222n., 322 and n.
overseas franchise, 296n., *and q.v.*
wages, 41n., *and q.v.*
mentioned, 208
countersign
by whom, 187-8
when, 169 and n.
and const. c'tee, 176n.
and executive decrees, 173, 189
in H.C.M., 304
and reference back, 177 and n.
Courant, Pierre (b. 1897, M.P. 1945, R.I. d. Seine-Inf. II, mayor of Le Havre), 255n., App. III
courtesy votes, 185n.
Courts
of Accounts, 255, **265, 266 and n.,** 404
admin., 407 *and see Conseil d'État*.
of Cassation, 302, 303n.
and H.C.M., **301-5,** 404

INDEX

Courts (*cont'd*)
  local, 241, 391
  not to be reorganized by decree-laws, 263
  and see Magistrates.
Couve de Murville, Jacques-Maurice (b. 1907, Amb. at Rome and Cairo), 264
credentials, in N.A., 192–3, 197n.
Creuse, dept. (cap. Guéret), 4, 311n.
Crimean War, 166
crises, ministerial (general), **177–87**, 225–33
  pol. function of, 399, 408–9 and nn.
  unimportance of, 374
  number of, in 3rd Rep., 10
  deputies' meditations upon, 218, 367 and n.
  harder to solve in 4th Rep., 313, 357–8, 375
  manœuvres in, 375
  'orange-peel,' 230
  and see instability.
crises, ministerial (specific)
  and Auriol, 1946...173
  series of, 1948...121–2
  new type of, 1949...36
  result from defeat in N.A., 1950–3...226–7
  of 1953...408–9
  and see individual P.Ms. (fall of cabinets).
Croix de feu, 12, 13, 108, 139
Croizat, Ambrose (1901–51, M.P. 1936, Com. d. Seine I), 331n., App. III
Crown, British, 166
Cube, Mr., 400
Cudlipp, Percy, 69n.
Curie, *see* Joliot-.
currency, 248, 392, *and see* devaluation; economic policy.
customs
  officers, strike of, 339
  treaties, 202n., 299
Czechoslovakia, 217n.

DAGAIN, Léon, (Soc. d.), 323n.30
Daily Herald, 69n.
Dakar, 194n.
Daladier, Édouard (b. 1884, M.P. 1919, P.M. 1933, Rad. d. Vaucluse)
  as young Rad., 11, 97n., 104
  and Coms, 45, 46, 192
  and Munich, 10, 46
  deported by Germans, 92
  party offices, post-war, 94, 98, 146, 147
  political position, post-war, 97, 102–3, 147–8 and n., 368, 411 and n.
  quoted, 99, 324n.
  mentioned, 111
Dansette, Adrien, 414n.

Darlan, Admiral Jean-François (1881–1942, M. of Marine 1940, named Pétain's successor 1941, chief of state Algiers November 1942, assassinated December), 386
Darnand, Joseph (Waffen SS major, sec.-gen. Vichy militia, executed 1945, aged 48), 306n.
Dassonville, Gaston (Com. d. Pas-de-Calais I), 355 and n.
Dauzat, Albert, 335n.
Dax, 192n.
Déat, Marcel (1894–?, Soc. and Neo-Soc. d. 1932–36, 1939–40, founded *Rassemblement National Populaire*, M. of Labour and National Solidarity 1944, disappeared in Germany), 6, 12, 61
Deauville, 98
Debré, Michel (b. 1912, M.P. 1948, R.G.R. and R.P.F. s. Indre-et-Loire), 102, 133, 264n., 344n.
Debû-Bridel, Jacques (b. 1902, M.P. 1948, R.P.F. s. Seine) quoted, 47n., 344n., 346n., 388n., 393n.
Declaration of war, 202, 274, 279
decree-laws and special powers, 253, **262–5**, 403, 406
  pre-war, 10, 168
  and const., 168, 291–2, 307
  Laniel's, 409, **412 and n.**
  Mayer's, 23, 409
  Reynaud's, 34, 35, 277, 291
decrees
  P.M. and, 189
  power to stop expenditure by, 256 and n., 412n.
Defence, and status of French Union, 296n.
Defence, C'tee of, and Council of National, 174
Defence c'tee
  of N.A., 204n., 234, 236n., 237, 239n., 245–7 and nn., 412n.
  of C.R., 412n.
Defence, M. of
  holders, 38, 188n., 189, 378, 384n.
  org., 388
  relation to P.M., 189, 377
  and provisional 12ths, 280, 413n.
  and parties, 377n., **378 and n.**, 380, 387, 388
  and political infiltration and attacks, 387, 392
Défense des contribuables, 149
Defos du Rau, Joseph (b. 1884, M.P. 1919, M.R.P. d. Landes), 207n.
Deixonne, Maurice (b. 1904, M.P. 1946, Soc. d. Tarn), 240
Dejean, Maurice, 410 and n.
Délégation des gauches, see gauches.

delegation of legislative power proposed: to c'tees of N.A., 237 and n.
to sections of N.A., 406
and see decree-laws.
Delmas, *see* Chaban-Delmas.
democracy
French conception of, 2, 4–5, 7, 33n., 154, **161-8**, 407
strength of, in France, 398, 407
' mass,' 343, 404
and see authoritarianism.
Denis, André (b. 1920, M.P. 1946, d. Dordogne ex-M.R.P.), 348 and n.*, 411 and n., 412n.
Departmental councils, *see* elections; local authorities.
departmental delegates in R.P.F., 128, 129nn.
departments of govt., *see* cabinet.
Dépêche de Toulouse, La (Rad. organ), 95
Déplat, *see* Martinaud-.
deportations by Germans, 302n.
deposit, electoral, 345 and n.
deputies, *see* constituency interests; overseas deputies; parliament, members of; party discipline.
Deschanel, Paul (1855–1922, M.P. 1885, Pres. Chamber 1898, Pres. Rep. January 1920, insane September 1920, s. 1921), 2, 170
Deux-Sèvres, *see* Sèvres, Deux-
devaluation
British 1949...37, 196
French 1948...33, 248, 383
French 1949...37, 196, 227
parl. consent unnecessary to, 209
développement, lois de, 254, 262n.
Diet, 1946 cabinet as, 381–2: *and see* cabinet; pigeons.
Diethelm, André (1896–1954, M.P. 1945, Cons.-Gaullist d. Vosges 1945–46, R.P.F. s. and d. Seine-et-Oise 1948–54), 125 and n., 356n., 413*, App. III
diplomatic service, 264
dirigisme, 21*, 55n., 332*, 339, *and see* economic policy.
discipline: of judges, 302–3
of politicians, *see* party discipline.
disjonction, 258 and n.
Disraeli, B., 166n.
dissolution
in 3rd Rep., 8, 155–6, 169, 178, 211
in const.
of Bayeux, 162 and n.
proposed by Socs., 165, 213
of 4th Rep., 180n., 211, 216, 220, **227-33**
first fortnight clause, 180n.
decided in cabinet meeting, 190
caretaker govt., *see* cabinet.

dissolution
of first N.A.
demanded by de Gaulle, 32, 121 and n., 195, 277–8
in 1951...195
threat of, as pol. weapon, 220, 355n., 406, 413
Reynaud demands power of, 1953... 408
distributive trades, 300
Dordogne, dept. (cap. Périgueux), 148, 348 and n.
Doriot, Jacques (1898–1945, M.P. 1924, expelled from Com. P. 1934, founded *Parti populaire français* 1936, fought against Russia 1941–42), 12
dosage, 380, 408*, 409*
dossiers, and H.C.M., 304
Doumer, Paul (1857–1932, M.P. 1888, Pres. Chamber 1905, stood Pres. Rep. 1906, s. 1912, Pres. Sen. 1927, Pres. Rep. 1931–32), 170
Doumergue, Gaston (1863–1937, M.P. 1893, s. 1910, P.M. 1913–14, Pres. Sen. 1923, Pres. Rep. 1924–31, P.M. 1934), 156, 366
Downing Street, S.W., 400
doyen d'âge, 198
drafting of bills, 250
Drago, Roland, quoted, 172n., 174n., 177n., 193n., 221n., 291n.
Dreyfus case, 6, 60, 107, 396, 398
Dreyfus-Schmidt, Pierre (b. 1902, M.P. 1945, Rad. and Prog. d. Belfort), 102
Drôme, dept. (cap. Valence), 85
Dubost, Antonin (1844–1921, M.P. 1880, s. 1897, Pres. Sen. 1906–20), 173n., 269
Duchet, Roger (b. 1904, M.P. (s.) 1946, R.I. s. Côte d'Or, mayor of Beaune), 110, 111 and n., 257n., 286, App. III
Duclos, Jacques (b. 1896, M.P. 1926, Com. d. Seine VI)
in parl., 51, 224, 231
in party, 50n., 366, App. VII
in prison, 57, 193n.
quoted, 194n.
Ducreux, Jacques (real name Tacnet) (1912–52, M.P. 1951, Rad. d. Vosges), 192
Duhamel, Georges, 335n.
Dulin, André (Rad. s. Charente-Maritime), 334n.
Dunkirk, 49n., 102, 349
Dupont, *see* Frédéric-Dupont.
Dupuy, Marceau (b. 1894, M.P. 1946, Rad. d. Gironde 1946–51), 354 and n.
Duverger, Maurice, quoted
on const.
assembly and parl. regime, 167n.
cabinet-making, 382n.
constitutionality, 290nn., 307n.
C.R., 272n., 282n., 334n.

INDEX

Duverger, Maurice, quoted
on const. *(cont'd)*
  electoral systems, 310n., 311 and n., 313n.
  H.C.M., 302n.
  High Court, 306n.
  parl. sessions, 195n.
  Preamble, 306–8nn.
  Presidency, 171n., 177n.
on parties
  two blocs, 311n.5
  characteristics, 87n., 394–5 and n.
  distribution
    age, 69nn., 84n., 100n., 112n.
    geog., 47n., 53n., 93n.
    occup., 53n.
  period of membership, 69n.
  internal divisions, 65nn., 80n., 367 and n.
  org., 48n., 63n., 64n., 95nn., 96n., 97n.
  strength, 52n., 68nn., 108n.
  relations with other orgs., 55n., 91n., 311 and n.
on peasantry and C.R. 272n., 334n.
Dyke, Vernon Van, 58n.

EARLE, Edward Mead, quoted, 47n., 138n., 332nn., 355n., 397nn.
eau de vie, 328n.
École nationale d'admin., 389n., 404
Economic Affairs c'tee of N.A., 240, 246 and n., 333
Economic Affairs, M. of, 189n., 264, 380 and n., 391–2
Economic Council (E.C.)
  in 3rd Rep., 298
  in 4th Rep., **297–300**, 388n.
  status, 191, 284n.
  rep. of agric. in, 332
  members rep. on party organs, 96, 147n.
  resolution on lack of statistics, 256n.
economic policy, 21–3
  currency, 248, 392
  deflation, 37
  of *inspecteurs des fin.*, 391
  and national income, 256, 393, 405 and E.C., 297
  subsidies, 38
  Auriol on, 175
  Pinay's, 42, 225n.
  Ramadier's, 32
  Reynaud's, 34, 360
  and see budget; devaluation; food policy; investment; wages; and each party separately.
economism, 57
Economist, The, 166n.
Education c'tee of N.A., 240–2 and nn., 246n., 248–9 and n., 330

Education, M. of
  budget in N.A., 246n.39, 413 and n.
  holders, 377n.
  and parties, 379 and n., 380, 381, **392**
Ehrmann, Henry W., 44n., 47n.
Einaudi, Mario, 77n.
Eisenhower, General Dwight D., 56
election expenses, 344–5 and n., 356n., *and see* party funds.
Élections législatives, Les, 113n., 130n., 206n., 315n.
election results
  1936 Chamber, 12, 45
  1945 C.A., 16, 119
  June 1946 C.A., 18, 112
  November 1946 N.A., 19, 152
  June 1951 N.A., 38–40, 109, 122, 125
  and see by-elections.
elections for departmental councils
  1945...93
  1948, postponed, 36, 74, 277, 384
elections, municipal
  October 1947...32, 120, 343
  April 1953...117, 123, 408
elections to second chamber
  1948 C.R., 36, 121, 122, 277, 319
  1952 C.R., 148
elections, caretaker cabinet during, 230–1
elections, pol. consequences
  of frequency, 28
  of imminence, 208, 241, 259
  opposition an asset at, 28, 394
  union of Left at, 9, 45, 311
electoral colleges, 270–1
electoral law, municipal, 32, 248, 365n.*
electoral law, overseas, 153, 208, 282n., 296n., 322
electoral law and 2nd chamber
  Senate, 158, 267
  C.R., **270–2**, 278, 346, and *q.v.*
electoral system
  British, applies in French Guiana, 443.
electoral systems, Chapters 19 and 21
  party views, **318–22**, and also
    M.R.P., 25, 32, 38, 87, 220, 223–4
    Rad., 37–8, 104, 220, 223–4
    Soc., 164, 360
    and see each party separately (*under sub-head* policy: const.)
  pol. effects
    on alliances, **312**, 320, **322–4**, 326, 346, **357–8**, 405
    on stability, **405**
    on static and modern France, **398**
  proportional representation, **313–7**, 322
  principle of, to favour strong parties, 345
  mechanical working of, **App. VI**
  notional result of (1951), 40, **317 and n.**, 325

electoral systems (*cont'd*)
proportional representation
party views on, 25, 32, 164, **318–22**
and alliances, 16–17, 357–8, 405
and party and personal voting, 359 *and see s. d. l. below.*
and wasted votes, 316 and n., 325 and n.
within parl. and in govt., *see* Proportional representation.
scrutin d'arrondissement, **309–14**
party views, 87, 104, **318–9**, 321
C.R. favours, 280 and n.
peasantry favour, 334 and n.
weakened C.P., 12, 311n.
and party alliances, 87, 164, 312, 357, 405
and party discipline, **154–5**, 326, 346, 359
and party and personal voting, 104, 347 and n., 356
and constituency interests, 104, 257, **328–9**
and wasted votes, 325 and n.
scrutin de liste
different forms of
distributing seats, 310, 316, 319, 320, 326n., 346, 357, 406
rigidity, **313–5**, 322, 344, *and see panachage*; preferential vote.
views on
of Gaullists, 319–20
of Goguel, 326n.
pol. effects
on party alliances, 326n., 406
on party disc., 352–3, 359
on party and personal voting, 257, **347–8**, 354, 359, 372–3
on constituency interests, 257, **328–9**, 349
use of lower places, 351
electoral laws of 1945–46, *see above, and also*
de Gaulle's, 119n., 315, 344
April draft, 17, 315, 345
October 1946...315 and nn., 316, 323, 344–5
electoral law of 1951
passing of, 190n., 208, 321–2, 360 and c'tee, 248n.
and C.R., 178n., 280 and n., 283, 285
and Com. obstruction, 199
interpretation disputed, 193, 445
effects of, *see above, and also*
effects of, on parties individually, 40, 122, 129–30, 148 and n., 317 and n., **322–6**
and see ballot; by-elections; *panachage*; preferential vote.
Élysée, 302, 304n.

employers' orgs., *see* Conseil national du patronat français; Petites et moyennes entreprises.
Encyclopedie politique de la France et du monde, 50n., 95nn., 96n., 319n.
Ensor, R. C. K., 303n.
Épinal, 18
équipes, in M.R.P., 83, 411n.
Esprit (Left Catholic review), 143
on Com. P., 44n., 45n., 47n.
on deputies occups., 206n.
on E.C., 299n.
on elec. geog., 57n., 85n.
on elec. system, 321n.
on parl., 209n., 275nn.
budget, 256n., 258n.*, 262n.*
c'tees, 251n.
on pol. and econ. power, 190n., 328n., 336n., 391n., 397n.
on Rad. P., 99 and n., 105–6 and nn.
Estèbe, Paul (R.I. d. Gironde I since 1951), 150n.
Études et conjoncture, 256n.
Eure, dept (cap. Evreux), 101n..
Eure-et-Loir, dept. (cap. Chartres), 191n.
Europe, Council of, 222n., 350
European affairs, 209, 402, 408
European army
and const., 308n.
and parties, 137, 360, 372, 411–2 and nn., App. IV
and v. of c., 218n., 221, 408, 413
European Coal and Steel Authority, *see* Schuman plan.
executions, 302n., 306n.
executive and P.M., 187, *and see* authority; cabinet; decrees.
expenditure, *see* budget; private members.
expense allowance of ds., 193
expenses, elec., 344
expulsions, *see* party discipline; purges.
ex-servicemen, 138, 219n., 328, 337

FABRE, M. H., 169n., 185n.
Fajon, Étienne (b. 1906, M.P. 1936, Com. d. Seine V), 50n., 176n.
family
allowances, 201n., 219n., 224, 241 and n., 249 and n., 260n., 331
agric., 219n., 333 and n., 337 and n.
civil servants', 260n.
in E.C., 299 and n.
associations
and E.C., 297
and politics, 69, 331
firms, 331–2 and nn.
M.R.P. as 'party of,' 165, 379
and R.P.F., 124n.
vote (and M.R.P.), 165

INDEX

fares
  in London, 400
  in Paris, 391
Fascism, 12, 46, 109, 115, 116n., 138–9
  and see Coty, F.; Darnand; Déat; Doriot; de la Rocque; *Croix de feu.*
Faure, Edgar (b. 1908, M.P. 1946, Rad. d. Jura)
  career, 34n., App. II, III, IV
  as P.M., 41, 181, 183n., 186n.*, 188n., 331*, 373n. 36
  use of v. of c., 217 and n., 220n., 241n.
  as critic, 244n.
  as c'tee chairman and M., 238n.
  as M., 409, 410n.
  quoted
    on budget, 22n., 237n., 254–7nn., 261 and n., 393*
    on const. and pol., 399n., 400n., 405n., 406n., 408–9n., 413n.
  mentioned, 100, 102
Faure cabinet, January-February 1952
  formed, membership, 41–2, 183n.*, 184n.46, 189n.64, 380
  and Finance c'tee, **244–6,** 260
  and parties, 41–2, 146, 372
  size of, 189n.64
  fall, 22, **42,** 219n., 226 and n., **245–6,** 256
Faure, Félix (1841–99, M.P. 1881, Pres. Rep. 1895–9), 170, 179n.
Faure, Maurice (b. 1922, M.P. 1951, Rad. d. Lot, sec. Rad. P.), 100
Faure, Paul (b. 1878, M.P. 1910, sec.-gen. Soc. P. 1921–38, on Vichy Nat. Council 1941–4), 61, 141, 149, 351
Fauvet, Jacques (pol. corr. of *Le Monde*)
  on insecurity of democracy, 410n.
  on elec. geog., 54n., 104n.
  on elec. law, 322n.
  on elec rivalries, 281n.
  on Parl.
    c'tees, 237n., 241n.22, 261nn.
    coulisses, 362n.
    C.R., 281n., 284n.
  on parties
    characteristics, 100, 138n., 145n., 368n.
    clientèle, 103, 104n., 130 and n., 149n.
    numbers, 52n., 68nn., 83n., 99n., 108n., 111n., 129n., 367n.
    org., 49n., 55n., 81n., 125n., 127n., 138n.
  on pressure-groups, 69n., 149n., 333n.
federalism, *see* Europe.
  imperial, 293
Fédération nationale des syndicats d'exploitants agricoles (F.N.S.E.A.), 332, 336n., 410n.

Fédération républicaine, 107, 108
federations, local party, 352
  Com., 49 and n.
  M.R.P., 80–2, 83, 348, 352, 367, 411
  Parti soc dém, 149
  Peasant P., 111n.
  Rad., 94, 98, 153, 348
  R.P.F., 123
  Soc., 63, 64–7, 69 and n., 72, 73n., 74, 352, 354, 360
  U.D.S.R., 144 and n.
Félix, Colonel (Jacques Chombart de Lauwe: b. 1905, M.P. 1945, P.R.L. d. Loire-Inf. 1945–51, stood as R.G.R.I.F. candidate 1951), 348n.
fellow-travellers, 141, 142 and n., 152, 346
féodalités
  pressure-groups, 340n.
  in R.P.F., 135n.
Ferhat Abbas (b. 1899, M.P. June-November 1946, U.D.M.A. leader), 152
Ferry, Jules (1832–93, M.P. 1869, P.M. 1880, stood for Pres. Rep. 1887, s. 1891, Pres. Sen. 1893, introduced *lois laïques*), 162n., 168, 170
Film Centre, National, 241
  festival, 246n.
  and see cine-clubs.
Finance, *see* budget; initiative, financial.
Finance c'tee, Chapter 15 and 16 *passim,* esp. **242–6,** *and also*
  of Chamber, 158, 160, 364
  of Senate, 243 and n.
  of N.A., 330, 333, 335
  of C.R., 262n., 265n.
  mentioned, 201n.
Finance, M. of
  and Parl., 259n., 260n., 262
  and parties, 377–83 (esp. **378**), 391–2
  Socs., 18, 22, 34, 35 and n., 181, 239n.14, 263n., 391
  power and policies of, 252, 255 264–5 and n., 391–2
  and tax evasion, 22
  holders
    and business, 331n.
    and Finance c'tee, 242 and n.
    and P.Ms., 188n., 242n., 377
    Mayer, 33, 41, 217, 221*, 243, 331n., 334, 384n.
    Petsche, 35n., 236n., 331n.
    Philip, 18, 391
    Pineau, 22*, 34, 35 and n.
    Pleven, 145n., 391–2
    Reynaud, 34, 35n., 382
    Schuman, 18, 33, 391
finances, loi de, see budgetary policy.
Finistère, dept. (cap. Quimper, *q.v.*), 74 and n., 88nn.
flagrant délit, 193 and n.

30—2

INDEX

Flandin, Pierre-Étienne (b. 1889, M.P. 1914, Pres. *Alliance dém* since 1932, P.M. 1934, Foreign M. 1936 and 1940–1, congratulated Hitler on Munich)
   ineligibility of, 111, 148 and n., 192n.
   as party leader, 108, 111n., 148
   cabinets, 188, 328 and n.
Fleurant-Agricola, 111
floating voters, 312, 329, **356**, 367, 399
Florenne, Yves, 361n.
Floret, *see* Coste-.
Flory, M., 178n.
fonctionnaires, *see* civil servants.
Fondation nationale des sciences politiques
   Cahiers de la, 54nn., 85n., 91n., 93n.
   Revue française de s.p., 71n., 101n., 113n., 131n., 276n., 283n.*, 318n., 325n.
Fonteneau, Jean, 84n.
Food, M. of, 388n.
food policy
   corn prices, 219n., 225
   min. resp. for, 188n.
   and peasants, 21, 174, 328
   rationing, 21, 55n., 332, 339
   speculation, 175
Force ouvrière, *see* trade unions.
Forces nouvelles (M.R.P. organ), 111n.
Foreign Affairs c'tee
   of N.A., 234, 236 and n., 237, 239nn., 242, 246, 412n.
   of C.R., 246n., 334n., 412n.
Foreign Affairs, M. of
   holders, 188n., **377**, 405n., 408
   and Coms., 378
   and other parties, 376, 377, 380, 383
   and P.Ms., 377
   diplomatic service, 264
Foreign Press Assoc., 175n.
forestry, 337
Fortnightly, The, 39n., 413n.
Foundation for Foreign Affairs, 206n.
Fourcade, Jacques (b. 1902, Pres. A.F.U. 1950–1, M.P. 1951, R.I. d. H-Pyrénées), 238n., 295, 348
Fourth Force, 24, 104, 110
Frachon, Benoît (b. 1892, sec.-gen. C.G.T. 1936), 52, 53n., 57
France
   Bank of, 324 and n., 331
   regions of, *see* regions.
France, *see* Mendès-.
franchise, *see* overseas franchise; woman suffrage.
Franchise c'tee of N.A., 201n., 237, 239n., 248 and n., 287
Franco, General Francisco, 12, 78
Frédéric-Dupont, Édouard (b. 1902, M.P. 1936, P.R.L., R.P.F. and A.R.S. d. Seine, Pres. Paris munic. council), 137

Frédérix, Pierre, 95n., 295n., 328n., 332n.
Free Democratic Party, German, 338
Free French, divisions among, 386
free vote, 384
freedom
   of association, 346
   of speech, 407
   and *statut des partis*, 345–6
freemasonry
   and army appointments, 387
   and Coms., 373
   and Rads., 91, 92, 99
   and Socs., 71, 387
French Union
   institutions of, **292–6**
   Assembly, *see* Assembly of French Union.
   High Council, 293 and n., 410n.
   Presidency, 169n., 293
   status of
     in const. and Preamble, 308, 410n.
     secession, etc., *see* self-government.
   mentioned, 205
   and see overseas France.
frères ennemis, 357, *and see* floating voters.
Front économique, 332
Front national, 47, 143
Front populaire, 12, 45–6, 348
   and Coms., 47, 52
   and Cons., 109
   and *Jeune République*, 77
   and Rads., 92, 97n., 104
   and Socs., 46, 61
   Auriol and, 173
   revival of?, 412
Frossard, Ludovic-Oscar (1889–1948, first sec.-gen. of French C.P., resigned 1922, M.P. 1928, Rep. Soc., M. under Pétain 1940, on Vichy Nat. Council 1941–4), 373
funds
   elec., *see* election expenses.
   party, *see* party funds.
   secret, 386

GAILLARD, Félix (b. 1919, M.P. 1946, Rad. d. Charente, u.-sec. to P.M. 1951–2), 102, 244n.
Galtier-Boissière, Jean, 6n.
Gambetta, Leon (1838–82, M.P. 1869, Pres. Chamber 1879, P.M. 1881), 170, 179
Gard, dept. (cap. Nîmes), 350n.
Gardey, Abel (b. 1882, M.P. 1914, s. 1924, Rad. d. Gers 1951–), 348
Garet, Pierre (b. 1905, M.P. 1945, M.R.P. and R.I. d. Somme), 238n., 348n.*, 380n.*, App. III
Garonne, river, 328n.
Garraud, J. M., 252n.

INDEX

gas and electricity industries, 263n.
Gauche
  signifies move to Right, 7
  indépendante, 142, 362n.
  républicaine, 7
  and see Left
gauches
  Cartel des, 61, 91, 103, 393
  Délégation des, 9, 159–60, 213, 247
  républicaines, Rassemblement des, *see Rassemblement*.
Gaulle, General Charles de (b. 1890, u.-sec. War under Reynaud 1940, Free French leader at Algiers 1943–4, P.M. and head of state 1944–6, R.P.F. leader 1947)
  career
    war, 13, 34n. 118, 119, 133–4, 386–7
    post-war, App. II, III, IV
  as P.M. and head of state, 13–17, 118
    elected, 183n.
    and admin., 266
    choice of Ms., 382
    M. of Defence, 378
    and elec. system, 315
    and pardons, 176
    rejects *coup d'état*, 17n.
    resigns, 17, 119, 387
    and *tripartisme*, 14–6, 119, 381, *also below*
    and Coms., 13–6, 47, 145n., 182n., 378, 382
    and Cons., 109, 133
    and M.R.P., 79
    and Rads, 93, 98, 119
    and Socs., 28, 62, 145n., 214
    and Auriol, 14, 17, 173
  feared as possible Pres. Rep., 170, 171n., 173n., 179, 180
  as R.P.F. leader
    founder, 20, 118, 120–1
    and org., 124–30, 368–9
    and dissolution of N.A., 32, 121 and n., 195
    and followers
      recruitment of, 215n., 348, 362
      friction with, 110, 122–3, 126, 135n.
      standing with, 409n., App. VII
    and Third force, 33, 218
    and business orgs., 136 and n., 340n.
    and Fascism, 138
  views
    on const., 14, 18–9, 118–20, **161–3**, 269, 288, 292
    on elec. and party systems, 315, 320, 324n., 344n.
  mentioned, 137, 198, 375
Gaulle, de, cabinets
  Algiers, 14
  1944...226n., 386, **391**
  1945...17 and n., 226n., 309, 344, 368, **378**

Gaulle, Pierre de (brother of above, M.P. 1948, R.P.F. s. and d. Seine I, ex-pres. Paris munic. council), 134n., 278, 347
Gaullist Union, 19, 120
Gaullists, *see* R.P.F.; Free French; Algiers; Gaulle, General Charles de.
  dissident, *see Action républicaine et sociale*.
Gay, Francisque (b. 1885, M.P. 1945, M.R.P. d. Seine I to 1951), 78, 365n., App. III
Gazier, Albert (b. 1908, M.P. 1945, Soc. d. Seine V), 331n., 388n., 393*, App. III
Generals, *see* Army; Boulanger; de Gaulle; MacMahon; Scandals.
Gennevilliers, 49 and n., 50, 52–3
George, Pierre, 54n., 91n., 113n.
Gerber, Philippe (M.R.P. s. Pas-de-Calais 1946–8), 275n., 277n.
German affairs, comm. for, 388
Germany, aggression by, 10, 46–7
Germany, comparisons with
  econ. interests of parties, 338
  food collection, 21
  nationalism of R.P.F. and S.P.D., 138
  Weimar Rep.
    dissolutions, 232
    moribund republics, 262
    national lists, 345
    Parteienstaat, 343 and n.
  mentioned, 138
Germany, French views on
  pre-war, 10, 12
  London agreements (1948), 220n.
  party views, 25, 75n.
  and see Europe.
Gers, dept. (cap. Auch), 348
Giacobbi, Paul (1896–1951, M.P. (s.) 1938, Rad. d. Corse)
  and const., 215n., 230n.
  and election prediction, 317n.
  and R.P.F. intergroup, 102, 126, 135*, 369*
  as M., App. III
Gingembre, Léon (b. 1904, leader of P.M.E.), 300, 331
Giraud, General Henri-Honoré (1879–1949, High Comm. North Africa 1942–3, C-in-C. 1942–4, M.P. June-November 1946, P.R.L.), 386 and n.
Gironde, dept. (two constituences: I Bordeaux *q.v.* and Western; II Eastern)
  constituencies, 322n., 354n.
  1951 election, 74n., 131, 145, 150n., 348, 354
Goguel, François, head of *service de la séance* of C.R., quoted
  deputies' occupations, 206n.
  E.C., 299n.

Goguel, François, quoted, (cont'd)
elec. geog.
  national results, 99 and n., 112nn., 129n., App. V
  and econ. geog., 54n., 70n., 71n., 114n., 131n.
  and parties, 54nn., 57n., 71n., 85nn., 101 and nn., 104n., 113nn., 131nn., Maps 1, 2 and 4
  of Paris, 71n., 85 and n., 113n., 131n.
elec. systems, 17n., 93n., 310n., 315n., 321n., **326n.**
parl.
  budget, 256n., 258n.
  business, 209n., 275nn.
  c'tees, 251n.
  decree-laws, 262n., 264n.
  parties, 204n.
  characteristics, 77n., 89n., 319n.
  clientèle, 149n.
  distribution, 47n., 93n., 347n.
  org., 50n., 95nn., 96n.
  two blocs, 311n.5
  pressure-groups (P.M.E.), 149n.
  taxation, 23n.
Gooch, R. K., 235n.
Gorse, Georges (b. 1915, M.P. 1945, Soc. d. Vendée to 1951, u.-sec. 1946 and 1949–50), 296, 388n.
Gouin, Félix (b. 1884, M.P. 1924, P.M. 1946, Soc. d. Bouches-du-Rhône II)
  career, 34n., App. II, III, IV
  Pres. C.A. and P.M., 17n., 19, 198, 381*
  elected P.M., 183n.
  and M. of Defence, 188n.
  and scandals, 306, 327n.
Gouin cabinet
  formed, membership, 17, 377, **382–3 and n.**, 392
  mutual recriminations, **392**
  and press law, 390
  fall, 226n.
Gourdeaux, Henri, 53n.
Government
  and N.A., Chapter 14
  participation in, *see* office; each party separately.
  and see authority; cabinet; instability; premiership.
grand electors, 270–1
Greece, const. of, 217n.
Grenoble, 36, 122, 129n.
Grévy, Jules (1807–91, M.P. 1848, Pres. of N.A. 1871–3, of Chamber 1876–9, of Rep. 1879–87), 169, 170, 173n., 179n.
groups, parl., *see* party groups; intergroups; Assembly, National (pressure-groups).
groupes d'entreprise, in R.P.F., 124

Grumbach, Salomon (1884–1952, M.P. 1928, Soc. d. Tarn 1945–6, s. elected by N.A. 1946–8), 274n.
Guadeloupe, dept. (cap. Basseterre), 191n., 294n., 323n.30, 443
Guérin, Maurice (M.R.P. d. 1945–51, High Court 1951), 257n., 305n.*, 306n.
Guesde, Jules (1845–1922, M.P. 1893, M. 1914–5), 60
gueuse, la, 396
Guiana, French (Guyane, dept. cap., Cayenne), 191n., 294n., 443
Guyon, Jean-Raymond (b. 1900, M.P. 1945, Soc. d. Gironde to 1951, chairman fin. c'tee 1947–51), 239n.*, 245*, 324*, 337n.*, 388n.

HADJ, *see* Messali.
Halévy, Daniel, 94n., 104n.
Halévy, Élie, 397n.
Hamon, Léo (b. 1908, M.P. (s.) 1946, M.R.P. s. Seine)
  off parl. c'tee, 412n.*
  on clerical question, 16n.
  on parl. life, 204n., 205n., 251n.
  on pressure-groups, 190n., 397n.
Harvard, 131n.
Hauriou, André (Soc. s.), 301nn.
Health c'tee of N.A., 201n., 204n. 239n., 241, 242n.22, 248n., 336
Health, M. of
  holders, 180n., 188n., 356n.*, 384n.
  and M. of Population, 189n.64, 379n.
  and parties, 378–9 and n.
Hénault, Pierre (P.R.L., R.P.F. and A.R.S. d. Manche 1948–), 337n.
Hérault, dept. (cap. Montpellier), 324, 328n., 349 and n., 444
Herriot, Édouard (b. 1872, M.P. 1919, P.M. 1924, Pres. of Chamber 1925, of N.A. 1947–54, of Rad. P.; Rad. d. Rhône I, mayor of Lyons)
  career, 61, 92, 199
  political position
  pre-war, 95, 97n., 147
  at liberation, 143
  post-war, in party, 97, 98n., 368, App. VII
  and Com., 143
  and Cons., 179n.
  and R.G.R., 147
  and R.P.F., 94, 98–9, 121n.
  as Pres. of N.A., 198, 199, 231, 279, 280nn., 290n.
  retires, 412
  views
  on overseas rep., 294
  on const., 172, 279, 280n.31, 308n.
  on elec. law, 323n.
  on E.D.C., 308n.
  on parl., 263n.
  on senators, 267n.

Herriot, Édouard
 views (*cont'd*)
  on Soc. party, 72n.
  mentioned, 111
Herriot cabinets (1924–6), 170n., 298, 328
Hervé, Pierre (b. 1913, M.P. 1945, Com. d. Finistère 1945–8), 353
Hesnard, O., 343n.
High Council of the French Union (H.C.F.U.), 293 and n., 410n.
High Council of the Magistrature (H.C.M.), **300–5**, 345, 404
High Court of Justice
 const., 203, 274, 302n., **305–6**
 exceptional, 306
Hitler, Adolf, 78, 109
hoarding, 248
Holland, 302n.
' horse-trading,' 384 and n., *and see* log-rolling.
Hôtel de Ville, 295
Houdet, Marcel, 134*, 135n.*, 150n.
House of Commons
 and elec. reform 1919...314n.
 and govt. 19th Cent., 166, 211, 214 and n.
 procedure, 200, 212, 250 and n.
 Speaker, 8, 198
 and see Britain, comparisons with.
House of Lords, 268, 273–4, 314n.
housing, 240, 241, 260n., 336, 405
 rent law, 177, 225n.
Hughes, H. Stuart, 138n.
Hugues, Émile, (Rad. d. Alpes-Maritimes), 333n.
Humanité, L' (Com. organ)
 attacks *dirigisme*, 55n.
 circulation, 391n.
 leaks to, 204n.
 under occupation, 46, 353
 quoted, 53n., 355n.
Husson, Raoul
 on voting figures, 16n., 99n., 112n., 316n., App. V
 bulletins modifiés, 315n.
 on deputies
  ages, 69n.
  occup., 70n., 84n., 101n., 112n., 206n.
  past careers, 86n.
 on C.R., party nomination to vacancy, 345n.

Illustration, L', 238n.
immobilisme, 36–7*, 190
Immunity c'tee of N.A., 194 and n., 239 and n.
immunity, parl., **193–4 and nn.**
 bill on, 177n., 291
 detachment of govt., 206, 230, 383
 of Malagasy ds., 239 and n.

impartiality
 Pres. of N.A's. departure from, 198
 preserving judicial, 305
 author's lack of, Preface
impeachment, 204, 302n., **305–6**, *and see* Moch.
incivisme
 meaning of, 3, 5
 econ., 22, 338, 407
 pol., 116, 313, 326, 348
 consequences of, 151, 225, 338, 341, 407
income, national, *see* economic policy.
income tax, introduction of, delayed by Senate, 268n., *and see* budget.
incontinence législative, 241n.22
Indépendants d'outre-mer, 152–3, 362n., *and see* overseas deputies.
independent candidatures, *see* candidatures, independent.
Independents (political group), *see* Republican Independents.
 lack of independence of, 111n.
India, French, 294n.
Indian Ocean territories, 294n.
Indo-China
 delegates to A.F.U. and H.C.F.U., 293–4
 Frenchmen of, rep. in C.R., 271n.
 High Comms. in, 386, 410n.
 trafic des piastres, 204n., 356n.
Indo-China, war in
 financial drain of, 253, 402
 not discussed in parl., 209
 and parties, etc., 24, 410 and n.
 Coms. 1947...19, 218, 383
 Coms. later, 56, 174, 355
 R.P.F., 135n., 138, 224, 296n.
 Auriol, 174
 Daladier, 148n.
 Mendès-France, 98
 Pleven govt. 1950...221 and n.
Indre, dept. (cap. Châteauroux), 101n., 143
Indre-et-Loire, dept. (cap. Tours), 351
industrial areas and politics
 and c'tee rep., 246n., 333
 and electioneering, 349, 352n., 353
 modern and static France, 396–8
 and parties
  Com., 53–4 and nn.
  Cons., 113–7 and nn.
  Left, 4
  M.R.P., 85 and n.
  Rads., 101 and nn., 104 and n.
  R.P.F., 131 and n., 136 and n.
  Soc., 69–72 and nn., 329
Industrial Production c'tee of N.A., 236n., 237, 242n.22, 246 and n., 335
Industrial Production, M. of
 Coms. and, 385n., *and see* Paul.
 and M. of Commerce, 379n.
 and c'tees, 246n., 333

Industrial Production, M. of (*cont'd*)
  holders, 350n., 353, 385n.
  and parties, 378–9, 380, 385n.
Industrial Revolution in France, 396–7
Industry
  backwardness of, 2, 253, 331 and n., 396–7, 405
  nationalized, *q.v.*
  workers control, and M.R.P., 83n.
ineligibility
  general rules, **191–2**, 271
  post-war political, **191–2 and nn.**, **198**, 351
  and parties
    Alliance dém., 148
    Cons., 117
    Parti soc. dém., 149
    Rad., 93
    R.G.R., 147
    R.P.F., 133
inflation, 22–3, 253
  expenditure met by, 257
information, *see* press
Information, secretaryship of, 390–1, 393
Information radicale, L', 97n.
initiative
  for Const. C'tee, 289
  financial
    of Senate, 159
    of C.R., 276, 279 and n.
    of private members, 256, 257–9 and nn., 276, 412n., *and see* constituency interests.
  legislative, *see* bills, introduction of.
inspecteurs des finances, 264, 391
inspecteurs généraux de l'administration en mission extraordinaire (I.G.A.M.E.) 404
instability, Govtl.
  in Britain, 19th Century, 165
  in 3rd Rep.
    principal causes, 27, **154–5**
    minor causes, 157–8, 211–3, 269
  in 4th Rep.
    principal causes, 5, **25**, **154–5**, 406
    minor causes, 21, 24–5, 36, 40, 253
    appearance not reality, 157, **374**, 380 and n., **399**
  cures for
    in const., 211–3, 216
    foreign, 161
    party, **161–5**, **213–4**
  gives power to bureaucracy, 10, 405
  and see crises; stability.
insurrection, duty of, 338
intellectuals, 140
  in Bayeux const., 162
  on E.C., 297–8
intelligence services, *see* secret services.
inter-groups
  Cons., 196
  R.G.R., 148, 196

inter-groups (*cont'd*)
  R.P.F., 20, 102, 121, 125, 134, 196–7, 369
  in C.R., 278
  A.P.L.E., 330
  Front économique, 332
Interior c'tee of N.A., 204n., 237, 239–42 and nn., 248 and n.
Interior, M. of
  and *affaire des généraux*, 387–8
  and Algeria, 240n.
  and dissolution, 230–1 and n.
  election forecasts, 317 and n.
  holders, 37, 178n., 188n.
  senatorial, 286
  parties and, 376, **377–8**, 379–81, 383, 385n.
  colonization in, 385, 386–7
  Rads., 11, 90
  and P.Ms., 377
  power, 2
International Labour Organization, 388n.
interpellations, 8, **157**, 202, 211, **212–3 and n.**
  on composition and policy, 181
  C.R. institutes, 279, 280n.31
  dealing with, 9, 200, 213, 225
  and party groups, 365
  and v. of censure, 224
investiture, **179–85**, 209n., *and see* premiership, elections to; cabinet, formation of.
investment
  agric., 333
  and E.C., 299n.
  Monnet plan, 23, 209
  and E.C., 298
  Coms. accept, 391
  as admin. reform, 404
  and nationalized industry, 333
  need for, 405
  new fund, 412n.
  reconstruction budget, 255
Irish elec. system, 313 and n.
Irish nationalist party, 199
Isère, dept. (cap. Grenoble, *q.v.*), 101n.
Isorni, Jacques (b. 1911, M.P. 1951, Pétain's counsel, Peas. d. Seine II), 117n., 150*, 192
Italy
  Fascist, 12, 46
  treaties with, 177, 299, 300
  mentioned, 20, 77n., 138

JACOBINS
  and Rad. tradition, 91
  and freedom of association, 308, 363
Japan, treaty with, 296, 353
Jaurès, Jean (1859–1914, M.P. 1885), 60, 91
Jean-Moreau, *see* Moreau.

INDEX 473

Jean, Renaud, *see* Renaud-Jean.
Jeancé, Henri, 256n.
Jeune République, 77, 78n., 141, 144, 411n.
Jeunesse ouvrière chrétienne, etc., 77, 78n.
Jews
and electorate, 351
under occupation, 302n.*, 406
and R.P.F., 139 and n.
joint committees, 236n.
Joliot-Curie, Frédéric, 55
Journal officiel, expansion of, 203, 209n.
Jouvenel, Bertrand de, 23n., 257n.8*, 397n.*
Jouvenel, Henry de (1876–1935, M.P. (s.) 1921, *Gauche dém.*, Amb. Rome 1934), 179n.
Jouvenel, Robert de, 103n., 328n., 335n., 373 and n., 388
judges, *see* magistrates.
of High Court, *q.v.*
judicial
review, 289, 306–7
system, *see* Courts.
juges d'instruction, 304
Juin, Marshal Alphonse, 410
Julien, Charles-André, 295–6
Jura, dept. (cap. Lons-le-Saunier), 101n.
justice
independence of French, 194n., 407
High Court of, const., 203, 274, 302n., **305–6**
High Court of, exceptional, 46n., 306 *and see* courts; magistrates
Justice and Legislation c'tee of N.A., 204n., 239n., 241, 242nn., 302, 304
Justice, M. of, 2, 304*, 349
and cabinet, 303–4
and H.C.M., 175, 301–5 and nn.
and Pres. Rep., 175
and P.M., 377 and n.
and press law, 390
and purge, 77, 134, 378
and parties, 377 and n., 378, 380 and n., 390
holders, 34, 240n.15, 304, 349
mentioned, 384n.

'KING's friends,' *see* office, participation in.
Kir, le chanoine Félix (b. 1876, M.P. 1945, R.I. d. Côte d'Or, mayor of Dijon), 348n.
Kœnig, General Pierre (b. 1898, of Bir Hakeim and Tunis, mil. gov. of Paris 1944–5, C.-in-C. Germany 1945–9, M.P. 1951, R.P.F. d. B-Rhin, chairman Defence c'tee of N.A.), 193, 239n.*, 350 and n., 445
Korean war, 23, 337

LABOULAYE, Lefebvre de (1811–83, M.P. 1871, s. 1880), 9
Labour c'tee of N.A., 240, 241 and n., 242n., 246, 249 and nn., 260n., 331
Labour, M. of
departmental disputes, 391
holders, 36–7, 371, 373 and n., 382n.
and parties, 378–9, 380
Labour Party, British, 400
Lacau, *see* Loustanau-.
Lachapelle, Georges, 311n., 313n.
Lacharrière, R. de, 293n.
Lacoste, Robert (b. 1898, M.P. 1945, Soc. d. Dordogne), 340, App. III
Lacroix, *see* Milliès-.
Laferrière, J., 167n.
laïcité, *see* anti-clericalism; Church schools.
Lake Success, 184n.
Lamennais, Robert de (1782–1854, M.P. 1848, ed. *L'Avenir* 1830, broke with Catholic Church 1834), 77
Lamps, René (b. 1915, M.P. 1945, Com. d. Somme), 200n., 354–5*
Landes, dept. (cap. Mont-de-Marsan), 337
Landes, Davis S., 332n.
Landry, Adolphe (b. 1874, M.P. 1910, R.G.R. s. Corsica 1946), 351
Languedoc, 94
Laniel, Joseph (b. 1889, M.P. 1932, R.I. d. Calvados)
career, 34n., 35n., Apps. II, III, IV
as P.M., 183n., 186n.*, 409 and n., 411–3 and nn.
stands for Pres. Rep., 414
position in own party, 111n.
and other parties, 361n., 394n., 409
Laniel cabinet
formed June 1953, membership, 111n., 183n.*, 184n.46, **380 and n.**, 409 and n.
and C.R., 281n.
and European army, 413
and Finance c'tee, 246n.37
and finance and special powers, 259n., **264n.**, 281n., 408*, **412 and n.**
size, 250n.
mentioned, 376n.1
Laos, 294, 410 and n.
Laribé, *see* Augé-.
La Rochelle, 240n.
La Rocque, Colonel Françis de (1885–1946, founded *Croix de feu*, on Vichy Nat. Council 1941, later deported to Germany), 108, 137, 148
Laurens, Camille (b. 1906, M.P. June 1946, Peas. d. Cantal)
and party split, 111, 112n., 379–80*
as M., 336n.*, App. III
and Vichy, 117n.

Laurens, Robert (brother of above, b. 1910, M.P. 1951, Peas. d. Aveyron), 336n.*
Laurent, *see* Raymond-.
Laval, Pierre (1883–1945, Soc. d. 1914, Cons. s. 1927, P.M. 1931 also 1935–6, 1940, 1942–4, executed 1945), 6, 95, 108, 306n., 327n., 373
Laval cabinets, 160, 298, 366
Lavandeyra, L. A., 54n.
lawyers
in N.A., 206 and n.
in C.R., 273
professors of law, in Const. C'tee, 289 and H.C.M., 301 and n., 302–3 and R.P.F., 137
' lawyer-peasants,' 113n.
leadership, political, better than voters deserve, 402
Lecœur, Auguste (b. 1911, M.P. 1945, Com. d. Pas-de-Calais II, purged from party secretariat 1954), 50 and n., 52
Le Corre, Darius (b. 1903), 142–3
Lecourt, Robert (b. 1908, M.P. 1945, M.R.P. d. Seine II, chairman parl. group)
pre-war activities, 78n.
mission d'information, 1948... 186 and n.
as M. of Justice, 304, 349, 350n., App. III
for Mendès-France, 1953...409n.*
quoted
on institutions, 209nn., 228n., 233n., 356n.
on politics, 356n., 405n., 406n.
Lécrivain-Servoz, Albert (b. 1898, M.P. 1945, M.R.P., R.P.F., ind., and Prog. d. Rhône II 1945–51), 362 and n.
Leenhardt, Francis (b. 1908, M.P. 1945, U.D.S.R. and Soc. d. Bouches-du-Rhône I), 144n.
Left
split on property and Communism, 7, 9, 27, 154
institutions hampering, 243, 267
Senate as obstacle to, 243, 267
few peasant ds., 333
Left and Right
comparison with Britain, 3, 4, 115
division less deep than that on Communism, 233
ministers from both equally distrusted, 154
prestige of Left superior, 7, **115n.**
Rads. balance between (3rd and 4th Reps.,) 89, 91, 93, 102, 103
R.P.F. and, 123, 135 and n.
and elec. coalitions, 154, 232, 310–2, 357
in drafting const., 167, 172, 227–9

Left and Right (*cont'd*)
and parl
role of c'tees (3rd Rep.), 235
and dissolution, 227–9
and 2nd Chamber, 172, 267
seating in chamber, 135 and n., 197
foreign and defence policy, 4, 12
legislation, *see* bills.
delegated, *see* decree-laws; delegation.
retroactive, 307n.
Le Havre, 240n.
Lemasurier, J., 292n.
Leopold, ex-King of the Belgians, 150
Léotard, Pierre de (Rad. d. Seine II), 148, 149
Le Puy, 198
Lespès, Henri (b. 1909, M.P. 1945, M.R.P. and R.P.F. d. Seine-et-Marne to 1951, High Court of Justice 1951), 134, 135n., 305n.*
Letourneau, Jean (b. 1907, M.P. 1945, M.R.P. d. Sarthe)
pre-war activity, 78n.
as M.-designate, 393*
as M., 379, 410*, App. III
Le Troquer, André (b. 1884, M.P. 1936, Blum's counsel at Riom, Pres. N.A. 1954, Soc. d. Seine III), 392*, 412, App. III
Levallois-Perret, 17n.
libel suits, 194 and n.
Liberal Party, British, 232
liberation, *see* Resistance; *tripartisme*.
Libération-Nord, 61, 143n., 385
Libérer et fédérer, 143n.
Lidderdale, D. W. S., quoted
general ref., 191n.
on authority in N.A., 207n.
on bills, 203n., 252n.
on *bureau*, 1948...231n.
on closure, 200n.
on c'tees, 234n., 235n., 238n.
Finance c'tee, 252n., 254n., 258nn., 265n., 266n., 276n.
on debate, 207n.
on obstruction and violence, 199n.
on party groups, 365n.15
on treaties, 202n.
on urgency procedure, 258n., 275n., 279n., 280n.31
on v. of c., 212n.
on voting methods, 197n.
Lille
elections in
1951...110, 130, 324
1952 by-election, 123n.
parl. rep. of (Senate), 267n.
R.P.F. in, 137n.
speeches and congresses at, 125n., 138n., 340n.
Limoges, 54n.
Limousins, 334

INDEX

Lipman, V. D., 306n.
list system of voting, *see* electoral systems (*s.d.l.*).
lobbies, making and unmaking of govts. in, 362n.
lobby
 China, 338, 400
 trade union, 339
 and see pressure-groups.
local administration, 404n., *and see* centralization; prefects
local authorities
 in const., **306 and n.**
 elections to, *q.v.*
 and elections
  of Senate, 158, 267
  of C.R., 270–2
  of Pres. Rep., 170n.
  of Pres. (Bayeux const.), 162
 and politicians, 272–3, 312, 349
 strikes of, 339
log-rolling, 252 and n., 328n., *and see* horse-trading; constituency interests.
Loire, dept. (cap. St. Étienne)
 Cons. of, 150n.
 1951 election in, 101n.
 1952 by-election in, 123n.
Loire, river, 70, 101–2, 114, 132, 324n.
Loire, Haute-, dept. (cap. Le Puy, *q.v.*), 74n., 192n., 394n.
Loire-Inférieure, dept. (cap. Nantes, *q.v.*), 101n., 348n.
lois laïques, 192n., *and see* anti-clericalism; Church schools.
London
 agreements on Germany, 1948... 220n.
 fares, 400
 de Gaulle govt. in, 389
loquacity of Com. ds., 200 and n.
Lorraine, 4, 54, 77, 260n.
lot, selection by, 364
Lot, dept. (cap. Cahors), 149, 348n.
Lot-et-Garonne, dept. (cap. Agen), 101n., 355
loterie nationale
 and lunatics, 205
 and Treasury, 265
Loustanau-Lacau, Georges (b. 1894, M.P. 1951, former *cagoulard*, Peas. d. B-Pyrénées), 200n.
Louvel, Jean-Marie (b. 1900, M.P. 1945, M.R.P. d. Calvados), 238n., 333*, App. III
Lozère, dept. (cap. Mende), 322n.
Lussy, Charles (b. 1883, M.P. 1936, Soc. d. Vaucluse, chairman parl. group), 215n., 371*, 409n.
Lüthy, Herbert, 55n.
Luxembourg, Palais du, 273
Luzon, Mgr. Cazaux, bishop of, 339
Lynskey tribunal, 327

Lyons
 ' cap. of the Republic,' 121n.
 Coms. of, 353
 congresses at, 62–3, 78, 84n., 141
 local politics of, 98, 121n., 147–8, 150n., 323n.30, 350
 parl. rep. (c'tees), 240
 Rad. newspaper, 95
 R.P.F. of, 137n.

MacMahon, Marshal Patrice de (1808–93, President of the Republic 1873–9), 7, 8, 156, 169, 178
Madagascar
 high comm. in, 388
 nationalist ds., 151–2, 176, 184n., 191n., 194, 239 and n. 15
 parl. rep., 294n.
 revolt of 1947...19, 152, 176
' Madagascar constitution,' 167
Madrid, 239n., 384
magistrates
 promotion of, 302, 303, 349
 qualities of, 407
 Resistance, 302n.
 security of tenure of, 303 and nn.
 and *parquet*, *q.v.*
 and see courts.
Magistrature, High Council of the (H.C.M.), **300–5** *and also*
 appoints judges, 189n.
 appoints to *commission* of High Court, 305
 election of, 203, 274
 Pres. Rep. and, 169n., 172, **175**
Maillaud, Pierre (1909–48, used pol. pseud. Pierre Bourdan, M.P. 1945, U.D.S.R. d. Creuse and Seine III), 10n., 390*, 397n., App. III
majority
 absence of, in electorate or Parl., 25–6, 313, 396, 402–3
 instability of
  in 3rd Rep., 9, 160, 268
  in 4th Rep., 357–8, 402–3
  in 1953...408, 412
 negative, in 3rd Rep., 8–9, 154
 problem of, in Parl., 27–8, 32, 154
 winning of, not a sufficient proof of parl. confidence, 178n., 221 and n.
majority, absolute (const. and parl.)
 in amending const., 182n., 287–8
 in appealing to Const. C'tee, 289, 291
 in electing Pres. Rep., 171 and n., 414
 in electing P.M., 19, 32, 38, 181–2, **183–5 and nn.**, 215
 proposal not to require, 185n.
 in ejecting govt., 215, 219 and n., 220, 225
 proposal not to require, **229–30**
 in impeachment, 305, 306

majority, absolute (const. and parl.) *(cont'd)*
  in overriding C.R., **276**, 277, 280n., 281, **283 and nn.**, 322n.
  proposal not to require, 285n.
  in parl. procedure, 207n., 222
  in c'tee, 208n.
majority, absolute (electoral)
  in 2-ballot systems, required on first ballot, 309, 310
  in 1919 electoral law, 310, 323n.
  in 1951 electoral law, 323–4 and nn., App. VI
majority, three-fifths
  in const. revision, 288
  in electing Pres. Rep., under April 1946 draft const., 170n.
majority, two-thirds
  in const. revision 288
  in H.C.M. elections, 301
  in High Court elections, 305
  in electing Pres. Rep., under draft const., 170n.
Malagasy deputies, *see* Madagascar.
Malignac, G., 336n.
Malraux, André (b. 1901, novelist and R.P.F. leader), 126n., 130, 134, 144, App. III
Malvy, Jean-Louis (1875–1949, Rad. leader, M.P. 1906, M. of Interior 1914–7, banished 1918, amnestied and chairman Finance c'tee 1924, M. of Interior 1926), 91
Manchester Guardian, quoted
  on social and econ. matters, 22n., 23n., 257n.8, 397n.
  on pressure-groups, 190n., 331n., 332n.
Mandel, Georges (1885–1944, real name Rothschild, Clemenceau's secretary, M.P. 1919, Pres. Ind. group 1932–40, M. of Interior under Reynaud 1940, chief advocate of further resistance, murdered by Vichy militia 1944), 364
maquis, 47 and n., 151n., 389, *and see* Resistance.
Marabuto, Paul, 332n., 368n.
Marcellin-Albert c'tee, 339
Marey, Georges, 174n.
marginal votes
  in 3rd Rep., 157
  of *colons*, 190 and n.
  and ' Madagascar const.', 167
  and U.D.S.R., 190n.
  in Britain and U.S.A., 399
  and see floating voters; I.O.M.
mariage (political), 133, 145, *and see* bigamy.
Marianne, 396
Marie, André (b. 1897, M.P. 1928, Rad. d. Seine-Inf. I)
  career, 34n., Apps. II, III, IV

Marie, André *(cont'd)*
  as P.M., **35**, 377
  consultations, 186 and n.
  choosing Ms., 35, 181
  meeting N.A. 180n.
  using v. of c., 35, 216, 220 and n., 277n.
  stands for P.M., 1953…184n., 409, 411
  as M. of Education, 104n., 377n.
  as M. of Justice, 34
  as conciliator, 33–4, 186 and n., 190 and n.
  on elec. system, 315n.
Marie cabinet, July-August 1948
  formed, membership, 34, 35, 184n.46, 377, 378n.
  significance, **34–5**, *and see* Reynaud law.
  and parties, 121n., 360
  fall, 22, 28, 34, 225, 226n., **227**, 263n.30*, **334**
' Marie constitution,' 35
Marin, Louis (b. 1871, M.P. 1905, R.I. d. Meurthe-et-Moselle to 1951)
  pol. position
    pre-war, 108
    1940–7…47, 109
    1947–53…239n.*, 348n., 354
  quoted, on c'tees, 238n.
Marine, M. of
  holders, 7
  admin. abuses, 265n.
Marine, Merchant, M. of, status, 189n.64
Marne, dept. (cap. Châlons), 339, 443
Marne, Haute-, dept. (cap. Chaumont), 101n.
Maroselli, André (b. 1893, M.P. (s.) 1935, Rad. d. H.-Saône 1945–51 and s. 1952–), 238n., 324, App. III
Marquet, Adrien (b. 1884, M.P. 1924, Soc. and Neo-Soc. d. Gironde, ex-mayor of Bordeaux, M. of Interior July-September 1940), 61
Marrane, Georges (b. 1888, M.P. 1946, Com. s. Seine, ex-mayor of Ivry), 180n., App. III
Marseilles
  local politics of, 130, 137n., 327n.
  parl. rep. of, 240 and n., 267n., 272
  speeches and congresses at
    R.P.F., 118n., 125n., 129n., 319n.
    U.D.S.R., 144 and n., 146
  strikes of 1947 in, 32
Martinaud-Déplat, Léon (b. 1899, M.P. 1932, admin. pres. Rad. P., Rad. d. Bouches-du-Rhône II since 1951), 179n., 366n., App. III
Martinet, Gilles, 72n.
Martinique, dept. (cap. Fort de France), 191n., 294n., 443

INDEX

Marty, André (b. 1886, M.P. 1924, ex-Com. d. Seine I), 16, 50 and nn., 199n., 368
Maspetiol, R., 336n.
Massif central, 54
Maunoury, *see* Bourgès-.
Mauriac, François, 47, 363, 411n.
Maurras, Charles (1868–1952, member of *Académie française* 1938–45)
  pol. views, 6, 7, 12, 396
  on purge, 77, 134 and n.
Mauvais, Léon (b. 1902, M.P. 1946, Com. s. Seine 1946–8), 50 and n.
Mayer, Daniel (b. 1909, M.P. 1945, sec.-gen. Soc. P. 1944–6, d. Seine II)
  position in party, 63, 360, 371
  as M., and resignation, 36–7, 371, 382, 391, 393n., App. III
  chairman Foreign Affairs c'tee, 239n.*
Mayer, René (b. 1895, M.P. 1946, Rad. candidate Charente 1945, d. Constantine since June 1946)
  career, 34n., Apps. II, III, IV
  as P.M., 42, 123, 153n., 183n., 408
  consultations, 186n.*
  choosing Ms., 183n.
  using v. of c., 217n., 408, 413 and n.
  stands for P.M.
    1949...37, 182
    1951...41, 183n., 185, 186n.
  as M. of Finance
    1947...33, 243, 262, 331n.
    1947 (special levy), 33, 106, 217, 218, 244n., 277, App. IV
    1951...41, 221*, 331n., 334
  as M. of Justice, 304–5
  and parties, 41, 185, 334, 361n.
  and interests, 41, 331n., 334, 340nn.
  quoted, 257n.8, 340nn.
  mentioned, 100, 102
Mayer cabinet, January-May 1953
  formed, membership, 153n., 183n.*, 184n.46, 189n.64, 356n., 376n., 380, 408
  first defeat in N.A., 240n.
  and finance, 245n., 256n., 259n., 264n., 281n.
  and C.R., 281n.
  fall, 23, **226** and n., 245n., 264n., 334, 408
mayors, 272, 339 and n.
maxima, loi des
  as weapon of govt., **258–9** and n.
  Bidault falls on, 1950...223, 260
  C.R. and, December 1948...280
mécontents, political, 348
Mediterranean coast, 54
melting-pot, parliamentary, 205
Melun, local by-election at (1949), 134, 135n., 150n.
Mendès-France, Pierre (b. 1907, M.P. 1932, chairman Finance c'tee 1953, Rad. d. Eure)

Mendès-France, Pierre (*cont'd*)
  career, 34n., 383 and n., 391–2, 409n., App. III
  resignation, 1945, 391–2, 409n.
  stands for P.M., 1953...184n., 337n., 408–11 and nn., 413, Apps. II, III, IV
  chairman Finance c'tee, 246n.37
  views, position in party, 98, 106, 363
Mendès-France c'tee report, *see Statistiques et études financières*
Menthon, François de (b. 1900, M.P. 1945, M.R.P. d. H.-Savoie, ex-chairman parl. group)
  as M. (Justice, and Econ. Affairs), 77*, 134*, 392*, App. III
  also, 78n., 237n., 350
Merchant Shipping c'tee of N.A., 236n., 237, 240 and n.
Merle, Marcel, 229n.
Messali Hadj (b. 1898, leader of M.T.L.D.), 152
métayers, 54
Métro, of Paris, 1, 71, 130
Meunier, Pierre (b. 1908, M.P. 1946, Prog. d. Côte d'Or), 142n.
Meurthe-et-Moselle, dept. (cap. Nancy, *q.v.*), 128, 143, 354
Meuse, dept. (cap. Bar-le-Duc), 114
Mexican war, 296n.
Meyer, Jacques, quoted, 212n., 215n., 217n., 219n., 223n.
Michelin factory, 57
Middleton, W. L., quoted, 267n., 310nn., 363n., 397n.
Midi, *see* regions of France.
Midol, Lucien (b. 1883, M.P. 1932, Com. d. Seine-et-Oise II), 239n.
militants, 326, 362
  and ds., 352, 356, **367–73**, 394
  and voters, 367, 372–3
  and see office, participation in; each party separately.
Millerand, Alexandre (1859–1943, Soc. M.P. 1885, M. 1899, Cons. P.M. 1920, Pres. Rep. 1920–4, s. 1925), 60, 169, 373
Milliès-Lacroix, M., 192n.
mining industry, *see* coal.
ministers
  benches for, 197
  impeachment of, 204 *and q.v.*
  and legislation, 187
  responsibility of, *q.v., and see* cabinet solidarity.
ministries, *see* cabinet.
missions d' information, 186 and n.
Mitterrand, François (b. 1916, M.P. 1946, pres. U.D.S.R. since 1953, d. Nièvre)
  career, 366n., 383 and n., 409 and n. 2, 410n., App. III

Mitterrand, François (cont'd)
quoted, on pol. practice and reform, 209n., 233n., 258n., 406n.
Moatti, René (b. 1905, M.P. 1951, R.P.F. d. Seine II), 139n.
Moch, Jules (b. 1893, M.P. 1928, Soc. d. Hérault)
  career, 34n., App. II, III, IV
  stands for P.M. 1949...37, 56, 182, **184 and n.**, 186n., 189n.64, 222n., **393**
  as M.
    of Defence, 38
    of Interior, **37**, 75, 386–7
    of Works and Transport, 385n.
  pol. position
    in own party, 66n., 360, 363, App. VII
    with non-Soc. voters, 66, 323n., 347, 444
    as conciliator, 190 and n.
  and constituency, 349n.
  impeachment proposed by Coms., 38, 88 and n., 178n., **306**
  quoted
    on Com. infiltration, 385n., 387n.
    on cost of air force, 393n.
    on Soc. P. machinery, 371
    on tax evasion, 22n.
Mollet, Guy (b. 1905, M.P. 1945, sec.-gen. Soc. P. since 1946, second chairman of c'tee on const., mayor of Arras, Soc. d. Pas-de-Calais II)
  career, 34n., App. II, III, IV
  stands for P.M. 1951: 38, 183n., 184n., 186 and n., 334
  offered P.M. 1953...413*
  conciliator, 1950...37 186 and n., 190 and n.
  position in party, 63, 66, 67, 371, 409n., 411, App. VII
  views, 1947...33, 262, 371
  views, 1953...409n., 411
monarchists, see royalists.
Monnerville, Gaston (b. 1897, M.P. Guyane 1932, s. Guyane 1946, s. Lot 1948, R.G.R., Pres. C.R. since 1947), 273n., 284n.
Monnet, Jean (b. 1888, assistant sec.-gen. League of Nations 1919–23, comm. in de Gaulle admin 1943–4, *comm.-gén. au plan* 1947–52, pres. High Authority European Coal and Steel Community 1952–), 391, 405
Monnet plan, *see* investment.
Monteil, André (b. 1915, M.P. 1945, M.R.P. d. Finistère)
  pol. position, 88n.
  on army appointments, 387n.
  keeps c'tee seat, 412n.*
Montel, Pierre (b. 1896, M.P. 1946, P.R.L. and R.I. d. Rhône I)
  and R.P.F. inter-group, 121n., 369*

Montel, Pierre (cont'd)
  c'tee chairman and M., 238n.
  vote *re* Moch, 184n.
  amendment on mil. budget, 245n.34*
Morazé, Charles, 54n.
Morbihan, dept. (cap. Vannes), 129n.
Moreau, Émile (died 1950, aged 82, Governor Bank of France 1926–30, Pres. Bank of Paris 1930–40), 328n.
Moreau, Jean (b. 1888, M.P. 1945, R.I. d. Yonne), 392, 409n.4*, App. III
Morocco
  status of, 152n., 293, 294
  Frenchmen in, rep. in C.R., 270, 271n.
  rep. in C.A., 191n.
  policy in, *see* Africa, North.
  Residents in, 405n.
Morocco, former Sultan Mohammed ben Youssef of, deposition of, 135n., 410–1
Moscow, *see* U.S.S.R.
Moscow conference of Foreign Ms., 1947...19–20
Moslems, Algerian, 152, 248
Mosley, Sir Oswald, 69n.
motorists, *see* petrol.
Mottin, Jean, quoted, **389–91**
Mouvement communiste français, 142
Mouvement de libération nationale (M.L.N.), 143
Mouvement du triomphe des libertés démocratiques (M.T.L.D.: Algerian nationalists), 152
Mouvement nationale judiciaire, 302n.
Mouvement républicain populaire (M.R.P.), Chapter 6, App. VII
  history
    forerunners, 77–8
    founded, 13, 78
    at liberation, 13–9, 78–9
    and de Gaulle, 14–6, 18, 20, 34, 79, 119
    recent drift to Right, 411–2 and n.
  clientèle
    numbers, 79, 83–4
    class basis, 83–4, 333, 351, 446
    cons. support, 19, 24, 34, 79
    left wing of, 34, 87, 240, 370, 411 and n.: *and see below, militants* and leadership
  discipline
    of deputies, 82–3, 121, 359–61 and n., 408–9 and n., 412n.
    of leaders, 360 and n., 408–9 and n.
    of *militants, see below*.
    of voters, 19, 24, 34, 79, 443n.
    and R.P.F., 132 and n.
    defiance of, 82–3, 132 and n., 348, 411 and n.
  militants
    and deputies, 82–3

Mouvement républicain populaire militants (cont'd.)
   and leadership, 36, 42, 80–3 and n., 85, 86, 87–8, 132, 204, 369–70, 411n.
   class basis, 84
   loyalty of, 74, 86, 318
   org., 79–83, 87, 367, 370
   funds, 80 and n., 365n.
   in Parl.
     in c'tees, 412n.
     in C.R., 278
     and ds.' salaries, 80 and n., 365n.
     group, 365
     and procedural reform, 209, 382–3
     and v. of c., 223
   participation in govt., 89, 189n., 379–80 and nn., 382–3, 385n., 394, 408, 447
   favours pact of majority, 394
   policy
     clerical, 24–5, 28, 88, 122, 331, 339, 356, 387
     colonial, 24, 151, 292, 405n., 411
     const.
        1945–6...16–9, 21, 79, 119, 164, 167, 171
        and E.C., 297, 298
        and elec. system, 25, 32, 38, 40, 87, 315 and n., 318–9 and n., 321, 351
        and H.C.M., 301
     and *statut des partis*, 345
     econ., 41, 246n., 264, 380, 393
     foreign and defence, 408, *and see* Europe; Schuman plan.
     T.U. and social, 24, 249 and n., 331, 410
   and rivals, 24–5
     Com., 62, 72, 119, 315
     Cons., 24, 79, 114, 380, 382
     Rad. 89, 94
     R.P.F., 32, 36, 79, 82, 87, 121, 132, 134, 319, 370, *and see above* (de Gaulle).
     Soc., 73–4, 88, 119, 122, 204n., 356
     Mayer, 185
     Pinay, 42, 88–9, 394n., 409
     Pleven, 178n.
     in 1953 crisis, 408, 411–2 and n.
   and scandals, 88, 204n.
   ex-M.R.P.
     Gaullist, 125n., 132, 134, 362
     Leftist, 142, 347, 362, 411 and n.
     generally, 348 and n., 350
M.R.P. journals
   L'Action fédérale, 80 nn.
   Forces nouvelles, 111n.
   M.R.P. à l'action, 84n.
M.R.P. *statuts nationaux*, 82n.
Mouvement unifié de la renaissance française (M.U.R.F.), 143
Mulhouse, 351

Munich treaty
   and Parl., 10, 196, 262
   and parties, 12, 46, 78, 92
municipal councils, *see* elections; local authorities.
Mussolini, Benito, 12, 78, 109
Mutter, André (b. 1901, M.P. 1945, P.R.L. and Peas. d. Aube), 323n.30, App. III
mystique
   of authority and discipline, 137
   Rad. lack of, 104
   of violence, absence of in R.P.F., 138

Naegelen, Marcel-Edmond (b. 1892, M.P. 1945, Soc. d. B.-Rhin 1945–51, B.-Alpes 1951– , gov.-gen. of Algeria 1948–51, stood for Pres. Rep. 1953), 192n., 350, App. III
Nancy
   Marin and, 348n.
   R.P.F. congress at, 125n., 127, 162n.*
Nantes, 83n., 87, 130, 370
Napoleon
   Emperor, 163
   Prince, 151n.
Naquet, Alfred-Joseph (1834–1916, M.P. 1871, s. 1882, later Boulangist, d. 1893), 179n.
nationalism
   of Right, 4, 115, 134, 138, 150
   Irish, 199
   and limitation of sovereignty, 308
   colonial, **151–2**, *and also*
     Indo-Chinese, 296n., 410
     Madagascan, 184n., *and q.v.*
     Moroccan, 410
     West African, 142
     and R.P.F., 135n., *and see* self-government.
nationality, dispute with Italy over, 177
nationalization
   and judicial review, 289
   and Preamble, 307 and n.
nationalized industries
   and eligibility for Parl., 192
   and E.C., 297
   and pol. interference, 263n., 385n., 388n.
   and audit, 266
   and investment, 281, 333
   and denationalization, 263
   and reorg. by decree, 34, 263, 412n.
   and see coal; railways.
navette, 276, 283, 285 and n.
navy, 7, 9, *and see* Marine.
Nazis, *see* Germany.
Nazi-Soviet pact, 12, 46, 48, 355
Nef, La, 72n., 334n., 405n.
Neo-Socialists, 12, 61, 359
Neumann, R. G., 322n., 385n.

neutralism, **140**–3
newspapers, *see* press.
Nièvre, dept. (cap. Nevers), 311n.
Noguères, Louis (b. 1881, Soc. d. Pyrénées-Orientales 1945–51, Pres. exceptional High Court), 46n., 354
Nonconformist conscience, 86
Nord, dept. (3 constituencies: I Dunkirk, *q.v.*; II Lille (cap. and *q.v.*) and Roubaix; III Valenciennes)
  elections in
    1951...70, 110, 130, 324
    1952 by-election, 123n.
  parl. rep.
    c'tees, 240
    constituencies, 315n., 349
    parties in
      Com., 49n., 50
      M.R.P., 356, 370n.
      Soc., 72
Normandy, 150, 240 and n., 328n.
North Africa, *see* Africa; Algeria; Morocco; Tunisia.
Norway, 302n.
notables, 93, 107, 114, 318

Observateur, L' (now *France-Observateur*: neutralist journal), 52n., 131n., 190n., 319n., 336n.
obstruction
  of H.C.M. by M. of Justice, 304 and n.
  parl., *see* Parliament.
Occidente, 139n.
occupation, foreign, and const. revision, 288
occupation, German
  censorship, 46, 389
  Coms. and, 46–7
  and Jews, 407
  lives lost (compared with purge), 302n.
  and Radicals, 92
Oceania, 184n., 294n.*
office
  acceptance of, parties keep control over members', 383
  chances of
    worse than in Britain, 250n., 376
    of c'tee chairmen, 238 and n.
    of conciliators, *q.v.*
    of critics, 244n.
    of Finance c'tee members, 242 and n
  participation in
    'permanent'
      by M.R.P., 89n., 394
      by Rads., 11–2, 106
      by 'king's friends,' 374–5
      I.O.M., 153
      Rep. Socs., 140, 148, 149
      U.D.S.R., 145 and n.

office
  participation in (*cont'd*)
    views on
      of voters, **447**
      of ex-ministers, 63, 371, 393 and n.
    and see militants and deputies; opposition; stability; each party separately.
Oise, dept. (cap. Beauvais), 101n., 272 and n.
Oloron, 257n.
opposition
  electoral advantage of, 28, 394
  permanent (untouchability), 358
  and see office.
opposition-mindedness, **447**
  of Finance c'tee, 242–3
  among Rads., 5, 7–8, 10, 103, 411n.
  among Socs., 72
  and see authority, distrust of; budgetary policy (resistance to taxation); *incivisme*; instability.
Oradour-sur-Glane, S.S. massacre at, 334, 335n.
oral question with débate, 279
Oran, 150
'orange-peel' crises, 230
order, exceptional measures for, in 1947 strikes, 177, 199, 277
  and see strikes.
organic laws
  for budget, 254
  for C.R., 269
Organisation civile et militaire (O.C.M.), 143n.
organized debate, 201 and n., 365
Overseas France, 294
  C.R., 270–1
  departments
    deputies of, 337n.
    elec. law, 443
    and see Guadeloupe, Guyane, Martinique, Réunion.
  deputies
    numbers and distribution of, **191n.**, 240, 296
    from Lyons, 323n.30, 362n.
    pol. importance of
      allegiance, party, 145–6, **151**–3
      bad party disc., 361
      marginal position
        (and const.), 167
        (and govts.), 152–3, 223n., 296 and n.
      metropolitan fear of being swamped by, 294
      mentioned, 140, 184n.
  franchise and elec. law, 153, 208, 282n., 296n., 322
Frenchmen, pol. rep. of, 270

INDEX 481

Overseas France (cont'd)
governors, high comms., Residents, etc.
   appointments, 189n., 350, 386, 388, 409n.2, 410 and n.
   charges against, 350n., 405n.
   power of, 405n., 410
   territories, and E.C., 297
Overseas France, M. of
   and parties, 379, 380, 386
   u-sec'ship and parties, 152n., 153n.
Overseas Territories c'tee of N.A., 236, 240 and n., 242n.22

PACIFIC territories, French, 294n.
pacifism, 140–3, 149, 282n.
   and see conscientious objectors.
Painlevé, Paul (1863–1933, M.P. 1910, P.M. 1917, Pres. Chamber 1924, stood for Pres. Rep. 1924), 140
Palais Bourbon, 45*, 295, 359, 373
Palewski, Gaston (b. 1901, M.P. 1951, de Gaulle's former *chef de cabinet*, R.P.F. d. Seine VI), 139n.
Palewski, Jean-Paul (brother of above, b. 1898, M.P. 1945, M.R.P. and R.P.F. d. Seine-et-Oise II), 139n.
panachage, **314,** 315, 320, 322, 323 and n., 347 and n., 348, 444–5
parachuting of deputies, 350
pardons
   and Auriol, 176
   demanded from M. of Justice, 349
   for High Court sentences, 306n.
   procedure for
      countersign, 169n.
      H.C.M. and Pres., 172, 175–6, 302 and purge, 302 and n.
Paris and suburbs
   concierges of, 335
   congresses at
      M.R.P., 83n.
      R.P.F., 125n.
   elections in
      1928...311n.
      1945–6...54nn., 85 and n., 101n., 143, 324n.
      1951
         Coms., 4, 54n., 57
         Cons., 112–3, 150
         M.R.P., 85 and n.
         Rads. and R.G.R., 101, 148, 149
         R.P.F., 130, 131 and n.
         Socs., 54n., 70, 71n.
         dissident Coms., 143
         ex-M.R.P. (neutralists), 347, 350
         mécontents, 348
         neutralists, 142 and n., 143, 347*, 350*
         non-voters, 324n.
         panachage, etc., in, 347, 350*
      by-elections, 110n., 123n, 131n.
      munic., 117, 130–1 and n., 134
P.P.F.

Paris and suburbs (cont'd)
   electoral campaign in, 356
   electoral law in, 322 and n., 324n., 443
   German entry into, 46
   munic. council
      M.R.P. candidates for, 80
      Pres. of, 134, 137*
      parties in
         Com., 45, 57, 311n., 350, 391n.
         Cons., 110n., 111n., 117
         Rads. and R.G.R., 90–1, 102, 104n., 148–9, 356
         R.P.F., 117, 120, 137n.
         U.D.S.R., 143
         and see elections *above*
   press, 389, 391n.
   trade unions, 71
   wage scales, 241 and n.
   mentioned, 54, 82, 86, 91, 94, 97, 121, 135n., 193 and nn., 222n., 241n., 266, 292–4, 342, 347–54, 387, 394, 399, 405n.
Paris basin, 131n., 132
Paris, Comte de, **150–1 and n.,** 340 and n.
Parisians (national as opposed to provincial personalities)
   deputies, 205
   and Rad. P., 96, 97
   and R.P.F., 121n., 126 and n.
   and Socs., 64n.
Parisot, M., 128
Parliament
   const. position of, Chapters 13 and 14 and pp. 10, 156–7, 187, 209–10, 235
   dissolution of lower house of, *q.v.*
   and finance, *see* budget; decree-laws; initiative; provisional twelfths.
   and legislation, *see* bills.
   members, personal and pol. position of
      camaraderie, 50–1, **205–6,** 251, 296 and n., 301n., 305 and n., **373, 388 and n.**
      constituency interests, *q.v.*
      irresponsibility, 219, 232, 242, 243, 372
      origins, local, 350–1
      origins, occup.
         3rd Rep., deputies, 4 and n., 206n.
         4th Rep., candidates, 40 and n. 84n.
         4th Rep., deputies, 84n., 206 and n.
         4th Rep., senators, 273
         and see each party separately.
      overseas, *q.v.*
      ' parl. proletariat,' 355n., 409 and n
      members, status of, **191–3 and nn.**
         and also
         eligibility, 151 and n.

31

Parliament
  members, status of, (cont'd)
    immunity, q.v.
    salaries, 365 and n.
    and C.R., 273
  officers
    bureau of N.A., 196 and n., 197–8, 230, 364n.
    bureau of C.R., 273
    bureaux, 194n.
    Presidents' Conference, q.v.
    Pres. of N.A., of C.R., see President.
    questeurs, 51n., 197–8
  procedure
    c'tees, q.v.
    debate
      disorder in, 199 and n.
      faults of, 200, 204, 207, 209 and n., 360
      oral question with (C.R.), 279
      organized, 201 and n., 365
      restricted, 200, 201n., 237, 409n.
    obstruction
      in N.A. debates, 177, 197, 199–200, 210, 321n.
      in C.R. debates, 277
      of parl. programme, 201, 208, 210
      reaction against, 199, 321n.
      weapons against, 200
    ordres du jour, 209n., 221n., and see Pres.' Conference.
    pol. effects of, 8–9, 157, 206, 211–3
    questions, 205 and n., 237 and n.
    reform, 208n. 53, 210, 406 and n., 409n.
    urgency, **208–9 and n.**
      and Const. C'tee, 289, **291**
      and C.R., **275 and n.**, 284
      and E.C., 297
      and expenditure proposals, 258 and n.
    vote, explanation of one's, 218
    voting, see below.
  sessions, sittings, **195–6**, 273–4, 282
    and also
    adjournment, clôture, 10, 291, 403
    convocation, 411
    dissolution, q.v.
  standing orders of N.A.
    and alternates in c'tees, 247 and n.
    and groups, 196
    and obstruction, 197
    and Pres.' Conference, 199n., 207
    and votes of censure, 224
    revision, debates, 200, 201n., 210
    and see Standing Orders
  standing orders of C.R., 276, 278
  time of
    govt.'s inability to control, 206, **208–10**
    H.C.M. baffled by lack of, 304

Parliament
  time of (cont'd)
    saving of, 200–1, and see under debate, above.
    waste of, by c'tees, 250
    waste of, by private members 258n.
  voting
    methods, 197
    public, to override C.R., 276
    public, on v. of c., 215
    scrutin public à la tribune, 197, 200, 222 and n., 224, 365
    secret
      for High Court, 305
      for impeachments, 305
      for Pres. Rep., 91, 170–1 and nn., 179n., 414
    inconclusive
      for H.C.M., 302
      for Pres. Rep., 414 and n.
Parliamentary Affairs, 380n.
parquet, 302–4 and nn.
Parti agraire, 111
Parti communiste internationaliste, 142
Parti démocrate populaire (P.D.P.), 77, 78 and n., 108
Parti républicain de la liberté (P.R.L.)
  formed, 14n., 35n.
  adherents, **109, 116,** 148
  tactics
    and Rads., 93
    and R.P.F., 135
    and govts. and policy, 223n., 245n., 383
Parti républicain et sociale de la reconciliation française (R.F.), 148
Parti républicain socialiste, 140, 148, 149
Parti social français, 108, 137, 139, 148
Parti socialiste démocratique, 141, 148, 149
Parties, 'national,' in 1951 elec. law, 322n.
Party discipline
  generally
    and acceptance of office, 383
    compared with Britain, **155,** 161–3, 166–7, 213–4 and n., 231–2, 356, 361, 400
    compared with Weimar Rep., 342–4
    monolithic, under tripartisme, 204, **342–5,** 355, **359–60, 381–2**
    later relaxation, **360–2**
    reasons why stronger since war, 346, 404
  electoral, Chapter 21
    lack of, in 3rd Rep., 310–2
    of voters
      'Republican,' 9, 45, 311 and n.
      personal and party voting, 443–5
      of Coms., 311 and n., 319, 443n.

Party discipline
electoral, (*cont'd*)
and deputies, 348, **351–6**
and elec. system, 314, App. VI
in Parl., Chapter 22
lax, in 3rd Rep., **154–8**, 164, 328
strict, under Combes, 9,159–60,213
under *tripartisme, see above.*
1947–53...360–1
lack of, in N.A., 207, 209
in c'tees, 239, 244, 247–9 and nn., 412n.
discipline de vote, 98, 359, 361 and n.
in Pres. election 1946...170, 171
and whips, 197, 232
and *statut des partis,* 345, *and q.v.*
and see each party separately.
Party funds
election expenses, 344–5n., 355n.
local and central, 63n., 80 and n., 94 and n.
and M.Ps.' salaries, 51 and n., 80, 365 and n.
other sources, 350n., 356n.
under *statut des partis,* 345
Party groups, **363–6**
chairmen of, in cabinet-making, 363–4, 382
and c'tee elections, 196, **236**
and inter-groups, 196–7, *and q.v.*
and party org., **366–73**
social contacts in, 205
and see militants and deputies.
Party organization, *see* each party separately.
party system, two-
equivalent of, in 3rd Rep., 232
advantages and dangers of, 233, 310, 401
Pas-de-Calais, dept. (2 constituencies:
I Boulogne *q.v.* and Calais *q.v.*;
II Arras (cap.) and Bethune)
1951 election in, 74n.
Coms. and, 49n., 50
parl. rep. (c'tees), 240
Socs. of, 64, 70, 73n.
' Passy,' Colonel (Armand Dewavrin), 386, 387
pastis, 87, 241, 336, 337n., 349, *and see* alcohol.
Patenôtre, Raymond (1900–51, M.P. 1928, newspaper owner), 95
Paul, Marcel (b. 1900, M.P. 1945–8, Com. d. H.-Vienne, resigned seat) as M., infiltration and scandals, 350n., 385n., 392*, App. III
and party, 57, 353
Paul-Boncour, Joseph (b. 1873, M.P. 1909, Soc. and Rep. Soc., P.M. 1932, Soc. s. 1946–8, elected by N.A.), 140
Peasant party, 14n., 35n., **109**, **111–2**, **113–4 and n.**, 117 and n.
discipline of, 361, 383

Peasant party, (*cont'd*)
militants and deputies, 112n.
policy, 117, 245n., 321, 333–4
and rivals
Coms., 109
R.P.F., 148n.
U.N.I.R., 150 and n.
Bidault, 223n.
Mayer, 41
splits, 111–2 and n., 113n.15, 380, **410n., 411n.**
peasantry
numbers and importance of, 2–3 and n., 396–7 and n.
class divisions among, 103, 410n.
Coms. and, *q.v.*
and const.
C.R., 334n.
E.C., 297–300
elec. law, 334 and n., 349 and n.
and econ. policy of govts., 35n., 248*, 410n., *and see below.*
and elections, leaders as asset in, 351
and food supply 1944–7...21, 174, 175, *and q.v.*
as pressure-group, 241, **332–4 and n.**, 337, 349 and n., 391, *and see* Agriculture, Confédération générale de l'
resistance to taxation, 5, 9, 22, 23 and n., *and see* Mayer (levy).
Pébellier, Eugene, senior (1866–1952, Peasant d. H.-Loire 1951–2), 198
Pébellier, Eugene, junior (son of above, b. 1897, M.P. 1936, ineligible until amnesty, Peas. d. H.-Loire since 1953, mayor of Le Puy), 192n., 198
Pébellier, Jean (brother of above, **Peas.** d. H.-Loire 1952–3, resigned seat when amnesty voted), no ref.
Peelites, 166
Pelletan, Camille (1846–1915, M.P. 1881), 7
Pensée française (in E.C.), 297, 299, 388n.
pensions
of deputies, 193 and n.
of ex-servicemen, 219n., 240 and n., 242
popularity of, in Parl., 201, 212
railwaymen's, 268n.
Pensions c'tee of N.A., 237, 240 and n., 242 and n., 260
Pensions, M. of
in Parl., 240n.
and parties, 378–9
Périer, *see* Casimir-.
Pernot, Georges (b. 1879, M.P. 1924, s. 1935, Vichy M. of the Family 1940, P.R.L. s. Doubs since 1946), 283*, 292n.
Perpignan, 102

Pétain, Marshal Philippe (1856–1951,
'chief of the French state' 1940–4)
pre-war, 6, 12, 386
in 1940...13, 14, 168
opponents, 61, 109
supporters, 351
Cons., 133, 150, 198
Rads., 92, 93
Socs., 61, 62, 69, 141, 149, 354
and see Vichy.
in 1941
Coms. and , 46
Comte de Paris and, 150
de Gaulle and, 133–4
post-war
imprisonment, 133
de Gaulle and, 133–4
supporters, 117n., 149–50, *and
see* Vichyites.
Pétain cabinets, **13**, 34n., 61, 92, 373
Petit, Claudius (Eugène Petit, named
Claudius in Resistance, b. 1907,
M.P. 1945, U.D.S.R. d. Loire)
position in party, 141, 144n.
position with voters, 347 and n.
as M., 379, App. III
quoted (on pressure-groups), 341n.51
Petit, Guy (b. 1905, M.P. 1946, u.-sec.
1952, M. 1953, Peas. d. B-Pyrénées,
mayor of Biarritz), 148, 340n.,
App. III
Petites et moyennes entreprises (P.M.E.)
and E.C., 300
and 1951 election, 149, 332
as pressure-group, **331–2**, 339–
40 and nn., 391
strike, 339
petrol (in politics)
alcohol used instead of fuel, 336
govt. defeats on, 219n., 225n., 243
and motorists as pressure-group,
322n., 335–6, 344, 348
rationing of, 220n., 280, 284n.
road hauliers, 329, 336, **337–8**
use of, in elections, 345n.
Petsche, Maurice (1895–1951, M.P.
1925, Ind. Cons. d. H.-Alpes)
career, 34n., 35n., 236n., Apps. II,
III, IV
stands for P.M. 1951...41, 183n.,
184n., 185, 186n.
as M. of Finance, 35n., 236n., 243,
331n., 378, 392*
as critic, 244n.
quoted, 259
petty bourgeoisie, 104, 328, 334, 339–40,
397, *and see Petites et moyennes
entreprises.*
Peyré, Roger, 327n., 387*
Peyret, Henri, 334n.
Peyroles, Mme. Germaine (b. 1902,
M.P. 1945, M.R.P. d. Seine-et-Oise
I 1945–51, lost seat, re-elected 1954)

Peyroles, Mme. Germaine (*cont'd*)
as vice-pres. N.A., 231*
quoted (on const. revision) 280n.31,
282n., 283n., 285n.
Pflimlin, Pierre (b. 1907, M.P. 1945,
M.R.P. d. B.-Rhin)
as M., App. III
resigns as M. of Agric., 336*, 391*
M.-designate, 393*
stands for Pres. N.A. 1954...412
philatelists, 350n.
Philip, André (b. 1902, M.P. 1945,
Soc. d. Rhône I 1945–51, first
chairman of c'tee on const.)
career as M., 18, 391, 392, App. III
position in party, 63
loses seat, 296n., 350, 388n.
appointed to E.C., 296n., 299n.,
388n.
piastres, traffic des, 204n., 356n.
Picasso, Pablo, 55
Pickles, Dorothy M., quoted
on Coms., 257n., 385n.
on institutions, 194n., 264n., 295n.,
296n., 299n.
on Preamble, 307n.
on social and econ., 23n., 397n.
Pickles, William, quoted, 85n., 101n.,
131n., map 2
pigeons
eating-, menace to liberty, 194n.9
homing-, menace to solvency, 262n.
olive-branch-bearing, menace to
peace, 55*
Pinay, Antoine (b. 1891, M.P. 1936,
s. 1938, on Vichy Nat. Council,
R.I. d. Loire)
career, 34n., Apps. II, III, IV
as P.M., 1952
nominated, 186n.
elected, majority, 33, 42, 123, 179n.,
205
cabinet-making, 383
also M. of Finance, 188n.
policy, **42**, 257n., 3$\underline{36}$
use of v. of c̄., 201, 217n., 219nn.,
220n., 241n.
nominated as P.M. 1953...409, 413
as M., 188n., 379, 392
popularity, 39, 116 and n., 406
position in party, 111n., 148,
409 and n.
and other parties
in 1951 election, 347n.
and M.R.P., 42, 88–9, 370n.,
394n., 409
and R.P.F., 24, 123, 127, 136,
185n., 369
and Socs., 225n., 379
and U.D.S.R., 146
quoted (on econ.), 257nn. 8 and 10,
340 and n.
Pinay cabinet, March–December 1952

Pinay cabinet, March-December 1952
  formed, membership, **42**, **111n.**, 183n.*, 184n.46, 185n., 189n.64, 380, 382–3
  abstention of, in parl. divisions, 383n.
  and C.R., 281n.
  and finance, **256 and n.**, 259n., 262–3, 264n.
  and Finance c'tee, 244, 260
  and parties, *see* Pinay.
  party discipline under, **361 and nn.**
  vote of censure against, 225n.
  fall, 22, **42**, 226 and n.
  mentioned, 357
Pineau, Christian (b. 1904, M.P. 1945, *rapp.-g.* Finance c'tee 1945–6, chairman 1946–7, Soc. d. Sarthe)
  as M. of Works and Transport, 391*
  as M. of Finance (2 days), 34, 35 and n., 181*, App. III
  as c'tee chairman and M., 238n.
  impeachment motion, 306
  quoted, 261*, 266n.
Pinto, Roger, quoted, 263nn., 264n., 292n., 307n.
Plaisant, Marcel (b. 1887, M.P. 1919, s. 1921, Pres. Foreign Affs. c'tee of C.R., R.G.R. s. Cher 1948–), 280n.31
plebiscites, *see* referendum.
Pleven, René (b. 1901, M.P. 1945, pres. U.D.S.R. to 1953, d. Côtes-du-Nord in 1st C.A. and since November 1946)
  career, 34n., Apps. II, III, IV
  as P.M., 37, 145, 146 (1st govt.), **41**, 183n. (2nd)
    consultations, 186n. (2nd)
    meeting N.A., 182 (1st), 183n. (2nd)
    resignation refused, 178 and n.
    use of v. of c., 217n., 223–4
  as M. of Finance, 145n., **391–2**
  pol. position, 33, **145**, 360, 391–2, **393n.**, 409n., 411
  as conciliator, 190 and n., 362, 383–4
  as critic, 146, 360
  and Mendès-France, 391–2, 409n.
  and R.P.F., 33, 145
  and voters, 347
  c'tee membership, 22n., 240n.19, 242n.
  quoted, 22n., 393n.
Pleven cabinet, July 1950-February 1951
  formed, membership, 37, 184n.46, 186n., 236n., 382
  significance, **145–6**
  and c'tees of N.A., 243–4, 248
  and finance, **255–6**
  and Moch's impeachment, 306
  tactics, 190 and n., 383, 384
  fall, **37–8**, **223–4 and n.**, 225, 226 and nn., 227

Pleven cabinet, August 1951-January 1952
  formed, membership, 41, 111, 183n., 184n.46, 189n.64, 380
  course, weakness, **41**, **190 and n.**, **331n.**, 334, 383
  econ. and fin. policy, 136, **256**, 262, 263n.
  and Finance c'tee, 244, 245 and n., 260
  resignation refused, 227
  Socs. and, 372 and n.
  fall, 22, **41**, 226 and n., 227, 244–5, 256, 262, **331 and n.**, 340*
Poincaré, Raymond (1860–1934, M.P. 1887, s. 1903, P.M. 1912–3, Pres. Rep. 1913–20, s. 1920, P.M. 1922–4 and 1926–9), 238n., 239, 328n.
Poincaré cabinet 1928 (and Rads.), 366
Poinso-Chapuis, Mme. Germaine (b. 1901, M.P. 1945, M.R.P. d. Bouches-du-Rhône I), 188n., 393n., App. III
Poinso-Chapuis decree, *see* Church schools.
police, 2, 88n., 194n.9, 265n.38, 386–7
Politica, quoted, *see* Pickles, William.
Political Quarterly, 267n.
Political Science Quarterly, 58n., 385n.
Political Studies, 191n., 193n., 361n.
politicians, low standing of, 402
Politique (pro-M.R.P. journal), quoted
  on institutions, 275n., 277n.*, 291n., 298n., 306n.
  on parl., const., 35n., 204–5nn., 251n.
  on party pol., 16n.,
  on pressure groups, 35n., 340n.
  on social security elections, 56n.
politique du clocher, la, 313, 329*, *and see* constituency interests.
polls, public opinion, *see* Sondages.
Populaire, Le (Soc. organ), 46n., 310n., 391n.
  quoted, 180n., 292n.
population
  numbers and distribution, 2–3
  birthrate, 402
  M. of, *see* Health.
postal workers, 332
Posts and Telegraphs, M. of
  status, 189n.
  and parties, 379 and n., 380n., 384n.
Pouët, *see* Tinguy du Pouët.
Pouillon, Jean, 318n.
pouvoirs, les, 91, 92, 318
pouvoirs publics, les, 284n.
powers, special, *see* decree-laws.
Prague, battle of, 20, 204, 218, 342
Preamble to constitution, **306–8**
  and constitutionality, 289
  and decree-laws, 307, 412n.
  and French Union, 410n.
Preamble to draft const., 17, 307
prefects
  appointment, 189n.

prefects (*cont'd*)
  and const., 189n., 306
  and local govt., 306, 404
  and politics, 191n., 230, 356n., 385n., 387
preferential vote, 314, **315 and n.**, 322, 344, **443-5**
Prélot, Marcel (b. 1898, M.P. 1951, ex-rector Strasbourg univ., R.P.F. d. Doubs)
  chairman Franchise c'tee, 239n.*
  member of Const. C'tee, 289, 291n.
  quoted
    on 3rd Rep., 212n.*
    on const., 35n., 167n.
    on Const. C'tee, 291n.
    on pressure-groups, 35n., 340n.
premiership
  const.
    in provisional regime, 179 and n.
    Soc. conception of, 164, 187
    in draft const., 172, 179
    in const. of 4th Rep., **187-90**, 213n.
    and caretaker cabinet for dissolution, 198, 230, 231 and n.
    executing laws, 187, 189
    in investiture debate, 209n.
    and v. of c., 215, 222-3, 232, *and see* individual P.Ms.; confidence
  pol.
    choice, in 3rd Rep.,178-9 and n., 181
    election, in 4th Rep., **179-85**, 201
    under *tripartisme*, 1945-7...381-2
    choosing Ms., 1947-53, 382-3
    resignation, 178n., *and see* Auriol.
    ' reinvestiture,' 1954,...411n.
  holders, origins of
    from previous cabinet, 380
    generation, 34 and n.
    previous office, 377 and n.
    party, 146, 378
    preference for conciliators, 190 and n., 362, 363, *and see* conciliators.
  office du président du conseil, 180n., 188 and nn., 404 and n.
presidencies (and Rad. P.), 100
President of Chamber, 8, 198 and n., 363
President of C.A., *see* Assemblies, Constituent.
President of C.R.
  subordinate to Pres. N.A., 273
  and Const. C'tee, 289
President of N.A.
  virtual vice-Pres. Rep., **198**-9, 273
  and *bureau*, 197
  caretaker govt. and at dissolution, 198, 228, 230, 231n.
  in choice of P.M., 172, 179
  on Const. C'tee, 289
  election of, 1954...412
  lacks authority of Speaker, 198, 200, **207 and n.**, 406

President of N.A. (*cont'd*)
  protest to Auriol against C.R., 279
President of the Republic, Chapter 12
  in const.
    Socs. favour abolition of, 164
    de Gaulle's conception, 161-3, 402-3
    eligibility, 151n.
    election
      method of, **170-1 and nn.**, 203, 274, 413-4
      govt. resigns upon, 19, 225, 226n. 411n., 413n.
  in 3rd Rep.
    personalities
      candidates, 156, 169-70
      preference for Pres. Chamber or Senate, 198n.
      weak incumbents, 156
    powers
      and cabinet-making, 178-9 and n., 363-4
      and *clôture*, 195
      and dissolution, 8, 211
  in 4th Rep.
    elections of, 1946 and 1953...19, 171 and n., 411, 413-4
    impeachment of, 204, 305
    powers, Chapter 12, 403, 414n.
    and Const. C'tee, 176, 274, 279, 288-91
    and C.R., 273, 291
    executive authority lost, 188
    and French Union, 169n., 293, 410 and n.
    and H.C.M., 169n., 172, 175-6, 301-4
    and messages to N.A., 273
    and pardons, 172, 302
    presiding in cabinet, 174, 190
    and reference back of bills, 172, 176-7 and n., 201n., 283, 291
    and resignation of P.Ms, 177-8 and n., *and see* Auriol.
    and v. of c., 221, 222n.
    and see Auriol.
President of Senate, 173n., 198n., 273
presidential govt., 161-2, 402-3
Presidents' Conference
  composition, 157, **199 and n., 206-7**, 235
  functions, 157, **199 and n.**, 200, 364-5
  and org. debates, 201 and n.,
  and urgency debates, 208
press, **389-91**
  freedom of, in Preamble, 307
  law of 1946...**389-91**
  ministerial resp. for, 188n.
  of parties
    in local politics, 95, 354
    in Rad. org., 95
    jobs on, disciplinary dismissals from, 359

press, (*cont'd*)
  petulance in ministerial crises, 367n.
Press c'tee of N.A., 241, 242n., 246n.
pressure-groups, Chapter 20
  instability gives power to, 405 and n.
  in Parl.
    groups in 3rd Rep., 197, **335–7**
    in c'tees, 240–1, 250, 251
    and E.C., 300
  and R.P.F., 138
  retard economic progress, 397
  A.P.L.E., 41 *and q.v.*
  C.G.A., 35n. *and q.v.*
  employers, 136 *and q.v.*
  trade unions, 35n., *and q.v.*
  and see constituency interests.
previous question, 200
Prigent, Robert (b. 1910, M.P. 1945, M.R.P. d. Nord II 1945–6, Nord I 1946–51), 78n., App. III
Prigent, *see* Tanguy-.
prime minister, *see* premiership; *and* prime ministers individually.
Priouret, Roger-A, quoted
  on Auriol as const.-maker, 173n.
  on C.R., 282n.
  on elec. system, 309n.
  on parties, 344 n., 360n., 393n.
    Com., 51n., 368n.
    Cons., 93n., 316n.
    Rad., 93n.
  on presidential election 1946…171n.
  on pressure-groups, 331n., 340n., 350n.
private members
  bills, *see* bills.
  expenditure proposals, *see* initiative, financial.
privileges and status
  of A.F.U. members, 294
  of E.C. members (lack of), 297
  of M.Ps., 191–4, *and see* Parliament, members of (immunity).
professorial chairs, 192n.
profit-sharing, 299
Progrès de Lyon, Le (Rad. journal), 95
Progressives, 141, 142, 152, 236, 362n., 409n., *and see* Cot.
projets de loi, 203n., *and see* bills.
proletariat, *see* workers.
  parl., *see* Parliament, members of.
promulgation of laws, 198, 274 and n., 275, 291
Pronteau, Jean (Com. d.), 356n.
property, rights of, in const., 307
proportional representation
  in elections, *see* electoral system.
  in govt. and admin., 321, 388
  Parl.
    principle of, **345**
    for A.F.U., 294
    and *bureau*, 197 and n., 230–1
    in caretaker govt., not required, 230n.

proportional representation
  Parl. (*cont'd*)
    for c'tees, 235, 238, 364 and n.
    for Const. C'tee, 289, 290
    and C.R., 36, 270–2 and n.
    for senators elected by N.A., 203
    for *bureau* of, 273
    and H.C.M. elections, 301, 345
    for High Court, 305, 306
    not for Pres. Conference, 207
propositions de loi, 203n., *and see* bills, private members.
prosecutors, public, *see* parquet.
Prot, Louis (b. 1889, M.P. 1936, Com. d. Somme), **354–5 and n.**
protectionism, 396–7
protectorates, 152n., 293, 294, *and see* Associated States.
Provence, 94
provisional regime, *see* constitution; *tripartisme.*
provisional twelfths, 253, 280, 413n.
proxy voting, 197 and n., 212, 222, 355, 361, 365
Public Administration, 191n., 265n.*, 266n.*, 306n., 404
public opinion polls, *see* Sondages.
Public Safety, C'tee of (in Revolution), 235
purge, post-war, **302 and n.,** 386
  attitudes to
    of Cons., 133
    of R.P.F., 133–4
    of Maurras, 77, 134
    by Coms., 386
  in govt. service, 386, 389
  and exceptional High Court, 306 and n.
  and M. of Justice, 378
  and pardons, 176, 306n., *q.v., and see* amnesty.
  in Parl. eligibility, 191–2
  in press, 389, 390
  in Rad. P. (absence of), 93
  in Soc. P. (severity of), 62, 69, 353–4
Pyrénées, Basses-, dept. (cap. Pau), 114, 150n., 351
Pyrénées, Hautes-, dept. (cap. Tarbes, *q.v.*), 146n., 322n., 347
Pyrénées-Orientales, dept. (cap. Perpignan, *q.v.*), 67, 150n., 354

Quai d'Orsay, 377, *and see* Foreign Affairs, M. of.
questeurs, 51n., 197–8
Queuille, Henri (b. 1884, M.P. 1914, s. 1935, Rad. d. Corrèze Nov. 1946)
  career, 34n., 35, Apps. II, III, IV
  as P.M., 34–8, (1st govt.), 102
  consultations, 186n. (2nd and 3rd)
  choosing Ms., 35 (1st), 181 (1st), **182** (2nd), 183 (3rd)

Queuille, Henri
as P.M. (cont'd)
meeting N.A., 180n. (1st), **181** (2nd)
and elec. reform, 322 (3rd)
use of v. of c., 201, 216, 217nn., 220 and n., 223n.
resignations, 178 and n. (1st and 3rd)
as M., 35n., 188n., 242n., 377 and n.
in own party, App. VII
and other parties, 146, 185n.
as conciliator, 190, 362
quoted, 55n., 257n., 338n., 358
Queuille cabinet, September 1948- October 1949
formed, membership, 34, 35, 184n.46, 189n.64
course, **35–7, 121–2**
and pol. *immobilisme*, 190, 263n., 384
and Finance c'tee, 243
fall, 22, 37, 190n., 225, 226n.
Queuille cabinet, 2–4 July 1950
formed, membership, 37, 184n.46, 189n.64*
fall, **37**, 181, 184n.46, 225, 226nn., 229, 230n., 360, App. IV
Queuille cabinet, March-July 1951
formed, membership, 38, 183n., 184n.46
and special powers, 262
resignation refused, 227
resigns, 41, 225, 226n.
Quimper, Auriol's speech at (1948), 168n., 174 and n.
quorum, in N.A., 200

RACIAL tolerance, 406
radiators, neglect of (pol. implications) 304n.
Radical party, Chapter 7, App. VII
history
in 3rd Rep., 4, 7–8, 11–12, 27, 99, 159, 160
'proconsular Radicalism,' 91, 102, 133
under Vichy, 92
in Resistance, 13
at liberation, 13, 92–3
and de Gaulle, 14–6, 93
enters office 1947,...19, 377
1947–53,...37–42, 94
clientèle, 4, 24, 90, 99–102, 104 and n., App. VII
discipline
of voters, 443n.
of deputies, 361 and n.
applications of, 97n., 98–9, 141–2, 147–8
discipline
laxity of, 98, 243 and n., 363

Radical party
militants
shortage of, 93
leaders and, 92, 96–8, 368
org., 94–9, 106, 141, 367
funds, 94 and n., **356n.**
in Parl.
groups, 19, 39
in Senate, 11, 90, 92, 268, 269, 281
and participation in govt., 11, 99, **105–6,** 198, 218n., 379–80 and nn., 383, 411n., 447
fear of govt, 5, 7–8, 10
policy
agric., 23, 103, 106
clerical, 25, 39, 41, 91, 103–4 and n., 330, 356
colonial, 24, 41, 187
and const.
1945–6...14, 21, 93, 105
and elec. law, 37–8, 40, 220, 311 314–5, 316 and n., 318, 321
and H.C.M., 301
and *statut des partis*, 346
econ., 23, 32, 37–8, 42, 98, 106
foreign and defence, 12, 98, 411
T.U. and social, 136
and rivals, 24–5
Coms., 14, 45–6, 92, 93, 98, 143, 412
Cons., 98, 100, 104, 108, 112–3, 114, 356
M.R.P., 89, 94
R.G.R., 140–1, 146 and n.
R.P.F., 42, 94, 98, 100, 102, 133, 136
Soc., 61, 71, 88, 91, 94, 98, 103–4, 412
U.D.S.R., 145
and scandals, 12, 91, 356n.
and press, 95, 390
ex-Radicals
Gaullist, 98–9, 102, 132, 348
Leftist, 102, 141, 142 and n.
other, 97n., 147–8
Radical journals, *L'Information radicale*, 97n.
Radical party statutes, 96n.
Radicaux et résistants de gauche,
railways
economies on, 241, 245
and rep. on coal board, 385n.
reorg. of, 22, 41, 262
workers on
bonus, 219n.
dismissals, 391
pensions, 268n.
T.U., and Pleven's fall, 331
Ralliement, 6
Ramadier, Paul (b. 1888, M.P. 1928, Soc. and Rep. Soc., mayor of Decazeville, Soc. d. Aveyron 1945–51, stood in Lot 1952)
career, 34n., 71, 183n.44, Apps. II, III, IV

INDEX

Ramadier, Paul (*cont'd*)
  as P.M.
    election, 19, 183n.
    consultations, 186n., 382
    and Soc. participation, 371, 372
    resignation refused, 178n.
    and colonization, 388
    and v. of c., 216, 218, 223 and n.
  as M. of Defence, 280*, 387 and n., 392*
  loses seat, 1951,...324, 388n.
  quoted
    on dissolution, 227n.45
    on H.C.M., 301n.
    on Thorez as colleague, 382n.
Ramarony, Jules (b. 1901, M.P. 1945, P.R.L. and Peas. d. Gironde 1945-51, Gironde II 1951-), 170n., 238n.
Ramette, Arthur (b. 1897, M.P. 1932, Com. d. Nord II 1945-51, s. Nord 1952-), 50
rapporteurs
  of c'tees, 158, 235, 238
    of N.A. and C.R., 277
    Finance c'tee
      rapp.-g., *see* Barangé.
      and Court of Accounts, 266
      other *rapps.*, 235, 239n., 241
    other c'tees, 241, 248, 288
  of const., *see* Coste-Floret.
  of E.C., 297
Rassemblement démocratique africain (R.D.A.), 142, 152
Rassemblement démocratique révolutionnaire (R.D.R.), 143
Rassemblement des gauches républicaines (R.G.R.), **147-9**
  strength, 19, 39
  class basis, 113
  and clericalism, 39
  and component groups
    Rad. critics of, 141, 147
    and Daladier, 98, 147-8
    and U.D.S.R., 144, 146 and n., 147
    and minor groups, 147 and n., 149, 351
    electoral conflict and co-operation, 146n., 148, 149, 351
  in Parl, 148, 196
  votes, 223n., 245n.
  and press law, 390-1
Rassemblement des groupes républicains et des indépendants français (R.G.R.I.F.), 149, 322n.
Rassemblement du peuple français (R.P.F.), Chapter 9, App. VII
  history
    founded, 20, 28
    1947-53...24, 32, 33n., 36-42
    and Cons. supporters, 119, 133, 369
    split, 24, 42, 126, 127, **136-7**, 139
    de Gaulle renounces, 126

Rassemblement du peuple français (*cont'd*)
  clientèle
    numbers, 120-2, 129
    class basis, 24, 116, 120, 124, 125, 130, 137, 138, 446
    geog. support, 130, 131 and n., 134
    strength in towns, 32, 113, 130-1
    and youth, 124n., 130, 137
  discipline
    structure, 126-9
    of voters, 369, 443n.
    of deputies, 361 and n.
    deputies and leadership, 121 and n., 125, 126, 129, 136-7, 368-9
    nat. and local orgs., 128, 134-5 and n., 350
    unsuccessful, *see below*. ex-R.P.F.
  militants
    and deputies, 122, 124, 368
    class basis, 130-1
  org., 123-30, 134
    authoritarianism of, 126-9, 135n., 350
    funds, 350n., 356n.
  in parl.
    groups, 125, *and see* inter-group.
    c'tee chairs, 239 and n.
    in C.R., 272, 278
    and seating, 7, 135 and n., 197
  and participation in govt., 123, 136, 185, 380, 408, 409, 447
  and investitures, 42, 184n., 185, 409 and n.
  policy
    and budget, 280-1
    clerical, 25, 122, 127, 134-5
    colonial, 24, 135n., 151
    const., *see* Const. of Bayeux *and* decree-laws, 264
      elec. laws, 40, 319-20 and n., 325, 357
      parl. procedure, 406
    econ., 25, 42, 121, 135, 221
    educational, 127
    foreign and defence, 25, 134, 137 245, 408
    T.U. and social, 124, 135, 136
  and rivals, 24-5
    Com. 32, 36, 57-8, 121, 122, 214, 131, 357 and n.
    Cons., 100, 111, 115, 117, 121, 136-7, 351 and n.
    M.R.P., 32, 79, 82, 87, 121, 132, 134, 319, 370
    Rad., 42, 94, 98, 100, 102, 133, **136**
    R.G.R., 148
    Soc., 63, 67, 74, 121, 134, 370
    U.D.S.R., 144
    Auriol, 174
    Comte de Paris, 150n.
    Mendès-France, 409 and n.
    Pleven, 33, 145, 190n.
    Thorez, 193

Rassemblement du peuple français (cont'd)
  and scandals, 356n.
  ex-R.P.F.
    expelled, 128, 129, 134
    resigned, 121 and n., 122n., 123, 129n., 132, 137 and n., 362
  R.P.F. organs
    L'Action ouvrière, 124n.
    Dossier du candidat, 124nn.
    Le Rassemblement, 17n., 124nn., 127n.
Rastel, Georges (b. 1910, M.P. 1951, unseated U.D.S.R. d. Eure-et-Loir), 191n.
Rau, *see* Defos du Rau
Raymond-Laurent, Jean (b. 1890, sec.-gen. P.D.P. 1924, Pres. Paris Munic. Council 1936–7, M.P. St. Étienne 1938, M.R.P. d. Manche), 78n.
Raynal, *see* Weill-.
réaction, la, 6, 12–3, 114–6, 117 and n.
rearmament
  pre-war, 45
  post-war, *see* army; budgets, military.
reconstruction, budgets for, 255, *and see* investment.
Reconstruction c'tee of N.A., 237n., 240–2 and nn.
Reconstruction and Town-planning, M. of : holders, 347*, 379
  and parties, 378–9, 380n.
Récy, Antoine de (b. 1913, M.P. 1946, Cons.-Gaullist and R.P.F. d. Pas-de-Calais II 1946–51), 184n.*, 191n.
reference back, *see* bills.
referendum
  of October 1945…14–6
  of May 1946…17–8, 164, 171, 269, 307, 343
  of October 1946…18–9, 343
  in Bayeux Const., 162, 403
  and const. revision, 202, 288 and n.
Réforme, La, 335n.
régime d'assemblée, *see* Assembly regime
regions of France
  Alpine, 113
  Anjou, 74, 330n.
  Basque, 334
  Central, 141
  East Central, 94
  Eastern Frontier and N.E., 4, 53, 54, 85, 88, 113, 131n., 132
  inland, 240n.
  Languedoc, 94
  Limousin, 334
  Massif central, 54
  Mediterranean coast, 54
  Midi, 4, 66, 205, 240n.19, 311, 339
  'modern and static,' 397–8
  North, conservative, 79
  Northern industrial, 54, 66, 74
  North-west, *see* West *below.*

regions of France (*cont'd*)
  Paris basin, 131n., 132
  Provence, 94
  Riviera, 333n.
  Southern half, 131–2, 141
  South, mountainous, 77
  South-west, 94, 101–2, 149
  West coast, 132, 141
  West and north-west
    church schools question in, **330n.**
    elec. importance of church schools in, 74, 88, 311
    rivalry between clerical parties, 329, 356, 357n.
    Cons. decline and revival, 113, 131–2, 137 and n.
    1951 election
      apparentement, 325, 326, 330
      and Com., 53
      and M.R.P., 85, 88 and n.
      and church pressure-group, **330**
  and see Alsace; Britanny; Cevennes; Champagne; Loire; Lorraine; Normandy; Parisians.
regionalism
  economic conflicts
    'modern and static,' 3, 397–8
    urban and rural, 267, 272, **332–4**, 337 and n.
    electioneering, 349, 353, 356
    among peasantry, 410n.
  religious and cultural conflicts, **329–30 and n.**, 334
    and elec. systems, 311, 326n.
    legal aspect (Alsace-Lorraine), 192n.
  racial, linguistic and national conflicts, **334–5 and n.**, 445
  mitigated by parl. and mil. melting-pots, 197, **205**, 400
  and see constituency interests.
regionalism and parties: electoral
  economic divisions
    Com., 53–4
    Cons., 113–4 and nn.
    M.R.P. 85 and n., 351, 356
    Rad., 91, 101n., 104 and n., 356
    R.P.F., 130–1 and n.
    Soc., 70–1 and n.
  hist. and geog.
    Com, 54
    M.R.P., 77, 85, 356
    Rad., 101–2 and n.
    R.P.F., 131–2
    Soc., 70
    Parti soc. dém., 149
  religious and cultural divisions
    Com., 53–4 and n.
    Cons., 113–4 and nn.
    M.R.P., 77*, 85, 88
    P.D.P., 77
regionalism and parties: internal
  Cons., 114 and n.

INDEX

regionalism and parties: internal (*cont'd*)
  M.R.P., 77, 81, 88, 337n.
  Rad., 91, 94, 95
  Soc., 66, 74, 81
regional commissioners, Com., 387
règlement, *see* Soc. P.; Standing Orders.
remainder, highest, 316, 442–3
Rémy, Colonel (pseud. of Gilbert Renault), 133 and n.
Renaud-Jean (b. 1877, M.P. 1924, Com. d. Marmande, Lot-et-Garonne, 1924–40), 355 and n.
Renaudel, Pierre (1871–1935, M.P. 1914, Soc., Neo-Soc. and Rep. Soc.), 61
Renault works, strike at (1947), 20, 368
rent law, 177, 225n.
Republic
  and generals, 7
  and Vichy, 13
  and opponents, 108, 115n.
  inviolability of, 288
Républicains populaires indépendants (R.P.F., ex-M.R.P.), 125
Republican Independents, 14n., 35n., 109, **111nn.**, 113, **114 and n.**, 117n.
  and A.R.S., 137
  discipline of, 111n., 361
Republican Socialists, 140, 148, 149
Resistance
  attacked by Maurras, 77, 134
  heroism in, and pol. and admin. jobs, 362, 385, 389
  ideals of, 414
  and magistrates, 302
  orgs., 47, 61, 143, 385
  pol. support, 13, 40, 73, 92, 119, 151n.
    and Coms., **46–8**, 50, 54n.
  and press, 389–90
  and see Free French.
responsibility of ministers, **167–8**, 174, **180 and n.**, 202
  collective, *see* cabinet solidarity.
  to Senate, 268–9
  to C.R., 274
restricted debate, 200, 201n., 237, 409n.
retroactive legislation, 307n.
Réunion, dept. (cap. St. Denis), 184n., 191n., 294n., 323n.30, 443
Revolution of 1789
  hist. significance of, 3, 6, 102
  Cons. regret, 6, 114
revolutionary tradition, 338, *and see* authoritarianism.
Revue des deux mondes, 328n.
Revue française de science politique, *see* Fondation nationale des s. p.
Revue juridique et politique de l'Union française, 293n.
Revue politique des idées et des institutions, 256n., 258n.*, 265n.*, 292n.

Revue politique et parlementaire
  on admin. and econ,. 336n., 385n., 388n.
  on E.C., 298n.
  on Parl., 198n., 257n., 280n.31
  on premiership, 180n., 213n.
Revue socialiste, 267n., 272n., *and see* Rimbert.
Reynaud, Paul (b. 1878, M.P. 1919, P.M. 1940, chairman Fin. c'tee 1951–3, R.I. d. Nord I since 1946)
  career, 34n., 108, Apps. II, III, IV
  stands for P.M. 1953...184n., 408, 411, 413
  M. of Associated States, 377n., 379n.
  M. of Finance, 34, 35 and nn., 121n., 263n., 360, 369, 382
  c'tee chairman (and M.), 238n., 239n., 245–6 and nn., 262n.
  pol. position
    and Coms., 192
    and Cons., 111 and n., 117, 363
    and M.R.P., 34, 360, 411
    and Socs., 34, 36
    and const. and finance, 258 and n., 259n., 262
  quoted, 340n.51, 405n.
Reynaud law of 17 August 1948... **262–4 and n.**, 266 and n., 277 and n., 291–2 and n., **412n.**, *and see* decree-laws.
Rhin, Bas-, dept. (cap. Strasbourg *q.v.*), parl. rep. of
  1951 dispute, 193, 445
  M.R.P. senator 1947...345n.
  absentees and foreigners, 350 and n.
Rhin, Haut-, dept. (cap. Colmar *q.v.*), 351, 367
Rhine, river, 328n.
Rhineland, Germans enter, 1936...10
Rhône, dept. (2 constituencies: I Lyons (cap. and *q.v.*), II remainder), 72, 101n.
Ribeyre, Paul (b. 1906, M.P. 1945, Peas. d. Ardèche), 367 and n., 383*, App. III
Ribière, Henri (b. 1887, Soc. d. Allier 1945–6)
  and U.D.S.R., 144n.
  and intelligence service, 387*
Rigal, Albert (Com. d. Loiret 1945–51, defeated 1951), 355 and n.
Right, *see* Left and Right; *and also*
  strength of, not based on votes, 12
  hostility of, to regime, 6, 12–3, 114–5
  in 3rd Rep., 107–8, 115, 363
  and Fascism, 12–3, 115
  weakness of, at liberation, 13
  and de Gaulle, 119
  and see authoritarianism, fear of; Conservatives; *réaction*, *la*.
rights, declaration of, *see* Preamble.

Rimbert, Pierre, quoted, 60n., 68–70nn.
riots
  in N.A., 199 and n.
  at Brest 1950...193n.
  at Grenoble, 1948...37, 122
  in Paris, February 1934...45, 108, 137
  in Paris, 1952...194n.9
  measures against, 404
  and see strikes.
Riviera, 333n.
road hauliers, *see* petrol.
Robespierre, Maximilien (1758–94), 63
Roclore, Marcel (b. 1897, M.P. 1945, R.I. d. Côte d'Or, defeated 1951), 238n., App. III
Rome, equated with Moscow, 364n.
Rossi, A., quoted, 13n., 44n., 46n., 48n., 55n., 355n.
Roubaix, 123n.
Rouen, 130
Rougier, Louis, 290n., 307nn.
Roure, Rémy, quoted, 323n., 337n., 340n.
Rousseau, *see* Waldeck-.
royalists
  deputies, 142n., 328n., 364
  and Comte de Paris, 149, **150–1 and n.**, 340 and n.
  and const. of 3rd Rep., 6, 155, 169
  and life senators, 1875...158–9
Russia, *see* Union of Soviet Socialist Republics.

SABOTAGE laws, 199, 224
Saint Étienne, 137n.
Saint-Maur-des-Fossés, 17n., 54n., 101n., 127
Saint Pierre et Miquelon, 294n.
Sait, Edward McChesney, 269n.
sanatorium, Soviet, 350
Sangnier, Marc (1873–1951, founded *Sillon* 1894, M.P. 1919–24, hon. pres. M.R.P., d. Seine III 1945–51),77, 141
Saône, Haute-, dept. (cap. Vesoul), 114, 131n., 150n., 323n.30
Saône-et-Loire, dept. (cap. Mâcon), 311n.
sapeurs-pompiers, 252n.
Sarraut, Albert (b. 1872, M.P. 1902, gov.-gen. Indo-China 1911–4 and 1916–9, s. 1926, P.M. 1933 and 1936, Pres. A.F.U. 1951), 95, 295
Sarraut, Maurice (brother of above, newspaper owner, murdered 1943), 95
Sarthe, dept. (cap. Le Mans), 311n.
Sartre, Jean-Paul, 143
Savoie, Haute-, dept. (cap. Annecy), 350
Sauvageot, André, 180n., 198n., 213n.
Sauvy, Alfred, 336n.
Sawyer, John E., 332n., 397nn.

scandals, general
  and Coms., 266n.38, 350n., 354–5, 392
  M.R.P. and, 88, 204n.
  and Rads., 12, 91, 356n.
  and R.P.F., 356n.
  and Socs., 72, 305–6, 327n., 350n., 387
  and c'tees of inquiry, 204n.
  and public opinion, 58, 402n., 447
  Mauriac regrets lack of, 363
scandals, particular
  admin (and Court of Accounts), 265–6 and n.
  Algerian wine, 72, 306, 327 and n.
  Begum's jewels, 88n.
  electoral corruption, 350n., 392
  of generals, 72, 88n., 204 and n., 306 and n., 327 and n., 387
  press corruption, 389, 390
  Stavisky, 92
  trafic des piastres, 204n., 356n.
Schauffler, Charles (1893–1951, P.R.L. d.), 51n.
Scheele, Geoffrey, 343n.
scholarships, 225n.
school medical service, 248n.
schoolteachers
  as pressure-group, 329
  rural, 330
  salaries of, 219n.
  and Rads., 90, 103
  and Socs., 70, 240, 329
Schuman, Robert (b. 1886, M.P. 1919, chairman Finance c'tee 1945–6, M.R.P. d. Moselle)
  career, 34n., 78n., Apps. II, III, IV
  as P.M., **33**, 183 n. (1st govt.), **34** (2nd)
  consultations, 186n. (1st), 182n., 184, 186 (2nd)
  tactics, 383
  use of v. of c., 216–7, 218, 220 and n.
  as M. of Finance, 18, 242n., 391
  as Foreign M., 188n., 377, 383 and n., 384n., 408
  and European policy, *see* European affairs, Schuman plan.
  and North Africa, 41, 190n., 405n.
  as c'tee member, 242n.
  position in party, App. VII
  and R.P.F., 88
  quoted (on proconsular policy-making), 405n., 410 and n.
Schuman cabinet, November 1947-July 1948
  formed, membership, 33, 184n.46, 262, 377, 378n.
  and Finance c'tee, 243, 244–5, 248
  and Marie, 190n.
  and Poinso-Chapuis decree, 188n.
  and U.D.S.R., 145, 360

Schuman cabinet, (cont'd)
  fall, 22, 24, **33**, 219n., **225 and n.**, 226 and n., 229, 230n., 244–5
Schuman cabinet, 5–7 September 1948 formed, membership, 34, 184n.46, 383*
  and Socs., 28, 184
  and U.D.S.R., 360
  fall, 22, **34**, 145, 181, 184n.46, 219n., 225, 226n., 229, 230n., **263n.**, 360, 378, App. IV
Schuman plan
  and Monnet, 391
  and pressure-groups, 341
  ratification, 41, 205, 221, 222n., App. IV
  and c'tees, 246 and n.
  and E.C., 299n., 300 and n.
Schumann, Maurice (b. 1911, M.P. 1945, broadcaster for Free French, ex-pres. M.R.P., d. Nord II, u.-sec. Foreign Affairs since 1951), 18, 78n., 266n., 411*
scrutin d'arrondissement, de liste, see electoral systems.
scrutin public à la tribune, 197, 200, 222 and n., 224, 365
Séances de la commission de la constitution of 1st C.A.
  on c'tees, 237n.
  on elec. system, 315n.
  on H.C.M., 301nn., 302n.
  on Pres., 172n., 176n.
  on *statut des partis*, 346n.
  of 2nd C.A.
  on const. revision and constitutionality, 287n., 290nn.
  on H.C.M., 301nn.
second ballot, see ballot (double).
second chamber, social function of, **397–8**, *and see* C.R.; Senate; single-chamber govt.
Second Republic, 170
secretary, local party, power of, 352
secret funds, 386
secret services, 386 and n., 387–8
secrétaires d'état, see under-secretaries.
Section française de l'internationale ouvrière (S.F.I.O.), see Socialist party.
Segelle, Pierre (b. 1899, M.P. 1945, Soc. d. Loiret), 382n., App. III
Seine, dept. (6 constituencies: I, Paris S; II, Paris N.W.; III, Paris N.E.; IV, banlieue S.; V, banlieue N.W.; VI, banlieue N.E.)
  1951 election in, 101n., 130
  elec. system in, 322n., 443
  parl. rep.
    c'tees, 240
    constituencies, 315n.
    C.R., 272
  parties in
    Com. org., 49n.

Seine, dept.
  parties in (cont'd)
    M.R.P., 351
    Socs., 73n.
    R.P.F., 136n., 137n.
  and see Paris.
Seine-Inférieure, dept. (2 constituencies: I, Rouen (cap. and *q.v.*) and eastern; II, Le Havre and western)
  1951 election in, 101n., 140
    disputed result, 193, 445
  1952 by-election, 123n.
Seine-et-Marne, dept. (cap. Melun, *q.v.*), 85n., 134, 135n., 137n., 351
Seine-et-Oise, dept. (2 constituencies: I, Mantes and N.; II, Versailles (cap and *q.v.*) and S.)
  1951 election in, 101n., 143
  electoral system in, 322n., 443
  parties of
    Cons., 111n.
    R.P.F., 136n., 137n.
    Socs., 73n.
self-government of colonies, 292, 296 308, 410n.
Senate, **158–60, 267–9, 397–8**
  status, power and outlook, 8–9, 156, 191, 273, 309
  ablest leaders attracted to, 159, 285
  abolition proposed, 90, 159, **173n.**
  and agric. 334n.
  c'tees of
    election of, by P.R., 235
    Army c'tee, 234
    Finance c'tee, 243
  C.R. not a revival of, 261, 282, 286
  decline of, inevitable at liberation, 403
  delaying tactics, 268, 274
  and dissolution, 8, 156, 169, 211, 227
  and finance, 252, 253, 261
  and overthrow of governments, 159, 226n., 268–9
  as political court, 274, 305
  Pres. of, *q.v.*
  and Pres. Rep., 171, 203
  Rads. in, 9, 11, 90, 92, 159, 160, 363
  traditions, 273, 274, 284
  in 1940...14
senators, *see* Parliament, members of.
  title revived by C.R., 274, 284n.
Senegal, Socs. of, 64
Senghor, Léopold-Sédar (b. 1906, M.P. 1945, Soc. and I.O.M. d. Sénégal), 153n, 296n.
separation of powers, 161–2, 211, 341
Serre, Charles (1901–53, M.P. 1946, M.R.P., R.P.F., ind., and Prog. d. Oran 1946–51, stood Dordogne 1951), 362 and n.
Servin, Marcel (b. 1918, M.P. 1946, Com. d. H.-Saône 1946–51, lost seat, party sec. 1954), 53
settlers, *see colons*.

494   INDEX

Sèvres, Deux-, dept. (cap. Niort), 74n.
Sharp, Walter Rice, quoted
  on justice, 303n.
  on laws of accounts, 265n.
  on log-rolling, 252n.
  on Senate, 267n., 268n., 272n.
shopkeepers, 328, 332, 339, 340, *and see Petites et moyennes entreprises*.
Siam, 296n., 410
Sicard, R., 404n.
Siegfried, André
  member of Const. C'tee, 289
  quoted
    on French politics generally, 5n., 6n., 115 and n., 367n., 397n.
    on Left and Right, 9n., 23n., 114, 115, 311n.5, 312n.
    on Rads. and ' king's friends,' 97n., 103 and n., 104 and n., 157nn.
    on Bonapartism, 132n., 163
    on Parl. 1945–7...360n.
Sieghart, M., 262n.
Sillon, Le (Catholic democratic journal), 77
single-chamber govt.
  and Assembly regime, 166n.
  Left favours, 163–4, 167, 269
  and provisional regime, 176
  and April draft const., 17, 269
sliding scale, *see* wages.
Social Democratic party, German, 138
social security system
  benefits, statistical status of, 394
  control of, by beneficiaries (and Coms.), 263n., 385
  employees of, bonus, 36–7, 220n.
  reorg. attempted
    by Reynaud, 1948...34
    by Pleven, 1952...41
    by Pinay, 1952...22–3
    by Laniel, 1953...412n.15*
Socialist Commentary, 55n.
Socialist party (S.F.I.O.), Ch. 5, App. VII
history
  in 3rd Rep., 9, 12, 60–1, 353
  under Vichy, 61, 141
  and Resistance, 13, 61, 385
  at liberation, 13, 16–20, 61–2, 353–4
  1947–53...32–4, 36–42
  and de Gaulle, 14–5, 20, 28, 62, 119
clientèle
  numbers, 60, 62, 68
  age structure, 68–9, 353–4
  class basis, 4, 24, 69–70, 72, 75, 446
  geog. support, 70–4
discipline
  of voters, 443n.
  of deputies, 121, 359, 360, 361, 409n.
  and deputies, loyalty, 75–6
  executive and deputies, 67–8, 213, **370-3**, 412n.

Socialist party,
  discipline (*cont'd*)
    nat. and local orgs., 63–6, 80, 354
    and youth org., 69
  militants
    and leaders, 60, 61, 66, 67, 72–3, 369, **370-3**
    intransigence of, **73-4**
  org., 63–9, 72–3 and n., 369, 371
  funds, 63 and n., 94n.
  in Parl.
    group, 365, 371–2
    and c'tees of N.A., 239n., 412n.
    and Senate, 269, 285
    and convoking N.A., 196n.
  and participation in govt., **29**, 32, 37, 40–1, 62, **71-3**, 75, 180, 183n., 225–6, **371-2 and n.**, 379–80 and nn., 382 and n., **394**, 408, 447
  and investitures, 183n., 184n., 185
  Blum cabinet, *q.v.*
  policy
    and civil service, 37, 219
    clerical, 10n., 25, 33, 73, 104, 356, 372
    colonial, 24, 32, 151
    and const., **164-5, 213-5**, *and also* 1945–6...16, 17–8, 21, 62, 164–5, 170
    and c'tee system, 235
    and decree-laws, 263
    and dissolution, 220, 228, 230n.
    and elec. law, 38, 40, 70, 315, 318, 320–2, 325
    and H.C.M., 301
    and premiership, 187
    and *statut des partis*, 345
    and v. of c., **213-5**, 219, 223
    econ., 37–8, 73
    foreign and defence, 12, 25, 46, 68, 221, 245, 411
    T.U. and social, 29, 33, 34, 37, 41–2
  and rivals, 24–5
    Coms., 44–6, 47, 62, 67, 92, 356–7, 394, 412
    Cons., 110, 356
    M.R.P., 73–4, 88, 119, 122, 240n., 356
    Rads., 61, 71, 88, 91, 94, 98, 103–4, 412
    R.P.F., 63, 67, 74, 121, 134, 370
    U.D.S.R., 62 and n., 73, 144–5
    P.S.U., 141
    R.D.R., 143
    Comte de Paris, 150n.
    Mendès-France, 409n.
    Petsche, 185
    Pinay, 184n.
    Pleven, 183n.
  and M. of Finance, 264
  and scandals, 72, 305–6, 327n., 350n., 387

INDEX

Socialist party (*cont'd*)
  ex-Socialists
    3rd Rep., 61, 353
    purged (Vichyites), 62, 69, 148–9, 353–4
    other, 69, 75–6, 142n., 149, 348, 354
Socialist party organs
  Bulletin intérieur, q.v.
  National Congress Reports, 63n., 64n., 65n., 66n., 68n., 69n., 70n., 285n., 365n.
  Règlement, 64, 66n., 69n.
Solal-Celigny, J., 214n., 217–23nn.
Somaliland, French, 294n.
Somme, dept. (cap. Amiens), 348n., 354, 380n.
Sondages (public opinion polls), **App. VII**
  on Blum cabinet, 22 and n.
  on elec. system, 318n.
  on voters and own parties, 58n., 86n., 105n., 367n.*, 447
  on voters and politicians generally, 402, 447
Soulier, Auguste, quoted on 3rd Rep.,
  on executive
    Presidency, 177n., 179nn., 227n.
    premiership, 179n., 180n., 188n., 190n.
    conciliators, 190n., 212n.
    dissolution, 156n., 228n., 230n.
    special powers, 262n.
    v. of c., 217nn.
  on Parl.
    c'tees, 238n., 243n., 250n.
    fall of govts., 212n., 226n., 227n., 328n., 366n.
    interpellations, 212n., 213n.
    sittings, 360n.
  on party system, 97n., 156n., 311n.5, 312n., 361n., 366n.
    elec. system, 311n.7
    pressure-groups, 328nn.
  on 412 Rep., Const. C'tee., 176n., 275n., 291n.
Sourbet, Jean (b. 1900, M.P. 1946, Peas. d. Gironde II, chairman parl. group, u.-sec. 1951), 238n.
Soustelle, Jacques (b. 1912, M.P. 1945, U.D.S.R. d. Mayenne 1945–6, R.P.F. d. Rhône I 1951– , ex-sec.-gen. R.P.F., ex-chairman parl. group)
  position in party, 144, App. VII
  as M., App. III
  and Resistance, 134 and n.
  quoted, on R.P.F. strength, 129n.
sovereignty, in const., 308
Spain
  French attitudes to, 12, 78, 239n., 354, 384 and n.
  mentioned, 106, 138

Speaker of House of Commons, 198, 207
special powers, *see* decree-laws.
Spinoza, Benedict, 6
stability
  of govt.
    and overseas deputies, 153
    and c'tees, 250
  of policy, 157, 374, 375–7, 380,
  and see instability.
Stalin, Marshal, 45
Standing Orders (*Règlement de l'Assemblée Nationale*), *see under* Parliament.
S.O. 5...197n.
  9, 10, 12...365n. 15
  13...197, 335 and n., 365n.15
  15...237, 247n., 365 and n. 15
  16...239n., 365n.15
  19...365n.15
  22...177n.
  24, 26, 29...234 and n.
  34...365n.15
  36–8...203n.
  38...197n.
  38 *ter*...365n.15
  38 *quater*...201n.
  39, 39 *bis*...365n.15
  48...258–9
  66 *bis*...365n.15
  68...258 and n.
  69...202n.
  79, 82, 83, 90, 92, 114...365n.15
' static France and modern France,' 398
Statistiques et études financières (M. of Finance report to *commission des comptes économiques et des budgets de la nation*, chairman M. Mendès-France), 23nn., 257n.8, 397n.
statut des partis, **345–6**
Stavisky, Serge Alexandre, 92
Strasbourg
  Council of Europe at, 222n.
  Com. congress at, 49
  M.R.P. congress at, 87, 370
  de Gaulle's speech at (1947), 20, 118, 120
  Pinay's speech at (1952), 340n.
  R.P.F. of, 137n., 350 and n.
straw, men of, 322n.
strikes
  in const., 307
  1938 general, 46
  1947 Renault, 20, 368
  1947 general, 32–3, 37, 141, 177, 199, 277
  1948 mining, 36
  1949, against Moch as P.M., 56
  1952, for liberation of Duclos, 57
  1953 summer, unofficial general, 410
  and Com. failures, 56–7, 367n.
  and Rads, 1906...91
  threat of, and party politics, 29, 139
  of non-working-class groups, **338–9**

strikes (cont'd)
  of taxpayers, 332
students
  allowance for, 241
  cheap fares, 391
  strike of, 339
'study groups,' parl., 335 and n.
Sturmthal, Adolf, 385n.
subscriptions, see funds.
substitutes, see alternates.
Sud-Ouest (newspaper), 151n.
Suel, Marc, 174n.
'super-prefects,' 404
Sûreté nationale, 88n., 266n.38
Switzerland, 403
syndicalism
  primæval, 60
  vestigial, 53n.
  patronal, 136n.
syndicat des sortants, 323, 394

TANGUY-PRIGENT, François (b. 1909, M.P. 1936, Soc. d. Finistère), 332, 379*, App. III
Tarbes, Auriol's speech at, 175 and n.
Tardieu, André (1876-1945, M.P. 1914, P.M. 1929, Cons.), 217n., 257n.
Tardieu cabinet, 1930, 160
Tarn, dept. (cap. Albi), 85, 150
Taylor, A. J. P., 343n.
taxation, see budgetary policy.
'Taxpayers' Defence' movement, 149
technocrats,
  in R.P.F., 130,
  and see inspecteurs des finances.
Teitgen, Henri (b. 1882, M.P. 1945, M.R.P. d. Gironde, lost seat 1951, on High Court 1951), 240n.15, 305n.*, 337n.
Teitgen, Pierre-Henri (son of above, b. 1908, M.P. 1945, pres. of M.R.P., d. Ille-et-Vilaine)
  career, 78n., 409n.2, App. III
  on party policy, 89n., 411
  as M. of Justice, 240n.15
  quoted, 320n., 340n., 409n.2
Temple, Emmanuel (b. 1895, M.P. 1936, R.I. d. Aveyron since November 1946), 184n., App. III
tenants and landlords, 277n.
Tenants' League (*Fédération des locataires*) and Com. P., 55 and n.
Terre Humaine (M.R.P. journal), 410nn., 411n.
'tertiary sector,' 397
Théry, Jacques, quoted
  on Assembly and parl. regimes, 167n.
  on cabinet, 180nn., 182n., 187n., 188n.
  and dissolution, 228n.
  and special powers, 264n.
  and v. of c., 214n.

Théry, Jacques, quoted (cont'd)
  on party system, 344n., 359, 360n.
  on premiership, 187n., 188n., 189n.
  and choice in emergency, 161n.
  on Presidency, 169n., 176n., 177n., 179n., 188n.
  on const. proposals
    de Gaulle's views, 161n.
    provisional regime, 168n., 176n.
    Soc. conception, 214 and nn., 228n.
Thibaudet, Albert, quoted
  on French politics generally, 114n., 329n.
  on Christian Democracy, 78 and n.
  on freemasonry, 71n.
  on the Left, 92n.
  on the Radicals, 91n., 97n., 100 and n., 102, 103 and nn.
  on the Right, 114n.
Thiers, Adolphe (1797-1877, P.M. 1836 and 1840, *chef du pouvoir exécutif* and Pres. Rep. 1871-3, s. 1876, later deputy), 169, 179n., 414n.
Third Force
  attitudes towards, of
    Auriol, 174
    Comte de Paris, 150
    Cons., 109
    Rads., 97
    U.D.S.R., 145
  basis and fortunes of, 16n., 32-3
  clericalism divides, 16n., 24, 88
  and Progs., 141
Third International, see Communist International.
Third Republic
  const., **154-61**
  and elec. and party systems, 232, 318, 366
    customs of, survive, 403
    instability, 190, 205, 211-3, **374**, *and see* majority.
    party groups, 363
  and executive
    Presidency, 176, 179n., 198n.
    premiership, 179n.
    clôture, 195
    decree-laws, 262-3
    dissolution, 227
    v. of c., 187, 212, 216
  Parl.
    c'tees, 235, 236, 242, 261
    finance, 253-4, 257n., 265
    members, 206
      and expenditure, 257n.
      and immunity, 193, 194
      overseas, 297
    Senate, 272
    sessions, 195
    and treaties, 202
  revision of, 287

INDEX

Third Republic (*cont'd*)
  historical
    origin, 6, 107, 155
    last years, 10, 11–2
    end, 12–3, 14, 168
    opinion in, 4, **8–9, 154–5, 159–61**, 168
  opinion on, 1945
    critics, 14
    supporters (Rads.), 14, 24, 165, 172
    Socs., 164
Thomson, Dr. David, quoted, 5n., 7n., 397n.
Thorez, Maurice (b. 1900, M.P. 1932, sec.-gen. Com. P., d. Seine IV)
  career, 34n., 52, Apps. II, III, IV
  stands for P.M. 1946...19, 360n., 394n.
  as M., 382n., 388, 392*
  position in party, 44–5 and n., 50 and n., 52, 368, App. VII
  and validity of election, 1951...193
  and voters, 347, 350, 444
  quoted, 45 and n.
  mentioned, 355
Thorez, Mme., *see* Vermeersch.
Tillon, Charles (b. 1897, M.P. 1936, Com. d. Seine VI, purged from party offices 1953, ex-mayor St. Denis), 16, 50 and n., 385n., 386*, App. III
timber, presidential, 414
Times, The, 194n., 257n., 331n.
Tinguy du Pouët, Lionel de (b. 1911, M.P. 1946, u.-sec. 1949–50, M.R.P. d. Vendée), App. III
  quoted, 256n., 258n., 265n.
Tito, Marshal, 142n.
tobacco-planters, 337n.
tomatoes, price of, as election issue, 354
Torrès, Henry (b. 1891, M.P. 1932, R.P.F. s. Seine since 1948), 139n.
Toulouse
  1951 election in, 130
  newspaper, *La Dépêche de*, 95
  Radical congress at, 1949...97, 99, 147, 368
tourist industry, and E.C., 298
Tours, Socialist congress at, 1920...44, 60, 68
towns
  and country, *see* regionalism.
  size of, *see* population.
trade unions (in general)
  and collective bargaining, compulsory arbitration, *see* wages.
  and E.C., 297–9
  and govt. depts., 378
  and Labour c'tee, 241n., 249 and n., 331
  and parties
    Com., 13, 20, 47, 56, 342, 368, 370, 385 and n.
    Cons., 34, 35n.
    M.R.P., 87, 240

trade unions (in general)
  and parties (*cont'd*)
    R.P.F., 124 and n.
    Soc., 28, 56, 240, 329, 370
  pol. consequences of growth of, 404
  as pressure group, 329, 331, 340
  and Vichy, 47
trade unions (particular)
  Catholic (*Confédération française des travailleurs chrétiens*), 24, 33, 71, 77, 314n.
  Confédération générale des syndicats indépendants, 124n.
  Confédération générale du travail (C.G.T.)
    appeal to Auriol, 177
    and Coms., 13, 74, 382
    leaders, 52, 53n.
    as pressure group, 341n.
    and Socs., 28, 71, 75, 392–3
    split, 1947...33
  C.G.T.-Force Ouvrière, 33, 56, 57, 71, 299, 340n., 392–3
Transport House, 400
Transport, M. of, *see* Works and Transport.
Transport policy, 392, *and see* fares.
treason
  and Malagasy ds., 194
  and Pres. Rep., 204, 305
Treasury, *see* Finance, M. of.
  accounts, 265 and n.
treaties
  and C.R., 274, 279, 285n.
  and E.C., 297, 299–300
  and Pres. Rep., 177 and n.
  ratification of, 201n., 202 and n., 220n.
  and see European Army; Schuman plan.
trêve scolaire, 88n.
tripartisme
  admin. changes under, 404
  cabinet (as diet), 190, 381–2, 384 ff.
  and elec. system, 315–7, 323
  ideals, 414
  and parl.
    class basis of N.A., 206
    disc., **204–5, 342–5,** 359, 374–5, *and see* party discipline.
    disc. relaxed, 183n., 360, 377
    second chamber unpopular, 269, 278n., 279, 281
  and peasantry, 332
  and purge, 302 and n., *and q.v.*
  supporters, divisions among, 357–8, 392
  opponents
    de Gaulle, 119–20
    P.M.E., 332
    Rad. and Cons., 19, 38, 40, 110
    U.D.S.R., 145
    universal unpopularity, 19

Trotskyists, 6–9, 143
Truman, Harry S., 116
Tunis, Bey of, 174
Tunisia
  status of, 152n., 293, 294
  Frenchmen of, rep. in C.A., 191n.
    in C.R., 270, 271n.
  Auriol and, 174
  N.A. debates on, 209 and n.
  policy in, 41–2, 181, 190n.
  Residents in, 386, 405n., 409n.2, 410 and n.
  and see North Africa.

UNDER-SECRETARIES
  and offices, 180n., 189n.64, 391
  and parties, 35n., 383, 388
unicameralism, *see* single-chamber govt.
Union démocratique du manifeste algérien (U.D.M.A.), 152
Union démocratique et socialiste de la résistance (U.D.S.R.), **143–6,** *also*
  nature of
    as small marginal party, 37, 140
    as party of *notables*, 347, 363, 366
    and overseas members, 152
  and candidates, 322n., 351
  discipline, 361, 383
  and elec. law., 315n., 321
  and rivals
    Rads., 93
    R.D.A., 142, 152
    R.P.F., 120n.
    Socs., 73, 144–5
    and Petsche, 236n.
  strength, 100n.
Union des chrétiens progressistes, 141
Union des républicains et résistants/progressistes, 141–2
Union nationale des indépendants républicains (U.N.I.R.), 150
Union of Soviet Socialist Republics
  domestic, 21, 200
  and international Communism, 44
  and French Coms., 46–7, 48, 50n., 382n.
  and de Gaulle, 13–4
  ' ni Rome ni Moscou,' 364
Union progressiste, 141–2, *and see* Progressives.
Union des républicains et d'action sociale (U.R.A.S.), 123
United States of America
  French attitudes to, 448
    Auriol's visit, 174
    Coms., 56
    de Gaulle, 14
    R.D.R., 143
    R.P.F., 136
    financial aid from, 253, 256, 257, 413n.

United States of America (*cont'd*)
  comparisons with
    concept of democracy, 406–7
    const. and Pres., 161, 162 and n., 177, 403
    history and politics, 396
    incivisme and pressure-groups, 5, 338, 400, 406–7
    Democratic party, 400, 414n.
    horse-trading and log-rolling, 399–400
    judicial review, 289
    non-voters, 407
    Pinay and Truman, 116
    parl. and congress, 198, 199, 201
    and candidates for Pres., 414
    and scandals, 327n.
    veto, Presidential, 177
universal suffrage, 397 *and see* woman suffrage.
university
  professors, 192n., 289
  rectors, 189n.
urgency procedure, *see* parl., procedure.

VAN DYKE, Vernon, 58n.
Vatican, 73, 77, 364*
Vedel, Georges, 167n.
Vélodrome d'hiver, 17n.
Vendée, dept. (cap. La Roche sur Yon), 74n., 99n., 137n.
Vermeersch, Mme. Jeannette (b. 1910, M.P. 1945, Com. d. Seine II), 199n.
Vermeil, Edmond, 343n.
Versailles, 203, 294, 295, 350n.
Vichy
  attitudes towards, of
    Coms., 46
    M.R.P., 78
    Peasants, 117
    Rads., 92
    R.P.F., 117, 133–4
    Socs., 61
    T.Us., 47
    Auriol, 173
    Faure, Paul, 149
    Flandin, 148
    Maurras, 6
  influence of
    on admin., 260, 275
    on Conservatism (discrediting of), 115
    on const. (Art. 94), 168
    on E.C. (suppression of), 298
  pol. significance of
    for Right, 6, 13, 108–9, 115
    for Left, 13
Vichyites
  and exceptional High Court, 306 and n.
  ineligibility of, 192 and n.
  R.P.F. and, 133–4

INDEX

Vichyites (cont'd)
  revival of, 117, 134
  and see Pétain.
Vie française, La, 331n.
Vienne, Haute-, dept. (cap. Limoges)
  Coms. of, 54n., 350n.
  M.R.P. of, 348
  Socs. of, 72, 74
Viénot, Mme. Andrée Pierre- (Soc. ex-d.) 349n.
Vietnam, 294, 296n., 410, *and see* Indo-China.
Vigier, Jean-Louis (b. 1914, M.P. 1951, R.P.F. and R.I. d. Seine III), 129 and n.
Villiers, Georges (b. 1899, mayor of Lyons 1941–2, pres. of C.N.P.F.), 257n.8
virements, 254, 263
Volta, Haute-, 191n.
Vosges, dept. (cap. Épinal, *q.v.*), 110n.
votes
  of confidence, *q.v.*
  preferential, *q.v.*
  wasted, 316 and n., 325 and n.
voting systems
  elec., *see* ballot; elec. system.
  parl., *see* ballot; parl. procedure.

Wages
  bonuses on, 36, 299, App. IV
  collective bargaining, compulsory arbitration, 37, 249 and n., 280n., 281, 299, 331 and n., 370, 371
  and Coms., 19–20, 368, 382
  and E.C., 298–9
  sliding scale for
    and C.R., 282, 285
    and govt., 41, 190n.
    and Labour c'tee, 241n., 249 and n.
    and parties, 41–2, 136, 148n., 249 and n., App. IV
Wahl, Nicholas, 131n.
Waldeck-Rousseau, René (1846–1904, M.P. 1879, s. 1894, P.M. 1899–1902), 170
Waldeck-Rousseau cabinet, 60
Waline, Marcel
  member of Const. C'tee, 290n.
  quoted
    on admin. colonization, 384n.
    on const. c'tee, 290nn.
    on C.R. and *navette,* 283n.
    on elec. system, 349n.
    on party system, 344n., 360n.
    on Preamble, 307nn., 308n.
Walter, Gérard, quoted, 44n., 48n., 50n., 60n., 311n.
war, declaration of, 202, 274, 279
War, M. of, admin. abuses in, 266n.38
Washington, D.C., 206n., *and see* U.S.A.

wasted votes, 316 and n., 325 and n.
Waterloo, 118
week-end, M.Ps.' lost, 349
Weill-Raynal, Étienne (Soc. d. Oise 1950–1, died 1951), quoted, 267n., 272n., 292n.
Weimar Republic, 343 and n., 345, *and see* Germany.
Weiss, J.-J. (1827–91, journalist and literary critic), 169n.
Werth, Alexander, quoted, 8n., 262n., 328n., 347n.
Wertheimer, Egon, 69n.
Weygand, Gen. Maxime (b. 1867, C.G.S. 1930, C.-in-C. May 1940, M. of Defence June-September 1940, gov. of Algeria 1941–2, deported by Germans), 386
wheat-growers, *see under* food policy; peasantry.
Williams, Philip, quoted
  on 1951 election, 39n.
  on 1953 crisis, 413n.
  on pol. function of crises, 383n., 399n., 408n.
  on Pres. in crises, 178n.
  on scandal of generals, 306n., 387n.
wine-growers, 335, 339, 410n.
wine, price of, as election issue, 349 and n., 354
women
  as electoral asset, 351
  equality of, in const., 307
  suffrage, 53, 93, 119, 309
    de Gaulle and, 119
    Senate and, 268n.
  and parties, 69, 84 and n., 147n., **446**
workers
  and C.R., 273, 282, 284
  and E.C., 297, 299
  and Labour c'tee, 241
  pol. weakness of, 397, 398
  and see trade unions; each party separately.
Works and Transport, M. of
  departmental disputes, 391
  holders, 42, 377n., 385n.
  and parties, 379 and n., 380
  successful policy of, 392*
Wright, Gordon, quoted
  on const.
    provisional regime, 168n.
    Auriol and C.A., 173n., 307n.
    M.R.P. and draft, 288n.
    Soc. conception, 214 and n.
    French Union, 293n.
    Preamble, 307nn.
    revision, 288n.
    statut des partis, 346n.
  on parties
    clashes between, 393n.
    and pol. individualism, 348 and n.

Wright, Gordon, quoted
  on parties (*cont'd*)
    strength of, in N.A., App. V
    Coms. and peasantry, 47n., 332n., 355n.
    and de Gaulle, 17n.
    M.R.P. membership, 79n.
  peasants and taxation, 23n.

YONNE, dept. (cap. Auxerre), 148, 150, 192n., 351, 352n.
youth
  in N.A.
    qualifications, 191, 198
    comparative, of M. Cachin, 198
youth (*cont'd*)
  and second chamber
    not in Senate, 158, 267
    not in C.R., 270
  and parties and orgs.
    Catholic, 77–8
    Com., 52–3, 55, 84
    Cons., 112
    M.R.P., 77–8, 83–4
    Rad., 97n., 100
    R.G.R., 147
    R.P.F., 124, 130, 137
    Soc., 68–9, 143
    internal disputes, 353, 354, 409
  courted and spurned, in 1953 crisis, 409
Youth, Arts, and Letters, abortive M. of, 188